Nationality and Population Change in Russia and the USSR

An Evaluation of Census Data, 1897-1970

Robert A. Lewis
Richard H. Rowland
Ralph S. Clem

 Published in cooperation with the
Program on Soviet Nationality Problems,
Columbia University

The Praeger Special Studies program—
utilizing the most modern and efficient book
production techniques and a selective
worldwide distribution network—makes
available to the academic, government, and
business communities significant, timely
research in U.S. and international economic, social, and political development.

Nationality and Population Change in Russia and the USSR

An Evaluation of Census Data, 1897-1970

Praeger Publishers   New York   Washington   London

Library of Congress Cataloging in Publication Data

Lewis, Robert A
    Nationality and population change in Russia
and the USSR.

    (Praeger special studies in international politics
and government)
    "Published in cooperation with the Program on Soviet
Nationality Problems, Columbia University."
    Bibliography: p.
    Includes index.
    1. Russia—Population. 2. Urbanization—Russia.
3. Minorities—Russia. 4. Russia—Census.
I. Rowland, Richard H., joint author. II. Clem,
Ralph S., joint author. III. Title.
HB3607.L47   301.32'9'47   76-6942
ISBN 0-275-56480-0

PRAEGER PUBLISHERS
111 Fourth Avenue, New York, N.Y. 10003, U.S.A.

Published in the United States of America in 1976
by Praeger Publishers, Inc.

Printed in the United States of America

This study of population change in Russia and the USSR has evolved over the past decade. At the outset, it was motivated by the general lack of knowledge of the population of the USSR, a modernizing, multinational state covering one-sixth of the earth's land surface, and by the importance of a knowledge of population processes to an adequate understanding of Soviet society, or any society. As the study progressed, however, our thinking changed considerably. The conceptual linkage between population change and modernization began to suggest itself as the principal framework around which demographic trends could be detailed and explained.

The study of modernization and population change and of their impact upon Soviet society has been neglected in both the West and in the USSR. In Western studies concerned with Soviet society, disproportionate attention has been devoted to Russian literature, biographies of politicians and literati, Communist ideology, political and diplomatic history, the totalitarian nature of Soviet society, Kremlinology, and the reporting and interpretation of current political events. In the USSR itself, ideological and political factors have hampered the objective analysis of Soviet society in terms of modernization and population change.

When one specializes in a region or country in any of the social sciences, there seems to be a natural inclination to treat that region as if it were a special or unique case in terms of societal processes, and this inclination is particularly strong if that region has a totalitarian government. This tradition is especially evident in the study of the USSR, in general, and in the study of its population, in particular. Indeed, Soviet Marxist demographers and many Western demographers who give undue weight to the totalitarian nature of Soviet society support this contention. However, it gradually became apparent to the authors that the processes being studied were largely universal: there were very few demographic surprises in the USSR and the relationships between modernization and population change were as strong in the USSR as in any other modernized or modernizing country. In other words, it became obvious that it was not directly the political system or ideology that explained population change in the USSR, but rather the degree to which the country or groups within Soviet society had modernized. Therefore, the authors began to strengthen the conceptual base of the study by drawing increasingly on demographic and other generalizations to a greater degree than had been anticipated.

At least some of the lack of systematic social scientific study of the USSR can be attributed to the scarcity of basic socioeconomic data. From the beginning of this study censuses were considered to be one of the best sources of data on any society, and, although national censuses have been taken in Russia and the USSR since 1897, they have been grossly neglected as a source of information for the study of Russian and Soviet society. Although the period covered by the censuses and the intervals between them are not entirely satisfactory, these censuses provide a large volume of basic population data for a major portion of the world for a significant period of time.

The authors have utilized the Russian and Soviet censuses extensively, although the enormous operational problems to be encountered in their use and the amount of time and effort required to solve these problems were not anticipated fully. There was almost a complete lack of territorial and definitional comparability among the first three censuses, which necessitated about a decade of data processing. Basic demographic data for the total, urban, and rural population from these censuses and appropriate censuses of surrounding countries have been reordered fundamentally into a set of comparable internal units for the present-day territory of the USSR, based upon consistent socioeconomic definitions. The resulting series of data constitutes the chief source of data for this study and the most complete series of socioeconomic data available for the USSR, an area generally lacking in such information. Even though the coverage of the data is not entirely comprehensive, it is hoped that this series will also be useful to others who are studying the USSR and are faced, as were the authors, with a lack of historical demographic and socioeconomic data.

With respect to the uniqueness of demographic processes in the USSR, the effectiveness of population policies is a central concern, because if the Soviet government could control population trends, general demographic concepts would have little or no explanatory power. Indeed, it is this ostensible "control" over demographic processes that has prompted Western scholars to attribute uniqueness to totalitarian societies. Thus, the authors decided that a major goal of this study should be to evaluate the extent to which demographic trends have coincided with announced or easily inferred population policies of the Soviet government, and, if this has not been the case, to investigate the factors that have contributed to the gap between policy and practice.

Finally, the authors also became convinced of the importance of attempting to assess the impact of population change on society by distinguishing the dominant demographic and geographic forces shaping Soviet society. In fact, it was thought that the ultimate goal of any population study should be the appraisal of the impact of population change on society. It became apparent that with a basic knowledge of demographic processes, one could make significant statements and

vi

guarded forecasts as to the current and future impact of population trends upon Soviet society. An investigation of these trends is necessary to anticipate and interpret the course of events in the USSR in the coming decades; if one can extrapolate from the experience of other societies, these demographic processes have far-reaching social, political, and economic consequences. For example, declining mortality and fertility, rapid urbanization, dramatic interregional migration, rising levels of education, the change from an agricultural to an industrial work force, and high rates of female participation in the work force have had an obvious and noteworthy effect upon modernizing societies.

In the Soviet context, as in many other countries, these demographic trends have an important ethnic dimension; that is, major differences exist among nationalities for all of these aspects of population change, differences that in other societies have exacerbated ethnic tensions. The critical importance of ethnicity in the USSR and its direct link to population change and modernization prompted the authors to treat this subject in the first volume of the study. Clearly, the USSR is just beginning to experience many of the problems generated by population change, such as depopulation in "European" rural areas where there are labor shortages, rapidly growing rural population in "non-European" areas where there is a labor surplus, and the mixing of nationalities resulting from internal migration. The final goal of this study, therefore, is to go beyond the descriptive and analytical stages to an assessment of the implication of population change for the society of the USSR.

ACKNOWLEDGMENTS

This study was supported by Grant HD 05585 of the Center for Population Research of the National Institute of Child Health and Human Development and was administered by the International Institute for the Study of Human Reproduction, Columbia University. This support is gratefully acknowledged; without it, the necessary data processing and background research would have been impossible.

The beginnings of this study of population change go back a decade to San Diego State College, where Robert Lewis and J. William Leasure received support from the National Science Foundation to develop the data-processing procedures and to investigate migration in Russia and the USSR. This support is also gratefully acknowledged, as is the contribution of Professor J. William Leasure of the Department of Economics, San Diego State University. In this beginning stage, Richard Rowland and Ralph Clem were undergraduate assistants, but after they came to Columbia University to pursue graduate work in the population geography of the USSR, they rapidly made the transition from student to colleague and therefore are coauthors of this study.

Over the years we have had many good assistants, but in particular we would like to express our appreciation to Nicholas Dima and Olga Acampora. We would also like to thank Jane Rowland for her prompt and truly excellent typing, particularly considering the large amount of statistical data in this volume. Richard Rowland, in addition to being coauthor, drew all the maps. We have learned much about population from A. J. Jaffe of the Bureau of Applied Social Research, Columbia University, and his influence is apparent throughout this study. Our association with the Program on Soviet Nationality Problems, Columbia University, and its director, Edward Allworth, has also stimulated our thinking.

CONTENTS

PART I: BACKGROUND MATERIALS TO THE SERIES

Chapter

LIST OF TABLES

xiv

LIST OF MAPS

The purpose of this study is to describe—by utilizing a time-series set of data based upon consistent definitions and comparable territorial units—and to explain—by reference to demographic and other concepts and generalizations wherever possible and conditions specific to the USSR where necessary—the changes in the numbers, geographic distribution, and socioeconomic and ethnic characteristics of the population of Russia and the USSR since the late nineteenth century. Furthermore, this study evaluates the success, or lack thereof, of Soviet government policies designed to influence the demographic behavior of its population, and assesses the implications for Soviet society resulting from the many and often dramatic population changes that have taken place in the Soviet Union over the past decades. The results of this study will be published in three volumes under the series title Population Change in Russia and the USSR: 1897-1970.

The present volume, the first in the series, is devoted to an investigation of the demographic and socioeconomic trends of the Soviet nationalities since 1897. In keeping with the series format, Soviet policies regarding the socioeconomic development of nationalities, as well as the implications for Soviet society stemming from the interaction of modernization, population change, and ethnicity, also will be discussed and evaluated.

The series begins with a volume focusing on nationalities and their relationship to population change because ethnicity is perhaps the fundamental demographic characteristic in terms of classifying the population in a multinational state such as the USSR. As detailed in Chapter 4, where the conceptual basis for this book is discussed, the very existence of a strong ethnic dimension in a society will condition the impact of modernization upon population change. This is so because nationalities generally stratify along socioeconomic lines, and population change relates primarily to differences in socioeconomic levels. Despite the critical importance of ethnicity for multinational societies, demographers usually have dealt with nationality groups in a very descriptive manner, if at all, and have not integrated concepts from the literature on ethnicity into their work. At the same time, scholars of ethnicity have overlooked largely the importance of demographic trends and the influences of these forces upon society.

In this volume the authors seek to integrate concepts from the nationality, demographic, and geographic literature to provide the framework for an exposition and analysis of the population of the ethnic groups of the Russian Empire and the USSR, and to assess the impact

xix

of these demographic trends for the present and future Soviet society. This integration of concepts is considered to be one of the methodological contributions of this volume to the study of ethnic processes in general; those familiar with the study of Soviet nationalities in particular should appreciate the value of the data that are the basis of the present work.

The second volume of the series will deal with population redistribution, and will focus on urbanization, migration, rural depopulation, differential natural increase, and the socioeconomic problems related to these processes. The third volume will be devoted primarily to an investigation of population growth and its societal consequences on an aggregate as well as a regional basis with emphasis on fertility and mortality, including population losses. Because demographic processes are so interrelated, throughout this study decisions have had to be made as to where a given subject should be discussed and the degree to which a particular process or trend is interrelated with other processes and trends. Therefore, the authors feel that it is necessary in this third volume to summarize and synthesize the chief population trends and processes that have been occurring in the USSR.

Because the conceptual framework of modernization and population change is relevant to the entire study, these central concepts are discussed in the first chapter of this volume. Likewise, the chapters on data procedures and on the basic geographic background of the USSR are, of course, apropos to this volume and to subsequent books as well. Extensive background material was not included in this or later volumes, as the broad outline of the geography, history, economics, and politics of the USSR is generally well known or readily available in other sources. By its very nature, the study of population is statistical, and this work is no exception. More data will be included here than is usual even in population studies, because Russian and Soviet demographic and socioeconomic data are not normally accessible to English-speaking scholars. Also, because there has been relatively little empirical work on the population of the USSR, major consideration will be placed on the description of population trends and their analysis. Inasmuch as the detailed discussions in many chapters are at times lengthy, technical, or not of interest to all readers, each chapter is prefaced with a summary discussion.

A universal, or general, approach to the analysis of population change in Russia and the USSR has been taken because the authors contend that population change relates primarily to modernization, and not directly to political or ideological systems or to cultural or historical factors unique to any one country. Essentially what has been done is to test empirically in the Soviet context relevant generalizations that, because of historical scholarly circumstances, have been formulated mainly in the West. In the broadest sense, the following questions have been posed: (1) What are the expected population trends and their correlates? (2) What patterns actually occurred and to what were they related? (3) How did the Soviet government affect these patterns? (4) What impact have these trends had upon Soviet society? All of these questions cannot be answered definitively, largely because of the lack of data and resources, which, to a greater or lesser extent, is the chief problem in all social research. The authors have attempted to restrict themselves to asking questions that are appropriate to the accuracy and coverage of the data, and, at times, as might be expected, have had to use variables that are not precisely representative of the phenomena or characteristics in question because of the nature of the information. Where general formulations did not explain the processes being studied, conditions specific to the USSR were investigated.

In the following sections of this introduction, topics related to three of the four general questions that were posed previously are discussed: what are the expected population trends and their correlates; how do government policies affect demographic behavior; and what impact do these demographic trends have upon Soviet society? The other general question to be considered, the actual demographic patterns and their correlates, will naturally be considered in the body of the appropriate volume. The expected population trends are derived from a brief discussion of the impact of modernization on population change and a survey of the demographic and ethnic literature.

Initially, however, it is pertinent that the methodology used be outlined. This is necessary to establish the logic of testing general formulations in the Soviet context, and also relates to the implications that can be drawn if the expected trends and their correlates are in operation in the Soviet Union.

GENERAL APPROACH

There has been a long-standing antiscientific tradition in the social sciences and history that maintains that societal phenomena are unique and thus not amenable to laws, largely because they are "culturally conditioned" and "historically determined."[1] This approach is antiscientific because the goal of science is to increase the level of generalization. Very frequently the USSR, in particular, and regions, in general, are viewed as unique entities.[2] In the West, most regional population studies treat their region or country as if it were unique, although they generally do not make their approach explicit. William Petersen, however, makes his approach very explicit in his well-known textbook on population, and bases his argument on a political or ideological distinction. He claims that demographic patterns are different

> in totalitarian societies, where the processes of
> fertility, mortality, and migration are significantly
> different from those typical in the West, because
> all institutions are essentially subordinated to the
> state and its ideological guide, the party. . . . Yet
> whatever the context, totalitarian population phe-
> nomena differ systematically from those in a nonto-
> talitarian country.[3]

Soviet Marxists also claim that there are political or ideological limitations to the explanation of demographic processes. Their
thinking is based on Marx's contention that each historical means of
production, identified for us unambiguously by the concept of historical materialism, has its own characteristic utilization of labor and
thus its own law of population.[4] Consequently, each historical system
should be studied separately in regard to population theory. Lenin,
as might be expected, agreed wholeheartedly with Marx in rejecting
the "abstract" or universal approach to demographic theory.[5] Thus,
Marxists believe that in the last analysis national productive relations
are the determining factors in a society's demographic behavior. For
this reason much emphasis is put on socioeconomic conditions in the
analysis of population, and in this respect the present study is in full
agreement. Soviet demographers also recognize that these determining factors are not absolute and that there are interrelationships between what they call the base and the superstructure of society. Therefore, they also acknowledge historical, religious, moral, and legal
influences, as well as biological and environmental ones.[6]

Soviet demographers seem to have no problem in defining the
population laws of capitalism, for Marx dealt with these in some detail
in Das Kapital. Even though a great deal has been written about them,
the formulation of these capitalist laws does not go much beyond Marx's
interpretations. Consequently, it seems incongruous to read a century later about such long-forgotten controversies as the Marxist debate with the Malthusians and Social Darwinists, as if they were current problems.[7]

In any case, the promise held out to us, that there will be revealed a "socialist law of population," is largely unfulfilled, even
though much has been written on the subject. Soviet demographers
acknowledge that they cannot define it with any precision.[8] Because
of the influence of Marxist ideology, they normally characterize the
socialist law of population in such broad economic terms as full employment and rational utilization of labor resources in socially useful
work—all this to result from the planned economy.[9] Some Soviet
demographers add such factors as improvement in the condition of
life and all-round development of the people.[10] In the past, rapid nat-

ural increase of the population was frequently ascribed to the socialist system, but recent sharp declines in fertility in the USSR and Eastern Europe have necessitated some revisions and reinterpretations.[11] That "communist" and "capitalist" fertility trends in developed countries are, on the evidence to date, very similar has caused some anxiety among Soviet demographers, but they normally maintain that these trends are the result of good factors in the Communist countries and bad factors in the capitalist countries.[12] They do not acknowledge that the processes of modernization and population change are similar in these countries, entirely independent of their political systems or any other ideological factors.

Because the validity of this antiscientific tradition has been refuted adequately by Fred Schaefer in geography, Carl Hempel in history, and Ernest Nagel, Adolph Grunbaum, and others in the social sciences in general, it is not necessary to consider these arguments in detail here.[13] Suffice it to say, with Nagel, that misconceptions frequently arise from the

> failure to distinguish between the question whether
> there is a structure of relations invariant in a class
> of systems and capable of being formulated as a com-
> prehensive theory (even if in highly abstract terms),
> and the question whether the initial conditions appro-
> priate for applying the theory to any one of the sys-
> tems are uniformly the same in all the systems. . . .
> Accordingly, the fact that social processes vary with
> their institutional settings, and that the specific uni-
> formities found to hold in one culture are not pervasive
> in all societies, does not preclude the possibility that
> these specific uniformities are specializations of rela-
> tional structures invariant for all cultures.[14]

One of the intentions of this study is to add empirical confirmation to some general hypotheses formulated in terms of just the kinds of uniformities and invariants to which Nagel here points the way. Consequently, the authors do not recognize geographic or ideological limitations to the demographic and geographic generalizations that are being tested. These demographic forces and processes appear to be universal; at least, there seem to be few demographic surprises to be found in the USSR. Furthermore, until other data from areas comparable with respect to these variables have been examined and tested it would be unscientific to refuse to extend, at least tentatively, our generalizations to a broader range. Uniqueness of phenomena is a conclusion that must be tested and verified. As a matter of scientific policy, one should only concede some peculiarity or uniqueness to a given nation or ideology if the data force it upon him. Since there are gross signs that modernization and population changes are occurring independent of political boundaries, and that their connections with other demographic variables are also independent, the most scientific attitude would be to hypothesize that the causal determinism is not "culture bound." To be scientific a hypothesis needs to be open to refutation, but this will mean that the more powerful hypothesis, being deliberately constructed so as to be based on a wider range of independent observations, will be more general. [15]

Since Marxism has been subjected to critique many times, there is no need to add to this literature. Suffice it to say that there is obviously considerable methodological disagreement between Soviet and Western demographers over what the initial conditions are that affect demographic behavior. The "historical systems" that the Marxists write about actually tend to be more political and ideological than descriptive of levels of modernization. Modernization and thus population change can occur under a variety of ideologies or political systems, and with respect to population change the results seem, on the basis of available evidence, to be very similar. Political systems are important only insofar as they affect modernization.

In any case, to restrict demographic generalizations a priori to "historical systems" without considerable verification is clearly unscientific, even though one of the chief claims of Marxism is that it is scientific. However, that Soviet demographers stress in their analysis socioeconomic conditions and take into account cultural variables make their approach to demographic problems tenable, regardless of the route they took to arrive at this position. In fact, much attention is given, at least in principle, to the interrelationship between population change and socioeconomic conditions in the Soviet demographic literature, even though there are relatively few studies in this literature subjecting this interrelationship to empirical test. The chief drawback of historical materialism with respect to the study of the population of the USSR by Soviet demographers is that its particularistic approach hinders the adoption of useful generalizations formulated in other developed areas and largely precludes international comparisons of population at roughly the same level of modernization and thus the testing of generalizations on an ever broader geographic basis.

As to the contention that totalitarianism results in uniquely different demographic processes, this simply cannot be confirmed in the Soviet context, no matter how much emphasis one puts on political terror, forced labor, forced settlement, and anti-Semitism—actions that are not necessarily unique to "Communist" societies. Although estimates to fit any degree of bias can be found, the population consequences of these events cannot be measured with any precision or "verified" from census data, because these consequences generally fall within the range of error of the Soviet censuses and vital statistics. However, even if one allows that significant losses occurred from these actions, these changes are very minor compared to the dominant population trends in the USSR. The Soviet government has been able to control mortality and international migration to a great degree, but has been unable to control fertility and internal migration. But this is one of the patterns that appears to be characteristic of governments in all developed countries. Despite the Soviet government's strong disapproval, Slavic fertility in the USSR is very probably currently below replacement, and the outstanding feature of internal migration in the USSR is that it does not conform to the needs of the economy. Once again the totalitarian model proves to be inadequate for analyzing Soviet society, further justifying the growing criticism of this approach to the study of the USSR.[16]

In brief, the authors' main concern is to clarify demographic processes in the USSR, because it is believed that an understanding of demographic processes is fundamental to the understanding of contemporary Soviet society, which is the ultimate aim. We do not wish to raise the question as to the feasibility of complete objectivity in the social sciences. However, that we take an empirical approach to the study of population change in the USSR, adopt a working hypothesis that demographic processes are more or less universal, and test accepted demographic generalizations in the Soviet context, at the very least, indicate that we are attempting to avoid subjectivity or ideology. We feel that this is important throughout the study, but particularly so in respect to the study of nationality, because much emotion and ideology have been apparent in its study, in the West as well as in the USSR, not to mention the obvious bias that can be found in the whole range of scholarship on the USSR. We might add in this regard that we are neither pro-Communist nor violently anti-Communist; we do not particularly dislike Russians or love Tadzhiks, Latvians, and so on, because we feel that we cannot afford this indulgence if we are to interpret honestly the Soviet scene. We acknowledge the achievements of the Soviet regime as well as its weaknesses and disabilities, in terms, of course, of our Western values. Our aim is simply to test, where possible, the universality of demographic processes in the Soviet context, while avoiding ideology and dogmatism as much as possible.

POPULATION CHANGE AND MODERNIZATION

The chief working hypothesis of this study is that people throughout the world tend to react in the same manner to the socioeconomic forces that influence their demographic behavior—whether they live under "capitalistic" or "communistic" regimes or anything in between.

Demographic processes are related largely to socioeconomic conditions, and not to the type of government under which they develop. Experience has shown that when the socioeconomic environment changes, demographic behavior changes. Consequently, to understand demographic processes in the USSR, one must relate Soviet developments to general demographic theory whenever possible, and through the general theoretical linkages make international comparisons of population trends and processes. In short, population changes in the USSR cannot be understood properly solely through studying the USSR. Therefore, every effort will be made in this study to apply demographic theory, which has incidentally developed mainly in the West, to the Soviet situation, both to illuminate the situation in the USSR and to test the universality of our generalizations. Another reason for relying heavily on Western demographic theory is that, until fairly recently, little demographic research has been done in the USSR, and the state of the art there still lags considerably behind that of the West.

An understanding of the demographic forces shaping Soviet society requires a knowledge of demographic processes, particularly of the relationship between modernization and population change. Unfortunately, this relationship has not been worked out in any great detail by demographers, although it is implicit or assumed in the works of many.[17] Because the relationship between population change and modernization is so central to our study, Chapter 1 is devoted to this subject.

POPULATION POLICY

Clearly, if the Soviet government were able to implement their population policies, a general approach to the study of the population of the USSR would be impossible because the Soviet government would have direct control over the population. However, the control of demographic behavior generally is very difficult, because in most instances it is complexly interrelated with a variety of other very stable socioeconomic trends. After studying some 300 socioeconomic trends for the United States and Europe, W. F. Ogburn concludes that the forces put into operation by modernization are strong, stable, and difficult to manage.[18]

Because of the preoccupation with the problems of population growth, the term "population policy" has come more and more to have a narrow meaning, in that it is thought of primarily in terms of reducing fertility. In this study a broader view is taken. Policies pertaining to mortality, migration (both international and internal), population distribution (including urbanization, suburbanization, rural depopulation, settlement, and colonization programs), and nationality will also be included within the scope of population policies. It is difficult, however, to know where to draw the line, because many social policies directly affect population. Notable examples include health, education, work force, military drafts, and economic policies. However, for the purposes of this study, population policy is defined as referring to the listed components of population. Nationality policies are particularly important in the Soviet context, as they are in most multinational states.

Some aspects of population are relatively easy to control. At least in the short run, mortality is relatively easy to control, because little personal initiative, expense, or social change are required, and everybody favors the idea of living longer. However, once an underdeveloped country has opted for death control, it is "locked in," for, in the absence of economic development or a decline in fertility, the standard of life will decline eventually until ultimately the death rate will rise again. International migration is also rather easy for governments to control, despite the fact that illegal immigrants have been numerous in the United States in the past few years.

Population variables that are closely interrelated with the socioeconomic environment are very difficult to control. This is the case with fertility, internal migration, urbanization, suburbanization, rural depopulation, and ethnic assimilation. And it seems that, in general, policies have not been successful, although it is difficult to determine what would have occurred in the absence of a policy or to differentiate long-term from short-term effects. The major exceptions are policies that were backed by considerable force, such as programs of genocide, forced labor, and forced settlement. Governments generally have not been willing to exert the necessary effort to change sufficiently the socioeconomic environment and thus population trends. One reason for this is that most governments want to preserve the status quo. D. V. Glass has documented the failure of the population policies designed to increase fertility in Western Europe in the 1930s.[19] The general failure of governments in the underdeveloped world to lower fertility without the necessary modernization is probably the most outstanding example of the failure of population policies to effect an all-embracing change in a demographic trend, at least in the short run.[20]

A number of countries have attempted to decentralize their populations, or to promote migration to underdeveloped parts of their countries, or to limit the population of certain cities. Most of these programs have met with very limited success. In the USSR, for example, despite the desires and the announced policies of the Soviet government, large cities continue to grow, Siberia recently has experienced a net outflow of population, and rapid rural depopulation in many "European" areas continues apace. Nor would it seem that pol-

icies to control population distribution have been much more successful in Australia or the United Kingdom. If you follow a demographic
trend, of course, your policy will be successful. In Japan the Eugenics Protection law merely legalized a trend, in that illegal abor-
tions were widespread before the law was enacted.[21]

An understanding of how socioeconomic processes affect demographic behavior surely would be beneficial and necessary for a rational policy, but would not necessarily guarantee success. To change
demographic behavior requires either coercion or a change in the socioeconomic environment sufficient to change demographic behavior.
Most policies have been unsuccessful largely because governments
have been unwilling to expend sufficient effort or expense to change
the socioeconomic environment to the extent that it would affect demographic behavior; a common misconception is that a policy results in
resolute action. Coercion requires great effort, too, and is, of course,
highly undesirable. It is often dangerous to reason from analog, but
it is instructive to consider the progress and difficulty in combating
racial discrimination, urban decay, environmental pollution, poverty,
and unemployment in relation to what we know about these problems.
It is also instructive to contemplate how very difficult or impossible
it would have been, if one were immortal and president, to maintain
U.S. fertility at colonial levels and to ensure that the population remained in rural areas in the face of the truly tremendous socioeconomic change that has occurred in the past century or so.

"Jawboning" or propaganda is usually insufficient to affect to
any appreciable degree demographic or human behavior. The assumption that a statement of policy or opinion of a political or religious
leader will affect to a significant degree demographic behavior should
be seriously questioned. What Moscow or the Pope has said or desires
is deemed by some to be very significant. An effect should be made
to ascertain what a government or a leader can control by edict or
declaration without making major changes in a society or using force,
and how people respond to authority, whether it be from fear or loyalty, when it is in their interest to act otherwise. The Catholic Church
has considerable religious authority and a well-developed information
network; yet in developed countries Catholic fertility is generally low,
despite papal edicts encouraging the contrary.

THE IMPACT OF POPULATION CHANGE
ON SOCIETY

To understand Soviet society, or any society, adequately, one
must understand the political, economic, geographic, social, and
demographic forces that are shaping that society and to which the gov-

ernment will react. Such an understanding would help us to anticipate and interpret the course of events in the USSR in the next decade or so—a task that has been relatively neglected, despite the considerable academic and governmental emphasis on Soviet studies over the past few decades.

Modernization activates demographic forces through population growth, redistribution, and changes in the composition of the population that play a major role in the processes of social change. The effect of a given population change on a society depends on how the population variables are interrelated to other variables related to modernization. These interrelationships result in major differences in the effects of population change between developed and underdeveloped societies and, to a limited extent, how the changes are perceived. Clearly the dramatic decline in fertility and mortality and the rise in life expectancy that have occurred in developed countries have had an immense impact on these societies and in particular on the lives of individuals, even though this impact very rarely has been acknowledged. The rapid population growth and the change in the age structure that have been caused by declining mortality and high fertility in underdeveloped countries are generating intense pressures in these societies.

Depending, of course, on socioeconomic conditions, population growth can result in obstacles to economic growth by affecting savings, investment, and dependency ratios; differential growth of various subpopulations has ethnic and political consequences in that tensions can result from the fact that all groups do not share equally in the advantages and disadvantages of population growth; increased demand for housing, education, employment, and health facilities can occur; growth in the size of bureaucracies in general and of such nongovernmental organizations as business firms, labor unions, political parties, and universities influences society; the need for more government services and more government regulations with the growth of population shapes a society; and changes in demand for services and in lifestyle as a population becomes older or younger have an economic impact. The massive redistribution of population involving rapid urbanization and rural depopulation that occurs with economic development obviously results in radical and fundamental cultural change encompassing all aspects of life.[22]

In the Soviet context, a number of demographic forces will have a discernible impact on Soviet society. These forces include a low and generally declining rate of population growth, sharp regional differentials in rates of population growth, low Slavic and generally moderate to high non-Slavic fertility, an aging "European" population, severe regional labor shortages resulting in part from the fact that migration is not meeting the needs of the economy, widespread rural depopulation in "European" areas, rapidly growing rural populations in many "non-European" areas, rapid urbanization, the maldistribution of population relative to industrial resources, the multinational character of the USSR and the differential mixing and integration of the nationalities into the modern society, and very high and increasing female work force participation rates.

The concept of "forces" or "processes" that "shape" a society may raise the specter of causal mechanisms at work that are independent of any human control, by individuals or even by governments. That they are measured as variables with some quantitative precision may heighten the anxiety of those, sometimes called "indeterminists," who deny determinism and who, for a mixture of reasons, shy away from thinking that anything so impersonal and uncontrollable might be at work shaping their societies.[23] The prospect of any type of determinism may also disturb those who suppose that all determinisms are as simplistic as those that have been based narrowly on environmental (or geographic) or economic factors. As Schaefer has pointed out, just because certain theories based on a narrow interpretation of determinism have been invalidated does not in any way invalidate the general concept of determinism as a means of scientific inquiry.[24]

The main principle of determinism, that all phenomena fall into causal patterns, is as valid for the social as it is for the physical sciences, despite claims for the uniqueness of the person, the complexity of things human, or the necessity of unencumbered moral judgment. The weakness of the argument against determinism in the social sciences has been repeatedly demonstrated.[25] Even if a strict sense of causal determinism such as Hempel's covering-law model of deductive-nomological explanation is insisted upon, there is no necessary conflict between saying that the forces of social change are deterministic and that the individual has both the ability and the right to choose freely.[26] This is particularly true with respect to probabilistic or statistical determinism (soft determinism), which is more appropriate to the social sciences. In either case, only certain outcomes are said to be determined, if certain conditions reach certain specifiable levels. Thus, just as in any scientific generalization, the outcomes are not being said to be necessary absolutely, but only relatively to those initial conditions. There is nothing requiring that the if-clauses of these conditional necessities be forced on us individually. In fact, as David Hume so rightfully notes, it is just those, from whatever motivation, fail to study these "necessities," who are also more likely to be subject to forces beyond their control.[27] Furthermore, social laws do not force upon us or prescribe to us any actions against our will; they merely describe how we behave as a rule under certain conditions. The only world, natural or social, in which policy can work is one organized according to cause-effect necessities, and intelligent policy must be based on knowledge, if and where this is possible, of these forces. One reason that population policies generally have been unsuccessful is that they normally have not been based on a sound knowledge of demographic processes.

No claim is being made that the demographic variables and processes studied here represent the exclusive or total determining factors in Soviet social change. As with any empirical study, it would be rash to claim some special privilege for one's own selection of variables. What is proper to claim is the power that these demographic variables and concepts have in forming working hypotheses of population change and its impact on society. But these working hypotheses must be tested, and they will be vindicated only to the degree they organize and systematize the data that they are applied to, much in the same way a theory systematizes empirical laws under it. Empirical generalizations must be tentative in the face of new experience. Any other attitude toward these instruments of research, which is all one is entitled to think his hypotheses are, is dogmatic.[28] After much refinement of these working hypotheses, and much intellectual effort, one may hope to arrive at something close to a theory in the way Hempel defines it: "a worthwhile scientific theory explains an empirical law by exhibiting it as one aspect of more comprehensive underlying regularities, which have a variety of other testable aspects as well, i.e., which also imply various other empirical laws."[29]

Nor do we claim that universal formulations can completely or always explain population change in the USSR. The initial conditions may differ significantly: often theory is inadequately formulated and frequently data are insufficient. Moreover, there are conditions specific to the USSR that explain aspects of population change. For example, migration theory cannot explain the forced resettlement of the Crimean Tatars; wars, famines, and collectivization have resulted in substantial losses of population and have affected population trends, although primarily in the short term. Long-term trends have been largely affected by the processes of modernization. What we do claim, however, is that the most reasonable approach is first to test general demographic concepts in the USSR to determine if, or to what extent, they explain the processes under investigation, and then to examine conditions specific to the USSR to explain further these processes.

NOTES

1. Some of the writers who have dealt with these unscientific tendencies include Adolph Grunbaum, "Causality and the Science of Human Behavior," in Readings in the Philosophy of Science, eds. Herbert Feigl and May Brodbeck (New York: Appleton-Century-Crofts, 1953), pp. 766-77; Carl G. Hempel, Aspects of Scientific Explanation

(New York: Free Press, 1965), pp. 231-43; Ernest Nagel, The Structure of Science (New York: Harcourt, Brace, and World, 1961), pp. 447-502; and Fred K. Schaefer, "Exceptionalism in Geography: A Methodological Examination," Annals of the Association of American Geographers 43 (September 1953): 226-49.

2. Schaefer, op. cit.

3. William Petersen, Population (London: Macmillan, 1970), pp. 17, 631.

4. Karl Marx, Capital, vol. 1 (New York: International Publishers, 1967), p. 632.

5. V. A. Boldyrev, Ekonomicheskiy Zakon Naseleniya pri Sotsializme (Moscow: Izdatel'stvo "Mysl'," 1968), p. 27.

6. Ibid.

7. B. Ya. Smulevich, Kritika Burzhuaznykh Teorii i Politiki Narodonaseleniya (Moscow: Sotsekgiz, 1959); D. I. Valentey, Reaktsionnye Teorii Narodonaseleniya Perioda Obshchego Krizisa Kapitalizma (Moscow: Izdatel'stvo Sotsial'no-Ekonomicheskoy Literatury, 1963).

8. Some of the more notable writings on this subject include Boldyrev, op. cit.; A. A. Dol'skaya, Sotsialisticheskiy Zakon Narodonaseleniya (Moscow: Sotsekgiz, 1959); Yu. N. Kozyrev, ed., Voprosy Marksistsko-Leninskoy Teorii Narodonaseleniya (Moscow: Izdatel'stvo Moskovskogo Universiteta, 1969); G. A. Slesarev, Metodologiya Sotsiologicheskogo Issledovaniya Problem Narodonaseleniya SSSR (Moscow: Izdatel'stvo "Mysl'," 1965); B. Ya. Smulevich, "K Voprosu o Zakone Narodonaseleniya," in Narodonaseleniya i Ekonomike (Moscow: Izdatel'stvo "Ekonomika," 1967), pp. 14-26; D. I. Valentey, ed., Marksistsko-Leninskaya Teoriya Narodonaseleniya (Moscow: Izdatel'stvo "Mysl'," 1971), pp. 4-47; and D. I. Valentey, Problemy Narodonaseleniya (Moscow: Vysshaya Shkola, 1961).

9. Boldyrev, op. cit., p. 52.

10. N. S. Esipov, "O Zakone Narodonaseleniya Sotsialisticheskogo Obshchestva," in Voprosy Marksistsko-Leninskoy Teorii Narodonaseleniya, ed. Yu. N. Kozyrev (Moscow: Izdatel'stvo Moskovskogo Universiteta, 1969), p. 34.

11. Boldyrev, op. cit., pp. 43-45.

12. Ibid., pp. 45, 75-96.

13. Grunbaum, op. cit.; Hempel, op. cit.; Nagel, op. cit.; and Schaefer, op. cit. For those interested in regions and regional studies, the Schaefer article is particularly instructive.

14. Nagel, op. cit., p. 462.

15. Karl R. Popper, "The Nature of Philosophical Problems and Their Roots in Science," in Plato's Meno, ed. Malcolm Brown (New York: Bobbs Merrill, 1970), pp. 129-30.

16. Alfred G. Meyer, "The Comparative Study of Communist Political Systems," Slavic Review 26 (March 1967): 3-12.

17. Some notable examples of studies on this time include Kingsley Davis, "The Theory of Change and Response in Modern Demographic History," Population Index 29 (October 1963): 346-67; Lincoln H. Day and Alice Taylor Day, "Family Size in Industrialized Countries: An Inquiry into the Social-Cultural Determinants of Levels of Childbearing," Journal of Marriage and the Family 31 (May 1969): 242-51; Calvin Goldscheider, Population, Modernization, and Social Structure (Boston: Little, Brown, 1971); Geoffrey Hawthorn, The Sociology of Fertility (London: Collier-Macmillan, 1970); David M. Heer, "Economic Development and Fertility," Demography 3, no. 2 (1966): 423-44; A. J. Jaffe, Population, Working Force, and Economic Growth: A Preliminary Outline, Centro Latinoamericano de Demografia (CELADE), S. 474/26 (Santiago, Chile, June 1970); Everett S. Lee, "Migration in Relation to Education, Intellect, and Social Structure," Population Index 36 (October-December 1970); 437-43; Irene B. Taeuber, "Demographic Modernization: Continuities and Transition," Demography 3, no. 1 (1966): pp. 90-108; and Joseph J. Spengler, "Values and Fertility Analysis," Demography 3, no. 1 (1966): 109-30.

18. William F. Ogburn, "Social Trends," reprinted in William F. Ogburn on Culture and Social Change, ed. Otis Dudley Duncan (Chicago: University of Chicago Press, 1964), pp. 104-09.

19. D. V. Glass, Population Policies and Movements in Europe (London: Frank Cass and Co., 1967).

20. Kingsley Davis, "Population Policy: Will Current Programs Succeed?" Science 158 (November 10, 1967): 730-39.

21. Tatsuo Honda, Population Problems in Post War Japan (Tokyo: Institute of Population Problems, 1967), pp. 11-13.

22. The following two recent works deal with the impact of population change on society in considerable detail: Neil W. Chamberlain, Beyond Malthus (New York: Basic Books, 1970); and Myron Weiner, "Political Demography: An Inquiry into the Political Consequences of Population Change," in Rapid Population Growth: Consequences and Policy Implications, ed. Roger Revelle (Baltimore: Johns Hopkins Press, 1971), pp. 567-617.

23. Grunbaum, op. cit.

24. Schaefer, op. cit.

25. Hempel, op. cit.; Nagel, op. cit.; and Schaefer, op. cit.

26. Hempel, op. cit.

27. David Hume, "Liberty and Necessity," in An Enquiry Concerning Human Understanding. I. Enquiries Concerning the Human Understanding and Concerning the Principles of Morals, ed. L. A. Selby-Bigge, 2d ed. (Oxford: Clarendon Press, 1902), pp. 80-96.

28. Willard Van Orman Quine, From a Logical Point of View (New York: Harper & Row, 1963), p. 44.

29. Hempel, op. cit., p. 444.

BACKGROUND MATERIALS
TO THE SERIES

1

MODERNIZATION AND
POPULATION CHANGE

This study proposes to describe and explain population change in Russia and the Soviet Union. Population change may be defined as changes in the numbers, geographic distribution, and characteristics of a population, including, for our purposes, the demographic trends of mortality, fertility, and migration, and such socioeconomic aspects as urbanization, work force participation, education, and the status of women. To describe and document demographic and socioeconomic trends may provide new and useful information, particularly if, as is the case in this study, such changes have not been known adequately before. To explain these changes, however, one requires a schema that will systematize the various elements of population change, link population change to social change in general, and incorporate concepts that provide a significant degree of explanation for the phenomena involved. The schema that best satisfies these requirements is the process of social change known as modernization.[1] Although it is clear that not all aspects of population change can be directly attributed to modernization (the effects of events such as war, famine, and mass or forced migration must be taken into account), this dramatic form of social change has had a profound impact upon the population of any society that has modernized.

It is not, however, the primary purpose of this study to investigate the interrelationships between population change and modernization. Rather, it is the authors' intention to draw from the demographic literature those concepts relating to the effects of modernization upon population change, briefly discuss the linkages between modernization and population change, and, finally, define broadly the relationships between modernization and the individual elements of population change (mortality, fertility, migration, urbanization, and so forth). We might

add at this point that modernization and population change are mutually
influencing, but the concern of this discussion is the effect of modernization on population change.

SUMMARY DISCUSSION

The process of social change known as modernization provides
a schema for the description and explanation of population change.
Population change is one aspect of modernization, which also includes
economic development, changes in social and political structure, and
changes in attitudes and values. Economic development, through the
creation of job opportunities in nonagricultural sectors, is the major
agent of population change. Clearly, however, modernization is not
the only force influencing population change; war, famine, forced or
mass migration, and assimilation must be taken into account.

Those elements of population change with which we are concerned are fertility, mortality, urbanization, migration, education,
work force, and the status of women. With modernization and economic development, dramatic changes occur among all elements of
population change. Mortality declines with improved agricultural
technology, food distribution, and public health. Fertility declines
as family size is controlled to facilitate the attainment of social and
economic aspirations, as the economic utility of children decreases,
as family structures realign, and as women enter the modern work
force. Urbanization takes place as people leave rural areas for job
opportunities in the cities. Substantial migration occurs, from rural-
to-urban places and from one region to another, because economic
development normally takes place in a few areas and in cities. Modernization and economic development are also associated with higher
levels of education, a shift from agricultural to nonagricultural employment, and the gradual integration of women into modern sectors.

The elements of population change interact with the other aspects of modernization and with one another. Thus, significant relationships exist between urbanization and fertility, fertility and the
status of women, the status of women and education, and so on. Finally, those demographic changes associated with modernization appear to have been virtually universal, occurring in all countries that
have modernized.

DETAILED DISCUSSION

The study of the process of social change known as modernization has developed into one of the primary focuses of the social

sciences. Indeed, the development of the various disciplines of the social sciences was largely coincidental with, and to different degrees influenced by, the transformation of society in Western Europe and the United States during the eighteenth and nineteenth centuries, a transformation that has served as the model for modernization. Because of this proximity, modernization studies for some time were concerned with documenting and identifying the "Western" model of modernization, which is understandable inasmuch as these were the first areas to modernize and the first countries for which extensive socioeconomic data were available.[2] This retrospective view has generated a large and useful literature on the background and effects of the modernization process, although much of the work is implicitly evolutionary and ethnocentric (with modernization equaling "Westernization") with respect to non-Western modernized societies such as Japan. A significant factor contributing to the continuing relevance and importance attached to the study of modernization is the increasingly critical social and economic situation of many contemporary developing countries. The apparent failure in effecting large-scale social and economic changes in these societies has resulted in the realization among scholars and planners that modernization is a far more complex process than originally thought, and that new dimensions must be added to the basic modernization model patterned after the Western European experience.[3]

Because modernization encompasses changes in virtually all aspects of society, there is a very real problem of defining this process of social change without being trivial, on the one hand, or tautological, on the other. Various scholars have viewed modernization from different perspectives, often from within the confines of academic disciplines or topical interests. Yet it appears there is a consensus that modernization is best defined broadly to include a number of more limited aspects of social change that can, in turn, be examined in greater detail. Thus, for our purposes, modernization is defined as that form of social change encompassing the changes in the economic, technological, demographic, political, social, and psychological aspects of human society that began in Western Europe around 1800. Briefly, these changes included significant increases in economic production (the Industrial Revolution), advances in technology and science (particularly the use of inanimate sources of power), consolidation of nation-states as forms of political organization, a realignment of family structures and a diminution of the importance of kinship, a change from ascriptive to achievement status, and increased motivation and achievement orientation. Demographic changes were integral to the modernization process. Furthermore, the recognition of the mutually reinforcing relationships among these aspects of modernization is included in the definition.

It is not feasible, given the state of knowledge concerning modernization and the complex interrelationships among its components, to attempt an analysis of all aspects of modernization, even when restricted to one country. Accordingly, we will extract concepts selectively from the vast literature on modernization that pertain directly to the demographic changes that are the focus of this study. We will discuss two of the major components of modernization relating to population change: economic development and the shift from ascriptive to merit or achievement systems and the "rationalization" of society. Other important features of the modernization process, such as the role of the political leadership in implementing social and economic change, will receive little attention here.[4]

It is not our intention, for example, to examine the motives of the Soviet government in the adoption of a system of forced, rapid industrialization and modernization. Rather, we are concerned with the resulting demographic changes brought about by modernization, regardless of the manner in which modernization was implemented. Indications are that these demographic changes are similar in all societies that have modernized, with differences being of degree and not of kind.

Economic development, largely through its most important constitutent, industrialization, is the driving force behind the modernization process, and is the basis for most population change. Economic development is used here in its broad sense of representing per capita increases in production and efficiency, changes in productive and market relationships, and structural changes in the economy.[5] Industrialization is viewed in this study as a more limited case of economic development, referring in particular to manufacturing and mining.

A number of reasons have been proposed to explain the origins of economic development, and, although there is no general agreement on this issue, the influence of technological change, personality traits and religion, political organization, demographic forces, natural resources, and social organization are generally accepted as contributing to one degree or another.[6] Whatever the origins of economic development, it is clear that the socioeconomic opportunities created by expanding economies have provided the motivation for substantial population change. As the individual's horizons are expanded by the perception of new opportunities, demographic behavior may be altered to facilitate the achievement of aspirations. If opportunities for social and economic advancement do not exist, there may be little reason to alter demographic behavior. Thus, fertility may be controlled because large families hinder the attainment of personal social and economic goals. The existence of economic opportunity in urban areas and certain regions has been the most important determinant of

migration. The influence of economic development upon the elements
of population change will be discussed in succeeding sections.

Modernization often has been characterized as consisting in
part of changes in sociopsychological behavior, the well-known shift
from ascriptive to achievement status and the increase in rational
achievement motivation.[7] We might object to the term "rational" if,
as is often implied, more traditional forms of behavior are, by definition, "irrational." In the case of demographic behavior, for example,
the traditional desire of a farmer in India to have four sons to support
him in his old age is eminently rational in the absence of social insur-
ance. We would suggest that with modernization, demographic behavior becomes rationalized to a new set of circumstances and opportunities, circumstances and opportunities engendered largely by economic development. Nevertheless, the transformation of social
values, attitudes concerning change, status, and behavior are clearly
integral parts of the modernization syndrome and influence other aspects of the process, such as economic development and population
change.

One crucial aspect of modernization and economic development
is that within a given society these forces are likely to influence different segments of society, and different regions of a country to greater
or lesser degrees. This differential impact of modernization is owing
primarily to existing systems of stratification or sanctions, to differences in institutions and attitudes regarding change, and to regional
differences in natural resources and other factors of production that
influence the allocation of investment and economic development. The
many opportunities for social mobility created by modernization, unless they are distributed on a reasonably equal basis to all segments
of society and regions of a country, may exacerbate tensions between
groups. This seems particularly true of multinational states, where
the benefits of society rarely are distributed equitably in the first
place. Thus, modernization may produce destabilizing forces in
previously stable societies, particularly if some groups perceive increased opportunities but, for various reasons, do not participate
fully in the modernization process.

In summary, modernization is a complex form of social change
involving economic development, technological change, population
change, changes in the political system, and a transformation of attitudes and values. Social institutions and structures become increasingly
differentiated, new roles are assigned to kinship and family, and status shifts from ascription to achievement.[8] All aspects of modernization are interrelated, with economic development assuming the primary role. Population change, as one aspect of modernization, is influenced for the most part by economic development and the socioeconomic opportunities generated thereby through the increased aspira-

tions of individuals to realize these opportunities. In the following
sections we will examine in greater detail the relationship between
modernization-economic development and the individual elements of
population change.

Urbanization

Of all the facets of population change associated with modernization, perhaps no other has been as dramatic and visible as the urbanization of human society. Although there is some disagreement
among scholars regarding the nature of urban-modern as opposed to
rural-traditional life-styles, nevertheless it is clear that urbanization
has had a strong impact upon society and particularly upon other demographic trends. Although cities have existed for centuries, the trend
toward urbanization began in Western Europe around 1800; the rate
at which the urban population has increased since that time has far
outstripped total population growth, and the high growth rate of the
urban population has accelerated consistently in relation to total population growth. Thus, the percentage of the world's population living
in urban areas has steadily increased since 1800; in 1800, 2.4 percent of the total population lived in cities of over 20,000; in 1850,
4.3 percent; in 1900, 9.2 percent; in 1950, 20.9 percent; and by
1970 the urban population had grown to 28.2 percent of the world's
population.[9] Urbanization has reached its highest levels in those
countries that have modernized; in Western Europe, the United States
and Canada, Japan, Australia, and New Zealand. Although international comparisons are difficult because of different definitions of "urban," it is safe to say that as of 1970 all of these modernized countries have over 65 percent of their populations in urban areas.[10]
Urban populations in contemporary developing countries range generally between 10 and 40 percent of the population, with levels inclined
to be lower in Africa and Asia and higher in Eastern Europe and Latin
America.[11] This section describes the relationships between urbanization and its correlates (principally economic development and industrialization), details the linkages between urbanization and other elements of population change, and, finally, examines the concepts concerning the impact of urban life upon society.

Initially, however, the distinction between urbanization and urban growth should be briefly considered because the two terms are often confused and they represent somewhat different processes. Urbanization can be defined as the process of population concentration
involving an increase in the percentage of the total population residing
in urban areas (that is, the level of urbanization) by whatever criteria
these urban areas are defined. Urban growth refers simply to an in-

crease in the urban population itself; urbanization takes this one step further by comparing urban growth with the change in the total or the rural population. It is, therefore, possible to have significant urban growth without urbanization, if rural population growth equals or exceeds urban growth.[12] Urbanization entails a structural change in the total population, with an increasing share of the populace living in cities and a decreasing share in rural areas. The social and economic impact of such a transformation upon society has been profound, as will be discussed.

The increasing levels of urbanization associated with modernization have been coincident with, and, to a large degree, brought about by, economic development and industrialization. At the outset we must note that this relationship, like virtually all social and economic relationships, is not a perfect one, and there are deviations from the positive correlation between increased urbanization and economic development-industrialization, both in a temporal sense and in regard to individual cities. In the initial stages of economic development, for instance, labor available in the cities may satisfy demand, delaying rural-to-urban migration. Labor intensity in the industrialization process is also an important factor in determining labor requirements and thus the rate of urbanization. Since urbanization is a finite process (100 percent is the limit) and economic development presumably is not, the relationship between the two processes diverges in later stages of modernization.[13] Yet the two processes of urbanization and economic development-industrialization have generally been complementary. Economic development, particularly industrialization, provided the impetus for urbanization by creating job opportunities that attracted migrants from rural areas.[14] The application of increasingly more advanced technologies and a higher degree of labor specialization supported higher levels of urbanization.[15] The concentration of population in cities aided economic development by providing adequate labor, both in numbers and with requisite skills, facilitating economies of scale, facilitating interindustry transportation, and providing large markets.[16] Thus, economic development-industrialization and urbanization have been mutually reinforcing trends, with each providing conditions that sustain the other.

Urbanization as an element of population change is linked with other demographic trends associated with modernization. Investigators have noted that fertility is lower in urban than in rural places,[17] and we have already noted that urbanization was caused in part by the migration of people from rural to urban areas. Both of these demographic phenomena are, in turn, related to the existence of socioeconomic opportunity in urban areas. Urban areas are the most modern areas, areas of maximum upward social mobility and opportunities for economic advancement, and, as people aspire to achieve these

higher levels, large families may stand in the way. Lower urban fertility is therefore an indicator of modernization in that lower fertility
entails an appraisal of the role of children, which takes into account
the aspirations of parents for socioeconomic achievement. Not to be
overlooked, of course, is the fact that children may have become economic liabilities in cities (particularly with the enactment of social
welfare legislation that reduced their labor value), whereas in rural
areas their labor had been an asset.[18]

Migration as an element of population change associated with
modernization has two facets: rural-to-urban migration, on the one
hand, and intraregional, interregional, and/or international migration,
on the other. The two are not mutually exclusive because a large
share of intraregional, interregional, and international migration is
also rural-to-urban. It is logical here to dichotomize the migration
component and to discuss rural-to-urban migration together with urbanization, and to consider migration in general in a later section.
Just as the existence of socioeconomic opportunities in the cities influenced fertility, so did it attract migrants from rural areas. As is
the case with most migration, the pull of job opportunities in urban
areas was usually combined with a push from rural areas resulting
from poor agricultural conditions, excessive population growth, mechanization of agriculture, and consequent decline in the demand for
rural labor—in short, a lack of opportunities in rural areas. In addition to job opportunities, the cities are also cultural, political, and
educational centers, and have an attraction beyond the purely economic. Rural-to-urban migration provided substantial shares of the
growth of cities associated with urbanization, supplementing to varying degrees the natural increase of the cities themselves. Indeed,
in-migration to cities was especially important in the past as many
cities were characterized by natural decrease due to high urban mortality.[19]

In addition to fertility and migration, urbanization has been
linked to other elements of population change, such as education and
the structure of the labor force. Educational levels attained by the
population are almost universally higher in urban than in rural areas.
The urban labor force is naturally concentrated in nonagricultural occupations; with advanced economic development and urbanization, the
service (tertiary) sector assumes increasing importance.

The impact of urbanization upon society has been profound, but
recent experience, particularly that stemming from the developing
countries, suggests that qualifications are required in the general
concepts concerning the nature of societal transformations associated
with urbanization. The dichotomy of so-called folk-urban ideal types
suggested by Robert Redfield and Louis Wirth,[20] among others, which
counterposed urban and rural societies in terms of values, goals, and

societal relations, has been called into question by others who point
to the maintenance of "traditional" practices and values in urban
areas and the existence of "nontraditional" traits in rural areas.[21]
Research in some urban areas has shown that rural in-migrants ease
their transition to urban life through various social institutions and
by residential congregation.[22] At this point it seems unclear as to
the exact means by which rural dwellers adapt to demographic behavior
that is more rational in an urban setting, although the availability of
education and socioeconomic opportunity is clearly a necessary factor.[23]
Urban residence is not always a sufficient condition to influence demographic behavior, but rather it must be combined with socioeconomic
opportunity, which, in the past (but not necessarily in contemporary
developing countries), was located mainly in the cities. Also it appears that at least two generations are required to complete the transition from rural to urban life. Thus, our view of cities as the centers of modernization may accord well with a retrospective analysis
of modern societies, but may need some modification for understanding those countries that are only now modernizing. Nevertheless,
urbanization is still a strong indicator of modernization.

Fertility and Mortality

Within the last century another change in human population dynamics has taken place that rivals urbanization in importance: the
transition from high to low fertility in modernized countries. Illustrative of the nature of the decline in fertility are historical data from
two modernized countries, one European and one Asian. In England
and Wales, the crude birthrate per thousand population fell from 34
in 1850 to 27 in 1900 and to 15 in 1950.[24] The crude birthrate in
Japan dropped from 36.1 in 1920 to 19.3 in 1955.[25] The current
(1971) crude birthrates in these countries are England and Wales,
16; Japan, 19.[26] By contrast, generally high levels of fertility characterize contemporary underdeveloped countries. For example, the
most recent data indicate that the crude birthrates in most of Asia,
Africa, and South America remain over 40 per thousand and in some
instances well above that level.[27]
    The nature and determinants of fertility are the most compli-
cated and least understood of the demographic process. Yet the fertility decline that occurred in the modernized countries perhaps can
be explained best by relating this dramatic trend to the broad social
and economic transformation of society associated with modernization.
Modernization and its components provide a reasonable framework for
examining the levels of and decline in fertility, as well as contributing
to an explanation of the phenomenon. As is the case with any facet of

population change, fertility trends have been influenced by social, cultural, and economic forces not associated with modernization, but in general the forces of modernization have no doubt accounted for the vast majority of the transition to low fertility. The decline in fertility in modernized countries must be examined together with levels of mortality because both trends are related to modernization and to one another, and, taken together, determine the rate of population growth. Therefore, a brief exposition of the trends in mortality will precede a more general discussion of modernization and fertility.

Mortality in all modern countries was universally high prior to the eighteenth century, although there were some local and temporal fluctuations around the high mortality levels, as well as socioeconomic class differentials.[28] After the mid-eighteenth century, declines in mortality began in Western Europe, with the timing of the declines varying from one country to another depending upon the spread of the determinants of lower mortality. The decline of mortality has been attributed to a number of factors, notably improvements in agricultural technology and production, higher standards of living, improved public health and sanitation, and the consolidation of governmental control over national territories, which facilitated improvements in commerce and transportation and reduced civil violence.[29] Although data documenting the decline in mortality are incomplete, it is illustrative to note that life expectancy at birth in Western Europe and the United States increased from between 30 and 35 years around 1700 to about 70 years in 1970.[30] Mortality levels among young children were generally the last to decline, probably because more pervasive social and economic changes were required to effect a decline in infant mortality.[31] In modern societies, mortality differentials often remain among socioeconomic classes and between racial and/or ethnic groups, reflecting the influence of the standard of living upon mortality.[32] Mortality levels have declined dramatically in underdeveloped countries since World War II, largely owing to the transfer of public health techniques and, in some instances, agricultural technology from more advanced countries. Significant declines in mortality may be achieved by this diffusion of technology without appreciable social and economic change.[33]

The growth of population is, as noted, a function of the levels of fertility and mortality (assuming, of course, no migration). Premodern societies maintained relatively stable populations by balancing high mortality with high fertility. The decline in mortality resulted, therefore, in dramatic population growth as long as the high rates of fertility persisted. In time, however, fertility also declined, establishing a new balance around low levels of fertility and mortality (not an exact balance, since fertility remains sufficiently higher than mortality to afford substantial population growth). This progression of mortality and fertility from high to low levels, with the fertility decline lagging behind declines in mortality in the sequence, is known as the "demographic transition." The concept of the demographic transition describes the general pattern of population trends that occurred in Western Europe and other modernized countries; an explanation for the decline in fertility depends upon knowledge of the social and economic determinants of human reproductive behavior.

Fertility and its decline were for many years viewed as determined by the availability and adoption of contraceptive devices and strategies. It now appears certain that, although knowledge of and access to the means for contraception is a useful and highly desirable social goal, contraception as an explanation for fertility decline is mechanistic and inconsistent with fact.[34] Substantial evidence exists that indicates that societies controlled fertility at least to some extent before the advent of modern contraception.[35] On the other hand, the availability of contraceptive devices in the underdeveloped world of today has failed to induce any significant reduction in the birthrate in these areas.[36] The question therefore devolves to why fertility is controlled, rather than how. Furthermore, premodern fertility differentials and the decline of fertility in all segments of modernized societies suggest that the transition to low fertility resulted from the intensification of fertility control in response to some stimulus—an adjustment rather than an innovation.[37]

It is becoming increasingly clear that the decline in fertility resulted from the restructuring of society that accompanied modernization, and that economic development was the prime mover in this process. Modernization and economic development, in effect, shift population into social groups where lower fertility is the norm: from rural to urban areas, farmer to industrial worker, lower to middle class, illiterate to educated.[38] Lower fertility is the norm in these groups, in part because of changes in social structure (kinship relationships), but more important because of the higher standards of living, upward social and economic mobility, and heightened aspirations engendered by industrialization and economic development.[39] Kingsley Davis has suggested that the high levels of population growth that resulted from the decline in mortality were incompatible with the desire to participate in the expanding economic sector associated with modernization. Thus, "Under a prolonged drop in mortality with industrialization, people in northwest Europe and Japan found that their accustomed demographic behavior was handicapping them in their effort to take advantage of the opportunities being provided by the emerging economy. They accordingly began changing their behavior."[40] D. V. Glass, however, in a critique of the Davis formulation, stresses rising aspirations rather than the decline in mortality.[41] Undoubtedly, both factors are influential.

The foregoing discussion should not convey the impression that modernization and its concomitants will necessarily cause a decline in fertility in some mechanistic fashion, nor is it true that all fertility declines were a result of modernization. Rather, we suggest that modernization-economic development is the usual process by which sufficient changes have been effected in the social and economic structure of society that, in turn, resulted in more intensive population control. Furthermore, if the extent of economic development is not such that, at the very least, significant socioeconomic opportunities are available, the relationship between modernization and fertility declines will no doubt be negated.[42] Thus, we can agree with Calvin Goldscheider:

> Some conditions—urbanization, industrial development, labor force participation of women, stabilization and reduction in mortality levels, education, among others—may bring about these institutional and structural changes, thereby generating pressures indirectly toward family size control. But they may not necessarily bring about these institutional changes. If urbanization reflects the relocation of kin groupings and does not disengage effectively kin control and power, if industrial development does not result in rising aspirations for mobility, if labor force participation of women does not provide alternative sources of prestige and status to women and does not result in releasing women from male or kinship domination, if educational advances are focused on specialized socioeconomic groups and not dispersed more widely throughout all segments of the population, if mortality reduction is brought about through medical and technological diffusion without changes in living standards, then it is likely that these specific changes will not result in the necessary pressures engendering fertility reduction.[43]

The chief point is that a minimum threshold of sustained economic development is required to bring about the necessary socioeconomic change that results in a decline in fertility.

The impact of changes in the levels of fertility upon society, as well as the implications behind the absence of such changes, is considerable. High fertility, when combined with low mortality, results in high rates of population growth, which historically have necessitated social and demographic responses. The most common response to population growth has been migration, both interregional and rural-

to-urban, and, with modernization, significant fertility control.[44]
High rates of population growth seriously impede economic development by requiring massive investments simply to maintain per capita
levels of capital, and strains upon the economy to provide adequate
education and health facilities for the expanding population are severe.[45]
Conversely, lower fertility (and hence a lower rate of population growth)
may facilitate economic development, as was apparently the case in
Europe during the Industrial Revolution.[46] Finally, regional differentials in population growth, often associated with unequal regional economic development, and differentials in fertility and population growth
among various social, economic, and ethnic groups result in changes
in the spatial distribution and composition of society, changes that
most societies must strain to accommodate.

Migration

The migration of population to cities and regions of industrial
growth is another aspect of population change that historically has
been associated with modernization and economic development. Migration, when defined as permanent or semipermanent changes in
residence (in contrast to nomadic wanderings or seasonal migrations),
is a useful indicator of population change and modernization; modernized societies have been characterized by significant geographic mobility. The volume of migration directly related to modernization and
economic development has been substantial, considering the totality
of rural-to-urban, intraregional, interregional, and international
movements.

It would be an oversight to omit rural-to-rural migration as an
important element in population change, because such movements
have been significant in the past. In many respects, however, these
movements have little in common with modernization, although the
declines in mortality associated with modernization may have prompted
out-migration. Our focus is modernization and population change;
therefore, rural-to-rural movements will be considered in this study
only briefly.

This study of migration, as well as the use of migration as an
indicator of modernization, centers around the economic motivations
behind the movement of population. We recognize, of course, that
countless folk through the ages, refugees or displaced persons, have
migrated in response to noneconomic forces, such as religious, racial, or political persecutions. We can take little account of them
here beyond the recognition and assessment of those movements of a
forced or idiosyncratic nature that fall within the scope of this study;
any explanation of these movements will be of an individual nature and

largely beyond the framework of our analysis. Other forms of migration, such as the premodern movements of peoples responding to population pressures or natural calamities, or the modern movement of retired persons and others to regions that offer environmental or cultural amenities, are likewise not the major concern here. The migration with which we are concerned—that which is economically motivated —has been the most important in modernized societies.

Migration related to modernization and economic development can be considered as a function of push-pull forces, or those conditions, largely economic, obtaining at the points of origin (push) and destinations (pull). Between the origin and potential destination are other considerations, termed "intervening obstacles" by Everett Lee, that impede movement to varying degrees and at different times for diverse classes of migrants.[47] There are other influences upon the decision to migrate, such as the availability of information concerning conditions at both the origin and destination and the inertia that mitigates against any move. Yet the basic conceptualization of migration as a balancing of conditions, particularly those relating to economic opportunities, provides the framework for discussing the majority of moves connected with modernization.

In historical perspective, the high rates of population growth in rural agricultural areas, brought about by declines in mortality during the initial stages of modernization, created a strong push force that resulted in out-migration. In many instances, poor conditions in agriculture exacerbated the pressure on the land, and eventually the mechanization of agriculture contributed to a labor surplus in rural areas. Combined with these push forces in rural areas were the pull forces of opportunity engendered by economic development and industrialization. The location of economic development was, for the most part, confined to urban areas, to specific regions, and to certain countries; thus, streams of migrants were directed along the economic gradient to cities and to developing regions and countries. The function of migration has been, therefore, to balance the supply of and demand for labor between rural and urban areas and among regions and countries, thereby facilitating economic development.[48] The well-documented experience of the United States and Japan is illustrative of the redistribution of population to areas of economic development.[49] Simon Kuznets has summarized this process as follows:

> Internal migration and the redistribution of population by residence among various parts of the country are a major way in which people respond to changing economic opportunities emerging in the course of economic growth. Not all internal migration is in response to economic growth; and not all the oppor-

tunities emerging in the course of growth require a
shift of residence to be converted into realized economic advances. But migration induced by growth
that promises greater opportunities has been sufficiently massive in the presently advanced countries
to warrant the view that the relation between population redistribution and economic development is
an important and indispensable link in the mechanism
of modern economic growth.[50]

Migration is a demographic phenomenon fraught with consequences for both the sending and receiving communities. Because
migration tends to be selective of certain groups within society—
young adults (at times, men predominate and, at other times, women),
persons with certain skills or qualifications—the age and sex structure of the population, as well as other aspects, at both origin and
destination of the migration stream are affected. Furthermore, the
movement of people from rural areas into cities, as well as from one
region of a country to another (particularly if different ethnic groups
or races are involved), is a potentially disjunctive process, as individuals are shifted into unfamiliar or even hostile social and economic
environments. The historical migration of individuals from areas of
lesser to greater opportunities, across natural and political boundaries, often in the face of uncertainty and physical danger, testifies
to the attraction of areas of economic development.

Education

The level of educational attainment is yet another characteristic
of a population that is associated with modernization; those countries
that have modernized are distinguished by educational levels considerably higher, both quantitatively and qualitatively, than the levels in
developing countries.[51] The education process is linked directly to
economic development, with education facilitating economic development and, in return, being stimulated by the demand for educated persons required by the expanding economy. There are, of course, important benefits to be derived from education in addition to those related directly to economic growth, such as the development of an in-
formed electorate and, on the personal level, the exposure to and appreciation of enriching knowledge and experiences. Yet the focus of
modernization studies that include an investigation of the education
process has been on the relationship between economic development
and education, perhaps because of the "applied" nature of many of
these studies.

It remains unclear whether education initially served to bring
about economic development or whether economic development created
the demand and incentive for and means of attaining higher and more
extensive education. It is clear, however, that education and economic
development are closely allied and mutually reinforcing. In a practical sense, an educated populace facilitates economic development by
providing workers with basic skills such as the ability to read, write,
and compute, as well as equipping them with concepts that make it
easier to grasp technical training on the job.[52] Also, a broad educational base contributes to advances in knowledge (particularly in research and technology) and to more efficient management and administration.[53] Economists have concluded that, although difficult to
measure, the contribution of education to economic growth has been
substantial.[54]

In addition to the role of schooling in economic development, the
education process is an integral part of social change in general, and
is related to population change in particular. The educational levels
of a population are associated with other demographic characterstics:
education is inversely related to fertility, and positively related to
some forms of migration, to the occupational structure, and with urbanization.[55] Hopefully, it is not trivial to point to the schools as instruments of social change, as environments in which young persons
become increasingly aware of wider social, economic, and intellectual
horizons.[56]

Education should not be considered in isolation, but rather as
one element of modernization and social change that influences demographic behavior in conjunction with other elements. For example,
as noted, educational levels within a society are generally inversely
related to fertility, but other variables associated with education no
doubt influence this relationship; educational attainment is positively
associated with income and urbanization, both of which are also inversely related to fertility. Thus, education may influence demographic
behavior, probably by enhancing aspirations and by providing the
means for attaining social and economic goals, but education alone
does not explain variations in other characteristics of a population.

Work Force

Another aspect of population change associated with modernization is the change in the composition of the work force. Basically,
the major change in the work force that accompanies economic development and modernization is the shift from agricultural to nonagricultural employment.[57] This movement out of agriculture into the nonagricultural work force, prompted in part by higher wages in the mod-

ern sector and often by poor conditions in rural-agricultural areas, is associated with economic development-industrialization and urbanization. It should be noted, however, that in some countries (New Zealand, for instance), a substantial shift out of agriculture resulted not so much from industrialization as from the development of specialized and modern agriculture.[58] At any rate, a high percentage of workers employed in nonagricultural pursuits is characteristic of modernized societies. Within the modern sector there will be a shift from secondary (manufacturing, blue collar) to tertiary (services, white collar) occupations as economic development progresses.[59]

Status of Women

The final aspect of population change associated with modernization is the change in the status of women within society. The principal feature among those facets of the changing position of women in modernizing societies with which we will concern ourselves is the increasing participation of females in the modern sectors of the economy. In developing societies there may be a relatively high level of work force participation by women, not only in the agricultural sector but also in lower level service jobs. As economic development progresses, however, more and more women enter the modern nonagricultural sectors. The prime mover in this process seems to be the increasing levels of education among women, education that enhances the desire for and facilitates the attainment of jobs in the expanding economy.[60]

The most important facet of work force participation by women with regard to other aspects of population change is the lower fertility among working women.[61] It is important here to distinguish between women employed in the modern economy and those working in agriculture and home (cottage) industries, because the latter form of employment is not necessarily linked with lower fertility.[62] The lower fertility among women employed in the modern sectors is probably attributable to the higher levels of education among these women, as well as to the aspirations and nonfamilial rewards (including financial gains) associated with such pursuits.[63] Finally, the lower fertility of working women may facilitate an early return to the work force as children enter school and require less direct supervision by the parents.[64]

PRELIMINARY PROPOSITIONS

It should be clear now that population change and its relationship to modernization is complicated, with all constituent elements being associated with one another through linkages that are not completely understood. The fact remains that in the great majority of cases, the impact of modernization, operating principally through economic development, has been to induce changes in the composition, rate of growth, and distribution of a given population. Although we can offer only tentative explanations for these changes, nevertheless, we can propose a normative model of demographic trends associated with modernization. The following propositions, based upon the more detailed, preceding sections, summarize the changes in demographic characteristics that can be expected in conjunction with modernization and economic development. Many of these propositions, or hypotheses, will subsequently be tested in the Soviet context, and their results will be used to provide explanations for population change in Russia and the USSR.

Proposition 1. Urbanization. The level of urbanization of a country will increase as modernization progresses.

Subsidiary Proposition 1a. Urbanization will be inversely related to fertility levels. Fertility will be lower in urban than in rural areas.

Subsidiary Proposition 1b. Urbanization will be positively associated with migration. There will be more migrants in urban than in rural areas.

Subsidiary Proposition 1c. Urbanization will be positively associated with levels of the nonagricultural work force. Urbanization has been linked to economic development; the growth of the nonagricultural work force is a good indicator of economic development; therefore, urbanization and the growth of the nonagricultural work force should be related. It goes almost without saying that most nonagricultural jobs are in cities.

Subsidiary Proposition 1d. Urbanization will be positively associated with higher levels of educational attainment. The level of education in the cities will be higher than in rural areas.

Proposition 2. Fertility and Mortality. The levels of fertility and mortality in a society will decrease as modernization progresses.

Subsidiary Proposition 2a. The level of fertility will be inversely related to the level of urbanization. Fertility will be lower in urban than in rural areas.

Subsidiary Proposition 2b. The level of fertility will be inversely related to the level of educational attainment. Areas of higher educational levels will be characterized by lower fertility.

Subsidiary Proposition 2c. The level of fertility will be inversely related to the level of female participation in the nonagricultural modern work force.

Proposition 3. Migration. With modernization there will be a substantial movement of persons from rural to urban areas and to regions of economic development.

Subsidiary Proposition 3a. Migration will be positively associated with urbanization. There will be more migrants in urban than in rural areas.

Subsidiary Proposition 3b. Migration will be positively associated with increases in the nonagricultural work force. If an increase in the nonagricultural work force is viewed as an indicator of the extent of economic development, then migration to areas of economic development should coincide with changes in the work force.

Proposition 4. Education. As modernization progresses, the levels of educational attainment of the population will increase.

Subsidiary Proposition 4a. The level of education will be positively related to urbanization. Educational levels will be higher in cities than in rural areas.

Subsidiary Proposition 4b. The level of education will be positively related to the percentage of the work force engaged in nonagricultural pursuits. Educational levels will be higher among workers in the nonagricultural sectors than among farmers.

Subsidiary Proposition 4c. The level of education will be inversely related to the level of fertility. Groups with higher levels of education will be characterized by lower fertility.

Proposition 5. Work Force. With modernization and economic development, there will occur a shift of workers out of agriculture and into nonagricultural pursuits.

Subsidiary Proposition 5a. The levels of participation in the nonagricultural work force will be positively associated with urbanization.

Subsidiary Proposition 5b. The percentage of the work
force in nonagricultural pursuits will be positively associated with migration.

Subsidiary Proposition 5c. As economic development
progresses, an increasing share of the nonagricultural work force will be in the tertiary
(service, white collar) sector.

Subsidiary Proposition 5d. Levels of participation in the
nonagricultural work force will be positively
associated with higher levels of education.

Proposition 6. The Status of Women. As modernization progresses,
women will enter into advanced sectors of society to an
increasing degree.

Subsidiary Proposition 6a. With modernization, women
will enter the nonagricultural work force to an
increasing degree.

Subsidiary Proposition 6b. The entrance of women into
the advanced work force will be positively associated with higher levels of education among
women.

Subsidiary Proposition 6c. The participation of women in
the nonagricultural modern sectors of the
economy will be inversely associated with
levels of fertility.

The propositions listed above may be applied to regions of a
country as well as to groups within a society. In other words, regions
of a country that have undergone modernization and economic development will be characterized by demographic features common to all
modernized areas (high urbanization, low fertility, higher educational
levels, in-migration, large nonagricultural work force), whereas
those regions lacking economic development will be characterized by
demographic features associated with modernizing or underdeveloped
areas (low urbanization, higher fertility, lower educational levels,
out-migration, large agricultural work force). Likewise, various
groups within a society, particularly ethnic groups, may be differentially integrated into the modernized sectors; therefore, these groups
will be characterized by demographic features commensurate with the
extent to which they participate in advanced society. In a later chapter several explanations are proposed for the differential integration
of various groups into the modern sector.

Finally, we should emphasize once again that the elements of
population change (fertility, mortality, migration, urbanization, education, work force) are influenced by more general forces of social

change such as modernization and, in return, demographic forces shape social change to some degree. Demographic characteristics, therefore, may be considered as indicators of the extent to which modernization and economic development have progressed. We do not, however, propose to label a group or region as modernized simply because its demographic characteristics resemble those of other societies or countries. It is clearly incumbent upon us to offer at least partial explanations or linkages whereby modernization has resulted in demographic change. In the foregoing sections we have discussed the relationships between modernization and the elements of population change, focusing primarily on the role of economic development, which, in our opinion, provides at least the core of these linkages. We would suggest that the interaction of the social and economic forces associated with modernization and economic development has resulted in identifiable and remarkably similar population change in virtually all instances and across cultural lines. The absence of substantial demographic change in the contemporary underdeveloped world (excepting, of course, declines in mortality) is very probably a reflection of the absence of the more general social and economic change that influenced population change in the West and in Japan. Thus, it would appear that modernization and economic development provide both an explanation for a significant share of population change and a convenient framework for analyzing these trends.

NOTES

1. This essentially is the approach suggested by Calvin Goldscheider, Population, Modernization and Social Structure (Boston: Little, Brown, 1971), Chap. 4.

2. Ian Weinberg, "The Concept of Modernization: An Unfinished Chapter in Sociological Theory," in Perspectives on Modernization, ed. Edward B. Harvey (Toronto: University of Toronto Press, 1972), pp. 3-8.

3. Charles Tilly, "The Modernization of Political Conflict in France," in Perspectives on Modernization, ed. Edward B. Harvey (Toronto: University of Toronto Press, 1972), pp. 50-51; and C. E. Black, The Dynamics of Modernization (New York: Harper & Row, 1966), pp. 5-9.

4. This topic has received substantial attention. See David E. Apter, The Politics of Modernization (Chicago: University of Chicago Press, 1965); and Black, op. cit., Chap. 3.

5. Wilbert E. Moore, The Impact of Industry (Englewood Cliffs, N.J.: Prentice-Hall, 1965), pp. 5-6.

6. On the importance of technological change, see Stanley A. Hetzler, Technological Growth and Social Change (London: Routledge and Kegan Paul, 1969). Concerning the influence of personality traits and religion, see David C. McClelland, The Achieving Society (Princeton, N.J.: Van Nostrand, 1961). On the role of the political system in initiating economic development, see Black, op. cit., Chaps. 3-6. Regarding social organization, see Everett E. Hagen, On the Theory of Social Change: How Economic Growth Begins (London: Tavistock, 1962); and Bert F. Hoselitz, Sociological Aspects of Economic Growth (New York: Free Press, 1960). Demographic forces facilitated economic development in modernized countries, just as these same forces impede economic growth in contemporary underdeveloped societies: Joseph J. Spengler, "Demographic Factors and Early Modern Economic Development," Daedalus 97 (Spring 1968): 433-46.

7. McClelland, op. cit., Chap. 10; Daniel Lerner, The Passing of Traditional Society: Modernizing the Middle East (New York: Free Press, 1958), Chap. 2; and S. N. Eisenstadt, Modernization: Protest and Change (Englewood Cliffs, N.J.: Prentice-Hall, 1966), pp. 7-11.

8. Regarding the concepts of "structural differentiation," see Neil J. Smelser, "Mechanisms of Change and Adjustment to Change," in Industrialization and Society, eds. Bert F. Hoselitz and Wilbert E. Moore (The Hague: UNESCO-Mouton, 1966), pp. 35-40.

9. United Nations, Bureau of Social Affairs, Report on the World Social Situation Including Studies of Urbanization in Underdeveloped Areas (ST/SOA/33), 1957, p. 114; 1970 estimate from United Nations, Department of Economic and Social Affairs, Growth of the World's Urban and Rural Population, 1920-2000 (ST/SOA/Series A/44), 1969, p. 58.

10. United Nations, Department of Economic and Social Affairs, Demographic Yearbook—1971, 1972, pp. 139-51.

11. Ibid.

12. Kingsley Davis, "The Urbanization of the Human Population," in Cities (New York: Knopf, 1969), pp. 4-5; and Robert A. Lewis and Richard H. Rowland, "Urbanization in Russia and the USSR: 1897-1966," Annals of the Association of American Geographers 59 (December 1969): 779.

13. Davis, op. cit., pp. 13-15.

14. Ibid., p. 13; and Adna Ferrin Weber, The Growth of Cities in the Nineteenth Century (Ithaca, N.Y.: Cornell University Press, 1963), Chap. 3.

15. Jack P. Gibbs and Walter T. Martin, "Urbanization, Technology, and the Division of Labor: International Patterns," American Sociological Review 27 (October 1962): 667-77; and William Fielding Ogburn, "Technology and Cities: The Dilemma of the Modern Metropolis," Sociological Quarterly 1 (July 1960): 139-53.

16. Bert F. Hoselitz, "The Role of Cities in the Economic Growth of Underdeveloped Countries," Journal of Political Economy 61 (June 1953): 195-208; and Weber, op. cit.

17. A. J. Jaffe, "Urbanization and Fertility," American Journal of Sociology 48 (July 1942): 48-60.

18. Ibid., pp. 58-60; and Goldscheider, op. cit., p. 150.

19. Weber, op. cit., Chap. 4.

20. Robert Redfield, "The Folk Society," American Journal of Sociology 52 (January 1947): 293-308; and Louis Wirth, "Urbanism as a Way of Life," American Journal of Sociology 45 (July 1938): 1-24.

21. Oscar Lewis, "Further Observations on the Folk-Urban Continuum and Urbanization with Special Reference to Mexico City," in The Study of Urbanization, eds. Philip M. Hauser and Leo F. Schnore (New York: Wiley, 1967), pp. 491-503; and Philip M. Hauser, "Observations on the Urban-Folk and Urban-Rural Dichotomies as Forms of Western Ethnocentrism," in The Study of Urbanization, eds. Philip M. Hauser and Leo F. Schnore (New York: Wiley, 1967), pp. 503-17.

22. Janet Abu-Lughod, "Migrant Adjustment to City Life: The Egyptian Case," American Journal of Sociology 67 (July 1961): 22-32.

23. Allan Schnaiberg, "The Modernizing Impact of Urbanization: A Causal Analysis," Economic Development and Cultural Change 20 (October 1971): 80-104.

24. E. A. Wrigley, Population and History (New York: McGraw-Hill, 1969), p. 195.

25. Irene B. Taeuber, The Population of Japan (Princeton, N.J.: Princeton University Press, 1958), p. 311.

26. United Nations, Demographic Yearbook—1971, pp. 127-28.

27. Ibid., pp. 125-29.

28. Wrigley, op. cit., Chaps. 3 and 4.

29. Harold F. Dorn, "Mortality," in The Study of Population, ed.Philip M. Hauser and Otis Dudley Duncan (Chicago: University of Chicago Press, 1959), p. 455; Philip M. Hauser, "World Population Growth," in The Population Dilemma, ed. Philip M. Hauser, 2d ed. (Englewood Cliffs, N.J.: Prentice-Hall, 1969), pp. 14-15; and Thomas McKeown, "Medicine and World Population," in Public Health and Population Change, eds. Mindel C. Sheps and Jeanne Clare Ridley (Pittsburgh: University of Pittsburgh Press, 1965), pp. 25-40.

30. Data on mortality levels in premodern Europe and the United States are, of course, incomplete and often of dubious accuracy. The data presented here for the period around 1700 are abstracted from Louis I. Dublin, Alfred J. Lotka, and Mortimer Spiegelman, Length of Life, rev. ed. (New York: Ronald Press, 1949), pp. 32-43. Estimates for 1970 are from United Nations, Demographic Yearbook—1971, pp. 746-65.

31. Goldscheider, op. cit., pp. 120, 124.

32. Dorn, op. cit., pp. 458-60.

33. Goldscheider, op. cit., pp. 114-24.

34. Kingsley Davis, "Population Policy: Will Current Programs Succeed?" Science 158 (November 10, 1967): 730-39.

35. Gosta Carlsson, "The Decline of Fertility: Innovation or Adjustment Process," Population Studies 20 (November 1966): 149-74; and A. J. Jaffe, "Differential Fertility in the White Population in Early America," Journal of Heredity 31 (September 1940): 407-11.

36. Davis, "Population Policy," op. cit.

37. Carlsson, op. cit., pp. 149-51, 172-74.

38. Goldscheider, op. cit., pp. 167-68; and Dov Friedlander, "Demographic Responses and Population Change," Demography 6 (November 1969): 359-65.

39. Goldscheider, op. cit., pp. 147-61. David Heer has suggested that although the "direct" effect of economic prosperity might be higher fertility, the "indirect" effects such as social mobility, education, and lower infant mortality outweigh the direct effect, resulting in overall lower fertility: "Economic Development and Fertility," Demography 3, no. 2 (1966): 423-44.

40. Kingsley Davis, "The Theory of Change and Response in Modern Demographic History," Population Index 29 (October 1963): 352.

41. D. V. Glass, "Population Growth and Population Policy," in Public Health and Population Change, eds. Mindel C. Sheps and Jeanne Clare Ridley (Pittsburgh: University of Pittsburgh Press, 1965), pp. 14-20.

42. Goldscheider, op. cit., pp. 152-56. This was, for some time, the case in England at the outset of the Industrial Revolution where, despite significant economic growth, the working population was "pauperized."

43. Ibid., pp. 160-61.

44. Davis, "The Theory of Change," op. cit.

45. Ansley J. Coale, "Population and Economic Development," in The Population Dilemma, ed. Philip M. Hauser, 2d ed. (Englewood Cliffs, N.J.: Prentice-Hall, 1969), pp. 54-84.

46. Spengler, op. cit.

47. Everett S. Lee, "A Theory of Migration," Demography 3, no. 1 (1966): 47-57.

48. A. J. Jaffe, "Manpower and Other Economic Contributions by Migrants: The United States Experience" (Paper presented at the Conference on Labor and Migration, Brooklyn College, New York, March 13-14, 1970), p. 17; and Simon Kuznets and Dorothy S. Thomas, "Internal Migration and Economic Growth," in Selected Studies of Migration Since World War II, Proceedings of the Milbank Memorial Fund (New York, 1958), pp. 196-211.

49. A. J. Jaffe and Seymour L. Wolfbein, "Internal Migration and Full Employment in the U.S.," Journal of the American Statistical Association, 40 (September 1945): 351-63; Hope T. Eldridge and Dorothy Swaine Thomas, Demographic Analyses and Interrelations, vol. 3. Population Redistribution and Economic Growth: United States, 1870-1950 (Philadelphia: American Philosophical Society, 1964); and Taeuber, op. cit., Chap. 7.

50. Simon Kuznets, "Introduction: Population Redistribution, Migration, and Economic Growth," in Hope T. Eldridge and Dorothy Swaine Thomas, Demographic Analyses and Interrelations, vol. 3. Population Redistribution and Economic Growth: United States, 1870-1950 (Philadelphia: American Philosophical Society, 1974), p. xxiii.

51. Frederick Harbison and Charles A. Myers, Education, Manpower, and Economic Growth (New York: McGraw-Hill, 1964), Chap. 3.

52. A. J. Jaffe, People, Jobs, and Economic Development (Glencoe, Ill.: Free Press, 1959), pp. 199-202.

53. Harold M. Groves, Education and Economic Growth (Washington, D.C.: National Education Association, 1961), pp. 16-19.

54. Harbison and Myers, op. cit., pp. 3-14.

55. On the relationship between education and fertility, see United Nations, Department of Social Affairs, The Determinants and Consequences of Population Trends (ST/SOA/Ser. A/17), 1953. Concerning education and migration, in particular the recent "brain drain" phenomenon, see G. Beijer, "Modern Patterns of International Migratory Movements," in Migration, ed. J. A. Jackson (Cambridge, Mass.: Cambridge University Press, 1969), pp. 11-59. The positive relationship between higher levels of education and occupational mobility is detailed in Otis Dudley Duncan and Robert W. Hodge, "Education and Occupational Mobility," American Journal of Sociology 68 (May 1963): 629-44. It is generally acknowledged that rural education is inferior, both in terms of facilities and the quality of education; see United Nations, Report on the World Social Situation, op. cit., pp. 64-65.

56. Jaffe, People, Jobs, and Economic Development, op. cit., p. 200; C. Arnold Anderson, "The Modernization of Education," in Modernization: The Dynamics of Growth, ed. Myron Weiner (New York: Basic Books, 1966), p. 90; and Harbison and Myers, op. cit., p. 2.

57. Wilbert E. Moore, "Changes in Occupational Structures," in Social Structure and Mobility in Economic Development, eds. Neil J. Smelser and Seymour Martin Lipset (Chicago: Aldine, 1966), pp. 200-04.

58. Simon Kuznets, "Quantitative Aspects of the Economic Growth of Nations. II. Industrial Distribution of National Product

and Labor Force," Economic Development and Cultural Change, Supplement to 5 (July 1957): 3–111.

59. Moore, op. cit., p. 203. Moore notes that the original formulation by Colin Clark, which stipulated a movement out of agriculture into manufacturing and eventually into services as economic development continues, has been altered in some cases, with direct movement out of agriculture and into services. See Colin Clark, The Conditions of Economic Progress, 2d ed. (London: Macmillan, 1951), pp. 395–439.

60. A. J. Jaffe, "Population, Working Force, and Economic Growth: A Preliminary Outline," Centro Latinoamericano de Demografia (CELADE), S. 474/26 (Santiago, Chile, June 1970): 5–6.

61. United Nations, Determinants and Consequences of Population Trends, pp. 88–89.

62. A. J. Jaffe and K. Azumi, "The Birth Rate and Cottage Industries in Underdeveloped Countries," Economic Development and Cultural Change 9 (October 1960): 52–63.

63. Judith Blake, "Demographic Science and the Redirection of Population Policy," in Public Health and Population Change, eds. Mindel C. Sheps and Jeanne Clare Ridley (Pittsburgh: University of Pittsburgh Press, 1965), pp. 41–69.

64. Jaffe, "Population, Working Force, and Economic Growth," op. cit., p. 6.

2

**DATA AND
METHODS**

Since the end of the nineteenth century, a relatively large volume of census data has been published for the Russian Empire and the USSR. National censuses were conducted in 1897, 1926, 1939, 1959, and 1970, and they are the chief sources of socioeconomic data for Russia and the USSR, even though the periods that they cover, the intervals between the various censuses, and the range of data collected are not entirely satisfactory. Nevertheless, data from these censuses have been used relatively little in the study of Russian and Soviet society, both inside and outside the USSR. Moreover, where they have been used, their use has been chiefly limited to aggregate data, that is, data for the country as a whole. This situation is also true in the study of population change, although there are a few exceptions.[1]

Aside from the general reluctance of many scholars to delve into numerous volumes of purely statistical data, the primary reason that these censuses have been used relatively little is very probably owing to the many data problems that one encounters in their use. The chief data problem is the lack of territorial and definitional comparability of data among the various censuses, which makes valid comparisons over time difficult. With respect to population change, population trends and their interrelationships cannot be measured over time. The authors have attempted to solve this problem, and the results of the work are 18 data matrices (19 regions by 50 to 100 variables), which comprise the basic data for the study and make possible the application of various demographic and statistical methods.

This chapter is devoted to a discussion of the procedures derived to solve the problem of the lack of territorial and definitional comparability, the operational definitions of demographic terms, the

major variables employed, and the methods utilized in this study.
In the ten years that we have been working on the problem of data
comparability, we have encountered an immense number of data problems, both large and small, related to the solution of this problem.
Because of limitations of space and time and our desire to avoid excessive tedium, we will not discuss all of these data problems. However, we feel that it is necessary to discuss in some detail our basic
procedures, so that our work can be evaluated and replicated as much
as possible.

SUMMARY DISCUSSION

The chief sources of data for this study are the Russian and
Soviet censuses of 1897, 1926, 1959, and 1970; all population data
used in this study are de facto.[2] Because the national territory of the
USSR has changed several times since the latter part of the nineteenth
century, the contemporary national territory differs from the national
territory in 1897 and 1926. Consequently, in order to provide even
aggregate data for the present-day national territory of the USSR, it
was necessary to gather data from East European censuses and other
sources for the border areas, that is, areas formerly outside but currently within the USSR.[3] Because the Soviet Union has a large, diverse
population, aggregate population data for the USSR are often too gross
to be meaningful. Moreover, frequent and drastic changes in the internal administrative divisions into which census and other data are ordered over the past century have made it very difficult to compare regional demographic and other data from one point in time to another.
For example, the number of major enumeration units in 1897 was
about 90; in 1926, about 190; and in 1959 and 1970, about 140. To
solve this problem it was necessary to reorder the data for each census into a common set of territorial units. For this purpose the
"major" (krupnyye) Soviet economic regions of 1961 were chosen
(Map 2.1). These regions were selected because 1959 and 1970 census units conform to them without adjustment, and because certain
other socioeconomic data pertinent to the analysis were presented in
these regions.
In order to allocate population data into comparable territorial
units (the economic regions), the authors have assumed that, except
for urban concentrations, population is evenly distributed within each
administrative unit; therefore, a variation in area would result in a
proportionate variation in population. The "rural" population and
rural population characteristics of the political divisions in 1897 and
1926 were allocated to the various economic regions on the basis of
the area of each administrative division that fits into the appropriate

economic region. All centers with a population of 15,000 and over were individually allocated to the appropriate economic region. By combining rural and urban components, it was possible to allocate the total population and total population characteristics into the economic regions for the various census years. Available tests indicate that the error involved in this procedure was not great.

Still another problem was the lack of comparable definitions of demographic and socioeconomic characteristics. With the exception of sex and age, definitions among the various Soviet censuses were not comparable. Therefore, it was necessary to make major statistical adjustments in order to obtain comparable data. The very best definition of a particular population characteristic was not always obtained, but the definitions utilized in this study are as nearly comparable as possible.

Thus, for the first time, comparisons over time based on comparable territorial units and definitions can be made for the present-day territory of the USSR employing a wide variety of census variables, which pertain primarily to nationality, urbanization, labor force, sex, age, fertility, and literacy. Specifically, 18 matrices have been generated, each containing roughly 50 to 100 demographic and socioeconomic variables for 19 regions for the census years of 1897, 1926, and 1959.

In order to enhance our analysis, we have applied various demographic and statistical methods to these matrices. In doing so, we have attempted to utilize the simplest methods possible given the particular task at hand. Of the methods, perhaps the most important is factor analysis, which, although complex, is necessary to our analysis. This method distinguishes clusters of highly interrelated variables (factors). From the application of this method to each of the 18 matrices, major demographic relationships in Russia and the USSR emerged. In addition, we utilize various locational indexes, such as the dissimilarity index and the coefficient of redistribution.

At the outset, we should emphasize that we have attempted to guard against any analytical interpretations that cannot be supported reasonably by our data. All social and economic data are, of course, approximations of reality, approximations that vary in accuracy according to the complexity of the phenomena to be observed and to the rigor with which information is collected. In this regard, census data are probably more accurate than most other social and economic data, because considerable efforts are taken to ensure the completeness and accuracy of the enumeration, fairly uniform procedures and methods exist that can be employed, and much of the information sought is rather straightforward. Nevertheless, we recognize the limitations of our data, particularly inasmuch as the original information required considerable modification. We are convinced, however, that the major

questions posed in this study can be answered to a significant degree
through an analysis of these data. After working with these data on
these questions for a long time and obtaining either expected or reasonable relationships, we are confident that the error in the data is
within tolerable limits. Indeed, we have checked all of our calculations and every effort has been made to be as accurate as possible.
To avoid rounding errors in our calculations, we have not rounded
the absolute data presented in the tables, but this does not mean that
we consider the data accurate to that degree. The compilation of a
set of data matrices , utilizing procedures described in detail in this
chapter, enables us to describe and explain population change in Russia
and the USSR to an extent that previously was not possible.

DETAILED DISCUSSION

The Problem of Territorial Comparability

Because population change in terms of its regional variation is
the prime interest, the first task was to order data into a consistent
set of territorial units so that regional comparisons over time could
be made and interrelationships established. The reason that this is
necessary is obvious, because if the boundaries of the territorial
units for which data are collected change from census to census, they
cannot be used to measure change over time. No enumeration unit in
any Russian or Soviet census had the same boundaries in all the census
years. Thus, it was necessary to select a consistent set of territorial
units and reorder the data in the various censuses into these units.

Careful selection of territorial units (regions) is important in
order to avoid biasing the data excessively. Unfortunately, there is
no one ideal set of regions with respect to the study of population
change; it would be desirable to have a different set of regions for each
component of population studied. Regions should be homogeneous in
terms of the problem studied, based on one factor or a combination
of factors, and delimited on a consistent basis, maximizing external
variation and minimizing internal variation. Unfortunately, the necessary population data are not available for the USSR, or most other
countries, in sufficient detail to permit the construction of a set of
regions for every analytical purpose. Consequently, the existing units
into which data have been collected must be used. Regionalization is
merely the spatial aspect of the classification problem, and there is
no adequate all-purpose multivariable set of regions for a country,
just as there is no all-purpose statistical or taxonomic interval. Furthermore, when comparisons are made over a long period of time, the

problem of establishing a set of homogeneous regions is virtually in-
soluble. Such dramatic socioeconomic change has occurred in all
areas of Russia and the USSR between 1897 and 1970 that it is impossible to delimit a set of regions that were homogeneous throughout
this period on the basis of any socioeconomic criterion.

Even though the "major" (krupnyye) Soviet economic regions of
1961 are not ideal with respect to the criteria that were discussed,
they were chosen as the basic statistical units for the study of population change in the USSR for the following reasons:

1. The Soviet government often presented a variety of socioeconomic data in these official units; in fact, much data from the 1959
census were presented in these units. It must be acknowledged, however, that our statistical work began about ten years ago, when these
regions were the official economic regions of the USSR, and subsequently their boundaries have been changed. To order data into a
more current set of economic regions would require an immense
amount of additional work; therefore, it was decided to continue to use
the 1961 regions. Furthermore, except for a few changes that have
occurred since 1961, the boundaries of the 1961 economic regions conform to those of contemporary administrative divisions; consequently,
additional data can be presented in these units easily and accurately.

2. Although these regions are somewhat gross and relatively
few in number, we have concluded that they do provide a satisfactory
picture of the regional variation of demographic characteristics.

3. These regions are relatively easy to work with. If we had
selected the approximately 140 krays, oblasts, and ASSRs of today,
the labor required to order data from each census into the 140 units
instead of 19 units would have been multiplied many times. This was
a primary consideration, because even ordering data into the 19 regions required an enormous amount of labor.

4. These are not true economic regions because they have been
delimited on the basis of political and administrative decisions and
include political administrative units in their entirety. Since nationality plays such a dominant role in the delimitation of political and administrative units, these regions are well suited for the study of the
nationalities. Because other population characteristics are closely
related to nationality, these economic regions are also very useful
for the study of Soviet population in general.

The following is a very brief description of the regions utilized
in this study (Maps 2.1 and 2.2):

1. The Northwest is a major industrial area of the RSFSR or
Russian Republic, which includes the city of Leningrad in its southwestern corner.

MAP 2.1

Economic Regions: 1961

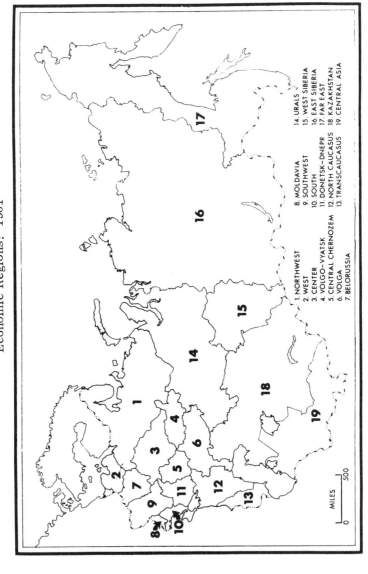

1. NORTHWEST   8. MOLDAVIA   14. URALS
2. WEST   9. SOUTHWEST   15. WEST SIBERIA
3. CENTER   10. SOUTH   16. EAST SIBERIA
4. VOLGO–VYATSK   11. DONETSK–DNEPR   17. FAR EAST
5. CENTRAL CHERNOZEM 12. NORTH CAUCASUS   18. KAZAKHSTAN
6. VOLGA   13. TRANSCAUCASUS   19. CENTRAL ASIA
7. BELORUSSIA

MILES
0   500

Source: Data compiled by the authors.

34

MAP 2.2

Administrative Units of Nationalities in the USSR

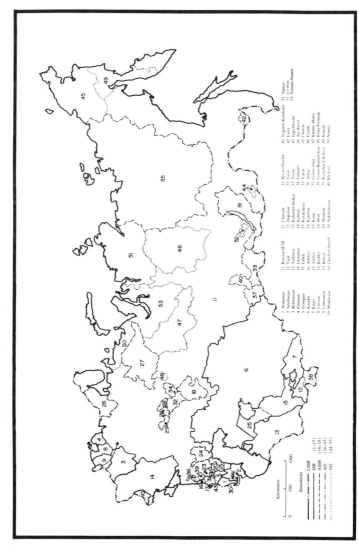

1 Armenian	11 Russian SFSR	21 Chuvash	31 Severo-Osetin	41 Nagorno-Karabakh	51 Taimyr
2 Azerbaijan	12 Tuik	22 Dagestan	32 Tatar	42 Evex	52 Ust Orda
3 Belorussian	13 Turkmen	23 Kabardin-Balkar	33 Tuvin	43 Inguš-Osetin	53 Yamalo-Nenets
4 Estonian	14 Ukrainian	24 Kalmyk	34 Udmurt	44 Aga-Buryat	
5 Georgian	15 Uzbek	25 Karakalpak	35 Yakut	45 Chukchi	
6 Kazakh	16 Abkhaz	26 Karelian	36 Adygs	46 Evenki	
7 Kirgiz	17 Adzhar	27 Komi	37 Gorno-Altay	47 Khanty-Mansi	
8 Latvian	18 Bashkir	28 Mari	38 Gorno-Badakhshan	48 Komi-Permyak	
9 Lithuanian	19 Buryat	29 Mordтом	39 Karachay-Cherkess	49 Koryak	
10 Moldavian	20 Checheno-Ingush	30 Nakhichevan	40 Khakas	50 Nenets	

Source: Edward Allworth, ed. Soviet Nationality Problems, (New York: Columbia University Press) 1971.
Drawn by: Richard H. Rowland

35

2. The West consists of the three Baltic republics of Latvia, Lithuania, and Estonia.

3. The Center is a major industrial region of the RSFSR centered upon the city of Moscow.

4. The Volgo-Vyatsk is the region of the RSFSR that is adjacent to the Center on the east, and includes the automobile manufacturing center of Gor'kiy.

5. The Central Chernozem is a major agricultural area of the RSFSR lying between the Center and the Ukrainian Republic.

6. The Volga is a region of the RSFSR straddling the middle and lower courses of the Volga River.

7. Belorussia coincides exactly with the Belorussian Republic.

8. Moldavia coincides exactly with the Moldavian Republic.

9. The Southwest is a major agricultural area that is in the western part of the Ukrainian SSR and includes the city of Kiev.

10. The South is in the southern part of the Ukrainian Republic, and is, in particular, on the northern littoral of the Black Sea and includes the Crimean Peninsula and the city of Odessa.

11. The Donetsk-Dnepr is the outstanding heavy industrial area of the eastern portion of the Ukrainian Republic.

12. The North Caucasus is a major agricultural area of the RSFSR lying to the north of the Caucasus Mountains.

13. The Transcaucasus consists of the three republics of Georgia, Armenia, and Azerbaydzhan, which lie south of the Caucasus Mountains.

14. The Urals is a major mining and manufacturing region of the RSFSR that extends along the slopes of the Ural Mountains.

15. West Siberia is a major industrial region of the RSFSR that includes the city of Novosibirsk and the mining and industrial area known as the Kuznets Basin.

16. East Siberia is the vast mineral-rich region of the RSFSR that includes Lake Baykal and such important cities on the Trans-Siberian Railway as Krasnoyarsk and Irkutsk.

17. The Far East is a large elongated area of the RSFSR that extends along the Pacific coast of the USSR and includes the city of Vladivostok in the extreme south as well as the Kamchatka Peninsula and the island of Sakhalin.

18. Kazakhstan coincides exactly with the Kazakh Republic.

19. Central Asia consists of the Uzbek, Turkmen, Tadzhik, and Kirgiz republics.

After selecting the regions to be utilized, the next problem was to derive a method for ordering data from each census into these 19 units. For 1959 and 1970 there was no major problem, since the total, urban, and rural populations are presented in units that fall completely into one region or another. Consequently, the following procedure concerns only 1897 and 1926.

The basic procedure involved has been developed and discussed in detail by J. William Leasure and Robert A. Lewis and need only be summarized here.[4] The first major step was to superimpose a map of the economic regions over a map of the political units for each census year. From this, a determination was made of the percent of the area of a given political unit that fell into a given region, that is, "area allocation." In addition, it was determined which urban centers (settlements with a population of 15,000 and over) of a given political unit fell into a given region.[5] Summation of the population in these centers resulted in the urban population of a given political unit that was allocated to a given region. The rural population (that is, the population not residing in centers of 15,000 and over) to be allocated to the given region was estimated on the assumption that this population was evenly distributed. Thus, the rural population of the unit was multiplied by the area allocation. Consequently, an estimate was made of the urban and rural and thus the total population of a given political unit that was allocated to a given region. The percentage that this allocated population comprised of the total population of the unit was termed the "population allocation." For example, in 1897, the population allocation of Chernigov Guberniya with respect to the Southwest region was 57.9. This means that an estimated 57.9 percent of the total population of that guberniya resided in the Southwest region.

Once the total, urban, and rural populations of each unit had been allocated to the appropriate regions, it was possible to estimate these populations for each economic region as a whole simply by a summation of all the allocated populations. It should be noted that these procedures were also applied to border areas (that is, areas within the USSR today that were outside the Russian Empire in 1897 and the USSR in 1926). This was accomplished after projecting data from these areas to the census dates we are concerned with. Thus, estimates of the total, urban, and rural populations for each of the 19 regions (and, consequently, for the entire present-day USSR) in 1897, 1926, and 1959 were derived.* Furthermore, we have made estimates of the total, urban, and rural populations in 1970 for the 1961 economic regions. Although the boundaries of some political units have changed since 1961, the changes have been so insignificant that we have regarded all 1970 political units as falling completely into one region or another.

---

*Since the publication of the Leasure and Lewis study (Population Changes in Russia and the USSR: A Set of Comparable Territorial Units), we have made some slight corrections in the total and urban population tables presented therein.

We realize, of course, that some of our procedures are not perfectly accurate. For example, the assumption of an even distribution of the rural population is rarely met in reality. Nonetheless, this assumption was made because the alternative task of determining more precisely the location of the rural population for an area as large as the USSR in more than one census year would have been enormous. Our relatively abbreviated procedure, in fact, took a great amount of time and effort. In addition, the assumption of uniform distribution, although not precisely accurate, does have considerable validity because of the dominantly flat terrain of the ecumene of the USSR. Also, available checks on our method tend to indicate that our error is not great.[6]

With these allocation procedures it was then possible to estimate the number of people according to various demographic characteristics for the total population of each region. This was accomplished by multiplying the number of persons in a given unit with a certain characteristic by the population allocation. For example, in 1926, Penza Guberniya contained 1,701,873 Russians and had a population allocation of 58.8 percent with respect to the Volga region. This means that 1,000,701 of its Russians (58.8 percent of 1,701,873) were allocated to this region. These procedures have been applied to the 1897 and 1926 censuses. For 1959 and 1970 the task was simpler because, as mentioned before, every unit virtually falls entirely within a given region. The original Leasure and Lewis study undertook this allocation of population characteristics for the work force, literacy, and Eastern Slavs. Subsequently, we have also applied the same procedures to males, females, various age cohorts, a number of specific non-Eastern Slavic nationality groups, and other characteristics. These characteristics will be discussed in more detail later.

For all of the characteristics, both those in the original Leasure and Lewis study and the subsequent ones, we have also incorporated as much data as possible from the censuses of adjacent countries for the border areas. This was generally accomplished by applying the characteristics of a border area from its census that was closest in time to the date of the appropriate Russian or Soviet census. For example, in 1930 the Ukrainian population was 11 percent of Bessarabia province in Romania. In 1926 an estimated 1,791,192 people of this province fell into Moldavia. Therefore, we estimated that in 1926, 197,031 Ukrainians (11 percent of 1,791,192) from Bessarabia were to be allocated to the South region.

Unfortunately, appropriate data could not always be found for the border areas. For example, no characteristics were available in 1897 and 1926 for the Tuva Republic, a part of East Siberia. Because we desired estimates of the characteristics for the entire population of each region in each year, we simply assumed that the char-

acteristics of the population for which we had data could be applied to
the entire population of the region; that is, we assumed that the characteristics of the population for which we had data could be applied to
the areas for which data were not available. Thus, in 1926, for example, 27.2 percent of the population of East Siberia for which we had
data (3,532,526) was aged 0 to 9 and the total population of the region
was 3,624,449. Therefore, we estimated the 0 to 9 population of the
entire population of the region to be 958,850 (27.2 percent of 3,624,449).
Obviously, these procedures for border areas are not perfect. Nevertheless, given the obstacles that anyone would encounter when try-
ing to achieve the goals we set, we believe that this procedure was
satisfactory.

In summary, by means of the allocation procedures just discussed, we have been able to allocate demographic characteristics
from various political units to the 19 economic regions. Summation
of the allocated figures to each region has enabled us to estimate the
population size of a whole host of demographic characteristics for the
total population of each region in each census year. Summation of
these regional totals has resulted in such estimates for the entire
present-day USSR in all four census years.

In addition, we have decided to derive similarly many of these
characteristics for the urban and rural populations of each region independently. Derivation of these characteristics for the urban and
rural populations involved a number of additional problems. The
prime theoretical procedure would be to assess the characteristics of
the urban settlement and rural settlements of each unit and then allocate these settlements and corresponding characteristics to the appropriate regions. However, this procedure could not be used because
data on the characteristics of all urban centers (settlements with
15,000 or more people) and all rural settlements (settlements with
less than 15,000 people) in each census were not always available.
For example, the 1897 census does not have any data for approximately
35 towns in the Russian Empire with more than 15,000 people because
they were not defined as urban in the census. The 1926 census does
provide much data for individual centers with a population of 15,000
and over. But the 1959 and 1970 censuses provide no characteristics
for any center of 15,000 and over, except for republic capitals Leningrad, Kaunas, and Sevastopol'. As might be expected, the lack of
data was even more pronounced for individual rural settlements.
These problems were also present for the urban and rural populations
of border areas. Consequently, other procedures had to be developed.

Although data are not available on the characteristics for all
urban centers based upon the 15,000 and over definition, such data
are usually available for the urban population of each unit based upon
the census definition of urban. Conceivably, utilization of these data
can be undertaken in more than one way.

One possible method involves the allocation of characteristics of the urban (census definition) population in terms of the allocation based upon the urban (15,000 and over) population. For example, assume a given unit had 100,000 Russians among its urban (census definition) population. In addition, assume that 40 percent of its urban (15,000 and over) population goes to a given region. It could thus be estimated that 40,000 Russians were allocated to the urban population of the given region. Although the census definitions of urban vary, we would at least be consistent in that the allocation would be based upon the 15,000 and over definition in all years.

This method, however, is somewhat deficient in that the allocation of the urban population based upon the census definition is often substantially different from that based upon the 15,000 and over definition. As a result, the allocated urban population of a characteristic often exceeded the allocated total population of the same characteristic, an incongruous situation. Thus, the only safe procedure seemed to involve allocation of the urban (census definition) characteristics of a given unit on the basis of the urban (census definition) population itself.

The determination of the percent of the urban (census definition) population of a given unit that was allocated to a given region, that is, "urban allocation," was quite difficult. The procedure involved was undertaken in the Leasure and Lewis study and was similar to that involving the 15,000 and over definition in that the location of all urban (census definition) centers had to be ascertained in order to determine into which region each center was to be allocated.[7] For the urban (15,000 and over) population this was relatively easy as the towns were relatively large and thus more likely to be found on available maps. However, since the urban (census definition) population very frequently includes hundreds of settlements with less than 1,000 people, it was very difficult to ascertain the location for all centers. Fortunately, in many cases a precise determination of a town's location was not necessary, because if a given unit was completely in a given region, this meant that 100 percent of the unit's total, urban, and rural populations was allocated to that region regardless of the urban definition involved. A prime example of this situation was Moscow Guberniya in 1897 and 1926 and Moscow Oblast in 1959 and 1970. In each case, 100 percent of the area of this province is in the Center. In fact, as mentioned before, in 1959 and 1970 all of the political units fell virtually completely into one region. Therefore, for these years a precise determination of the location of individual towns was not necessary at all.

In most cases for 1897 and 1926 a precise determination of the location of urban (census definition) settlements was necessary in order to allocate appropriately the urban (census definition) population of a given unit to a given region. Such a determination was undertaken

by using a variety of maps. In some cases it was not possible to find
the location of a given city on the map, and some educated guesses
were required. For example, knowledge of which minor civil division
(for example, uyezd) the town was located in was utilized to infer the
region into which the town was to be allocated. For the most part,
these cases had relatively little significance since the percent of the
urban (census definition) population of a given unit that was located in
these small centers was quite insignificant. In short, we can say with
some confidence that the urban (census definition) population allocations are quite valid.

The results of these procedures are included in Table 1 of the
Leasure and Lewis study[8]; it shows the percent of the urban (census
definition) population of a given unit that was allocated to the given region (urban allocation). Investigation of this table reveals that no urban allocations are presented for border areas. We have computed
these percentages subsequently. Because many urban (census definition) centers in these border areas were not listed separately, and because it was extremely difficult to ascertain the location of those that
were listed separately, it was virtually impossible to estimate the urban allocation with a procedure similar to that used for Russia and the
USSR. Therefore, a substitute procedure was necessary.

Because we had already derived a list of all centers in border
areas with an estimated population of 15,000 and over in 1897 and 1926,
we decided to make use of this set of data. From this list, we could
determine the percent of the urban (15,000 and over) population of a
given border unit that fell into a given region. This was, in short, the
urban allocation based upon the 15,000 and over definition. Consequently, we decided to allocate characteristics of the urban (census definition) population of border units on the basis of the percent of its urban (15,000 and over) population that fell into a given region. This
procedure was selected, in spite of the aforementioned problems
that might ensue, because of the lack of any reasonable alternatives.

Eventually, the characteristics of the urban (census definition)
populations were allocated to the appropriate economic regions. Summation of the allocated figures for each region resulted in an estimate
of the characteristics of the urban (census definition) population of each
region. However, we were not satisfied to stop at this point, since we
still desired an estimate of the characteristics of the urban (15,000
and over) population, that is, for our comparable definition of urban.
Because the vast bulk of the urban (census definition) population is located in urban (15,000 and over) centers, we assumed that characteristics of the urban (census definition) population could be applied to the
urban (15,000 and over) population.[9] For example, in 1926, 37 percent of the urban (census definition) population of the Southwest were
Ukrainians and the urban (15,000 and over) population of that region

was 2,214,145. This meant that the estimated number of Ukrainians in the urban (15,000 and over) population of that region was 819,234.

After the demographic characteristics for the urban (15,000 and over) population of each region were derived, the characteristics of the rural population could be easily derived. This was accomplished by simply subtracting the number involved in the urban (15,000 and over) population from that of the total population. For example, in 1926 the total number of Ukrainians in the Southwest was 15,863,594 and the urban (15,000 and over) number of Ukrainians of the same region was 819,234. This meant that the number of Ukrainians in rural areas of the Southwest was 15,044,360. These procedures were applied for as many variables as possible in 1897, 1926, 1959, and 1970.

The Problem of Definitional Comparability

The other major problem confronting our investigation is the lack of definitional comparability of demographic terms from one census to the next. Therefore, we attempted to derive characteristics that are as comparable as possible from one census to another. Leasure and Lewis undertook this task for work force categories (total work force, industry, and agriculture), literacy, and certain nationalities (Eastern Slavs).[10] We have expanded these original data in a number of ways. First, because border areas were not included, we subsequently made estimates for these areas using the sources and procedures previously discussed. Second, we derived a tertiary or service sector for the work force simply by subtracting the industrial (secondary) and agricultural work forces from the total work force. Although our tertiary sector includes construction work, it is still largely composed of service occupations. Also, we generated a host of other demographic variables, including sex, age, and other nationalities.

More specifically, we have estimated the number of people having the following characteristics for the total population of each region in 1897, 1926, 1959, and, as much as possible, 1970:

● sex: males and females separately
● urban size: urban population (15,000 and over definition) residing in centers of 15,000 to 99,999 and 100,000 and over
● work force: total work force, agricultural work force, industrial work force, and tertiary work force
● age: cohorts 0 to 9, 10 to 19, 0 to 19, 20 to 39, 40 to 59, 20 to 59, 60 and over, 0 to 19 and 60 and over, and females 20 to 49
● literacy: literate population aged 10 to 49 and total population aged 10 to 49
● nationality: see the lists on pages 45 and 47

A number of comments are necessary to clarify these characteristics. First, our investigation was limited to these characteristics
because we were primarily concerned with characteristics that could
be found in all three of the 1897, 1926, and 1959 censuses. Recall
that our investigation began well before the first published results of
the 1970 census, but we are completing our series with the results
of the 1970 census. Such characteristics as educational levels and
more precise work force categories simply could not be investigated
in all three censuses. There are no educational data in the 1926 census or more specific work force data in the 1959 census that we could
use in our regional framework.

In fact, work force data as a whole presented a number of problems. First, the work force data we have utilized for 1959 are actually for 1961, since not even these gross sectors can be derived by
economic region in 1959.[11] In addition, work force data are not based
upon the same concepts. Whereas the 1897 and 1926 data are based
upon the gainfully employed concept, 1959 (1961) data are presented
on the basis of the average annual number of workers. Also, because
we have excluded dependents who work, our agricultural work force
tends to be somewhat smaller. But in spite of these deficiencies,
such work force data are being employed in this study because work
force data are crucial to any demographic study. Furthermore, our
major focus is upon regional variations, and the work force variables
we have developed adequately portray regional variations in the work
force.

Our array of age cohorts is largely determined by the age cohorts presented in the 1959 census. Whereas the 1897 and 1926 censuses present data for single years of age by appropriate political
unit, the 1959 census does not present such data by these units (that
is, krays, oblasts, and ASSRs). Only the cohorts 0 to 9, 10 to 19,
20 to 24, 25 to 29, 30 to 34, 35 to 39, 40 to 44, 45 to 49, 50 to 54,
55 to 59, 60 to 69, and 70 and older are presented by these units in
1959. The primary cohorts we were interested in were 0 to 9, 0 to
19, 20 to 39, 20 to 59, 60 and older and females 20 to 49. The cohorts 0 to 9 and females 20 to 49 were necessary to allow us to derive
child-woman ratios in all three censuses; although the 0 to 4 cohort
is usually used in this measure of fertility, the 0 to 9 cohort had to
suffice. The 0 to 19, 20 to 59, and 60 and older cohorts were derived
because we wanted dependency ratios for all three census years.
Once again, for obvious reasons we could not use the more conventional
cohorts of 0 to 14, 15 to 64, and 65 and older. Finally, the 20 to 39
cohort was selected as a comparable indicator of migration. Although
the 1897 and 1926 censuses contain place-of-birth data, no migration
data, per se, are included in the 1959 census. Because the bulk of
migrants are usually young adults, the 20 to 39 age cohort was selected

as an indicator, albeit a very crude one, of migration for each region.
The remaining cohorts of 10 to 19 and 40 to 59 were gathered simply
because they were easy to calculate after deriving the cohorts we
were primarily concerned with. The age cohort for the literate population also deserves attention. Although it is customary to use the
population 10 and older, our upper limit of 49 was necessitated by
the fact that this is the upper limit provided in the 1959 census.

Finally, the nationality data require considerable clarification
because, with perhaps the exception of work force data, these data
provided the greatest obstacles to comparability from one census to
another. The first consideration is to determine how precise the Soviet census definition of nationality is. Nationality can be broadly
defined as a sense of community characterized to different degrees by
such variables as language, territory, history, culture, religion,
and national character. Because the importance of these component
variables differs considerably from one nationality to another, it is
impossible to use them in a census to define nationality, even if data
on these variables were available. If there were a uniquely correct
definition of nationality, uniquely correct data could be gathered according to this definition. In the absence of this definition, the best
way to determine nationality for our purposes is through self-identifi-
cation. Soviet census takers asked each person's nationality in the
1926, 1939, 1959, and 1970 censuses. The 1897 census, however, provides data only by native language.

Moreover, how the nationality question is asked or worded and
the sort of instructions given to the census taker can also bias the responses. In the 1926 census the question was asked, "To what sub-
nationality (narodnost') do you belong?" In the 1939, 1959, and 1970
censuses, the query concerned the nationality (natsional'nost') to
which the person belonged. In this sense, nationality refers to nation
(natsiya), and not every ethnic group officially has acquired the status
of natsiya or natsional'nost'. At least in theory these two are defined
in terms of literary language, economy, territory, history, and number (at least 300,000). To prevent confusion and error on this point,
a very penetrating Soviet analysis of the subject had recommended
that both terms (narodnost' and natsional'nost') be used in the 1970
census, but the recommendations were not heeded by the government.[12]
In the census question about spoken language, it was also recommended
that the term "conversational language" (razgovornyy yazyk) be used
in place of "native language" (rodnoy yazyk), which can be confused
with the language of one's nationality. This suggestion was also re-
jected.

Instructions to the census takers for the 1897 census were weak
in failing to provide instructions with respect to the native language
question. The 1926 census supplied fairly detailed instructions re-

specting both the nationality and native language questions. The 1959
census was weaker than that of 1926 but still stronger than that of
1897.[13] The "disappearance" of several rather populous Soviet nationalities between 1926 and 1959 has been blamed on inadequate census instruction, changes in the wording of the key question, and some
census takers' lack of knowledge about ethnic terminology and the ros-
ter of Soviet nationalities.[14] Despite these shortcomings, tsarist and
Soviet censuses provide a wealth of reasonably accurate data about the
nationalities of the country.

The major problem, however, concerned the specific nationalities to be investigated. The main difficulty is the fact that, as mentioned before, the number of listed nationalities often varies from one
census to the next. Thus, it is not possible to investigate each and
every specific nationality found in one census throughout all of the remaining censuses. For example, the Sarts and "Turks without distribution," the latter being about the most unusual "nationality" listed in
any of the censuses, are found only in the 1897 census and, consequently, cannot be investigated as such in all the subsequent censuses.
This situation, combined with our desire for simplicity, led us to focus
our investigation on a relatively limited number of groupings, some of
which involve supraethnic groupings listed below:

1. Eastern Slavs (with data provided for Russians, Ukrainians, and
   Belorussians separately)
2. Turkic language and/or Muslim religion, that is, Turkic-Muslims
   (with data provided for Iranian language, Turkic language, Muslim
   religion, and Tatars separately)
3. Mobilized, or Advanced, Europeans, that is, Jews, Georgians,
   Armenians, Latvians, and Estonians (with data provided for Jews
   separately)
4. Other major nationalities:

   a. Finnic peoples excluding Estonians
   b. Lithuanians
   c. Moldavians and Romanians

The criteria utilized for establishing these groupings were, in
general, socioeconomic level, language, and religion. Grouping 1
(Eastern Slavs) and each of its three components (Russians, Ukrainians, and Belorussians) are included because of their numerical importance. Grouping 2 (Turkic language and/or Muslim religion) consists of any group that is either Turkic speaking or Muslim or both
(for example, Uzbeks, Kazakhs, Tatars). For convenience, hereafter this grouping will be referred to as Turkic-Muslims. With this
grouping we have first sought to combine the large bloc of Turkic-
speaking peoples together, especially because the changing census

definition of specific Turkic groups frequently makes it very difficult
to investigate one specific nationality throughout all censuses, as
Appendix A and the previous discussion concerning Sarts and "Turks
without distribution" testify to. Most of these Turkic groups are also
Muslims and comprise the bulk of Muslim peoples in the USSR. However, there are Muslim groups that are non-Turkic but have socioeconomic levels that are relatively similar to the Turkic peoples (for
example, Tadzhiks, Chechens, Avars). Therefore, we have decided
to combine these people with the Turkic peoples to form Grouping 2.
In addition to this one large bloc, we have also gathered data for the
following subgroupings separately: persons who speak an Iranian
language, persons who speak a Turkic language, Muslims, and Tatars.
Tatars are the only single nationality of Grouping 2 to be investigated
separately because of their relatively advanced status as compared to
the other nationalities of Grouping 2.*

Grouping 3 (Mobilized Europeans) consists of five groups (Jews,
Georgians, Armenians, Latvians, and Estonians) who are major non-
Slavic peoples of European USSR with relatively high socioeconomic
levels. Obviously, there is no uniformity of religion or language
within this group. In addition, because of the importance of the Jews,
in particular, we are also investigating them separately. Although the
Mobilized Europeans are similar in terms of socioeconomic characteristics, this category turned out to be the least satisfactory in terms
of population change. Rather than desegregating this category and re-
running our computer programs, we dealt with these groups individually where necessary in our analysis of their population change.

Grouping 4 consists of three subgroupings of other major nationalities. These three subgroupings will only be investigated separately and not all together. Grouping 4a (Finnic peoples excluding Estonians) includes another major bloc of linguistically related nationalities within the Soviet Union (for example, Mordvinians, Mari, Karelians). Estonians are not included here since they belong more logically
in Grouping 3. Groupings 4b and 4c (Lithuanians and Moldavians and
Romanians) are being investigated because of the political importance
of the nationalities involved. Both Lithuanians and Moldavians have

---

*Exemplifying the problems of investigating individual nationali-
ties in all censuses, the presentation of Tatars in 1897 caused some
difficulties. In the Transcaucasus provinces, the group listed as
Tatars actually was composed mostly of Azeri. Therefore, because
in subsequent censuses Tatars were about 1 percent of the combined
Tatar and Azeri population in this region, we have estimated the 1897
Tatar population of this region to be 1 percent of the listed "Tatar"
population.

republic status but are not included in Groupings 1 to 3, as are the remaining 13 nationalities with such a status. Romanians are included with Moldavians because they are virtually the same nationality.

Because these groupings and subgroupings often overlap (for example, peoples speaking a Turkic language overlap greatly with those who are Muslims), we have decided to focus our attention on ten mutually exclusive groupings in particular. In doing so, we can avoid repetitious discussions of many groupings that otherwise would occur. The ten groupings involved are as follows:

- Russians
- Ukrainians
- Belorussians
- Tatars
- Turkic-Muslims (that is, Turkic-Muslims excluding Tatars or non-Tatar Turkic-Muslims)
- Jews
- Mobilized Europeans (that is, Mobilized Europeans excluding Jews or non-Jewish Mobilized Europeans)
- Finnic peoples (that is, Finnic peoples excluding Estonians)
- Lithuanians
- Moldavians and Romanians

Hereafter three of the ten groupings will, for convenience, be referred to by the name of the larger grouping of which they are the largest part: the Turkic-Muslims excluding Tatars will be referred to simply as Turkic-Muslims; the Mobilized Europeans excluding Jews, as Mobilized Europeans; and the Finnic peoples excluding Estonians, as the Finnic peoples. Appendix A shows the specific nationalities in each census that comprise the ten groupings.

In summary, the system of nationalities we are using is somewhat arbitrary, especially since it does not include all the nationalities in the Soviet Union. The excluded nationalities, however, are minor in terms of relative size. In 1959 and 1970 no excluded nationality comprised even 1 percent of the total Soviet population. Our groupings include the major nationalities, and account for well over 90 percent of the population in any census. In addition, not only are our groupings often logical in terms of linguistic and religious criteria but they also are generally consistent with groupings arrived at by utilizing an objective statistical taxonomic technique based primarily on socioeconomic criteria.[15]

These, then, are the major demographic characteristics we have extracted for the total population of the economic regions. The same characteristics were also extracted for the urban and rural populations separately with the following exceptions. First, because the

1959 census does not provide appropriate work force data for the urban and rural populations, the work force categories investigated for the total population could not be similarly examined for the urban and rural populations. However, this problem was partly alleviated, as will be seen in the subsequent discussion on variables. Also, urban size classes were obviously not determined for the rural population.

In conclusion, with the exceptions noted, we have estimated these characteristics for the total, urban, and rural populations of the 19 economic regions in 1897, 1926, 1959, and, as much as possible, 1970. It should be kept in mind that these data are only estimates and contain a number of deficiencies. In particular, we have made no effort to correct obvious but rather small errors in the figures as published in the census. For example, in Muslim areas in 1897 there is almost certainly an underenumeration of children aged 0 to 1. We did not undertake any procedures to correct these figures because, for our study, we are concerned with the 0 to 9 age cohort, and even a corrected to 1 population would comprise only a small proportion of this cohort; and a brief investigation revealed that regional patterns of variables based on the 0 to 9 age cohort were virtually the same whether the 0 to 1 cohort was corrected or not. In short, as far as our analysis is concerned, correction of this and of many other minor errors would not be worth the time and effort.

Also, it should be remembered that the population of characteristics in regions containing border areas are relatively deficient. Such problems in these areas as the lack of available data, the different census dates, the different definitions of terms, and the different languages of presentation undoubtedly make these estimates less reliable. Nevertheless, we did attempt to overcome these border area obstacles as much as was reasonably possible.

Nevertheless, in spite of the deficiencies discussed, we do have a high degree of confidence in our data. Given the enormous task involved, we actually are, in fact, quite proud of what we have achieved: a capability for the first time to investigate changes in a wide array of demographic characteristics for Russia and the USSR based on a comparable national territory and set of territorial units and on a roughly comparable set of definitions.

Variables

On the basis of the procedures just discussed, we have been able to generate a wide array of demographic and socioeconomic variables for the total, urban, and rural populations for 1897, 1926, and 1959. In addition, we have computed changes in these variables for the periods 1897-1926, 1926-59, and 1897-1959. Although we are processing

1970 data as they are published and 1970 data are used in this study, we have not been able as yet to gather all the demographic characteristics that we have processed for 1897, 1926, and 1959 because the data are not yet available. Therefore, this discussion will be primarily concerned with the 18 matrices of demographic variables we have generated based upon the 19 economic regions in each of these three census years. Thus, for each of the three census years there is a separate matrix for the total, urban, and rural populations, accounting for nine "static" matrices. In addition, separate matrices were developed for the total, urban, and rural populations for each of the three intercensus periods, accounting for an additional nine "dynamic" matrices.

There are a number of reasons for generating these matrices of variables. First, the static matrices allow us to assess regional variations in particular variables in each census year. Second, the dynamic matrices allow us to assess changes in regional variations of particular variables from one census to another. Finally, the presence of variables all based upon the same number of cases (here, 19 regions) allows us to examine basic demographic relationships. Thus, with these matrices major demographic patterns and processes in Russia and the USSR can be described and analyzed to a considerable extent.

For the three static matrices concerned with the total population, 90 variables have been generated. These variables can be separated into four main categories: distribution, composition, level of urbanization, and specialized. Distribution variables involve the regional distribution of each characteristic, namely, the percent of the total national population of each characteristic that was located in each region. For example, the distribution of Russians refers to the percentage of the total Russians in the nation who lived in the Northwest region, the West region, and so on. Composition variables concern the relative importance of each characteristic in each region, namely, the percent of the total population of a region comprised by each characteristic. For example, the composition of Russians revealed what percent of the total population of the Northwest region was Russian, what percent of the West region was Russian, and so on. Variables involving levels of urbanization serve as an indication of the degree of modernization of a given population group (nationality, age group, and so on); specifically these variables involve the percent of the total population of a characteristic in a region that resided in urban centers. For example, the level of urbanization of Russians revealed what percent of the total number of Russians in the Northwest region resided in urban centers, what percent of the total number of Russians in the West region resided in urban centers, and so on. Finally, specialized variables are those that did not fall into the other three categories.

Examples of specialized variables calculated for each region are the child-woman ratio and the literacy rate. Appendix B lists the 90 variables comprising the static matrices for the total population.

A number of comments are necessary concerning these variables, especially the specialized variables. The distribution, composition, and level of urbanization variables are fairly understandable, entailing three perspectives on the demographic characteristics we have been able to compile. (Variable 32, percent of the total population residing in urban centers, has been classified as a composition variable, but could also be classified as a level of urbanization variable.)

Individual specialized variables are included for a variety of reasons. Variable 84 (child-woman ratio) was derived as an indicator of fertility. Although this index is crude, especially with our somewhat unconventional cohort for children, it is the best indicator of fertility we could derive, given the constraints of our goals, in that it is the only index of fertility that can be obtained for all economic regions in all three census years. Variable 85 (sex ratio) is also a composition variable, because it correlates exactly with the percent of the male total population. Variable 83 (percent of females aged 20 to 49) is simply a by-product of variables 84 and 85. Since we knew the total number of females and the number of females in the reproductive years, it was possible to calculate variable 83 as an indicator of the reproductive potential of the female population. Variables 86 to 88 were calculated to reveal the work force structure of each region. Variable 89 (literacy rate) was calculated to serve as an index of educational levels. In spite of its deficiencies in this respect, this is the only index of educational levels that can be obtained for all economic regions in all three census years. Finally, variable 90 (population density) was calculated because it is a conventional measure of population distribution, albeit a very crude one, particularly in relation to our large regions; and it was easily obtainable.

These 90 variables are the major variables we have been able to generate given the constraints of our data and our goals. Unfortunately, a number of other possible variables could not be calculated at all. An additional number, although available, could not be calculated for all three census years or for the economic regions. Many of these will be interwoven into our study when appropriate, because even though the 90 variables provide the basis for our study, it would not be reasonable to confine our work solely to these variables alone.

The other 15 matrices of data are largely dominated by these 90 variables, although each varies somewhat from this basic 19 x 90 matrix. Variables derived for the urban and rural static matrices are listed in Appendixes C and D. Generally, they are similar to the variables in the total matrices, with some exceptions. As with the total matrices, distribution, composition, and specialized variables

could be similarly derived for the urban and rural matrices. Of
course, for the urban matrices, except for the work force variables,
distribution refers to percent of the total national urban population of
each characteristic that was located in each region, and, again, except for the work force variables, composition refers to the percent
of the urban population of region comprised by each characteristic;
an analogous situation applies to the rural population, except, of
course, for the replacement of the term rural for urban. And in both
matrices specialized levels are completely confined to the urban and
rural populations, respectively, with the exception of the work force
variables.

As is evident, however, there are a number of differences
among the total, urban, and rural matrices. Most notable is the
fewer number of variables in the urban and rural matrices (55 and 50
variables, respectively). This difference is owing mainly to the absence of the 24 level of urbanization variables from the urban and
rural matrices. Such variables, of course, involve the total population only.

Another reason for the fewer variables in the urban and rural
matrices is the fact that, as mentioned before, work force variables
could not be gathered for the urban and rural matrices because appropriate data were not presented in the 1959 census. However, because
we desired some work force indicators for these matrices, we consequently added variables from the total matrices. The industrial and
tertiary work forces were added to the urban matrices and the agricultural work force was added to the rural matrices. Especially noteworthy is variable 54 (percent of the total nonagricultural work force
in industry) of the urban matrices. This is the best indicator available as to the industrial or service orientation of cities in all three
census years. Of course, the underlying assumptions of these additions are that the two nonagricultural sectors were exclusively confined to urban areas and the agricultural sector was exclusively confined to rural areas. Such assumptions obviously have their deficiencies, but the additions were made nonetheless.

In summary, we have generated three static matrices for each
of the three census years of 1897, 1926, and 1959. For each year, a
total, urban, and rural matrix has been developed, with the total matrix consisting of 90 variables, the urban matrix consisting of 55 variables, and the rural matrix consisting of 50 variables. (It will be
noted that these matrices do not contain individual variables concerned
with Jews, non-Jewish Mobilized Europeans, Tartars, and non-Tatar
Turkic-Muslims. This is because, as will be seen, these matrices
were developed in order to be subjected to factor analysis and, unfortunately, we decided to single out these four groupings only after
we had completed the factor analyses. Nevertheless, the variables
focusing on these four groupings will be utilized in our study.)

On the basis of these nine static matrices, nine corresponding dynamic, or change, matrices were calculated for 1897-1926, 1926-59, and 1897-1959. For the most part, these dynamic matrices simply consist of the absolute change in the respective percentages or ratios found in the static matrices. For example, the total dynamic matrix for the 1897-1959 period includes 90 variables, which represent the differences resulting from the subtraction of the percentages and ratios in the1897 total static matrix from the corresponding percentages and ratios in the 1897 total static matrix from the corresponding percentages and ratios in the 1959 total static matrix. (Absolute change was preferred over percentage change for a number of reasons. First, it was easier to calculate. Second, the degree of change as measured by percentage change is often distorted by a low base figure [this became especially apparent when measuring the increase in the level of urbanization of some of the nationality groupings; see Chapter 5]. Also, absolute change served as the basis for the calculation of other locational measures, which will be discussed in the section on methods. In addition, we have found it to be a useful indicator of change in the past [see Lewis and Rowland, "Urbanization in Russia and the USSR: 1897-1966," pp. 779-80]. Furthermore, as Table 5 of the Lewis and Rowland study suggests, regional patterns based on absolute change in a percent or ratio are often roughly similar to those based upon percentage change. Finally, as will be seen, we are especially interested in the correlations between these "dynamic" variables, and, from what we can surmise, it makes little difference whether the variables being correlated involve absolute change or relative change. For example, we found that from 1897 to 1959 the correlation between the absolute change in the level of urbanization and the absolute change in the percent of the population in the industrial work force was not substantially different from the correlation between the percentage change in urbanization and percentage change in industrialization. Thus, the results appear to be approximately the same regardless of whether absolute change or percentage change is the measure.)

Thus, for the dynamic matrices concerned with the total population the variables could be classified as redistribution,* change in composition, change in level of urbanization, and change in specialized indicators. Similar to the situation regarding the static matrices, the urban and rural dynamic matrices consist of the same types of variables except for the fact that they did not include changes in the

---

*The reader should keep in mind that the redistribution variables are concerned not only with migration but are also a function of natural increase and migration.

level of urbanization. The variable numbers for the dynamic matrices correspond to those listed in the appendixes for variables of the static matrices (therefore, additional appendixes for the dynamic matrices are unnecessary).

In addition to the 90 variables for the total dynamic matrices, the 55 variables for the urban dynamic matrices, and the 50 variables for the rural dynamic matrices, we have added variables concerning the average annual percentage change in the total, urban, and rural populations because they are basic indicators of change. The total, urban, and rural growth rates were all added to the total dynamic matrices, resulting in a final total of 93 variables. The urban growth rates were added to the urban dynamic matrices (leading to a final total of 56 variables) and the rural growth rates were added to the rural dynamic matrices (resulting in a final total of 51 variables). It should be noted that we did not include variables concerned with the percentage change in the absolute population of each characteristic because these types of variables are largely represented by the redistribution variables. For instance, regional variations in the growth of the Russian population are virtually identical to regional variations in the redistribution of the Russian population.

In conclusion, we have generated 18 matrices of data for the 19 economic regions with each matrix consisting of roughly 50 to 100 variables. Thus, for the first time an extensive array of demographic variables has been derived for Russia and the USSR generally based upon a comparable national territory and set of territorial units and upon roughly comparable definitions of each variable. Results will be presented throughout the volumes of this series whenever appropriate.

Methods

In order to extract additional information, we have applied a number of methods to the matrices. The major methods include factor analysis, rank correlation, the dissimilarity index, and the coefficient of redistribution.

Factor analysis is utilized in this study to simplify our extensive array of data and to seek out the relationships among the variables.[16] This commonly used technique essentially involves the following steps. After the variables have been standardized and intercorrelated, the intercorrelation matrix is subjected to factor analysis, and usually five to ten major clusters of highly intercorrelated variables emerge. A factor is essentially any one of these clusters and can be thought of as an artificial variable that represents a number of other variables. In short, factor analysis typically reduces a large number of variables to a few artificial variables, or factors.

A final step is then to derive standardized scores for each unit or observation (factor scores). This is accomplished by weighting factor score coefficients (estimates of the loadings) by standardized scores for each variable.

These factors can then be "rotated" to achieve the maximum degree of association of variables with the factors. The rotation utilized here is the varimax criterion. This rotation is especially advantageous, because the rotated factors are more distinct from one another, a feature that aids the authors' desire to obtain distinct clusters of variables. In the unrotated version, factors often were more similar in that a particular variable was often highly loaded upon more than one factor (a loading is, in effect, a correlation coefficient between a factor and a variable). Therefore, in the unrotated version, factors are generally less distinct from one another.

Another advantage of the rotated version is that it facilitates the naming of the factors. A factor's name is usually arbitrarily determined on the basis of those variables most highly loaded upon it. Loadings in the rotated factors were, in general, more polarized than those in the unrotated factors; that is, the highest loadings on a particular rotated factor were usually very high, while those on a particular unrotated factor were more moderate. Thus, rotated factors had the advantage of being easier to name because there was much less doubt about which were the major variables comprising the factor.

An additional reason for using factor analysis is that it allows a simplification of cartographic procedures. Instead of mapping every variable individually, the mapping of one factor essentially accomplishes the mapping of the many individual variables that are highly loaded upon or related to that factor. It should also be noted that the types of factor analyses utilized here are rank correlation factor analyses. Rank correlation is being used primarily to avoid problems created by highly skewed variables. Therefore, all the data were ranked and ordinal data served as the input into the factor analysis program.[17]* Pearsonian correlation coefficients of ordinal data are basically identical to Spearman rank correlation coefficients. The 5 percent confidence level for an N of 19 is 0.461.

Finally, a few comments are necessary on the number of cases and the dimensions of the matrices. We realize that 19 cases is not an ideal number, especially for an area as large as the Soviet Union and especially since much spatial variation is masked by these gross

---

*Although we actually utilized a principal components analysis program, we use the term "factor analysis" in this study for purposes of simplicity and conventionality. In addition, we would like to thank Barry Appelman, consultant at the Columbia University Computer Center, for helping us derive a ranking program.

units. Nevertheless, given, once again, the constraints upon our study, it was the most feasible solution.

Furthermore, additional checks on the correlation results based on the 19 regions tend to support their validity. For example, one of the authors replicated a significant portion of the variables and analysis utilized here, employing instead 1926, 1959, and 1970 data ordered into the 141 census units of 1959; statistical results were essentially the same as in our study.[18] Thus, approximately the same results occurred when the number of cases was either 19 or more than 100. In addition, as will be seen, the correlations based on the 19 regions tend, in general, to be quite explicable. Thus, we feel that the use of only 19 regions has not produced greatly distorted results.

The matrix dimension problem involves the fact that in all 18 matrices the number of variables greatly exceeds the number of cases. R. J. Rummel has expressed the fact that there may be problems associated with such dimensions.[19] In particular, he says that, "when the interest is in inference from sample results to universal factors . . . the number of cases should exceed the variables."[20] However, this situation is not applicable to our work, since we are using data for the entire population and not just a sample. Furthermore, Rummel notes that, "when the interest is only in describing data variability, then a factor analysis will yield such a description regardless of variables exceeding cases in number."[21] Since we are using factor analysis for describing relationships, it seems that the dimensions of our matrices are no problem. In addition, Rummel cites a number of studies, including two by himslef, in which factor analysis was applied to a matrix in which the number of variables greatly exceeded the number of cases.[22] Finally, perhaps the best testimony to the validity of our approach is the fact that our factors are logical and generally conform to clusters that one would predict from a brief survey of the intercorrelation matrix.

In summary, rank correlation factor analyses of each of the 18 matrices will serve as a major set of methods in our study. Results of these analyses will be presented throughout the discussion whenever appropriate.

The dissimilarity index and the coefficient of redistribution are similar in many respects: they both measure the locational patterns of a given characteristic, they both are based ultimately upon our distribution variables, and they both are calculated in the same manner.

The dissimilarity index measures the relative degree of locational segregation of a characteristic at one point in time.[23] It is calculated by comparing the percentage distribution of that characteristic with the percentage distribution of the total population or some other relevant characteristic. (The dissimilarity index is being used here in its broadest context in that it involves a comparison with both the total population or some other relevant characteristic. Unless stated otherwise, the dissimilarity index will be used in the former sense in this study; that is, a comparison of the distribution of a given characteristic with that of the total population.) In computing this index, the percentages of the distribution of one characteristic are subtracted from those of another. The absolute value of the sum of either the positive or negative differences serves as the dissimilarity index for that characteristic. (An alternative and virtually identical means of calculation is to sum the absolute value of all positive and negative differences and divide this sum by two.) This value can range from 0 to 100. (When one characteristic is compared to the total population, a value of 100 is impossible, as it is not possible for the location of a characteristic to be completely separate from that of the total population. However, if one characteristic is compared to another characteristic this upper limit of 100 is possible, because it is possible for locations of two characteristics [say, ethnic groups] to be completely separate from one another.

A value of 0 occurs when the distribution of the characteristic is the same as that of the total population or some other relevant characteristic (that is, the differences are 0, so the the sum of the differences has to be 0). A value of 100 or almost 100 represents a high degree of segregation in that the spatial distribution of the given characteristic is completely different from that of some other relevant characteristic or the total population, respectively. For example, consider the following hypothetical case of the dissimilarity index for nationality X based upon five regions:

Region	Population	Nationality X	Nationality X – Total Population
A	10	80	+70
B	30	5	−25
C	30	0	−30
D	20	0	−20
E	10	15	5
Total (percent)	100	100	+=75

Thus, the dissimilarity index for nationality X based on this regional framework is 75, which is indicative of the fact that nationality X is highly segregated from the total population.

The coefficient of redistribution measures changes in the distribution of a characteristic. It is calculated in a manner similar to that of the dissimilarity index. Here, however, the percentage distribution of a characteristic at one point in time is compared with that of the same characteristic at another point in time. The absolute value of the sum of either the positive or negative differences represents the coefficient of redistribution, and can vary in value from 0 to 100, with 0 indicating no redistribution and 100 indicating complete redistribution. Again, considering the hypothetical example of nationality X at two different points in time (T_1 and T_2) based upon five regions, we have:

Region	T_1	T_2	$T_2 - T_1$
A	10	80	+70
B	10	5	-5
C	5	0	-5
D	5	0	-5
E	70	15	-55
Total (percent)	100	100	+=70

Thus, the coefficient of redistribution for nationality X between T_1 and T_2 is 70, which suggests that the locational patterns of this nationality have changed quite dramatically.

Both the dissimilarity index and the coefficient of redistribution should become more meaningful when actually put into practice. They will be used quite extensively throughout the study whenever appropriate, especially in the discussion of the distribution and redistribution of nationalities.

NOTES

1. For example, see Frank Lorimer, The Population of the Soviet Union: History and Prospects (Geneva: League of Nations, 1946); and Chauncy D. Harris, Cities of the Soviet Union (Chicago: Rand McNally, 1970).

2. Russian Empire, Tsentral'nyy Statisticheskiy Komitet Ministerstva Vnutrennikh Del, Pervaya Vseobshchaya Perepis' Naseleniya Rossiyskoy Imperii, 1897 G., 89 vols.; USSR, Tsentral'noye Statisticheskoye Upravleniye SSSR, Vsesoyuznaya Perepis' Naseleniya 1926 Goda, 66 vols.; USSR, Tsentral'noye Statisticheskoye Upravleniye pri Sovete Ministrov SSSR, Itogi Vsesoyuznoy Perepisi Naseleniya 1959 Goda, 16 vols; and USSR, Tsentral'noye Statisticheskoye Upravleniye pri Sovete Ministrov SSSR, Itogi Vsesoyuznoy Perepisi Naseleniya 1970 Goda, 7 vols. Data from the census of 1939 will not be used to any great extent because very little information was published for major statistical enumeration units (that is, oblast and ASSR) below the republic level.

3. For a list of these censuses and other sources, see footnote 3 of Robert A. Lewis and Richard H. Rowland, "Urbanization in Russia and the USSR: 1897-1966," Annals of the Association of American Geographers 59 (December 1969): 777.

4. J. William Leasure and Robert A. Lewis, Population Changes in Russia and the USSR: A Set of Comparable Territorial Units (San Diego, Calif.: San Diego State College Press, 1966).

5. This urban criterion is the comparable urban definition we have utilized in all our studies. For a more detailed discussion of the reasons for using this criterion, see Lewis and Rowland, op cit., 777-79; and ibid., pp. viii-xi.

6. For example, see Leasure and Lewis, op. cit., pp. xi-xii. In addition, one of the authors has independently allocated 1926 data into the 141 census units of 1959, and when he aggregated his data into the 19 regions, the results confirmed the validity of the allocation percentages for the 19 regions. The difference was usually less than 1 percent. See Ralph S. Clem, "Population Change and Nationality in the Soviet Union, 1926-1970" (Ph.D. diss., Columbia University, 1975). Also, as will become apparent later, the results of our work generally tend to conform to expected patterns.

7. Leasure and Lewis, op. cit., pp. ix-x.

8. Ibid.

9. The most recent estimates of the 15,000 and over population of each region in 1897, 1926, 1939, and 1959 can be found in Lewis and Rowland, op. cit., p. 782.

10. For a detailed discussion of these characteristics, see Leasure and Lewis, op. cit., pp. 38-41.

11. For a detailed discussion of these 1961 data, see ibid., pp. 38-40.

12. S. Bruk and V. Kozlov, "Voprosy o Natsional'nosti i Yazyke v Predstoyashchey Perepisi Naseleniya," Vestnik Statistiki, no. 3 (1968): 32-37.

13. For a comparison of the questionnaires and instructions concerning the 1897 and 1926 censuses, see N. Ya. Vorob'yev, Vsesoyuznaya Perepis' Naseleniya 1926 G. (Moscow: Gosudarstven- noye Statisticheskoye Izdatel'stvo, 1957), pp. 83-104.

14. Bruk and Kozlov, op. cit., p. 35.

15. Ralph S. Clem and Steven I. Gordon, "Nationality Classification for Geographic Research," Proceedings of the Middle States Division, Association of American Geographers (1972), pp. 44-50.

16. For a good discussion of this technique, see R. J. Rummel, Applied Factor Analysis (Evanston, Ill.: Northwestern University Press, 1970).

17. The factor analysis program utilized (BMD-X72) is de- scribed in BMD, Biomedical Computer Programs: X-series Supple-

ment, ed. W. J. Dixon (Berkeley, Calif.: University of California Press, 1970), pp. 90-103.

    18. Clem, op. cit.

    19. Rummel, op. cit., pp. 219-20.

    20. Ibid., p. 220.

    21. Ibid.

    22. Ibid.

    23. For a good discussion of this index, see U.S. Department of Commerce, Bureau of the Census, The Methods and Materials of Demography, by Henry S. Shryock and Jacob S. Siegel and Associates, I (Washington, D.C.: Government Printing Office, 1971), p. 262.

3

GEOGRAPHIC
BACKGROUND

Because we are especially concerned with spatial patterns of population, we feel that it is necessary to describe briefly the geographic background of the USSR. This discussion will focus on those elements that are salient to a discussion of population, in that detailed discussions of the geography of the USSR are easily available in other sources[1] and this study is demographically oriented. Major elements to be discussed include areal size, location, topography, climate, soils, natural vegetation, natural resources for industry, and economic patterns. Because our intention in this discussion is to provide background information for those with little knowledge of the USSR, we will emphasize the broad, general influences of the geographic background on population distribution. More detailed relationships will be investigated in the various parts of this study. Of course, we do not mean to imply in this discussion that the natural environment and the location of resources are the determining factors in population distribution or change. They must, of course, be viewed in their societal context.

NATURAL ENVIRONMENT

Areal Size

The USSR is by far the largest state in the world. With an area of 8,650,000 square miles, it alone accounts for roughly one-sixth of the land surface of the earth and is more than twice as large as each of the next largest states: Canada, China, the United States, and Brazil. In fact, the combined area of the two eastern regions of East

Siberia and the Far East alone exceeds that of the coterminous United
States. Another reflection of this immense area is that in terms of
longitude, the USSR extends about 170 degrees, or almost half around
the earth in the middle latitudes.

Such a large areal size influences demographic patterns of the
Soviet Union in a number of ways. First, its large size increases
the probability that the USSR will have a relatively large population
and contain a relatively wide diversity of peoples (particularly considering the extent of its inhabitable area). Its population of approximately one-quarter of a billion, which ranks third among nations of
the world, and the presence of more than 100 nationalities are reflec-
tions of this situation. In addition, the large areal size entails unparalleled distances of internal migration. Such distances in the Soviet
Union can exceed 6,000 miles, thus frequently exceeding distances of
international migration in other parts of the world.

Location

With respect to location, the outstanding characteristic of the
USSR is its high latitudinal position. Its latitudinal position ranges
from nearly 36 degrees to almost 78 degrees north, excluding the
islands in the Arctic Ocean, with the vast majority of the country lying north of the forty-fifth parallel, the parallel on which Minneapolis
is located.

This locational position is primarily responsible for the generally severe climate of the Soviet Union. About two-thirds of the country is covered by tundra and taiga. Most of the country experiences
a mean temperature of 32°F or below at least 30 days per year. In
addition, virtually the entire country receives snowfall, and only about
10 percent of the area is regarded as arable. Furthermore, only
about 1 percent of the area of the USSR has a warm temperate climate.
In contrast, this climatic type dominates such areas as Europe, the
eastern United States, northern India, southeastern China, and Japan,
thus including a relatively great share of the world's population.
Thus, the climatic type that is apparently the most conducive to dense
human settlement is virtually absent from the USSR.

A major demographic implication of this climatic situation is
the fact that the USSR as a whole is relatively sparsely inhabited.
Whereas the population density for the land area of the world is roughly
75 people per square mile, the corresponding figure for the USSR is
less than half—only 28 people per square mile. A more detailed discussion of the relationship between climate and population, especially
the spatial patterns, will be presented in the following sections.

Topography

In addition to a generally severe climate resulting from its high
latitudinal position, the landform structure of the Soviet Union also
exhibits a high degree of uniformity. The country consists primarily
of a vast plain surrounded by higher and more rugged landforms on the
southern and eastern peripheries. The plain is a continuation of the
enormous lowland that begins in France and England and extends on
through northern Germany and Poland and then into the USSR. In the
Soviet Union this plain rarely exceeds 1,000 feet in elevation and extends roughly halfway across the country up to the Yenisey River in
East Siberia. The only major break in this flat surface are the Ural
Mountains, which form the border between the Northwest and Urals
regions and extend southward through the southwestern portion of the
latter region. This break is relatively insignificant, however, since
elevations generally are less than 3,000 feet and the highest peaks
are, like the Appalachians, only slightly above 6,000 feet. Consequently, the Urals are no major barrier to transportation and communications.

The presence of this vast expanse of lowlands has influenced
population distribution by facilitating agricultural development, transportation, and communications, thereby promoting a relatively high
degree of settlement. Map 3.1, which shows the "ecumene," or inhabited area, of the USSR in a simplified manner, indicates that the
vast majority of the Soviet population does in fact reside within this
physiographic zone. In addition, this immense plain very probably
has tended to neutralize the barrier to migration of the vast distances
existing within the present-day boundaries of the USSR, particularly
in earlier periods.

To the east and south of this great plain lie areas of considerably
higher elevation. To the east, the land surface rises to peaks in excess of 10,000 feet. To the south, even higher elevations are reached.
In the Caucasus chain, which forms the boundary between the North
Caucasus and Transcaucasus regions, elevations rise to above 18,000
feet, while in the Pamirs, in the southeastern portion of Central Asia,
elevations of more than 24,000 feet are encountered. These mountainous zones not only discourage local settlement but also tend to reduce
the extent of settlement in the great plain. By blocking the movement
of warm moist air from the more southerly oceans, the mountain
ranges contribute to the high degree of aridity that plagues much of
the interior plain. In fact, the vast majority of the USSR receives
less than 20 inches of precipitation annually. In contrast, nearly all
of Europe and about one-half of the United States (excluding Alaska)
receive more than 20 inches of precipitation annually.

MAP 3.1

USSR: Major Areas of Settlement

AREAS WITH A RURAL DENSITY OF 10 PERSONS
OR MORE PER SQUARE KILOMETER (25 PERSONS OR MORE PER SQUARE
MILE). THESE AREAS ALSO CONTAIN MOST OF THE URBAN POPULATION
OF THE USSR. CITIES WITH A POPULATION OF 1,000,000 AND OVER
IN 1970 ARE SHOWN ON THE MAP.

Source: Based upon: Malyy Atlas SSR (1973) pp. 9-10; and Chauncy D. Harris, Cities of the Soviet Union (1970), p. 11.

63

Climate, Soils, and Natural Vegetation

As implied, the two chief traits of the climate of the USSR are the relatively high degree of coldness and aridity. In this section the climatic conditions of the USSR will be discussed in greater depth, especially with regard to the spatial patterns. In addition, soils and natural vegetation conditions will be discussed because they both are so highly associated with climatic conditions.

Although low temperatures generally dominate Soviet climatic conditions, given the considerable latitudinal extent of the country, significant regional variations do exist. The highest temperatures, of course, are generally recorded in the most southerly regions of the country, Central Asia and the Transcaucasus, and these regions, along with part of the Crimean Peninsula of the South region, contain most of the very few areas of the USSR that have a warm, temperate climate. The Transcaucasus, in fact, contains the only area of the Soviet Union (and this area is very limited in size) with a humid subtropical climate, a climatic type mild enough to allow for the growth of tea and citrus fruits, which, incidentally, dominates the southeastern portions of the United States and China. However, even though Central Asia and the Transcaucasus contain these warm temperate areas, they both contain substantial areas of more severe temperature conditions; for example, major portions of both regions experience mean temperatures of 32°F or below for more than 30 days a year. These values, of course, generally increase with an increase in latitude. Portions of the Arctic coast in East Siberia and the Far East, in fact, have more than 270 days with this range of mean temperatures. In addition, in parts of East Siberia temperatures of below -90°F have been recorded.

These regional patterns of temperatures help explain the major sparsely populated zone that extends throughout the northern portion of the USSR (Map 3.1). This population void generally coincides with the more familiar natural regions of the tundra and taiga. The tundra is a generally treeless zone extending along the entire Arctic coast of the USSR in a narrow belt usually 100 to 300 miles wide. The taiga, in contrast, is a vast coniferous forest, which generally coincides with the subarctic climatic zone and comprises the remainder and bulk of this northern population void. In both regions soil conditions are an additional major impediment to settlement, tundra soils and the podzols of the taiga being relatively poor for agriculture. Furthermore, reflecting the high latitude of these natural regions, virtually all of the tundra and the eastern half of the taiga is subject to permafrost (conditions in which the soils are either permanently or semipermanently frozen).

Whereas temperatures generally decline toward the north, precipitation values in the USSR generally show an opposite spatial trend. Although parts of the mountainous regions along the southern and eastern peripheries receive the highest amounts of precipitation in the USSR (more than 40 inches per year), precipitation values actually generally decline from the northwest to the southeast. Annual values of between 20 and 40 inches are experienced in the West region (the Baltic republics) and adjacent areas. In contrast, in much of Central Asia and Kazakhstan annual totals of less than 8 inches are recorded; in fact, values of less than 4 inches annually are characteristic over wide portions of these regions. These low precipitation values are instrumental in the sparsely population character of much of these two regions. Nevertheless, although these regions are generally very sparsely populated, they do contain the most densely populated rural areas in the USSR. These dense agglomerations of settlement are based primarily on the major rivers flowing from the mountain chains on the southern periphery. Such rivers as the Tedzhen, Murgab, Amu-Dar'ya, Zeravshan, and Syr-Dar'ya have, in fact, supported irrigation agriculture since well before the time of Christ. Today, irrigation systems in these regions account for the bulk of the cotton produced in the Soviet Union.

Between the sparsely populated zones of the extremely cold north and extremely dry south lies an intermediate zone. Especially since it is somewhat warmer than the area to the north and somewhat moister than the area to the south, it is relatively favorable for agriculture in the Soviet context; in fact, it contains the bulk of the arable land in the Soviet Union. Because of such conditions and because of its spatial pattern, it has often been termed the Fertile Triangle, with the base of the triangle being on a line roughly from Leningrad to Odessa and the sides extending from these two cities to Novosibirsk in Siberia.

Within the Fertile Triangle, the north-to-south climatic transition can be further evidenced in terms of a northern and southern portion. The northern portion of the Fertile Triangle, especially the northwest portion, dominates the West region, the southwestern corner of the Northwest region, Belorussia, the northern part of the Southwest region, and the Center, as well as substantial parts of the Volgo-Vyatsk and Ural regions. It is characterized by humid continental climate, mixed forests, podzolic soils, and an agricultural emphasis on flax, potatoes, oats, and rye.

The southern portion dominates Moldavia, the Ukraine, the Central Chernozem region, the North Caucasus region, the Volga region, the extreme southwestern part of the Ural region, northern Kazakhstan, and a significant part of West Siberia. This portion generally consists of the steppe and forest-steppe natural regions. The steppe is the largest in area of the two and is generally a semiarid region dominated by grassland vegetation. The forest-steppe, as its name implies, is a grassland zone with trees interspersed; not surprisingly, it is a transitional zone between the mixed forests to the north and the steppe to the south. The southern portion of the Fertile Triangle also contains the famous and relatively fertile chernozem (black earth) soils, and has an agricultural emphasis on wheat, sugar beets, corn, and sunflowers.

Partly because of the relatively favorable conditions for agricultural development, this triangular region contains the vast majority (approximately 75 percent) of the Soviet population (Map 3.1). The share of the Soviet population residing within the Fertile Triangle has declined, however, a decline that can be observed on the basis of our 19 economic regions. The Fertile Triangle contains either all or a significant share of the populated area of 15 of these regions. Central Asia, the Transcaucasus, East Siberia, and the Far East are the only regions that do not contain areas that fall within the Fertile Triangle. Therefore, for demographic purposes, the other 15 regions can be used as a surrogate for the Fertile Triangle. Investigation reveals that the percentage of the Soviet population residing in these 15 regions, in fact, has declined from 89.9 percent in 1897 to 81.2 percent in 1970. Nevertheless, despite the rapid industrialization and urbanization of the USSR in recent decades and despite the rapid population growth in areas outside the Fertile Triangle, the distribution of population is still largely based upon spatial patterns of areas that are suitable for agriculture, reflecting the inertia effect of agricultural resources.

It should be kept in mind, however, that this so-called Fertile Triangle is highly favorable for extensive settlement primarily only in the Soviet context. As might be gathered from the preceding discussion, a major limitation of this area is that where soils are more fertile there is less rainfall and vice versa. In many other areas of the world, the environmental conditions of the Fertile Triangle would be regarded as marginal. For example, in the United States, the humid continental and steppe climates are located primarily in the North Central states and Great Plains. In fact, no major region of the USSR is comparable to the Corn Belt or Cotton Belt of the United States in that there are no major regions in the USSR that have both a long growing season and sufficient precipitation. Consequently, population densities in the Fertile Triangle are somewhat lower than those in other major agricultural areas in the world, even if mechanization is taken into account.

Natural Resources for Industry

The industrial resource base of the USSR presents an almost completely opposite picture from that of the agricultural resource base. Whereas the Soviet Union has a relatively poor environment for agriculture, it has perhaps the best natural resource base for industry of any country, a circumstance that is enhanced by its large territorial size. Virtually every major mineral resource is found in the USSR, and usually in abundance. This wide variety and abundance of mineral resources has been a major factor in the rapid industrialization of the Soviet Union, a process that has received top priority in the Soviet economic plans beginning in the late 1920s. Perhaps most importantly the Soviet Union is the world's leading producer of coal, iron ore, and manganese, the three major inputs into the production of steel. This situation has greatly enhanced the particular Soviet policy of rapidly expanding the heavy industrial sector. In recent years, in fact, the USSR has led the world in the production of steel. In addition, the USSR ranks second in the production of petroleum, natural gas, copper, gold, and nickel, and its petroleum reserves are surpassed only by those of Saudi Arabia.

The location of the industrial resources has both advantageous and disadvantageous aspects with respect to the distribution of the population. Fortunately, the Fertile Triangle includes many outstanding mineral deposits. The exploitation of these deposits has been enhanced by a nearby supply of labor and, in turn, has further enhanced settlement in the Fertile Triangle. Two major mineralized zones are particularly worthy of mention, especially because they have given rise to some of the most important industrial regions in the USSR. It should be noted, however, that some very important industrial regions in the USSR have virtually no local natural resource base; outstanding in this respect are the urban-industrial regions centered on Moscow (Center) and Leningrad (Northwest), which are based mainly on market, labor, and transportation advantages and are principally oriented toward the machine-building industries. One major mineralized zone is composed of the Volga and Urals regions. The Volga region and the southwestern portion of the Urals region contain the outstanding petroleum-producing area in the country. These oil fields now account for well over half of the petroleum produced in the USSR. In addition, the Ural Mountains themselves are one of the outstanding mineralized zones in the world. Nearly all major minerals are located within this area, with iron ore and copper being particularly important. As might be expected, the Volga and Ural regions have emerged as major areas of the chemical, steel, and machine-building industries.

However, perhaps the most important mineral zone within the Fertile Triangle is the Donetsk-Dnepr region of the eastern Ukrainian SSR. This region is the foremost producer in the USSR of coal, iron ore, and manganese, and the major deposits of each (the Donbas, Krivoy Rog, and Nikopol', respectively) are all within 300 miles of each other. Perhaps nowhere else in the world is there such a close

proximity of major deposits of these main raw material inputs for the
production of steel. Not surprisingly, the Donetsk-Dnepr is the leading steel-producing region in the USSR, accounting for more than one-
third of the national production.

Unfortunately for the Soviet Union, however, the resource location pattern of the Donetsk-Dnepr is more of an exception than a rule.
Although the Fertile Triangle does include some noteworthy mineral
deposits, a number of major mineral deposits are situated well beyond
this major zone of settlement. Outstanding in this respect is the Asian
part of the USSR. Although the European part of the country contains
the bulk of the Soviet population, the Asian part contains the bulk of the
reserves of a number of important industrial resources, particularly
coal and hydroelectric power. In addition, these more remote areas
contain substantial supplies of petroleum and natural gas, as well as
many other important minerals. All in all, the areas outside the Fertile Triangle are a veritable mineral storehouse.

The ensuing locational disparity between major areas of settlement and major areas of mineral wealth is one of the major geographic
problems facing Soviet planners. A prime demographic response to
this locational disparity has been a substantial migration to the remote
regions, especially Siberia. In fact, although the tundra, taiga, and
desert regions are still very sparsely populated, the presence of major
mineral deposits within these regions has led to a number of new major
mining settlements. The classic example is the city of Noril'sk, which
is located north of the Arctic Circle in the northwestern portion of
East Siberia. From its founding in the mid-1930s, this city has grown
to a population of well over 100,000, largely on the basis of substantial
deposits of nickel, copper, and cobalt.

Recently, however, migration to the remote eastern regions has
changed somewhat in that net out-migration has begun from some of
these regions. This problem will be investigated in greater depth in
the second volume of this series. Suffice it to say here that the whole
question of effectively settling the mineral-rich regions beyond the
Fertile Triangle is a major example of the interplay between the natural environment and the distribution of population in the Soviet Union.

Summary

The previous sections have sought to distinguish the major elements of the natural environment of the USSR, especially in terms of
their individual effects on the distribution of population. As a summary
of these relationships, it might be useful to reverse the sequence of
discussion, namely, a brief description of the population distribution
and the environmental factors involved in such a distribution.

Map 3.1 shows the distribution of population in the USSR. From the map it is possible to distinguish one major area of settlement and three minor areas of settlement. Together these areas comprise the ecumene of the USSR. In addition, two major areas that are largely uninhabited can also be distinguished.

The major area of settlement is the so-called Fertile Triangle, which extends from the western border of the USSR into northern Kazakhstan and West Siberia. This zone contains roughly three-fourths of the Soviet population. Environmental conditions promoting relatively appreciable settlement here include a generally flat landscape; the best large-scale combination of adequate temperatures and precipitation in the USSR; the relatively rich chernozem soils in the southern portion; and some major mineral deposits, especially in the Donetsk-Dnepr, Volga, and Urals regions.

The three minor areas of appreciable settlement include the oases of Central Asia and southern Kazakhstan, the Transcaucasus region, and the string of settled areas extending through the Trans-Siberian Railway zone from West Siberia to the southern part of the Far East region. The oases of Central Asia and southern Kazakhstan are based primarily on the major rivers flowing northward from the southern peripheral mountainous areas and on relatively favorable temperatures for agriculture. Both environmental features in this region help sustain irrigation agriculture and the highest rural population densities in the USSR.

The Transcaucasus region has a number of environmental advantages for settlement. As with Central Asia and southern Kazakhstan, relatively favorable temperatures and rivers from nearby mountains provide the basis for irrigation agriculture here also. Unlike the major populated areas of Central Asia and southern Kazakhstan, however, a great share of the settled area of the Transcaucasus, especially the western portion, is favored by annual precipitation totals that often exceed 40 inches per year.

Although settlement in the Trans-Siberian Railway zone is based mainly on the presence of the railway itself, environmental factors also have exerted some influence. Outstanding here are the existence of substantial mineral deposits, especially coal, and a considerable potential for the production of hydroelectric power. In addition, although the subarctic climate of the zone generally impedes agricultural development, some local basins do support agricultural settlement.

Finally, the two major areas of sparse settlement reflect the two major climatic impediments of the Soviet Union. In the vast, sparsely populated zone that covers most of the northern and eastern USSR, extremely low temperatures are the major barrier to settlement. In contrast, extreme aridity is the principal environmental re-

striction to settlement in the less extensive sparsely populated area
in Central Asia and Kazakhstan. Although both population voids are
more settled than in the past because of the recent exploitation of substantial local mineral deposits, they serve as classic examples of the
primary impact of the environment upon population patterns in the
USSR.

REGIONAL ECONOMIC DEVELOPMENT

Agriculture

Throughout the course of Russian and Soviet history, the conditions and geographic expansion of the rural economy have had a profound impact upon society. Significant developments within the agricultural sector have taken place even within the last 25 years, developments that have resulted in substantial population change and have had
important implications for Soviet society. Perhaps because of the im-
posing industrial and economic stature of the Soviet Union, we tend to
overlook the fact that until very recently (1961 by Soviet estimates)
the majority of the country's population was rural.

The theme of this study is modernization and its relationship to ·
population change; in this regard, economic development based upon
urban-industrial activities is clearly the most important element influencing population change. Yet, agricultural pursuits, which generally are not included in studies of modernization, certainly have
played a role in effecting population change (particularly migration),
and no study of population change in Russia and the USSR would be
complete without an assessment of trends and changes in rural population characteristics and redistribution. Accordingly, this section will
consider briefly the broad outline of Russian agrarian history, and
examine the conditions of agriculture in that country, including regional
characteristics, that contributed to population change. The main
thrust of change in Russian agriculture, at least in terms of population change, took place before the period covered by this study (1897-
1970). However, because of the importance of these changes, such as
the migration of Russians, Ukrainians, and Belorussians to agricultural lands beyond their traditional homelands, lands inhabited largely
by non-European peoples, we are constrained to note briefly these
trends and suggest the societal implications deriving therefrom.

The most important aspect of population change associated with
the agrarian history of Russia has been the migration of agriculturists
to new lands. This historical migration, away from established,
densely populated regions in central European Russia, resulted from

the general impoverishment of the rural population. The woeful conditions of agrarian life in Russia resulted, in turn, from inadequacies of the natural environment and the limitations imposed by the rural social and economic systems.

In addition to the limitations imposed by the natural environment, the social organization of rural areas, together with economic conditions, severely limited agricultural productivity. Landholdings among the vast majority of peasants were decidedly inadequate and fragmented. Agricultural technology and practices in Russia were backward, and the conservative and fatalistic peasantry resisted innovations. Until the end of the nineteenth century, regional specializations in crop production were not feasible because of the lack of a transportation network; each region, indeed, each farm, had to be self-sufficient. Following the abolition of serfdom in 1861, conditions did not improve markedly for most peasants, as redemption payments for allotted lands taxed or even exceeded the resources of most households.[2] Finally, one must add to the long list of rural shortcomings the oppressive social climate in which a few rich landowners were supported in grand style by many poor peasants, where brutalities designed to keep the populace in line were commonplace, and where frequent peasant uprisings were put down with strong punitive measures.[3]

The combination of poor agricultural resources and unfavorable social and economic conditions acted as strong push forces out of the traditional Russian regions to new agricultural land. Population growth in the older, central regions brought about increasing pressures on the land, pressures that historically were alleviated by out-migration to the frontiers and the resulting expansion of acreage. As George Pavlovsky stated: "Wherever the Russian frontier was moved, its extension was followed or, not unfrequently, even preceded by Russian settlers."[4] As the Muscovite state and later the Russian Empire expanded into and secured the areas along the middle and lower Volga, the Ukrainian and North Caucasian steppe, and Siberia, peasants and cossacks were attracted to the prospects of new, better land and somewhat greater personal freedom. Thus, the most fertile areas in the forest-steppe transition zone were eventually settled by agricultural colonists; these flat, open lands had been depopulated by nomads following the Tatar invasion.

The major historical changes in agriculture and the redistribution of rural population that fall within the scope of this study are the migrations to Siberia and Kazakhstan. The first major migration of agricultural settlers to the steppe areas of West Siberia and northern Kazakhstan occurred mainly in the last decade of the nineteenth and first decade of the twentieth centuries. Migration to areas east of the Urals during this period alone is estimated at 6.5 million.[5] Relatively good agricultural land was the lure, with the beginning of the Trans-

Siberian Railroad (1892) and the promulgation of the Resettlement Act (1899) providing additional inducements.[6] Analysis of migration data in the 1897 tsarist census and the 1926 Soviet census reveals high rates of rural in-migration to the North Caucasian, West Siberian, and Kazakh steppe, with the migration stream shifting more to the latter two regions by 1926. These same data indicate that the core regions of European Russia provided the bulk of out-migrants.[7]

In addition to the large-scale migration to West Siberia and Kazakhstan in the pre-Soviet period, more recent rural in-migration into these areas resulted from the expansion of acreage associated with the Virgin and Idle Lands Program (1954-56). As a result of this agricultural development scheme, rural population increased significantly, particularly in northern Kazakhstan.[8]

In summary, the historical redistribution of the rural population resulted from poor agricultural conditions in the central Russian regions and the general impoverishment of the peasants. In the period preceding the growth of industry, this migration was directed mainly to new agricultural lands incorporated into the expanding Russian state, although some migrants moved to cities in developing industrial regions as well. In later periods, agricultural migration became numerically less important as rural out-migrants moved primarily to cities. The impact of rural population redistribution has been significant, particularly since the majority of the migrants were ethnic Russians (and, to a lesser extent, Ukrainians, Belorussians, and Mordvinians), and the colonized areas were mainly non-Russian. Rural population pressures continue to confront the Soviet government with serious problems, although now the high densities occur in non-Russian areas.[9]

Industry

The rapid expansion of the capitalist economy during the last decades of the tsarist regime and the tremendous industrialization drive and economic growth of the Soviet Union are, in the aggregate, generally widely known and certainly well documented. Not so well known are the geographic patterns that resulted from this economic growth, patterns that evolved through a combination of the inherent location of natural resources; previously existing population distribution; government development schemes; and the economic, political, and technological conditions prevalent during different historical periods. It is not our intention here to examine in detail the economic history of Russia and the USSR, or to analyze those features of the economy that are peculiarly Russian or Soviet. Rather, we propose simply to present chronologically the economic development of the various regions of the Russian Empire and the USSR, citing aggregate economic trends only insofar as they shed additional light upon changes in the economic geography of the country.

Our reasons for undertaking this brief survey include, as we noted earlier, the belief that regional changes in population character- istics can best be understood by linking these changes to economic de- velopment. The linkages between economic development and the var- ious aspects of population change (such as urbanization, migration, and fertility) have been detailed in an earlier chapter; in this section we should like to summarize those major regional economic trends that will be utilized to explain much of the population change that has occurred in Russia and the USSR.

The Tsarist Period

Industrial development in the Russian Empire is generally con- sidered to have begun in the early decades of the eighteenth century during the reign of Peter the Great. As a means of supporting his military adventures, Peter imposed heavy taxation upon the populace and encouraged the development of the war materiel industries, in par- ticular, textiles and iron production. In this regard, two regions of the empire experienced significant industrial growth during the Petrine period: the Center region around Moscow, based on textiles and metallurgy, and the Urals region, based upon iron and copper produc- tion. The development of the iron industry in the Urals, utilizing local ores and charcoal for smelting, was perhaps the most dramatic development, in that industry existed in the Center region before Peter. In fact, the increase in production of the Urals made Russia the world's leading producer of iron during most of the eighteenth century. Metal- lurgical centers founded in the Urals during the Petrine period, includ- ing Yekaterinburg (Sverdlovsk) and Nizhniy Tagil, continue to this day to be major iron and steel producers. [10]

During the next century and a half, industrial expansion occurred principally in the two established regions, with the Northwest region (around St. Petersburg, or Leningrad) also assuming increasing impor- tance. Some new mining centers in Siberia were developed, but the Urals dominated both mining and smelting, particularly in the key iron industry (the Urals accounted for 83 percent of total Russian pig iron production in 1860). [11] The textile sector was further expanded in towns and cities of the Center region by the growth of the cotton indus- try; such cities as Ivanovo, Kostroma, and Vladimir supplemented Moscow as centers of linen and cotton manufacturing. It should be noted that a significant, indeed, often a majority, of industrial produc- tion during this period was centered on cottage industries, particularly in the textile sector. [12]

During the latter decades of the nineteenth century, Russian industry, especially heavy industry, witnessed another major geographic shift. While the Urals iron production remained dependent upon charcoal for smelting, innovations abroad (in particular, the use of coking coal) had advanced iron production in the countries of Western Europe well beyond the Russian level. In the 1880s and 1890s, encouraged by the demand for iron products (principally from the expanding railroads) and backed by foreign capital, intensive economic development began in the eastern Ukraine (Donetsk-Dnepr region), based on the large reserves of coking coal in the Donets Coal Basin, or Donbas, and a major source of iron ore at Krivoy Rog.[13] By 1913, 67 percent of the Russian pig iron production was in the Donetsk-Dnepr region, and the Urals share had declined to 20 percent of the total production.[14] This area, centered around cities such as Donetsk, Voroshilovgrad, Makeyevka, and Kramatorsk, continues to be the major iron and steel region of the Soviet Union.

By the beginning of the First World War, there had occurred significant economic development in the Russian Empire. On the eve of the Revolution, the major areas of industrial production were the Northwest region, the Center region, the Urals, and the eastern Ukraine (Donetsk-Dnepr region). Additionally, petroleum production in the Caucasus region, mainly around Baku, had developed to a large degree. It is difficult to assess the economic legacy that the tsarist government bequeathed to its successor. Although underdeveloped in comparison with the major powers of Western Europe, the Russian economy had experienced appreciable growth in the last decades of the nineteenth century. In particular, as a result of large government investments, the basic railroad network had been laid. At any rate, the economic-geographic patterns that evolved in Russia persist to this day.

The Early Soviet Period

During World War I and during the consolidation of power by the Bolsheviks, the economy of the fledgling Soviet Russia was devastated by military action and the general reign of violence of the civil war period. Following the extraordinary measures enacted by the Soviets (the period of so-called War Communism), Lenin initiated in 1921 a program of economic reconstruction (the New Economic Policy, or NEP), which included concessions to capitalists and in particular to peasants. The general success of the NEP is attested to by the recovery of industrial and agricultural production to prewar levels by 1926.[15]

The Bolsheviks, however, viewed the NEP as a temporary phenomenon that, in the long run, was antithetical to socialism and reinforced the enemies of the working class. Thus, plans were being worked out in the mid-1920s to expand the economy and embark upon a centrally directed program of industrialization that would strengthen the Soviet state against both foreign and domestic enemies. Within the Bolshevik ranks, however, there was considerable disagreement as to both the pace of future industrialization and the means by which to finance it. Clearly, industrial expansion was, of necessity, reliant upon savings from the agricultural sector, but there existed alternative methods, ranging from coercion to market and consumer goods incentives, for extracting the needed funds from the rural economy.[16] The Soviet industrialization debate certainly had noneconomic overtones; Stalin utilized internal dissension within the Party as one means of consolidating political power. Yet the final outcome of the development controversy—rapid, forced industrialization, emphasis on producer goods and heavy industry, and the collectivization of agriculture —resulted in dramatic changes in the economic geography of the Soviet Union. The emphasis upon heavy industry and producer goods naturally influenced the location of investment to regions where this form of manufacturing was most reasonably undertaken. Essentially, as in any developing country with limited investment funds, there was a tension between the expansion of existing centers of production and the economic development of more underdeveloped regions. In most instances, investment into established manufacturing regions was economically more desirable, as these regions contained skilled labor and a supporting infrastructure. Also, the existing centers of production were mainly in the European USSR and thus closer to markets, thereby lowering transportation costs. To expand into frontier regions often necessitated large capital outlays for physical plant and transportation lines, as well as the importation of labor. Although many of the frontier areas shared a definite advantage in terms of raw material quantity and quality, their peripheral location in relation to populated areas required long, expensive hauls of goods to markets.

Noneconomic factors, such as defense considerations, the desire for regional self-sufficiency, and the program to develop non-Russian nationality areas, dictated large-scale investment in eastern regions. The nature of economic development (the emphasis on heavy industrial or producer goods) during the first two five-year plans resulted in a major expansion of coal, iron and steel, and copper production in the Urals, West Siberia, and Kazakh regions. Iron ore from the Urals was utilized, together with coking coal from the vast reserves in West Siberia (the Kuznets Coal Basin, or Kuzbas), by means of incredibly long shipments (1,400 miles) of both iron ore and coal to newly established iron and steel plants at both ends of the haul (the famous Ural-Kuzbas Combine).[17] In the Kazakh Republic, large coal deposits near Karaganda were developed during this period, and the mining and smelting of copper, lead, and zinc increased significantly.[18] The

tremendous economic growth of the Soviet economy, in general, and
of the eastern regions, in particular, is reflected by the fact that this
period (1926-39) witnessed the greatest growth of urban population in
Soviet or Russian history, or, for that matter, of any country of the
world. Of the three regions of the Soviet Union in which cities increased in size by three times during this period, two (the Urals and
West Siberia) were in the east. The growth of such cities as Magnito-
gorsk in the Urals, Novokuznetsk and Novosibirsk in West Siberia,
and Karaganda in Kazakhstan, is virtually unparalleled.[19]

Although the most impressive alterations of the economic landscape during the early Soviet period took place in the east, development continued in the established industrial regions in the European
USSR. The iron and steel industry in the Donetsk-Dnepr region was
modernized and expanded, and it was in this region that one of the landmark projects of early Soviet development, the dam and hydroelectric
station on the Dnepr at Zaporozh'ye, was constructed. Indeed, the
Donetsk-Dnepr was one of the three regions of the country in which
the urban population trebled between 1926 and 1939, an indicator of
the fact that economic growth did not take place only in the east during this period.[20]

World War II and the Postwar Soviet Period

With the invasion of the USSR in June 1941, the Soviet government undertook a massive relocation of industrial enterprises from
areas in the west that were threatened by the German advance to relatively more secure regions in the east. Over 1,300 major enterprises,
together with personnel, were relocated, primarily to the Urals, Siberia, Kazakhstan, and Central Asia. Following the war, these plants
remained in the east, the net effect being a shift in Soviet industrial
production from west to east. The reconstruction of war-damaged industries in the west, particularly the heavy manufacturing region of
the eastern Ukraine (Donetsk-Dnepr), has somewhat restored the
prewar balance, but the eastern regions still account for a significantly
larger share of total Soviet production than before the German invasion.[21] The regional distribution of pig iron production, an excellent
indicator of heavy industrial output, is illustrative of this shift from
west to east and the later shift back to the west. In 1940, or the last
prewar year, 71 percent of pig iron production was located in the European USSR (the west) and 28 percent of production took place in the
Urals and Asiatic USSR (the east). In 1945 the shift of production to
the east resulted in an increase for this area to 76 percent of pig iron
production, whereas the share of the west declined to 24 percent. By
1965, however, the balance of production had shifted back to the west
with the restoration of its industrial capacity, with the result that the

west accounted for 62 percent and the east for 38 percent of production in that year.[22]

As is the case with the majority of Soviet industry, the more recent development of the Urals, Kazakhstan, and Siberia has been based on abundant mineral resources, huge supplies of energy, and heavy manufacturing (especially iron and steel). As noted earlier, the eastern regions contain natural resources significantly disproportionate to their share of the population, and Soviet planners have long favored a shift in population and production to the east to utilize more fully these high quality and relatively low cost resources. The development in the eastern regions begun in the 1930s was greatly enhanced by World War II and continued through much of the postwar period. The Soviet government has devoted substantial shares of total investment to the eastern regions, embarking upon development of hydroelectric stations, thermal electric stations utilizing very low cost coal, power-oriented industries. It appears, however, that recently the pace of development in the east may have been reduced, perhaps as a result of a general unwillingness on the part of the populace to relocate permanently to the harsh eastern regions and to the low rate of return on investment in these areas.[23]

In addition to the rapid development of the east, another area, the Volga region, has experienced dramatic industrial growth since the war. The rapid expansion of industry in the Volga region is directly attributable to the change in fuel consumption within the Soviet economy from coal, firewood, and peat to petroleum and natural gas, and to the shift in petroleum production from the established Caucasus fields to the relatively recently developed Volga-Urals fields. In 1940 coal, firewood, and peat accounted for 79 percent of Soviet fuel consumption, with petroleum and natural gas equaling only 21 percent. By 1965 coal, firewood, and peat had declined to 48 percent of fuel consumption, whereas petroleum and natural gas had expanded to account for 52 percent.[24] This increased importance of the petroleum/natural gas sector was concomitant with a geographic shift in petroleum production from the Baku and Groznyy fields in the Caucasus, where large-scale production began in the late 1800s, to the Volga-Urals fields, which expanded rapidly in the postwar years. In 1940 the Caucasus and North Caucasus fields produced over 85 percent of Soviet petroleum, while the Volga-Urals accounted for only 6 percent. In 1965, however, whereas the Caucasus produced 17 percent of total petroleum, the Volga-Urals now accounted for 72 percent.[25] This dramatic shift in and emphasis on petroleum production obviously greatly enhanced industrial development in the Volga region, particularly in the Tatar and Bashkir ASSRs and in Kuybyshev Oblast. Chemical industries have developed in the Volga region in conjunction with the petroleum production, and major hydroelectric stations on the Volga and Kama rivers have further contributed to the development of the region.[26] This tremendous industrial development, combined with the central position of the region (relative to the European and Asian portions of the USSR), portends further economic expansion in this region.

The recent shift to petroleum and natural gas as fuel sources, combined with an expanding chemical industry, has favored industrial development in the western European USSR. Petroleum and natural gas are reasonably transportable via pipelines, and refineries and chemical plants dependent on petroleum can be located near established market areas in the west. This development has provided the impetus for economic growth in Latvia, Lithuania, and Belorussia, which receive natural gas and petroleum by pipelines from the Dashava gas fields in the Ukraine and the oil fields in the Tatar ASSR.[27]

Within recent years, increased emphasis has been placed by the Soviet government on the further economic development of regions in the heavily populated west, at the expense of the eastern regions. In addition to the previously mentioned labor and investment shortcomings of the eastern regions, they are far removed from markets for their industrial production. Indications are that Soviet planners are becoming more inclined to locate large industrial enterprises in the western regions with their large markets, skilled labor supply, and well-developed economic infrastructure. Recent developments in the key iron and steel industry may herald this trend. Although significant growth within the iron and steel industry in the east has taken place recently, the primary attention is being given to expansion in the European West.[28]

Summary

In summary, the regional industrial development of Russia and the USSR can be outlined as follows: During the tsarist era, industry developed early in the Center and Urals regions and later in the Northwest and Donetsk-Dnepr regions; during the early Soviet period, there was significant development in the east, particularly in the Urals, West Siberia, and Kazakhstan, but also in the west; and the German invasion necessitated the relocation of industry to the east, but, following World War II, the western regions were rebuilt to virtually their prewar position. Development in the eastern regions (the Urals, West Siberia, East Siberia, and Kazakhstan), although of massive proportions, has been of late superseded by the increased attention to the west and, in particular, to the Volga region.

NOTES

1. Examples of more comprehensive surveys of the natural environment of the USSR include Paul E. Lydolph, Geography of the U.S.S.R., 2d ed. (New York: Wiley, 1970), pp. 3-21; and James S. Gregory, Russian Land, Soviet People (New York: Pegasus, 1968).

2. George Pavlovsky, Agricultural Russia on the Eve of the Revolution (New York: Howard Fertig, 1968), Chaps. 2, 4, and 7.

3. Geroid Tanquary Robinson, Rural Russia Under the Old Regime, rev. ed. (Berkeley, Calif.: University of California Press, 1972), in particular Chaps. 6 and 7.

4. Pavlovsky, op. cit., p. 21.

5. Donald Treadgold, The Great Siberian Migration (Princeton, N.J.: Princeton University Press, 1957), pp. 33-34.

6. Ibid., Chap. 3; see also George J. Demko, The Russian Colonization of Kazakhstan: 1896-1916 (The Hague: Mouton & Co., 1969), Chap. 3.

7. J. William Leasure and Robert A. Lewis, "Internal Migration in Russia in the Late Nineteenth Century," Slavic Review 27 (September 1968): 375-94; and J. William Leasure and Robert A. Lewis, "Internal Migration in the USSR: 1897-1926," Demography 4, no. 2 (1967): 479-96.

8. See W. A. Douglas Jackson, "The Virgin and Idle Lands of Western Siberia and Northern Kazakhstan: A Geographic Appraisal," Geographical Review 46 (January 1956): 1-19; and W. A. Douglas Jackson, "The Virgin and Idle Lands Program Reappraised," Annals of the Association of American Geographers 52 (March 1962): 69-79. Over 100 million acres were brought under cultivation in conjunction with this scheme, increasing total Soviet agricultural land by about 30 percent. Rural in-migrants to the Virgin and Idle Lands were estimated at about 250,000; the vast majority were, no doubt, Russians and Ukrainians.

9. See Neil C. Field, "Land Hunger and the Rural Depopulation Problem in the USSR," Annals of the Association of American Geographers 53 (December 1963): 465-78.

10. W. H. Parker, An Historical Geography of Russia (Chicago: Aldine, 1969), pp. 112-20; and Maurice Dobb, Soviet Economic Development Since 1917, rev. ed. (New York: International Publishers, 1966), pp. 55-57.

11. Parker, op. cit., p. 242.

12. Peter I. Lyashchenko, History of the National Economy of Russia to the 1917 Revolution (New York: Macmillan, 1949), pp. 265-304, 333-36.

13. Dobb, op. cit., pp. 57-58; and Lyashchenko, op. cit., pp. 538-42.

14. Parker, op. cit., p. 297.

15. Dobb, op. cit., pp. 97-207.

16. Alexander Erlich, The Soviet Industrialization Debate, 1924-1928 (Cambridge, Mass.: Harvard University Press, 1960), pp. 1-98.

17. Theodore Shabad, Basic Industrial Resources of the U.S.S.R. (New York: Columbia University Press, 1969), p. 37.

18. Ibid., pp. 284-308.

19. Chauncy D. Harris, Cities of the Soviet Union (Chicago: Rand McNally, 1970), pp. 299-304.

20. Ibid., p. 303.

21. Lydolph, op. cit., pp. 474-75.

22. Shabad, op. cit., p. 38 (Table 10).

23. Leslie Dienes, "Investment Priorities in Soviet Regions," Annals of the Association of American Geographers 62 (September 1972): 437-54.

24. Shabad, op. cit., p. 6 (Table 1).

25. Ibid., pp. 14-15 (Table 5).

26. Ibid., pp. 124-34.

27. Ibid., pp. 201-13.

28. Theodore Shabad, "Soviet Lists Plans to Expand Iron and Steel Industry," New York Times, 3 April 1971, p. 2; Theodore Shabad, "Soviet Starting Production in Largest Blast Furnace," New York Times, 20 February 1973, p. 43; and "Germans Join in $1-Billion Pact to Equip a Soviet Steel Plant," New York Times, 23 March 1974, p. 1.

II

NATIONALITY AND
POPULATION CHANGE
IN RUSSIA AND THE USSR

CHAPTER

4

POPULATION CHANGE
IN MULTINATIONAL STATES

Chapter 1 discussed the general relationships between modernization and the major aspects of population change. This chapter will
examine the impact of modernization upon the population of multinational states, in general, and the USSR, in particular, in order to
provide a conceptual framework for the analysis of ethnic processes
in the USSR. The historical expansion of the Soviet Union will be examined and a survey made of Soviet nationality policy, as well. The
central point in this discussion, and the theme of this study, is that
modernization affects various ethnic groups in multinational states to
different degrees or at different times. Therefore, for reasons suggested below, individual nationalities in multinational states normally
are characterized by different levels of modernization (as measured
by demographic and socioeconomic indicators), reflecting the degree
to which these nationalities have been integrated into modern sectors
of society. Modernization in multinational states is a potentially destabilizing force, in that it often results in a realignment of nationalities in systems of ethnic stratification, while at the same time bringing
about heightened awareness of inequalities and increased aspirations
among groups. We will have more to say about the societal implications of modernization and population change in multinational states in
Chapter 10.

GENERAL PATTERNS

If, within multinational states, various nationalities are distinguished by different levels of modernization, the inquiry naturally devolves to the question: Why do some nationalities modernize to a

greater extent, or sooner, than others? We suggest here that the answer to this important question is twofold: political-military dominance over other groups permits favoritism toward the dominant nationality and the imposition of sanctions against minorities; and some nationalities, because of certain aspects of their culture, are more likely to take advantage of the opportunities created by economic development. We should stress that these factors are not mutually exclusive. Taken individually or in combination, where appropriate, these proposed explanations should further our understanding of how modernization influences population in multinational states.

The first proposed explanation for the evolution of different levels of modernization in multinational states is straightforward: military conquest and domination. This situation is basically that of colonial areas that were eventually absorbed into a larger country or that became independent under the control of the colonist element. Examples of the first type would include the American Southwest and the annexation of Tibet by China. The second type would include Australia, New Zealand, and South Africa. In all of these instances, the indigenous ethnic groups were overcome by other, sometimes racially distinct, groups employing more technologically advanced military force. The ascendancy of the dominant group is perpetuated by the garrisoning of troops and later by political means and the imposition of social and economic sanctions.[1]

In many contemporary countries, significant and clearly well-intentioned efforts have been made to provide for the social and economic advancement of previously disadvantaged groups; in other well-known examples this is not at all the case. In all of these cases, the nature and magnanimity of the dominant group notwithstanding, the original indigenous populations are characerized by lower levels of modernization than the dominant group. In other words, the original inhabitants are less educated, more rural, have higher fertility (and often higher mortality), occupy lower level jobs, and are normally less geographically mobile. Although it is difficult to document many of these examples with empirical data—this situation is, after all, not one that most countries prefer to publicize—some illustrations may be offered.

The American incorporation of Mexican lands into the United States, in particular the area now defined as the state of New Mexico, is a prime example of the conquest-incorporation type. Before overt military action in these territories, American traders and some farmers established themselves in the region, a presence that was to serve a useful function when hostilities broke out between the United States and Mexico in 1846. The actual military conquest of the region was virtually uncontested; the Americans already in the area influenced the Hispano officials and population against resistance. Following the

takeover and the establishment of the American political regime, outsiders entered the area to take jobs in the expanding mining industry
and as farmers and cattlemen. The cities, even the old historical
Hispano cities such as Albuquerque, became Anglo strongholds. Thus,
the majority of the modernized society (urban-industrial) became
Anglo; what indigenous folk entered the nonagricultural sector did so
at the lower levels.[2]

The settlement of New Zealand by European colonists is illustrative of the conquest-independence type. As the colonists, seeking agricultural land, expanded into areas inhabited by the indigenous population (the Maori), tensions between the two groups increased until
fighting erupted in the 1860s. The military victory over the Maori
assured the colonists of control; eventually New Zealand became independent within the British Commonwealth. Committed to a nondis-
criminatory policy, the New Zealand government has attempted through
various programs to integrate the Maori into modern society, and not
without some success. Yet the indigenous population remains less
modernized than the European population of the country.[3]

The reasons why indigenous populations remain relatively nonmodernized (relative to the dominant group) include such factors as
discrimination in education and employment and, in some cases, even
more rigid controls such as apartheid. Karl Deutsch has suggested
that nationalities that share "social communication" with dominant
groups in society have an advantage over other nationalities that are
outside these channels.[4]

> As an alignment with a center and a leading group,
> nationality offers to its members the possibility of
> vertical substitutions unbroken from any one link
> to the next. In a competitive economy or culture,
> nationality is an implied claim to privilege. It em-
> phasizes group preference and group peculiarities,
> and so tends to keep out all outside competitors.[5]

In addition to the barriers imposed by the dominant group against
their integration into modernized society, minority groups may not attempt to increase their participation in the modern sectors for some
time. The "reference group" for the minorites remains traditional
and nonmodern, and they do not consider the values and rewards of
the dominant group of any relevance or use. This isolation from modernized society will eventually be reduced as succeeding generations
are drawn into modern economic and educational sectors. Ethnic
stereotypes, often reinforced in multinational situations by differences
in skin color or language, contribute to a continuation of the dominant
group's ascendancy.[6]

Interestingly, the dominant position enjoyed by one group in a multinational state may be eroded by the loss of political and military power, such as occurred in Finland during the nineteenth century. Finland, until 1809, was a part of the kingdom of Sweden, and the Swedish minority controlled the towns and virtually all aspects of social, economic, and cultural life. With the establishment of Finland as a virtually autonomous duchy of Russia, the movement of Finns into urban areas and more advanced economic and social sectors accelerated until, in the latter half of the century, the character of the country became Finnish rather than Swedish.[7] Clearly, the change in political control was not the sole consideration in the erosion of Swedish hegemony, but this shift enabled the Finns to gain control of the political apparatus and to establish their language and culture as the dominant form.[8]

The idea that some ethnic groups possess certain cultural features that facilitate their integration into modernized society is not a new one, nor is it to be construed as an implication that "natural" differences contribute to the socioeconomic levels of nationalities. When technological change and economic development create new societal roles, competition for these roles results, competition that will be based (barring discriminatory sanctions) on skills and achievement orientation. The culture of some ethnic groups may incorporate values that encourage the entry of their members into modernizing roles.[9] History provides us with numerous cases of ethnic groups that, from the onset of modernization, rapidly entered the expanding educational institutions and the advanced work force, and broke local ties to pursue advancement in developing areas. Indeed, many of these same groups dominated nonagricultural sectors in premodern societies. Examples of such groups are the Jews of Eastern Europe; the Armenians, Lebanese, and Greeks of the eastern Mediterranean and Middle East; the Indians of East Africa; and the Chinese of Southeast Asia. There are, of course, considerations other than cultural traits to be taken into account. For instance, many of these groups experienced population pressures that necessitated out-migration to nonagricultural areas.

Yet the popular conception of some groups as achievers is supported by social-psychological research, principally that concerning Jews in the United States.[10] Researchers have noted that aspects of Jewish culture, for example, the respect for education and the emphasis on individuality, may contribute to the high achievement levels of Jews in American Society—the most "modern" of all societies.

In summary, we suggest that two factors influence the entrance of ethnic groups into modernizing society: the extent to which society is dominated by one or more nationalities and the cultural traits of individual nationalities. We have focused our attention upon cases of conquest-incorporation or conquest-independence to illustrate the first factor.

There are means (other than direct conquest of one group or groups by another) through which ethnic groups with differential levels of modernization reside within one country. In Belgium and Yugoslavia, multinational countries were created from dissolving empires. In both of these instances, one or more ethnic groups occupied, from the outset, disproportionately large shares of modern society, principally owing to the differential influence of other, outside societies.[11] The unequal levels of modernization in Yugoslavia and Belgium have resulted in ethnic tensions as previously disadvantaged groups seek a more equitable distribution of the rewards of advanced society.[12]

Whatever the circumstances under which ethnic groups are combined in multinational countries, there seems to be a universal situation in which one or more groups modernize earlier than others. We have posited that the reasons for this phenomenon are political and cultural, or, in the case of Belgium and Yugoslavia, owing to the combination of groups that have been differentially influenced by modernization. The impact of modernization upon population change and the reciprocal influence of population change upon modernization are such that in multinational states the timing of initial modernization is of paramount importance. Simply put, nationalities that, for whatever reason, modernize early control the emerging modernized sectors of the economy and society and are generally reluctant to share this position with groups that modernize later. However, with continued modernization it can be hypothesized that in most instances ethnic stratification will eventually be evaded, and all ethnic groups will have similar socioeconomic characteristics.

The principal impact of modernization upon population change in multinational states is through population growth and migration. The majority of population growth within the last two centuries has resulted from the declines in mortality associated with the early stages of modernization. This fact suggests that the timing of declines in mortality within a multinational state would be critical, since those groups that experienced declines in mortality would be the first to experience rapid population growth. In turn, rapid population growth, assuming a static agricultural technology and intensive land use, results in out-migration. Out-migration from rural areas experiencing population growth can take several forms: migration to cities (local and interregional), migration to other rural areas, or international migration. All of these responses have occurred historically, but with economic development, the expansion of opportunities in cities has drawn increasing numbers of migrants to urban areas. Furthermore, agricultural resources are finite, and as population growth continues, migration to rural agricultural areas becomes somewhat less of an option.

Clearly, forces other than population growth influence migration.
As detailed in Chapter 1, migration is strongly influenced by pull factors, which can be equated roughly with jobs. Also, other factors
have influenced the extent to which population can be supported in a
given area; land tenure systems, mechanization of agriculture, new
crops, and various natural calamities combine with population growth
to define population pressure upon resources. Of particular importance, however, is the fact that modernization results in both population growth and increased economic opportunities.

The migration aspect calls attention to the importance of the
location of economic development in multinational states. If opportunities are available in local urban centers, migration will be intraregional; if not, migration will be interregional or international. Since,
in most multinational states, certain regions of the country are identified with different nationalities, economic development may result
in the influx of outsiders into nationality areas if the indigenous population cannot, for one reason or another, meet the demand for qualified workers. Economic development as an ongoing process may continue to effect a redistribution of nationalities even if the indigenous
population becomes highly modernized. Modernization, among other
things, normally results in lower rates of population growth, and if
economic development creates more jobs than the low fertility-mod-
ernized indigenous population can meet satisfactorily, either in-migration or slower economic growth must result. In the long term, increased indigenous fertility would be a remote possibility. Appreciable increases in labor productivity can, of course, alleviate labor
shortages.

We will examine international migration and its effects on the
distribution of nationalities, although at first glance international migration may seem irrelevant to the Soviet example. International migration, excluding refugee or forced movements, is determined by
the same basic forces that shape all migration, that is, the balancing
of economic opportunities between relatively deprived and affluent
areas. Thus, the relevance of international migration becomes one
of scale, although even much international migration (such as that in
contemporary Western Europe) entails shorter moves than much internal migration in the Soviet Union (owing to the latter's enormous
geographic size). One important aspect of international migration is
that it increases the total population of a country, whereas internal
migration redistributes some total population but does not add to that
total. [13] However, in multinational states where different nationalities
occupy specific regions (and particularly when those regions are formally identified, as in a federation), one can view internal migration
on the regional scale as being generally similar to international migration in that net in-migration results in added increments to the re-

gion's population. When we refer to the effect of migration as adding increments to the population, we are, of course, concerned mainly with added increments to the labor force (and most migration is just that). In short, people move primarily for jobs. If internal migration results in the influx of workers of one nationality into traditional regions of another group, the effects on society should be broadly analogous to that of foreign immigration. Clearly, distinctions of citizenship, minority rights, and the like are normally different in the international and internal migration cases, and international migration is considerably easier to control. We would not want to make light of these or other considerations, yet we believe that a valid case can be made for examining the common features of international migration and internal migration in multinational states, and the effects thereof on society.

Within the broad field of international migrations and nationalities, the Unites States and Western European examples are illustrative of how ethnic group distributions are influenced by economic development. During the period of heavy immigration into the United States from Europe, the destinations of immigrants were strongly influenced by the location of economic opportunities; that is, immigrants were drawn to jobs in regions of economic growth and to cities. Temporal and spatial changes in economic growth in the United States resulted in the concentration of immigrants in certain areas. Since immigrants arrived from different European countries at different periods, the various immigrant groups are generally concentrated in whatever area experienced economic growth at the time of their arrival.[14] The attraction of cities for immigrants was dramatic, inasmuch as jobs in the burgeoning nonagricultural sectors of the economy were naturally located in urban areas. Although it is difficult to characterize in general terms the vast and multifaceted immigration to the United States from Europe, it is probably safe to say that a general lack of economic opportunities in Europe and population pressures on agricultural resources, combined with the demand for workers in the United States, were the major forces involved. Other motivations, such as flight from religious or political persecution are well known but are of lesser importance, and will not be dealt with here. In summary, the U.S. experience suggests that given economic development in different areas at different times, immigration will react to the location of opportunities, and various ethnic groups, thus, will be distributed largely in response to the creation of new, surplus jobs.

Recent Western European international migration is similar to the U.S. example in that migrants are moving from countries with low levels of opportunities to countries that offer better opportunities. Broadly, the migration is from Italy, Yugoslavia, and Turkey, north and west to Germany, Sweden, and France. Immigrants into France

from North Africa are also important. In France, for example, in
1968 immigrants accounted for 5.3 percent (2.6 million) of the total
population, up from 3.9 percent (1.8 million) in 1962; estimates of the
foreign population in France in 1972 put the immigrant population at
3.4 million (6.5 percent of the total population).[15] Thus, in France
the immigrant population is rapidly accounting for an increasingly
larger share of the total population, inasmuch as the French themselves have a low rate of population increase. It is just this low rate
of natural increase, combined with expanding economies in the countries of Western Europe, that creates the demand for workers in addition to those provided by the indigenous population. Many of the countries that supply immigrants into France are characterized by high
levels of population growth and/or economies that do not provide sufficient job opportunities. This differential level of population growth
and economic opportunity no doubt accounts for the bulk of the foreign
immigration into France; the immigrants are seeking jobs in an economy that offers greater opportunities than their homelands. Most frequently, the immigrants take the unskilled and undesirable jobs. Population growth in France apparently is insufficient for meeting labor
force requirements, and population growth in the countries of emigration almost certainly exceeds the expansion of job opportunities in
those areas. As was the case in the United States, extensive foreign
immigration has resulted in serious social problems in Western Europe.

Internal migration within multinational states can result in the
transfer of population from one nationality area to another, with generally the same societal effects as international migration. The principal consideration here is one of scale, as we discussed earlier. The
impact of such migrations on society in multinational states varies according to the historical, demographic, and legal status of nationality
areas. If, for instance, a certain area had been traditionally occupied
by a given nationality for a long period of time, that nationality comprised a large majority of the region's population, and the area was
legally and administratively defined in an ethnically federated state,
we might expect strong identification by the titular nationality with
the region as a homeland. An influx of other nationalities, even other
nationalities of a federal state, could result in increased tensions
among groups. Increments into the indigenous labor force from other
nationality areas could, depending on the ability of the local economy
to absorb the newcomers, bring about competition among nationalities
for jobs, education, housing, and other social activities. Much of the
historical conflict among nationalities, including the more violent
forms (riots, massacres, pogroms), can be explained by the competition for economic opportunities in difficult times.[16] Thus, internal
migration within multinational states is a potentially disjunctive force,
and merits our serious attention.

Again, the United States is an example of how differential regional economic growth, together with observable population pressures, results in the redistribution of ethnic groups, this time through internal migration. The initial large-scale migration of American blacks to areas of economic opportunities in the northern cities resulted from the drastic curtailment of European immigrants during World War I. The pressing need for new entrants into the expanding wartime labor force was combined with pressures on agricultural resources in the South caused by the boll weevil infestation and the mechanization of agriculture and relatively rapid population growth.[17] This combination of economic growth and the resultant job opportunities in the North, and pressures against resources and a lack of opportunity in the South, was largely responsible for initiating the internal migration of the blacks.

We have stated that in the initial stages of modernization, mortality declines result in population growth. The timing and impact of modernization upon nationalities in a multinational state are also important in relation to fertility, the other component of population increase. As nationalities enter the modernizing sectors, fertility, after a period, will decline. This decline in fertility with modernization is, as discussed in a preceding chapter, a result of increased aspirations and socioeconomic opportunity, declines in infant mortality, higher levels of education, urbanization, and the employment of women in the modern economy.

Because some nationalities are not integrated into modern society until relatively late, for reasons suggested earlier, fertility remains high among these groups. At the same time, these relatively nonmodernized groups have experienced dramatic declines in mortality, declines owing not so much to social and economic change but rather to the diffusion of other determinants of low mortality, such as public health measures. This situation is directly analogous to that obtaining in present-day underdeveloped countries, where diffusion of some determinants of low mortality, but not the more pervasive changes required to effect declines in fertility, has resulted in rapid population growth. The result of continued high fertility and declines in mortality among less modernized ethnic groups in multinational states is the same as among underdeveloped countries: rapid population growth.

Several examples will serve to illustrate the sequential impact of modernization upon fertility among ethnic groups in multinational states. In New Zealand the relatively nonmodernized Maori are experiencing rapid population growth because of continued high fertility (a crude birthrate in 1961 of 46.4 per 1,000) and low mortality (8.3 in 1961). Fertility and population growth rates among the dominant white population (which is considerably more modernized) is about half that of the Maori.[18] In Yugoslavia, population growth in the more modern-

ized Croatian and Slovenian republics is substantially slower than in
the less modernized Montenegrin and Macedonian regions.[19] In virtually every multinational country for which we have data, identical
patterns are in evidence: population growth among relatively less
modernized ethnic groups exceeds that of the more modernized groups.

In conclusion, the impact of modernization upon nationalities in
a multinational state will probably be (or has been) sequential. Politically or militarily dominant nationalities will modernize earlier, as
will groups that are characterized by strong achievement orientations.
Other groups will modernize later, depending upon their status within
society. The population change associated with modernization likewise
will occur sequentially among groups as they modernize. Population
growth will result in out-migration from rural agricultural areas to
cities and to developing regions. Population growth and fertility among
groups will decline as these nationalities modernize.

Assimilation

Just as population change is not determined solely by modernization, so population change in a multinational country may result from
factors not normally considered as demographic. In a multinational
country, assimilation often contributes to changes in the numbers,
distribution, and characteristics of ethnic groups. By assimilation,
we refer to changes in ethnic identity, the general case of which is the
identification by individuals among ethnic groups of lower socioeconomic
status with dominant or more advanced ethnic groups. Ethnic identity
is based upon the individual's psychological bonds with a group defined
by race, religion, or national origin. These ethnic characteristics
are normally taken in combination, and the relative importance of each
of the elements may vary from one situation to the next.[20]

The study of assimilation is concerned with the circumstances
under which an individual redefines those elements upon which ethnicity is based. In other words, what characteristics of the individual's original ethnic group and what exogenous forces acting upon the
individual within the socioeconomic milieu combine to facilitate or impede changes in ethnic identity? Brian Silver, in a penetrating analysis of ethnic identity and its correlates in the Soviet Union, suggested
that characteristics of ethnic groups themselves (such as geographic
distribution, religion, economic activities, and affinities with respect
to dominant groups in language, culture, and history), taken together
with government policies that influence ethnic characteristics (territorial delimitations, language and literary policies, and legal and administrative use of nationality identifications), largely determine the
extent to which ethnic group identity is reinforced.[21] Government

policies regarding language, in particular, language instruction and the medium of instruction in schools, seem to be important for the maintenance of ethnic identity.[22] The availability of social and economic institutions, such as clubs, churches, and mutual aid societies, and the extent to which groups congregate on the microlevel (residential segregation), have been shown to be important factors that influence assimilation.[23] Government policies often have an effect upon these factors as well as upon education and language.[24] Intuitively, given the characteristics of ethnic groups and the nature of policies affecting those characteristics, the length of time during which a group is exposed to assimilatory forces would be an obvious consideration.

In addition to those government policies that affect directly such ethnic correlates as religion and language, other, broader social and economic changes influence changes in ethnic identity. Deutsch refers to "social mobilization" as a process of social change wherein groups become urbanized, are employed in nonagricultural pursuits, attain higher levels of education, are exposed to and are capable of absorbing mass media, and incur a number of other changes. According to this concept, assimilation is more likely to occur among those groups that are "mobilized," that is, more modernized, primarily owing to increased contacts with other groups in the urban environment.[25]

Assimilation perhaps is best conceived as a continuum, with ethnic groups adopting new languages and other cultural vestiges earlier and not attaining complete acceptance by the dominant group and surrendering all original ethnic identification until much later. Milton Gordon has characterized this assimilation continuum as "cultural assimilation," or the earlier stages of assimilation involving changes in language, dress, and the like, and "structural assimilation," which entails acceptance into primary group associations (such as clubs, social cliques, and so on). Once structural assimilation is attained, even more sensitive barriers, such as sanctions against intermarriage, prejudice, and discrimination, will eventually be eliminated.[26] It is clear that ethnic identity is a durable, emotional, and persistent phenomenon that is frequently difficult to measure precisely; and particularly when ethnicity coincides with other social and economic characteristics, it is an important force in multinational countries (a fact dramatically demonstrated by the revival of ethnic identification in the United States).[27] Despite the persistence of ethnic identity in many instances, assimilation often has resulted in significant alterations in nationality populations, a phenomenon that will be illustrated in this study.

POPULATION CHANGE IN MULTINATIONAL
STATES: THE SOVIET EXAMPLE

There is little conceptual work from which to formulate hypothetical patterns of modernization and population change in a specific multinational state, such as the USSR. We can, however, at least sketch the broad outline of the extent to and sequence in which the various Soviet nationalities can be expected to be integrated into modernized society. In other words, it is our purpose here to draw upon the conceptual framework detailed in the preceding section to identify those ethnic groups in the tsarist and Soviet states that would be expected to modernize early in the process, and to discuss briefly the reasons why. From these expected patterns we will be able to analyze, in later chapters, those aspects of population change among groups that are directly related to modernization, such as urbanization, migration, and natural increase.

It appears from historical comparisons that the nationality that controls political-military power is likely to dominate modernized society. In this regard, we can unequivocally state that in the tsarist and Soviet contexts the Russians are the dominant nationality. The Soviet Union is, for all intents and purposes, the successor state to the Russian Empire, an empire created through the extension of Russian military power over weaker, non-Russian areas. During the period of civil war that followed the Revolution of 1917, the fledgling Soviet state attempted, with a good deal of success, to retain those non-Russian lands formerly controlled by the tsar.[28] Following a comparatively brief period between the two world wars wherein the USSR was somewhat truncated, the Soviets regained virtually all areas that were within the Russian Empire at its zenith, as well as some areas that were never part of the empire.* The expansion of the Soviet Union into non-Russian areas, such as the Baltic states, Galicia, and Moldavia, was, of course, brought about by the same means as tsarist expansion: force of arms. Thus, the Soviet Union is a state created by the conquest of non-Russian areas by Russians, in much

---

*Following World War II, the only former tsarist territories not within the Soviet Union were Finland, the former tsarist provinces in Poland proper, and the Kars area ceded to Turkey. Now within the Soviet Union, and never within the Russian Empire, were the East Prussian territory now known as Kaliningrad Oblast, areas in the western Ukraine (Galicia) and Bukovina, the area now known as Zakarpatsk Oblast, the Tuva area, and the Kuril Islands. Additionally, important territories were taken from Finland, and tsarist losses in the Far East (southern Sakhalin) were regained.

the same fashion as the United States expanded into regions originally controlled by Indians and Mexicans. In such states, on the basis of historical comparison, we might reasonably expect the conquering nationality to be in the ascendancy.

In addition to the strictly military-political preeminence of the Russians, other, more subtle features of Soviet society reinforce the dominant group's position. Foremost among these features is the overwhelming use of the Russian language in education, industry, government, and the media; Russian is also the language of command in the Soviet armed forces. Russian is the medium of instruction in most institutions of higher learning (although some of the nationalities with Union Republic status do have native language instruction at the university level), and within the universities, Russian dominates the scientific and engineering disciplines.[29] Russian is the lingua franca of industry, particularly in the technical, management, and scientific fields.[30] The predominance of the Russian language in the media is illustrated by the fact that in 1970, with Russians accounting for slightly over 50 percent of the Soviet population, over 80 percent of books, magazines, and newspapers published in the USSR in that year were in Russian.[31]

We should make clear at this point that we do not regard the predominance of the Russian language as an evil phenomenon; indeed, there is a strong case to be made on the grounds of efficiency for using a single language in a diverse multinational state. The Soviet government has sponsored extensive development of non-Russian languages (often to the point of creating alphabets and grammars). And, although the Russian language predominates, there does exist an impressive record of education and publishing in non-Russian languages. Yet the fact that Russian is the principal language of the Soviet Union greatly facilitates the entrance of Russians into the modernized sectors, into the better jobs and higher education. Non-Russians suffer from an inherent competitive disadvantage because of the language barrier, not unlike the problems encountered by immigrants to the United States. Bilingualism, of course, might provide a partial solution to the language barrier, although the quality of Russian language instruction in non-Russian areas has been the subject of frequent criticism in the Soviet press. By 1970 some 55 million, or 48.7 percent, non-Russians either declared Russian as their native language or stated that they had a fluent command of Russian as a second language.

Bilingualism or the ability to speak Russian fluently reduces to some extent the barriers for non-Russians who seek to enter the Russian-dominated modernized sectors. There remains, however, an even more subtle, pervasive, and difficult to evaluate barrier, that of ethnic or racial discrimination, It would be naive, as well as contrary to historical precedents, to assume that Russians do not dis-

criminate against other ethnic groups, particularly those of different
races and religions. Such features of multinational societies as ethnic
stereotypes, aversions to different skin color, and alleged superiority
of certain nationalities are not unknown in Soviet society. The most
obvious indicator of ethnic discrimination in the Soviet Union is the
long-standing official portrayal of Russians as wise, industrious "big
brothers" who unselfishly extend the hand of assistance to the poor,
underdeveloped nationalities of the USSR. These glorifications of the
Russians as teachers and humanitarians often reach dizzying heights.
Thus, an Uzbek poet could write (in 1965): "You are kind, you are
truly great, you are human a hundred times o'er! Oh how dear you are
to me, my own, my Russian brother—elder brother!"[32] These and
other methods extolling the seemingly endless virtues of the Russians
are characteristic of racist ideologies in general.[33]

Specific instances of discrimination against non-Russians are
difficult to locate, given the nature of the Soviet press. In an earlier
period in Soviet history, however, ethnic discrimination was sought
out and publicized, and revealed that non-Russians received lower pay
than Russians and were treated badly by Russian supervisors, that
ethnic slurs were common, and even physical violence against non-
Russians was not unknown.[34] Unfortunately, we have no objective information with which to evaluate the present state of ethnic relations
in the USSR, but it is our contention that ethnic animosities and discrimination almost certainly exist. This contention has received
some support from our conversations with Soviet citizens during our
travels in the USSR.

It appears, then, that the Russians would be expected to dominate
modernized society within the USSR just as they dominate Soviet society
in general. This domination is facilitated by features of Soviet society
such as the use of Russian as the lingua franca and is based to some
unspecifiable degree upon ethnic and racial discrimination.

In addition to the Russians, we might expect other nationalities
to be integrated into modernized society, but for different reasons.
The characterization of ethnic groups and their cultures as achievement oriented is, as we have noted, admittedly based upon insubstan-
tial evidence and even less conceptual reasoning. Nevertheless, the
examples of such ethnic groups as Jews, Armenians, Indians, and
Chinese, which have, despite minority status and varying degrees of
discrimination, occupied disproportionately large shares of advanced
society in many different settings, leads us to conclude that certain
groups do possess an achievement syndrome. The ability or inclination of such groups to achieve is, of course, often related to the necessity for achievement, a necessity dictated by population pressures and
a lack of opportunity in their homelands or to various social and economic sanctions that have the effect of forcing them into the modernized
sectors.

There are a number of Soviet nationalities that might properly be referred to as achievement oriented: Jews, Armenians, Georgians, Latvians, Estonians, and Tatars.[35] Perhaps the prime example of the achieving minority in the tsarist and Soviet contexts has been the Jews. Forced by the restrictive policies of imperial government to reside in towns within a certain geographic region of the Russian Empire (the Pale of Settlement), the Jews, of necessity, had to adopt an urban way of life. At the same time, it appears that population growth resulted in pressures against the scanty economic opportunities available within the Pale; many Jews emigrated from this area to the United States. Following the Revolution, legal restrictions against the Jews were lifted, and they flocked to other areas of the country (mainly to cities) and, more important, entered the universities in large numbers.[36] It should also be noted that a disproportionately large number of Bolsheviks in Russia were Jews, giving them at least some access to political power in the emerging Soviet state.[37] Combined with the documented achievement orientation of Jews elsewhere, these historical circumstances would indicate a prominent place for Jews in the modernizing sectors of Soviet society.

To a lesser but still significant extent, and for basically the same reasons, ethnic groups other than the Jews would be expected to have modernized relatively early in the Soviet context. The Armenians, victims of this century's most devastating genocide excepting the Nazi crimes of World War II, have been highly integrated into advanced Soviet society. Occupying a position in the Middle East analogous to that of the Jews in Eastern Europe (merchants, urban dwellers), the Armenians may also be characterized as achievement oriented and likely to enter the modernized sectors in large numbers. The Georgians, like the neighboring Armenians, have a lengthy history and, at the time of the Bolshevik Revolution, were possessed of an advanced intelligentsia and political infrastructure. Furthermore, there had been some industrialization in nineteenth-century Georgia, and the indigenous Georgians accounted for large shares of the urban population in their homeland.[38] Finally, both Georgians and Armenians held important posts in the Bolshevik, Menshevik, and other socialist parties; Stalin was, of course, a Georgian. (Among other prominent Caucasian political figures in early Soviet history were the Armenians Shaumian and Mikoyan and the Georgians Ordzhonikidze and Mdivani.)

The Baltic peoples present a slightly different picture of national development than do the Jews, Armenians, and Georgians. The Latvians and Estonians, whose homelands were within the tsarist provinces (gubernii) of Liflyand, Kurlyand, and Estlyand, for centuries were mainly rural dwellers, peasants in the system of large agricultural estates dominated by a German nobility. During the latter half of the nineteenth century, nationalism spread among both the Latvians and

Estonians, encouraged at first by a Russian government seeking to
limit the influence of the Baltic Germans. Latvians and Estonians began a movement into cities, and indigenous literary and political cir-
cles expanded.[39] Although it is difficult to establish an achievement
syndrome among Latvians and Estonians, one can point to the strong
impact of Western culture in this region, including the influence of
Protestantism, as likely to promote modernization among these two
nationalities.[40]

    The Tatars are the final nationality, and the only non-European
group, which, based upon our criteria, one might expect to modernize
relatively early. By the late 1800s, the Tatars (principally those known
as the Kazan', or Volga Tatars) were the most advanced economically
and politically of all the non-European peoples. Conquered in the earliest phase of Muscovite expansion, the Tatars reconciled themselves
to their position and profited from their geographic location by serving
as intermediaries in the brisk trade between the Slav and Muslim
worlds.[41] Consequently, the Tatars acted in virtually the same capacity in the Muslim areas of the Russian Empire as did Jews, Armenians, Greeks, Chinese, and Indians in other parts of the world,
that is, as urbanized merchants and bourgeoise. In this regard,
Richard Pipes cites a survey taken in the early 1800s that "revealed
that the Tatars owned one-third of the industrial establishments in the
Kazan province, and controlled most of the trade with the Orient."[42]
Additionally, the Tatars were the intellectual, cultural, and political
leaders among Muslims of the Russian Empire and later of the Soviet
state; the most prominent Muslim Communist, Sultan Galiyev, was a
Tatar.

    One additional consideration must be taken into account, that of
the sequence in which the various nationalities can be expected to
modernize. We have emphasized that the groups discussed here would
be expected to modernize relatively early, relative, that is, to the
remainder of nationalities that do not have access to political-military
power or are not characterized by the achievement orientation or socioeconomic position conducive to modernization. Clearly, there is a
time lag in the modernization of ethnic groups in multinational states,
with the delayed integration of the late modernizers determined by the
length of time necessary to prepare these groups for participation in
advanced society and the degree to which their participation is required.

    Education appears to be the principal means by which the inte-
gration of nationalities into modern sectors is facilitated, and the necessity for the eventual integration of all groups results from work force
requirements. The improvement and extension of education seems to
be the most readily implemented of all aspects of social change associated with modernization. Increased levels and quality of education

are popular social goals to which few would object. Thus, as education becomes widely available to nationalities that were previously characterized by relatively low educational levels, their integration into modernized society will be facilitated.

It is perhaps ironic that modernization may result in the inability of the modernized population to provide the entrants into the labor force required by an expanding economy. With the onset of modernization, population growth is likely to be appreciable, owing to continuing high fertility and the lower rates of mortality coincident with the early stages of economic development. As groups become modernized, however, fertility normally declines, resulting in lower rates of population growth. As long as population growth was high, the early modernizing groups could provide sufficient manpower for the work force, but with the lower growth rates associated with modernization, additional workers may be needed, at least for unskilled jobs. In later stages of economic development, therefore, the modernized areas or groups will require labor inputs from areas and groups that are modernizing later, thereby encouraging the entrance of these previously less advanced groups into advanced sectors. This would seem to be the case particularly in the labor intensive Soviet economy.

In summary, there are a number of Soviet nationalities that, based upon available generalizations and historical comparisons, would be expected to modernize early in relation to the majority of groups. Russians, the nationality dominating Soviet society in the military-political sense, are clearly the most important of the modernizing groups. Other ethnic groups, such as the Jews, Armenians, Georgians, Latvians, Estonians, and Tatars, have been able to modernize relatively early because of achievement orientation, social and economic circumstances, and some political influence. Other nationalities, outside of the modernization process in the early stages (Ukrainians, Belorussians, Uzbeks, Buryats, Bashkirs, and others), may make significant gains in later stages as their qualifications become improved and the need for their services grows.

THE HISTORICAL DEVELOPMENT OF THE MULTINATIONAL SOVIET STATE

The Expansion of the Russian Empire

The expansion of the Russian Empire[43] from its origins as the Muscovite principality subordinate to Tatar suzerainty to the transcontinental world power of today within a span of roughly 400 years is certainly one of history's landmark developments. In this section we

will briefly outline the expansion of the Russian Empire, primarily
from the sixteenth century to the Revolution, with an emphasis on the
incorporation of diverse ethnic groups, which resulted in the formation of a multinational state.

The territorial acquisitions of the various tsars and their importance in the changing international political and economic scene
have been dealt with at length elsewhere; Peter the Great's desire for
an outlet on the Baltic and the long-standing Russian ambition for control of the Dardanelles are characteristic of the historical military
and diplomatic maneuverings of the Russian state. This expansion of
the expire, for whatever reasons—military security, trade, agricultural land, protection of coreligionists, or manifest destiny—took place
across territories inhabited to one degree or another by peoples who
shared one major characteristic: they were all non-Russians. Admittedly, many ethnic Russians did inhabit frontier areas prior to their
de jure control by the empire as traders, cossacks, fugitive serfs,
and the like, but they were clearly in the minority. The conquest of
non-Russian lands resulted in the incorporation of a wide range of
peoples into the tsarist empire, as well as the proliferation of Russians
into these territories. The social and political consequences of the
formation of an ethnically diverse state have been of great importance
both to the Russian Empire and to its successor, the Soviet Union.
Recent events in the contemporary USSR indicate that the greatest impact of multinationality in that country is still to come.

Origins

Although the origins of the Slavs are unclear, it is known that
by the ninth century A.D. they inhabited large areas in western parts
of the mixed-forest and forest-steppe zones of what is now European
Russia. Two cities, controlling the lucrative north-south trade routes,
emerged as centers of government and commerce within this zone of
Slavic settlement: Kiev (to the south and west), on the Dnepr River,
and Novgorod (to the north and east), near Lake Ilmen. During the
period of their expansion into present-day European Russia, the Slavs
encountered indigenous groups, principally Finnic tribes, many of
which were eventually absorbed. During the period before the Mongol
invasions, the Slavs were in contact with various peoples surrounding
their zone of settlement: Volga Bulgars, Khazars, Pechenegs, Polov-
tsy, Poles, Lithuanians, and the Finnic peoples of the northern coniferous forests. The Mongol invasions of the thirteenth century resulted
in great reductions in the area and population of the Slavic principali-
ties, and arrested for over two centuries the expansion of the Russian
state. Furthermore, the period of the Tatar yoke witnessed incursions
into previously Slavic-controlled areas by rising powers in the West;

Swedes, Germans, and Lithuanians occupied former Russian lands.
Gradually, beginning in the fourteenth century, power in the Russian
lands was consolidated under the Grand Duchy of Moscow, whose
grand dukes had taken advantage of privileges vested in them by the
Tatars. By the middle of the sixteenth century, the Muscovite principality was sufficiently powerful to reverse the centuries-old pattern
of nomadic invasions, and to begin its own expansion at the expense
of its former overlords.

The Middle Volga

The first move toward territorial enlargement by the resurgent
Russian state was against the khanate of Kazan', one of three khanates
of the former Golden Horde (the other two being the khanates of As-
trakhan' and Crimea). In a campaign that ranks among the most important in Russian history, Tsar Ivan IV (the Terrible) took the Tatar
fortress at Kazan' (1552), thereby opening the Volga and Kama region
to Russian expansion. By assuming control of the lands of the Kazan'
Khanate, large numbers of non-Russian peoples were incorporated
into the Russian state, but only after several years of pacification and
punitive expeditions. These peoples included various Finnic and Turkic
groups: Mari, Mordvinians, Udmurts, Chuvash, and, of course,
Kazan' (or Volga) Tatars. Following the defeat of the Kazan' Tatars,
the Russians moved down the Volga, conquering the khanate of Astrak-
han' (1555) and gaining control of the Volga from its headwaters to the
Caspian Sea. In addition to the obvious military and trade ramifications
of the conquest of the Volga region, it was significant for our purposes
that this expansion resulted in the first major incorporation of non-
Russian peoples into the Muscovite state, and the pattern of Russian
conquest, agricultural settlement, administration, and economic exploitation was established.

Siberia and the Pacific

Following the defeat and subjugation of the Kazan' Khanate, the
Russians quickly pushed beyond the Urals and into Siberia, principally
in quest of furs and certain other commodities. Encountering mainly
Siberian tribes, many of which were still characterized by Stone Age
culture, the Russians brushed aside resistance and established a system of fur tribute collection in the annexed lands. From the Urals to
the Pacific, non-Russian peoples were added to the empire, including
the Komi, Siberian Tatars, Yakuts, Buryats, and the various Siberian
tribes. The beginning of the expansion into Siberia is traditionally
marked by the conquest of Sibir' by the cossack Yermak (1581), and
by the end of the seventeenth century the Russians controlled the lands

from the Urals to the Sea of Okhotsk. Russian imperial expansion in the Far East was completed by the acquisition from China of lands in the basin of the Amur River and the coastal region known as the Maritime (Primor'ye) Province by the treaties of Aigun (1858) and Pekin (1860), and the acquisition of southern Sakhalin from the Japanese in exchange for the Kuril Islands. These later territorial gains resulted in the incorporation of still other groups, including Koreans and Chinese. Although not as important numerically as groups in other areas conquered by the Russians, the peoples of Siberia and the Far East have assumed added political importance with the recent increase in tensions between the Soviet Union and China.

The Urals

The Russian conquest of Kazan' brought the Muscovite principality into contact, and eventually conflict, with a large nomadic group in the southern Urals, the Bashkirs. Although Russian expansion to the east toward the Pacific proceeded at a phenomenal rate, the Bashkirs and other powerful groups stood in the way of any movement south toward the Kazakh steppes. At one time or another the various nomadic groups, including Bashkirs, Nogays, Kalmyks, and Kazakhs, entered into loose vassalage with the Russian Empire, but the nomads considered these arrangements to be pragmatic and temporary. Eventually, encroachment by cossacks and Russian settlers into nomadic grazing lands resulted in open warfare. The most serious of these frontier wars was the Bashkir War (1735-40), which was prompted by Bashkir fears of Russian annexation as manifested in the construction of the Russian post at Orenburg (1735). By the middle of the nineteenth century, the Russians had pushed the frontier, marked by a series of forts and military posts, south to the northern edge of Kazakh territory. The lands occupied in the southern Urals and along the northern littoral of the Caspian Sea included nomadic groups other than Bashkirs, among them Kalmyks and Nogays.

The West

Territorial gains achieved by the Russian Empire in the west were less spectacular but, at the time, more important, than the gains in the east. The acquisition of territories in the west required more sophisticated military and diplomatic methods than did those in the east, and some of the campaigns, such as those of Peter I (the Great), were costly in terms of casualties and finances. The largest annexations came at the expense of Poland, which was the successor to Lithuania as Russia's principal antagonist in the west. In 1667 Poland ceded to Russia territory including the important cities of Kiev and

Smolensk. Since 1654 the Ukrainian Zaporozhian cossacks, controlling the area around the middle course of the Dnepr River, had maintained a loose alliance with the Russians. In 1708 the cossacks allied
themselves with Charles XII of Sweden, and, at the Battle of Poltava
(1709), their combined forces were defeated by the Russians under
Peter I. Subsequently, the Ukrainian lands and population were incorporated into the Russian Empire. Thus, a reunion of lands formerly under Eastern Slav control prior to the Mongol invasions of
the thirteenth century was effected. However, the intervening centuries had resulted in the development of the Ukrainians separate from
the Russians, the Ukrainians having been under a more Western influence through Lithuanian and Polish domination. This incorporation
of Ukrainian lands into the Russian Empire was viewed by many
Ukrainians not so much as a reunion but as an annexation.

During the latter part of the eighteenth century and the early
years of the nineteenth century, additional lands along the western
border of the empire were annexed following the partitions of Poland
and wars with Turkey and the Crimean Tatars. It was during this
period that Russian access to the Black Sea was secured, opening
vast areas of the Ukrainian and North Caucasian steppe to agricultural
settlement. Also, Bessarabia was taken from Turkish control in 1812.
These western acquisitions were of significant importance to the evolution of the multinational Russian Empire in that large numbers of
non-Russians were incorporated; these groups included Ukrainians,
Belorussians, Poles, Lithuanians, Jews, Romanians, Moldavians,
and Crimean Tatars.

The Baltic Area and Finland

In the early decades of the eighteenth century, Tsar Peter I,
in a series of campaigns against the Swedes, succeeded in incorpor-
ating large areas along the eastern littoral of the Baltic Sea into the
Russian domain. These areas were inhabited by peoples known today
as Estonians and Latvians, together with smaller groups and a ruling
class composed mainly of Germans. Other gains during this period
included Karelia and parts of Finland, which resulted in the incorporation of many Karelians and Finns into the empire. Finland in its entirety was annexed as a grand duchy in 1809.

The Caucasus and Transcaucasus

Beginning with the reign of Peter I in the early eighteenth century, Russian's expansion across and beyond the Caucasus range proceeded whenever its two antagonists in this region, Persia and the
Ottoman Empire, were not capable of strong resistance, and when

troops were not needed for the more important conflicts in the west. Russian expeditions pushed south, skirting the Caucasus by taking Derbent along the Caspian Sea (1722), and seized Baku, in what is to-day the Azerbaydzhan SSR, from the Persians in 1723. Later, how-ever, during the ascendancy of the Persian military conqueror Nadir Shah, the Russian government found it prudent to return Derbent and Baku (1735).

Russian expansion into the region began anew in 1783, when, by the Treaty of Georgievsk, a Russian protectorate was established over the kingdom of Georgia. The Christian Georgians, seeking assistance against the Muslim Turks, actively sought Russian protection, and finally, in 1801, Georgia was formally annexed into the Russian Em-pire. Almost continuous warfare against both the Turks and Persians in the first years of the nineteenth century, culminating in the Treaty of Gulistan (1813), gained for the Russians most of the western littoral of the Caspian Sea (including, again, Derbent and Baku). In 1826, war again broke out between Russia and Persia, and again the cessation of hostilities witnessed new gains by the Russians, including the southern area of present-day Azerbaydzhan (as far south as the Lenkoran low-land) and eastern Armenia and Nakhichevan' (as far south as the Araks, or Araxes, River). Thus, the southern frontier of the empire in the Caucasus region was now completed (with minor adjustments in later years), and two peoples with ancient backgrounds, the Georgians and Armenians, as well as a major Muslim group, the Turkic Azeri, were incorporated into the Russian Empire.

To the rear of the Transcaucasus front, however, in the reaches of the Caucasus range itself, a host of smaller mountain peoples con-fronted the Russians with what may have been the most stubborn re-sistance encountered by the expanding empire. Russian penetration into the Caucasus itself, although somewhat facilitated by friendly Christian groups such as the Ossetians, met with strong opposition from Muslim peoples, most notably the Cherkess (Circassians) to the west and the Avars and Chechens to the east. The Russians, by push-ing lines of fortified positions farther into the mountains and by con-ducting punitive expeditions against the mountain peoples, made some territorial gains, but also gained the enmity of the mountaineers. Campaigns against the Cherkess lasted from approximately 1830 to the final collapse of resistance in 1864. Campaigns against the groups in the eastern Caucasus took place between approximately 1820 to 1859. During the period 1836 to 1859, forces of the mountain peoples were led by the Imam Shamil, whose talents for mountain warfare were particularly troublesome for the Russians. The eventual mili-tary subjugation of the peoples of the Caucasus brought under Russian control a vast array of ethnic groups (the Caucasus region is one of the most ethnically diverse in the world), including the Cherkess, Ossetians, Chechens and Ingush, Avars, Lezgins, Dargins, Abkhaz, Kabardinians, Balkars, Kumyks, and many other groups.

Kazakhstan and Central Asia

The last major regions to be incorporated into the Russian Empire were Kazakhstan and Central Asia. Russian contact with the nomadic Kazakhs dated back to the end of the seventeenth century. Eventually a loose vassalage system evolved, wherein various khans of the three Kazakh hordes recognized Russian suzerainty (although at times this relationship wore thin). By the end of the eighteenth century the Russians, mainly through the use of cossack bands, had constructed lines of forts along the northern steppe perimeter of Kazakh territory from Gur'yev on the Caspian Sea to Ust'-Kamenogorsk near the Altay Mountains. By the middle of the nineteenth century, this fortified line had been moved considerably to the south in the Kazakh steppe area, and another line had been extended along the foothills of the mountain ranges that border southern Kazakhstan. Thus, by the middle of the nineteenth century, Kazakh lands had been virtually encircled by Russian-fortified lines. More important, however, was the in-migration of Russian agricultural settlers into the fertile steppe areas. The Kazakh economy, and indeed its entire way of life, based largely on nomadic herding, was seriously threatened by incursions on grazing lands by Russian farmers. This clash of competing land-use systems naturally led to the outbreak of hostilities between the Kazakhs and Russians, most notably the revolt led by Kenesary Kasim (1836-46) and the widespread rebellion in 1916.

With the Kazakh steppe region annexed into the empire, the Russians opened the last major phase of expansion by commencing a series of campaigns against the Muslim peoples of Central Asia. The region known today as Central Asia (formerly West Turkestan) stretches from the Caspian Sea in the west to the Pamir and Tyan'Shan' mountains in the east, between the lands of the Kazakhs to the north and Iran and Afghanistan to the south. The Russians had been engaged in reciprocal trade with various areas of Central Asia for some centuries prior to their conquest of the region in the last half of the nineteenth century; they had, in fact, attempted on at least two prior occasions to extend military power into the area, with both ventures ending in failure. On the eve of the Russian conquest, Central Asia was divided into three khanates: Khiva in the west, Bukhara in the center, and Kokand in the east. The first of the khanates to fall to Russian expansion was Kokand, the landmark being the fall of Tashkent in 1865 (the khanate of Kokand was abolished in 1876). In 1868, the ancient city of Samarkand was taken from the khanate of Bukhara, and in the same year a treaty was concluded that reduced the Bukharan Khanate to a

vassal state of the empire. In 1873, military expeditions against the
khanate of Khiva forced it into similar vassalage to the tsar. The last
campaign of the Central Asian expansion was against the Turkmens,
culminating in the battle of Gok Tepe in 1881, after which the majority
of Turkmen lands came under Russian control (the area around the
important city of Mary, or Merv, was annexed in 1884). With the exception of some minor territorial adjustments, the Central Asian region was now completely under Russian control, either by direct annexation or through vassalage agreements, and several large Muslim
ethnic groups became subjects of the tsar, including Uzbeks, Tadzhiks, Kirgiz, Turkmens, and Karakalpaks.

The Territorial Consolidation
of the Soviet Union

With the collapse of the tsarist government in 1917, the territorial composition of the country was altered, particularly along the
western frontier.[44] Following the revolutions of that year, several
nationalities took advantage of the erosion of power to secede from the
Russian state. Thus, Finland, Estonia, Latvia, and Lithuania became
independent countries. Also, large areas formerly within the Russian
Empire were incorporated into the post-World War I Polish state,
and Bessarabia was annexed by Romania. The Soviet government did
not willingly accede to these territorial losses (indeed, Red troops in
many instances attempted to regain control forcibly of the secessionist areas), but the general condition of military instability that prevailed during the civil war years limited the extent to which the Bolsheviks could exert their authority in the borderlands. During the
civil war period, Soviet forces did succeed in maintaining control of
vitally important non-Russian areas, usually against the expressed
wishes of the indigenous population. Thus, Central Asia, the Far East,
the majority of the Ukraine, the non-Russian areas in the Volga and
Ural regions, and the Transcaucasus remained within the Soviet state.
Throughout the early decades of Soviet power, in other words,
in the 1920s and 1930s, the secessionist states enjoyed independence.
With the ominous approach of World War II, however, these territories
fell victim to the expansion of the future antagonists. In 1939 Germany
and the Soviet Union occupied Poland, with the Soviets regaining much
of the territory in Poland formerly controlled by the tsarist government. In 1940 Soviet troops occupied Estonia, Latvia, and Lithuania,
and forced Romania to return Bessarabia and to cede northern Bukovina. The border realignments that followed World War II confirmed
the prewar Soviet gains, as well as granting the USSR additional territories in East Prussia and Czechoslovakia. Interestingly, most of

these postwar accessions were never within the Russian Empire. Of the territories in the west that were lost by the fledgling Soviet state, all, with the exception of Finland and some of the former tsarist holdings in Poland, were regained. Even in the case of Finland, the Soviets imposed important territorial concessions in the Arctic and in Karelia. Finally, following World War II, the Soviet Union regained territories that had been ceded to Japan after the Russo-Japanese War (1904-05), including the southern half of Sakhalin. In addition, Japan relinquished control of the Kuril Islands, which had by agreement between the Russian Empire and Japan been under Japanese control since the mid-nineteenth century.*

Thus, the Soviet Union as it is presently constituted bears a remarkable resemblance in territorial composition to the former Russian Empire. Indeed, the Soviet holdings are more extensive than the lands controlled by the tsars, and include the full range of nationalities that were brought under Russian dominance during the expansion of the empire.

SOVIET NATIONALITY POLICY

Soviet authorities have contended that nationality problems, so openly manifested under the tsarist regime, were "solved" following the October Revolution of 1917 by the application of Leninist Soviet nationality policy.[45] Although it is difficult to identify a clear set of implemented policies that can be termed "nationality policies," some programs of the Soviet government pertaining directly to the nationalities can be defined. According to Soviet usage, nationality policies are those policies aimed at solving the "nationality question." This formulation, of course, requires a definition of the nationality question, and it is illustrative of the conceptual difficulties involved in examining Soviet nationality policy to note that the definition of the nationality question has changed through the years.[46] Changes in the Soviet conception of the nationality question and in Soviet nationality policies have resulted from various Marxist-Leninist theoretical interpretations and from the course of internal and external historical events affecting the USSR. In this regard we shall briefly discuss the theoretical background of Soviet nationality policies and detail the more important historical events that influenced the treatment of nationalities in the USSR. Finally, we will identify those policies that have been

---

*We have attempted here to outline only the major territorial changes; we recognize that there have been a number of lesser changes along the entire Soviet border.

linked to a solution of the nationality question, policies we are able to
evaluate in light of our empirical findings.

It has been contended that Marx, who is the original source of
virtually all aspects of Soviet social, economic, and political theory,
provided precious little advice pertaining to nationality problems for
his socialist successors. It is clear that societal relations based on
ethnicity were not the central focus of Marx (or of Engels); the Marxist theory of historical political-economic change, of course, was
predicated upon economic class conflict and its social correlates. It
is equally clear, however, that Marx did not ignore nationality and its
implications, but rather provided what he considered to be a viable
solution to ethnic problems: the elimination of class conflict and
economic exploitation of one group by another through the victory of
the proletariat. As Lenin stated, "Marx had no doubt as to the subordinate position of the national question as compared with the 'labour
question.' But his theory is as far from ignoring national movements
as heaven is from earth."[47]

Marx viewed human nature as composed of two broad sets of
traits, one set being common to all men and another set a temporary
manifestation of the common traits conditioned by natural, social,
and economic conditions.[48] Nationalities, according to Marx, were
likewise based on the influences of the natural and economic setting.[49]
Implicit in this approach to human nature and nationality is the assumption that changes in the forces that influence these traits will result
in changes in the manifestations of human nature, or of nationality.
Human nature reached its fullest expression under socialism, Marx
contended, and the elimination of economic exploitation provided the
opportunity for removing animosities between national groups. Thus,
the most important contribution by Marx to Soviet nationality theory
is, in our opinion, the contention that nationality, like other human
traits, is subject to change through the application of policies that affect the economic and social environment. It should be noted that
Marx conceived of nationalism in the current sense as a temporary
phenomenon, but he did not view the socialist world as without nationalities.[50] Rather, the era of socialism would bring about fraternal
relations among the proletariat of all nations emerging as "proletarian
internationalism."[51]

The first major attempt to implement a viable socialist program
that included recognition of ethnic ambitions within a multinational
country was the movement led by the Austrian Social Democrats Otto
Bauer and Karl Renner.[52] Marx and Engels had a particular lack of
regard for the smaller nationalities of the ethnically variegated Austro-
Hungarian Empire, believing that the consolidation of these groups
was historically progressive (for the formation of large economic
units), and was to be preferred to the fragmentation of the country into

small nation-states.[53] The latter decades of the nineteenth century witnessed, however, rising nationalist tendencies among Czechs, Serbs, Croats, and other groups within the Austro-Hungarian Empire, a concrete political problem with which the Marxists had to reconcile themselves. At the Congress of Bruenn in 1899, representatives of the socialist parties of Austria-Hungary debated measures that would grant, within a socialist framework, degrees of cultural autonomy for the various nationalities.[54] This compromise between the theoretical, international aspects of Marxism and the very real nationality situation in Austria-Hungary, known generally as national-cultural autonomy, set the precedent for the active consideration by socialists of nationalist sympathies in other multinational countries, most notably in the Russian Empire.

The Russian Empire around the turn of the century was also the scene of rising nationalist movements among the non-Russian nationalities. Historically, the treatment of non-Russian groups within the empire had been a function of the nature (voluntary annexation, military conquest, acquisition through treaties) and chronology of their incorporation, as well as their level of socioeconomic and cultural development.[55] For example, the nationalities of the Volga region and Siberia, incorporated during the earliest expansion of the Muscovite state, were considered fully integrated into the empire, with very few administrative distinctions drawn between them and the Russians. Other, more advanced nationalities, incorporated during later military campaigns in the west (Finns, Poles, Baltic peoples), were administered almost as federated areas with varying degrees of local autonomy. The tsarist government intended to achieve a high degree of social, economic, and political uniformity among the non-Russians through more or less evolutionary processes; uniform administration and a uniform way of life for all peoples would lead to a uniform national population.[56] Political and administrative centralism was a principle from which very few nationality deviations would be tolerated (the Grand Duchy of Finland being the most noteworthy).[57]

The assassination of Tsar Alexander II in 1881 and the accession to the throne of Alexander III signaled the beginning of a strong, repressive, reactionary regime; repression and reaction applied as well to the nationalities, as the imperial government initiated a determined Russification policy. The period between 1881 and 1917 was marked by sanctions against nationalities in language, literature, education, religion, politics, and at times by physical violence—this was the time of pogroms against Jews and Armenians.[58] Unfortunately for the tsarist regime, nationalism among non-Russians was on the rise during this same period, prompted in part by hostility toward the government's repressive Russification measures. Over the longer term, however, nationalism among these ethnic groups resulted from the

general social and economic development in the Russian Empire during the latter half of the nineteenth century, during which time urban,
educated elites were formed among the nationalities, together with
heightened or incipient cultural developments and an awakening of
ethnic awareness. These non-Russian nationality elites provided a
base of support for revolutionary ideas.[59]

> Faced by the rejection of its drive for uniformity
> in way of life, the government turned to an active
> policy of Russification in the second half of the nine-
> teenth century, just at the time when self-awareness
> was beginning to take hold of the nationalities. The
> stubbornness and myopia expressed in this policy
> paved the way for the mass disaffection of the na-
> tionalities that proved a very strong element in the
> collapse of the imperial regime.[60]

Responding to the increasing ethnic tensions in the Russian Empire, various political factions, among them the Marxist Social Democrats, began devoting serious attention to the nationality situation.
During the first decade of this century, most of the liberal political
parties adopted platforms that embodied concessions to the nationalities
of Russia, although the extent of these concessions varied widely. In
1903, for example, the Social Democrats advocated several important
points concerning the nationalities, including measures of regional
autonomy, equality of all nationality groups, language and education
rights, and the right of nations to self-determination.[61]
       Lenin, in the Marxist vein, viewed nationality and nationalism
as secondary to the class struggle. Emphasizing the economic benefits to be realized in large, centralized states, he was opposed generally to the fragmentation of existing states or to decentralized, federal structures. Furthermore, Lenin saw ethnic assimilation as progressive (with the stipulation that forced measures be excluded), and
he had little use for small ethnic groups that, he believed, could be
assimilated into larger groups.[62] As a shrewd judge of political realities, however, he began to realize the significance of the heightened
ethnic sentiments in Russia, and saw in the various nationalist movements potential allies for the proletariat in the upcoming struggle with
the regime.
       Equally important for a consideration of Lenin's thinking on na-
tionality policies was the fact that within the Social Democratic party
there existed rival factions that threatened the stability of the socialist
movement, factions that by their nature were illustrative of the intellectual tension between Marxism and nationalism. To the left within
the Party stood those (most notably Rosa Luxemburg) who would toler-

ate very few concessions to the nationalities, and, in particular, were strongly opposed to political secession. Opposing this faction were the Mensheviks, of whom many were from the Caucasian nationalities and advocates of some form of national-cultural autonomy akin to the concept of Bauer and Renner. Lenin saw the leftist position as politically ill-advised in light of the realities of the nationalist fomentation in Russia, and was against the Menshevik stance on ideological grounds (believing in centralism and assimilation). Clearly, a formula was required to demonstrate to the nationalities that the Social Democrats had a viable program for the elimination of ethnic oppression and to provide a solution for the intra-Party conflict surrounding nationality. The solution was Lenin's elaboration of the concept of self-determination, adopted by the Russian Social Democratic Labor party at its Second Congress in 1903.

Beginning in 1913, Lenin published a series of articles that amounted to his major works on nationality, and in which he explained in great detail his principle of self-determination. The development of nation-states was, according to Lenin, a concomitant of the rise of capitalism, because large, uniform polities were required for the market and productive forces inherent therein. The process of consolidation of nation-states had largely been completed in Western Europe, but the multinational empires of Eastern Europe and Asia had only entered this historical phase around 1905. Thus, it would be contrary to the progressive tendency of the formation of nation-states (through bourgeois-democratic revolutions) for the Marxists to oppose self-determination.[63] There was, therefore, a theoretical as well as a practical basis for the principle of self-determination.

Lenin encountered serious criticism from both the left and right wings of the Party on this principle, the left insisting that he was aiding the fragmentation of the Russian Empire into a host of small states and the right condemning self-determination as vague.[64] Self-determination to Lenin was not at all vague; he stated explicitly that it stood for the right of nations to secede from the Russian state and form independent political entities.[65] With regard to the leftist criticism that self-determination would result in fragmentation, it is clear that Lenin believed that the nationalities would not secede and, in the event, sufficient qualifications were included in the principle to justify active intervention to prevent secession. Self-determination was a right, Lenin stated, and to advocate the right did not mean the same as advocating self-determination itself. "To accuse those who support the right of self-determination, i.e., the freedom to secede, of encouraging separatism, is as stupid and hypocritical as accusing those who advocate freedom of divorce of encouraging the destruction of family ties."[66] Recognizing the right of nations to self-determination, Lenin said, would engender trust between the nationalities and the so-

cialist movement and reduce rather than promote the danger of secession.[67] Furthermore, Lenin obviously believed that the nationalities
would not actually secede because economic forces militated against
fragmentation and the masses were aware of this fact; with the right
to self-determination assured (removing ethnic oppression and animosities), economic considerations would promote consolidation into the
larger proletarian state.[68]

There can be little doubt that Lenin ever intended to honor self-
determination, as evidenced by the qualifications included in his formulation and, of course, by the events themselves. The most important qualification was that the interests of the proletariat, being more
"progressive," would always take precedence over national interests.
Also, the proletariat of the non-Russian nationalities were required
to demand union with the dominant proletarian state, thereby counter-
acting any dissolution. Lenin was extremely vague as to what groups
or classes had the right to opt for secession, and no general formula
pertaining to all nationalities, places, or times was ever enunciated.[69]
In the final analysis, Lenin's formulation and interpretation of the
principle of self-determination was sufficiently unclear and qualified
as to cover virtually any eventuality that ensued. The concept fur-
nished the Social Democrats with a powerful political slogan that
Lenin utilized just as he had stated on several occasions: a tactical
alliance that furthered the interests of the proletariat and nothing
more.

The revolution of February 1917 catapulted the nationality situation into a critical political and military problem. From the outset,
the provisional government was unwilling to take determined measures
to placate nationality unrest, beyond the removal of formal restrictions against various groups and the pronouncement of equality for all
citizens regardless of their ethnic, religious, or racial background.[70]
As the internal order of the former Russian Empire disintegrated by
degrees into civil war, those nationalities so inclined were presented
with the opportunity for secession; other groups that had in the past
advocated only local autonomy found it necessary in light of events to
adopt some form of self-rule to maintain order and to protect themselves from foreign military intervention or from the designs of
neighboring nationalities. Civil unrest took on nationality dimensions
in non-Russian areas, particularly in the North Caucasus, Caucasus,
and Central Asia, with indigenous nationalities taking to arms against
Russian city dwellers, troops, and agricultural settlers. Many non-
Russian nationalities saw in the fluid political-military situation the
chance to regain lands or privileges that Russians had preempted during the ancien regime.[71]

The years 1917 and 1918 witnessed the secession from the Russian state of Lithuania, Latvia, Estonia, and Finland, together with

the occupation of Poland by Germany and the annexation of Bessarabia by Romania. In addition, large territories were controlled by White military forces, notably in Siberia. The slogan of self-determination had proved a disaster for Lenin and the Bolsheviks, intent in reality for economic and other reasons to maintain a large state generally synonymous with the tsarist empire, and it became increasingly clear that the slogan needed additional theoretical and pragmatic qualification. Lenin, therefore, together with Stalin (who was emerging as the principal Bolshevik spokesman on nationality problems), began to stress the qualifications built into the original, pre-Revolutionary concept of self-determination. National self-determination, Stalin wrote in early 1918, could not stand in the way of the development and interests of the proletariat.

> There are cases when the right of self-determination
> conflicts with another, a higher right—the right of
> the working class that has come to power to consoli-
> date that power. In such cases—this must be said
> bluntly—the right of self-determination cannot and
> must not serve as an obstacle to the working class
> in exercising its right to dictatorship.[72]

With a theoretical justification in hand, the Bolsheviks rapidly moved to establish military and political power in the non-Russian areas. Secessionist regimes in the Ukraine, Belorussia, the Caucasus, and Central Asia were defeated and their territories reincorporated into the Russian state through combinations of force of arms, treachery, and the granting of temporary concessions.[73] The Bolsheviks found it expedient to conclude alliances with certain nationalist groups during the civil war, particularly since the White forces held the nationalities in contempt and virtually forced them into cooperation with the Reds.[74] Following their consolidation of power, the vast majority of the pragmatic concessions granted to the nationalities were unilaterally abrogated by the Bolsheviks.

The force of nationalism had shown itself to be stronger than Lenin and the Bolsheviks had foreseen; more than a force to be exploited in the struggle for proletarian hegemony, nationalism proved to be a phenomenon that required some concessions, or at least the appearance of concessions. The federal concept of government began to suggest itself increasingly as the non-Russian areas were incorporated into the proletarian state, despite the previous outspoken animosity of Lenin and others for this decentralized form of government. Stalin justified the adoption of a federal state largely on pragmatic grounds, stating that, in light of the outright secessions by some nationalities, federation was a step toward unity, a move toward a cen-

tralized state, and was an expedient course in the face of strong nationalist sentiments that the Bolsheviks had underestimated. Most important, however, was the fact that the decentralized state structure
was more than balanced by a Communist party that was highly centralized and, in reality, in complete control of the state apparatus.[75]
Lenin had consistently insisted on a unitary, highly disciplined Communist party, a point from which he granted no real exceptions. According to the principle of "democratic centralism," each echelon of
the Party was required to carry out orders from the next higher echelon without question, and subject to appeal only after execution of the
orders. With the centralized Party in firm de facto control of the federal state organs, local autonomy and decision making largely became
a fiction.[76]

The final result of the years of revolution, civil war, and nationality insurrection was the evolution of the Union of Soviet Socialist
Republics, formally created by the Soviet Constitution of 1924 as a
federation of nominally independent republics and other ethnic units
with varying degrees of status within the federal structure. Although
the status of some nationality units has been altered through the years,
and although some nationalities have had their titular units abolished
altogether, the basic federal structure remains. In 1971 the official
Soviet administrative structure delimited 15 union republics, 20 autonomous republics, 8 autonomous oblasts, and 10 national okrugs, with
one nationality comprising the titular group of each unit in almost all
cases (Map 2.2).[77]

In general, the status of a nationality within the federal structure,
as reflected by the level of its titular unit, is determined by the size
of the group, by the proportion the titular group constitutes of the
unit's population, and by its geographic location. The latter criterion
is particularly important in distinguishing between Union and Autonomous
republics; since the former possess, at least theoretically, the right
to secede from the USSR, proximity to an international border is a logical necessity. The status of a nationality unit is not entirely without
meaning, inasmuch as nationality rights in education, publishing, and
some other activities are a function of the level of the unit within the
federal hierarchy.

Several periods can be delimited regarding policies toward the
non-Russian nationalities since the establishment of Soviet authority
in the early 1920s. During the early years of Soviet rule, until the
end of the 1920s, policies toward the nationalities in general were
liberal and encouraging, just as this period witnessed the growth of
art and literary forms, campaigns against illiteracy, new developments
in education, and a broad expansion of socialist ideals.[78] Major efforts at integrating the indigenous population into the Soviet system, including the Communist party, were made, but not without resistance

from the Russians who looked down on the other nationalities.[79] The Communist party, having relied on the urban, industrial proletariat for its strength, was overwhelmingly Russian (72 percent in 1922), largely because the vast majority of the urban proletariat was Russian.[80]

Following the advent of Stalin to complete control of the Soviet system, treatment of the nationalities became increasingly less generous. Beginning around 1928, or at the time of the inception of the industrialization and collectivization drives of the first plan period, concessions made to the non-Russians were curtailed, the political careers of those non-Russian Communists who advocated real federal relations between the republics and the center ended, and eventually most of the nationality elites were eliminated by the purges and executions of the 1930s.[81] The reasons for this shift from friendly to hostile treatment appear to have been due to Stalin's belief that a centralized, uniform state was preferable to a federal (in the real sense), ethnically heterogeneous state. This desire for centralism, which Stalin demonstrated early on, was perhaps encouraged by the external threat of fascism, and, in the course of events, Stalin placed the Russian nationality in a clearly privileged position when confronted with the possible defeat of the Soviet Union during World War II.[82] Excesses committed against some non-Russian nationalities (especially those who allegedly collaborated with the Nazis) by the Soviets during the war are well documented and illustrate the tenuous nature of nationality rights in the USSR.[83]

Following the death of Stalin, most of the nationalities that had been deported during the war years were allowed to return to their homelands, and their nationality units were re-created, although usually in somewhat altered form. From 1953 to 1958 there ensued a period of relative liberal policies toward the nationalities. In 1959, however, the Soviet government once again began to implement policies that adversely affected the non-Russian nationalities, particularly in the education and language fields.[84] The most prominent issue during this period was the reforms in language instruction in Soviet schools promulgated by Khrushchev in 1958-59, the so-called Thesis 19 proposals. Basically, these proposals were aimed at the erosion of non-Russian languages and at the same time were intended to strengthen the position of the Russian language as the lingua franca of the USSR.[85] Beyond the obvious connotations of language policy in a multilingual modernizing country and the benefits to be derived from a single language of internationality communication, the widespread adoption of Russian has been viewed by Soviet theorists as a prelude and prerequisite to ethnic assimilation.[86] It is perhaps illustrative of the importance of language to ethnic identification that the implementation of the school and language reforms met with virtually unprecedented resistance from non-Russian government and Party officials.[87]

The official position with regard to ethnic assimilation is obviously an important and sensitive issue. The basic theoretical framework within which the government operates is the well-known "flourishing" (rastvet) and "coming together" (sblizheniye) process, during which the nationalities will develop their cultural and socioeconomic traits as a prelude to an eventual "merging" (sliyaniye) into a unitary "Soviet people."[88] It is the timing of this process that has been the subject of debate among Soviet scholars and officials.[89] During the Khrushchev regime the Soviet government and the Party stressed a more rapid assimilation of non-Russian nationalities, but during the later 1960s the official line advocated a more gradual evolution with a prolonged future for nationality traits. The extent to which the government and Party leaders interpret signs of ethnic change as representing the progress of the nationalities along the continuum toward the eventual merger may well determine the future of nationality rights and the federal form of government in the Soviet Union.

Soviet Industrial Location Policies and the Nationalities

Soviet nationality policy has been variable and at times somewhat vague, and thus it is difficult to test its effects. One aspect of nationality policy in the USSR, in other words, a policy bearing directly upon the nationality question, has been clearly stated and can be empirically tested: this is the explicit and long-standing policy that calls for the economic development of formerly backward regions inhabited chiefly by non-Russians. This policy is one of the principles of Soviet industrial location and derives from Lenin's nationality policy and Marxist doctrines that socialist and Communist society must be highly industrialized and egalitarian.[90] The goal of the Soviet government has been to eliminate the economic and cultural backwardness of nationality areas, and thus the backwardness of nationalities resident therein.

Because this policy has been in existence since the Tenth Party Congress in 1921, and the country has experienced rapid economic development, it might be expected that by now regional differentials in industrialization and economic development would be relatively slight. In fact, Soviet authors frequently claim that the problem of economic equalization has been basically solved, and that the differences that exist in regional national income can be accounted for by such factors as differences in the taxation of commodities, commodity prices, the structure of industry, and the importance of agriculture in the regional economy, and that the equalization of services is not adequately taken into consideration.[91] To substantiate further this claim they generally point to relative increases in regional industrial production and national income. Whether there has been significant industrial equalization of non-Russian areas and to what extent the various nationalities have benefited from the equalization that has occurred are, of course, central considerations of our investigation of ethnic stratification in the USSR. In short, has practice conformed to policy in regional economic development?

Locational policy and practice in the USSR before World War II has been analyzed by I. S. Koropeckyj, who concludes that defense considerations were of the highest priority among the locational principles and the industrial equalization of underdeveloped non-Russian areas was of the lowest priority.[92] Other locational principles are purely economic in nature and include the location of industry closer to sources of raw materials and consumers, the development of specialized industries in each economic region (which should also be as economically self-sufficient as possible), the even distribution of industrial production throughout the country, and the elimination of the differences between cities and rural areas in terms of industrial and agricultural development. The strong emphasis on defense considerations resulted in investment mainly in established western areas, where returns were the greatest, and the establishment of new industrial centers in the east, mainly in the Urals and West Siberia, areas inhabited chiefly by Russians. Even though economic development is a high priority in the USSR, the building of socialism and communism is a higher goal, and thus defense considerations, including the shift of industry to the east, took precedence over economic considerations in the interwar period.

To support his contention that industrial equalization of backward areas had the lowest priority, Koropeckyj presents data that show that in all non-Russian republics, except the Ukraine and Azerbaydzhan, per capita investment shares were well below population shares in 1926 and 1939, and that in terms of number of industrial workers per 1,000 population and per capita industrial output, the non-Russian republics were generally far behind the RSFSR. Thus, the regional disparities in industrial development that existed in the prerevolutionary period were perpetuated. Although there was some improvement between 1926 and 1939 in terms of the number of industrial workers, the situation worsened in terms of per capita industrial output. That heavy industry received the bulk of the investments between 1926 and 1939 and that, except for the Ukraine, conditions favorable for the development of heavy industry were generally absent in the non-Russian republics, in part account for the relative lack of development in non-Russian areas.

In the postwar period, based on the union republics, Koropeckyj finds a slight leveling in net material production and industrialization

between 1950 and 1958, but a reversal of this trend in the 1960s.
Within the RSFSR, however, he found a trend toward the reduction of
interregional inequality in the postwar period. [93]

Leslie Dienes has studied regional investment priorities in the
USSR since World War II, and has gathered data on regional economic
growth that can be used to evaluate the extent to which industrial
equalization of non-Russian areas has occurred since World War II. [94]
His conclusion is that even though industrial dispersion is a major goal
of Soviet planners, dispersion into new areas has been highly selective,
with the bulk of the investment outside of the traditional western centers going to the Urals, the Kuzbas-Novosibirsk area, the middle
Volga, and south central Siberia. Dienes further states:

> The inescapable conclusion is that, despite a greater
> cost consciousness on part of planners, Soviet re-
> gional investment policy in the past decade has not
> been guided mainly by questions of profitability and
> economic efficiency. Capital was not allocated among
> regions to equate their marginal costs and/or prod-
> ucts. Labor, which has turned out to be more immo-
> bile than expected, was not employed to the level
> where marginal output approached its marginal cost.
> Regional investment allocation evidently was guided
> by strategic considerations, and by a strong desire
> to develop the vast Asian hinterland, particularly
> Siberia, with its wealth of mineral resources. [95]

The indexes in Table 4.1 show that there was still considerable
regional disparity in industrial and economic development in the 1960s.
In terms of per capita industrial employment, the Baltic and the
Donetsk-Dnepr were the only regions outside the RSFSR that were
above the national average; within the RSFSR the Central Chernozem
and the North Caucasus were the only regions below the national average. The other indexes substantiate the pattern of regional inequality
in development, particularly in non-Russian areas. It would also
seem that there has been relatively little improvement in per capita
industrial employment and per capita industrial output since 1939. [96]
Furthermore, industrial development within the RSFSR has been in
areas chiefly inhabited by Russians. Judging from the index of per
capita state investment, it appears that there has been no major recent effort toward industrial equalization of non-Russian areas. In
short, even though there has been considerable economic development
and significant improvement in the standard of living in non-Russian
areas, industrial equalization has not been achieved to any appreciable
extent.

TABLE 4.1

Indexes of Development of Soviet Regions*

Region	Industrial Employment per 1,000 Population (1965)	Per Capita Industrial Output (1965)	Per Capita Fuel Consumption (1965)	Agriculture and Food Industries as a Percentage of Total Agricultural and Industrial Output (1962)	Per Capita National Income (1968) 100 = 1,017 Rubles	Index of per Capita State Investment 1959–67 USSR = 100
Northwest	174	148	122	24	132.3	174
West	114	123	87	47	111.9	110
Center	150	165	92	22	133.3	128
Volgo–Vyatsk	123	102	77	27	119.5	80
Central Chernozem	72	81	85	62	88.2	77
Volga	103	102	111	41	90.9	129
Belorussia	76	66	62	50	97.1	74
Moldavia	45	51	40	79	84.1	54
Southwest	63	60	41	63	91.1	58
South	80	87	54	62	104.0	113
Donetsk–Dnepr	125	122	187	34	113.5	118
North Caucasus	79	81	73	56	90.0	96
Transcaucasus	60	64	60	57	60.7	83
Urals	142	138	195	27	114.7	132
West Siberia	107	83	135	38	105.6	143
East Siberia	100	84	171	37	91.3	197
Far East	109	103	142	47	107.2	207
Kazakhstan	60	49	57	67	73.1	157
Central Asia	40	45	56	71	61.1	77
USSR total	100	100	100	—	100.0	100

*These data are for the current Soviet economic regions, and, thus, sometimes do not correspond to the regions used in this study, although the differences between the two sets of regions are not great.

Source: Leslie Dienes, "Investment Priorities in Soviet Regions," Annals of the Association of American Geographers 62 (September 1972): Tables 1 and 3. For explanatory notes, see sources to Tables 1 and 3.

119

Moreover, in recent years there apparently has been little equalization of income in the USSR. After an extensive analysis of the available income data by republic, Gertrude Schroeder found that, aside from the Baltic republics, non-Russian republics had income levels below, and frequently significantly below, that of the RSFSR. She concludes with respect to levels of living that

> In 1961 the gradual evening out of these differences was explicitly declared to be a part of the program for building communism. The evidence, judging from the data for the 1960's, does not support the fact that this statement had been one of the instructions to planners and consequently had served as a guide to the allocation of resources and the distribution of budget funds. In fact, this admittedly incomplete evidence suggests that the richer republics may be getting richer and the poorer ones may be getting poorer.[97]

In addition, Rodgers has recently concluded that

> Despite professed socialist goals of balanced economic growth in regional development and subsidization of national minorities, micro-regional employment inequalities still persist. . . . Between 1955 and 1965 there was remarkably limited evidence of the implementation of the equality principle. If there is a conscious regional economic planning policy in the USSR, it appears to support growth rather than equity.[98]

Maintaining that measures of regional inequality seriously understate the degree of inequality among nationalities in the USSR, Silver investigated socioeconomic indicators for the 15 union-republic nationalities between 1926 and 1959. He concludes that

> The preceding analysis has revealed a mixed pattern of relationships between sociocultural development and equality among Soviet nationalities. Measured in absolute terms, the increase in levels of education, numbers of skilled workers, and female access to formal education have been enormous, as has the reduction in the incidence of early marriage. Birth rates, too, have shown substantial change over time, although not always in the expected direction.

Thus, if one were to focus primary attention on
the amount of change one would have to conclude
that almost universal progress toward modernization has characterized the sociocultural development of union republic nationalities. But the initial expectation of a decline in the relative differences of socioeconomic development among the
nationalities has not always proved correct. In
general, those aspects of social relations most amenable to planned change over a relatively short time-
span (such as access to education) have shown the
greatest change and the greatest reduction in internationality variation. Least susceptible to planned
change have been certain practices once supported
by strong religious sanctions—those relating to
marriage, fertility, and female status in general.[99]

The next question that is relevant to our investigation is to what
extent the various nationalities have benefited from the industrialization that has occurred in non-Russian areas. That industry is established in a non-Russian area does not necessarily mean that indigenous
non-Russians are employed in the plants as managers or workers and
thus receive the benefits of higher wages and urban amenities. In
fact, Russians, Jews, and other "European" nationalities have migrated
to the cities of non-Russian areas in large numbers and frequently comprise a large proportion, if not a majority, of the urban population and
the urban work force. Most frequently, they take the best jobs because
they have higher educational levels. Although we cannot document precisely the extent to which the non-Russians have benefited from industrialization in their nationality areas, available data indicate that in
most instances the indigenous nationalities have not shared proportion-
ality in the benefits of industrialization. This subject will be discussed
in greater detail in the following chapters.

Soviet writers have stressed the economic development of non-
Russian areas as indicative of the nonexploitative nature of the socialist federal system. Furthermore, higher socioeconomic levels for
all nationalities, higher levels engendered by economic development
and industrialization, are viewed as a necessary condition for the
elimination of ethnic animosities and the smooth merging of groups
into the future Soviet people. On the occasion of the fiftieth anniver-
sary of the founding of the USSR, Leonid Brezhnev, First Secretary
of the Soviet Communist party, announced that the goal of attaining
equalization among the nationalities had been achieved, and, therefore,
Leninist nationality policy had been vindicated.[100] Whether or not
this equalization has indeed been achieved, whether or not all nation-

alities have benefited approximately equally from the advances of the
Soviet economy, and whether or not the nationalities have been integrated fully into the modernized sectors of society remain to be seen
from analyses of empirical data. We intend to cast additional light
upon this important subject in succeeding chapters of this study.

NOTES

1. Tamotsu Shibutani and Kian M. Kwan, Ethnic Stratification:
A Comparative Approach (New York: Macmillan, 1972), pp. 122-31
and Chap. 9.

2. D. W. Meinig, Southwest: Three Peoples in Geographical
Change, 1600-1970 (New York: Oxford University Press, 1971), Chaps.
4, 6, and 8.

3. Keith Jackson and John Harre, New Zealand (New York:
Walker, 1969), pp. 41-48, 153-66. Regarding the level of modernization, in 1961 about one-third of the Maori lived in urban areas,
whereas about two-thirds of non-Maoris lived in cities and towns.
Significant changes in the occupational structure of the Maori population have occurred since World War II; there are now more Maori in
manufacturing than in agriculture, but still more Maori remain in
agriculture than the comparable percentage for non-Maoris. See New
Zealand, Department of Statistics, Population Census, 1961, 8.

4. Karl W. Deutsch, Nationalism and Social Communication,
2d ed. (Cambridge, Mass.: Massachusetts Institute of Technology
Press, 1966), pp. 96-104. In the concept of "social communication,"
Deutsch includes language as well as broader aspects of culture, such
as habits, associations, and preferences. "It [social communication]
consists in the ability to communicate more effectively, and over a
wider range of subjects, with members of one large group than with
outsiders." See p. 97.

5. Ibid., p. 102.

6. Shibutani and Kwan, op. cit., Chaps. 2-4.

7. Deutsch, op. cit., pp. 130-33.

8. John H. Wuorinen, Nationalism in Modern Finland (New York:
Columbia University Press, 1931), pp. 1-28.

9. Shibutani and Kwan, op. cit., pp. 139-48.

10. Fred L. Strodtbeck, Margaret R. McDonald, and Bernard
C. Rosen, "Evaluation of Occupations: A Reflection of Jewish and
Italian Mobility Differences," American Sociological Review 22 (Octo-
ber 1957): 546-53; Bernard C. Rosen, "Race, Ethnicity, and the
Achievement Syndrome," American Sociological Review 24 (February
1959): 47-60; and Nathan Hurvitz, "Sources of Middle Class Values of
American Jews," Social Forces 37 (December 1958): 117-23.

11. Regarding Yugoslavia, see Jack C. Fisher, Yugoslavia: A Multinational State (San Francisco: Chandler, 1966). Fisher attributes differential levels of modernization in Yugoslavia primarily to the impact of different foreign occupations, mainly by Austria-Hungary and the Ottoman Empire. In the case of Belgium, the Walloons modernized earlier than the Flemings, due to the influence of France. See Cynthia H. Enloe, Ethnic Conflict and Political Development (Boston: Little, Brown, 1973), pp. 118-21.

12. Enloe, op. cit., pp. 113-21.

13. A. J. Jaffe, "Manpower and Other Economic Contributions by Migrants: The United States Experience" (Paper presented at the Conference on Labor and Migration, Brooklyn College, New York, March 13-14, 1970), p. 13.

14. David Ward, Cities and Immigrants (New York: Oxford University Press, 1971), pp. 51-83.

15. Odile Rabut, "Les Etrangers en France," Population, no. 3 (May-June 1973): 620-24.

16. Shibutani and Kwan, op. cit., pp. 378-83.

17. Karl E. and Alma F. Taeuber, Negroes in Cities (Chicago: Aldine, 1965), pp. 11-14.

18. New Zealand, Population Census, 1961, 8.

19. In the more modernized Croatian and Slovenian republics, the crude rates of natural increase in 1970 were 3.9 per 1,000 and 5.9 per 1,000, respectively, whereas the same rate in Montenegro was 13.6 per 1,000 and in Macedonia natural increase equaled 15.6 per 1,000. See Yugoslavia, Savezni Zavod za Statistiku, Statisticki Godisnjak Jugoslavije, 1973 (Beograd, 1973), p. 350.

20. Milton M. Gordon, Assimilation in American Life: The Role of Race, Religion, and National Origins (New York: Oxford University Press, 1964), pp. 23-30.

21. Brian D. Silver, "Ethnic Identity Change Among Soviet Nationalities: A Statistical Analysis" (Ph.D. diss., University of Wisconsin, 1972), pp. 9-10.

22. Ibid., pp. 43-75.

23. Raymond Breton, "Institutional Completeness of Ethnic Communities and the Personal Relations of Immigrants," American Journal of Sociology 70 (September 1964): 194-205; and Stanley Lieberson, "The Impact of Residential Segregation on Ethnic Assimilation," Social Forces 40 (October 1961): 52-57.

24. For a review of research concerning immigrant groups, see Charles Price, "The Study of Assimilation," in Migration, ed. J. A. Jackson (Cambridge: Cambridge University Press, 1969), pp. 181-237. At this point it may be instructive to note that the vast majority of research concerning assimilation pertains to immigrant groups, primarily in the United States, Canada, Australia, and Great Britain. In

most respects, the immigrant situation with regard to assimilation is similar to that obtaining among nationalities in multinational countries, with the important exception of those ethnic groups in multinational states that reside within their own nationality area or homeland. Otherwise, government policies (such as those concerning the provision of native-language schools) toward immigrants and national minorities alike probably influence these groups to a similar extent.

25. Deutsch, op. cit., pp. 123-27. "Social mobilization" is composed essentially of elements that we have earlier included in our conceptualization of modernization. Deutsch also recognized that social mobilization may proceed at a faster rate than assimilation, in which case ethnic identity might be reinforced among educated, nonassimilated individuals. Furthermore, he noted that assimilation could take place among rural dwellers (the "underlying population"), but hypothesized that the rate of assimilation would be considerably slower than among mobilized urbanites. See p. 163.

26. Gordon, op. cit., pp. 70-81.

27. Regarding both the durability of ethnicity and the relationship of ethnicity to economic activity, see Nathan Glazer and Daniel Patrick Moynihan, Beyond the Melting Pot: The Negroes, Puerto Ricans, Jews, Italians, and Irish of New York City, 2d ed. (Cambridge, Mass.: Massachusetts Institute of Technology Press, 1970).

28. See Richard Pipes, The Formation of the Soviet Union, rev. ed. (New York: Atheneum, 1968), Chaps. 2-5. The only areas lost to the Soviets after the civil war were Finland, the former tsarist provinces in Poland, the Baltic states, Bessarabia (Moldavia), and parts of western Belorussia and Ukraine that were incorporated into Poland. A small area, around the city of Kars, was ceded to Turkey.

29. Silver, op. cit., pp. 43-64; and Yaroslav Bilinsky, "Education of the Non-Russian Peoples in the USSR, 1917-1967: An Essay," Slavic Review 27 (September 1968): 431-34.

30. Jacob Ornstein, "Soviet Language Policy: Continuity and Change," in Ethnic Minorities in the Soviet Union, ed. Erich Goldhagen (New York: Praeger, 1968), p. 136.

31. USSR, Tsentral'noye Statisticheskoye Upravleniye pri Sovete Ministrov SSSR, Narodnoye Obrazovaniye, Nauka i Kultura v SSSR (Moscow: Izdatel'stvo "Statistika," 1971), pp. 363, 370, 378-79. To obtain the total number of magazines and newspapers printed in Russian, we assumed that all issues published outside the RSFSR in other than the language of the titular republic were in Russian. This, of course, results in a slight, but not critical, overestimate of the Russian language publications.

32. Robert Conquest, Soviet Nationalities Policy in Practice (New York: Praeger, 1967), p. 91. The quote is attributed to the Uzbek poet Gafur Gulyam.

33. The Russians as "elder brothers" is a prominent theme in Soviet nationality policy. See, for instance, Teresa Rakowska-Harmstone, Russia and Nationalism in Central Asia (Baltimore: Johns Hopkins Press, 1970), pp. 80-90. For a more general discussion of race ideologies and their function, see Shibutani and Kwan, op. cit., pp. 241-49.

34. Conquest, op. cit., pp. 54-55.

35. For another approach to the characterization of Soviet nationalities, see John A. Armstrong, "The Ethnic Scene in the Soviet Union," in Ethnic Minorities in the Soviet Union, ed. Erich Goldhagen (New York: Praeger, 1968), pp. 3-32. Essentially, Armstrong's representation of these six nationalities is identical to our approach. In his scheme, Jews and Armenians are termed "Mobilized Diasporas," whereas Georgians, Latvians, and Estonians are referred to as "State-nations." Although Tatars are included with the less-advanced "Colonials," their unique role as intermediaries is acknowledged.

36. By 1927, Jews constituted 13.5 percent of students in higher education and 1.8 percent of the population. See Nicholas DeWitt, Education and Professional Employment in the USSR (Washington, D.C.: Superintendent of Documents, 1961), pp. 358-60.

37. In 1922, Jews comprised 5.2 percent of Communist party members, with a significantly higher membership rate per population than Russians (Pipes, op. cit., p. 278). The total number of Russians in the Party was, of course, much larger than the Jewish figure. Many outstanding Bolsheviks were Jews, including Trotsky, Kaganovich, Radek, Zinoviyev, and Sverdlov.

38. See David Marshall Lang, A Modern History of Soviet Georgia (New York: Grove Press, 1962), Chaps. 5-9.

39. Hugh Seton-Watson, The Russian Empire, 1801-1917 (Oxford: Oxford University Press, 1967), pp. 414-15, 496-98, 609-10.

40. For a general background on the culture of the Baltic nationalities, see Stephen P. Dunn, Cultural Processes in the Baltic Area Under Soviet Rule (Berkeley, Calif.: University of California Press, 1966), pp. 3-16.

41. Alexandre Bennigsen and Chantal Lemercier-Quelquejay, Islam in the Soviet Union (London: Pall Mall Press, 1967), pp. 26-27, 37-39, 109, 126-27.

42. Pipes, op. cit., p. 12.

43. As background information for this section, we have drawn selectively upon a number of sources, most importantly Edward Allworth, ed., Central Asia: A Century of Russian Rule (New York: Columbia University Press, 1967); Alton S. Donnelly, The Russian Conquest of Bashkiria, 1552-1740 (New Haven, Conn.: Yale University Press, 1968); Michael Hrushevsky, A History of Ukraine (New Haven, Conn.: Yale University Press, 1941); W. H. Parker, An His-

torical Geography of Russia (Chicago: Aldine, 1969); and Hugh Seton-Watson, op. cit.

44. Sources utilized for information contained in this section included Conquest, op. cit.; Pipes, op. cit.; and the very helpful International Boundary Study Series issued by the Geographer, Department of State, U.S. Government.

45. The contention that problems associated with nationality in the USSR have been solved by the advent and growth of socialism in that country, and by the application of Soviet nationality policy, is a pervasive theme in official and scholarly publications. For an expression of the position of the Soviet government regarding the solution of the nationality question, see L. I. Brezhnev, O Pyatidesyatiletii Soyuza Sovetskikh Sotsialisticheskikh Respublik (Moscow: Izdatel'stvo Politicheskoy Literatury, 1973).

46. See Edward Allworth, "Restating the Soviet Nationality Question," in Soviet Nationality Problems, ed. Edward Allworth (New York: Columbia University Press, 1971), pp. 1-21.

47. V. I. Lenin, "O Prave Natsiy na Samoopredeleniye," Sochineniya, 4th ed., vol. 20 (Moscow: Gosudarstvennoye Izdatel'stvo Politicheskoy Literatury, 1948), p. 406.

48. Solomon F. Bloom, The World of Nations: A Study of the National Implications in the Work of Karl Marx (New York: AMS Press, 1967), pp. 1-32.

49. Ibid., pp. 15-22.

50. Ibid., Chap. 2.

51. Ibid., p. 27.

52. Pipes, op. cit., pp. 21-27.

53. Bloom, op. cit., pp. 43, 200-02.

54. Pipes, op. cit., pp. 24-25.

55. Marc Raeff, "Patterns of Russian Imperial Policy Toward the Nationalities," in Soviet Nationality Problems, ed. Edward Allworth (New York: Columbia Uuniversity Press, 1971), pp. 22-42.

56. Ibid., pp. 33-38.

57. Seton-Watson, op. cit., pp. 267-74.

58. Ibid., pp. 485-505; and Pipes, op. cit., pp. 6-7.

59. Seton-Watson, op. cit., pp. 271-72, 409-18, 485-505; and Pipes, op. cit., pp. 9-21.

60. Raeff, op. cit., p. 38.

61. Pipes, op. cit., pp. 32-33.

62. Alfred D. Low, Lenin on the Question of Nationality (New York: Bookman, 1958), Chap. 2.

63. V. I. Lenin, "Kriticheskiye Zametki po Natsional'nomu Voprosu," op. cit., pp. 3-34; and Lenin, "O Prave Natsiy na Samoopredeleniye," pp. 367-424. These important works, together with other articles by Lenin on the nationality question, are translated and

collected in V. I. Lenin, Questions of National Policy and Proletarian Internationalism (Moscow: Progress Publishers, 1970).

64. Pipes, op. cit., pp. 41-49.

65. Lenin, "O Prave Natsiy na Samoopredeleniye," pp. 367-72.

66. Ibid., p. 393.

67. Ibid., p. 392.

68. Pipes, op. cit., pp. 44-46; and Low, op. cit., Chap. 4.

69. Low, op. cit., Chap. 4.

70. Pipes, op. cit., pp. 50-51.

71. Ibid., Chap. 2.

72. J. V. Stalin, Works (Moscow: Foreign Languages Publishing House, 1953), p. 270.

73. Pipes, op. cit., Chaps. 3, 4, and 5.

74. Conquest, op. cit., pp. 21-25.

75. Ibid., pp. 25-47; and Pipes, op. cit., pp. 108-13.

76. See Leonard Schapiro, The Communist Party of the Soviet Union (New York: Vintage Books, 1964), in particular, Chap. 13. In 1941, an extensive collection of Communist party documents was seized by advancing units of the German army at Smolensk. This archive, which was captured later in Germany by American forces, illustrates dramatically the control of the decision-making apparatus and of government organs by the Party. See Merle Fainsod, Smolensk Under Soviet Rule (New York: Vintage Books, 1958).

77. USSR, Prezidium Verkhovnogo Soveta, SSSR: Administrativno-Territorial'noye Deleniye Soyuznykh Respublik, 1971 (Moscow: Izdatel'stvo "Izvestiya Sovetov Deputatov Trudyashchikhsya SSR," 1971).

78. Conquest, op. cit., Chap. 3; and Roman Szporluk, "Nationalities and the Russian Problem in the U.S.S.R.: An Historical Outline," Journal of International Affairs 27, no. 1 (1973): 28-29.

79. Conquest, op. cit., pp. 53-55.

80. Pipes, op. cit., p. 278. Although the Party was dominated numerically by Russians, membership relative to population was actually much higher for some nationalities (Jews, Latvians, Georgians, Poles, Estonians, and Ossetians). Furthermore, the leadership of the Party was mainly non-Russian.

81. Szporluk, op. cit., pp. 29-31.

82. Hans Kohn, "Soviet Communism and Nationalism: Three Stages of a Historical Development," in Soviet Nationality Problems, ed. Edward Allworth (New York: Columbia University Press), pp. 57-61.

83. For example, see the well-documented work on the tribulations of the Volga Germans, Crimean Tatars, and Caucasian peoples in Robert Conquest, The Nation Killers: The Soviet Deportation of Nationalities, 2d ed. (New York: Macmillan, 1970).

84. Szporluk, op. cit., p. 36.

85. Yaroslav Bilinsky, "The Soviet Education Laws of 1958–1959 and Soviet Nationality Policy," Soviet Studies 14 (October 1962): 138–57.

86. There is a very extensive Soviet literature on the desirability and characteristics of the assimilation process and the bases of national identity. We would refer the reader to the following works as an introduction: M. S. Dzhunusov, "Natsiya kak Sotsial'no-Etnicheskaya Obshchnost' Lyudei," Voprosy Istorii, no. 4 (April 1966): 16–30; T. Yu. Burmistrova, Teoriya Sotsialisticheskoy Natsiy (Leningrad: Izdatel'stvo Leningradskogo Universiteta, 1970); A. I. Kholmogorov, Internatsional'nyye Cherty Sovetskikh Natsiy (Moscow: Mysl', 1970); and V. I. Kozlov, Dinamika Chislennosti Narodov (Moscow: Mysl', 1969).

87. Bilinski, op. cit.; and Vernon V. Aspaturian, "The Non-Russian Nationalities," in Prospects for Soviet Society, ed. Allen Kassof (New York: Praeger, 1968), pp. 168–75.

88. See Grey Hodnett, "What's in a Nation?" Problems of Communism 16 (September–October 1967): 2–15.

89. Grey Hodnett, "The Debate over Soviet Federalism," Soviet Studies 18 (April 1967): 458–81.

90. I. S. Koropeckyj, Locational Problems in Soviet Industry Before World War II (Chapel Hill, N.C.: University of North Carolina Press, 1971), pp. 55–56; and V. Rutgayzer, "Torzhestvo Leninskoy Natsional'noy Politiki v Ekonomicheskom Stroitel'stve," Kommunist, no. 18 (December 1968): 24–35.

91. Rutgayzer, op. cit., pp. 30–35.

92. Koropeckyj, op. cit., pp. 51–80.

93. Ibid., pp. 74–77.

94. Leslie Dienes, "Investment Priorities in Soviet Regions," Annals of the Association of American Geographers 62 (September 1972): 437–54.

95. Ibid., 446; and I. S. Koropeckyj, "Equalization of Economic Development in Socialist Countries: An Empirical Study," Economic Development and Cultural Change 21 (October 1972): 79–80.

96. Koropeckyj, Locational Problems, p. 76.

97. Gertrude E. Schroeder, "Regional Differences in Incomes and Levels of Living in the USSR," in The Soviet Economy in Regional Perspective, ed. V. N. Bandera and Z. L. Melnyk (New York: Praeger, 1973), p. 193.

98. Allan Rodgers, "The Locational Dynamics of Soviet Industry," Annals of the Association of American Geographers 64 (June 1974): 226, 238.

99. Brian Silver, "Levels of Sociocultural Development Among Soviet Nationalities: A Partial Test of the Equalization Hypothesis," The American Political Science Review 68 (December 1974): 1632–33.

100. Brezhnev, op. cit.

5

URBANIZATION

Because this study is concerned with the modernization of Soviet nationalities and urbanization is a prime indicator of modernization, it is appropriate that the urbanization of the nationality groupings should be the first topic to be discussed. Urbanization, especially its meaning and association with economic development and modernization, has previously been discussed in sufficient detail, and need only be summarized here. To reiterate, urbanization is the process of population concentration that involves an increase in the percent of the total population residing in urban centers (that is, level of urbanization) and is normally highly associated with social change, economic development, and modernization. Therefore, it is very useful in assessing the degree of modernization of a given nationality. In multinational states there are usually differentials in the levels of urbanization among various ethnic groups, differentials that generally reflect the degree to which groups have been integrated into the modernized society. Of course, there are instances where urbanization is not a good indicator of differential modernization. For example, it appears that in the later stages of urbanization, the level of urbanization becomes much less useful as an indicator of differential modernization, since modernization and economic development can continue to increase, while urbanization, as defined here, is a finite process. For example, in the United States, because most ethnic groups are highly urbanized, urbanization is not a good indicator of socioeconomic stratification along ethnic lines. However, since the Soviet Union is not as highly urbanized as the United States, such problems do not exist to any great extent. Furthermore, even casual observation leads one to conclude that differential levels of urbanization in the USSR in the time period investigated here are generally indicative of differential levels of modernization and economic development. This will be increasingly apparent elsewhere in this study.

For a number of reasons it is logical to hypothesize that the Russians, in particular, would experience a relatively high degree of urbanization. First of all, they, being the dominant group, hold the most powerful positions in Soviet society and, accordingly, there might be a tendency for them to direct a disproportionate share of the Soviet capital investment to the major region of Russian settlement, the RSFSR. That such a tendency, in fact, has existed is suggested by the fact that the RSFSR has generally received well over 60 percent of the capital investment in the Soviet period (excluding investment in kolkhozes), although it always was a smaller percentage of the population within the present-day boundaries of the USSR in all of the four census years, and Russians have never been more than 55 percent of the population of Russia and the USSR in the four censuses. An additional condition favoring a high degree of Russian urbanization is that the greatest share of the most important mineral deposits in the USSR are located within the RSFSR, especially in Siberia, the Ural Mountains, and the Volga-Urals region. Furthermore, major areas of the RSFSR traditionally have experienced considerably rural overpopulation and out-migration. Thus, the dominant position of the Russians, coupled with the presence of substantial areas of industrial resources and rural overpopulation in their republic, could account for the very high degree of Russian urbanization.

Also, it is reasonable to expect a high degree of Russian urbanization in non-Russian areas, because such areas frequently are dominated by more traditional groups who cannot provide the required skilled labor for modern urban-industrial activities. Thus, an inflow of the more modernized Russians to fill this labor shortage can be expected. Such a migration is fraught with further potential repercussions, including assimilation and ethnic tensions.

Finally, in addition to the dominant Russians, other nationalities would conceivably participate in the urbanization process to a greater extent than the more traditional groups. Such ethnic groups as the Jews in the European USSR, Tatars in Central Asia, Armenians and Georgians in the Transcaucasus, and Latvians and Estonians in the Baltic area are characterized by achievement orientation and, particularly in the case of Tatars, a status as middlemen between the Russians and non-Russian nationalities.

In conclusion, these are the major patterns that one would expect to find in an investigation of the urbanization of Soviet nationalities. These and other patterns of the urbanization of Soviet nationalities will be discussed in greater depth in this chapter.

SUMMARY DISCUSSION

Although other regions of the world have higher levels of urbanization, the Soviet Union and most of its major nationality groupings
have been urbanizing faster than any other major region in the world
during recent decades, reflecting the planned rapid industrialization
of the USSR during this period. Indeed, most nationality groupings in
the USSR have surpassed the second-ranking world region (Latin
America) with respect to urbanization increase.

However, despite the fact that all nationality groupings have urbanized substantially, there are significant variations in the degree of
urbanization of the groupings. Not unexpectedly, Russians have, with
the exception of the Jewish population, had the greatest level of urbanization and the greatest increase in that level between 1897 and 1970,
especially in the Soviet era (1926-70). The Jews have had both a
greater level of urbanization and a greater increase in that level between 1897 and 1970. Jewish urbanization, however, has been highly
influenced by some unusual factors that are not necessarily associated
with modernization, and during the Soviet era the Jewish increase was
surpassed by many other groupings, especially the Russians. In addition, Tatars have experienced significant urbanization, particularly in
comparison with other non-European groups. Of the remaining groupings, Ukrainians, Belorussians, Mobilized Europeans, and Lithuanians
have generally experienced a moderate rate of urbanization, while the
Finnic peoples, Turkic-Muslims, and Moldavians and Romanians generally had low rates of urbanization. It should be noted, however, that
in recent years, Lithuanians and Belorussians have urbanized at a rate
comparable to the Russians, but the Russians have maintained their
rapid rate for almost a half century, not just during the last decade.
Indeed, very few, if any, peoples in human history have urbanized as
rapidly as the Russians in the Soviet era. That in 1970 the Russian
level of urbanization was more than twice that of the large bloc of
Turkic-Muslim peoples is illustrative of the considerable ethnic differentials in levels of urbanization within the USSR.

The high degree of Russian urbanization has been related to a
number of factors. Russians are the dominant group in the Soviet
Union, and, not unexpectedly, the Russian republic has received a
disproportionate share of the total amount of Soviet capital investment,
which has been primarily directed toward the industrial sector, thereby
enhancing the industrialization and urbanization of the Russian homeland.
The rapid industrialization of the RSFSR and the consequent rapid urbanization of the Russians have also been promoted by the fact that the
RSFSR is very rich in mineral resources for industrialization and has
traditionally included substantial areas of rural overpopulation, especially in European Russia. In addition, within the RSFSR, Russian ur-

banization has been appreciable in many areas where non-Russian groups are more numerous in terms of total population, but in virtually every non-Russian nationality unit in the RSFSR, Russians have been the most numerous nationality in the cities.

Russian urbanization also has been quite significant outside the RSFSR. Like most groups, Russians are more urbanized outside the RSFSR than within it. Although Russians have never been more than one-fifth of the total population of the area outside the RSFSR, they have generally accounted for roughly one-third of the urban population and urban growth of these non-Russian regions. Major areas where Russians are relatively numerous in urban centers, even a majority in many instances, include the Kazakh and Kirgiz SSRs, nearby portions of the Uzbek SSR, the Crimea, the eastern region of the Ukrainian SSR, and some individual cities in other republics, especially the capital cities. The eastern Ukraine (Donetsk-Dnepr) is the principal region of Russian urban settlement outside the RSFSR in terms of the absolute number of urban Russians. At the other end of the spectrum, the Transcaucasus stands out as the region where Russians comprise a very low proportion of the urban population.

These patterns suggest that the relative presence of Russians in cities of the non-Russian republics is inversely related to the level of advancement of the indigenous nationality. Namely, the more underdeveloped the indigenous group, the greater the need for Russians in urban-industrial activities requiring higher levels of education and skills. This relationship was demonstrated statistically after the Baltic republics were excluded. Latvians and Estonians upset the expected inverse relationship because, although they are highly educated, there has been a significant influx of Russians to cities of Latvia and Estonia. This has occurred because the Latvian and Estonian populations have been growing so slowly that the increase in the indigenous work force has not been able to satisfy the labor requirements of their expanding economies. Russians, thus, have benefited not only from the industrialization of the RSFSR but also from much of the industrialization of non-Russian areas. Therefore, industrialization of these areas has not solely benefited the indigenous group but has also benefited the Russians, in many cases much more than the indigenous group.

The influx of Russians to cities of non-Russian areas has had many repercussions. First of all, it has enhanced the Russification of non-Russian groups because of the greater contacts between Russians and non-Russians in these cities. This Russification, or, in many instances, complete assimilation of non-Russian urban dwellers, is yet another factor contributing to the increase of Russians in urban areas. In addition, because these cities are frequently Russian in nature, they pose a somewhat unfamiliar cultural environment to the indigenous groups, thus impeding local rural-to-urban migration. The migration

of indigenous groups to cities in their nationality areas has also been
impeded because Russians take up many of the jobs in the cities. Finally, there generally has been little local rural population pressure,
owing to higher mortality until recently in non-European rural areas.

In many non-Russian areas, however, especially in Turkic-Muslim areas such as Central Asia, mortality has been greatly reduced
and fertility is still very high, resulting in accelerated population
growth. Because the vast majority of the indigenous Turkic-Muslim
population resides in rural areas, rural population pressure, therefore, has been heightened significantly. This pressure undoubtedly
will not be eased by increasing opportunities in rural areas, especially
since these areas are so highly dependent upon irrigation. Indeed,
increased opportunities in rural areas in most parts of the USSR appear to be very limited, not an unusual situation for a modernized
country. Thus, it appears that the major response will be mass out-
migration from these rural areas to all parts of the USSR, marking a
major departure from the past, as traditionally these nationalities
have been highly immobile. The societal implications of such migrations are dramatic, warranting a separate discussion in Chapter 10.

In summary, with respect to the four major questions of this
study, the following statements can be made:

1. Because Russians are the dominant group, we would expect
them to experience the greatest degree of urbanization of any of the
nationality groupings. In addition, appreciable urbanization would be
expected for the Jews, Tatars, and Mobilized Europeans.

2. Results of our analysis revealed that for all practical purposes, Russians did experience a greater degree of urbanization than
any other grouping, with regard to both the level of urbanization and
change in that level, especially in the Soviet era. The Jews and
Tatars also urbanized considerably, but the Mobilized Europeans did
not urbanize as much as expected.

3. Although these urbanization patterns were not the direct result of specific Soviet policies, government economic policies did
have a considerable indirect influence; outstanding in this respect has
been the policy of rapid industrialization and disproportionate capital
investment in the RSFSR.

4. Aside from the obvious modernizing influence of the urbanization process, many implications for Soviet society as a whole are
noticeable, especially with respect to the urbanization of various nationalities outside their homelands. Economic development in non-
Russian areas frequently has entailed an influx of Russians to the cities
of such areas. The presence of Russians in these cities has enhanced
the Russification of non-Russian nationalities and impeded the local
rural-to-urban migration on the part of the indigenous groups, although

their lack of appropriate skills and the lack of appreciable rural population pressure in the past are perhaps the prime reasons for the
meagerness of such a migration. It appears, however, that this situation may be reversed and that a substantial migration of non-Russians,
particularly Central Asians, to cities in Russian areas is likely.
Rapid population growth is occurring in the rural areas of Central
Asia, greatly increasing population pressure. Substantial out-migration from these rural areas seems inevitable, because opportunities
in local cities appear quite limited and there apparently will be a great
demand for outside labor, particularly low-skilled labor, in cities of
the Russian areas. Thus, a substantial migration of dominantly
Turkic-Muslim peoples to such cities is highly probable. If these
peoples eventually comprise a substantial share of the population of
cities that were dominantly Russian in the past, an increase in ethnic
tensions most likely will occur.

DETAILED DISCUSSION

An investigation of the process of urbanization in Russia and the
USSR is of singular importance because, since around the turn of the
century, the Soviet Union has been urbanizing at a rate not only above
the world average but also generally above the rate of any other major world region.[1] These patterns can be documented on the basis of
the conventional urban definition in studies concerned with world urbanization, namely, settlements of 20,000 or more people. According to this definition, the level of urbanization of the Russian Empire
in 1897 was roughly on a par with that of the world in 1900, 9.4 and
9.2 percent, respectively.[2] By 1970, however, the Soviet level of
urbanization based upon the same definition had increased to 44.3
percent, whereas the world average had increased to only 28.2 percent.[3] Also, UN estimates for the 1920-70 period indicate that the
USSR was urbanizing faster than any of the other seven major world
regions. Between 1920 and 1970 the percentage point change in the
Soviet level of urbanization was 33; the next closest, or second-
ranking, region was Latin America, with a percentage point increase
of 24.*

Because the urbanization process in Russia and the USSR has
been so rapid and because there have been significant differentials by
nationality grouping in the USSR, the urbanization of many individual

---

*As mentioned before, percentage point change is our major indi-
cator of the change in the level of urbanization. To repeat, it simply
involves the subtraction of the earlier percent from the later percent.

Soviet nationalities has far exceeded the urbanization of the total world population. Our analysis of Soviet urbanization, of course, is based upon a slightly different urban definition, namely, settlements of 15,000 and over. Table 5.1 shows the levels of urbanization according to our definition for the nationality groupings in each of the four census years; Table 5.2 reveals the percentage point changes in these levels, and Table 5.3 shows the average annual percentage point changes. In addition, Table 5.4 reveals the level of urbanization for every nationality in 1970 based upon the census definition of urban. These tables will serve as the basis for discussion for the remainder of this chapter.

Because of no other alternatives, the levels for 1897 and 1926 are based upon the summations of the total and urban populations for each grouping from the 19 regions. The 1959 and 1970 percentages presented in these tables are based upon the census summary data. The same procedure used for individual regions was followed here in that the nationality composition of the total urban population (census definition) was applied to the total urban population (15,000 and over definition) in order to estimate the population of each grouping that resided in settlements of 15,000 and over for the USSR as a whole.

It is interesting to note that in measuring the change in the level of urbanization of the nationality groupings, the use of percentage point change instead of percentage change is especially beneficial. We noted in an earlier chapter that percentage point change was preferred over percentage change, partly because the latter is often distorted by a low base figure. Because the early urbanization levels of many groupings were very low, use of percentage change would, consequently, result in a distorted high rate of urbanization. For example, if the level of urbanization of a grouping increased from 2 percent in 1897 to 6 percent in 1970, this would result in a percentage change of 200 percent, even though the grouping remained overwhelmingly rural and traditional. If the level of urbanization of another grouping increased from 20 percent in 1897 to 60 percent in 1970, this would also result in a percentage change of 200 percent, even though this second grouping was transformed from being predominantly rural and traditional to predominantly urban and modernized. The distortion embodied in the percentage change measure should be apparent. According to this measure, both groupings urbanized (or modernized) at the same rate (200 percent), even though the first grouping remained predominantly rural and traditional, while the second grouping was transformed from being predominantly rural and traditional to being predominantly urban and modern. When percentage point change is used, the more significant increase in the level of modernization of the second grouping emerges—in this case, 40 percentage points for the second grouping versus four percentage points for the first grouping. Therefore, percentage point change appears to be an especially preferable measure

TABLE 5.1

Level of Urbanization by Nationality Grouping: 1897–1970

Grouping	1897	1926	1959	1970
Russians	13.0	16.1	46.0	56.3
Ukrainians	4.7	7.3	31.3	40.1
Belorussians	2.2	5.8	26.2	36.1
Tatars	8.9	11.1	36.9	45.6
Turkic-Muslims	5.0	6.3	18.6	22.8
Jews	34.4	53.0	77.4	78.5
Mobilized Europeans	12.3	20.0	36.5	46.3
Finnic peoples	1.7	3.4	20.4	27.4
Lithuanians	2.3	7.2	27.4	38.0
Moldavians and Romanians	4.1	7.3	10.3	16.0
USSR Total	9.9	13.3	38.2	46.6

Sources: See Chapter 2, footnotes 2 and 3.

of the increase in the level of urbanization or modernization of a grouping.

Average annual percentage point change simply involves the percentage point change divided by the number of years in the period. For example, a percentage point increase of 40 over an 80-year period would entail an average annual percentage point change of 0.50. Because the 1926 census was taken in December while the others were taken in January, the length of the intercensal periods were not always whole numbers. The corresponding lengths for the six periods are 1897–1926, 29.9 years; 1926–59, 32.1 years; 1897–1959, 62.0 years; 1959–70, 11.0 years; 1926–70, 43.1 years; and 1897–1970, 73.0 years. Note that, although the word "rate" usually refers to percentage change, in this study it will be used to refer to either percentage change or percentage point change.

With the use of these tables it is possible to illustrate the urbanization of individual nationality groupings in comparison to the urbanization of the world as a whole. The comparison will involve the closest approximation of overall periods: the 1926–70 period for the USSR and the 1930–70 period for the world.[4] Although the urban criterion differs slightly (being 15,000 and over for the USSR figures and 20,000 and over for the world), the comparison can still be made, especially since the vast majority of the Soviet population in centers of 15,000

TABLE 5.2

Percentage Point Change in the Level of Urbanization by Nationality Grouping: 1897–1970

Grouping	1897–1926	1926–59	1897–1959	1959–70	1926–70	1897–1970
Russians	3.1	29.9	33.0	10.3	40.2	43.3
Ukrainians	2.6	24.0	26.6	8.8	32.8	35.4
Belorussians	3.6	20.4	24.0	9.9	30.3	33.9
Tatars	2.2	25.8	28.0	8.7	34.5	36.7
Turkic–Muslims	1.3	12.3	13.6	4.2	16.5	17.8
Jews	18.6	24.4	43.0	1.1	25.5	44.1
Mobilized Europeans	7.7	16.5	24.2	9.8	26.3	34.0
Finnic peoples	1.7	17.0	18.7	7.0	24.0	25.7
Lithuanians	4.9	20.2	25.1	10.6	30.8	35.7
Moldavians and Romanians	3.2	3.0	6.2	5.7	8.7	11.9
USSR total	3.4	24.9	28.3	8.4	33.3	36.7

Sources: See Chapter 2, footnotes 2 and 3.

TABLE 5.3

Average Annual Percentage Point Change in the Level of Urbanization by Nationality Grouping: 1897-1970*

Grouping	1897-1926	1926-59	1897-1959	1959-70	1926-70	1897-1970
Russians	0.10	0.93	0.53	0.94	0.93	0.59
Ukrainians	0.09	0.75	0.43	0.80	0.76	0.48
Belorussians	0.12	0.64	0.39	0.90	0.70	0.46
Tatars	0.07	0.80	0.45	0.79	0.80	0.50
Turkic-Muslims	0.04	0.38	0.22	0.38	0.38	0.24
Jews	0.62	0.76	0.69	0.10	0.59	0.60
Mobilized Europeans	0.26	0.51	0.39	0.89	0.61	0.47
Finnic peoples	0.06	0.53	0.30	0.64	0.56	0.35
Lithuanians	0.16	0.63	0.40	0.96	0.71	0.49
Moldavians and Romanians	0.11	0.09	0.10	0.52	0.20	0.16
USSR total	0.11	0.78	0.46	0.76	0.77	0.50

*Average annual percentage point change equals total percentage point change (see Table 5.2) divided by the number of years in the corresponding intercensal period.

Sources: See Chapter 2, footnotes 2 and 3.

TABLE 5.4

Level of Urbanization by Nationality: 1970*
(census definition of urban)

90.0-100.0

JEWS (97.9)
Tats (97.1)
Karaimy (96.7)

80.0-89.9

Khalka-Mongols (88.2)
Peoples of India and
  Pakistan (87.8)
Assyrians (81.9)

70.0-79.9

French (74.2)
Slovaks (71.8)

60.0-69.9

KOREANS (68.1)
RUSSIANS (68.0)
ARMENIANS (64.8)
GREEKS (61.1)
Finns (60.5)
Czechs (60.3)

50.0-59.9

GYPSIES (56.7)
[USSR total (56.3)]
Vepsy (55.7)
ESTONIANS (55.1)
TATARS (55.0)
OSSETIANS (53.3)
LATVIANS (52.7)
Iranians (52.6)
Izhortsy (52.2)
Afghans (52.1)
Shortsy (51.1)

40.0-49.9

UKRAINIANS (48.5)
Laks (47.9)
LITHUANIANS (46.7)

GERMANS (45.4)
POLES (45.2)
KARELIANS (44.9)
GEORGIANS (44.0)
BELORUSSIANS (43.7)
Orochi (41.8)
KUMYKS (40.3)

30.0-39.9

AZERI (39.7)
INGUSH (38.7)
Kurds (38.6)
BULGARIANS (37.3)
HUNGARIANS (36.5)
KOMI (36.5)
MORDVINIANS (36.1)
KALMYKS (35.9)
Abkhaz (34.5)
Nivkhi (33.9)
Yukagiry (33.8)
GAGAUZ (33.2)
UDMURTS (32.1)
TURKMENS (31.0)
UYGURS (30.9)
KARAKALPAKS (30.5)
LEZGIANS (30.5)
Lapps (30.0)

20.0-29.9

Albanians (29.4)
CHUVASH (29.1)
Balkars (28.4)
Eskimos (27.5)
KAZAKHS (26.7)
BASHKIRS (26.6)
Mansi (26.1)
Nanaytsy (26.0)
TADZHIKS (26.0)
Khakas (25.7)
UZBEKS (24.9)
ROMANIANS (24.8)
BURYATS (24.6)

Negidal'tsy (24.0)
KABARDINIANS (23.9)
Itel'meny (23.4)
KOMI-PERMYAKS (22.9)
DARGINS (22.7)
Dungane (22.6)
Aleuts (22.4)
CHECHENS (21.8)
Adyge (21.6)
Circassians (21.1)
Koryaks (21.1)
YAKUTS (21.1)
MARI (20.5)
MOLDAVIANS (20.4)

10.0-19.9

Udegeytsy (19.0)
AVARS (18.7)
Nganasany (18.7)
Chukchi (17.7)
Abaza (17.6)
TUVINIANS (17.1)
Eveny (16.9)
KARACHAY (16.4)
Tabasarany (16.2)
Ul'chi (16.0)
Udiny (15.9)
Evenki (15.3)
Khanty (15.3)
Sel'kupy (14.9)
Altays (14.7)
KIRGIZ (14.6)
Tofy (14.5)
Nentsy (13.4)
Dolgany (12.7)
Nogays (12.6)
Tsakhury (11.7)
Kety (11.4)

0.0-9.9

Beludzhi (9.9)
Aguly (3.6)
Rutul'tsy (1.5)

*Nationalities with a population of more than 100,000 are indicated with capital letters.

Source: 1970 Soviet census (see Chapter 2, footnote 2).

and over is located in centers of 20,000 and over. In 1970, for example, 95.1 percent of the Soviet population in centers of 15,000 and over was located in centers of 20,000 and over. Also, as the tables indicate, the 1970 Soviet levels of urbanization based on the 15,000 and over and 20,000 and over definitions were nearly equal (46.6 and 44.3 percent, respectively). Thus, the two definitions are virtually identical.

Our data reveal that between 1926 and 1970 every nationality grouping except Moldavians and Romanians urbanized well above the world average of 0.30 percentage points per year. As Table 5.3 suggests, the majority of the groupings urbanized at a rate more than twice that of the world, and faster than the second-ranking major world region, Latin America.

Even in the most recent period, these trends have been maintained. Between 1960 and 1970 the world urbanized 0.30 percentage points per year. Not only was the Soviet Union still the top-ranking world region in this regard but, as Table 5.3 suggests, every nationality grouping again, save one, urbanized above the world average between 1959 and 1970. The exception in this period were the Jews, who are so highly urbanized that it is difficult for their level of urbanization to increase substantially. Also, as before, the majority of groupings urbanized at a rate more than twice that of the world and significantly faster than that for the second-ranking major world region or, in this case, regions (North America, Oceania, and Latin America).

This truly dramatic urbanization of Soviet nationalities should be kept in mind during subsequent discussions, because our concern will be with differences in urbanization and modernization among the individual nationality groupings and between Russians and non-Russians, in particular. Therefore, many groupings necessarily will have a relatively low increase in their level of urbanization in the Soviet context, although such an increase may be high by world standards.

In order to analyze the process of urbanization among the Soviet nationality groupings, the following framework will generally be adhered to.[5] Urbanization will be analyzed first in terms of the differential change between the urban and total (or rural) populations of the given grouping, because any change in the level of urbanization is due to the rate of change of the urban population vis-a-vis the total (or rural) population. In particular, an increase in the level of urbanization is always because the rate of urban population change has exceeded that of the total (or rural) population. It is imperative that the reader be aware of the difference between the change in the level of urbanization, on the one hand, and the change in the urban population, on the other hand, and does not confuse the two. The former involves the change in the percent of the total population comprised by the urban population, which we define as urbanization, whereas the latter involves the change only in the urban population itself, which we define as urban growth. As will become apparent later, some groupings, especially Turkic-Muslims, have experienced considerable urban growth, but only a small increase in their level of urbanization, because their total and rural populations also have increased considerably, thus impeding a higher level of urbanization. Therefore, the reader should not be perplexed by the fact that a grouping may have experienced rapid urban growth but has not experienced a comparatively significant increase in urbanization. Table 5.5 has been added to partly clarify the situation. It includes a brief summary of the change in the level of urbanization of each grouping and the changes in their urban and rural populations.

The differential change between the urban and total (or rural) population, in turn, can be analyzed in terms of three conditions that theoretically promote a situation where the rate of urban population change exceeds that of the total (or rural) population: urban natural increase exceeding rural natural increase, net rural-to-urban migration, and reclassification of settlements from rural to urban status. Because the first condition has occurred rarely in human history and the third has been generally insignificant, the emphasis will be on net rural-to-urban migration. Rural-to-urban migration has an especially profound, double-barreled impact on urbanization, because it not only increases the urban population but also simultaneously reduces the rural population. It should be pointed out that data deficiencies will usually make a rigorous analysis of these three situations impossible; most groupings, however, experienced such rapid urban growth that rural-to-urban migration had to be of very great significance. The final level of analysis will involve an investigation of various socioeconomic conditions (especially industrialization, education, and rural population pressure) and natural conditions, if any, that influenced the above processes. The nationality groupings will be discussed in the same sequence as shown in the tables.

Russians

The rate of Russian urbanization since the turn of the century and particularly since the inception of the five-year plans very probably has been surpassed by few, if any, populations in human history. The Russian urbanization process has been so spectacular that the number of Russians residing in cities today is roughly 50 million more than would be the case if the Russian level of urbanization in the mid-1920s still persisted. Overall, the number of Russians residing in cities has increased by approximately 60 million since the period im-

TABLE 5.5

Brief Summary of Changes in the Level of Urbanization and Changes
in the Components of Urbanization by Nationality Grouping: 1897-1970

Grouping	Percentage Point Change in Level of Urbanization	Percentage Change in	
		Urban Population	Rural Population
Russians	High +	High +	Moderate-low +
Ukrainians	Moderate +	High +	Low +
Belorussians	Moderate +	High +	Low +
Tatars	Moderate-high +	High +	Moderate-high +
Turkic-Muslims	Low +	Moderate-high +	Moderate-high +
Jews	High +	Low +	High -
Mobilized Europeans	Moderate +	Moderate-low +	Moderate +
Finnic peoples	Moderate-low +	High +	Moderate-low -
Lithuanians	Moderate +	High +	Low +
Moldavians and Romanians	Low +	Moderate-low +	Moderate-high +

Note: + denotes increase; - denotes decrease.

Sources: 1897 Russian census; 1970 Soviet census; and various
foreign sources (see Chapter 2, footnotes 2 and 3).

mediately preceding the era of the five-year plans with their emphasis
on rapid industrialization. Although Russians have comprised only
about one-half of the population of Russia and the USSR since the turn
of the century, they have generally accounted for roughly three-fifths
to two-thirds of the country's urban population and urban growth.
Russians are now about as urbanized as such advanced regions as
Western Europe and Japan, which represents a sharp change from as
recently as the 1920s, when the Russian level of urbanization was
roughly comparable to that of Latin America.[6]
  Between 1897 and 1970 Russians experienced the second highest
percentage point increase in the level of urbanization (43.3) of any
nationality grouping in the USSR; only the Jews surpassed them in this
respect (Table 5.2). The Jewish increase (44.1), however, was only

slightly higher than that of the Russians, and, as will be seen later, Jewish urbanization was highly related to many factors not necessarily associated with modernization. Furthermore, during the Soviet era (1926-70), the Russians had the highest percentage point increase in the level of urbanization of any grouping, and the average annual percentage point increase in the Russian level of urbanization in all three post-1926 periods was higher than that of any grouping in any period, except for Lithuanians between 1959 and 1970 (Table 5.3).

The Russians also have been relatively highly urbanized in all four census years, reflecting, of course, their relatively high degree of modernization (Table 5.1). Of the groupings, they ranked second in 1897, 1959, and 1970 and third in 1926, and, along with Jews, they were the only grouping to have a level of urbanization above the national average in all four census years. In fact, aside from the Russians and Jews, only one other grouping was ever above the national average: the Mobilized Europeans in 1897 and 1926.

The most obvious explanation for the rapid urbanization of the Russian population is that the rate of growth of the Russian urban population has greatly exceeded that of the Russian total and rural populations. Between 1897 and 1970 the Russian urban population increased nearly ten times (905.8 percent), but of the ten major groupings, the Russians ranked only sixth in this respect, which partly reflects the low base urban populations of the five higher groups. During the same period, however, the Russian rural population increased by only 16.7 percent. All of this increase occurred in the 1897-1926 period, and in the three post-1926 periods the Russian rural population declined. Thus, during the Soviet era, Russian urbanization has followed the classic model of many Western countries in that urban growth has been accompanied by rural decline.

The major share of this relatively rapid increase of the Russian urban population probably has been owing to net rural-to-urban migration. The relative importance of net rural-to-urban migration cannot be assessed with any precision for any grouping because of the lack of appropriate data. However, estimates have been made that indicate that between 1926 and 1970, 56.3 percent of the total increase in the urban population (census definition) of the USSR was caused by net rural-to-urban in-migration.[7] During the same period, based upon the 15,000 and over urban definition, Russians accounted for nearly two-thirds (66.3 percent) of the total Soviet urban population growth. Therefore, because the bulk of the Soviet urban growth was Russian urban growth and the bulk of the Soviet urban growth was due to net rural-to-urban migration, it seems logical to conclude that net rural-to-urban migration was a prime factor in the rapid urbanization of the Russian population. In addition, the fairly high average annual percentage increase in the Russian urban population (4.0) during this pe-

riod suggests that rural-to-urban migration had to be of great importance. Finally, traditionally Russian regions were the areas of extensive rural depopulation, indicating again rural out-migration.

The appreciable degree of Russian rural-to-urban migration and
urbanization can be explained conveniently in terms of the push-pull
model. The push has consisted primarily of the existence of rural
overpopulation and lack of opportunities in the major areas of Russian
rural settlement in central European Russia. The pull primarily has
involved the expanding opportunities associated with the rapid industrialization that has occurred in Russia and the USSR, especially the
RSFSR. Elsewhere we have demonstrated statistically that the urbanization in Russia and the USSR has been closely linked, as might be
expected, to industrialization, especially in the post-1926 period.[8]

Once again, because Soviet urbanization has been so dominated
by Russians, it is logical to expect a strong relationship between Russian urbanization and Soviet industrialization. This is borne out by
rank correlations for various periods based on the 19 economic regions
between the percentage point change in the level of urbanization of
Russians and the percentage point change in the percent of the total
population comprised by the industrial work force. The rank correlation coefficients for the periods 1897-1959, 1926-59, and 1959-70
were 0.651, 0.640, and 0.521, respectively, each of which suggests
a fairly strong relationship between Russian urbanization and Soviet
industrialization.[9]

Although the processes of industrialization and urbanization
have occurred principally within areas of Russian settlement (the Center, Northwest, Urals, Volga, and Siberia), the process of Russian
urbanization, as hypothesized, has extended well beyond such areas.
Russian urbanization has occurred both in non-Russian units within
the RSFSR and in the remaining 14 republics. Within the RSFSR, there
are currently 31 non-Russian nationality units (16 ASSRs, five autonomous oblasts, and ten national okrugs). In 1970 Russians were the
largest nationality in the urban population of 30 of these 31 units, and
outnumbered, usually very substantially, the titular group or groups
of the corresponding unit. In 27 of the 30 units Russians comprised a
majority of the urban population; even in the three units in which they
did not comprise a majority of the urban population (Kalmyk ASSR,
Severo-Osetin ASSR, and Chuvash ASSR), Russians still accounted
for over 40 percent of the urban population. Furthermore, in the
Dagestan ASSR, the one unit in which they did not outnumber the titular
group in urban centers, Russians were outstanding from another perspective; although Russians did not outnumber the peoples of Dagestan
taken as a whole, they outnumbered by far all of the individual nationalities in this group and accounted for more than 30 percent of the urban population of this ASSR.

The dominance of Russians among the urban population of the non-Russian nationality units of the RSFSR is also evident on the basis of individual cities. Although nationality data for individual cities are not published in the 1959 and 1970 census volumes, except for the 15 republic capitals and Leningrad in both years and Sevastopol' and Kaunas in 1959, such data occasionally appear in various books and articles. A study by V. V. Pokshishevskiy, for instance, indicates that Russians typically comprised well over one-half of the population of many cities in the non-Russian units of the RSFSR in 1959;[10] for example, Russians accounted for 75.2 percent of the population of Izhevsk, the capital and principal city of the Udmurt ASSR, and 74.1 percent of the population of Volzhsk in the Mari ASSR.

Similar patterns are evident in the Tatar ASSR, where data for individual cities are also available. Although the Tatars are a relatively advanced nationality, Russians have played a significant role in the substantial modernization of this ASSR, a process that has been highly associated with the presence of major oil fields. Russians accounted for 54.7 percent of the urban growth (census definition) of the Tatar ASSR between 1926 and 1970 and comprised 57.9 percent of its urban population in 1970.

A survey of the work force in three cities of the Tatar ASSR in the late 1960s provides additional insights.[11] The cities investigated were Kazan', Almet'yevsk, and Menzelinsk, the first two of which were the largest cities in the ASSR in 1970, although Kazan' was by far the largest with a population approximately ten times that of Almet'yevsk. Not surprisingly, in 1968 Russians comprised roughly 50 percent or more of the population of each of the three cities (61.9, 48.0, and 62.1 percent, respectively), and over one-half of the surveyed workers in each city (61.4, 52.8, and 60.6 percent, respectively). As might be expected, they usually comprised even higher shares of occupations requiring greater skills. For example, in Kazan', Russians comprised 71.8 percent of the scientific and technical workers and 71.0 percent of the managers of collectives, social organizations, and state organizations. The relatively high participation of Russians in jobs requiring higher levels of education reflects the fact that the indigenous Tatars, their relatively advanced status notwithstanding, still do not have an educational level equal to that of the Russians. For example, according to the 1970 census, 4.5 percent of Russians aged ten and over had a completed higher education, whereas the corresponding figure for Tatars in the RSFSR, the largest single unit for which educational data for the Tatars were available, was only 2.2 percent. Consequently, as a result of the substantial modernization of the Tatar ASSR and the relatively lower education of the indigenous work force, Russians have moved in and have received a large share of the benefits accruing from the rapid economic development of this non-Russian area.

Many of these same processes have also been in operation outside the RSFSR. The significant role played by Russians in the modern sectors of the economies of the non-Russian republics is reflected first of all in their relatively high level of urbanization outside the RSFSR. As Table 5.6 reveals, the five economic regions where Russians attain their highest levels of urbanization are all outside the RSFSR (the Donetsk-Dnepr, the Transcaucasus, Central Asia, Belorussia, and the West). In 1970 the level of urbanization of Russians inside the RSFSR was 55.9 percent, whereas outside the RSFSR the level was 64.3 percent. When the census definition of urban is utilized, the percentages are even higher; indeed, in 1970, by this definition four out of every five Russians (80.2 percent) who lived outside the RSFSR were residents of urban centers. But Russians are not unique in this respect. Most nationalities are more urbanized outside their homeland than within it. This, of course, is owing to the fact that those persons who migrate out of the homeland tend to be more educated, motivated, and advanced and consequently tend toward settlement in urban areas.[12]

More important for our investigation is the relative importance of Russians in the total and urban populations of the non-Russian areas. Although Russians never comprised even one-fifth of the total population of the area outside the RSFSR in any of the four census years, they have generally accounted for more than one-fifth and often more than one-third of the urban growth and urban population of this area (Tables 5.7 to 5.9). Only in the 1897-1926 period did Russians fail to account for less than 30 percent of the urban growth and urban population of this area outside the RSFSR, and they have consistently comprised a higher percent of the urban population than of the total population of every economic region and republic outside the RSFSR (Tables 5.7 to 5.9).

Although Russians, of course, do not dominate the urban population outside the RSFSR as they do in the non-Russian nationality units within the RSFSR, in some units their dominance is roughly equal to that in the RSFSR. In two republics, Kazakhstan and Kirgizia, Russians actually comprised a majority of the urban population in 1970. Furthermore, this dominance was usually widespread throughout both republics. In 16 of the 18 units of the Kazakh SSR (with Alma-Ata city and oblast considered separately), Russians were the largest nationality, thus outnumbering the native Kazakhs, and in 13 of these 16 units Russians constituted a majority of the urban population. In addition, as was the case in an analogous situation in the RSFSR, Russians comprised more than 40 percent of the urban population of the three other units (Aktyubinsk, Turgay, and Chimkent oblasts) and more than 30 percent of the urban population of the two units (Gur'yev and Kzyl-Orda oblasts) where they were not the largest nationality in urban cen-

TABLE 5.6

Russian Level of Urbanization by Economic Region: 1970

Region	Percent	Region	Percent
Northwest	62.2	South	58.2
West	63.9	Donetsk-Dnepr	72.7
Center	62.9	North Caucasus	48.8
Volgo-Vyatsk	48.2	Transcaucasus	71.2
Central Chernozem	33.2	Urals	61.3
Volga	58.2	West Siberia	57.8
Belorussia	64.6	East Siberia	48.4
Moldavia	55.7	Far East	54.8
Southwest	62.4	Kazakhstan	56.5
		Central Asia	67.9
USSR total	56.3		

Source: 1970 Soviet census (see Chapter 2, footnote 2).

ters. In the Kirgiz SSR Russians were the largest urban nationality in four of the five units (with Frunze and rayons of republic subordination considered separately). In three of the four units, Russians also were a majority of the urban population, and in the remaining unit, Osh Oblast, Russians still accounted for more than 30 percent of the Urban population. Only in Naryn Oblast, which lies in the high, remote Tyan-Shan Mountains and which has a very small urban population, did Russians comprise a relatively insignificant proportion in the cities (12.9 percent).

Although Russians were not as dominant in the urban centers of the remaining 12 republics, they have been fairly prominent in certain units. In the Crimean Oblast, the famous resort region of the Ukraine, Russians were a majority of the urban population in 1970. This, together with the large number of Russians in Odessa, accounts for the South region ranking third after Kazakhstan and Kirgizia in terms of the percentage of Russians in its urban population. The Crimea is a Russian exclave in that in 1970 Russians accounted for 67.3 percent of the total population and 72.9 percent of the urban population. Furthermore, although the Crimea was the only political unit outside the RSFSR and the Kazakh and Kirgiz SSRs where Russians constituted a majority of the urban population in 1970, in a few other units Russians were the largest urban nationality, albeit not in a majority; these included: three units in the Uzbek SSR, which, not surprisingly, are ad-

TABLE 5.7

Russian Urban Growth in Area Outside the RSFSR: 1897-1970

Period	Russian Urban Growth as a Percentage of the Total Urban Growth	Average Annual Percentage Increase in Russian Urban Population
1897-1926	12.7	0.9
1926-59	37.5	4.7
1897-1959	33.4	2.9
1959-70	30.2	3.7
1926-70	34.2	4.5
1897-1970	32.1	3.0

Sources: See Chapter 2, footnotes 2 and 3.

jacent or very close to the Kazakh and/or Kirgiz republics (Syrdar'in Oblast, Tashkent city, and Tashkent Oblast); and the capital cities of Riga in the Latvian SSR, Dushanbe in the Tadzhik SSR, and Ashkhabad in the Turkmen SSR. In addition, in two other units, Voroshilovgrad Oblast and Donetsk Oblast of the eastern Ukrainian SSR heavy manufacturing region, Russians accounted for more than 40 percent of the urban population in 1970, although they were outnumbered by the indigenous Ukrainians.

Data for individual cities also attest to the importance of Russians in urban centers outside the RSFSR. Pokshishevskiy's study indicates that Russians comprised more than half the population of many cities in 1959, most of which, not unexpectedly, were in the Kazakh SSR and nearby areas of the Uzbek SSR.[13] Major examples include cities associated with mining activities in central Kazakhstan: Karaganda, 74.4 percent; Dzhezkazgan, 56.7 percent; and Balkhash, 56.6 percent. In addition, a map in a study by V. I. Naulko reveals that Russians were roughly a majority of the population of many major cities in the Ukrainian SSR in 1959.[14] This map reveals that, as might be expected, Russians were most noticeable in many cities of the Crimea and the Donbas. In the Crimea, Russians comprised over 70 percent of the population of such major cities as Kerch' (81 percent), Feodosiya (80 percent), Sevastopol' (77 percent), Yalta (73 percent), Simferopol' (71 percent), and Yevpatoriya (71 percent). In the Donbas they accounted for approximately one-half of the population of such major cities as Makeyevka (52 percent), Donetsk (51 percent), Gorlovka (47 percent), and Lugansk (now Voroshilovgrad) (47 percent).

TABLE 5.8

Russians as a Percentage of the Total and Urban Populations of Economic Regions Outside the RSFSR: 1897–1970

Region	1897		1926		1959		1970	
	Total	Urban	Total	Urban	Total	Urban	Total	Urban
West	5.9	20.8	6.3	6.6	17.1	27.3	19.1	27.7
Belorussia	5.3	17.4	5.6	12.8	8.2	19.4	10.4	19.7
Moldavia	8.5	28.7	11.8	26.4	10.2	30.4	11.6	28.2
Southwest	4.9	26.5	2.3	7.4	6.0	16.7	6.7	15.4
South	19.6	43.5	19.0	39.9	30.9	44.1	34.0	43.6
Donetsk–Dnepr	18.1	33.7	14.6	32.2	26.1	33.8	29.1	35.5
Transcaucasus	4.3	17.0	5.7	17.7	10.2	18.4	7.9	13.5
Kazakhstan	16.0	52.4	22.0	53.8	42.7	57.6	42.4	58.4
Central Asia	2.2	9.1	5.8	23.3	16.4	36.7	15.1	33.2
Non-RSFSR total	8.5	26.4	8.6	21.1	17.8	32.0	19.0	31.4

Sources: See Chapter 2, footnotes 2 and 3.

TABLE 5.9

Russians as a Percentage of the Total, Urban, and Capital City Populations by Republic Outside the RSFSR: 1959 and 1970

(census definition of urban)

Republic (Capital)	1959			1970		
	Total	Urban	Capital	Total	Urban	Capital
Ukrainian (Kiev)	16.9	29.9	23.0	19.4	30.0	22.9
Belorussian (Minsk)	8.2	19.4	22.8	10.4	19.7	23.4
Estonian (Tallin)	20.1	30.8	32.2	24.7	33.9	35.0
Latvian (Riga)	26.6	34.5	39.5	29.8	38.0	42.7
Lithuanian (Vil'nyus)	8.5	17.0	29.4	8.6	14.5	24.5
Uzbek (Tashkent)	13.5	33.4	43.9	12.5	30.4	40.8
Kirgiz (Frunze)	30.2	51.8	68.6	29.2	51.4	66.1
Turkmen (Ashkhabad)	17.3	35.4	50.3	14.5	29.0	42.7
Tadzhik (Dushanbe)	13.3	35.3	47.8	11.9	30.0	42.0
Kazakh (Alma-Ata)	42.7	57.6	73.1	42.4	58.4	70.3
Georgian (Tbilisi)	10.1	18.8	18.1	8.5	14.7	14.0
Armenian (Yerevan)	3.2	4.5	4.4	2.7	3.5	2.8
Azerbaydzhan (Baku)	13.6	24.9	34.8	10.1	18.3	27.7
Moldavian (Kishinev)	10.2	30.4	32.2	11.6	28.2	30.7

Sources: 1959 and 1970 Soviet censuses (see Chapter 2, footnote 2).

The substantial Russian presence in individual cities outside the RSFSR for which data are available is also indicated by the fact that they have generally comprised a higher proportion of the capital city of a given republic than generally of the entire urban and total populations of the same republic (Table 5.9). The only exceptions to these patterns are Kiev, Tbilisi, and Yerevan, where in both 1959 and 1970 Russians constituted a smaller share of the capital city's population than they did of the total urban population. Of the three cases, only the Kiev difference is sizable enough to warrant comment. The main explanation for the Kiev situation is that Russians, as just mentioned, accounted for relatively high shares of the urban population in other portions of the Ukrainian Republic, especially the Crimea and the Donetsk-Dnepr region.

Furthermore, in 1970, Russians typically accounted for more than one-fourth of the population of the majority of the capital cities. In fact, they even comprised more than one-half of the population of two of the 14 capital cities; not surprisingly, these two cities were the capitals of the Kazakh and Kirgiz republics (Alma-Ata and Frunze, respectively). In addition, they comprised more than 40 percent of the population of four other capitals: Ashkhabad in Turkmenistan, Riga in Latvia, Dushanbe in Tadzhikistan, and Tashkent in Uzbekistan.

Because each SSR capital is without exception the largest city of its republic, these patterns reflect the especially high orientation of Russians to relatively large cities outside the RSFSR. This orientation has also been studied by Pokshishevskiy. Citing the cases of the Lithuanian and Tadzhik SSRs in 1959, he notes that, generally speaking, the larger the city, the greater the share of the population that is Russian. For example, in both republics Russians typically accounted for more than 20 percent of the population of cities of 50,000 and over, but less than 10 percent of the population in cities of less than 10,000 people. [15]

Outside the areas just noted, Russians were a smaller proportion of the urban population in 1970 (Tables 5.8 and 5.9). In many areas they comprised between 25 and 40 percent of the urban population; these included the West region as a whole and the Latvian and Estonian SSRs in particular (only the Lithuanian SSR was below 25 percent); the Moldavian SSR; the Ukrainian SSR as a whole and the Donetsk-Dnepr region in particular (the percentage for the South region was, of course, above 40 percent, while that for the Southwest region was below 25 percent); and Central Asia in general and the Uzbek, Tadzhik, and Turkmen republics in particular (in the Kirgiz SSR, of course, the proportion was over 50 percent).

There are two areas in which Russians comprised less than 25 percent of the urban population, each consisting of three contiguous political units: a bloc on the western border consisting of the Lithuanian

and Belorussian SSRs and the Southwest region of the Ukrainian SSR;
and the Transcaucasus region as a whole and each of its three constituent republics in particular (Georgia, Armenia, and Azerbaydzhan). As Tables 5.8 and 5.9 indicate, the very lowest percentages
were found in the Transcaucasus. On the basis of economic regions,
the Transcaucasus ranked the lowest and on the basis of the 15 republics, Armenia ranked by far the lowest; only Lithuania had a smaller
percentage than Georgia and Azerbaydzhan. When Baku is excluded,
the Azerbaydzhan SSR actually had a lower percent (9.2) than the
Lithuanian SSR and, for that matter, the Georgian SSR. Baku is a
major oil-producing region, and it has traditionally accounted for a
relatively large share of the Russian urban population in the Transcaucasus; in 1970 this one city alone accounted for 41.2 percent of all
urban Russians in the Transcaucasus.

Many of these patterns suggest that, as implied at the beginning
of this chapter, the relative importance of Russians in the urban centers of non-Russian areas might be inversely related to the relative
level of advancement of the indigenous groups. The patterns of the
Georgian and Armenian SSRs certainly support this contention in that
the indigenous nationalities are two of the most highly educated groups
in the USSR, and Russians comprise very meager shares of the urban
populations of these republics.

In order to test this hypothesis in a more rigorous fashion, a rank
correlation was run on the basis of 1970 data between the educational
level of the 14 republic nationalities (defined here as the percent of the
population aged ten and over who had a complete or incomplete higher
or secondary education) and the percentage of the urban population of
each of the 14 republics comprised by Russians. Results reveal that
the hypothesis was not necessarily supported in that the rank correlation was -0.184; that is, although an inverse relationship was, as hypothesized, present, it was not very strong.

Further investigation reveals that the three Baltic nationalities
and republics were the prime contributors to the low relationship. Latvians ranked third in education, but the Latvian SSR ranked third in
terms of the percentage of Russians in its urban population; Estonians
and the Estonian SSR ranked fifth and fourth, respectively; and Lithuanians and the Lithuanian SSR ranked 13th in both cases. The Latvian and
Estonian cases are similar in that while the indigenous group is highly
educated, Russians still comprised a relatively large share of the urban
population. In fact, as Table 5.9 reveals, the Latvian and Estonian
SSRs, along with the Belorussian SSR, were the only non-Russian republics where Russians increased their share of both the republic urban
population and the population of the republic capital between 1959 and
1970. This was due to the fact that Latvians and Estonians have had
very slow population growth, primarily because of prolonged low fer-

tility. Therefore, the indigenous population has not been able to provide the required workers, and Russians, accordingly, have moved in
to provide the necessary labor.[16]

Lithuanians present a somewhat different picture. Although they
have the lowest educational level of any of the republic nationalities except for Moldavians, there have not been many Russians in Lithuanian
cities. This may be partly explained by the fact that in recent years
the Lithuanians have been modernizing rapidly; in the last decade the
educational level of Lithuanians has risen at a rate greater than that
of any other republic nationality. Therefore, the demand for Russians
has not been substantial. In addition, the fact that the Lithuanian population has been growing more rapidly than the Latvian and Estonian
populations reduces the need for Russians in the Lithuanian SSR as compared to the Latvian and Estonian republics.

Because of the deviance of the Latvian, Lithuanian, and Estonian
cases the relationship was tested again, this time excluding the three
Baltic republics. A rank correlation coefficient of -0.616 tends to support the hypothesis that Russians comprise a higher percentage of the
urban population in more traditional areas, at least in non-Russian republics outside of the Baltic.

This inverse relationship between the degree of modernization of
a non-Russian nationality and the presence of Russians in the modern
sector of the homeland of these nationalities has been suggested in
other studies. With regards to Central Asia, in particular, Ann Sheehy
notes that, although considerable labor reserves exist in areas of Central Asia that are largely dominated by indigenous peoples,

> there are acute shortages of labor in the large cities
> and new industrial towns, on various construction
> projects, and in the sovkhozes on newly reclaimed
> land. [These shortages exist,] . . . because of
> the native peoples' relatively low mobility and lack
> of industrial skills. . . . As a result there is a con-
> tinuing influx, from outside the region, of Russians,
> and others who find local living and working condi-
> tions, except in Turkmenistan, more attractive than
> in Siberia and the other labor-deficit areas from
> which they often come. It is indicative of the short-
> age of skilled labor that special inducements or wage
> coefficients are still being offered for working in
> certain parts of Central Asia. . . . When a new in-
> dustry or a project such as a hydroelectric power
> station is involved, the organization may well have
> to bring in a certain number of its own skilled
> workers. But it may also choose to bring in many

more of its own workers than are absolutely necessary rather than lose time training indigenous workers on the spot, particularly since there may be a
shortage of qualified instructors who speak the ver-
nacular. The temptation to recruit any skilled Russian laborers who come to the region of their own
accord in preference to the unskilled Central Asians
is also very great. The result is that any major new
industrial development almost inevitably leads to an
influx of Russians [underscoring ours]. This can
be seen clearly in the latest census results, which
show that [for example] between 1959 and 1970 the
Russian population of Bukhara Oblast (exploitation
of natural gas and gold deposits) increased by
60,000 or 124 per cent, . . . compared with an
average increase in the Russian population in the
country as a whole by only 13 per cent.[17]

A study by V. I. Perevedentsev indicates many of the same patterns. This study, in particular, concerns ethnic patterns at two nodes
of modern economic activity in the Tadzhik SSR in the mid-1960s: the
Dushanbe integrated textile mills and the construction site of the Nurek
hydroelectric plant.[18] He notes that Russians comprised more than
one-half of the personnel at both sites (55.7 and 51.8 percent, respectively); in contrast, the indigenous Tadzhiks comprised only 15.2 and
27.8 percent, respectively.[19] Perevedentsev implies that one of the
major factors underlying these patterns is the frequent lack of necessary job skills among the native Tadzhiks.[20]

Pokshishevskiy has also commented on these relationships, and
maintains that the Russian share of the population will increase in
areas where the local work force is insufficient in terms of qualified
personnel and cannot be trained fast enough to keep pace with local
economic growth.[21] He also provides data from the 1959 census that
further document the association between the industrialization of non-
Russian areas and the influx of Russians. First of all, he classified
the administrative centers of ASSRs and autonomous oblasts, both
within and beyond the RSFSR, into three types: rapidly industrializing,
moderately industrializing, and slowly industrializing. Not surprisingly,
the average Russian share of the population of each group declined
from groups 1 to 3—73.5, 45.4, and 27.1 percent, respectively.[22]
In addition, he classified 33 cities of non-Russian nationality units in
the USSR into two types, industrial and less industrial, and indicated
the ethnic composition of each. Once again, it is not surprising to find
that on the average Russians comprised a higher share of the population of industrial cities than they did of the cities with a less-developed
industrial structure (54.7 and 35.7 percent, respectively).[23]

Perevedentsev suggests that cultural factors are also important in the migration of Russians to cities in non-Russian areas because such a migration is facilitated by the familiar ethnic environment of the cities, since such cities are often highly Russian in culture.[24] In short, the migration of Russians to cities in non-Russian regions also partly involves a self-generating mechanism.

The highly Russian culture of such cities, however, often tends to further impede the migration of the indigenous peoples to cities in their homelands. As Sheehy notes:

> Although it is true that many undertakings do not
> make as much effort as they might to recruit and
> train local labor, it is also true that the Central
> Asians have shown themselves somewhat reluctant
> to leave the rural areas for the republican capitals,
> the new industrial towns, and the big construction
> projects, where most of the jobs are. What deters
> them is that these towns and construction sites are
> largely Russian or at least Russianized and therefore
> present an alien ethnic environment. Moreover,
> their knowledge of Russian, the language often used
> in the factory, is generally very poor. In 1970
> only some 15 to 20 per cent of Uzbeks, Tadzhiks,
> Turkmens and Kirghiz claimed to have a good com-
> mand of the language.[25]

Perevedentsev again notes similar patterns in his study concerned with two nodes of modern economic activity in the Tadzhik SSR. In particular, he suggests that the migration of Tadzhiks to these nodes is impeded by the fact that Russian is the language of communication, but the local Tadzhiks know little Russian; because the number of Tadzhik engineering and technical personnel is insignificant, it is difficult to overcome this situation since there are, consequently, few persons who are capable of giving instruction in Tadzhik at the training school for the construction project.[26] In addition, he suggests that local migration is impeded by the fact that the tradition of early marriage and large families among the Muslim Tadzhiks impedes the substantial participation of Tadzhik women in the textile mill, an industry that typically employs relatively large numbers of females; the difficulties of the Tadzhiks in adjusting to the different environment of life within a factory; and the fact that the influx of Russians greatly limits the number of jobs available to the indigenous population.[27] Thus, a complex chain of events is put into operation. The deficiencies of the indigenous work force prompts an influx of Russians, and the resulting Russianization of the cities further en-

hances an in-migration of Russians and impedes an in-migration of
indigenous peoples.

The impact of the influx of Russians has extended well beyond
the influence of impeding local rural-to-urban migration. The substantial presence of Russians in cities of non-Russian areas has been
a major force for the Russification of non-Russian peoples. This process is indicated by the fact that the share of non-Russians who consider Russian to be their native language is invariably higher in urban
centers than in the rural areas. Brian Silver has suggested that the
presence of Russians in cities and the higher levels of social mobilization among non-Russian urban dwellers interact to increase levels of
linguistic Russification.[28]

In 1970, according to the census definition of urban and rural,
while 22.1 percent of the non-Russian urban population considered
Russian to be their native language, the corresponding percentage for
the non-Russian rural population was only 3.7 (Table 5.10). In addition, according to the 1970 census, non-Russians who did not consider
Russian to be their first language but who considered Russian to be a
second language comprised 46.9 percent of the non-Russian urban
population, while the corresponding figure for rural areas was once
again lower (29.7 percent). In 1970 more than two-thirds (69.0 percent of the non-Russian urban population considered Russian to be
either their native language or a second language, which was more
than twice the corresponding proportion for rural areas (33.4 percent).
Since the Russification process has tended to be relatively high in
cities, it would seem reasonable to assume that assimilation has been
another factor in the rapid urban growth and urbanization of the Russian population. The size of the Russian urban population has been enhanced by the fact that very probably greater proportions of the urban
non-Russians, as opposed to the rural non-Russians, have changed
their nationality to Russian, particularly other Slavs, Jews, and Finnic peoples. These figures, of course, include non-Russians inside
the RSFSR.

In the republics beyond the RSFSR the great rural-urban differential is still noticeable. In particular, in 1970, 17.3 percent of the
non-Russians in cities beyond the RSFSR considered Russian to be
their native language, but only 2.0 percent of the rural non-Russian
population of the same area did likewise. In addition, 45.2 percent of
the non-Russians in cities beyond the RSFSR considered Russian to
be a second language, while the corresponding percentage for the non-
Russian rural population of the same area was only 24.1. In total,
62.5 percent of the non-Russian urban population beyond the RSFSR
considered Russian to be either their native language or a second
language, whereas in rural areas the comparable figure was only
26.1 percent. Altogether, in 1970 nearly three-fourths (74.1 percent)

TABLE 5.10

Linguistic Russification by Non-Russian Grouping and Non-Russian
Total, Urban, and Rural Populations: 1970
(census definition of urban and rural)

	Percentage of Population with Russian as		
Grouping	Native Language	Second Language	Native or Second Language
Ukrainians	14.3	36.3	50.6
Belorussians	19.0	49.0	67.9
Tatars	10.2	62.5	72.8
Turkic-Muslims	2.0	28.4	30.4
Jews	78.2	16.3	94.5
Mobilized Europeans	4.6	29.2	33.8
Finnic peoples	19.0	63.6	82.6
Lithuanians	1.5	35.9	37.4
Moldavians and Romanians	4.2	35.8	40.0
Total non-Russians	11.6	37.1	48.7
Urban non-Russians	22.1	46.9	69.0
Rural non-Russians	3.7	29.7	33.4

Source: 1970 Soviet census (see Chapter 2, footnote 2).

of the urban population outside the RSFSR was comprised either by
Russians or by non-Russians who considered Russian to be their native language or a second language. Thus, the in-migration of Russians to cities in non-Russian areas has been a major force for the
Russification of non-Russian peoples.

Although the in-migration of the indigenous population to local
cities has not been that substantial in the past, this situation will probably change in the future. Because the indigenous rural population in
many non-Russian areas is still increasing at a rapid rate and because
the agricultural resources of such areas will not be sufficient to accommodate this increase (especially in the irrigation-based rural areas
of Central Asia), the increasing population pressure in the rural areas
of these regions will undoubtedly promote a substantial increase in the
indigenous urban population in the future. This subject is explored in
greater depth in Chapter 10.

This process seems, in fact, to be in operation already. As Tables 5.8 and 5.9 indicate, whereas the Russian share of the population in cities outside the RSFSR increased between 1926 and 1959, it generally declined between 1959 and 1970. As Table 5.7 indicates, this was not due to any great reduction in the growth rate of Russians, whose urban population continued to increase at a fairly rapid rate in areas outside the RSFSR (3.7 percent per year). Instead, the prime factor in the decline of the Russian share was that the non-Russian urban population was growing even faster in these areas (4.0 percent per year).

As Tables 5.8 and 5.9 reveal, the Russian share experienced relatively great declines in the Transcaucasus and Central Asia. The Transcaucasus, as has been mentioned previously, has always been a region where Russians comprised a low proportion of the urban population, partly owing to the generally high educational levels of the indigenous nationalities, especially Georgians and Armenians. In fact, although the Russian urban population still continued to increase in the Transcaucasus between 1959 and 1970, it just barely increased (only 8.1 percent for the entire period), and in the cities of Tbilisi and Yerevan there was an absolute decline in the number of Russians. A prime factor appears to be net out-migration. In 1970, for example, data indicate that the only republics in which more people moved from urban centers of the republic to the RSFSR than from the RSFSR to the urban centers of the republic were Georgia and Azerbaydzhan, and Armenia had the lowest net in-migration of any of the remaining republics.[29] In other words, assuming that the migrants to and from the RSFSR were primarily Russians, it appears that there has been a net out-migration of Russians from cities of the Transcaucasus or, at best, very little net in-migration. Urban patterns of the Transcaucasus nationalities, of course, will be discussed in greater depth in subsequent sections.

The Central Asian situation is much more typical of the Russian and non-Russian urban growth patterns in non-Russian areas. Unlike the Transcaucasus, the declining share of Russians in local cities is not caused by a lack of substantial net in-migration but by the very rapid rate of urban growth among the indigenous nationalities, a rate that more than offsets the continuing rapid increase of Russians. This is probably related to the higher fertility of the indigenous population and increasing rural-to-urban migration resulting from growing pressures on the land.

In summary, excluding Jews, Russians, as hypothesized, have experienced the greatest degree of urbanization of all the major nationalities in Russia and the USSR. Furthermore, they have participated to a significant extent in the urbanization process of most areas outside the RSFSR, especially because of the relative lack of trained workers in the indigenous labor force. Major repercussions of the influx of Russians to urban centers of non-Russian areas include increased Russification of non-Russian nationalities and an impeding of local rural-to-urban migration partly because of the highly foreign (that is, Russian) nature of many of the cities and the fact that Russians take many of the available jobs in the cities. In short, Russians have not only benefited to a great extent from the economic development of their own areas of settlement but they have also benefited greatly from the economic development of non-Russian areas. Non-Russian groups, in turn, have not benefited as much as might be expected from the development of their own areas. In more recent years, however, the indigenous urban population has been increasing fairly rapidly in non-Russian areas. The factors behind this trend, the question as to whether or not this trend will be of long-range duration, and additional implications concerning the relations between Russians and non-Russians, especially those concerning who will benefit from economic development will be discussed in Chapter 10, which is concerned with the implications of population change in the multinational Soviet Union.

Ukrainians

The Ukrainians have been considerably less urbanized than the Russians throughout the 1897–1970 period. Whereas the majority of Russians now reside in urban areas, the Ukrainian rural population still outnumbers its urban population by some 8 million people. Furthermore, while the Russian level of urbanization is now roughly comparable to that of such highly developed areas as Western Europe and Japan, the Ukrainian level is more on a par with those of such lesser industrialized regions as southern Europe, Eastern Europe, southern Africa, and mainland Middle America.[30] With respect to the major indicators of urbanization, Ukrainians generally were below the national average and ranked around the median (Tables 5.1 to 5.3). Between 1897 and 1970 their level of urbanization increased by 35.4 percentage points, which was the fifth highest increase of the ten nationality groupings, and was slightly below the national increase and well below the increase for the Russians (Table 5.2). Between 1926 and 1970 the Ukrainian increase was relatively high, but was again below both the national and Russian increases. Only in the 1959–70 period did Ukrainians have an increase above the national average, and even then they still ranked around the median. The Ukrainians also occupied a position around the median with respect to the level of urbanization in the four census years and were always below the national average, and, of course, below the Russians (Table 5.1). The 1970 level of urbanization of Ukrainians is in accordance with these general patterns.

The Ukrainian level of 40.1 percent was the fifth highest of the groupings, and was about six percentage points below the national level and 16 points below the Russian level.

But although the Ukrainians occupied such a mediocre position with respect to urbanization in the Soviet context, it should not be forgotten that they have still achieved an appreciable increase in the level of urbanization. This was owing primarily to a combination of rapid urban growth (1,338.9 percent between 1897 and 1970) coupled with slow growth of the rural population (only 5.5 percent for the entire 1897-1970 period). Like the Russians, Ukrainians also have experienced an absolute decline in their rural population in the post-1926 period. Not unexpectedly, the biggest loss in the Ukrainian rural population occurred between 1926 and 1959, the period of collectivization and World War II, both of which hit the Ukraine especially hard. Over four-fifths (86.5 percent) of the decline in the Ukrainian rural population between 1926 and 1970 occurred between 1926 and 1959, when their rural population declined by more than 7 million, or more than one-fifth (-22.8 percent).

That the Ukrainian urbanization process has not been more appreciable is perhaps somewhat surprising, particularly in light of the fact that the Ukrainian SSR has been an outstanding region of mining and manufacturing. The Donetsk-Dnepr region, in fact, now ranks as one of the top two or three industrial regions in the USSR. The lack of a more appreciable Ukrainian rural-to-urban movement has been owing partly to the absence of severe and chronic rural population pressure in the Ukraine. Major reasons for this relatively low rural population pressure will be discussed in Chapter 6. They include the extensive population losses in Ukrainian rural areas in association with collectivization, famine, and World War II; the relatively low fertility of rural Ukrainians; the comparatively abundant agricultural resources of the Ukraine; and the late agricultural colonization of the Ukraine. In addition, somewhat analogous to the case of Central Asia, the local rural-to-urban migration of Ukrainians has probably been impeded by the fact that the cities of the Ukraine actually have been appreciably non-Ukrainian in nature. Jews and Poles have comprised a sizable share of the population of cities in the western Ukraine, and, as suggested in the previous section, the presence of Russians has been especially noticeable in cities of the southern and eastern Ukraine. Another major reason for the less than expected Ukrainian migration to local cities has been the relatively low educational levels of the Ukrainian populace; again, as elsewhere in the USSR, the deficiencies of the indigenous labor force have impeded rural-to-urban migration.

Similarly, this situation has led to a considerable influx of Russians into the Ukraine. Although the previous section dealt particularly with the migration of Russians to cities in dominantly Turkic-Muslim areas, it should be remembered that the Ukraine has been the prime area of Russian urban settlement outside the RSFSR. Between 1897 and 1970 over two-fifths (42.5 percent) of the growth of the Russian urban population outside the RSFSR occurred in the Ukraine. This percentage has been remarkably stable, especially in the three post-1926 periods; for example, the corresponding percentages for the 1926-59 and 1959-70 periods were 43.9 and 41.1, respectively. In the pre-1926 period of 1897-1926 the Ukraine accounted for a some-what lower proportion (34.4 percent) of Russian urban growth outside the RSFSR; also during this period the Russian share of the population of Kiev declined by more than half (54.4 to 24.5 percent).

These patterns were related in part to the fact that there was probably an overenumeration of Russians in the Ukraine in 1897. First of all, Russification policies of the tsarist government in its last dec-ades were believed to have encouraged large numbers of non-Russians (especially Ukrainians) to declare themselves to be Russians.[31] In ad-dition, the nationality criterion in 1897 was native language and even today Ukrainians comprise well over 40 percent of all non-Russians who consider Russian to be their native language. Also, since the share of non-Russians who consider Russian to be their native language has been much higher in urban areas than in rural areas, this also undoubtedly promoted a relatively high number of "Russians" in urban centers of the Ukraine in 1897. Thus, the relative reduction of urban Russians in the Ukraine between 1897 and 1926 was undoubtedly re-lated to an overenumeration of Russians in cities of the Ukraine in 1897. In fact, in 1897, Russians comprised almost two-thirds of the urban population of the Ukraine. Although that percentage declined in subsequent years, by 1970, despite the substantial Russian movement to other republics, almost one-half (45.1 percent) of the Russian ur-ban population outside the RSFSR was still found in the Ukraine.

As was discussed in the previous section, Russian urbanization in the Ukraine has been particularly high in the South and Donetsk-Dnepr regions. Although the Russians have comprised a higher share of the urban population of the South than in the Donetsk-Dnepr, the Donetsk-Dnepr has been the major region of Russian urban settlement in the Ukraine from other perspectives. In 1970, of the 19 economic regions, the Russian level of urbanization reached its greatest extent in the Donetsk-Dnepr (72.7 percent). In addition, by 1970 the Donetsk-Dnepr still had a larger Russian urban population than any other eco-nomic region outside the RSFSR and alone comprised 29.1 percent of the entire Russian urban population outside the RSFSR and 64.5 per-cent of the Russian urban population in the Ukraine. The great pres-ence of Russians in the Donetsk-Dnepr has been related, of course, to the substantial mineral wealth and subsequent industrialization of this area since the latter decades of the nineteenth century and to the inabil-

ity of the relatively less modernized and more rural Ukrainians to provide the necessary labor for the rapid industrialization of the region.
As such, the Donetsk-Dnepr region serves in some ways as a fore-
runner to the process of Russian urbanization in non-Russian areas.

However, although the Ukraine has been subjected to a great influx of Russians for a relatively long time, the Ukrainian experience,
unfortunately, cannot be used as a reliable model for predicting what
might happen in other areas, especially Central Asia, in the future.
Its usefulness as such a model is primarily limited by the fact that
the Ukraine is one of the major industrial areas in the USSR and, thus,
has substantial job opportunities, and it has not experienced the degree
of rural population pressures that the Central Asians will be experiencing in the future. Thus, even though a significant number of
Ukrainians have migrated to the predominately Russian rural areas,
a massive flight of rural Ukrainians to cities in Russian areas has
not occurred, a pattern that probably will be a major response of the
Central Asian nationalities in the future. In fact, 80.9 percent of the
urban Ukrainians in 1970 still resided in the Ukraine.

Within the Ukraine, the regional patterns of Ukrainian urbanization are somewhat similar to those of Russians. Ukrainians do comprise a much higher share of the urban population of the Southwest region than of the South and Donetsk-Dnepr regions because there are
relatively few Russians in the less industrialized Southwest (Russians,
for example, accounted for only 22.9 percent of the population of Kiev
in 1970). Yet the major focus of Ukrainian urbanization has been the
Donetsk-Dnepr region. In 1970, despite the fact that Kiev of the Southwest region had more than 1 million Ukrainians, the greatest total for
any single city in the USSR, the Donetsk-Dnepr region had more than
6 million urban Ukrainians, by far the highest total of any of the 19
economic regions. In particular, the Donetsk-Dnepr accounted for
42.9 percent of all urban Ukrainians in the USSR and 53.0 percent of
all urban Ukrainians in the Ukraine. Also, the Ukrainian level of urbanization has been much higher in the Donetsk-Dnepr than it has in
the South and Southwest; in 1970, respective levels of urbanization
were 53.2, 38.2, and 23.6 percent. Thus, although the industrialization of the Donetsk-Dnepr has especially benefited Russians, it has
also had a discernible modernizing influence on the indigenous Ukrainians.

Although the Ukrainian urban population is still highly concentrated in the Ukraine, the urbanization of Ukrainians outside the RSFSR
has not been insignificant. First of all, like most nationalities, Ukrainians are much more urbanized and educated outside their homeland
than within. In addition, many Ukrainians have participated as a
"sputnik" people of the Russians in the urbanization of the USSR, both
in terms of migrating to major areas of industrialization in the RSFSR

and migrating to cities in such regions as Kazakhstan and Central
Asia. Indeed, Kazakhstan had the largest Ukrainian urban population
of any economic region outside the Ukraine in 1970. This migration,
however, has not been out of desperation as it would be among the
Central Asian nationalities. Instead, it has primarily involved a movement of relatively advanced Ukrainians. This is reflected by the fact
that urban Ukrainians of the RSFSR actually have higher educational
levels than do urban Russians in the same republic. In 1970, for example, 5.7 percent of such Russians (census definition of urban) who
were aged 10 and over had a completed higher education. The comparable figure for urban Ukrainians in the RSFSR was 9.2 percent, a
proportion that was also well above the corresponding figure of 5.2
percent for urban Ukrainians in the Ukraine.

Belorussians

The urbanization of the Belorussians represents a further step
downward from that of the Russians and Ukrainians. As recently as
1959 the Belorussian level of urbanization was comparable to that of
such developing countries as Peru, Ecuador, Morocco, and Algeria.[32]
However, since 1959, the Belorussians have been urbanizing at one of
the fastest rates in human history. In fact, whereas only 2 million
Belorussians resided in cities in 1959, this number increased by more
than 1 million during the next decade.

The Belorussians generally have ranked low with respect to the
major indicators of urbanization (Tables 5.1 to 5.3). Although their
level of urbanization increased by 33.9 percentage points between
1897 and 1970, this increase was relatively low, and fell slightly below the national average and nearly ten percentage points below the
Russian increase. Between 1926 and 1970 the Belorussian increase
was once again below the national and Russian increases.

Furthermore, the Belorussian level of urbanization in the four
census years was also quite low in all cases (Table 5.1). In 1897 and
1926 Belorussians ranked next to last in this respect, having an especially low level of only 2.2 percent in 1897. By 1959 and 1970 the
Belorussians ranked somewhat higher, but still in 1970 their level of
urbanization was more than ten percentage points below the national
level and more than 20 points below the Russian level.

However, although Belorussians have had a relatively low degree
of urbanization, from some perspectives it has been quite appreciable.
First of all, although the increase in their level of urbanization ranked
only seventh between 1897 and 1970, there was a substantial clustering
of the third through seventh positions (Table 5.2). Therefore, the Belorussian increase was only less than three percentage points below that
of the third-ranking group, the Tatars.

Thus, Belorussians experienced a fairly significant increase in urbanization in the overall 1897-1970 period. This increase has been due to a very rapid rate of urban growth and, to a lesser degree, to a low rate of rural growth. Of the ten groupings, in the six intercensal periods, Belorussians never ranked less than fourth with respect to the rate of urban growth and were always above the national average. In fact, along with Lithuanians, Belorussians were the only grouping to have an urban growth rate above the national average in all six periods. As will be seen, the similarities between the urbanization of these two groups does not stop here. In the overall 1897-1970 period the Belorussians' urban growth rate of 2,544.2 percent was surpassed only by the Lithuanians, and in two periods, 1926-70 and 1926-59, Belorussians ranked first. This rapid urban growth, of course, partly reflects a very low base urban population, in that although the total Belorussian population in 1897 was more than 5 million, the Belorussian urban population was only about 100,000. The considerable increase in the Belorussian level of urbanization also has been enhanced by very slow rural population growth. Between 1897 and 1970 the Belorussian rural population increased by only 4.2 percent and in none of the six intercensal periods did it grow by more than 6 percent over the entire period. Furthermore, in the 1959-70 period, it finally experienced a decline.

This rural population decline in the 1959-70 period, combined with continued rapid urban growth, resulted in a rate of urbanization that was one of the fastest of any group in human history. Of the groupings, only Lithuanians and Russians had a greater percentage point increase in the level of urbanization during this period and just barely so (Table 5.2). More important, the average annual percentage point increase in the level of urbanization for Belorussians during this period (0.90) was among the very highest for any grouping in any period (Table 5.3). In fact, of the groupings, only Lithuanians in the same period (1959-70) and Russians in the three post-1926 intercensal periods experienced a greater increase.

Other trends underline the very rapid urbanization experienced by Belorussians in recent years. First, of the 19 regions, Belorussia had the highest percentage increase in its level of urbanization between 1959 and 1970. In addition, many individual cities in the Belorussian SSR have been experiencing very rapid growth recently. Outstanding in this respect in terms of both size and growth has been the city of Minsk, the capital of the Belorussian Republic. Between 1959 and 1970 its population nearly doubled as it increased from 509,489 to 916,949. By 1972 the population of Minsk was almost 1 million (996,000) and at this writing its population is undoubtedly over a million. Not surprisingly, this was the most rapid growth experienced by any Soviet city with more than 500,000 people in 1959 and by any of the republic capi-

tals except Frunze, which is considerably smaller. In addition, of the
34 cities in the Belorussian SSR that had a population of 15,000 or
more in 1970, every one increased in population between 1959 and
1970, an intercensal period in which for the first time a very large
number of Soviet cities were experiencing population decline (approximately 100 cities, primarily in the Urals region and eastward).
Furthermore, most of these cities of Belorussia experienced rapid
growth. Well over one-half of them had a population increase of more
than 50 percent between 1959 and 1970, and even the slowest growing
city of Belorussia increased its population by 20 percent. Outstanding
cities in this respect included Novopolotsk and Soligorsk, both of which
had no population in 1959 according to the 1970 census and had a population of roughly 40,000 by 1970, and Svetlogorsk and Zhodino, whose
population increased by roughly seven and three times, respectively,
between 1959 and 1970.

   This rapid urbanization has been stimulated by the considerable
capital investment and industrialization in the Belorussian SSR during
the 1960s. For example, whereas capital investment and industrial
production in the USSR approximately doubled between 1960 and 1970
(according to Soviet estimates), in the Belorussian Republic they approximately tripled.[33] A particularly important aspect of this rapid
industrialization has been the development of chemical industries
based upon oil from the Volga fields and natural gas from Dashava in
the western Ukraine.[34] Many of the most rapidly growing cities in
Belorussia reflect this development. Novopolotsk, for example, now
has one of the largest oil refineries in the USSR.[35] All of these patterns, of course, reflect the increased attention given to the industrialization of the western USSR in more recent years.

   Although the rapid urbanizations of the Belorussian Republic and
Belorussians are clearly closely related, they are not completely synonymous. Despite the fact that the Belorussians accounted for the
bulk of the urban growth of Belorussia between 1959 and 1970, the recent rapid industrialization of the republic has, as might be expected,
also resulted in an influx of Russians. In fact, between 1959 and 1970
the Russian level of urbanization had a greater percentage point increase in the Belorussian SSR than it did in any of the other 19 economic regions. Furthermore, the rate of Russian urban growth in the
Belorussian SSR was so fast that Russians actually slightly increased
their percent of the urban population of the republic between 1959 and
1970 (Table 5.9). This increase becomes more significant in light of
the facts that the Russian percentage was declining in a majority of
the other republics and the Belorussians were also experiencing very
rapid urban growth. Yet the Russian rate of growth was great enough
to generally offset the Belorussian growth; in fact, in only two other
republics (Moldavia and Kazakhstan) did Russians experience a faster

rate of urban growth (census definition) between 1959 and 1970. Actually, both Belorussians and Russians increased their share of the urban population of Belorussia, even though Belorussians grew slightly faster, because the non-Russian and non-Belorussian groups were growing at a somewhat slower aggregate rate. Virtually the same patterns were evident in the city of Minsk, except Belorussians were growing even faster here than they were within the total urban population (census definition) of Belorussia.

Thus, in recent years, Belorussians have been experiencing very rapid urbanization in association with the rapid industrialization of their homeland. As might be expected, however, Russians have also benefited greatly from this development as indicated by the very rapid urbanization and urban growth of Russians in the Belorussian Republic.

Tatars

Although not to the extent of Russians and Jews, the Tatars have experienced a relatively high degree of urbanization, especially in relation to other Turkic-Muslims. Whereas the non-Tatar Turkic-Muslim level of urbanization is comparable to that of many underdeveloped areas of the world (as will be discussed in the next section), the Tatar level is roughly similar to an area such as southern Europe.[36] Although southern Europe is the least urbanized major region of Europe, it is certainly more advanced than most countries commonly referred as underdeveloped.

In all six intercensal periods and in all four census years, the degree of urbanization of Tatars was higher than that of the non-Tatar Turkic-Muslims (Tables 5.1 to 5.3), which supports our contention that they should be considered separately. In fact, based upon our estimates the Tatar level of urbanization was exactly twice that of the non-Tatar Turkic-Muslims in 1970. The urbanization of Tatars also has been fairly considerable from other perspectives. Between 1897 and 1970, of the ten groupings, only the Jews and Russians had a greater percentage point increase in the level of urbanization. Furthermore, in the Soviet era (1926-70) only Russians surpassed the Tatars in this respect, and the Tatars and Russians were the only groups to have an increase above the national average in all of the three Soviet intercensal periods. In addition, although the Tatar level of urbanization has always been below the national average, it has only been slightly below, usually by one or two percentage points, and it has been relatively high in the sense that the Tatars were always among the top-five groupings (Table 5.1). The Tatar level of urbanization in 1970 exemplifies these patterns in that by this date a level of 45.6 percent had been reached, exactly one percentage point below the national level.

Like the Eastern Slavs, the rapid urbanization of the Tatars
between 1897 and 1970 has been enhanced by very rapid urban growth
(1,210.9 percent). In fact, during the 1926-59 and 1926-70 periods,
only Belorussians had a higher rate of urban growth than the Tatars.
Unlike the Eastern Slavs, however, the Tatars have yet to experience
rural population decline in any of the six intercensal periods. In fact,
of the ten groupings, Tatars had a relatively high rural growth rate
in four periods, including 1897-1970, and in the 1926-59 period their
rate was the highest. Nevertheless, although the Tatar rural population did not decline, it also did not grow rapidly (only by 52.6 percent
over the entire 1897-1970 period), a situation that has contributed to
the rapid urbanization of the Tatars.

Many aspects of the urbanization of Tatars have been discussed
elsewhere, since one of the few detailed studies on Russian urbanization in non-Russian areas has focused upon the Tatar ASSR. This
discussion emphasized the fact that the economic development of the
Tatar Republic has resulted in an influx of Russians and, consequently,
has substantially benefited the Russian population. It should be pointed
out, however, that the local Tatar population has benefited to an appreciable extent also. First of all, two detailed studies on the Tatar ASSR
both indicate that the Tatars have experienced a substantial degree of
social mobility.[37] In addition, although the Tatar level of urbanization
in the Tatar ASSR is relatively low compared to both Russians in the
republic and Tatars outside the republic, from other perspectives it
is relatively high. In 1970 the level of urbanization (census definition)
of Tatars in the Tatar ASSR was 38.6 percent. In comparison, other
major Turkic-Muslim groups had considerably lower levels. For example, the levels of urbanization (census definition) of Uzbeks in the
Uzbek SSR and Kazakhs in the Kazakh SSR were only 23.0 and 26.3
percent in 1970, respectively. Thus, compared to other Turkic-Muslims, Tatars generally have experienced a relatively high degree of
modernization in their homeland.

However, as Tatars are among the most dispersed nationalities
in the USSR, they are one of the few major groups in the USSR in
which the vast majority of their urban and total populations are outside their titular unit. In fact, in 1970 over four-fifths (81.8 percent)
of the Tatar urban population (census definition) was located outside
the Tatar ASSR. Also, based upon the census definition of urban, the
level of urbanization of Tatars outside the Tatar ASSR in 1970 was
more than 20 percentage points higher than that of Tatars within their
republic (60.7 versus 38.6 percent, respectively).

Although Tatars achieve their highest levels of urbanization in
many regions to the west (for example, the Central and Northwest regions), their numbers are most significant in urban centers to the
south and east, especially the Urals and Central Asia, which together

in 1970 accounted for nearly one-half (47.8 percent) of the entire Tatar
urban population in the USSR. The Urals region has been particularly
outstanding. In 1970 the Urals contained more urban Tatars than any
other economic region, even more than the Volga region, the Tatar
"homeland" on the basis of economic regions. In particular, in 1970
the Urals accounted for 30.8 percent of the urban Tatars, whereas the
Volga accounted for 24.8 percent. Within the Urals region the major
area of Tatar settlement has been the Bashkir ASSR, which in 1970
accounted for 42.2 percent of the urban Tatars in the Urals. In fact,
although Russians outnumbered both groups combined, Tatars actually
outnumbered the Bashkirs in the urban population of the Bashkir ASSR
and accounted for 22.2 percent of this population.

Tatar urbanization has also been very significant in another
area of appreciable Turkic-Muslim settlement, Central Asia. In 1970,
17.0 percent of the Tatar urban population was located in Central Asia,
a figure that was surpassed only by the Urals and Volga regions. Also,
only in the Volga did the Tatars comprise a higher share of the urban
population. In 1970 Tatars comprised 9.0 percent of the urban population of the Volga, while in Central Asia and the Urals they accounted
for 7.6 and 7.5 percent, respectively. Although Central Asia in recent years has contained the largest share of the Crimean Tatars, who
cannot be distinguished from Volga Tatars in the recent censuses, a
great share of the Tatars in Central Asia are Volga Tatars, since
they have greatly outnumbered the Crimean Tatars and, consequently,
have comprised the vast majority of the Tatar population as a whole
(see Chapter 6). Within Central Asia the urban Tatars have been primarily located in the Uzbek SSR. In 1970 nearly three-fourths (73.4
percent) of the Tatar urban population (census definition) in Central
Asia was located in this republic, where the Tatars also accounted
for a relatively high 9.7 percent of the urban population.

Some aspects of Tatar urbanization resemble those of Russian
urbanization, although on a lesser scale. Similar to Russians, Tatars
have also migrated to urban centers of many non-Tatar areas, partly
because, somewhat like the Russians, they are more advanced than
the indigenous population. In this case, however, the advanced group
is more culturally similar to the indigenous groups in that both groups
are Turkic-Muslims. In short, the role played by Russians with respect to non-Russians appears to be duplicated, albeit at a lower level,
by the more modernized Tatars with respect to the non-Tatar Turkic-
Muslims.

Turkic-Muslims

The Turkic-Muslims, excluding Tatars, have been among the
least urbanized nationality groupings in the USSR. Even today the num-

ber of Turkic-Muslims residing in rural areas exceeds the number
residing in urban areas by 17 million people, a differential not even
approached by any of the other groupings. Furthermore, as recently
as 1959 their level of urbanization was comparable to that of the
Philippines.[38] Moreover, the Turkic-Muslims evidently are not even
as urbanized as their brethren in the so-called Muslim World, that is,
northern Africa and southwest Asia.[39]

The Turkic-Muslims have ranked with the Finnic peoples and the
Moldavians and Romanians as the nationality groupings having consistently low values with respect to the major indicators of urbanization
(Tables 5.1 to 5.3). Between 1897 and 1970 the level of urbanization of
the Turkic-Muslims increased by 17.8 percentage points, or less than
one-half the national average, and roughly 25 percentage points below
the Russian increase (Table 5.2). This relatively slow urbanization
was not confined to one period but was uniform in all six periods. In
the periods 1897-1970 and 1926-70 plus three of the four remaining
periods, the Turkic-Muslims ranked next to last in this respect and in
the other period (1897-1926) they ranked last. In addition, in every
period except 1959-70 the increase in their level of urbanization was
less than one-half the national increase.

Furthermore, in all of the four census years, their level of urbanization was well below the national average and was less than one-
half that of Russians (Table 5.1). In fact, in 1970 the Russian level
of urbanization was over 30 percentage points, or nearly 2.5 times
higher than that of the Turkic-Muslims, clearly demonstrating the
sharp difference in the standards of living between these two major
Soviet nationality groupings. In addition, except for 1897, the level
of urbanization of the Turkic-Muslims was always less than one-half
that of the national average, and of the ten groupings they ranked eighth
in 1926 and ninth in both 1959 and 1970. In these two most recent
census years, only the Moldavians and Romanians had a lower level of
urbanization.

The low urbanization of the Turkic-Muslims is not confined to
only a few component nationalities, but rather is generally characteristic of all the major representatives of this grouping (Table 5.4).
Even after a prolonged period of Soviet rule, the major Turkic-Muslim
nationalities (100,000 and over in population) all had a level of urbanization (based upon the census definition of urban) that was between 25 and
55 percentage points below that of the Russians. For example, in 1970
the level of urbanization of the Uzbeks, by far the largest single Turkic-
Muslim nationality, was more than 30 points below the national level
and more than 40 points below the Russian level. The only such group
with a level within 20 percentage points of the national average were
the Kumyks and Ingush, as well as the Azeri, who happen to be located
in a region containing the Baku oil fields; in fact, in 1970 almost exactly

one-third (33.7 percent) of the urban Azeri (census definition of urban)
in the USSR were located in the city of Baku alone. It should be pointed
out that some very small Turkic-Muslim nationalities do have urbanization levels above that of the Kumyks, who had the highest level in
1970 of any of the major Turkic-Muslim nationalities. These include
the Tats, Karaimy, Iranians, and Shortsy, as well as the Laks. The
Tats and Karaimy are particularly outstanding, since their urbanization levels (census definition) were well over 90 percent in 1970 (97.1
and 96.7, respectively). The greatest share of the Tats are found in
the city of Baku and the Dagestan ASSR, while the Karaimy are located
principally in the Ukraine, especially the Crimea. But none of these
nationalities with an urbanization level above the Kumyks is really significant in terms of numbers (in 1970 there were only 17,000 Tats and
5,000 Karaimy), and the conclusion that every Turkic-Muslim nationality
has a low level of urbanization, thus, is almost universally valid.

The major immediate factors underlying the relatively small
increase in the level of urbanization of the Turkic-Muslims have been
the relatively slow increase in their urban population and the relatively
rapid increase in their rural population. Once again, it should be kept
in mind that these two patterns are being assessed in the Soviet context and consequently are perhaps somewhat exaggerated. Between
1897 and 1970 the urban population of the Turkic-Muslims grew by
845.0 percent, certainly a substantial increase. However, this rate
of increase was low compared to most of the other groupings, and only
in the 1959-70 period did the Turkic-Muslim rate of urban growth rank
higher than fifth. During this most recent period, only the Moldavians
and Romanians had a higher rate of urban growth (88.3 versus 77.9
percent over the entire intercensal period).

But this not insignificant urban growth of the Turkic-Muslims
has been greatly offset by the relatively rapid increase in their rural
population. In fact, this grouping, along with the Tatars, Moldavians,
and Romanians, were the only ones to have an increasing rural population in all six periods. Also, the Turkic-Muslims had the second highest rate of rural population increase between 1897 and 1970, with only
the Moldavians and Romanians surpassing them in this respect.

Furthermore, in recent years, when the rural population of most
groupings has been declinining, the rural population of the Turkic-Muslims has not only been increasing but actually increasing at a more
rapid rate than in the past! These patterns have been manifested in a
number of ways. First, of the ten groupings, they had the highest rate
of rural population increase in both the 1926-70 and 1959-70 periods.
Second, during the 1897-1926 and 1926-59 periods their rural population was growing at a rate of only 0.3 percent per year, but between
1959 and 1970 this rate of growth accelerated to 2.9 percent per year.
All in all, roughly two-thirds (68.3 percent) of the total increase in the

rural population of the Turkic-Muslims between 1897 and 1970 occurred in the 1959-70 period.

In addition, the Turkic-Muslims have been responsible for much
of the rural population growth in the USSR. Between 1897 and 1970
they accounted for approximately three-fifths (58.8 percent) of the
USSR rural population growth. In more recent years, since the rural
population of most of the other major groupings has been declining,
the relative importance of the rural growth of the Turkic-Muslims
has been very difficult to measure statistically in a comprehensible
form. For example, between 1926 and 1959 the total rural population
of the USSR declined by roughly 16 million people, while at the same
time that of the Turkic-Muslims was increasing by roughly 1.6 million. Then between 1959 and 1970 the USSR total increased by only
approximately 30,000, while that of the Turkic-Muslims increased by
roughly 6.6 million, or more than 200 times the national rural growth;
thus, if the Turkic-Muslims were excluded, the USSR as a whole,would
have been undergoing a fairly substantial decline in its rural population
during recent years.

The great acceleration in the rural population increase of the
Turkic-Muslims has occurred by a process not unlike that that has led
to rapid population growth in the predominately rural underdeveloped
countries of the world as a whole. This rapid population growth has
been caused primarily by a sharp reduction in the death rate, which,
in turn, has been due to the diffusion of advanced death controlling
techniques from developed countries to underdeveloped countries.
Similarly, such techniques have also been transferred from the more
developed portions of the USSR to the more underdeveloped portions,
such as Central Asia, areas that are, of course, dominated by the
Turkic-Muslims.

The implications for Soviet society of the high rates of population
growth among the Turkic-Muslims, contrasted as they are with the
generally slow growth among the European nationalities, are potentially the source of the most serious and far-reaching problems that
the USSR will face in coming decades. Nowhere is this problem more
evident than in Central Asia, where the greatest share of Turkic-Muslims is located. Although the implications stemming from the rapid
growth of the rural population of Central Asia are discussed at considerable length in Chapter 10, the importance of future trends and
their relationship to urbanization warrant a summary at this point.

As mentioned earlier, the vast majority of the population growth
among the Turkic-Muslims is taking place in rural areas, a situation
that naturally results from the fact that these nationalities are overwhelmingly rural dwellers. The impact of this dramatic rural growth
upon Soviet society will depend primarily upon the extent to which the
local rural and urban economies can absorb the expanding population.

The most serious ramifications of population growth in rural areas of
Central Asia involve the large increments to the work force that must
be accommodated. In order to examine this situation in a systematic
way, we have proposed a number of alternative "solutions" that might
either singly or in some combination represent a likely scenario for
future demographic trends. These alternatives are then evaluated for
feasibility and consequences.

Faced with growing pressure upon agricultural resources, historically societies have been forced to choose among three possible
courses: further agricultural development, slower population growth,
or out-migration. In the case of Central Asia, the possibility of expanding agricultural production to accommodate rural population pressures and the rapid expansion of the work force seems to be an in-
feasible solution, principally because of finite resources, the costly
nature of increasing the irrigated acreage upon which agriculture in
this area is based, and the mechanization of farming, which actually
reduces labor requirements. Slower rates of population growth present
only a long-term answer inasmuch as future generations of workers
are already born and, barring a catastrophe of immense dimensions,
over the next two decades will enter the work force. In addition, it
is very difficult to promote birth control in such rural, traditional
areas as the Turkic-Muslim areas of the USSR, as the experience in
underdeveloped areas has demonstrated. Out-migration from rural
areas, which will siphon off excess labor, appears to be the only likely
possibility; indeed, this has been the response that most societies have
made under similar circumstances.

Given that out-migration in large numbers from rural areas of
Central Asia is the probable trend for the future, the question then
becomes one of the potential destinations of these migrants. Again, a
number of alternative possibilities present themselves: emigration
to foreign countries, migration to rural areas in other regions of the
USSR, local rural-to-urban migration, and migration to Soviet cities
outside Central Asia.

It seems improbable that large-scale emigration from the Soviet
Union will occur in the future. The migration of Central Asians to
other rural areas within the Soviet Union is a limited possibility, limited because although these other agricultural regions are often areas
of labor shortages, the labor shortages are in themselves a manifestation of out-migration from these areas resulting from poor conditions
and a lack of opportunities. The attraction of these areas for migrants,
then, is not great.

By far the most feasible solutions are those that entail a movement from rural areas in Central Asia to either local or distant cities.
Rural-to-urban migration has been the typical response to rural population pressures in recent times, largely because with modernization

most economic opportunities develop in cities. It appears that the
most likely course of events will involve a combination of these two
migratory flows. Because of the large number of potential in-migrants
from rural areas, and because of the insufficient economic opportunities in the cities of Central Asia, which are already dominated by Russians and other outsiders, the local urban areas almost certainly will
not be able to absorb the total volume of movement from the farms.
Thus, migration of a substantial number of Central Asians to cities in
other regions of the USSR within the coming decades is a strong possibility, particularly since there are considerable labor shortages in
many of these cities. Cultural differences between Central Asia and
other, more "Western" regions of the Soviet Union may ameliorate
this trend somewhat, but there are certainly enough historical precedents that suggest these differences alone will not stop economically
motivated migration.

The movement of Central Asians to both local and distant cities
will have major disjunctive implications. As the pressures upon economic opportunities increase, the Central Asians may well look with
increasing disfavor upon the large numbers of Russians and other nationalities in the modern sectors of Central Asian society. Likewise,
the movement of culturally and physically distinct nationalities to territories beyond their homelands generally has resulted in increased
ethnic tensions. There is no reason to expect that the reactions of
Russians to a large Turkmen presence in Leningrad will be any different than that of white New Yorkers to the growing Puerto Rican populations, of Londoners to Indians and Pakistanis, or of the French in Mar-
seille to North Africans. Clearly, the impact of these demographic
forces will have a major influence upon the future of Soviet society.

Jews

The Jews are by far the most highly urbanized nationality grouping in the USSR. In fact, the Jews of the Soviet Union are among the
most urbanized people in the world, and, excluding such "city-states"
as Hong Kong, West Berlin, and Singapore, are very probably more
urbanized than any country in the world. [40]
The exceedingly high degree of Jewish urbanization is very evident in Tables 5.1 to 5.3. Between 1897 and 1970 they had the greatest percentage point increase in the level of urbanization of any grouping (44.1 percentage points), although they were less outstanding between 1926 and 1970, ranking only seventh (Table 5.2). In addition,
their level of urbanization was the highest of any grouping in all four
census years, and they were, along with Russians, the only grouping
to have a level of urbanization above the national average in all four

census years (Table 5.1). In 1970 almost four-fifths (78.5 percent)
of the Soviet Jews resided in urban centers, a level that was more
than 30 percentage points above the national average and even more
than 20 percentage points above the Russians. Furthermore, when the
census definition of urban is utilized, the Jewish level of urbanization,
of course, has been even higher (Table 5.6). By 1970 virtually all
(97.9 percent) of the Soviet Jews resided in urban centers based upon
this criterion, and, of the roughly 100 other listed nationalities in the
USSR, not one had a higher level of urbanization than the Jews in 1970,
not even the very small nationalities. This situation, of course, reflects the outstanding position of Jews in the Soviet Union with respect
to their level of modernization.

　　However, as mentioned earlier, Jewish urbanization patterns
require considerable elaboration, because Jewish urbanization has
not been entirely associated with modernization; that is, it has been
greatly influenced by forces not necessarily associated with modernization. Their high level of urbanization has been greatly influenced by
political rather than socioeconomic forces, and the substantial increase in their level of urbanization has not been associated with significant urban growth. Both of these topics will be discussed separately.

　　The very high level of Jewish urbanization in Russia and the
USSR was greatly enhanced by tsarist policies. Jewish settlement was
restricted largely to the western borderlands of the Russian Empire
(discussed in greater depth in Chapter 6). Moreover, within this restricted area of settlement, Jewish residence was generally limited to
urban areas, in particular, and a considerable degree of overcrowding
and poverty were characteristic of such areas.[41] Tsarist law, however, did not rigorously define an urban center with respect to Jewish
residence. Determination of such an urban center was left to the dis-
cretion of local police and administrative authorities.[42] Thus, Jews
lived in settlements that were not legal cities, and many in particular
resided in small market towns.[43] Consequently, in 1897 "only" about
one-half (49.4 percent) of the Jewish population of the Russian Empire
resided in legal cities, which formed the basis of the census definition
of urban; and, according to the 15,000 and over definition, we have estimated that roughly one-third (34.4 percent) of the Jewish population
resided in urban centers within the present-day boundaries of the
USSR. But, although Jewish residence was not restricted to legal
cities, the Jewish level of urbanization was well above that of other
major nationalities and for the country as a whole, and Jews were the
second-largest single nationality in urban centers at this time. In
particular, they dominated many urban centers of the western borderlands of the empire, forming Jewish islands in a sea of Ukrainians,
Belorussians, Moldavians, Lithuanians, or Poles. The peak was

reached in the city of Berdichev near Kiev, where Jews comprised over three-fourths (77.1 percent) of the population in 1897. Thus, the consistently high level of urbanization of the Soviet Jews was greatly enhanced by a somewhat artificial situation, and although these residential restrictions have been removed in the Soviet era, this high level of urbanization has been maintained.

The factors underlying the substantial increase in the level of urbanization of the Jews were also quite unusual. As mentioned before, this increase was due more to a substantial decline in the Jewish rural population than to a significant increase in the Jewish urban population. In each of the six intercensal periods, the Jews had the lowest rate of both urban and rural population change, except for the 1897-1926 period, when their rate of urban growth ranked next to last. Overall, between 1897 and 1970, the Jewish urban population increased by only 13.9 percent, whereas the total urban population of Russia and the USSR increased more than nine times. Furthermore, in three periods (1926-59, 1926-70, and 1959-70) the Jewish urban population actually declined, the only instance where the urban population of any grouping ever declined; in fact, no other grouping ever came close to experiencing an urban population decline in any of the six intercensal periods. Because this decline in the Jewish urban population occurred after 1926, it is difficult to attribute it to the extensive emigration of Jews in the last decades of the Russian Empire. Instead, World War II and assimilation must be cited as the main causes, and of these, World War II must be regarded as the prime factor, because nearly all (86.3 percent) of the Jewish urban population decline between 1926 and 1970 occurred in the 1926-59 period.

Still, a not insignificant share of the decline in the Jewish urban population also must be attributed to the fact that a substantial number of Jews have undoubtedly changed their nationality to Russian. That many Jews would be so assimilated is suggested by the fact that the Jews are the most Russified nationality in the Soviet Union, in that in 1970 over three-fourths (78.2 percent) of the Soviet Jews considered Russian to be their native language. Of the roughly 100 other nationalities of the USSR, only the Karaimy, who are Jewish by religion but speak a Turkic language, had a higher percentage (82.1), but they are insignificant since they numbered less than 5,000.

As the Jewish level of urbanization always increased, this means that the Jewish level of urbanization often increased despite the absence of urban growth. Such a situation has been rare in modern urban history. One of the few times it occurred was in Ireland in the nineteenth century.[44] Similar to the Irish experience, a major catastrophe was also at play in the Jewish experience, one that particularly befell the rural population, but with war rather than famine being the principal reason.

The rate of decline in the Jewish rural population has been by far the greatest experienced by any of the nationality groupings. Although the rural population of most of the groupings declined in more recent years, the Jews were the only grouping to experience such a decline in all six intercensal periods. Overall, between 1897 and 1970 the Jewish rural population declined by 83.7 percent, or from almost 3 million to less than 500,000. World War II was the prime contributor to this decline as indicated by the fact that well over one-half (59.7 percent) of the decline occurred in the 1926-59 period.

Although the Jewish urban population also declined during the 1926-59 period, the Jewish rural population felt the impact of the war to an even greater extent because the major areas of Jewish rural settlement fell within the zone of German occupation. In 1897 over 90 percent of both the Jewish urban and rural populations resided in the six regions (West, Belorussia, Moldavia, Southwest, South, and Donetsk-Dnepr) that contained parts of the Jewish Pale of Settlement. By 1926 these regions contained less than 80 percent (77.7) of the Jewish urban population, but still contained over 90 percent (90.6) of the Jewish rural population. Thus, in the years just prior to World War II, unlike urban Jews, virtually all of the rural Jews within the present-day boundaries of the USSR were found in these same six regions, which all fell within the war zone. The result was not unexpected. Virtually 100 percent of the decline in the Jewish rural population between 1926 and 1959 occurred in this bloc of regions. Of the total decline of the Jewish rural population between 1897 and 1970, well over one-half of this decline occurred within these six regions during the 1926-59 period. Of the six regions involved, the Southwest (that is, the northwestern Ukraine) was outstanding in this respect, reflecting the fact that it had by far the largest Jewish population prior to World War II. This region alone accounted for more than one-half of the total decline in the number of rural Jews between 1897 and 1970 and between 1926 and 1959.

As a result of the impact of World War II on the Jewish rural population, the Jewish level of urbanization experienced its biggest increase during the 1926-59 period. As Tables 5.2 and 5.3 reveal, this level increased by 24.4 percentage points, or 0.76 percentage points per year.

However, despite these overall patterns of increase in the Jewish level of urbanization, the rate of Jewish urbanization has not been that outstanding in the Soviet era. Unlike the other groupings, nearly one-half (42.2 percent) of the percentage point increase in the Jewish level of urbanization occurred in the 1897-1926 period. In addition, whereas Jews had the greatest percentage point increase in the three periods beginning with 1897, in the three post-1926 periods their increase has ranked much lower. In fact, between 1959 and 1970 the

Jews had the smallest percentage point increase of any grouping. Because urbanization is a finite process in that the level of urbanization can never exceed 100 percent, this most recent trend in Jewish urbanization is to be expected. Any group that is as highly urbanized as the Jews cannot experience a continued great increase in the level of urbanization.

Thus, the patterns of Jewish urbanization within Russia and the USSR have been unusual. But in spite of the fact that such essentially nonmodernizing forces as residential restrictions and war have greatly increased Jewish urbanization, it should not be doubted that the high level of Jewish urbanization is indicative of a very high level of modernization. A brief glance at nationality educational differentials quickly puts such doubts to rest (see Table 9.4).

Mobilized Europeans

Although fairly highly urbanized, the Mobilized Europeans have not experienced the degree of urbanization one might expect from such advanced peoples. This situation is best exemplified by the Georgians, who are less urbanized than the other three nationalities in this grouping (Latvians, Estonians, and Armenians), but, with the exception of the Jews, are the most educated nationality in the USSR. All in all, Mobilized Europeans are about as urbanized as the Tatars, and, thus, about as urbanized as a region like southern Europe. In fact, the level of urbanization of the Mobilized Europeans did not increase significantly between 1897 and 1970 (Table 5.2). They had a percentage point increase that ranked fairly low and was below the national average (Table 5.2). A similar situation also characterized the 1926-70 period. Moreover, in only two of the six intercensal periods (1897-1926 and 1959-70) did the Mobilized Europeans have an increase that was above the national average. As these patterns imply, the Mobilized Europeans experienced a relatively small increase in the 1926-59 period, a period of very rapid urbanization in the USSR. This pattern will be discussed in greater depth later.

However, the Mobilized Europeans have had relatively high levels of urbanization. As mentioned earlier, aside from the Jews and Russians, they were the only other grouping ever to have a level of urbanization above the national average, achieving such a position in 1897 and 1926, when they ranked third and second, respectively (Table 5.1). But, although they ranked relatively high in 1959 and 1970, in both of these years their level of urbanization was slightly below the national average. These patterns reflect the increasing demographic importance of the Transcaucasus nationalities, especially Georgians (Table 5.1).

That the level of urbanization of Mobilized Europeans did not increase to a greater extent can be attributed to the combined effects of a slow urban growth rate (primarily among Estonians and Latvians) and a fairly stable rural population size (among Georgians and Armenians). Although their urban population grew by more than seven times (615. 0 percent) between 1897 and 1970, of the ten nationality groupings, they ranked very low in this respect, with only the Jews having a lower rate of increase, and they never ranked among the top-four groupings in any of the six periods.

The slow rate of urban growth for this grouping is attributable primarily to the Latvians and Estonians, especially during the 1926-59 period. As mentioned before, this period was one of relatively slow urbanization on the part of the Mobilized Europeans. Indeed, of the groupings they ranked eighth with respect to both the percentage point change in the level of urbanization and rate of urban growth. In fact, as Table 5.2 reveals, whereas the bulk of the 1897-1970 percentage point increase in the level of urbanization of nearly all of the groupings occurred between 1926 and 1959, less than half of the 1897-1970 increase for the Mobilized Europeans occurred during this period.

This relatively slow pace was not unrelated to the fact that two of the four component nationalities (Latvians and Estonians) were outside the USSR during much of this period and did not benefit to any great extent from the emphasis on very rapid industrialization within the boundaries of the Soviet Union during this period. That their urban growth rates were not that high during this period is manifested in a number of ways. It is, of course, difficult to compare the urban growth rates of Latvians and Estonians with those of other nationalities during this period since most of the Latvians and Estonians were in their respective independent nations and most were not enumerated in the 1926 Soviet census. However, both countries did take censuses in 1925 and 1926, respectively, and although their urban definitions were not the same as the Soviet definition, it is possible to conclude that between 1926 and 1959 the urban population of each group roughly doubled. In comparison, our estimates suggest that the urban population for the present-day USSR almost quadrupled. The slow urban growth of Latvians and Estonians is reflected in the urbanization and urban growth patterns of the West region during the 1926-39 period, when Latvia and Estonia were independent nations. Of the 19 economic regions, the West region ranked 18th with respect to both percentage point increase in the level of urbanization and rate of urban growth. Interestingly, the only region to rank lower in both cases was Moldavia, a region that was also primarily outside the USSR during this period.

The relatively slow rate of Latvian and Estonian urban growth, of course, also reflects their low fertility levels. As mentioned previously, Russians have moved into Latvia and Estonian cities partly to

provide the necessary workers, because even though the Latvians and
Estonians are quite advanced, their rate of population growth has apparently not been great enough to supply the necessary labor. As suggested previously, the trends among the Georgians and Armenians have
been somewhat different in that, although they are relatively advanced,
their growth rates have been evidently sufficient to prevent a substantial influx of Russians.

The Georgians and Armenians are primarily responsible for the
lack of a substantial rural population decline of the Mobilized Europeans,
a situation that also has prevented relatively substantial gains in the
level of urbanization of this grouping. Of the ten nationality groupings,
the Mobilized Europeans generally ranked higher with respect to the
rural growth rate than to the urban growth rate. This pattern is exemplified by the 1897-1970 period. During this period their urban
growth rate ranked only ninth, but their rural growth rate (16.5 percent for the entire period) ranked fifth and was above the national average. Furthermore, in five of the six periods their rural growth rate
ranked among the five highest, and in none of the six periods did they
experience substantial rural depopulation. That such a depopulation
has yet to occur primarily reflects the influence of the Georgians and
Armenians. Based upon the census definition, even as recently as
the 1959-70 period, when many other nationalities were experiencing
rural population decline (especially such other relatively advanced nationalities as Russians, Jews, Latvians, and Estonians), the rural
population of the Georgians and Armenians still continued to increase.
During this period the Georgian rural population increased by almost
100,000, or 5.7 percent, and the Armenian rural population increased
by over 40,000, or 3.6 percent. These patterns are substantiated by
data from the 1970 census, which indicate that Georgians and Armenians and their respective republics are still experiencing very low
levels of rural-to-urban migration.[45]

Rural conditions that account for the lack of a more substantial
rural out-migration of the Georgians will be discussed to a greater
extent in Chapter 6. Especially important in this regard has been the
high degree of labor intensiveness in rural areas of Georgia. This
migration has been further impeded by the fact that the opportunities
in local cities are somewhat limited, as Georgia has received a relatively small amount of investment and, consequently, is not highly
industrialized. For example, in 1970, although Georgia contained
1.9 percent of the USSR population, it received only 1.4 percent of
the total Soviet capital investment and contained only 1.2 percent of
the total number of Soviet industrial workers.[46] In addition, between
1960 and 1970 of the 15 republics, only four others had a lower growth
rate of industrial production than Georgia, and, not surprisingly, the
Georgian rate was below the national average.[47] Therefore, the

Georgian level of urbanization essentially has been greatly impeded by
the lack of more substantial opportunities in local urban centers and
a relatively high demand for labor in rural areas. Because the Georgians have comprised a relatively large share of the total population
of the Mobilized Europeans (more than one-third in 1970, for example),
this has tended to impede the urbanization process for the grouping as
a whole.

Finnic Peoples

The Finnic peoples generally have experienced a relatively low
degree of urbanization as compared to most other groupings. Even
though there are more than 3 million Finnic peoples in the USSR today,
barely 2 million reside in urban centers. Furthermore, their current
level of urbanization is comparable to such areas as the Caribbean islands, northern Africa, and southwest Asia. [48]

In fact, the Finnic peoples have experienced a low degree of urbanization in every period and in every year (Tables 5.1 to 5.3). In
particular, of the ten groupings, their index of urbanization never
ranked higher than seventh in any of the four census years or six intercensal periods. No other grouping had such uniformly low values.
With regard to percentage point change in the level of urbanization
from 1897 to 1970 and from 1926 to 1970, the Finnic peoples ranked
very low (Table 5.2). Furthermore, not once did their increase exceed
the national average.

Similarly, their level of urbanization was always below the national average in all four years, ranking tenth or last in 1897 and 1926
(their level of 1.7 percent in 1897 was the lowest of any grouping in
any year!) and eighth in 1959 and 1970 (Table 5.1). In 1970 their
level of urbanization was almost 20 percentage points below the national
average and almost 30 percentage points below the Russian level.

When individual Finnic nationalities are investigated, the pattern
of uniformly low urbanization again emerges (Table 5.4). In 1970
every Finnic nationality except the Finns, Vepsy, and Izhortsy, who
are all very insignificant in terms of population size, had a level of
urbanization (census definition of urban) well below the national level.
Indeed, the level of every Finnic group save the Finns, Vepsy, and
Izhortsy was more than ten percentage points below the national average. Mordvinians, the largest Finnic nationality, were, in fact, almost exactly 20 points below.

Paradoxically, despite their low degree of urbanization, the
Finnic peoples have experienced rapid urban growth and substantial
rural population decline. Between 1897 and 1970 the Finnic urban
population increased by more than 18 times (1,740.9 percent), and only

the Lithuanians and Belorussians had a higher rate of urban growth. The Finnic urban growth rate, in fact, generally ranked very high, and in five of these six periods was above the national average. However, like Lithuanians and Belorussians, this rapid urban growth is greatly distorted by a low base figure. In 1897 the Finnic urban population totaled only about 50,000, with only the Lithuanians having a smaller total of the ten groupings, and in 1926 the Finnic urban population of roughly 125,000 was the lowest of any grouping. Therefore, almost any increase in the Finnic urban population would result in a great percentage increase.

However, these growth rates would have been even higher had not the Finnic peoples been so relatively highly Russified. As mentioned before, in 1970, 22.1 percent of the non-Russian nationalities in urban areas considered Russian to be their native language; in contrast, the corresponding figure for the Finnic peoples was almost twice as high (39.2 percent). This suggests that a substantial number of urban Finnic peoples have probably changed their nationality to Russian. Without this high degree of Russification, the number of urban Finnic peoples would probably have been more than the approximate total of 900,000 in 1970, based upon our estimates. In short, the rapid urban growth of the Finnic peoples would have been even more rapid had not a substantial number of urban Finnic peoples changed their nationality to Russian, although this situation would probably not greatly alter the basic patterns of Finnic urbanization and urban growth.

The high degree of Russification of the Finnic peoples is also partly caused by the close proximity between Finnic and Russian areas of settlement. Most Finnic areas of settlement are completely surrounded by Russians, and Russians typically dominate such areas. In 1970 Russians outnumbered the titular Finnic nationality in all five Finnic ASSRs within the USSR (Karelian, Komi, Mari, Mordvinian, and Udmurt). Of course, Russians were even more preponderant in urban centers of these Finnic units and, in fact, comprised nearly three-fourths (71.1 percent) of the urban population of these five ASSRs combined. For example, in the city of Izhevsk, an industrial city in the Udmurt ASSR, one of the more industrialized Finnic areas, Russians comprised more than three-fourths (75.2 percent) of the population in 1959.[49] Thus, local economic development in these units once again appears to have greatly benefited the Russians, and the indigenous peoples have not benefited as greatly as might be expected, thus reducing their expected rate of urban growth. In addition, this situation also has tended to promote the very high degree of Russification of the urban Finnic peoples, thus impeding a more rapid rate of Finnic urban growth and urbanization.

Another factor dampening the degree of Finnic urbanization has been the numerical dominance of this grouping by the highly rural Mordvinians. In 1959 and 1970, for example, Mordvinians were the largest Finnic nationality and alone accounted for roughly two-fifths of the total and urban populations of the Finnic grouping. Between 1959 and 1970 many Finnic nationalities had a percentage point increase in their level of urbanization that was above the national increase of 8.4 based upon the census definition. These included the Udmurts (9.9) and Mari (8.8), the second- and third-largest Finnic groups. The Mordvinians' level increased by only 7.0 percentage points, resulting in an overall Finnic percentage point increase of 7.8, which was below the national average.

A more rapid rate of Finnic urbanization did not occur despite the fact that the Finnic rural growth rate was as low as its rate of urban growth was high. Between 1897 and 1970 the Finnic rural population declined by 15.8 percent, and, of the ten groupings, only the Jews had a greater percentage decline. Furthermore, the Finnic rural population declined in five of the six periods, experiencing an increase only between 1897 and 1926. All of the decline took place after 1926, and, although the Finnic rural population declined between 1959 and 1970, most (91.3 percent) of the post-1926 decline of roughly 1.1 million occurred between 1926 and 1959. The majority of this decline took place in the Northwest region, reflecting the removal of the largely rural Finnish population from the Vyborg area to Finland (see Chapter 6).

Lithuanians

The Lithuanian pattern of urbanization has been similar to that of the neighboring Belorussians, although the Lithuanians generally have experienced somewhat greater urbanization. Lithuanian urbanization prior to the 1960s was generally low, but during the last decade it has been spectacular. In fact, between 1959 and 1970 Lithuanians urbanized at a rate comparable to that of Russians between 1926 and 1959. Accordingly, the Lithuanian urbanization process in the last decade or so has been among the fastest in the history of the world. Indeed, whereas it took roughly three and a half decades (1926-59) for the Lithuanian urban population to grow by about 500,000, it took only the approximate decade between 1959 and 1970 for it to increase by nearly the same amount (400,000).

Tables 5.2 and 5.3 reveal that the percentage point increase in the Lithuanian level of urbanization was generally moderate to high.

From 1897 to 1970 and from 1926 to 1970, of the ten groupings it
ranked fourth in this respect, although this increase was slightly below
the national increase. Moreover, between 1959 and 1970 the increase
in the Lithuanian level of urbanization surpassed that of all of the other
groupings; in fact, based upon the census definition of urban, it exceeded that of all of the individual nationalities of the USSR with more
than 1 million people in 1970, including, of course, the remaining 14
SSR nationalities. Not surprisingly, the next highest increases were
experienced by the neighboring Belorussians and the Poles, a significant number of whom are located astride the Lithuania-Belorussia
boundary. In addition, the average annual percentage point increase
in the Lithuanian level of urbanization during this period was the highest ever attained by any grouping in any period (Table 5.3).

But, although the Lithuanians have urbanized rapidly, they have
yet to attain a very high level of urbanization. Of the ten groupings,
they never ranked higher than sixth, achieving such a position in 1959
and 1970 (Table 5.1). Even though their level increased greatly from
2.3 percent in 1897 to 38.0 percent in 1970, their 1970 level was still
almost ten percentage points below the national average and nearly 20
points below the Russian level.

This rapid urbanization of the Lithuanians has been promoted by
a low rate of rural population growth. Between 1897 and 1970 the
Lithuanian rural population increased by only 5.0 percent overall. In
addition, like many other groupings, their rural population actually
declined in the three post-1926 periods.

The major immediate explanation, however, for the fairly rapid
urbanization of the Lithuanians has been an extremely high rate of urban growth. Between 1897 and 1970 the Lithuanian urban population
increased by over 27 times (2,642.2 percent), a rate unsurpassed by
any other grouping. In fact, the Lithuanians also ranked first in two
other periods (1897–1926 and 1897–1959) and never ranked lower than
fourth. Furthermore, along with the Belorussians, the Lithuanians
were the only grouping to have an urban growth rate in excess of the
national average in all six periods. However, like the Belorussians
and Finnic peoples, this rapid urban growth is partly the result of a
very low base figure. Indeed, in 1897 the Lithuanians had the lowest
urban population (roughly 37,000) of any grouping. The rapid urbanization that occurred between 1959 and 1970 was related to rural population decline (–2.2 percent) and continued rapid urban growth (58.9
percent, or 4.2 percent per year), although ironically the Lithuanian
rank with respect to the urban growth was lower in this period than it
was in some other periods.

As with Belorussians, the rapid urban growth and urbanization of Lithuanians in recent years is manifested in a number of other respects. For example, between 1959 and 1970, whereas the urban population of the USSR increased by 41.2 percent, that of the Lithuanian SSR increased by 71.1 percent. In addition, as in the Belorussian Republic, every city in the Lithuanian SSR with a population of 15,000 and over in 1970 increased its population between 1959 and 1970. Furthermore, every city increased rapidly in that each one increased its population by at least one-third, with the slowest growing town of Lithuania increasing its population by "only" 34 percent. Although the Lithuanian SSR did not contain such extremely rapidly growing towns as did the Belorussian Republic, one city, Alitus, did more than double its population.

As in Belorussia, considerable capital investment and industrialization evidently have been the major stimuli to the rapid urbanization of the Lithuanians during the 1960s. Whereas capital investment and industrial production in the USSR roughly doubled between 1960 and 1970, in Lithuania they more than tripled, according to Soviet estimates.[50] Furthermore, Lithuania was the leading republic with respect to percentage increase in total investment of the 15 republics; only the Kirgiz SSR had a greater rate of increase in industrial output.[51] Again, similar to the Belorussian SSR, the expansion of local chemical industries has been particularly notable. The connection of the Lithuanian SSR via pipelines with major oil and natural gas fields has facilitated their development. For example, in 1961 a pipeline from the Dashava natural gas fields in the western Ukraine reached Lithuania.[52]

Not unexpectedly, the urbanization of the Lithuanian SSR and Lithuanians, although greatly interconnected, has not been completely synonymous. As elsewhere, including the other Baltic republics and the Belorussian Republic, the rapid industrialization of the Lithuanian SSR during the 1960s has resulted in an appreciable influx of Russians, and between 1959 and 1970 the Russian urban population (census definition) of the republic increased by 28.0 percent. However, as Table 5.9 suggests, this influx was not great enough to prevent a decline in their percentage of the urban population of Lithuania. This implies that the Lithuanians themselves were increasing at a much more rapid rate; indeed, the Lithuanian urban population (census definition) of the Lithuanian SSR increased by 59.2 percent between 1959 and 1970, and Lithuanians accounted for more than four-fifths (81.4 percent) of the urban growth (census definition) of the republic during this period. As Tables 5.8 and 5.9 reveal, only in the Transcaucasus republics were there comparatively fewer Russians in local urban centers.

That the influx of Russians to cities of the Lithuanian Republic has not been greater is strange in light of the low educational level of

the Lithuanians and the relatively important role of Russians in urban
areas of the other Baltic republics and adjacent Belorussia. One census indicator of educational level is the percentage of the population
aged 10 and over that had a higher or secondary education, complete
or incomplete. Based upon this index, of the 15 SSR nationalities,
Lithuanians ranked last in 1959 and next to last in 1970 (see Table
9.4). Consequently, a very substantial influx of Russians might be
expected in order to supply the required skilled personnel necessary
for the industrialization process.

That such an influx has not transpired can be attributed to many
factors. First of all, although the Lithuanians have a relatively low
degree of education on the basis of the above indicator, their position
is really not that inferior. Between 1959 and 1970 the increase in their
educational level, based upon the above indicator, was the greatest of
any of the 15 SSR nationalities (see Table 9.4). In addition, when
higher education, per se, is investigated, the Lithuanian position is
much more favorable. For example, in 1970, of the 15 SSR nationalities only six others had a greater level of higher education, as measured by the percentage of the population aged 10 and over with a complete or incomplete higher education. Thus, the lack of a greater influx
of Russians to urban centers of Lithuania can be partly attributed to
the fact that the Lithuanians themselves apparently have been able to
supply a substantial number of the necessary skilled personnel.

It was noted, however, that some of these educational conditions
have not prevented a relatively great influx of Russians to Latvia and
Estonia. The chief difference in this regard is that the Lithuanian
population has been growing at a more rapid rate than the Latvian and
Estonian populations. Between 1959 and 1970 the Lithuanian population
increased by 14.6 percent, whereas the Latvian and Estonian populations
increased by only 2.2 and 1.9 percent, respectively. Therefore,
whereas the highly educated Latvians and Estonians have been unable
to provide the necessary skilled labor because of their low growth
rates, it appears that the more rapidly growing Lithuanians have been
able partly to meet more adequately their labor requirements, despite
their lower overall educational levels as compared to their two Baltic
neighbors. Thus, despite their lower educational levels, it appears
that the Lithuanians have been able to provide a great share of the
skilled work force necessary for the rapid industrialization of their
republic because of a number of factors: their educational levels have
been increasing rapidly, they have a relatively greater number of people with a higher education, and their rate of population growth has
not been extremely low, especially when compared to the growth
rates of the neighboring Latvians and Estonians.

Moldavians and Romanians

It is very appropriate that the Moldavians and Romanians should
be the last grouping to be discussed with respect to urbanization, because, generally speaking, they have experienced the least urbanization
of any grouping. Even today the Moldavian and Romanian rural population outnumbers their urban population by nearly 2 million people,
a sizable differential for a grouping that does not even have a population of 3 million. The current Moldavian and Romanian level of urbanization is roughly comparable to that of such major underdeveloped
regions of the world as Southeast Asia and middle south Asia, which
includes India, Pakistan, and Bangladesh.[53]
     From 1897 to 1970 and 1926 to 1970 they had the lowest percent-
age point increase in the level of urbanization of any of the ten groupings (Table 5.2). Indeed, their increase was roughly 25 points below
the national average and 30 points below the Russian increase. In addition, the Moldavian and Romanian increase was the lowest of any
grouping in two other periods, and was always low and usually well
below the national average in all periods.
     Furthermore, the Moldavian and Romanian level of urbanization
has always ranked very low (Table 5.1). This was especially so in
1959 and 1970, when their level was roughly 30 points below the national
level and 35 to 40 points below the Russian level. In these two years
no other grouping had a level of urbanization below the Moldavians and
Romanians, not even the Turkic-Muslims! Moreover, the Moldavian
and Romanian level of urbanization has been below that of most of the
individual Turkic-Muslim groups. In 1970 roughly one-fifth (20.4
percent) of the Moldavians and Romanians resided in urban centers
according to the census definition of urban. Reference to Table 5.4
reveals that this level was lower than that for all major Turkic-Muslim nationalities except for the Avars, Tuvinians, Karachay, and Kirgiz. Thus, in a country with significant areas of both Western and
non-Western cultures, it is somewhat ironic that the lowest level of
urbanization among the major nationality groupings is experienced by
a Western-oriented grouping. The low degree of urbanization of the
Moldavians and Romanians is also reflected on the basis of the 19
economic regions. The Moldavian region (which is synonymous with
the Moldavian SSR) had the lowest level of urbanization of any region
in 1970, and the percentage point increase in its level of urbanization
was the lowest of any region between 1897 and 1970.
     The very low increase in the Moldavian and Romanian level of
urbanization has been due, first of all, to a combination of comparatively slow urban growth and relatively rapid rural growth. Only the
Jews had a lower urban growth rate between 1897 and 1970, and in
four of the six periods the Moldavians and Romanians ranked eighth

or ninth in this respect. As implied before, a relatively low rate of
Moldavian and Romanian urban growth was especially characteristic
of the 1926-59 period. During this period, only the Jews had a lower
rate of growth, actually a decline, and whereas the total urban population of the present-day USSR more than tripled, that of the Moldavians
and Romanians increased only by 60.7 percent. This slow urban
growth apparently was especially characteristic of the 1926-39 period.
During this period, the urban population of the Moldavian SSR actually
declined, the only instance where the urban population of an economic
region ever declined in any of the post-1897 intercensal periods. Like
the Latvian and Estonian republics, Moldavia was largely outside the
USSR during this period, being primarily in Romania, and consequently
did not benefit from the very rapid industrialization occurring within
the USSR during this period. Furthermore, the Romanian government
deemphasized industry in Bessarabia, the province that comprises
most of the present-day Moldavian SSR.[54] Therefore, it is no wonder
that the Moldavians and Romanians within the present-day boundaries
of the USSR experienced such little urban growth and urbanization during this period.

As might be expected, the Moldavian and Romanian urban growth
increased substantially with the annexation of Bessarabia and northern
Bukovina to the Soviet Union in the early 1940s. In both the 1939-59
and 1959-70 periods the urban growth rate of the Moldavian SSR was
well above the national average. Furthermore, between 1959 and 1970
the Moldavian and Romanian urban growth rate was the highest of any
grouping, and the urban growth rate of the Moldavian SSR was the
highest of any economic region, a significant turnaround from the
1926-59 period. This rapid urban growth in the 1959-70 period undoubtedly has been due to the fact that the percentage increase in both
capital investment and industrial production in the Moldavian SSR was
well above the national average between 1960 and 1970.[55]

However, low base figures have contributed to the rapidity of the
increase in the urban population, capital investment, and industrial
production, and the urbanization of both the Moldavian Republic and
the Moldavians and Romanians between 1959 and 1970 was not great.
On the basis of the percentage point increase in the level of urbanization, the Moldavian SSR ranked 11 among the 19 economic regions,
and Moldavians and Romanians ranked eighth among the ten groupings.
A major contributor to the low degree of urbanization is the comparatively poor natural resource base of Moldavia for industrialization.
This is reflected by the fact that the industrial structure of this republic is dominated by food-processing industries to a much greater extent than the industrial structure of any other republic.[56]

Perhaps the primary explanation for the meager urbanization of
the Moldavians and Romanians is that they experienced relatively rapid

rural population growth in all six periods. Between 1897 and 1970
their rate of rural growth (89.4 percent) was the highest of any grouping. In addition, they always ranked very high in this respect, ranking first also in the 1897-1926 period, and their rate of rural population growth was above the national average in all six periods, the only
grouping to do so. The lack of a more appreciable out-migration from
rural areas of the Moldavians and Romanians has been due not only
to the limited local industrial resource base and consequent urban opportunities but also to the relatively favorable agricultural environment. Of the 15 SSRs, Moldavia, along with the Ukraine, are the only
ones where both arable land and sown acreage covers more than half
the area of the republic; in contrast, only about one-tenth of the USSR
as a whole is regarded as arable.[57]

NOTES

1. For more detailed discussions of Soviet urbanization in general, see Chauncy D. Harris, Cities of the Soviet Union (Chicago:
Rand McNally, 1970); Chauncy D. Harris, "Urbanization and Popula-
tion Growth in the Soviet Union, 1959-1970," Geographical Review 61
(January 1971): 102-24; Robert A. Lewis and Richard H. Rowland,
"Urbanization in Russia and the USSR: 1897-1966," Annals of the Association of American Geographers 59 (December 1969): 776-96; Robert A Lewis and Richard H. Rowland, "Urbanization in Russia and the
USSR: 1897-1970," in The City in Russian History, ed. Michael F.
Hamm (Lexingon, Ky.: University Press of Kentucky, in press); D.
I. Valentey, V. V. Pokshishevskiy, and B. S. Khorev, eds., Prob-
lemy Urbanizatsii v SSSR (Moscow: Izdatel'stvo Moskovskogo Universiteta, 1971); and B. S. Khorev, Problemy Gorodov (Moscow: Izdatel'stvo "Mysl'," 1971). Note that the Harris book contains an excellent and very comprehensive bibliography of publications in Russian,
English, and other languages concerned with aspects of Russian and
Soviet urbanization.

2. The world figure for 1900 was derived by Kingsley Davis and
Hilda Hertz, "Patterns of World Urbanization for 1800-1950," in
United Nations, Bureau of Social Affairs, Report on the World Social
Situation Including Studies of Urbanization in Underdeveloped Areas
(ST/SOA/33), 1957, p. 114.

3. The world figure for 1970 was estimated by the United Na-
tions in United Nations, Department of Economic and Social Affairs,
Growth of the World's Urban and Rural Population, 1920-2000
(ST/SOA/Series A/44), 1969, p. 58. The validity of these projected
UN estimates are verified at least in the case for the Soviet Union, be-
cause the UN estimated level of urbanization for the USSR in 1970 of

42.7 percent was very close to the actual percent from the 1970 Soviet census (that is, 44.3 percent).

4. Data for the world as a whole and major world regions can be found in United Nations, op. cit., pp. 31, 58.

5. For a good discussion of some of the elements of this framework, see Kingsley Davis, "The Urbanization of the Human Population," in Cities (New York: Knopf, 1970), pp. 10-12.

6. United Nations, op. cit., pp. 31, 58, 122.

7. B. Ts. Urlanis, Rost Naseleniya v SSSR (Moscow: Statistika, 1966), p. 34; and Izvestiya, April 19, 1970, p. 1.

8. Lewis and Rowland, "Urbanization in Russia and the USSR: 1897-1966," 790-92; and Lewis and Rowland, "Urbanization in Russia and the USSR: 1897-1970."

9. For a discussion on the derivation of industrial data for 1970, see Lewis and Rowland, "Urbanization in Russia and the USSR: 1897-1970."

10. V. V. Pokshishevskiy, "Etnicheskiye Protsessy v Gorodakh SSSR i Nekotoryye Problemy ikh Izucheniya," Sovetskaya Etnografiya, no. 5 (1969), p. 13.

11. O. I. Shkaratan, "Etno-Sotsial'naya Struktura Gorodskogo Naseleniya Tatarskoy ASSR," Sovetskaya Etnografiya, no. 3 (1970), pp. 3-16.

12. It should be noted that a certain unknown proportion of this migration by more highly educated persons is "forced" migration in that college graduates can be assigned to areas outside their homeland for three years after graduation; for example, see Yaroslav Bilinsky, "Assimilation and Ethnic Assertiveness Among Ukrainians of the Soviet Union," in Ethnic Minorities in the Soviet Union, ed. Erich Goldhagen (New York: Praeger, 1968), p. 155. Many, however, return home after they have fulfilled this obligation.

13. Pokshishevskiy, op. cit.

14. V. I. Naulko, Geografichne Rozmishchennya Narodiv v URSR (Kiev: Naukova Dumka, 1966).

15. Pokshishevskiy, op. cit., p. 14.

16. V. V. Pokshishevskiy, "Urbanizatsiya i Etnograficheskiye Protsessy," in Problemy Urbanizatsii v SSSR, ed. D. I. Valentey, V. V. Pokshishevskiy, and B. S. Khorev (Moscow: Izdatel'stvo Moskovskogo Universiteta, 1971), p. 60.

17. Ann Sheehy, "Some Aspects of Regional Development in Soviet Central Asia," Slavic Review 31 (September 1972): 559-61.

18. V. I. Perevedentsev, "O Vliyanii Etnicheskikh Faktorov na Territorial'noye Pereraspredeleniye Naseleniya," Izvestiya Akademii Nauk SSSR, Seriya Geograficheskaya, no. 4 (1965), pp. 31-39.

19. Ibid., p. 35.

20. Ibid.

21. Pokshishevskiy, "Etnicheskiye Protsessy v Gorodakh SSSR," op. cit., p. 10.

22. Ibid., pp. 11-12.

23. Ibid., pp. 12-13.

24. Perevedentsev, op. cit., p. 37.

25. Sheehy, op. cit., p. 561.

26. Perevedentsev, op. cit., pp. 35-36.

27. Ibid., pp. 36-37.

28. Brian D. Silver, "Ethnic Identity Change Among Soviet Nationalities: A Statistical Analysis" (Ph.D. diss., University of Wisconsin, 1972).

29. Vestnik Statistiki, no. 11 (1971), p. 84.

30. United Nations, op. cit., pp. 121-22.

31. For example, see Pokshishevskiy, op. cit., p. 59.

32. United Nations, op. cit., p. 105.

33. USSR, Tsentral'noye Statisticheskoye Upravleniye pri Sovete Ministrov SSSR, Narodnoye Khozyaystvo SSSR v 1970 G. (Moscow: Izdatel'stvo "Statistika," 1971), pp. 140, 488. (Hereafter, for all Narodnoye Khozyaystvo citations only the title and page numbers will be given.)

34. Theodore Shabad, Basic Industrial Resources of the U.S.S.R. (New York: Columbia University Press, 1969), pp. 201-06.

35. Ibid., p. 203.

36. United Nations, op. cit., pp. 121-22.

37. Shkaratan, op. cit., pp. 8-11; and Yu. V. Arutyunyan, "Opyt Sotsial'no-Etnicheskogo Issledovaniya," Sovetskaya Etnografiya, no. 4 (1968), pp. 8-13.

38. United Nations, op. cit., p. 105.

39. Ibid., pp. 121-22.

40. Ibid., pp. 104-06, 121-22.

41. Avrahm Yarmolinsky, The Jews and Other Minor Nationalities Under the Soviets (New York: Vanguard Press, 1928), pp. 25, 28; and Victor Berard, The Russian Empire and Czarism (London: David Nutt, 1905), p. 127.

42. Berard, op. cit., p. 133.

43. Ibid., p. 132; and Yarmolinsky, op. cit., pp. 25, 29.

44. Adna Ferrin Weber, The Growth of Cities in the Nineteenth Century (New York: Macmillan, 1899), pp. 64-65.

45. Vestnik Statistiki, no. 2 (1973), pp. 87-89.

46. Narodnoye Khozyaystvo SSSR v 1970 G., op. cit., pp. 159, 488.

47. Ibid., p. 140.

48. United Nations, op. cit., pp. 121-22.

49. Pokshishevskiy, "Etnicheskiye Protsessy v Gorodakh SSSR i Nekotoryye Problemy ikh Izucheniya," op. cit., p. 13.

50. Narodnoye Khozyaystvo SSSR v 1970 G., op. cit., pp. 140, 488.

51. Ibid.

52. Shabad, op. cit., pp. 207–08.

53. United Nations, op. cit., pp. 121–22.

54. A. L. Odud, Moldavskaya SSR (Moscow: Gosudarstvennoye Izdatel'stvo Geograficheskoy Literatury, 1955), pp. 62, 78.

55. Narodnoye Khozyaystvo SSSR v 1970 G., op. cit., pp. 140, 488.

56. Ibid., pp. 166–67.

57. Ibid., pp. 291, 300.

6

REGIONAL DISTRIBUTION
AND REDISTRIBUTION

Regional population distribution and redistribution are relevant
to a discussion of the modernization of Soviet nationalities because,
as mentioned earlier, more modernized peoples tend to be more mobile or migratory. Accordingly, it is logical to hypothesize that the
more advanced nationality groupings of the Soviet Union will have experienced the greatest interregional migration and dispersal. In particular, we would expect this pattern to be especially characteristic
of Russians, Tatars, Jews, and Mobilized Europeans. The testing
of this hypothesis will be carried out in the following sections, although, as will be seen, such an undertaking is difficult because of
data problems, particularly because our indicator of redistribution is
not solely a function of migration.

Migration can take many forms. For example, on the basis of
a regional framework, such as the one utilized in this study, movement can be either intraregional (local) or interregional (distant),
with both movements typically being rural-to-urban. In this chapter
the emphasis will be upon the interregional migration of the nationality
groupings. Chapter 5 was concerned primarily with the urbanization
and rural-to-urban migration of the groupings, which involves both
intra- and interregional movements. Therefore, this chapter will
not deal specifically with the urban aspects of interregional movements.

SUMMARY DISCUSSION

Although the total population of Russia and the USSR has experienced appreciable interregional redistribution, only a relatively few
nationality groupings have undergone substantial interregional migra-

tion and dispersal since 1897 and 1926. Foremost in this respect
were the Russians, Jews, and Tatars. This high degree of dispersal
is not unexpected given their relatively high degree of modernization.

The redistribution of Russians, of course, entailed mainly an
eastward dispersal from their traditional homeland in the western
USSR. Major factors involved included rural overpopulation and the
presence of turmoil in much of the western areas and the expansion
of opportunities in the eastern regions, especially with the rapid industrialization of this area during the Soviet era. The dominant position of the Russians within imperial and Soviet society enabled them
to take advantage of these opportunities, even when development occurred in non-Russian areas. As a result, the fairly highly dispersed
Russians became even more dispersed.

The Jews also experienced a significant eastward shift. They
shifted primarily from the Jewish Pale in the west, an area to which
their residence was generally limited during the tsarist era, particularly to such highly urbanized regions as the Center (Moscow), Northwest (Leningrad), and Central Asia. Much of this eastward shift was
caused by the substantial decline of the Jewish population in the Pale,
a decline that was, in turn, related to foreign emigration and especially to population losses associated with World War II. Nevertheless, there was also a significant migration of Jews to regions of economic development.

Like the Russians and Jews, the Tatars also shifted eastward.
In particular, they gravitated primarily from the Volga and South regions, the "homelands" of the Volga and Crimean Tatars, to the Urals
and Central Asia. Although part of this movement involved the forced
deportation of Crimean Tatars during World War II, the eastward migration of the more populous Volga Tatars was of great significance.

Thus, as expected, nationality groupings experiencing the greatest degree of interregional migration and dispersal were primarily
the more modernized ones. Although the distribution of the total population of the USSR generally has experienced an eastward shift since
1897 and 1926, the more advanced Russians, Jews, and Tatars were
the only groupings whose population distribution experienced an appreciable shift in this direction; as implied in Chapter 5, they moved eastward primarily in association with expanding urban-industrial activities in this area, partly because the indigenous work force of this
area had not been sufficiently advanced to provide the required labor
for such activities. Although most of the other groupings also experienced an eastward shift after 1897, these shifts were not as substantial, which is surprising in light of the fact that so many of these
groupings were subjected to war in their western homelands (especially Ukrainians, Belorussians, Lithuanians, and Moldavians and
Romanians).

The remaining seven groupings under investigation generally did not experience a high degree of interregional migration and dispersal. Undoubtedly, the lack of a more substantial dispersal was partly related to the fact that the individual nationalities have a great attachment to their homeland areas, especially now that these areas have been given official status in the Soviet era, and in many instances there has been sufficient economic development to absorb surplus labor. However, this does not mean that substantial out-migration will never occur from such areas. If local living standards deteriorate sufficiently, such a migration may transpire. In addition, the lack of a more appreciable dispersal of these groupings also partly reflects the fact that they are generally much less modernized than the Russians, Jews, and Tatars.

The major exception to this contention were the highly advanced Mobilized Europeans. Although they experienced a high degree of redistribution based upon the coefficient of redistribution, very little interregional migration of this grouping actually occurred. This grouping experienced a substantial relative shift from the West or Baltic region to the Transcaucasus, a shift primarily due to the relatively high population growth of Georgians and Armenians as compared to Latvians and Estonians. In 1970 roughly 90 percent or more of the population of each of the four nationalities of this grouping was still located in its respective economic region and, usually, republic. The lack of dispersal of the Latvians and Estonians can be primarily explained by the high level of economic development and substantial job opportunities existing within their titular republics, a situation that has been enhanced by their very slow rate of population growth. Nationalistic feelings also are undoubtedly of considerable importance.

The lack of dispersal on the part of Georgians and Armenians is more difficult to explain, particularly since their republics are not among the most economically developed areas of the USSR. Nevertheless, certain attributes of their economies seem to impede substantial out-migration. These include a very labor-intensive system of agriculture that helps absorb much of the local work force, participation in a number of illegal activities, and moderate levels of economic development. In addition, being highly educated peoples, the Georgians and Armenians are better able to respond to job opportunities in the modern sectors of their homelands than are, for example, the Central Asian nationalities. However, this situation may change in the future, since the Georgian and Armenian populations have been growing rather rapidly in recent years, although the rate of growth is apparently declining. Thus, increasing population pressure may occur, stimulating out-migration from these areas.

The other groupings that experienced comparatively little interregional migration and dispersal were, as to be expected, the less advanced peoples of the USSR. Some of these groupings did have a certain amount of redistribution based upon the coefficient of redistribution, but deeper investigation revealed that the degree of interregional migration and dispersal within the USSR was apparently not great, at least not as significant as in the cases of the Russians, Jews, and Tatars. Outstanding in this respect were the Finnic peoples. Their population shifted mainly eastward from the Northwest region. However, this shift was not due to a major eastward migration of Finnic peoples of the Northwest region but was, instead, primarily related to the evacuation of more than 400,000 Finns from this region to Finland in the early 1940s.

Three other less advanced groupings also experienced a noticeable redistribution in their population based upon the coefficient of redistribution: Turkic-Muslims, Ukrainians, and Moldavians and Romanians. The Turkic-Muslims shifted primarily from Kazakhstan to Central Asia. This redistribution was not, as might be surmised, due to a mass migration of Kazakhs to Central Asia. Instead, it was related to the great population losses experienced by the Kazakhs in the 1910s and 1930s caused by the considerable chaos in Kazakhstan during these periods and to the very high fertility of the major Central Asian nationalities. All in all, the less modernized Turkic-Muslims are still, as to be expected, among the least mobile peoples in the USSR, a situation that may change somewhat in the future as their very rapid rate of population growth results in increased population pressure and, in turn, migration.

The Ukrainian and Moldavian-Romanian groupings were similar in that they both tended to become noticeably more concentrated in their homelands. In both cases the share of their populations residing in the Ukraine and Moldavia, respectively, has increased appreciably. The increased concentration of Ukrainians in the Ukraine is of special interest because it appears to be related primarily to a high degree of Russification in areas outside the Ukraine. In particular, the formerly large rural Ukrainian populations of the adjacent North Caucasus and Central Chernozem regions have declined enormously, apparently because thousands of Ukrainians now declare themselves to be Russians. A similar process, in fact, apparently reduced the Ukrainian population, especially the rural Ukrainian population, of many other dominantly Russian regions. Thus, the Ukrainian population probably actually dispersed to a greater extent than our measures indicate, but such a movement was apparently not highly associated with modernization, and it is doubtful if it approached the degree of dispersal of the Russians, Jews, and Tatars.

Finally, we come to the opposite end of the spectrum, that is, to two groupings that were very highly concentrated in 1897 and 1926 and have tended to remain so: the Lithuanians and the Belorussians.

The vast majority of the population of each of these groupings was and continues to be found in their respective economic regions and republics (or areas approximating their present-day republics). The Lithuanians, in particular, presented the most extreme picture of high concentration and negligible redistribution. Of all the groupings, they had the highest dissimilarity index in all four census years and the lowest coefficient of redistribution in all six intercensal periods. In addition to their both being less advanced peoples, another factor tending to impede the interregional dispersal of the Lithuanians and Belorussians has been the great increase in the level of economic development of Lithuania and Belorussia in recent years.

In summary, with respect to the four major questions of this study, the following statements can be made:

1. Because the Russians are the dominant nationality, and because the Tatars, Jews, and Mobilized Europeans are socioeconomically and culturally well suited for modernized society, we would expect these groups to have experienced a relatively high degree of interregional migration and dispersal, with the remaining, less advanced minority groupings experiencing no substantial migration and dispersal.

2. Results revealed that, except for the Mobilized Europeans, such patterns did, in fact, occur. Indeed, of the ten groupings, the Russians, Tatars, and Jews are now the three most dispersed nationality groupings in the USSR.

3. Generally speaking, the distribution and redistribution patterns of the nationality groupings have not been the product of governmental policies directly aimed at their creation. However, there have been some exceptions to this generally valid conclusion, for example, the Jewish Pale of Settlement of tsarist Russia and the eastward deportation of many nationalities in World War II. Furthermore, many governmental policies have had an indirect influence, especially those concerned with regional patterns of industrial investment. For example, the eastward migration of Russians is obviously an indirect result of the policy aimed at rapid industrialization of eastern regions.

4. The interregional redistribution of Soviet nationalities involves many implications for Soviet society as a whole. First of all, it has affected the nationality composition of individual regions. Outstanding in this respect has been the impact of the redistribution of Russians. In virtually every region outside the traditional areas of Russian settlement, the Russian share of each region's population increased since 1897 and 1926. Also, as was discussed in Chapter 5, the migration of Russians has been to urban areas in particular, and this has involved additional implications.

DETAILED DISCUSSION

During the past century, the spatial distribution of the population of Russia and the USSR has undergone appreciable change. Although it has been reduced somewhat in recent years, the most notable change has been an overall shift toward the more easterly regions of the country. The overall west-to-east shift has been related, on the one hand, to extensive population decline associated with war, rural overpopulation, and out-migration in the west, and, on the other hand, to the expansion of both industrial and agricultural economic opportunities, relatively high fertility, and appreciable in-migration in the east. As will be seen, most of the individual nationality groupings have tended to shift eastward, although only a relatively few, notably the Russians, have done so to any substantial degree.

An investigation of the regional distribution and redistribution of the population of Russia and the USSR, as a whole, and of individual Soviet nationalities, in particular, entails a number of problems. The difficulties involved in such an investigation of both the total population and the population of individual nationalities are often similar, but there are also additional complexities peculiar to an examination of the nationalities. The problems concerning the total population will be discussed in greater depth in a later book concerned with general population redistribution in Russia and the USSR. At this point, only those problems associated with the study of nationalities will be discussed, although they may also be applicable to the total population.

Perhaps the outstanding difficulty involved in this investigation of the regional distribution and redistribution of the Soviet nationality groupings is the fact that we are concerned mainly with the interregional migration of these groupings, but appropriate data for a rigorous assessment of these patterns are lacking. Only in the 1926 and 1970 censuses are data available on the migration of individual nationalities, and these data are not extensive. Consequently, in order to assess the regional distribution and redistribution of the nationality groupings, we have had to utilize other indicators that could be derived for all groupings in each census year and each intercensal period. These indicators have been discussed in depth before and need only be summarized here. They include the percent of the population of a given grouping residing in each region, that is, the regional distribution of the population of a grouping; the percentage point change in that percent from one year to another; the coefficient of redistribution; the dissimilarity index; and the change in the dissimilarity index.

The first indicator is the basic index with the other four being derivations from this first index. The second index simply reveals the change, either positive or negative, in the percent of a given nationality residing in a given region, that is, the redistribution of each grouping on the basis of individual regions. The coefficient of redistribution is a summation of the positive values in the second index, and indicates the overall magnitude of the regional redistribution of a grouping. The dissimilarity index compares the distribution of a given grouping (that is, the first index) with that of the total population. As such, it suggests the degree of regional segregation or concentration of a grouping with respect to the total population; the higher the dissimilarity index, the more segregated or concentrated is the grouping in comparison to the total population. Finally, the change in the dissimilarity index suggests whether a group is becoming more concentrated or more dispersed with respect to the total population; a high positive value indicates increasing segregation or concentration, while a high negative value suggests increasing integration or dispersion. These indexes are included in Appendix Tables E.1 to E.10 and Tables 6.1 to 6.3.

Although these five indicators are useful for our analysis, they have a number of deficiencies. First, since they all involve the first index, the regional distribution of a nationality grouping, they all suffer from the fact that there are difficulties in measuring that distribution in all four census years. Such difficulties have been alleviated as much as possible, and revisions have been incorporated in the appropriate tables used in this study.

For example, for 1897 our allocation system had to be revised somewhat because it sometimes distorted the regional distribution of a nationality. According to our system, if, say, 30 percent of the total population of a given political unit fell within a given region, then 30 percent of the population of each characteristic, including each nationality, would likewise fall into that region. In some cases, this was an inappropriate procedure, because a given nationality may have been very concentrated in one part of that unit; that is, our system would say that 30 percent of the population of a given nationality would go to a given region, when in fact, most of that population would fall completely in another region.

For example, take the case of Kazan' Guberniya, which was essentially cut in half by a north-south trending boundary between the Volgo-Vyatsk region to the west and the Volga region to the east. Two main non-Russian nationalities that inhabited this guberniya were the Tatars and Chuvash. Consequently, because 63.8 percent of the total population of Kazan' Guberniya fell into the Volga region, we, accordingly, allocated 63.8 percent of, for example, the Tatar population to the Volga. Data for uyezdy, the first-order subdivision of a guberniya, revealed, however, that the overwhelming majority of the Tatar population actually resided in the eastern half of the guberniya, that is, the Volga region. Thus, our system allocated too many Tatars to the Volgo-Vyatsk and too few Tatars to the Volga. Similarly, the Chuvash

TABLE 6.1

Coefficient of Redistribution by Nationality Grouping: 1897–1970

Grouping	1897–1926	1926–59	1897–1959	1959–70	1926–70	1897–1970
Russians	5.8	15.8	18.8	2.8	17.7	21.0
Ukrainians	9.1	13.4	15.3	1.9	13.8	15.1
Belorussians	9.4	7.6	10.9	4.0	8.6	9.9
Tatars	15.8	23.1	30.7	2.3	24.2	31.8
Turkic–Muslims	7.9	10.4	16.4	2.6	11.5	17.4
Jews	14.3	34.7	46.7	2.7	36.1	48.3
Mobilized Europeans	7.8	15.5	20.9	3.9	18.8	24.5
Finnic peoples	9.8	25.7	20.4	4.8	25.5	21.7
Lithuanians	2.5	3.4	1.3	0.7	3.4	1.3
Moldavians and Romanians	3.4	15.8	15.9	1.7	16.3	16.5
USSR total	5.0	10.3	14.3	3.9	12.9	16.9

Sources: See Chapter 2, footnotes 2 and 3.

were highly concentrated in the west or Volgo-Vyatsk, but our system
allocated too many Chuvash to the Volga and too few to the Volgo-
Vyatsk.

Therefore, we have revised the original estimates of the regional
distribution for those nationality groupings whose distribution patterns
seemed to be distorted; for 1897 these included the Belorussians,
Tatars, Finnic peoples, Lithuanians, and Moldavians and Romanians.
These revisions were carried out in a fairly rough manner by examining the more specific location of the appropriate nationalities on the
basis of uyezdy and readjusting the regional distribution percentages.

For 1926 this problem was not as serious, because the political
units of 1926 more closely approximated those of the economic regions.
Therefore, unlike 1897, a large share of the 1926 units fell completely
into one region, so the problem of the subdivision of a unit was not as
great. In 1926 Kazan' Guberniya no longer existed; instead, the Tatar
and Chuvash ASSRs had been formed. Thus, the Chuvash ASSR encom-
passed the major part of the Chuvash population that formerly fell into
the western half of Kazan' Guberniya. Because the Chuvash ASSR fell
completely into the Volgo-Vyatsk region, our allocation system placed
this Chuvash population in the Volgo-Vyatsk region in the first place,
and hence no revision was necessary. The only major problem area
in 1926 was the distribution of Moldavians and Romanians with respect
to Moldavia and the Southwest and South regions. Our system allocated
too few Moldavians and Romanians to Moldavia. This was corrected by
investigating the location of the grouping by the subdivisions of the
province of Bessarabia in Romania in 1930, a unit that comprised the
bulk of present-day Moldavia.

Thus, for 1897 and, to a certain extent, for 1926, we have had
to make revisions in the original estimates of the regional distribution
of certain nationalities. Although these estimates are still not completely accurate (it would take a lifetime to make very precise estimates), the results are still essentially valid.

Problems of a different nature existed for 1959 and 1970. Because every unit fell completely into a given region there was no problem in the allocation of the available data. The problem, instead, involved the fact that, except for Russians and Ukrainians, the population
of a given nationality was not listed for each and every unit. For each
unit only the most populous nationalities in that unit were listed, with
the remaining nationalities being grouped together in an anonymous
"others" category. Therefore, for example, in 1970, the number of
Belorussians was not indicated for roughly ten units, even though
there were probably at least a few Belorussians in most of these units.
In general, this was no major problem in that these gaps were minor,
and we were still able to account for well over 90 percent of the population of each grouping.

A minor technical problem still existed, however. Our index of regional distribution involves the population of a grouping residing in a given region divided by the total population of that grouping for the USSR as a whole. For 1959 and 1970 two figures were available for the total population of the non-Russian and non-Ukrainian groupings: that available in the summary tables of the censuses and that which was the summation of the populations of the grouping for the 19 regions, a sum that was slightly lower than the total population as indicated in the census summary tables. We opted for the second figure (summation of the regional populations), primarily so that the percentages for each region would add up to virtually 100 percent and thus would be consistent with the procedures for 1897 and 1926. If we had used the census summary figure, the summation for the Turkic-Muslims would have been only about 96 percent. Consequently, because we have calculated changes in these percentages between each and every census year, we felt that consistency was necessary for all four years.

Actually, these problems are of very minor significance. The major patterns of distribution and redistribution would still emerge regardless of the basis for calculating the percentage regional distributions in 1959 and 1970. For example, according to our estimates, 97.7 percent of the Lithuanians resided in the West region in 1970. However, according to the 1970 Soviet census, 95.7 percent of the Lithuanians resided in this region. Thus, the difference in the results is inconsequential. We have pointed out these differences primarily to counter questions that may arise concerning differences between our figures and the percentage distributions listed in the census. Thus, these deviations are due to slight differences in the methods employed.

Perhaps the prime deficiency of our various indexes of distribution and redistribution is not so much these minor technical problems but the shortcomings with respect to their ability to measure what we want measured. We are particularly interested in investigating the interregional migration of each grouping, as our theme involves modernization and migration. However, such data generally are not available. Although our indicators of distribution and redistribution are certainly influenced by interregional migration, they are not exclusively a function of migration. Instead, they are determined by migration plus regional differences in natural increase and, as will be seen, ethnic assimilation. In short, the patterns of the regional redistribution of a grouping are highly related to patterns of regional population growth rates of that grouping, which are, in turn, a function not only of migration but also of fertility, mortality, and assimilation.

Our indicators may suggest that a given grouping has experienced a great degree of redistribution, when, in fact, very little migration has occurred. For example, the Mobilized Europeans have experienced a significant relative shift from the West region to the Transcaucasus. This has not meant that there has been a mass migration of Latvians and Estonians to the Transcaucasus. Rather, it reflects the fact that the Georgian and Armenian populations have been growing much more rapidly than the Latvian and Estonian populations, illustrating the importance of the natural increase component in the redistribution analysis. Hence, a higher proportion of the total Mobilized European population now resides in the Transcaucasus and, accordingly, a lower proportion now resides in the West. Although a redistribution of the population of this grouping has certainly occurred, this shift has not been because of migration.

On the other hand, although a substantial redistribution based upon our indexes does not necessarily mean that substantial interregional migration has occurred, substantial interregional migration most likely will be translated into a high degree of redistribution on the basis of our indicators. For example, as will be seen, the well-known interregional migration of Russians is reflected in our indicators.

Despite these problems, our indexes will have to suffice. Indeed, they are the most complete and rigorous data available concerning the regional distribution and redistribution of the Soviet nationalities over a fairly long period. As much as possible we will try to assess the importance of migration in any substantial amount of redistribution that is suggested by these indexes.

The framework for this chapter involves the following sequence of topics, that is, each grouping will be treated in terms of the following: First, the coefficient of redistribution will be examined to assess the extent of overall redistribution. This will be followed by a discussion of the dissimilarity index and changes therein in order to assess the degree of concentration or dispersal of the grouping. Then the regional patterns of redistribution will be discussed. Finally, attention will be given to the factors involved in the patterns, with special emphasis on the role of migration.

Russians

As is to be expected, the Russians have experienced appreciable dispersal, particularly from their traditional areas of settlement in the west to regions farther east, where between 1897 and 1970 the Russian population increased by roughly 25 million. In addition, whereas about 93 percent of the Russians resided in western regions in 1897, only 78 percent did so in 1970. So great has been the eastward shift that if 93 percent of the Russians still resided in the western USSR, the number of Russians residing in this area would exceed the actual Russian population by roughly 20 million.

TABLE 6.2

Dissimilarity Index by Nationality Grouping: 1897-1970

Grouping	1897	1926	1959	1970
Russians	37.2	36.2	29.4	29.9
Ukrainians	57.4	57.2	66.3	67.1
Belorussians	77.4	78.5	80.5	77.0
Tatars	59.6	66.3	57.6	55.5
Turkic-Muslims	66.8	65.7	63.6	62.5
Jews	60.2	52.0	31.8	31.2
Mobilized Europeans	81.4	83.1	88.1	87.2
Finnic peoples	64.3	65.9	65.9	63.7
Lithuanians	93.1	92.2	95.5	94.9
Moldavians and Romanians	79.8	81.5	86.8	85.7

Sources: See Chapter 2, footnotes 2 and 3.

A great share of the Russian dispersal has been to non-Russian
areas; between 1897 and 1970 the Russian population outside the RSFSR
increased by more than 15 million. As a result, more than 21 million
Russians now reside in the 14 non-Russian republics, and Russians
comprise nearly one-fifth of their total population. In addition, nearly
10 million Russians live in the "non-Russian" nationality units of the
RSFSR, and Russians now account for nearly one-half of their total
population.

The patterns of Russian distribution and redistribution can also
be examined in terms of the special indicators (see Tables 6.1 to 6.3).
These indicators suggest that the Russians have experienced a moderate
amount of redistribution and have been highly and increasingly dispersed.
That the Russians experienced a relatively moderate degree of redistribution is indicated by the fact that of the ten groupings, the Russian
coefficient of redistribution ranked fifth in both the 1897-1970 and 1926-
70 periods, and ranked either fourth or fifth in three of the other four
periods (Table 6.1). That their coefficient of redistribution was not
even higher as compared to other groupings was partly related to the
very large population of the Russians. For many of the groupings to
experience a high coefficient of redistribution, a shift of only a few
hundred thousand people is required. But, in the case of the Russians,
a shift of many millions of people is required to affect substantially
their overall distribution. Obviously, it is much more difficult for
the Russians to have a high coefficient of redistribution. Also, the

TABLE 6.3

Change in Dissimilarity Index by Nationality Grouping: 1897–1970

Grouping	1897–1926	1926–59	1897–1959	1959–70	1926–70	1897–1970
Russians	-1.0	-6.8	-7.8	0.5	-6.3	-7.3
Ukrainians	-0.2	9.1	8.9	0.8	9.9	9.7
Belorussians	1.1	2.0	3.1	-3.5	-1.5	-0.4
Tatars	6.7	-8.7	-2.0	-2.1	-10.8	-4.1
Turkic-Muslims	-1.1	-2.1	-3.2	-1.1	-3.2	-4.3
Jews	-8.2	-20.2	-28.4	-0.6	-20.8	-29.0
Mobilized Europeans	1.7	5.0	6.7	-0.9	4.1	5.8
Finnic peoples	1.6	0.0	1.6	-2.2	-2.2	-0.6
Lithuanians	-0.9	3.3	2.4	-0.6	2.7	1.8
Moldavians and Romanians	1.7	5.3	7.0	-1.1	4.2	5.9

Sources: See Chapter 2, footnotes 2 and 3.

Russian coefficient did not attain higher levels because the Russians were relatively highly dispersed in the first place, and could not experience a radical change in their distribution, except in the very unlikely event that appreciable concentration would occur.

The great dispersion of the Russians is further manifested by the fact that the Russians had the lowest dissimilarity index in all four census years (Table 6.2). Furthermore, even though the Russian dissimilarity index was very low in 1897, it still experienced a substantial further decline, suggesting an increased dispersal. Only the Jews had a greater decline between 1897 and 1970, and only Jews and Tatars had a greater decline between 1926 and 1970 (Tables 6.2 and 6.3). Only during the 1959-70 period did the Russian dissimilarity index fail to decline. This lack of decline can be attributed to several factors: because the dissimilarity index involves the distribution of the total Soviet population, the fact that this population was shifting to non-Russian areas with high rates of natural increase, especially Central Asia, meant that Russians were becoming more segregated with respect to the total population; the former dispersal of Russians, especially to the east, has greatly diminished, a topic that will be discussed in greater depth later; and because the Russians were so highly dispersed in the first place, it is difficult for them to experience continued substantial dispersion.

The Russian dissimilarity index is, of course, somewhat biased by the fact that Russians comprised roughly a majority of the population of Russia and the USSR. Since the dissimilarity index compares the distribution of the population of a given grouping with that of the total Soviet population, the Russian dissimilarity index will be quite low because the Soviet distribution is so highly influenced by the Russian distribution.

However, it should not be doubted that the Russians have been relatively highly dispersed and have tended to become even more dispersed since 1897 and 1926. The high dispersal of Russians can also be seen from other perspectives. First of all, as Appendix E reveals, the main region of Russian settlement in all four years, the Center, never comprised more than 26 percent of the Russian population. In contrast, usually well over 26 percent of the population of most of the other nine groupings has been concentrated in one region. For example, in 1970 the Center contained less than 20 percent of the Russian population, whereas, with the exception of Jews, well over 20 percent of the population of every other grouping was concentrated in one region. Also, in 1970, eight regions contained at least 5 percent of the Russian population. For all of the remaining groupings except Jews the corresponding number of regions was much smaller. Thus, the high dispersion of Russians is also in evidence on the basis of these regional perspectives.

TABLE 6.4

Percentage of Russians Residing in Traditional Regions
of Russian Settlement: 1897-1970

Region	1897	1926	1959	1970
Center	25.6	25.4	20.5	19.5
Central Chernozem	12.2	11.7	7.3	6.7
Urals	11.9	11.0	12.0	11.6
Volga	11.4	10.8	8.3	8.4
Northwest	10.4	10.9	8.7	8.7
Volgo-Vyatsk	8.7	7.1	5.5	4.9

Sources: See Chapter 2, footnotes 2 and 3.

That the Russian population has been dispersing is also quite
evident from Appendix E, Tables 6.3 to 6.6, and Maps 6.1 to 6.5,
which indicate that the Russian population has generally shifted eastward from its homeland in the western USSR. In particular, between
1897 and 1970, outstanding regions with a large percentage point decline in their percentage of the total Russian population were all in
the western USSR: the Center (-6.1), the Central Chernozem (-5.5),
the Volgo-Vyatsk (-3.8), the Volga (-3.0), and the Northwest (-1.7);
similar regional variations also existed during the Soviet era (1926-
70).

Another way of documenting this dispersal is to focus on the traditional regions of Russian settlement. Table 6.4 shows the percent-

TABLE 6.5

Percentage of Russians Residing in Eastern Regions: 1897-1970

Region	1897	1926	1959	1970
West Siberia	3.0	6.1	7.6	7.3
East Siberia	2.5	3.3	4.9	5.1
Far East	0.3	0.9	3.1	3.4
Kazakhstan	1.4	1.7	3.5	4.3
Central Asia	0.2	0.6	2.0	2.3

Sources: See Chapter 2, footnotes 2 and 3.

TABLE 6.6

Percentage Point Change in the Share of the Total Population Residing
in the Five Eastern Regions by Nationality Grouping:
1897-1970 and 1926-70*

Grouping	1897–1970	1926-70
Russians	15. 0	9. 8
Ukrainians	3. 9	-0. 8
Belorussians	4. 5	-1. 7
Tatars	12. 7	15. 7
Turkic-Muslims	5. 0	1. 0
Jews	9. 7	8. 4
Mobilized Europeans	0. 7	-0. 7
Finnic peoples	7. 6	4. 6
Lithuanians	0. 4	0. 2
Moldavians and Romanians	1. 1	0. 7
USSR total	11. 6	8. 5

*Calculated by the summation of the five individual percentage
point changes as found in Appendixes E.9 and E.10.

Sources: See Chapter 2, footnotes 2 and 3.

age of the Russian population residing in the six regions (Center, Central Chernozem, Urals, Volga, Northwest, and Volgo-Vyatsk), that
were the prime regions of Russian settlement in 1897 and 1926, prime
in the sense in that these regions had the six largest Russian populations and thus the six largest shares of the Russian population. As
Map 6.1 reveals, these regions form one bloc, in that each region
was contiguous with at least one of the other five regions. These regions both collectively and usually individually contained a smaller
proportion of the Russian population in 1970 than they did in 1897,
1926, or 1959 (Table 6.4). All together they contained more than four-
fifths of the Russian population in 1897, but by 1970 they accounted
for only three-fifths of that population. If this bloc of six regions still
contained four-fifths of the Russians, their Russian population would
exceed the actual Russian population by roughly 25 million.

It should be remembered that, although a substantial out-migration of Russians has occurred from all of these regions to other regions,
intraregional migration has also been significant. In particular, the
rapid industrialization of the Center, Urals, Volga, and Northwest re-

MAP 6.1

Regional Distribution of Russians: 1897

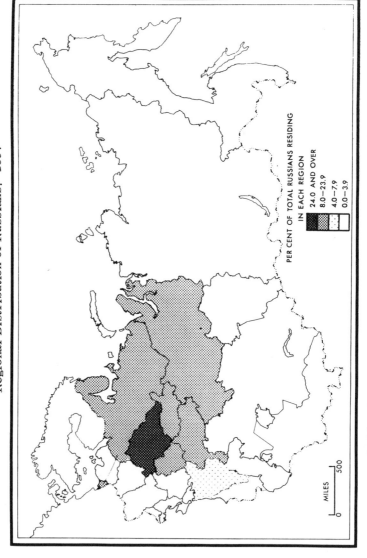

PER CENT OF TOTAL RUSSIANS RESIDING
IN EACH REGION

24.0 AND OVER
8.0—23.9
4.0—7.9
0.0—3.9

MILES
0   500

Source: Data compiled by the authors.

MAP 6.2

Regional Distribution of Russians: 1926

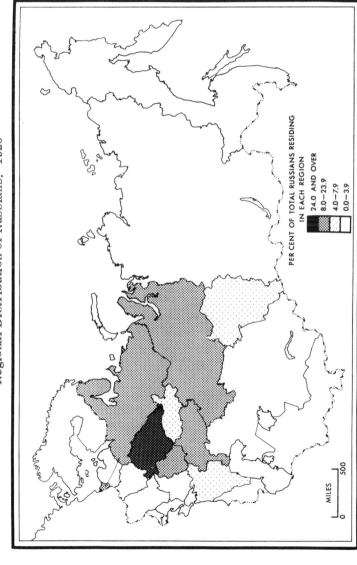

PER CENT OF TOTAL RUSSIANS RESIDING
IN EACH REGION

24.0 AND OVER
8.0 — 23.9
4.0 — 7.9
0.0 — 3.9

MILES
0   500

Source: Data compiled by the authors.

209

MAP 6.3

Regional Distribution of Russians: 1959

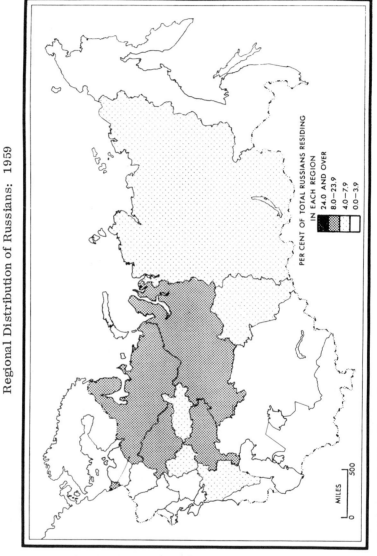

PER CENT OF TOTAL RUSSIANS RESIDING
IN EACH REGION

24.0 AND OVER
8.0—23.9
4.0—7.9
0.0—3.9

MILES
0   500

Source: Data compiled by the authors.

MAP 6.4

Regional Distribution of Russians: 1970

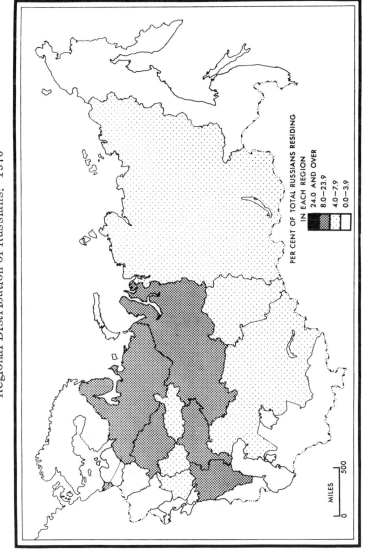

PER CENT OF TOTAL RUSSIANS RESIDING
IN EACH REGION

24.0 AND OVER
8.0—23.9
4.0—7.9
0.0—3.9

MILES
0   500

Source: Data compiled by the authors.

MAP 6.5

Regional Redistribution of Russians: 1897–1970

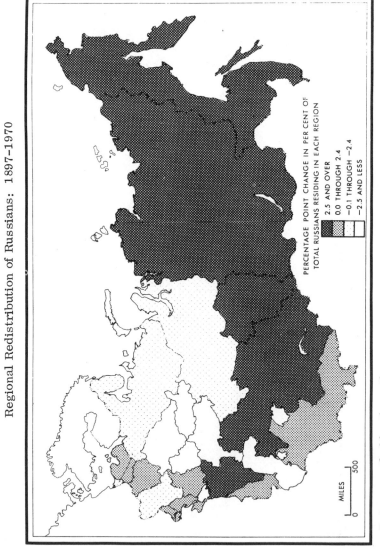

PERCENTAGE POINT CHANGE IN PER CENT OF
TOTAL RUSSIANS RESIDING IN EACH REGION

2.5 AND OVER
0.0 THROUGH 2.4
−0.1 THROUGH −2.4
−2.5 AND LESS

MILES
0   500

Source: Data compiled by the authors.

212

gions has promoted a substantial local rural-to-urban migration of
Russians. These movements, however, did not add to the Russian
population of the respective regions; consequently, they have not been
able to stop the shift in the Russian population away from these regions.

The Russian population, of course, has shifted primarily toward
the east. Between 1897 and 1970 outstanding regions with a large increase in their percentage of the total Russian population were all
in the eastern USSR (except for the North Caucasus): West Siberia
(4.3 percent), the Far East (3.1 percent), the North Caucasus (3.1
percent), Kazakhstan (2.9 percent), East Siberia (2.6 percent), and
Central Asia (2.1 percent). Roughly similar regional variations
existed between 1926 and 1970, although West Siberia was not as outstanding in this period. In fact, every eastern region had an increase
in its share of the Russian population in both the 1897-1970 and 1926-
70 periods. That the shift was eastward is further indicated by Table
6.5, which shows the percentage of the Russian population residing in
the five eastern regions. Both collectively and individually these regions contained a higher share of the Russian population in 1970 than
they did in 1897 and 1926. All together they contained less than one-
tenth of the Russian population in 1897, but by 1970 they accounted
for over one-fifth of that population. Of course, this means that the
share of the Russian population residing in the 14 remaining, or
"Western," regions declined from over 90 percent in 1897 to less than
80 percent in 1970.

The Russians were not alone in this eastward movement in that
the share of the population of all the other groupings residing in the
eastern regions also increased during one or both of these periods
(see Appendix E and Table 6.6). However, of the ten groupings, no
other grouping except Tatars and Jews experienced a substantial percentage point increase in the share of its population residing in the
east, a fact that will become obvious throughout the remainder of this
chapter.

The eastward shift of the Russian population, of course, is
partly related to regional variations in war losses. Because the western areas have suffered more than eastern areas in this regard, population losses in the western areas have been much higher. Consequently, this has tended to lessen the growth of the Russian population
in the west.

However, migration also has been of crucial importance in the
west-to-east shift of the Russian population. This migration has been
discussed in Chapter 5 and will be discussed in greater detail in a
subsequent volume devoted to population distribution and redistribution
in the USSR. Consequently, it will be considered only briefly here.
This migration primarily has been due to rural overpopulation in the

west and expanding opportunities in the east. Rural impoverishment
was especially characteristic of the Russian areas of European Russia in the late nineteenth century. Major factors contributing to this
impoverishment included a rapidly growing population, a decline in
per capita land area, high taxes, redemption payments, agricultural
technological backwardness, deficiencies of the communal system, and
a relatively poor natural environment for agriculture.[1] As a result,
the predominantly Russian gubernii encircling Moscow Guberniya
were characterized by a relatively high degree of out-migration, according to the 1897 census.[2] Even in more recent years, Central
European Russia has still been a major area of rural out-migration.[3]

Increased opportunities in the east have occurred in both the
agricultural and industrial sectors. Russian migration to agricultural
areas has been associated with the increased exploitation of virgin and
idle land east of the Urals, both in the pre-Soviet period and the Soviet
era, especially around the turn of the century and since the mid-1950s
in northern Kazakhstan and West Siberia. Increased opportunities in
the east have been even greater in industry. These opportunities have
arisen primarily in the Soviet period in association with the governmental policy of industrializing the mineral-rich east.

During recent years this migration to the east has been reversed
somewhat. The Soviet government is having difficulty keeping people
in the east once they have moved there, and net out-migration from
some eastern areas has occurred recently. That West Siberia has been
a prime area of net out-migration is reflected in Table 6.5. Between
1959 and 1970 the share of the Russian population residing in West
Siberia declined, the only case where an eastern region had a declining
share of the Russian population in any intercensal period, although, as
Table 6.4 reveals, the Urals, which is often regarded as an "eastern"
region, experienced a similar decline. The main point is that, as hypothesized, the relatively advanced and dominant Russians have experienced an appreciable degree of population redistribution, a redistribution that has been one of dispersal and one highly related to migration.

The impact of the dispersal of Russians has been profound. For
example, it has brought changes in the nationality composition of most
regions. In every region beyond the six traditional regions of Russian
settlement, the percent of the regional population comprised by Russians increased between 1897 and 1970, a trend that occurred also between 1926 and 1970, with the exception of Moldavia (see Table 6.7).
Other implications of this dispersal are discussed in Chapters 5 and 10.

Ukrainians

The Ukrainian population has experienced relatively little dispersal from its homeland. Between 1897 and 1970 the enumerated

Ukrainian population beyond the Ukrainian Republic did not increase at all, for all practical purposes, totaling slightly more than 5 million in each census year. At the same time, the Urkainian population of the Ukrainian Republic has increased by more than 16 million. Thus, the Ukrainians actually have become relatively more concentrated in their homeland, despite the tremendous war losses in this area.

These patterns are reflected in Tables 6.1 to 6.3, which suggest that the Ukrainians have not experienced a high degree of redistribution, and that what redistribution has occurred has been primarily one of concentration rather than dispersal, thus tending to concentrate further a population that already was not highly dispersed. That Ukrainians have not redistributed to a relatively great extent is suggested by the fact that of the ten groupings their coefficient of redistribution ranked eighth in the 1897-1970 period and seventh in the 1926-70 period, positions they held in three of the remaining four periods; in no period did they rank higher than fifth (Table 6.1).

The fairly high degree of concentration of the Ukrainian population is revealed in Tables 6.2 and 6.3. Table 6.2 suggests that the Ukrainian population actually has been relatively highly dispersed, especially because its dissimilarity index was relatively low in 1897 and 1926, ranking ninth and eighth among the ten groupings. However, the Ukrainian dissimilarity index actually was relatively high in these two years in that it was always over 50 and was generally much closer to the fifth ranking grouping than to the lowest ranking grouping (that is, Russians). Furthermore, by 1959 and 1970 the Ukrainian dissimilarity index had increased to the high 60s and ranked fifth in both cases. Thus, the Ukrainian population actually has been much more concentrated than a cursory ranking of the groupings would tend to suggest.

That the Ukrainian population has become increasingly concentrated is indicated further by Table 6.3, which shows that the Ukrainian dissimilarity index increased considerably. Indeed, in four periods (1897-1970, 1926-70, 1897-1959, 1926-59, and 1959-70), the Ukrainians had the highest positive change in their dissimilarity index of any of the ten groupings. This indicates that the Ukrainian population, in general, has been concentrating to a greater degree than any other grouping.

The high degree of Ukrainian concentration involves the Ukrainian Republic itself (see Map 6.6). Generally speaking, roughly 80 percent of the Ukrainian population resided in this republic in all four census years, with the Southwest always accounting for slightly less than one-half of the Ukrainian population, the Donetsk-Dnepr for roughly one-fourth to one-third, and the South for less than one-tenth (see Appendix E and Table 6.8). Despite the general stability of these proportions, however, the three regions of the Ukrainian Republic collectively and individually had a higher share of the Ukrainian population

TABLE 6.7

Russians as a Percentage of the Total Population by Economic
Region: 1897–1970

Region	1897	1926	1959	1970	Percentage Point Change 1897–1970
Northwest	72.4	83.9	86.6	86.6	14.2
West	5.9	6.3	17.1	19.1	13.2
Center	93.3	96.0	94.5	94.1	0.8
Volgo-Vyatsk	78.5	78.4	76.4	75.2	-3.3
Central Chernozem	82.0	84.3	96.0	96.4	14.4
Volga	65.0	69.4	75.6	75.4	10.4
Belorussia	5.3	5.6	8.2	10.4	5.1
Moldavia	8.5	11.8	10.2	11.6	3.1
Southwest	4.9	2.3	6.0	6.7	1.8
South	19.6	19.0	30.9	34.0	14.4
Donetsk-Dnepr	18.1	14.6	26.1	29.1	11.0
North Caucasus	44.8	42.6	76.4	72.3	27.5
Transcaucasus	4.3	5.7	10.2	7.9	3.6
Urals	72.4	73.7	73.3	73.2	0.8
West Siberia	84.1	77.4	85.3	87.6	3.5
East Siberia	66.6	72.8	80.4	81.3	14.7
Far East	43.6	47.2	81.2	84.9	41.3
Kazakhstan	16.0	22.0	42.7	42.4	26.4
Central Asia	2.2	5.8	16.4	15.1	12.9
USSR total	44.4	47.5	54.6	53.4	9.0

Sources: See Chapter 2, footnotes 2 and 3.

MAP 6.6

Regional Distribution of Ukrainians, Belorussians, Mobilized Europeans, Finnic Peoples, Lithuanians, and Moldavians and Romanians: 1970

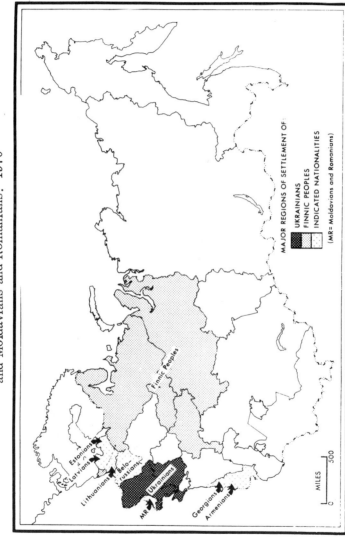

Source: Data compiled by the authors.

TABLE 6.8

Percentage of Ukrainians Residing in the Three Regions of the
Ukrainian SSR: 1897–1970

Region	1897	1926	1959	1970
Southwest	46.6	44.3	47.8	47.3
Donetsk-Dnepr	23.9	26.4	30.8	30.7
South	7.4	5.8	7.7	8.6

Sources: See Chapter 2, footnotes 2 and 3.

in 1970 than they did in 1897 and 1926. In particular, between 1897
and 1970, the share of the Ukrainians residing in the Donetsk-Dnepr
region increased by 6.8 percentage points, the share in the South increased by 1.2 points, and the share in the Southwest increased by
0.7 points. In absolute terms, the Ukrainian population of these three
regions increased by roughly 7 million, 2 million, and 8 million persons, respectively. These increases can be explained partly by the
increased tendency between 1897 and 1926 of Ukrainians to declare themselves as Ukrainians and by the change in the definition of "nationality"
between the tsarist and Soviet periods. In the 1897 census nationality
was defined by native language; since many Ukrainians declare Russian
as their native tongue, there was no doubt an underenumeration of
Ukrainians in the tsarist census. However, even between 1926 and
1970 similar regional variations were in evidence in that these three regions experienced the greatest increases in the share of the Ukrainian
population during this period also. Indeed, between 1926 and 1970 the
Ukrainian population of the Donetsk-Dnepr, South, and Southwest regions increased by roughly 3 million, 1.5 million, and 3.5 million,
respectively. These trends are truly astonishing, especially considering that the Ukrainian population losses associated with war and collectivization have been especially heavy in the Ukrainian Republic itself.
    Even more astonishing is the fact that, as Appendix E and Table
6.8 indicate, the increased concentration of the Ukrainians occurred
primarily between 1926 and 1959, a period that included collectivization, famine, and World War II. Although the Ukrainian population did
not decline in each of the three Ukrainian regions between 1926 and
1959, it increased only very slowly and altogether the Ukrainian population of the Ukrainian Republic increased by only 17.4 percent, or
0.5 percent per year between 1926 and 1959. Therefore, the increasing concentration of the Ukrainian population in the Ukrainian Republic
during this period was not due to rapid growth of the Ukrainian popula-

tion, and, consequently, it was evidently not due to a mass influx of Ukrainians back to this republic.

Deeper investigation suggests that this increased concentration was caused primarily by the rapid decline of the Ukrainian population in two regions outside the Ukrainian SSR. The regions in question are two regions of the RSFSR that are adjacent to the Ukrainian Republic: the North Caucasus and the Central Chernozem. As Appendix E reveals, both regions were the prime areas of Ukrainian settlement in regions beyond the Ukrainian Republic in 1897 and 1926. In 1926, for example, they accounted for 8.7 and 4.7 percent of the total Ukrainian population, respectively, figures unsurpassed by any other region outside the Ukrainian SSR. Indeed, the North Caucasus actually had more Ukrainians than did the South region, one of the three regions of the Ukrainian Republic. By 1959, however, the North Caucasus and the Central Chernozem contained only 1.0 and 0.8 percent of the Ukrainian population, percentages roughly duplicated in 1970. Between 1926 and 1959 the predominantly rural Ukrainian population in the North Caucasus declined by 88.2 percent, or from more than 3.1 million to less than 400,000; in the Central Chernozem the decline was by 82.9 percent, or from more than 1.6 million to less than 300,000. In short, between 1926 and 1959 the large Ukrainian population of the North Caucasus and Central Chernozem regions declined by roughly 4 million people and had largely vanished.

Russification was almost certainly the reason for this reduction. It has been noted, for example, that the growth of the Russian population of the USSR perhaps has been partly due to the assimilation of other peoples, in particular, the Ukrainians of the Kuban' area and other portions of the North Caucasus region.[4] Indeed, the Soviet Ukrainian author Ivan Dzyuba notes that during the 1930s Ukrainian cultural and educational centers in the North Caucasus were "dispersed by the Terror," and defenders of the "Ukrainian character" were wiped out. According to Dzyuba, many Ukrainians in this area have been afraid to admit to being Ukrainians ever since.[5] The propensity toward the Russification of Ukrainians in the North Caucasus was apparent in the 1926 census also. In the "North Caucasus Kray" in the 1926 census, a region roughly similar to the North Caucasus region of this study, nearly one-half (42.9 percent) of the Ukrainians considered Russian to be their native language. In comparison, corresponding figures for the USSR as a whole (1,926 boundaries) and the USSR outside the Ukrainian SSR (1,926 boundaries) were only 12.6 and 33.1 percent, respectively. Inasmuch as linguistic shifts are highly related to ethnic assimilation, additional credence is given to the Russification hypothesis.

A similar pattern was not apparent at this time in the Central Chernozem region, however. In the "Central Chernozem region" of the 1926 census, a region roughly similar to the Central Chernozem region of this study, only 10.3 percent of the Ukrainians regarded Russian as their native language.

By 1959, however, a very high degree of Russification in the Central Chernozem region was apparent. In that year 75.3 percent of the Ukrainians in the Central Chernozem regarded Russian as their native language, a truly incredible figure given the fact that the vast majority of the Ukrainians in this region still resided in rural areas. Not unexpectedly, this figure was well above the national average of 12.2 percent and the average for the USSR outside the Ukrainian Republic of 48.4 percent. The North Caucasus region continued to have a relatively high percentage of Ukrainians speaking Russian as their native language (57.5) in 1959. These patterns suggest a strong tendency toward Russification, and it appears that the great decline in the Ukrainian population of the North Caucasus and the Central Chernozem regions was probably due to the fact that the bulk of the Ukrainians in these regions simply declared themselves to be Russians in the 1959 and 1970 censuses. This high degree of Russification apparently resulted from the fact that the Ukrainian rural population resided for quite a long time among a more numerous Russian population.

A similar type of Russification probably has been responsible for the lack of a substantial increase in the enumerated Ukrainian population of many other regions. Between 1926 and 1959 the Ukrainian population also declined considerably in West Siberia, the Volga, and Kazakhstan. Like the North Caucasus and Central Chernozem, these regions were areas where large Ukrainian rural populations resided for a long time within major areas of Russian rural settlement.

It is worthwhile to emphasize that this Russification has occurred primarily in rural areas. This situation is quite unusual in that the Russification of most non-Russian nationalities actually has been much greater in urban areas than in rural areas (see Chapter 5). But in the above cases, where a Ukrainian rural population was exposed for a fairly long time to a large Russian population, an extremely high degree of rural Russification has occurred. Indeed, in 1970 the percent of rural (census definition) Ukrainians in the RSFSR considering Russian to be their native language was, amazingly, almost equal to the corresponding percentage for the Ukrainian urban (census definition) population of the RSFSR (55.6 and 58.2 percent, respectively)!

Thus, one of the reasons for the lack of dispersal of the enumerated Ukrainian population has been the high degree of Russification of the Ukrainians residing beyond the Ukrainian Republic itself. It appears that more substantial numbers of Ukrainians did move eastward, but such movements were not apparent in the census data, because by the time a later census was taken, many Ukrainians decided to declare themselves as Russians.

However, although a greater migratory dispersal of the Ukrainians actually occurred than census data would at first indicate, such a movement was not necessarily highly associated with modernization, because it involved mainly a rural-to-rural movement. In addition, even if the Ukrainians who dispersed still declared themselves to be Ukrainians, it is quite unlikely that the Ukrainian population would have a degree of dispersal, as measured by the indexes used in this study, which would be comparable to that of Russians and Jews.

All in all, the Ukrainians have tended to remain fairly highly concentrated in their homeland. That there has been no significant dispersion of this population appears to be also primarily the result of the following factors: the comparatively low educational level of the Ukrainians, which impedes their migration toward major areas of modern economic development outside the Ukrainian Republic; the presence of substantial opportunities within the Ukrainian SSR itself, including those resulting from the relatively good, in the Soviet context, local agricultural resource base and significant local industrialization (in 1970, the Ukrainian SSR was the leading republic with respect to the percent of total arable land, and it contained a greater number of industrial workers than any other republic save the RSFSR[6]; the lack of chronic rural population pressure, due not only to the fairly good agricultural resource base but also to low rural fertility, to the extensive loss of life associated with collectivization, famine, and war, and to the fact that it was colonized rather late (it is interesting to note, however, that although such an indicator is not a completely valid measure of rural population pressure, the rural population per unit of arable land of the Ukrainian Republic was lower than that of most other republics [Table 6.9]); and attachment to the Ukrainian homeland. It must be acknowledged, however, that all groups have a strong attachment to their homelands. Nevertheless, economic and demographic conditions can impel people to leave their homelands, regardless of their nationalistic feelings; witness, for example, the millions of Europeans who left their homelands during the past two centuries.

Belorussians

The Belorussians have shown no great tendency to disperse and, consequently, have remained very highly concentrated in Belorussia itself. These patterns are reflected in Tables 6.1 to 6.3 and in Map 6.6. That the Belorussians have not redistributed to any great extent is indicated by the fact that during the 1897-1970 and 1926-70 periods, only one grouping, the Lithuanians, had a lower coefficient of redistribution (Table 6.1). They have remained highly concentrated

TABLE 6.9

Number of Rural Inhabitants per Sown Hectare by Republic: 1970
(census definition of rural)

Republic	Number	Republic	Number
RSFSR	0.4	Turkmen SSR	1.8
Ukrainian SSR	0.7	Tadzhik SSR	2.4
Belorussian SSR	0.8	Kazakh SSR	0.2
Estonian SSR	0.6	Georgian SSR	3.3
Latvian SSR	0.6	Armenian SSR	2.5
Lithuanian SSR	0.7	Azerbaydzhan SSR	2.1
Uzbek SSR	2.1	Moldavian SSR	1.3
Kirgiz SSR	1.5		

Sources: 1970 Soviet census (see Chapter 2, footnote 2); and
Narodnoye Khozyaystvo SSSR v 1970 G., p. 300.

also because their dissimilarity index always has been relatively high
(approximately 80) and has changed very little, either in one direction
or another (Tables 6.2 and 6.3), and the percentage of the Belorussian
population residing in Belorussia remained remarkably high and stable, being 81.2 in 1897, 82.9 in 1926, 84.4 in 1959, and 80.7 in 1970.
Except for Lithuanians, no other grouping was so highly and so consistently concentrated in one region.

As with Ukrainians, this consistently high concentration is even
more remarkable considering the fact that the growth of the Belorussian population in Belorussia has been slow, primarily because it
fell within the fighting zone during both world wars. In addition, similar to the Ukrainians, rural Russification appears to have contributed
to the lack of dispersal. In particular, the Belorussian population
has declined substantially since 1926 in West Siberia and East Siberia,
predominately Russian regions that contained relatively large Belorussian rural populations in 1926. It thus appears that, like the Ukrainians,
large numbers of Belorussians in these regions have changed their
nationality to Russian. Such a high tendency toward Russification is
suggested by the fact that, similar to the Ukrainians, the Belorussian
rural population of the RSFSR in 1970 was very highly Russified in
that more than one-half (53.7 percent) of this population (census definition) considered Russian to be its native language. Thus, it seems
that a more substantial number of Belorussians actually moved to
Russian areas. However, as with the Ukrainians, it should be remem-

bered that such a movement was not that highly associated with modernization, since it was oriented toward rural areas. Furthermore, it is doubtful that the Belorussian indicators of dispersal would be comparable to those of the Russians and Jews even if many of these Belorussians had not changed their nationality to Russian.

Other major factors in the slight dispersal of the Belorussian population are again quite similar to those mentioned for the Ukrainians. These include a relatively low educational level; alleviation of rural population pressure due to appreciable population losses associated with wars (this is reflected in the fact that the majority of the republics had a higher rural population per unit of arable land than Belorussia in 1970 [Table 6.9]); and increased local opportunities with the rapid industrialization of Belorussia during the 1960s (see Chapter 5).

Tatars

The Tatars have dispersed to a much greater extent than most other groupings. In fact, between 1926 and 1970 the Tatar population residing outside the Tatar "homeland" (Tatar ASSR and Crimean Oblast) increased by roughly 3 million. In contrast, the Tatar population within this homeland area increased by only 200,000, with that of the Crimean Oblast being virtually reduced to nothing. As a result, whereas almost one-half of the Tatars resided in the two "homeland" units in 1926, by 1970 only slightly more than one-fourth lived in these areas.

The great dispersal of the Tatars is also reflected by the indicators in Tables 6.1 to 6.3. They reveal that the Tatars have experienced a significant amount of redistribution, especially a high degree of dispersion, patterns not unexpected given their relatively high degree of modernization, particularly in comparison to the other Turkic-Muslims. The high degree of redistribution is indicated by the fact that of the ten groupings, the Tatar coefficient of redistribution was surpassed only by the Jews between 1897 and 1970 and only by the Jews and Finnic peoples between 1926 and 1970 (Table 6.1). Indeed, in only one period (1959-70) did the Tatar coefficient of redistribution fail to rank first, second, or third among the ten groupings. By this latest period appreciable redistribution was not to be expected, because the Tatar population had already become relatively highly dispersed.

The dispersal of the Tatar population is suggested by their generally relatively low dissimilarity index and by the general decline in that index (Tables 6.2 and 6.3). Although the Tatar dissimilarity index has not been as low as that of the Russians and, more recently, the Jews, it did rank eighth in every year save 1926. In short, the Tatar population has been relatively highly dispersed. Furthermore, the Tatar dissimilarity index has declined, often substantially, indicating a continued dispersal of this population. Indeed, only three groupings had a greater decline between 1897 and 1970, and only one (Jews) had a greater decline between 1926 and 1970.

Appendix E, Table 6.6, and Maps 6.7 to 6.11 reflect this dispersal on the basis of individual regions. Like the Russians, an eastward shift has been in evidence. Between 1897 and 1970 regions in which the share of the Tatar population declined most substantially were the Volga (-11.8 percentage points) and the South (-6.3); similar patterns existed for 1926-70 in that these two regions occupied the exact same positions. Because the Volga and South regions contained the homelands of the Volga and Crimean Tatars, respectively, this suggests a dispersal from the Tatar homeland. Whereas in 1897 and 1926 these two regions combined comprised slightly more than one-half of the Tatar population, by 1970 they comprised only roughly one-third of this population. That relatively few Tatars resided in their homeland is further reflected by the fact that in 1970 only slightly more than one-fourth of the Tatars lived in the Tatar ASSR; no other nationality with its own SSR or ASSR had such a small proportion of its total population residing in the political unit bearing its name. Also, less than 7,000 Tatars resided in the Crimean Oblast in the same year.

The considerable eastward shift of the Tatar population is reflected in Table 6.10. Only the Russians had a greater increase in the share of its population residing in the five eastern regions collectively between 1897 and 1970, and between 1926 and 1970 the Tatars had the greatest increase. As will be discussed below, Central Asia was the most significant eastern region in this regard.

That the Tatar population has shifted eastward is also exemplified by the fact that between 1897 and 1970 the share of the Tatar population residing in individual regions increased to its greatest extent in the Urals (13.6 percentage points) and Central Asia (12.0); these two regions also occupied the two leading positions between 1926 and 1970. However, only Central Asia can be regarded as a truly new area of Tatar settlement, since the Urals has always contained a high proportion of the Tatar population. Indeed, except for the Tatar ASSR, no ASSR, oblast, or kray had a larger Tatar population in 1970 than did the Bashkir ASSR of the Urals region.

It appears that migration has been the prime factor in this dispersal of the Tatar population. The Crimean Tatars were, of course, forced to migrate to the east following their alleged collaboration with the Germans during World War II, thus accounting for the decline in the South region and for a part of the Central Asia increase.[7]

MAP 6.7

Regional Distribution of Tatars: 1897

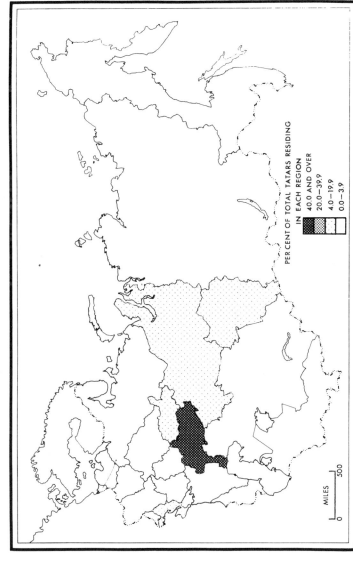

PER CENT OF TOTAL TATARS RESIDING
IN EACH REGION

40.0 AND OVER
20.0—39.9
4.0—19.9
0.0—3.9

MILES
0   500

Source: Data compiled by the authors.

225

MAP 6.8

Regional Distribution of Tatars: 1926

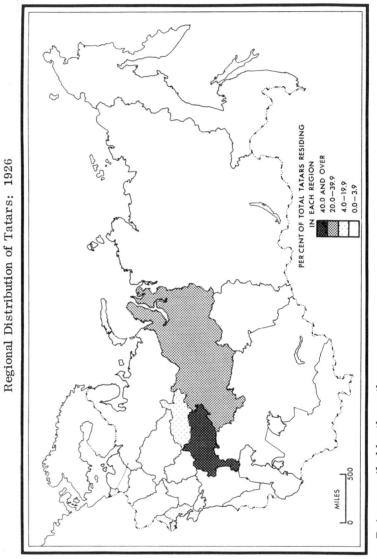

PER CENT OF TOTAL TATARS RESIDING
IN EACH REGION

40.0 AND OVER
20.0—39.9
4.0—19.9
0.0— 3.9

MILES
0   500

Source: Data compiled by the authors.

226

MAP 6.9

Regional Distribution of Tatars: 1959

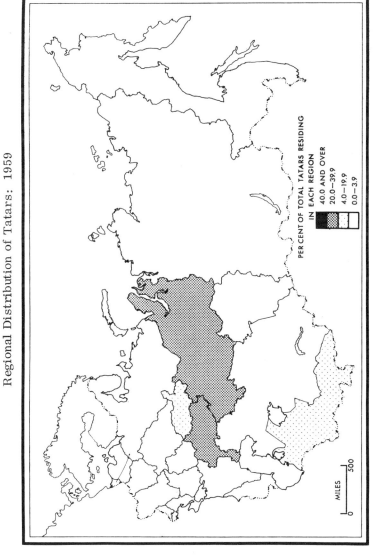

PER CENT OF TOTAL TATARS RESIDING
IN EACH REGION

40.0 AND OVER
20.0—39.9
4.0—19.9
0.0—3.9

MILES
0 500

Source: Data compiled by the authors.

227

MAP 6.10

Regional Distribution of Tatars: 1970

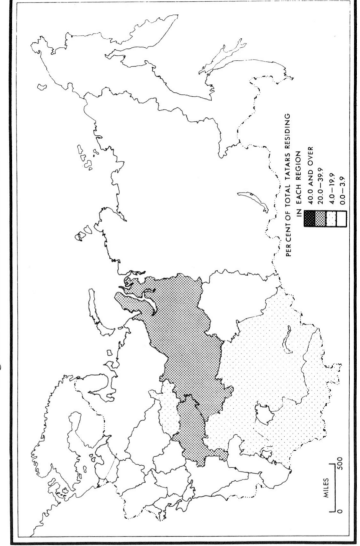

Source: Data compiled by the authors.

MAP 6.11

Regional Redistribution of Tatars: 1897–1970

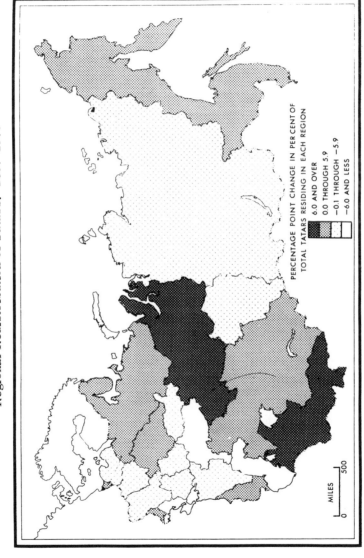

PERCENTAGE POINT CHANGE IN PERCENT OF
TOTAL TATARS RESIDING IN EACH REGION

6.0 AND OVER
0.0 THROUGH 5.9
−0.1 THROUGH −5.9
−6.0 AND LESS

MILES
0   500

Source: Data compiled by the authors.

229

TABLE 6.10

Percentage of Tatars Residing in Main Regions of Tatar Settlement:
1897-1970

Region	1897	1926	1959	1970
Volga	45.0	50.5	34.5	33.2
Urals	18.0	26.0	32.1	31.6
Volgo-Vyatsk	9.9	5.1	4.4	4.0
South	6.4	6.2	0.0	0.1
Central Asia	0.7	1.3	12.0	12.7

Sources: See Chapter 2, footnotes 2 and 3.

It appears, however, that the Crimean Tatars did not account
for most of the total shift of the Tatar population to Central Asia, and,
accordingly, the migration of the Volga Tatars was of relatively great
importance. It should be noted, first of all, that between 1926 and
1959 the Tatar population of Central Asia increased very rapidly
from 38,902 to 587,915, or by an estimated 549,013. It is difficult
to assess the Crimean Tatar share of this increase because none of
the four censuses presents data for Crimean Tatars, per se. Particularly crucial is the fact that the 1959 and 1970 censuses do not indicate how many Crimean Tatars lived in Central Asia. We do know,
however, that the Tatar population of the Crimean ASSR in 1926 was
179,094. Also, according to figures presented by Robert Conquest,
the Crimean Tatar population numbered roughly 202,000 in 1936 and
220,000 to 230,000 on the eve of deportation in 1944.[8] He notes that
a considerable number of the Crimean Tatars died during the deportation period, both during the roundup and on the trains to the east.[9]
Conquest has assessed the various estimates of these losses and concludes that the "Crimeans appear to have risen once more to about
their pre-war number."[10]
    This conclusion seems to be generally valid in light of the sub-
stantial losses involved. Although not all of the Crimean Tatars were
shipped to Central Asia, it seems reasonable to conclude that there
were roughly 200,000 Crimean Tatars in Central Asia in 1959. Assuming that there were virtually no Crimean Tatars in Central Asia
in 1926, this obviously means that the Crimean Tatar population of
Central Asia increased by roughly 200,000 between 1926 and 1959.
(That most of the Tatars in Central Asia in 1926 were Volga Tatars
and not Crimean Tatars is suggested by place-of-birth data from the

census. According to these data, the number of people residing in Central Asia who were born in the Tatar ASSR was many times as great as those residing in Central Asia who were born in the Crimean ASSR. For example, in Tashkent Okrug, the political unit of Central Asia containing the largest number of Tatars in 1926, 5,014 people were born in the Tatar ASSR, while only 319 were born in the Crimean ASSR.) However, the total Tatar population of Central Asia increased by roughly 550,000 over the same period. Therefore, it appears that the Volga Tatar population of Central Asia increased by roughly 350,000.

Assuming that the Volga Tatars accounted for virtually all of the 39,000 Tatars residing in Central Asia in 1926, this means that the Volga Tatar population of Central Asia increased roughly nine times, or roughly 7 percent per year between 1926 and 1959. Such a rate could obviously only be attained by a great amount of net in-migration. Even if the Crimean Tatar population of Central Asia in 1959 was, say, 300,000, this would still mean that the Volga Tatar population increased by 250,000, that is, more than six times, or approximately 6 percent per year. Such a rate would still suggest a very substantial net in-migration of Volga Tatars to Central Asia.

The main concern here is not a precise estimate of the number of Crimean Tatars in Central Asia but rather that a sizable part, perhaps even the majority, of the rapid increase in the Tatar population in Central Asia can be attributed to the migration of Volga Tatars to Central Asia in response to economic opportunities. If this contention is agreed upon, it can be concluded that a large proportion of the shift of the Tatar population to Central Asia can be attributed to voluntary migration. In short, the relatively modernized Tatars, as expected, have experienced a relatively high degree of voluntary geographic mobility, a movement particularly oriented to urban areas (see Chapter 5).

Turkic-Muslims

Not unexpectedly, the relatively less modernized Turkic-Muslims have experienced notably little population redistribution. In fact, over 90 percent of their population resided in their major traditional regions of settlement in all four census years. In regions beyond those of traditional settlement, their population increased by well under 1 million people between 1897 and 1970, a rather small figure for a grouping that increased by roughly 16 million overall and now numbers more than 30 million.

This low degree of geographic mobility is reflected in Tables 6.1 to 6.3. The inappreciable redistribution is indicated by the fact

that the coefficient of redistribution for the Turkic-Muslims ranked
only sixth in the 1897-1970 period and only eighth in the 1926-70 period; in fact, it ranked either sixth or eighth in all six periods (Table
6.1).

Tables 6.2 and 6.3 suggest that the Turkic-Muslim population
has been relatively highly dispersed and has shown a trend toward
even slightly greater dispersion. Table 6.2 reveals that their dissimilarity index was around the seventh highest. The relatively high degree of dispersion suggested by this index, of course, reflects the
fact that the Turkic-Muslim grouping is an amalgam of many nationalities that are not necessarily concentrated in one region. However,
this grouping has not been nearly as dispersed as the Russians and,
more recently, the Jews. Table 6.3 reveals that, although their dissimilarity index has remained roughly the same, it has declined
slightly. The conclusion that this indicates a significant dispersal of
the Turkic-Muslims is somewhat misleading, as will be seen.

Appendix E, Table 6.11, and Map 6.12 reveal that, for the
most part, the regional redistribution of this grouping almost exclusively has involved their two main regions of settlement, Central
Asia and Kazakhstan. Indeed, between 1897 and 1970 Central Asia
had by far the biggest increase of any region in its share of the Turkic-
Muslims (14.1 percentage points), while Kazakhstan had the biggest
decline (-9.6); both regions occupied similar positions between 1926
and 1970. In short, the main shift in the Turkic-Muslim population
has involved a shift from Kazakhstan to Central Asia.

It appears that this shift has not been due to a mass migration
of Kazakhs to Central Asia. Although between 1926 and 1959 the
Kazakh population of the Central Asian region increased by 65.0 percent, this represents an increase of only 1.6 percent a year, a rate
that can be explained almost entirely by the natural increase of
Kazakhs already residing in Central Asia. Instead, the prime explanation for the great decline experienced by Kazakhstan was the great
reduction in the Kazakh population. This decline was, in turn, related
chiefly to increased interaction between the Kazakhs and the Russians.
During the last years of tsarist Russia, an extensive Russian colonization of the steppes of Kazakhstan occurred. This colonization upset
the economy of traditionally nomadic Kazakhs because they were expelled from the best grazing lands and, in many cases, had to undertake a sedentary existence.[11] In addition, in 1916 the government
attempted to mobilize the Kazakhs for labor at the front, even though
traditionally this nationality had been exempt from military service.[12]
As a result of altered economic and military conditions, the Kazakhs
revolted. This revolt was suppressed by the government, leading to a
substantial emigration of Kazakhs to adjacent Chinese territory.[13]

TABLE 6.11

Percentage of Turkic-Muslims Residing in Main Regions of
Turkic-Muslim Settlement: 1897-1970

Region	1897	1926	1959	1970
Central Asia	34.8	40.8	47.9	48.9
Kazakhstan	25.1	22.3	14.9	15.5
Transcaucasus	12.4	11.7	14.5	14.7
Urals	10.7	6.4	5.8	4.9
North Caucasus	8.1	8.1	7.5	8.1
Volgo-Vyatsk	4.0	4.3	3.8	2.8
Volga	2.3	2.9	2.2	1.9

Sources: See Chapter 2, footnotes 2 and 3.

The largest decline in the Kazakh population, however, took
place during the 1930s. During this period a further colonization of
the Kazakh steppe occurred, this time in the form of Soviet collectivization. The Kazakhs again were expelled from much of their best
grazing lands and forced to abandon their traditional nomadic life.[14]
Many responded by slaughtering their livestock and emigrating to
China.[15] All in all, due to the deteriorating food situation and emigration, the Kazakh population of the USSR declined from almost 4 million in 1926 (most of whom resided in Kazakhstan) to barely more than
3 million in 1939.[16] Taking natural increase into consideration, it
has been estimated that the Kazakhs actually suffered a loss of 1.5
million people.[17]

These trends are reflected by the fact that the total Turkic-
Muslim population of Kazakhstan declined between both 1897 and 1926
and between 1926 and 1959. The former decline was only roughly
20,000, while the latter was nearly 700,000. Hence, it is not surprising that the share of the Turkic-Muslims residing in Kazakhstan
declined during both of these periods, especially between 1926 and
1959.

If the great increase in the share of Turkic-Muslims residing
in Central Asia cannot be explained by a mass influx of Kazakhs, how
can it be explained? This increase was due mainly to comparatively
rapid population growth of the major Central Asian nationalities
(Uzbeks, Tadzhiks, Kirgiz, and Turkmens). Based upon our estimates for the present-day boundaries of the USSR, the population of
the four Central Asian nationalities collectively increased by 44.4

MAP 6.12

Regional Distribution of Turkic–Muslims: 1970

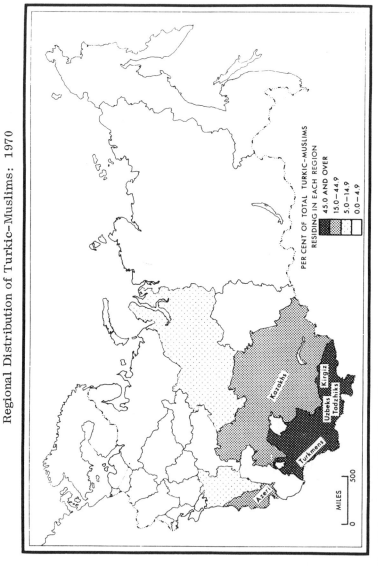

PER CENT OF TOTAL TURKIC–MUSLIMS
RESIDING IN EACH REGION

45.0 AND OVER
15.0–44.9
5.0–14.9
0.0–4.9

Kazakhs

Kirgiz

Uzbeks

Tadzhiks

Turkmens

Azeri

MILES

0   500

Source: Data compiled by the authors.

234

percent between 1926 and 1959, with the Uzbeks having the highest rate in particular (50.9 percent).* In contrast, the remaining Turkic-Muslims in the USSR increased by only 31.4 percent excluding Kazakhs and by only 16.0 percent including Kazakhs.

Aside from the Kazakh situation, the comparatively high rate of growth of the major Central Asian groups appears to have been related, in turn, to their relatively high fertility; the fact that many Turkic-Muslims in the North Caucasus region experienced substantial losses in association with their deportation in World War II; and their location.

The relatively high fertility of the major Central Asian nationalities is reflected by the available nationality child-woman ratios from the 1959 census. Table 7.9 reveals that each of the four major Central Asian nationalities had a higher child-woman ratio than every other major Turkic-Muslim nationality except for the Kazakhs, Chechens, and Ingush. Their high fertility notwithstanding, these latter three groups still experienced meager, if any, population growth between 1926 and 1959. The Kazakh situation has already been discussed. The Chechens and the Ingush, two nationalities that reside along the northern slopes of the Caucasus Mountains, suffered population losses, like the Crimean Tatars, in their deportation during World War II. Between 1939 and 1959 the population of the Chechens, by far the largest of the two groups, increased by only about 10,000, from 408,000 to 419,000. A similar fate also befell two other Turkic-Muslim groups of the North Caucasus region, the Karachay and Balkars.[18] Not surprisingly, as Table 6.11 reveals, the North Caucasus share of the total Turkic-Muslim population declined between 1926 and 1959, a trend further intensified by the relatively low fertility of other groups of this region, especially, as Table 7.9 reveals, the Avars, Dargins, and Kumyks. All of the deported nationalities of the North Caucasus, however, were allowed to return to their homelands in the late 1950s.

The low fertility of the Turkic-Muslims outside Central Asia in comparison to that of those within Central Asia also helps to explain the generally declining share of the Turkic-Muslim population residing in other regions besides Kazakhstan and the North Caucasus. As Table 6.11 indicates, this trend is especially characteristic of the Urals, the Volgo-Vyatsk, and the Volga regions. The Chuvash, who had the lowest child-woman ratio of any Turkic-Muslim nationality in 1959 (Table 7.9), particularly influenced the Volgo-Vyatsk (the location of the Chuvash ASSR) and Volga declines. The Bashkirs

---

*The Uzbek population of 1926 here consists of three nationalities listed in the 1926 census: Uzbeks, Kurama, and Kipchaks. Similarly, the Tadzhiks consist of the Tadzhiks and Yagnobtsy.

heavily influenced the decline in the Urals region, the home of the
Bashkir ASSR. This decline has been related not only to the relatively
low fertility of the Bashkirs but also to population losses associated
with conflict in the early twentieth century and to apparent assimilation.
Substantial population losses occurred during the Civil War in 1920
when the Soviets conquered the Bashkir lands.[19] As a result, the
Bashkir population of Russia and the USSR declined from roughly 1.5
million in 1897 to 1 million in 1926.*

In addition, it appears that a large share of the Bashkir population has been assimilated not by the Russians, but by the Tatars, their
more advanced and culturally similar neighbors. Indeed, in 1959
more than one-third (35.3 percent) of the Bashkirs considered Tatar
to be their native language, a partial reflection of, as touched upon
in the previous section, the sizable Tatar population in the Bashkir
ASSR; in fact, in 1970, there were actually more Tatars than Bashkirs
in the Bashkir ASSR!

Finally, location also has seemingly played a significant role
in the relatively rapid growth of the major Central Asian nationalities.
Being located on the southern periphery of the USSR, they have not
been subjected to the great pressures placed upon the indigenous
groups of other Turkic-Muslim areas; that is, those pressures associated with the Russian colonization of Kazakhstan and Bashkiria and
the German invasion route through the North Caucasus.

The only region outside Central Asia to experience a notable
increase in its share of the Turkic-Muslims has been the Transcaucasus, one of the main regions of Turkic-Muslim settlement (Appendix
E and Table 6.11). In both the 1897-1970 and 1926-70 periods, the
number of the Turkic-Muslims residing in this region increased, being surpassed only by Central Asia in the extent of the percentage
point increase, although Central Asia did have a much higher increase.
The Transcaucasus increase reflects the relatively rapid growth of
the Azeri, the main Turkic-Muslim nationality of this region. Indeed,
between 1926 and 1959 the Azeri population of the present-day USSR
increased by 64.2 percent, which was even faster than the Uzbeks, the
most rapidly growing Central Asian nationality during this period.
This partly reflects the fairly high fertility of the Azeri, as Table 7.9
suggests. In addition, like the Central Asians, their location has
favored a relatively high growth rate in that they also reside primarily
on the southern periphery of the USSR and have avoided population
losses due to Russian colonization and war.

---

*The Bashkir population of 1897 and 1926 consists of three na-
tionalities as listed in each census: Bashkirs, Mishars, and Teptyars
in 1897 and Bashkirs, Mishars, and Teptyars in 1926.

In summary, the population of the Turkic-Muslims has shifted to Central Asia and the Transcaucasus primarily because of the rapid growth of the major indigenous Turkic-Muslim peoples of these regions. In turn, such growth has been related to the relatively high fertility of these peoples and to the peripheral location of these regions, which has helped to minimize population losses associated with Russian colonization and German invasion. Accordingly, a combination of relatively low fertility, population losses associated with conflict and deportation, and assimilation accounted for a generally declining share of the Turkic-Muslim population residing in most of the other major regions of settlement of this grouping outside Central Asia and the Transcaucasus—Kazakhstan, the North Caucasus, the Urals, the Volgo-Vyatsk, and the Volga.

Despite these regional shifts, however, the Turkic-Muslim population has experienced very little migration, especially migration not associated with turmoil. It should not be concluded that the decline in the dissimilarity index for the Turkic-Muslims represents a significant dispersal on their part. Rather, it reflects the fact that the distribution of Turkic-Muslims has been becoming more similar to that of the total Soviet population because the rapidly growing Turkic-Muslims are themselves comprising an increasing share of that total population.

Other indicators testify to the low geographic mobility of the Turkic-Muslims. An investigation of Table 6.11 reveals that well over 90 percent of the Turkic-Muslims resided in the same seven regions in all four census years. In addition, the six major Turkic-Muslim nationalities that have SSR status still tend to be highly concentrated in the economic region that includes the republic bearing their respective names. Particularly outstanding are the four major Central Asian nationalities and the Azeri. In 1970 roughly 95 percent or more of the population of each of these nationalities resided in Central Asia or the Transcaucasus, respectively. Only the Kazakhs have a relatively smaller proportion, but even here roughly 80 percent of this population was found in Kazakhstan. Furthermore, at least three-fourths and usually more than four-fifths of the population of each of these six nationalities were found in their respective SSRs.

The low mobility of the Turkic-Muslims is also reflected in the available migration data from the 1970 census.[20] According to these data, 5.7 percent of the total population of the USSR in 1970 was "migrants," that is, generally speaking, people who changed their place of residence in the previous two years. Corresponding percentages are listed for 44 major nationalities, including 25 Turkic-Muslim groups. With the exception of three small nationalities of Siberia (Yakuts, Khakasy, and Tuvinians), every Turkic-Muslim nationality had a percentage below the national average. Furthermore, some of

these groups had the very lowest percentages of all the 44 nationalities.
Except for Georgians and Armenians, every nationality with a percentage below 2 percent was a Turkic-Muslim nationality. These included
Uzbeks, the single largest Turkic-Muslim nationality, Azeri, Turkmens, Karakalpaks, and Abkhaz, with the Azeri having the lowest
percentage of any of the 44 nationalities.

The low mobility of the Turkic-Muslims reflects their less modernized status (for example, low education); their general lack, until
recently, of rapid population growth and consequent heightened rural
population pressure; and the lack of more substantial local urban opportunities (see Chapters 5 and 10). Thus, the Turkic-Muslims, as
might be expected, have experienced little interregional migration and
dispersal. There will be more migration in the future, however, in
that rapid population growth and increasing rural population pressure
probably will promote substantial out-migration from rural areas,
especially in Central Asia (see Chapter 10).

Jews

The Jews have experienced an exceptionally high degree of population redistribution in the USSR. From a grouping that was previously
highly confined to the western borderlands of the Russian Empire, they
have come to be one of the most dispersed Soviet nationalities.
Whereas most Jews formerly resided in the western borderlands,
only roughly one-half do today. Indeed, if most of the Jews still resided in this extreme western portion of the USSR, the Jewish population of this area would exceed the actual present-day number of Jews
in this area by roughly 1 million, a not inconsiderable population when
it is remembered that only 2 million Jews remain in the USSR today.

The radical change in the geographic distribution of the Jewish
population is dramatized further in Tables 6.1 to 6.3. A very high
degree of redistribution is indicated by the fact that the Jews always
had a relatively high coefficient of redistribution (Table 6.1); they
had the highest coefficient of any of the ten groupings during the 1897-
1970 and 1926-70 periods, as well as two other periods (1926-59 and
1897-1959). In one other period (1897-1926) they ranked second and
in the one remaining period (1959-70) they still ranked as high as
fifth. Similar to the Tatars, their relatively lower coefficient of redistribution in the 1959-70 period reflects the fact that they are now
so highly dispersed that further appreciable redistribution is not
probable.

The high degree of Jewish dispersal also is substantiated by
Tables 6.2 and 6.3. First of all, the Jewish dissimilarity index
never ranked higher than seventh (Table 6.2). In fact, in 1959 and

1970 only the Russians had a lower index, and the Jewish index almost equaled that of the Russians. Thus, the Jews were almost as dispersed as the Russians. Russians and Jews stand alone in this respect in that none of the other eight groupings had a dissimilarity index that was within 20 points of that of Jews. Furthermore, in all periods except for 1959-70, the Jews had by far not only the greatest change but also the greatest negative change in the dissimilarity index, indicative of a sizable dispersal. Whereas the dissimilarity index of the other nine groupings never changed by more than 11 points in any intercensal period either positively or negatively, and for all practical purposes remained much the same, that of the Jews declined by almost 30 points between 1897 and 1970 and by more than 20 points between 1926 and 1970.

The dispersal of the Jews attains added significance when it is realized that the Jews were even more concentrated or segregated in 1897 than previously implied. Although only three other groupings had a lower dissimilarity index in 1897, the Jewish dissimilarity index was actually comparatively high in that it was roughly 60 and was closer to the second ranking grouping (Mobilized Europeans) than it was to the tenth ranking grouping (Russians).

Furthermore, the Jews were highly concentrated in that their residence was largely confined to a very small portion of the Russian Empire, in particular in dominantly non-Russian areas. This confinement of Jewish settlement was but one example of many anti-Semitic actions by the tsarist government during the latter decades of its existence. In particular, Jewish residence was restricted to a bloc of 25 gubernii in the extreme western borderlands of the empire, including the ten Polish gubernii and 15 other gubernii collectively known as the Jewish Pale of Settlement.[21] The overall success of this policy is indicated by the fact that in 1897, 94.9 percent of the Jewish population of the Russian Empire resided in these 25 gubernii. Although more than one-fourth of the gubernii of the Russian Empire was involved, the 25 gubernii, especially those of Poland, were very small and thus Jewish settlement was very highly concentrated in a relatively small area of the empire.

It is somewhat difficult to delineate the Jewish Pale and Poland on the basis of the economic regions, because the western borderland area is one of the few areas where the international boundary of tsarist Russia differed substantially from that of the present-day USSR. Most significant is the fact that the ten Polish gubernii now lie primarily and usually completely outside the present-day USSR. Hence, for the most part, the Jews residing in these gubernii in 1897 are not included in any of the 19 economic regions. This loss was partially offset by the inclusion in the economic region structure of those Jews residing outside the Russian Empire in 1897 in the provinces of Galicia

and Bukovina of Austria-Hungary, parts of which are now in the USSR.
The six regions listed in Table 6.12 serve as the best approximation
of this main area of Jewish residence that can be made on the basis
of the economic regions, although they exclude areas within the Pale
and Poland (especially the Polish gubernii) and include areas that did
not fall within this zone (especially Galicia, Bukovina, much of the
West region).

Because each of the six regions involved is contiguous to at
least one of the remaining five regions, they form a bloc. For convenience, hereafter this bloc will be referred to as the "Pale," although it does not coincide exactly with the actual former Pale. As
Table 6.12 indicates, well over 90 percent of the Jewish population in
1897 resided in this modified "Pale." Thus, although the Jewish population was spread out among six economic regions, it was actually
concentrated in one comparatively small region, as Map 6.13 also
readily attests to. Furthermore, it is noteworthy to add that based
on the 19 economic regions, the dissimilarity index of the Jews with
respect to the Russians was 86.9, more than 25 points above the Jewish dissimilarity index with respect to the total population (Table 6.2).
Thus, not only was the Jewish population highly concentrated but, as
was the intention of the tsarist government, the Jews were largely
excluded from the main areas of Russian settlement.

The great dispersal of the Jews can also be seen in Appendix E,
Table 6.12, and Maps 6.12 to 6.16. They reveal that the share of
Jewish population residing in the "Pale" has declined substantially.
In fact, whereas more than 90 percent of the Jewish population resided
in these six regions collectively in 1897, by 1959 and 1970 only slightly
more than one-half of the Jewish population could be found in this bloc

TABLE 6.12

Percentage of Jews Residing in Regions Approximating the Jewish
Pale: 1897-1970

Region	1897	1926	1959	1970
Southwest	43.5	38.4	18.8	17.4
Belorussia	21.1	15.8	7.1	7.0
West	11.0	7.6	3.1	3.1
South	8.4	10.0	8.4	8.1
Donetsk-Dnepr	5.5	8.3	11.9	11.0
Moldavia	4.2	3.7	4.5	4.6

Sources: See Chapter 2, footnotes 2 and 3.

MAP 6.13

Regional Distribution of Jews: 1897

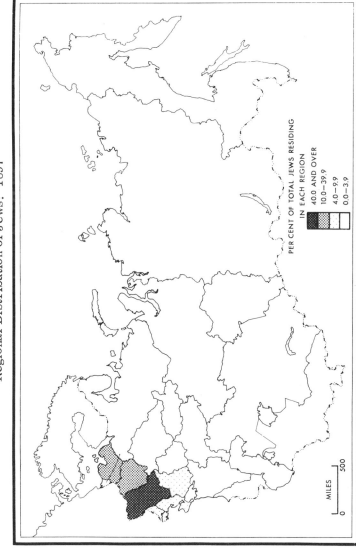

PER CENT OF TOTAL JEWS RESIDING
IN EACH REGION

40.0 AND OVER
10.0—39.9
4.0—9.9
0.0—3.9

MILES
0   500

Source: Data compiled by the authors.

241

MAP 6.14

Regional Distribution of Jews: 1926

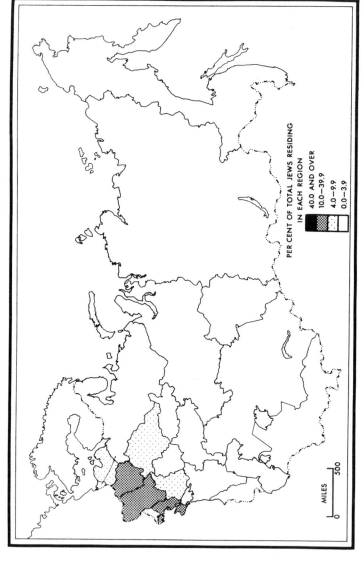

Source: Data compiled by the authors.

242

MAP 6.15

Regional Distribution of Jews: 1959 and 1970

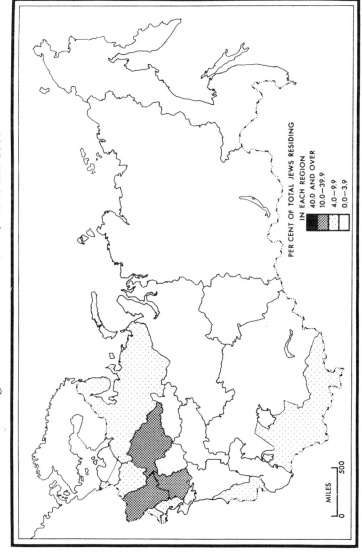

PER CENT OF TOTAL JEWS RESIDING
IN EACH REGION
40.0 AND OVER
10.0—39.9
4.0—9.9
0.0—3.9

MILES
0   500

Source: Data compiled by the authors.

243

MAP 6.16

Regional Redistribution of Jews: 1897–1970

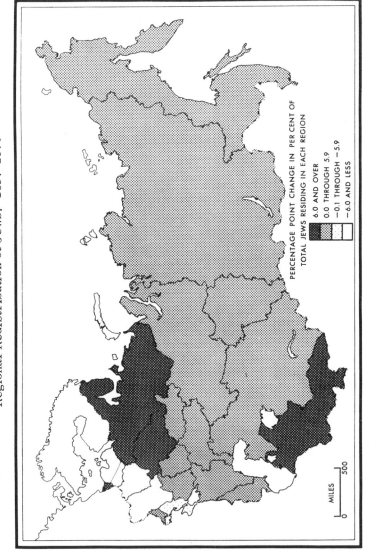

PERCENTAGE POINT CHANGE IN PER CENT OF
TOTAL JEWS RESIDING IN EACH REGION

6.0 AND OVER
0.0 THROUGH 5.9
−0.1 THROUGH −5.9
−6.0 AND LESS

MILES
0   500

Source: Data compiled by the authors.

244

of regions. Indeed, the share of the Jewish population residing in individual regions between 1897 and 1970 declined to its greatest extent in individual "Pale" regions. Outstanding were the Southwest (-26.1), Belorussia (-14.1), and the West (-7.9). These same three regions occupied the same ordinal positions between 1926 and 1970.

The regions that experienced the greatest increase in their share of the Jewish population between 1897 and 1970 were the Center (13.2 percentage points), the Northwest (7.3 percent), and Central Asia (6.0 percent); these same three regions experienced the greatest increases between 1926 and 1970 also. As Appendix E reveals, by 1970 two of these regions comprised a larger share of the Jewish population than did some regions within the "Pale," namely, the Center and Northwest, which accounted for 15.1 and 8.8 percent of the Jewish population in 1970, ranking second and fourth, respectively, in this regard. In fact, in 1970 nearly one-fifth of the Soviet Jews were found either in Moscow or Leningrad, including urban settlements subordinated to their city soviets, and in each city Jews were the second most populous nationality. Only the Southwest had a higher percentage (17.4) than the Center and only the Southwest and Donetsk-Dnepr (11.0) had higher percentages than the Northwest. The Donetsk-Dnepr was the only "Pale" region to experience a substantial increase in its share of the Jewish population between both 1897 and 1970 and 1926 and 1970. The big shift of the Jewish population toward such highly urbanized and industrialized regions as the Center, Donetsk-Dnepr, and Northwest reflects the disproportionate participation of Jews in modern urban-industrial activities in the USSR (see Chapter 5).

Thus, the Jewish population has shifted eastward. At first glance, this may seem to be a misleading statement. First, because Jewish residence was so highly concentrated in the extreme western portion of Russia and the USSR, any substantial shift in their population within the USSR would necessarily be eastward. In addition, although the major regions (the Center and Northwest regions) to which the Jewish population shifted are east of most of the "Pale," they can hardly be regarded as eastern regions of Russia and the USSR as a whole. Nevertheless, the Jews did experience a substantial eastward shift even when the five most easterly regions of the USSR are used as the criterion for "east" (Table 6.6). Indeed, of the ten groupings, only the Russians and Tatars experienced a greater eastward redistribution.

Furthermore, it is probable that the dispersal of the Jews was even greater than indicated by the measures used in this study because of the high degree of Russification of the Jewish population. As Table 5.10 suggests, the Jews are probably the most Russified of all Soviet nationalities. Not unexpectedly, they reach very high levels of Russification in the RSFSR; in 1970, for example, 87.8 percent of the Jews in the RSFSR considered Russian to be their native language as compared to the corresponding figure of "only" 78.2 percent for the entire USSR. Therefore, it seems reasonable to conclude that a relatively large number of Jews in the RSFSR changed their nationality to Russian. Consequently, as with the Ukrainians and Belorussians, this has tended to reduce the actual number of Jews residing in the east.

It is interesting to note that, as implied above and as Appendix E indicates, the Far East was not the prime eastern region involved in the eastward shift of the Jews, because in 1970 only about 1 percent of the Jews resided in this region. One might have expected the Far East to be more significant in this regard because it contains the Jewish Autonomous Oblast, the political unit established for Jews in 1934. That this unit has been of virtually no significance to the Soviet Jews is reflected by the fact that in 1970 only 11,452 Jews resided here. This accounted for less than 1 percent of all Soviet Jews and, in fact, for only 6.6 percent of the population of the Jewish A. O. itself.[22]

The eastward dispersal of the Jewish population, of course, has been related to the great population losses in the "Pale" associated with foreign emigration and especially with the tremendous local devastation during World War II. The emigration of Jews was especially pronounced during the 1897-1926 period. In fact, an estimated 1.25 million Jews emigrated from Russia between 1898 and 1914.[23]

However, the major Jewish losses occurred during the 1926-59 period, the period including World War II. Not surprisingly, the Jewish population in all six regions of the "Pale" declined between 1926 and 1959; in fact, it declined in all six regions during the 1897-1970 and 1926-70 periods. The greatest declines were experienced by the Southwest (from 1,875,000 in 1897 to 370,000 in 1970), Belorussia (from 911,000 to 148,000), and the West (from 475,000 to 66,000). All in all, the Jewish population of the "Pale" declined by roughly 2.3 million, or 66.7 percent between 1926 and 1959; by almost 3 million, or 73.1 percent between 1897 and 1970; and by more than 2.3 million, or 68.3 percent between 1926 and 1970, not taking into consideration natural increase.

It might be gathered from such patterns that the eastward movement of Jews was more artificial than real, because it may be surmised that regions east of the Pale experienced an increase in their share of the Jewish population not because of substantial Jewish inmigration, but as a result of losses in the western areas. In general, however, although the tremendous Jewish losses in the "Pale" certainly promoted increasing percentages in other regions, it appears that much of this increase was due to migration and an actual increase in the Jewish population in the more easterly regions. In fact, the Jewish population increased in absolute numbers in all but two of the 13 regions beyond the "Pale" in both the 1897-1970 and 1926-70 periods and in all but three of these 13 regions between 1926 and 1959, the main period of the Jewish population decline.

This substantial increase in the Jewish population in areas beyond the "Pale" has been related particularly to migration. During World War I a large number of Jews were evacuated from the "Pale" to more easterly regions and apparently they never returned to the west.[24] With the removal of legal barriers to Jewish migration, the migration of Jews from overcrowded towns in the "Pale" to cities in more easterly regions continued in the Soviet era.[25] Alec Nove and J. A. Newth note that 324,000 Jews migrated from the west to the east between 1926 and 1939.[26] Accordingly, the Jewish population of the Ukraine and Belorussia declined between 1926 and 1939, while that of the RSFSR increased rapidly from 589,000 to 948,000.[27] This movement continued when many Jews were evacuated to the east during World War II.

Another reflection of the Jewish migration to the east was the very rapid growth of the Jewish population in many of these regions. In particular, in four regions (Urals, Far East, Kazakhstan, and Central Asia), the Jewish population roughly tripled or more than tripled between 1926 and 1959; indeed, in the Far East and Kazakhstan it increased by about seven times. A tripling over such a time period entails an average annual rate of increase of approximately 3.5 percent. Such a rate could generally be accomplished only by the existence of net in-migration. This is especially true in the case of the Jews, because they have had relatively low fertility and, consequently, low natural increase.

Thus, the Jews have experienced a substantial amount of migration and dispersal, a not unexpected movement given the high degree of modernization of the Jewish population. According to Soviet education data, Jews are far and away the most advanced major nationality in the USSR. For example, in 1970 the proportion of Jews with a higher education (complete or incomplete) was at least twice the corresponding proportion for the Georgians, the next most highly educated major Soviet nationality. Their high degree of modernization was dramatized even further in Chapter 5, which was concerned with urbanization.

Although the dispersal of the Jews was partly related to factors not necessarily associated with the process of modernization, it still was similar to the redistribution that would be expected from a relatively advanced group under peacetime conditions. In particular, Jewish migration involved a flow from small overcrowded towns in the "Pale" to large urban-industrial agglomerations beyond their traditional region of settlement, especially Moscow, Leningrad, and the Donets Basin.[28] Such a migration involved a substantial degree of modernization, and would be expected under normal conditions (see Chapter 5).

Mobilized Europeans

Despite the fact that they are relatively advanced and highly educated (see Table 9.4), the Mobilized Europeans have dispersed to a small degree. Indeed, most of the Georgians, Latvians, and Estonians still reside in their own republic, while most of the Armenians are still either in their own republic or in the adjacent republics of the Transcaucasus. However, because the Georgians and Armenians have been growing much more rapidly than their Baltic counterparts, the Mobilized European population has shifted greatly from the West region to the Transcaucasus.

Many of these patterns are reflected in Tables 6.1 to 6.3. In general, these tables suggest that the Mobilized Europeans have experienced relatively substantial redistribution, but it has been a movement entailing increasing concentration of an already highly concentrated population. That this grouping redistributed to a fairly substantial extent is indicated by the fact that of the ten groupings it had the third highest coefficient of redistribution between 1897 and 1970, a position it also occupied in the 1897-1959 and 1959-70 periods (Table 6.1).

The high degree of concentration of the Mobilized Europeans is indicated by Tables 6.2 and 6.3. Of the ten groupings they had the second highest dissimilarity index in all four years (Table 6.2). In addition, their dissimilarity index increased during the 1897-1970 period and in most of the other periods (Table 6.3). Only two other groupings had a greater increase in their dissimilarity index between 1897 and 1970, suggesting that the Mobilized European population has become increasingly concentrated.

Appendix E and Table 6.13 reveal that the distribution and redistribution of the Mobilized Europeans have involved primarily the two regions comprising their "homeland": the Transcaucasus and the West. These two regions combined, in fact, contained roughly 90 percent or more of the Mobilized Europeans in all four census years (Map 6.6). Furthermore, not only has this grouping been highly concentrated in these regions but, generally speaking, each of the four component nationalities has been highly concentrated in its own republic. In 1970 over 90 percent of the Georgians, Latvians, and Estonians resided in their three respective republics. In the same year roughly five-eighths of the Armenian population resided in the Armenian Republic. However, the bulk of the remaining Armenians resided in the adjacent Transcaucasus republics of Georgia and Azerbaydzhan, particularly in the Nagorno-Karabakh Autonomous Oblast, an Armenian exclave in the Azerbaydzhan Republic, and in the cities of Tbilisi in the Georgian Republic and Baku in the Azerbaydzhan Republic. Thus, in 1970 roughly 90 percent or more of the population of each of the four component nationalities resided in the economic region containing its republic.

Although this grouping was highly concentrated in all four years, the share of the Mobilized Europeans residing in their "homeland" increased from roughly 90 percent in 1897 and 1926 to roughly 95 percent in 1959 and 1970 (Appendix E and Table 6.13). In particular, the substantial redistribution and increasing concentration of the Mobilized Europeans have been toward the Transcaucasus. Between 1897 and 1970 the share of the Mobilized Europeans residing in the Transcaucasus increased by 22.5 percentage points, by far the greatest increase experienced by any region. This increase was largely at the expense of the West region, whose share of the Mobilized Europeans declined by 17.1 percentage points between 1897 and 1970. The Transcaucasus and the West also had by far the greatest increase and decrease, respectively, between 1926 and 1970. Thus, although this grouping has redistributed to a great extent according to the coefficient of redistribution, a dispersion from traditional regions of settlement has not been involved.

This increasing concentration contradicts a previous hypothesis. Because the Mobilized Europeans are relatively advanced, it was hypothesized that they should become increasingly mobile and dispersed. As is obvious from the previous discussion, this has not occurred to any great degree. In fact, substantial migration has not even been involved extensively in the shift of this grouping from the West to the Transcaucasus, as evidenced by the fact that in 1970 the Latvian and Estonian populations of the Transcaucasus region each numbered less than 3,000. This shift in the Mobilized European population, instead, has been due almost exclusively to differential rates of natural increase on the part of the component nationalities. Indeed, based upon our estimates for the present-day USSR, the Georgian and Armenian populations increased appreciably during the 1926-70 and 1926-59 periods, whereas the number of Latvians and Estonians actually de-

TABLE 6.13

Percentage of Mobilized Europeans Residing in Main Regions of
Mobilized European Settlement: 1897-1970

Region	1897	1926	1959	1970
Transcaucasus	47.3	51.3	66.5	69.8
West	42.4	38.7	29.1	25.3

Sources: See Chapter 2, footnotes 2 and 3.

clined in both periods, although they both did increase slightly between 1959 and 1970 (see Table 7.10).

These differential rates of population growth are primarily related to differential rates of fertility and war losses. Latvians and Estonians, being more highly educated and urbanized at a much earlier stage than most Soviet nationalities, were among the first nationalities of Russia and the USSR to experience low fertility (see Chapter 7). This is reflected by the fact that during the last decades of tsarist Russia, the gubernii of Kurlyand, Liflyand, and Estlyand, the primary units of Latvian and Estonian settlement, generally had the lowest birthrates of any of the 50 gubernii of European Russia, the only gubernii for which such data were typically available.[29] Whereas the crude birthrates of most gubernii were in the 40s and 50s during this period, the crude birthrate of these three gubernii was usually in the 20s or low 30s.[30]

The relatively low fertility of Latvians and Estonians is also apparent in more recent data. For example, in 1959 the child-woman ratios (that is, children aged 0 to 9 per 1,000 females aged 20 to 49) for the Latvians and Estonians were 0.612 and 0.638, respectively (see Table 7.9). These were the lowest ratios of any nationality in the USSR for which appropriate data are available. In contrast, the child-woman ratios for Georgians and Armenians were appreciably higher (0.905 and 1.240, respectively), although they were not as high as the ratios for many other nationalities, especially Turkic-Muslim nationalities.

In addition, as is obvious from the western locations of these two nationalities, the Latvians and Estonians suffered greater losses in association with wars. Thus, the shift of the Mobilized European population from the West to the Transcaucasus has been due primarily to the more rapid natural increase of the Georgians and Armenians as compared to that of the Latvians and Estonians, which, in turn, has been primarily related to the lower fertility and more substantial war losses experienced by the latter two groups. The Mobilized Europeans, thus, have experienced virtually no interregional migration. As mentioned, this is quite surprising given the fact that they are highly advanced peoples and, theoretically, would be more mobile.

What factors might account for the fact that the component nationalities of the Mobilized Europeans have not dispersed from their homelands to any great extent? An outstanding and obvious factor is that the Latvian and Estonian republics typically have had comparatively high levels of economic development. For example, according to the 1970 census, no other republic had a higher percentage of its work force engaged in the complex of manufacturing, construction, transportation, and communications than did Estonia and Latvia. In both cases more than 50 percent of the work force (52.4 and 50.9, respectively) was found in these occupations, and the RSFSR was the only other republic to exceed this percentage. In addition, available data reveal that the Estonian and Latvian republics have the highest levels of per capita national income of any of the 15 republics; in 1970 their income levels were more than 40 percent above the Union-wide average, and well above the levels for the next highest republics.[31] Also, during the period 1959-67 the per capita amount of state investment in the Latvian and Estonian republics was above the Union-wide average, while during the same period it was below the Union-wide average in the majority of the republics outside of the RSFSR.[32] Furthermore, since the Latvian and Estonian populations have been growing so slowly, sufficient job opportunities have evidently existed in these republics. In fact, there has been a significant influx of Russians to the Latvian and Estonian republics, due in part to the fact that the indigenous groups have been growing so slowly that they have not been able to supply the necessary workers (see Chapter 5). Consequently, apparently there has been no great need for the Latvians and Estonians to move to other republics on the basis of economic conditions. Undoubtedly, the lack of such a migration also has been due to the dislike on the part of the Latvians and Estonians for Russians. Indeed, nationalistic feelings have been relatively high in the Latvian and Estonian SSRs, particularly since the Latvians and Estonians traditionally have been more culturally advanced than the Russians, and particularly since Latvia and Estonia were independent nations during the interwar period but were then reincorporated into the USSR.

Thus, the attraction of Latvians and Estonians to their respective republics can be explained in large part by a high degree of nationalism and a favorable local economic and demographic situation, favorable in the sense that sufficient job opportunities apparently exist in these republics. From another perspective, the situation is not so favorable, because the resulting influx of Russians has tended to increase ethnic friction. Indeed, there are indications that many Latvians and Estonians favor slower rates of economic growth in their republics so as to lessen the influx of Russians.[33]

The attraction of Georgians and Armenians for their own republics represents a slightly different picture, and is more difficult to explain. In particular, the economic and demographic situations are not as favorable as they are in the Latvian and Estonian republics. First of all, the Georgian and Armenian republics have not been as advanced economically as the Latvian and Estonian republics. Whereas the Estonian and Latvian republics were the two leading Soviet republics with respect to the share of the work force engaged in manufacturing, construction, transportation, and communications in 1970, with each being above 50 percent in this regard, corresponding per-

centages for the Armenian and Georgian republics were only 43.2 and
32.1, respectively, both of which were below the Union-wide average.
Indeed, only four other republics had a lower percentage than the
Georgian SSR. In addition, whereas the per capita levels of national
income of the Estonian and Latvian republics were unsurpassed by
any other republics in 1970 and were, consequently, well above the
Union-wide average, corresponding levels for the Georgian and Armenian republics were substantially below the USSR average, in both
cases being roughly 70 percent of the Union-wide norm; indeed, only
Azerbaydzhan and the dominantly Turkic-Muslim republics of Central
Asia had a lower level than the Georgian Republic.[34]

Furthermore, whereas the rate of investment has been relatively high in the Latvian and Estonian republics, the per capita amount
of state investment in the Georgian SSR during the 1959-67 period was
well below the USSR average, and, although such investment in the
Armenian SSR was above the Union-wide figure during the same period,
it was just barely above this average and was well below the level for
the Latvian and Estonian republics, as well as most regions of the
RSFSR and Kazakhstan.[35] Moreover, as the Georgian and Armenian
populations have been growing more rapidly than those of the Latvians
and Estonians, we might expect population pressure to be greater in
these republics. Indeed, the Georgian and Armenian republics have
the highest rural population per unit of arable land of any Soviet republic (Table 6.9), and reported per capita incomes on collective farms
in both republics are apparently not above the USSR average.[36]

In short, on the basis of relative conditions of economic development and population growth, the Georgian and Armenian republics appear to be less attractive than the Latvian and Estonian republics.
Therefore, there seems to be good reason to expect an out-migration
of Georgians and Armenians. However, despite these conditions, the
Georgians and Armenians remain as two of the most immobile nationalities of the Soviet Union. In fact, according to available data
from the 1970 census, Georgians and Armenians were, along with a
few relatively less modernized Turkic-Muslim nationalities, the only
nationalities in which less than 2 percent of the population of the nationality were migrants.[37] (See the previous section on Turkic-Muslims for a brief definition of "migrant.") Georgians and Armenians,
thus, have experienced relatively little interregional migration or
local rural-to-urban migration (see Chapter 5).

Why, then, have the Georgians and Armenians tended to remain
primarily in their own republics? First of all, it should be mentioned
that, although the conditions of population growth and economic development are less favorable in the Georgian and Armenian republics
than in the Latvian and Estonian republics, such conditions in the
Georgian and Armenian republics do not appear to be that severe, es-

pecially as compared to the situation facing other regions of the USSR. In particular, the Georgian SSR and especially the Armenian SSR are more economically developed than, for example, Central Asia, and the fertility rates and growth rates of the Georgians and Armenians are not nearly as high as those of the major Turkic-Muslim peoples of Central Asia.

In addition, although reported incomes in the Georgian and Armenian republics are not that high, it should be pointed out that the enterprising Georgians and Armenians often supplement their incomes with illegal activities.[38] The classic example is that of the Georgians taking fruits and vegetables to Moscow and selling them at a substantial profit. The Soviet government has responded by cracking down on such activities, but, as one reporter notes, "it will be no easy task to make the Caucasus walk the straight and narrow."[39]

Other factors appear to be especially responsible for continued concentration of Georgians and Armenians in their homelands. In both republics the agricultural sector is characterized by a relatively high degree of labor intensiveness. Indeed, in 1970 both republics were always above the USSR average with respect to number of man-days required for a given unit of output of some major agricultural commodities.[40] For example, whereas it took 0.26 man-days to produce 1 centner (approximately 220 pounds) of grain (excluding corn) on collective farms in the USSR as a whole, the corresponding number of man-days for the Georgian and Armenian republics were 0.82 and 1.07.[41] This relatively high degree of labor intensiveness partly reflects the fact that the highly mountainous topography of both republics impedes the mechanization of agriculture. Although the Georgian and Armenian republics together contained more than 3 percent of the rural population (census definition) of the USSR in 1970, they accounted for less than 2 percent of all tractors of the USSR.[42]

Georgian agriculture, in particular, is relatively highly oriented toward such very labor-intensive specialty crops as citrus fruits and tea.[43] It is estimated, for example, that the production of tea requires at least 400 to 450 man-days of labor per hectare, whereas such a conventional crop as wheat requires only 10 to 12 man-days.[44] In order to gather just 1 kilogram of tea leaves, it is necessary to pick 3,000 young sprouts by hand![45] Also, although reported per capita collective farm incomes in the Georgian Republic are not high as compared to the Union-wide average, they also are not low. According to available data for 1966, they were, in fact, equal to the USSR average, although a significant share of this income comes from private plots.[46] In addition, local agricultural production has increased fairly substantially in recent years; for example, state purchases of tea leaves grown in the Georgian SSR increased by 65 percent between 1960 and 1970.[47] Also, agricultural wages in the USSR

have increased appreciably in the post-Stalin era, and the Georgian
Republic has probably benefited to a great degree from the fact that
major improvements have been made in recent years in the incomes
of workers on collective farms (for example, pension rights and guar-
anteed monthly wages), the major type of agricultural system in this
republic.[48] Thus, although the Georgian SSR does not have an out-
standingly attractive agricultural system, the great demand for agricultural workers, the absence of comparatively low agricultural incomes, increased agricultural production, improvements in wages,
and the existence of lucrative black market activities tend to continue
to keep thousands of Georgians on the farms.

Reported agricultural incomes are not as favorable in the Armenian Republic. In fact, according to the data for 1966, only two
other republics had a lower per capita income on collective farms.[49]
However, when the economies of the Georgian and Armenian republics
are taken as a whole, that of the Armenian Republic is seemingly
somewhat more attractive. First of all, the Armenian Republic is
more industrialized than the Georgian Republic and, consequently, is
not as dependent upon agriculture. Also, although per capita national
incomes in the Georgian and Armenian republics were both roughly
only 70 percent of the Union-wide average in 1970, the income level
for the Armenian SSR was somewhat higher than that for the Georgian
SSR (74 percent of the Union-wide average as opposed to 67 percent,
respectively).[50] In addition, like the Georgians, Armenians are
known to participate in illegal activities.

Furthermore, although the Georgian and Armenian republics
are not among the most economically developed republics of the USSR,
when local industrialization does occur, the indigenous peoples are
relatively better able to take advantage of the job openings. In many
other non-Russian republics, the indigenous peoples, being relatively
less modernized, are not able to respond greatly to increased job
opportunities associated with local industrialization. Instead, an influx of Russians typically occurs. But, because Georgians and Armenians are so highly educated, they are able to take advantage of
such opportunities, a situation that is reflected in the small number
of Russians in these two republics. Thus, as compared to many indigenous peoples of other non-Russian republics, job opportunities
resulting from local economic development are relatively high for
the Georgians and Armenians, from this perspective at least. Consequently, despite the fact that the Georgian and Armenian republics
are not major areas of economic development in the USSR, certain
attributes of their economic system tend to impede a mass out-migration to other republics.[51] In fact, as of yet there apparently has not
been an appreciable decline in living standards in these republics.

In addition, environmental and historical-cultural factors may also inhibit such a migration. The Transcaucasus region is one of the more pleasant regions of the USSR, environmentally speaking. Although such relative conditions do not necessarily make out-migration impossible (witness the migration of Puerto Ricans to New York City or of Indians and Pakistanis to Great Britain, for example), it could impede such a movement. Furthermore, the Georgians and Armenians probably have a great attachment for their homelands.

However, this does not mean that substantial out-migration will never occur from these areas (witness the migration of Greeks to Western Europe, for example), especially since the Georgian and Armenian populations are still growing fairly rapidly. Indeed, between 1959 and 1970 they increased by 1.7 and 2.2 percent per year, respectively. These relatively high growth rates will be reflected in years to come in increases in the size of the work forces and in the number of new entrants to the work forces in the Georgian and Armenian republics. In fact, whereas many regions and republics will be experiencing declines between 1980 and 1990, substantial increases will continue to occur in these two republics (see Tables 10.1 and 10.2). Furthermore, as previously suggested, the Armenian SSR and especially the Georgian SSR have not received disproportionately high shares of Soviet capital investment, and there appears to be no tendency to change this situation substantially in the near future.[52] According to the 1971-75 plan, "scheduled cutbacks in the rate of growth of investment are especially steep in . . . Armenia."[53] Consequently, given future demographic and economic trends, it remains to be seen whether the economies of these two republics can continue to absorb projected increases in the size of the local work force.

According to Eugene Kulischer, societies facing increased local population pressure have three alternative means of response: economic development, birth control, and emigration (that is, out-migration, be it to another area within the country or to another country).[54] Given the future demographic and economic trends in the Georgian and Armenian republics, it would seem that the third response, out-migration to other republics, might finally come into operation, at least more so than it has in the past.

In summary, despite their high level of development, the Mobilized Europeans have tended to remain primarily in their homelands. The attraction of Latvians and Estonians to their homelands is relatively easy to explain. Both republics have a high level of economic development and substantial job opportunities, especially since the Latvian and Estonian populations are growing so slowly. The attraction of Georgians and Armenians to their homelands is more difficult to explain, primarily because these republics have a considerably lower level of economic development and both nationalities are in-

creasing in size fairly rapidly. Such an attraction seems to be particularly related to the fact that labor intensive systems of agriculture
are significant in these republics and thus are able to absorb much of
the work force, and levels of economic development, although not high,
are not as low as, say, those of the Central Asian republics. Furthermore, many Georgians and Armenians are able to make a livelihood
from various illegal activities. Most important, in both republics the
standard of living has apparently not yet declined and, thus, there
has been no substantial stimulus for out-migration. Obviously, most
members of all four nationalities must feel that a migration to other
republics would entail a decline in their overall standard of living,
although the Georgians and Armenians may be faced with greater pressures in the future to migrate to other republics.

Finnic Peoples

    The Finnic peoples have experienced a very high degree of re-
distribution, but have occupied an intermediate position with respect
to the degree of concentration or dispersion (Tables 6.1 to 6.3).
That the Finnic peoples have redistributed substantially is indicated
by the fact that their coefficient of redistribution was high in every
period (Table 6.1). Of the ten groupings, it ranked fourth in the overall 1897-1970 period and never occupied a lower position in any other
period. Indeed, the Finnic coefficient of redistribution ranked either
first or second in the three post-1926 periods.
    That the Finnic nationalities have occupied an intermediate po-
sition with respect to the degree of concentration or dispersion is revealed by Tables 6.2 and 6.3. Tables 6.2 reveals that the Finnic dissimilarity index ranked sixth among the ten groupings in all four census years, being in the mid-60s in every case; consequently, as Table
6.3 reveals, virtually no change occurred in this index. In short, the
Finnic peoples were not especially highly concentrated or dispersed
in the first place, and have tended to remain that way.
    Appendix E and Table 6.14 shed light on this pattern of substan-
tial redistribution, but little concentration or dispersion. They suggest that this pattern has been due primarily to the fact that the substantial redistribution in the Finnic population chiefly has involved
four regions (Northwest, Volgo-Vyatsk, Urals, and Volga) that have
been the main regions of settlement for this grouping in all four years
(Map 6.6). Generally speaking, the redistribution has been from
the Northwest and Volga to the Urals and Volgo-Vyatsk. In particular,
between 1897 and 1970 the number of Finnic peoples residing in the
Northwest and Volga regions declined by 13.9 and 3.3 percentage
points, respectively, while that of the Urals and Volgo-Vyatsk in-

creased by 10.5 and 2.8 percentage points, respectively. These four regions occupied similar positions between 1926 and 1970, although the decline of the Volga and the increase of the Volgo-Vyatsk were both even more pronounced. But because these increases and decreases primarily involved the major regions of Finnic settlement, they more or less offset each other. Thus, no increased concentration or dispersion occurred, in that in all four census years, roughly 90 percent of the Finnic population resided in these four regions, as Tables 6.2 and 6.3 also suggest.

But, nevertheless, appreciable interregional shifts did occur. In general, it appears that interregional migration was a comparatively minor factor in these shifts. First of all, the great decline in the percentage of the Finnic peoples residing in the Northwest region did not involve a mass migration of the local Finnic peoples to the Urals or Volgo-Vyatsk. Instead, this decline can be largely attributed to two other factors: the movement of Finns out of the Vyborg area (that is, the Karelian Isthmus) and other areas back to present-day Finland; and a high degree of Russification of some of the local Finnic peoples.

As Appendix E and Table 6.14 reveal, the decline in the share of Finnic peoples residing in the Northwest region occurred almost exclusively between 1926 and 1959. In fact, during this period the Finnic population of the Northwest declined by 62.3 percent, from an estimated 1,096,150 in 1926 to 412,866 in 1959. The relatively large Finnic population of this region in 1926 is due to the fact that portions of the present-day Northwest region, especially the Vyborg area, were in Finland at this time and, consequently, contained a substantial Finnish population. According to our estimates, 437,313 Finns resided in that portion of Viipurin or Vyborg Province that fell into the present-day Northwest region. An estimated additional 57,059 Finns resided in those portions of Oulu and Kuopio provinces that also fell into the present-day Northwest region. When such portions of these three provinces of Finland were annexed to the USSR after the Russo-Finnish War, most of the Finns in these areas moved to Finland. According to Eugene Kulischer, 415,000 Finns were evacuated from the Karelian Isthmus during the winter war of 1939-40 and after the Finnish defeat.[55] As a result, by 1970 only 19,897 Finns resided in Leningrad Oblast, that is, the present-day oblast containing the Karelian Isthmus or Vyborg area. In fact, in 1970 there were only 84,750 Finns in the entire USSR.

Another factor promoting the decline in the Finnic population of the Northwest region has been an apparent high degree of Russification, although this factor is obviously of secondary importance when compared to the Finnish losses associated with the war and boundary changes. Particularly noteworthy in this respect are the Karelians

TABLE 6.14

Percentage of Finnic Peoples Residing in Main Regions of
Finnic Settlement: 1897-1970

Region	1897	1926	1959	1970
Northwest	28.1	29.6	14.4	14.2
Volgo-Vyatsk	23.4	18.1	28.1	26.2
Urals	23.0	21.8	34.2	33.5
Volga	16.2	21.4	13.6	12.9

Sources: See Chapter 2, footnotes 2 and 3.

and remaining Finns. According to the 1970 census, 36.8 percent of
the Karelians and 42.5 percent of the Finns in the USSR considered
Russian to be their native language. These figures are well above the
Union-wide average for all non-Russians of 11.6 percent. This re-
flects, of course, the fact that the Karelians and Finns, like most
Finnic peoples, are located primarily within areas of appreciable
Russian settlement, especially the northern half of European USSR.
In addition, the Karelians have had a relatively low fertility rate, not
only in comparison to other Finnic nationalities, as Table 7.9 and
Chapter 7 suggest, but also in comparison to most other major Soviet
nationalities. The Karelian population of the USSR, in fact, did decline between both 1926 and 1959 and between 1959 and 1970, as did,
of course, the Finnish population.

　　As mentioned, the share of the Finnic population residing in the
Volga region also experienced an appreciable decline, although this
percentage point decline was not nearly as great as that experienced
by the Northwest region. Similar to the situation of the Northwest,
the bulk of the decline in the Volga also occurred between 1926 and
1959. Indeed, during this period, the Finnic population of the Volga
region declined by 50.7 percent, almost as much as that of the Northwest.

　　The Volga decline primarily reflects the influence of the Mordvinians. Although the Mordvinian ASSR is in the Volgo-Vyatsk region
and not in the Volga region, in 1970 roughly 30 percent of the Mordvinians resided in this region, and Mordvinians accounted for over 90
percent (91.9) of the Finnic population of this region. Like the Finns
and Karelians, the Mordvinian population of the USSR also declined
between both 1926 and 1959 and 1959 and 1970. As with the Finns
and Karelians, this decline apparently has been due in part to a high

degree of Russification. In 1970, for example, over one-fifth (22.1 percent) of the Mordvinians considered Russian to be their native language. Like the Finns and Karelians, this reflects the fact that Mordvinians reside primarily in areas dominated by Russians.

At the other end of the spectrum, the Urals and Volgo-Vyatsk experienced relatively great increases in their percentage of the Finnic peoples. A major factor in both cases appears to have been the relatively rapid growth of the major local Finnic groups: Udmurts in the Urals and Mari in the Volgo-Vyatsk. While other Finnic nationalities, such as the Karelians, Finns, and Mordvinians, have been declining in population since 1926, the population of both the Udmurts and Mari increased between 1926 and 1959 and between 1959 and 1970. As Table 7.9 suggests, this reflects their somewhat higher fertility as compared to that of the other major Finnic peoples. As a result, between 1926 and 1959, the major period of the shift of the Finnic peoples toward the Urals and Volgo-Vyatsk, the Finnic population of these two regions actually increased. That the share of the Finnic peoples residing in the Volgo-Vyatsk region, in particular, generally increased rather than declined is somewhat surprising given the fact that this region contains the "homeland" of the Mordvinians, the population of which, as mentioned before, has declined since 1926. That this decline did not have a more substantial impact on the Volgo-Vyatsk region is partly due to the fact that only relatively few Mordvinians actually reside in the the Mordvinian ASSR. Indeed, in 1970 less than one-third of the Mordvinians resided in their "homeland." Except for the Tatars, no other nationality with its own SSR or ASSR had such a low percentage of its population residing in the political unit bearing its name. This reflects the fact that Mordvinians have generally been one of the most dispersed nationalities in Russia and the USSR, with significant pockets of settlement in all of the more easterly regions of the RSFSR even before the turn of the century.

However, although the Finnic population of the Urals and Volgo-Vyatsk regions increased, it should be pointed out that the rate of increase was not inordinately high. In fact, despite the tremendous loss of life in the USSR as a whole during this period, the total population of the present-day USSR actually increased at a slightly higher rate than the Finnic population of the Urals and Volgo-Vyatsk, as did, of course, the total population of many of the other groupings. Although the total population of the USSR increased by only 24.5 percent between 1926 and 1959, the Finnic population of the Urals and the Volgo-Vyatsk increased by even lower rates of 21.1 and 19.7 percent, respectively. On an average annual basis, this means that the Finnic population of these two regions increased by only 0.6 percent per year in both cases. Consequently, the big shift in the Finnic population to the Urals and Volgo-Vyatsk regions cannot be explained to any great extent by migration.

Thus, despite the substantial regional redistribution of the Finnic peoples—a redistribution that primarily involved only the traditional regions of Finnic settlement—relatively little interregional migration of the Finnic peoples actually occurred. This is not surprising in light of the fact that the Finnic peoples are relatively less modernized, and would, thus, hypothetically, not experience substantial
migration. Although there was an appreciable migration of Finns to
Finland, this movement was not an interregional movement within the
USSR; also, it was related to the peculiarities of war and boundary
changes and not to the normal forces of modernization.

Lithuanians

The Lithuanians represent the most extreme situation of a grouping that has remained very highly concentrated in one small portion of
the USSR. In all four census years over 90 percent of the Lithuanians
resided in the same comparatively small area. These patterns are
evident in Tables 6.1 to 6.3, which clearly indicate that the Lithuanians
have experienced virtually no redistribution and have tended to remain
very highly concentrated. The lack of any substantial redistribution
is indicated by the fact that the Lithuanians had the lowest coefficient
of redistribution of any of the ten groupings in all six intercensal periods (Table 6.1). That the Lithuanians have tended to remain highly
concentrated is reflected by Tables 6.2 and 6.3. Table 6.2, in fact,
reveals that the Lithuanian dissimilarity index was as high as its coefficient of redistribution was low in that of the ten groupings the
Lithuanians had the highest dissimilarity index in all four years. In
fact, the Lithuanian dissimilarity index was over 90 in all four census years, a level no other grouping reached in even one of the four
years. Thus, the Lithuanians represent the most extreme case of a
grouping that has been and tended to remain very highly concentrated.
Not surprisingly, this concentration has especially involved the
West region, the region containing the Lithuanian SSR (Appendix E).
In each of the four census years over 95 percent of the Lithuanians
resided in this region. As Appendix E indicates, no other grouping
was as highly concentrated in one region, once again reflecting the
extreme concentration of the Lithuanians.
Moreover, within the West region, roughly 90 percent or more
of the Lithuanians has been particularly concentrated in the Lithuanian
SSR or a roughly equivalent area. In 1897 the equivalent area consisted primarily of portions of Kovno, Vil'no, and Suvalk Gubernii;
in 1926 it consisted of the independent state of Lithuania and in 1959
and 1970 it consisted, of course, of the Lithuanian SSR.

Major factors involved in the lack of a dispersal of the Lithuanian population include the following. To begin with, Lithuanians have tended to be relatively nonmodernized, as suggested by such indicators as level of education and urbanization. On this basis alone, one would not expect a high degree of mobility. Second, the Lithuanians typically have been nationalistic and resentful of the Russians, consequently have had a high degree of attachment to their homeland.[56] In addition, in more recent years, urban-industrial opportunities in the Lithuanian Republic have been expanding very rapidly, further tending to motivate Lithuanians to stay in their homeland (see Chapter 5).

Moldavians and Romanians

The Moldavians and Romanians also have not experienced any substantial population dispersion. In fact, they actually have become somewhat more concentrated in Moldavia itself, which now accounts for over four-fifths of the Moldavian and Romanian population of the USSR. These patterns are reflected in Tables 6.1 to 6.3, which suggest that the Moldavians and Romanians have experienced relatively little redistribution, and that that has occurred has primarily involved an increased concentration of a population already fairly highly concentrated. That this grouping has not redistributed to a very great extent is indicated by the fact that its coefficient of redistribution between 1897 and 1970 was only the seventh highest among the ten groupings (Table 6.1). In fact, in no period did the Moldavian and Romanian coefficient of redistribution ever rank higher than fourth in this regard.

Tables 6.2 and 6.3 reveal that the Moldavians and Romanians have been relatively highly concentrated and increasingly so. Table 6.2 indicates that the Moldavians and Romanians had the third highest dissimilarity index in all four census years. As this index has increased to a certain extent (Tables 6.2 and 6.3), this suggests that the Moldavian and Romanian population has become increasingly concentrated.

Appendix E and Table 6.15 indicate the regional aspects of these patterns. They reveal that, as with many of the other groupings, the bulk of the redistribution primarily has involved traditional major regions of settlement, in this case Moldavia and the adjacent Southwest and South regions of the Ukraine. These three regions, in fact, were the leading regions of Moldavian and Romanian settlement in all four census years, and together contained over 95 percent of the Moldavian and Romanian population in each year, with Moldavia containing the vast majority of this population.

In particular, as Tables 6.2 and 6.3 also suggested, the redistribution has been primarily one of increasing concentration, in that

TABLE 6.15

Percentage of Moldavians and Romanians Residing in Main Regions
of Moldavian and Romanian Settlement: 1897-1970

Region	1897	1926	1959	1970
Moldavia	70.0	70.0	85.0	84.4
Southwest	14.0	17.0	8.1	7.1
South	14.0	11.2	5.6	5.4

Sources: See Chapter 2, footnotes 2 and 3.

Moldavia experienced by far the greatest increase of any region in
its share of the Moldavian population between 1897 and 1970 (14.4
percentage points). The South and the Southwest regions both, accordingly, experienced by far the greatest declines (-8.6 and -6.9
percentage points, respectively). Roughly similar patterns existed
between 1926 and 1970 also. .

It is difficult to explain this increased concentration of the Moldavian and Romanian population. As Appendix E and Table 6.15 reveal, this shift from the Southwest and South to Moldavia occurred
primarily between 1926 and 1959. Whether or not migration is primarily responsible for this increased concentration of the Moldavians
and Romanians is beside the point. The main point is that the Moldavians and Romanians certainly have not experienced substantial
out-migration from their traditional area of settlement in the USSR.
This lack of dispersal is to be expected. Like many of the other
groupings included in this study, the Moldavians and Romanians are
less modernized (see Table 7.9). Therefore, a low degree of mobility
and dispersion is to be expected. Furthermore, Moldavia is one of
the best agricultural areas of the USSR, being one of but two Soviet
republics (the Ukraine is the other) in which a majority of its area is
arable land.[57] Hence, this would further tend to impede a more substantial out-migration of this grouping.

NOTES

1. For good discussions of the plight of the Russian peasantry,
see Geroid Tanquary Robinson, Rural Russia Under the Old Regime
(New York: Macmillan, 1932), pp. 94-116; and George Pavlovsky,
Agricultural Russia on the Eve of the Revolution (London: George
Routledge and Sons, 1930), pp. 61-146.

2. For a discussion of these migration patterns, see J. William Leasure and Robert A. Lewis, "Internal Migration in Russia in the Late Nineteenth Century," Slavic Review 27 (September 1968): 379-82.

3. For example, see V. I. Perevedentsev, "Sovremennaya Migratsiya v SSSR," in Narodonaseleniye i Ekonomika (Moscow: Izdatel'stvo "Ekonomika," 1967), p. 106.

4. Narody Yevropeyskoy Chasti SSSR, vol. I (Moscow: Izdatel'stvo "Nauka," 1964), p. 22.

5. Ivan Dzyuba, Internationalism or Russification? 2d ed. (London: Weidenfeld and Nicolson, 1968), p. 188.

6. Narodnoye Khozyaystvo SSSR v 1970 G., pp. 159, 291.

7. See Robert Conquest, The Nation Killers: The Soviet Deportation of Nationalities (New York: Macmillan, 1970).

8. Ibid., pp. 64-65.

9. Ibid., p. 162.

10. Ibid., pp. 160-62.

11. Richard Pipes, The Formation of the Soviet Union, rev. ed. (New York: Atheneum, 1968), p. 83; Eugene M. Kulischer, Europe on the Move (New York: Columbia University Press, 1948), p. 32; and George J. Demko, The Russian Colonization of Kazakhstan: 1896-1916 (The Hague: Mouton & Co., 1969), pp. 197-98.

12. Pipes, op. cit.; and Kulischer, op. cit.

13. Pipes, op. cit., pp. 83-84; and Kulischer, op. cit.

14. Kulischer, op. cit., pp. 100-01.

15. Ibid., p. 101.

16. Ibid.

17. Ibid.

18. For a discussion of the deportation of these North Caucasus nationalities, see Conquest, op. cit.

19. Pipes, op. cit., p. 167.

20. Vestnik Statistiki, no. 2 (1973), pp. 87-88.

21. James Mavor, An Economic History of Russia, II, 2d ed., rev. (New York: Russell and Russell, 1925), p. 207; Victor Berard, The Russian Empire and Czarism (London: David Nutt, 1905), p. 127; and Avrahm Yarmolinsky, The Jews and Other Minor Nationalities Under the Soviets (New York: Vanguard Press, 1928), pp. 25-26.

22. For a discussion of this lack of movement to the Jewish A. O., see Chimen Abramsky, "The Biro-Bidzhan Project, 1927-1959," in The Jews in Soviet Russia Since 1917, ed. Lionel Kochan (London: Oxford University Press, 1970), pp. 62-75.

23. S. Ettinger, "The Jews in Russia at the Outbreak of the Revolution," in The Jews in Soviet Russia Since 1917, ed. Lionel Kochan (London: Oxford University Press, 1970), p. 21.

24. Kulischer, op. cit., p. 31.

25. Ibid., p. 108.

26. Alec Nove and J. A. Newth, "The Jewish Population: Demographic Trends and Occupational Patterns," in The Jews in Soviet Russia Since 1917, ed. Lionel Kochan (London: Oxford University Press, 1970), p. 136.

27. Kulischer, op. cit., p. 109. These figures are based upon the boundaries of 1926 and 1939.

28. Ibid., pp. 109-10.

29. A. G. Rashin, Naseleniye Rossii za 100 Let (Moscow: Gosudarstvennoye Statisticheskoye Izdatel'stvo, 1956), pp. 167-68.

30. Ibid.

31. Gertrude E. Schroeder, "Regional Differences in Incomes and Levels of Living in the USSR," in The Soviet Economy in Regional Perspective, ed. V. N. Bandera and Z. L. Melnyk (New York: Praeger, 1973), pp. 168-69.

32. Leslie Dienes, "Investment Priorities in Soviet Regions," Annals of the Association of American Geographers 62 (September 1972): 442.

33. For example, see V. Stanley Vardys, "Geography and Nationalities in the USSR: A Commentary," Slavic Review 31 (September 1972): 568; Bernard Gwertzman, "Protest on Soviet Laid to Latvians," New York Times, 27 February 1972, p. 11; Hedrick Smith, "Estonians Retain Identity but Mix More with Russians," New York Times, 28 December 1973, p. 2; and "Latvians Chided for Nationalism," New York Times, 21 March 1971, p. 17.

34. Schroeder, op. cit.

35. Dienes, op. cit.

36. Schroeder, op. cit., p. 178.

37. Vestnik Statistiki, no. 2 (1973), pp. 87-88.

38. "The Great Russian Ripoffsky," Newsweek, 20 August 1973, pp. 38, 43; "Soviet Officials Outfox Crafty Fruit Smugglers," New York Times, 15 January 1974, p. 2; and Hedrick Smith, "Pravda Assailing Soviet Georgians," New York Times, 19 November 1973, p. 6.

39. Smith, op. cit., p. 6.

40. Narodnoye Khozyaystvo SSSR v 1970 G., p. 403.

41. Ibid.

42. Ibid., p. 375.

43. V. Sh. Dzhaoshvili, Naseleniye Gruzii (Tbilisi: Izdatel'stvo "Metsniyereba," 1968), pp. 35, 36, 82, 97; and Robert G. Jensen, "Soviet Subtropical Agriculture: A Microcosm," Geographical Review 54 (April 1964): 186.

44. F. F. Davitaya, Gruziya (Moscow: Izdatel'stvo "Mysl'," 1967), p. 117.

45. Ibid.

46. Schroeder, op. cit., p. 178.

47. Narodnoye Khozyaystvo SSSR v 1970 G., p. 338.

48. David W. Bronson and Constance B. Krueger, "The Revolution in Soviet Farm Household Income, 1953-1967," in The Soviet Rural Community, ed. James R. Millar (Urbana, Ill.: University of Illinois Press, 1971), pp. 214-58; and Murray Feshbach and Stephen Rapawy, "Labor Constraints in the Five-Year Plan," in U.S. Congress, Joint Economic Committee, Soviet Economic Prospects for the Seventies, Joint Committee Print (Washington, D.C.: Government Printing Office, 1973), p. 513.

49. Ibid.

50. Schroeder, op. cit.

51. Hedrick Smith, "Moscow Allows Armenia Its Nationalism," New York Times, 20 December 1971, p. 8.

52. James H. Noren and E. Douglas Whitehouse, "Soviet Industry in the 1971-75 Plan," in U.S. Congress, Joint Economic Committee, Soviet Economic Prospects for the Seventies, pp. 223-24.

53. Ibid.

54. Kulischer, op. cit., p. 319.

55. Ibid., pp. 264-66.

56. "200 Lithuanians Reported Jailed," New York Times, 14 June 1972, p. 5.

57. Narodnoye Khozyaystvo SSSR v 1970 G., p. 291.

7

**POPULATION
GROWTH**

Change in the rate of total population growth in a society is determined primarily by changes in fertility and mortality and thus natural increase, which as previously indicated, are related to modernization. Likewise, levels of fertility and mortality of an ethnic group are indications of the degree of modernization of that group. In this chapter we will investigate population growth of the nationality groupings between 1897 and 1970 by relating it generally to the level of modernization of each grouping. Consequently, we will not undertake a detailed analysis of the determinants of fertility and mortality, because our chief interest for the purposes of this study is to ascertain differences in fertility, mortality, natural increase, and assimilation of the various nationalities. Our discussion of the growth of the total population of the USSR will be brief and descriptive, because our intention is only to provide background information, and we plan to analyze fertility and mortality in much greater detail in a later volume. Because there has been relatively little immigration and emigration, we will treat the USSR as a more or less closed system, although emigration between 1890 and 1915 has been estimated at 3.3 million, and emigration and repatriation of aliens between 1914 and 1926 at about 2 million. There was also a relatively insignificant amount of emigration during World War II.[1]

The population growth of the nationality groupings will be analyzed largely in terms of the demographic transition. According to this formulation, as modernization progresses, populations move through from three to five stages, as variously defined, that are described in terms of fertility and mortality. In short, with the transition from a preindustrial agricultural economy to a modern urban-industrial economy, populations go through a transition from relatively high birth- and death rates and a consequent slow rate of natural

increase to relatively low birth- and death rates and relatively slow
natural increase. First the death rate declines and after a varying
period of time the birthrate declines, which results in an expansion
and then a slowing of population growth.[2]

SUMMARY DISCUSSION

Even though the Soviet population in the aggregate has gone
through the demographic transition, not all nationalities in the USSR
have completed the transition from high to low death and birthrates.
Although it is difficult to establish exactly when a population completes
the transition, because this formulation is loosely defined and in the
Soviet context vital rates by nationality are not available, as might be
expected, the various nationality groupings have gone through the
transition at different rates and at different times. As we have already pointed out, nationalities modernize at varying rates. The
Latvians, Estonians, and very probably the Jews achieved relatively
low levels of fertility, mortality, and natural increase before World
War II, and even if they had not suffered substantial population losses
as a result of war and emigration, these populations would have grown
relatively slowly. Actually, the Latvians and Estonians barely increased their population between 1897 and 1970, and the Jews declined
by over 2 million.

The Russians, Ukrainians, and Belorussians, who comprised
74 percent of the Soviet population in 1970, reached the last stage of
the demographic transition in the 1960s. Largely because of losses
through war and famine, the Ukrainians and Belorussians grew relatively slowly, not experiencing the expected expansion of their populations in the second stage of the transition. The Russians grew
faster, having a moderate rate of increase between 1897 and 1970,
primarily because of appreciable Russification of other nationalities,
mainly Ukrainians, Belorussians, and Jews. The Tatars are the
only Turkic-Muslim group that has undergone appreciable modernization, and currently they probably are about to enter the last stage of
the transition. They are the only grouping to grow faster than the
Russians between 1897 and 1970 because of the expected expansion and
decline in their rate of growth since 1926. Moreover, losses as a
result of war and famine were probably less than those of the Eastern
Slavs.

The Georgians and Armenians appear to be approaching the
last stage of the demographic transition, although both groups still
grew fairly rapidly between 1959 and 1970. By 1926 mortality of the
Georgians was probably already declining but fertility was moderately
high; their population has been increasing until fairly recently. Cur-

rently, their population is characterized by low mortality and fairly low fertility. By 1926 the death rate of the Armenian population had already begun to decline and had reached a fairly low level by 1940, but the birthrate did not begin to decline substantially until the 1960s, when it declined sharply. As a result of a prolonged period of relatively high fertility and low mortality the Armenian population has grown rapidly since 1926. This nationality is now approaching the last stage of the transition.

The Finnic peoples only recently have completed the transition from high to low death and birthrates. Both fertility and mortality were relatively high before World War II, but had declined to low levels by 1971. In Lithuania, mortality and fertility had declined to moderate levels by 1940, and thereafter fertility more or less stabilized until 1960 and mortality continued to decline during this period. In the 1960s fertility declined to a moderately low level. Thus, in terms of fertility and mortality, the Lithuanians have been one of the more modernized groups at least for the past three decades. The Moldavians and Romanians more than doubled their population between 1897 and 1970, largely because mortality had declined considerably and fertility remained high until after World War II. By 1970 fertility had declined to a fairly low level.

The Turkic-Muslim population is the only grouping that has not progressed far in terms of the demographic transition. Currently their population is growing very rapidly, because mortality has declined considerably, particularly since World War II; fertility decline, however, seems to be in its initial stages. Fertility among the various Turkic-Muslim nationalities grades from high to moderate. The Central Asian groups, the Kazakhs, the Azeri, and some of the North Caucasus groups, have very high fertility and have experienced very little decline in fertility, although there are indications that a general decline might occur in the near future. Other Turkic-Muslim groups along the Volga, in the North Caucasus, and in Siberia have moderate levels of fertility and probably are experiencing a fertility decline. In short, some of the Turkic-Muslim nationalities are in the second stage of the transition, while others have progressed somewhat further.

With respect to the four major questions of this study, we can make the following statements:

1. As to the expected patterns, previously we have hypothesized that the most modernized groupings were the Russians, Jews, Mobilized Europeans, and Tatars, and we would expect these groups to have gone through the demographic transition first and to have the lowest birth- and death rates.

2. As to the patterns that occurred, the empirical evidence only partially confirms our hypotheses. Mortality, which requires

relatively little socioeconomic change, has gone down for all groups, although not at the same time and at the same rate. The Jews, Estonians, and Latvians experienced similar declines somewhat later. These groups have the lowest fertility in the USSR, and currently are below replacement in terms of net reproduction. The Georgians and Armenians, however, have experienced fertility decline relatively recently, and their fertility levels are currently significantly above those of the Jews, Estonians, Latvians, and Russians. The fertility of the Ukrainians and Belorussians is much lower than would be expected based upon other indicators of modernization, as is that of the Lithuanians, Moldavians and Romanians, and the Finnic peoples. Tatar fertility did not decline as early as expected, even though at present it is probably fairly low.

We plan to investigate fertility decline in the USSR in much greater detail in a later volume, so deeper insights into the processes of fertility decline must await this future study. Suffice it to say at this juncture, among the indicators of modernization, fertility is the one variable that is probably the most difficult to effect and that nationalities vary considerably in terms of fertility decline and their resistance to the forces of modernization, probably largely because of cultural reasons. A central problem in the study of Soviet fertility is why there has been a significant decline in rural Slavic areas, whereas most Turkic-Muslim rural areas have maintained high levels of fertility.

3. An appraisal of the effect of Soviet governmental policy on the growth of population must also await our future study. We can, however, point out that the general governmental policy of modernizing the USSR has had a major impact on the growth of the Soviet population.

4. The impact on society of the differential growth of population by nationality is discussed in Chapter 10.

DETAILED DISCUSSION

Total Population Growth

Between 1897 and 1970 the population of the contemporary territory of the USSR almost doubled and grew at a rate of 0.9 percent per year (Table 7.1). The modest growth of the Soviet population in this century is the result of large population losses primarily because of war and the decline in natural increase. Direct and indirect losses of population as a result of wars, famines, and economic disorganization are huge and approach 90 million people. The higher rates of population growth between 1926 and 1939 and 1959 and 1970 can be explained largely by the absence of war. Furthermore, natural increase rates were also relatively high during much of the 1926–39 period, thus contributing to relatively rapid growth and offsetting losses from famine, collectivization, and forced labor. Khrushchev has estimated that 10 million or more perished in jails or camps during the Stalin era.[3]

During this century crude birthrates have declined more than crude death rates, and thus crude natural increase has declined (Table 7.2). The most rapid decreases in rates of birth, death, and natural increase occurred following World War II. In 1969 the crude birthrate reached its lowest point, 17.0 per 1,000, and the natural increase rate was 8.9 per 1,000. Since 1969 the crude birthrate has been rising slowly, as has the crude death rate since 1964. In 1971 the crude birthrate was 17.8 per 1,000, the crude death rate was 8.2, and the natural increase rate was 9.6.

TABLE 7.1

Population Growth in the USSR: 1897–1970

Year	Population (in millions)	Average Annual Percentage Increase in Population
1897	125.0	—
1926	167.7	1.0
1939	193.1	1.2
1959	208.8	0.4
1970	241.7	1.4
1897–1970	—	0.9

Sources: See Chapter 2, footnotes 2 and 3.

It must be noted, however, that the data in Table 7.2 vary greatly in reliability. The data for the prerevolutionary period are probably fairly complete, judging from their magnitude. The chief problem is that their coverage includes only European Russia. The 1926 data suffer from both underregistration and lack of complete coverage of even the Soviet population within the 1926 boundaries, and have been adjusted several times by Soviet officials.[4] Regional crude birth- and death rates have been published for 1940 and 1950 and for most years since the late 1950s. An investigation of these data, how-

TABLE 7.2

Crude Birth-, Death, and Natural Increase Rates in Russia and the
USSR: 1896-1972

Years	Birthrate	Death Rate	Natural Increase Rate
1896-1900*	49.5	32.1	17.4
1901-05*	47.7	31.0	16.7
1926-28	44.2	21.8	22.4
1937-40	36.0	17.9	18.1
1951-55	26.2	9.1	17.1
1956-60	25.2	7.5	17.7
1961-65	21.0	7.2	13.8
1966-70	17.4	7.8	9.6
1971-72	17.8	8.4	9.4

*European Russia

Sources: Narodnoye Khozyaystvo SSSR v 1970 G., p. 47; Narodnoye Khozyaystvo SSSR v 1964 G., p. 34; and Vestnik Statistiki, no.
12 (1973), p. 76.

ever, reveals that in some areas there have been unexpected sharp
rises in fertility, most notably in parts of Central Asia and the Transcaucasus, and many rather backward areas have very low death rates.
In fact, it has been reported that until the 1950s, underregistration
of births in Central Asia was between 10 and 25 percent, and that
both births and deaths are still being underreported.[5] Similar problems very probably exist in other "non-European" areas. Nevertheless, one can probably safely assume that birth and death registration
in more recent years is almost complete, and despite underregistration of births and deaths in this century, the general trend of declining
rates of births, deaths, and natural increase is correct.

The crude birthrate, of course, is an inadequate measure of
fertility because it does not take into account changes in age and sex.
A better measure is gross and net reproduction rates that are standardized for age, and indicate the number of daughters born to women
in the reproductive years. There has been a linear decline in fertility
since 1897, but there have been major variations during time of war
and economic reorganization (Table 7.3). An investigation of gross
reproduction rates for individual years since 1950 indicates that fertility was fairly stable during the 1950s, declined steadily during the

TABLE 7.3

Maternal Reproduction Rates in Russia and the USSR: 1897-1972

Years	Gross	Net
1897*	3.29	1.60
1926	2.64	1.72
1938-39	2.14	1.44
1958-59	1.37	1.26
1961-62	1.30	1.21
1963-64	1.23	1.14
1964-65	1.20	1.13
1965-66	1.20	1.13
1969-70	1.18	1.13
1970-71	1.20	1.15
1971-72	1.20	1.15

*European Russia.

Sources: Frank Lorimer, The Population of the Soviet Union: History and Prospects (Geneva: League of Nations, 1946), p. 131; D. I. Valentey, ed., Osnovy Teorii Narodonaseleniya (Moscow: Izdatel'stvo "Vysshaya Shkola," 1973), p. 266; and Vestnik Statistiki, no. 12 (1973), p. 75.

1960s, and rose very slightly after 1970. According to published age-specific rates, upward of two-thirds of all births currently occur to women below age 30, and fertility has increased slightly since the late 1950s in age groups 15 to 19 and 20 to 24, but has declined appreciably in other age groups. Women aged 20 to 29 have the highest fertility.[6]

Despite the low level of fertility in the USSR, there are appreciable regional variations in fertility. In 1970, 78.6 percent of the Soviet population lived in republics where the crude birthrate was below 16 per 1,000, and included the following Union republics: RSFSR, the Ukraine, Belorussia, Latvia, and Estonia.[7] Over much of this territory fertility was below the level of replacement of the population. In the period 1963-64 the net reproduction rate of the population of the Ukraine was reported to be below 1, and in 1964-65 in Belorussia it stood at 1.02.[8] Fertility in Latvia was well below replacement in the period 1965-66,[9] as was very probably the case in Estonia. Judging from the low crude birthrates and the gross reproduction rates for the 1970-71 period (Table 7.4), one can conclude that fertility was

TABLE 7.4

Maternal Gross Reproduction Rates by Republic: 1971-72

Republic	Rate
RSFSR	0.99
Ukrainian SSR	1.02
Belorussian SSR	1.13
Uzbek SSR	2.78
Kazakh SSR	1.62
Georgian SSR	1.26
Azerbaydzhan SSR	2.07
Lithuanian SSR	1.15
Moldavian SSR	1.27
Latvian SSR	0.97
Kirgiz SSR	2.40
Tadzhik SSR	2.97
Armenian SSR	1.53
Turkmen SSR	2.85
Estonian SSR	1.05

Source: Vestnik Statistiki, no. 12 (1973), p. 75.

below replacement in the RSFSR, the Ukraine, Latvia, and Estonia and only slightly above replacement in Belorussia and Lithuania. There is also a significant urban-rural differential in fertility; in 1971-72 the urban gross reproduction rate for the USSR was 0.97 and the rural was 1.62.[10]

On the other hand, in 1970 the 8.3 percent of the total Soviet population that lived in Central Asia had crude birthrates above 30 per 1,000 but below 35, and in terms of births per thousand, women aged 15 to 44 had a fertility rate over twice that of the Union-wide average.[11] The fertility rate of the indigenous population of Central Asia approximates that of underdeveloped areas. Between 1959 and 1970 the Uzbeks, Turkmens, and Tadzhiks grew at an average annual rate of 3.9 percent and the Kirgiz grew 3.7. Crude death rates varied from 5.5 to 7.4 per 1,000 during this period for these republics. If one accepts the upper limit of seven deaths per 1,000 total population because of underregistration, this yields an average crude birthrate for this 11-year period in the mid-40s for these nationalities. The lower reported crude birthrates largely reflect the presence of Russians and other "European" populations that have much lower fertility. Gross reproduction rates also reflect this significant fertility

differential (Table 7.4), approaching an average of about six children
even with a significant proportion of Russians living in these areas.
The apparent rise in fertility in Central Asia in the past decade will
be analyzed in the author's volume on fertility. Suffice it to say at
this juncture, changing socioeconomic conditions in the past decade
would not seem to promote a rise in fertility, declining infant mortality has probably affected child-women ratios appreciably, and more
complete birth registration has affected crude birthrates.

Lithuania, Georgia, Moldavia, Armenia, Kazakhstan, and Azerbaydzhan, in terms of crude birthrates, fall between 16 and 30 and
account for 13.1 percent of the Soviet population. Their gross reproduction rates are also intermediate (Table 7.4).

Mortality also has declined significantly from about 32 deaths
per 1,000 population at the beginning of this century to about 8 in the
1970-71 period (Table 7.2). Since the middle 1960s the crude death
rate has been slowly rising, largely because the population is becoming older, although in the past few years age-specific death rates
have been rising slightly particularly for men over 25 years of age.[12]
After age 15, female death rates are significantly lower than male.
Regionally, there is much less variation in crude death rates than in
crude birthrates. The highest crude death rates are in Latvia and Estonia, slightly over 11 per 1,000 in 1970, because of an older population and the lowest are in Armenia, 5.1 per 1,000.[13] The crude
death rates in most republics range between 6 and 9 per 1,000.
There is a slight urban-rural differential; standardized rates by age
in 1971-72 were 7.9 per 1,000 in urban areas and 8.4 in rural.[14]
Because of the decline in mortality, the expectation of life has increased from 32 years in 1897 to 70 years in 1969. There is a significant differential between men and women; in 1969 life expectancy
at birth for women was 74 years, whereas for men it was 65 years.[15]

Since the late 1920s dramatic economic, technical, and social
changes have occurred in the USSR, and associated with this fundamental transformation of Soviet society, the country has gone through
the demographic transition.[16] This pattern, which is common to all
developed countries, is the transition from high to low birth- and
death rates. To date, Soviet fertility has been studied relatively little and adequate data are generally lacking. The decline in fertility
in the USSR is a very complex phenomenon and difficult to explain
adequately. Among the many factors, however, that account for this
decline are rapid urbanization; rising educational levels; a very high
rate of female participation in the work force, which is particularly
influential in the modernized sectors of the economy; an adverse sex
ratio because of male losses during the war, although currently this
factor is of little importance; changes in the proportion of women in
the reproductive ages; a sharp decline in infant mortality; shortages
of services and housing; and a general rise in material aspirations.

In short, the processes of modernization result in a general desire for smaller families, although different groups within the society are affected to a greater or lesser degree. The legalization of abortion and the increasing availability of contraceptives have provided the means to limit family size once the motivation for smaller families developed. Mortality is easier to explain, generally being primarily related to economic development and the availability of modern medicine.

As a result of war, epidemics, and famine, the USSR has suffered enormous population losses in this century. These losses complicate the analysis of virtually all aspects of population change, particularly between the two intercensal periods in which wars occurred. The losses can only be approximated because of the lack of data. For much of this century vital statistics are nonexistent or defective, and the normal errors in censuses preclude making anything but a crude approximation of the population losses. For the period 1914–26 Frank Lorimer used available vital statistics, the 1897 and 1926 censuses, and the scant data on emigration and war losses to estimate the total loss of population from war, famines, epidemics, emigration, and birth deficit. He estimates the total loss for this period at 28 million, but labels his estimate as merely an approximation. Using the 1926 and 1939 censuses and estimating natural increase from vital statistics for the beginning and end of this intercensal period, he estimates the loss of population from forced industrialization, the collectivization of agriculture, and the settlement of nomads at about 5.5 million. Once again, he points out the approximate nature of this estimate.[17]

Population losses during World War II were even greater than during the earlier period. Although there are no exact data as to direct losses as a result of war, they have been estimated at 20 to 22 million, including indirect losses (birth deficit) at not less than 50 million.[18] If one accepts the official natural increase rate of 1939 and 1950, and assumes that in the absence of a war the population would have grown during this period at the median rate, there is a deficit of about 53 million people. If these crude estimates are accepted, the total population loss in this century, both direct and indirect, would be about 87 million people, a truly staggering figure.

Population Growth by Nationality Grouping

The growth of the various nationality groupings between 1897 and 1970 can be described fairly precisely, but there are insufficient data to analyze the growth with any precision. The chief factors underlying the differential growth of the nationality groupings are mortality (including war, epidemic, and famine losses), fertility, emigration, and assimilation. There are no data on mortality by nationality, and even the rough estimates of war losses cannot be distributed evenly, because obviously the occupied areas, and the Jewish population, in particular, suffered disproportionately high losses.

Fertility data by nationality can be obtained only from data on age distribution, from which child-woman ratios can be calculated on the basis of the ratio between children under 10 years of age to women aged 20 to 49. The normal procedure in calculating child-woman ratios is to use children under 5 years of age instead of under 10, but data for children under 5 were not available in all censuses. This measure, however, cannot be converted with any precision to a measure of fertility that could be used for estimating the growth of a nationality, even if mortality data were available. Child-woman ratios are also greatly affected by infant mortality, assimilation, and the usual census problems associated with enumerating young children (that is, underenumeration). Infant mortality is still relatively high in the USSR, and there are significant regional variations. Infant mortality stood at 167 per 1,000 in 1939 and declined to 81 in 1950 and 25 in 1970.[19]

Regionally there is considerable variation; in 1971 the infant mortality rate in Vil'nyus (Lithuanian SSR) was 11 per 1,000 and in Dushanbe (Tadzhik SSR) it was 46.[20] Rural levels very probably are higher and more variable. Child-woman ratios of nationalities that are experiencing considerable assimilation are particularly low, because children very probably are declared as Russians, particularly where there is considerable intermarriage, which results in extremely low child-woman ratios. For example, in the RSFSR in 1970 the child-woman ratio for the Jewish population was 286 per 1,000 women aged 20 to 49 and only 6.2 percent of the Jewish population was below age 10. This is incredibly low fertility and must reflect assimilation. Data on intermarriage are scarce, but in 1969 in Khar'kov 32.6 percent of the Jewish women who married that year married non-Jewish men, mainly Russians and Ukrainians.[21] In 1959 the urban Karelians and Mordvinians also registered extremely low fertility as measured by the child-woman ratio.[22]

In terms of appraising loss or gain of a nationality through assimilation, if a person completely assimilates to another nationality there is no direct measure of this change in identity, even though there are data on nationality and native language that can be used as an indicator of assimilation processes. Data on emigration are also scant, and only very crude estimates can be made. In the analysis of population growth by nationality grouping, an attempt is made to appraise the relative importance of these factors, even though data are lacking to do this with precision.

Russians

The Russians were by far the largest grouping in all census
years, and they increased their proportion of the total population from
about 44 percent in 1897 to about 55 percent in 1959 (Tables 7.5 and
7.6). There was a slight decline in their share of the total population
between 1959 and 1970. Aside from the Tatars, no other grouping
grew as fast as the Russians between 1897 and 1970; the Russian population increased by 132 percent, or 1.2 percent annually. There was
very little variation in the growth of the Russians in the various intercensal periods in that they were above the USSR average in all periods
except the 1959-70 period (Tables 7.7 and 7.8). Despite substantial
population losses, the Russian population maintained a 1.2 percent
growth rate between 1897 and 1926, largely because of a relatively
high rate of natural increase and assimilation. This growth rate is
underestimated because, in the 1897 census, there were no data by
nationality, only by native language. Therefore, considerable numbers of non-Russians were included as Russians in 1897 but not in the
1926 census, when both nationality and native language data were collected. For example, in 1926 about 6.5 million non-Russians spoke
Russian as their native language; Ukrainians, Belorussians, and Jews
accounted for 90 percent of those in this category. Assuming that the
same proportion of the population were non-Russians speaking Russian
as their native language in 1897 as in 1926, the annual growth rate of
the Russians would be about 1.5 percent instead of 1.2, and there
would have been almost 5 million fewer Russians in 1897.

Between 1911 and 1913 political units in the traditional Russian
areas of European USSR had crude natural increase rates generally
ranging between 14 and 18 per 1,000; crude birthrates were generally
in the 40s.[23] According to reported crude birth- and death rates in
1926, these areas generally had crude natural increase rates between
20 and 25 per 1,000, with crude birthrates still generally in the 40s,
although deaths were apparently underregistered.[24] These rates of
natural increase were undoubtedly depressed by the appreciable out-
migration that has occurred in these areas since the middle of the
nineteenth century, so these rates may be considered to be a minimum
estimate of natural increase for the total Russian population.

Assuming that these natural increase rates were generally
characteristic, it is obvious that the overall growth rate of the Russians between 1897 and 1926 was considerable below these rates.
This lower overall growth rate can be accounted for largely by direct
war losses, the birth deficit associated with the war, famine, and
epidemics, and emigration. Lorimer estimates military deaths in
Russia and the USSR between 1914 and 1926 at 2 million, birth deficit
at 10 million, civilian deaths at 14 million, and emigration at 2 mil-

TABLE 7.5

Nationality Groupings as a Percentage of the Total Population:
1897-1970

Grouping	1897	1926	1959	1970
Russians	44.4	47.5	54.6	53.4
Ukrainians	19.4	21.4	17.8	16.9
Belorussians	4.5	3.6	3.8	3.7
Tatars	1.9	1.7	2.4	2.5
Turkic-Muslims	12.1	10.1	10.3	12.9
Jews	3.5	2.4	1.1	0.9
Mobilized Europeans	3.9	3.6	3.8	3.8
Finnic peoples	2.3	2.2	1.5	1.4
Lithuanians	1.3	1.2	1.1	1.1
Moldavians and Romanians	1.0	1.2	1.1	1.2

Sources: See Chapter 2, footnotes 2 and 3.

lion.[25] The Russian population probably suffered losses proportionately greater than those of the total Soviet population. Apparently,
millions of people died in the famine of 1921, which was centered
along the Volga, an area predominantly peopled by Russians.[26] Population losses in European USSR because of epidemics, which generally
are related to famines, have been estimated at 3.3 million between
1914 and 1923.[27] Conversely, the Russian population was probably
somewhat augmented by assimilation; 9.6 percent of the non-Russian
population spoke Russian as their native language in 1926, which indicates that there must have been some assimilation.

Between 1926 and 1959 the Russian population continued to grow
faster than the USSR average (Table 7.8), but below their estimated
rate of natural increase. By 1960 natural increase in the traditional
Russian areas of European USSR had declined to about 15 per 1,000,
with crude death rates ranging between 7 and 8 per 1,000.[28] The
Russian population undoubtedly suffered great losses during World
War II, even though it is impossible to estimate them. Between 1926
and 1939 the total USSR population grew at the rate of 1.2 percent
annually, even though there were major population losses associated
with collectivization, the settling of the nomads, and the Ukrainian
famine. Between 1939 and 1959, however, the total USSR population
grew only 0.4 percent annually. Relative to the total population that
grew 0.7 percent per year, the Russians grew more rapidly between
1926 and 1959, 1.1 percent per year, and this can probably be accounted for largely by assimilation.

TABLE 7.6

Total Population by Nationality Grouping: 1897-1970

Grouping	1897	1926	1959*	1970*
Russians	55,513,302	79,668,661	114,113,579	129,015,140
Ukrainians	24,274,727	35,800,313	37,252,930	40,753,246
Belorussians	5,676,047	6,106,795	7,913,488	9,051,755
Tatars	2,320,748	2,924,948	4,967,701	5,930,670
Turkic-Muslims	15,118,442	16,868,292	21,412,000	31,096,267
Jews	4,308,460	4,090,694	2,267,814	2,150,707
Mobilized Europeans	4,856,213	6,102,347	7,867,017	9,241,651
Finnic peoples	2,879,210	3,703,773	3,124,266	3,282,748
Lithuanians	1,609,887	1,960,144	2,326,094	2,664,944
Moldavians and Romanians	1,303,464	2,030,079	2,320,505	2,817,286
USSR total	125,042,841	167,665,835	208,826,650	241,720,134

*In 1959 and 1970, except for Russians and Ukrainians, figures in this table should not be used for the pro-cedures discussed in Appendix E. The 1959 and 1970 figures in this table represent the entire populations of all groupings as taken from census summary tables. However, the procedures in Appendix E are based on and should utilize populations that are summations of the 19 economic region totals. Except for Russians and Ukrainians, these summations are less than the census summary figures. Thus, for the eight other groupings in 1959 and 1970, the following figures should be used in association with Appendix E: B (7,739,771 and 9,036,891); T (4,885,567 and 5,903,871); TM 20,688,950 and 30,625,999); J (2,124,956 and 2,118,630); ME (7,585,035 and 9,013,659); FP (2,859,975 and 3,150,306); L (2,220,186 and 2,610,061); and MR (2,221,541 and 2,729,434).

Sources: See Chapter 2, footnotes 2 and 3.

TABLE 7.7

Percentage Change in the Total Population by Nationality Grouping: 1897–1970

Grouping	1897–1926	1926–59	1897–1959	1959–70	1926–70	1897–1970
Russians	43.5	43.2	105.6	13.1	61.9	132.4
Ukrainians	47.5	4.1	53.5	9.4	13.8	67.9
Belorussians	7.6	29.6	39.4	14.4	48.2	59.5
Tatars	26.0	69.8	114.1	19.4	102.8	155.6
Turkic-Muslims	11.6	26.9	41.6	45.2	84.3	105.7
Jews	-5.3	-44.6	-47.4	-5.2	-47.4	-50.1
Mobilized Europeans	25.7	28.9	62.0	17.5	51.4	90.3
Finnic peoples	28.6	-15.7	8.5	5.1	-11.4	14.0
Lithuanians	21.8	18.7	44.5	14.5	36.0	65.5
Moldavians and Romanians	55.7	14.3	78.0	21.4	38.8	116.1
USSR total	34.1	24.5	67.0	15.8	44.2	93.3

Sources: See Chapter 2, footnotes 2 and 3.

TABLE 7.8

Average Annual Percentage Change in the Total Population by Nationality Grouping: 1897–1970

Grouping	1897–1926	1926–59	1897–1959	1959–70	1926–70	1897–1970
Russians	1.2	1.1	1.2	1.1	1.1	1.2
Ukrainians	1.3	0.1	0.7	0.8	0.3	0.7
Belorussians	0.3	0.8	0.5	1.2	0.9	0.6
Tatars	0.8	1.7	1.2	1.6	1.6	1.3
Turkic-Muslims	0.4	0.7	0.6	3.4	1.4	1.0
Jews	−0.2	−1.9	−1.0	−0.5	−1.5	−1.0
Mobilized Europeans	0.8	0.8	0.8	1.5	1.0	0.9
Finnic peoples	0.9	−0.5	0.1	0.4	−0.3	0.2
Lithuanians	0.7	0.5	0.6	1.3	0.7	0.7
Moldavians and Romanians	1.5	0.4	0.9	1.7	0.8	1.1
USSR total	1.0	0.7	0.8	1.4	0.9	0.9

Sources: See Chapter 2, footnotes 2 and 3.

In a multinational state, the population growth of individual nationalities is a function not only of the usual demographic components (fertility, mortality, and migration) but also of ethnic assimilation.* Assimilation may contribute significantly to the growth of certain nationalities (those to which people are assimilating) or, conversely, assimilation may retard growth or even result in absolute declines among ethnic groups that are losing adherents. It has long been recognized that the process of ethnic assimilation in the USSR is a dynamic one, and much attention has focused upon the announced programs of the Soviet government that advocate and encourage the merger of nationalities.[29] It appears, however, that the magnitude of ethnic change in the Soviet Union, as well as certain determinants of the process, has not been fully appreciated. Our estimates, admittedly based upon incomplete data and employing simplifying assumptions, indicate that since 1926 a minimum of between 4 and 6 million non-Russians assimilated to the Russian nationality. Furthermore, our data disclose that the majority of those non-Russians who changed their ethnic identity to Russians were rural dwellers, in contrast to most accepted generalizations concerning assimilation, which stress the importance of the urban, modernized sector for assimilatory processes.

Assimilation in the Soviet context involves principally, but not entirely, the shift from non-Russian nationalities to Russians. (We must also take note of the fact that considerable assimilation other than Russification has taken place in the Soviet Union, or, in other words, assimilation from one non-Russian group to another. This assimilation has resulted largely from the consolidation of smaller tribal groups into the larger nationalities, and has occurred primarily among the Turkic-Muslim groups. Such changes in ethnic group identity are not directly our concern here, inasmuch as the losing and gaining groups are both within our larger nationality groupings; assimilation in these cases therefore has no effect on the growth of the total grouping.[30]) This process, entailing a change in ethnic identity, is generally referred to as "Russification," in contrast to "Sovietization," which involves the broad process of modernization and industrialization, and "Russianization," which refers to the proliferation of Russian language and culture.[31] These three elements, in this formulation, are interdependent, with Russianization and Sovietization hypothetically promoting Russification.

A great deal of emphasis has been placed upon the linguistic affiliations of Soviet nationalities, with the adoption by non-Russians of the Russian language as the native tongue (rodnoy yazyk) seen as

---

*See Chapter 4 for the conceptual basis of this section and definition of terms regarding ethnic assimilation.

the primary indicator of Russification.[32] Soviet censuses provide considerable data for various geographic units cross-tabulated by nationality and native language, age and sex, and urban-rural residence. These data provide the basis for most inferences concerning ethnic assimilation in the USSR. In this regard the shift of non-Russians to the Russian language must be considered as an intermediate step along the assimilation continuum, and not as complete Russification. Indeed, the major shortcoming of the reliance upon language affiliation data as an indicator of Russification is that once complete Russification has taken place, the individual declares himself as a Russian and "disappears" into the mass of that nationality. Therefore, language affiliation provides insights into the process or determinants of Russification, but because of the nature of these data there are no reasonable methods of estimating the actual numbers of individuals who have become completely assimilated.

Data available for the first time, derived in conjunction with this study, provide another means of investigating the process of Russification. More important, these data enable an estimate of the magnitude of ethnic change in the Soviet Union. Essentially, our procedure involved historical comparisons of various nationality populations on the oblast and equivalent-level scale between the census years 1926, 1959, and 1970. Our attention focused on those units within the RSFSR and Kazakhstan, because preliminary investigation revealed that war losses and population transfers in the Baltic republics and in the Belorussian, Ukrainian, and Moldavian SSRs were of such dimensions as to obscure the ethnic changes caused by assimilation. The Transcaucasian and Central Asian republics likewise were excluded from our analysis because of the relatively insignificant Russification that has occurred in these areas.

With a time series for each nationality in each oblast of the RSFSR and Kazakhstan, we simply summed population declines to arrive at an estimated loss due to assimilation. Thus, if the Ukrainian population of Saratov Oblast declined from about 223,000 in 1926 to 112,000 in 1959, which in fact it did, we would estimate the loss due to Russification at approximately 111,000. This procedure has obvious drawbacks, which at once overestimate and underestimate the number of persons who actually assimilated. For example, it is, of course, possible that some persons may have moved to other areas of the Soviet Union, accounting for part of the decline. Furthermore, various calamities, such as famines and natural disasters, together with losses during World War II, would further reduce the population of any nationality caught up in these events. Most of the areas included in the present analysis were beyond the zone of German occupation; although there would naturally have been military losses from these areas, civilian deaths would certainly not have been as severe as in the occupied territories to the west. In this regard we take note of all nationality population trends within a given unit in order to judge the reliability of each estimate; if all groups declined during a certain period, the case for assimilation would be open to doubt. On the other hand, simply utilizing the absolute decline for each ethnic group to estimate assimilation does not take into account natural increase among the groups, and almost certainly results in an underestimate of the numbers actually involved. Furthermore, it is likely that an unknown number of non-Russians moved into these areas in advance of German forces, again adding to the population of these groups. It would be much too convenient to suggest that these factors would effectively balance out. Rather, we would ask the reader to keep them firmly in mind when evaluating our estimates.

As with the majority of conceptual studies of assimilation, those focusing upon ethnic change in the Soviet Union have stressed the impact of modernization as the primary determinant of assimilation.[33] Clearly, the urban environment, in particular, appears, at least on the basis of language affiliation, to play a very important role in the assimilation process, with those non-Russians in cities being considerably more prone to adopt Russian as the native tongue. These formulations agree with those concepts propounded by Karl Deutsch and others that suggest increased ethnic contacts and interethnic communication in urban areas break down nationality barriers and promote assimilation. Conversely, these same concepts point to rural areas as areas of generally low rates of ethnic assimilation.[34]

Another major determinant of assimilation in the USSR is the area in which members of the various nationalities reside. The Soviet Union is a federation of ethnically based territorial units, and each nationality derives certain cultural and educational benefits within but not outside its particular republic, autonomous republic, or autonomous or national okrug. It is generally agreed that the maintenance of cultural and social institutions is critical to nationality vitality, and that the lack of schools, clubs, mutual aid societies, and media access in one's native language may result in an erosion of ethnic identity.[35] The educational system appears to be of primary importance; in the Soviet Union, schools are provided in the native language only within the nationality homeland itself.[36] Thus, assimilatory pressures can be expected to be strongest outside the individual nationality's homeland.

Our analysis revealed that while modernization-urbanization is no doubt a major contributing factor in the assimilation-Russification process in the Soviet Union, the vast majority of those who apparently changed from non-Russian to Russian nationality did so in rural areas and were, in general, from the less-urbanized nationalities. The influence of residence outside one's own nationality area, which effectively eliminates many of the reinforcing elements of ethnic identity, emerged as the principal determinant of Russification. Finally, as one might expect, an element of time lag is evident in the patterns of Russification, with those areas of longest historical settlement of non-Russians in Russian regions providing the majority of those persons assimilating. The process of assimilation is generally measured in generations, therefore, those areas in which a number of generations of non-Russians have been removed from their homeland would be the areas in which Russification would be expected to be most intense.

Specifically, the overwhelming share of non-Russians who assimilated to Russians appears to have been approximately 3 to 4.5 million rural Ukrainians, who, between 1926 and 1959, "disappeared" from areas of historic Ukrainian agricultural settlement along the Kursk-Belgorod-Voronezh-Rostov-North Caucasus axis, in the area around Saratov, and in West Siberia. An examination of language-affiliation data from the 1926 Soviet census revealed that Ukrainians residing in rural areas (the number of urban Ukrainians in these areas was very small, usually less than 10 percent of the total) in these regions had relatively high levels of linguistic Russification. In the North Caucasus region in 1926, for example, approximately 43 percent of Ukrainians declared Russian as their native language. Levels of linguistic Russification in other areas were lower than in the North Caucasus, however, at times reaching only 10 percent. In the seven units in which Ukrainians experienced the greatest population declines between 1926 and 1959 (Rostov, Kursk, Belgorod, Voronezh, and Saratov oblasts and Krasnodar and Stavropol krays), the number of Russians increased significantly in all but two (Kursk and Saratov oblasts). Thus, war losses would not explain the entire Ukrainian decline, unless the losses affected the Ukrainians disproportionately, large numbers of Russians moved to these areas after World War II and before 1959, or the Russians had very high rates of natural increase that enabled them to replace the war losses. The first possible explanation seems unlikely, the second unrealistic in light of migration and regional development studies, and the third we know to be untrue (the Russians were characterized by moderate fertility at this time); therefore, Russification appears to be the principal cause of the decline in the Ukrainian population in these units.

The Russification of rural Ukrainians from these rural, agricultural regions has been noted previously, but the magnitude has not been appreciated.[37] Several authorities have attributed the Russification of Ukrainians in the North Caucasus and Central Chernozem to the lack of Ukrainian cultural institutions, most of which were closed by the Soviet regime in the 1930s (this area is outside the Ukrainian Republic).[38] The decline in Ukrainian population in many

units between 1959 and 1970 lends additional support to the Russification explanation, there having been no war or known catastrophe during
this later period that might account for the losses. In all units in
which Ukrainians declined by more than 5,000 between 1959 and 1970,
the number of Russians increased significantly (by an amount much
greater than the Ukrainian decline). Many of the units in which large
Ukrainian declines were noted during this period were agricultural
areas of predominantly rural Ukrainian settlement (the Central Chernozem, West Siberia, and Far East regions), which were also characterized by high rates of linguistic Russification (generally over half
of the Ukrainians in these areas declared Russian as their native
language).

With regard to the aforementioned time-lag element, the large
Ukrainian rural population in Siberia and the Far East, originating
mainly from the great agricultural migrations to these regions around
the turn of the century, became the focal area of Russification during
the period 1959-70. Although a few units in West Siberia witnessed
a decline in the Ukrainian population during the earlier 1926-59 period
(particularly in Altay Kray and Novosibirsk Oblast), the losses in the
east between 1959 and 1970 were proportionately greater and occurred
on a much wider scale. The Ukrainian population declined in 11 of
the 18 units of West Siberia, East Siberia, and the Far East between
1959 and 1970; in these three regions alone the Ukrainian losses
amounted to over 165,000, accounting for the majority of the Ukrainian
decline in the RSFSR. Thus, the principal area of Russification of
Ukrainians shifted to the eastern regions during the later period, a
reflection of the more recent settlement in these areas in relation to
the earlier settled areas adjoining the Ukrainian homeland (such as
the areas around Kursk, Belgorod, Voronezh, and the North Caucasus) where the majority of assimilation took place in the earlier 1926-
59 period.

Interestingly, however, there were several units in the Urals
and Siberia, areas of large-scale economic development and of sharp
increases in the numbers of Ukrainians during the earlier 1926-59
period, in which the number of Ukrainians declined significantly during the later 1959-70 period. This suggests that the modernization-
urbanization-Russification process has resulted in the assimilation of
Ukrainians in these areas. Furthermore, this trend indicates that
Russification indeed may operate at a faster rate in the urban-industrial setting than in rural areas, since Ukrainian migration to these
areas is relatively recent, dating only from the 1930s.

In addition to the Ukrainians, a number of other non-Russian
groups apparently have provided large numbers of persons who assimilated to Russians. These include, between 1926 and 1970, some
100,000 Karelians (residing near Kalinin, or Tver), 120,000 Mord-

vinians (primarily from the Volga area), 100,000 Belorussians (mainly in West Siberia), and smaller numbers of Mari, Udmurts, Chuvash, Poles, Germans, and other groups. Because of their catastrophic war losses, it is not possible to estimate Jewish assimilation to Russians between 1926 and 1959 but it can be surmised that considerable Russification occurred. By our estimates, during the period 1959-70, it appears that more than 50,000 Jews in the RSFSR and Kazakhstan changed their ethnic affiliation to Russian, and the Jewish population of the total USSR declined by 117,000. We would remind the reader once again that inasmuch as these estimates do not include any allowance for natural increase, but only those cases where ethnic populations declined on an oblast scale, the number of persons who actually assimilated in fact must have been much larger.

These assimilation patterns suggest that policies of the Soviet government regarding education and cultural activities are effective in promoting Russification. At issue, however, is whether these policies, such as those limiting native language educational facilities to nationality units, are specifically intended to facilitate Russification or are merely the result of administrative or financial efficiencies.

In summary of this point, it would seem that the process of ethnic change known as Russification has resulted at a minimum in the assimilation of approximately 4 to 6 million non-Russians to the Russian nationality. By far, the largest constituent part of this total was accounted for by Ukrainians, mostly rural dwellers in areas historically dominated by Russians. The assimilation that has taken place since 1926 has apparently resulted from the lack of ethnic cultural institutions for non-Russians in Russian areas. The long historical association of most of these nationalities with the Russians, as well as close linguistic affinities between the Russians and other Slavic groups, such as Ukrainians, Belorussians, and Poles, no doubt has facilitated the Russification process.

Population growth has been slow among those nationalities that are losing adherents to the Russians, with many groups experiencing absolute declines. Between 1959 and 1970 the number of Jews, Mordvinians, Poles, Karelians, and Finns declined by a combined total of over 380,000; language affiliation data suggest that most of this decline can be attributed to Russification (although some Poles apparently shifted to Ukrainian). Assimilation compounds the low rates of natural increase characteristic of those groups that are becoming Russified, and losses to assimilation often account for sizable shares of a nationality's population. For example, the approximately 4 million Ukrainians who assimilated to Russian since 1926 would amount to 10 percent of the present-day Ukrainian population of the USSR. It is obvious from the foregoing discussion that assimilation has increased the Russian population and resulted in losses for many other nationalities.

The analysis of historical population trends in the Soviet Union always entails a certain amount of hazardous estimation. The difficulty of arriving at a reasonably accurate estimate of the extent of Russification is doubly troublesome because of the nature of the assimilation process itself and such complicating factors as migration and natural increase. Our estimate of the Russification of from 4 to 6 million non-Russians must, by the limited methodology employed, be considered a minimum figure, because no natural increase of the groups was taken into account. Thus, even a very small increase in a large non-Russian group, an increase considerably below expected levels, would exempt this group from our estimates. Furthermore, the estimates utilized herein were drawn solely from the RSFSR and Kazakhstan, and substantial Russification no doubt has taken place in other areas (such as the cities in the Belorussian and Ukrainian republics).

The impact of Russification upon the growth of individual Soviet nationalities suggests that assimilation is a factor in any study of population trends in a multinational state. Within the Soviet context further research concerning the demographic and socioeconomic correlates of Russification is necessary in order to include more precise estimations of the numbers involved. Clearly, additional emphasis upon ethnic change as a factor in demographic analysis is warranted.

It would seem reasonable to assume that the Russian growth rate should not have been above the USSR average. That it grew faster is very probably owing largely to assimilation. Although the Russian population probably did not suffer proportionately as great war losses as did the Ukrainians and Belorussians, whose territories were totally occupied, Russian war losses must have been great, considering that much of western Russian areas were occupied and their losses at Leningrad alone approach a million people. There was some emigration of Russians during World War II, but it affected the growth rate of Russians very slightly, because of the large number of Russians relative to the very small number of immigrants. Eugene Kulischer has estimated the total number of nonrepatriable displaced persons from the USSR at 300,000, and most of these were very probably not Russian. This figure excludes ethnic Germans, German refugees from East Prussia, and Poles.[39]

On the basis of natural increase, the Russian population probably did not grow significantly faster than other nationality groupings between 1926 and 1959. Very probably mortality declined first in European USSR. In the 50 gubernii of European Russia, the crude death rate declined from 36 per 1,000 population in the period 1891-95 to 27 in the period 1911-14; for roughly the same territory it had declined to about 20 by 1929.[40] By 1940 the reported crude death rate for the USSR was 18 per 1,000, but there must have been considerable underreporting.[41] Many nationality areas, particularly in the North Caucasus, Transcaucasus, and Central Asia, had death rates much below the Union-wide average, and many nationality areas in the west, where reporting was presumably better, registered death rates much above the USSR average. By 1959 the crude death rate for the USSR had declined to 7.6 per 1,000, but reported crude death rates in the Transcaucasus and Central Asia were still well below the Union-wide average.[42] From the scant available data, it can very probably be assumed that mortality declined first among the "European" population of the USSR, particularly in the west, and as medical facilities were made available, mortality decline spread to the other nationality areas. That the Turkic-Muslim group grew slowly between 1926 and 1959 and very rapidly between 1959 and 1970 would seem to support this contention.

Child-woman ratios are the only data available on fertility by nationality (Table 7.9). According to this measure, in 1926 fertility was uniformly high with relatively little variation by nationality; infant mortality as well as variations in fertility are reflected in this indicator of fertility, which very probably accounts for the lower levels among some of the Turkic-Muslim groups. By 1959 the Russian child-woman ratio was about 70 percent of the level in 1926; thus, mortality decline among the Russian population and other European groups was accompanied by a significant decline in fertility. Between 1959 and 1970 Russian fertility continued to decline, according to the child-woman ratio. It can probably be assumed that at first mortality declined faster than fertility among the "European" population and the East Slavs grew faster than the other nationality groups, but as mortality declined throughout the USSR and Slavic fertility declined, the situation reversed itself, because fertility has remained at moderate to high levels among many of the "non-European" nationalities.

Between 1959 and 1970 there were no significant war losses or emigration of the Russian population, and they grew at 1.1 percent per year, or about 13 percent in these 11 years, which was very probably above their natural increase rate. That they grew faster than was expected is because of assimilation. Between 1960 and 1970 the average rate of natural increase for the RSFSR was 9.5 per 1,000.[43] The crude birthrate declined from 23 to 15 per 1,000 and the crude death rate rose from 7 to 9 per 1,000, resulting in a very slow rate of natural increase in 1970. In both 1959 and 1970 Russians comprised 83 percent of the population of the RSFSR, and 86 percent of the Russians lived in the RSFSR in 1959, while 84 percent lived there in 1970. The non-Russian population in the RSFSR generally has higher fertility than the Russians, particularly the nationalities along the Volga, in the North Caucasus, and in Siberia. The Russian population outside the RSFSR, although younger because of migration, is

TABLE 7.9

Child-Woman Ratio by Major Nationality: 1926, 1959, and 1970
(number of children 0 to 9 per woman 20 to 49)

Nationality	1926	1959	1970
Karelians	1.335	0.702	0.482
Latvians	—	0.612	0.675
Estonians	—	0.638	0.677
Ukrainians	1.354	0.714	0.691
Russians	1.233	0.863	0.727
Belorussians	1.486	0.836	0.759
Lithuanians	—	0.823	0.859
Georgians	1.483	0.905	0.933
Tatars	1.432	1.105	1.002
Mordvinians	1.432	0.933	1.015
Ossetians	1.931	0.998	1.032
Komi	1.266	1.052	1.044
Moldavians	1.377	1.190	1.099
Udmurts	1.248	1.131	1.105
Chuvash	1.339	1.037	1.154
Armenians	1.575	1.240	1.203
Mari	1.202	1.146	1.310
Bashkirs	1.441	1.431	1.540
Buryats	1.043	1.460	1.563
Kabardinians	—	1.537	1.584
Balkars	—	1.698	1.616
Yakuts	1.410	1.494	1.622
Kalmyks	1.200	1.646	1.741
Kumyks	—	1.504	1.848
Tuvinians	—	1.728	1.853
Avars	—	1.334	1.967
Azeri	1.794	1.711	2.082
Kazakhs	1.261	1.896	2.213
Lezgians	—	1.722	2.214
Dargins	—	1.427	2.249
Chechens	1.805	2.204	2.257
Ingush	2.180	2.042	2.265
Turkmens	1.384	1.809	2.384
Uzbeks	1.134	1.878	2.401
Tadzhiks	1.257	1.782	2.422
Kirgiz	1.134	1.885	2.445

Note: The child-woman ratio is defined here as the number of children aged 0 to 9 per woman aged 20 to 49. For 1926 and 1959 the appropriate age groups could be extracted directly from the census. For 1970 appropriate age groups were not available by nationality; 0 to 10 instead of 0 to 9, and total population aged 20 to 49 and not females 20 to 49. In order to estimate the number of children aged 0 to 9, the 0 to 10 population was multiplied by 0.9, it being assumed that 90 percent of the 0 to 10 age group would be in the 0 to 9 age group. In order to estimate the number of females 20 to 49, the total population 20 to 49 was multiplied by 0.52, since females constituted 52 percent of the total 20 to 49 population of the USSR.

Sources: 1926, 1959, and 1970 Soviet censuses (see Chapter 2, footnote 2).

largely urban, and therefore probably does not have higher fertility
than the Russian population within the RSFSR. In fact, the 9.5 per
1,000 figure is probably an overestimate of the Russian natural increase rate; probably 9 per 1,000 would be a more reasonable estimate of Russian natural increase since 1959. If one assumes a 0.95
percent average annual increase, there would be about 2.4 million
fewer Russians than were enumerated in the 1970 census, and if one
assumes a 0.90 percent rate the "deficit" is about 3 million. The
amount of assimilation of non-Russians probably falls somewhere
within this range, even though these are very crude estimates.

Thus, the Russian population has gone through the demographic
transition. By the turn of the century, crude death rates were declining in Russian areas; by 1926 they were at moderate levels. Fertility
remained high until some time after 1926, and by 1959 crude birthrates for the Russian population were in the low 20s and the crude
death rate was low. After 1959 Russian fertility continued to decline,
and currently is at a very low level.

Prior to the publication of the results of the 1970 census, there
was much speculation among those interested in Soviet nationality problems about the possibility that the Russian population would no longer
be a majority of the Soviet population. This issue and its possible
psychological or political impact on the Russians or the Soviet leadership have been raised repeatedly in professional meetings. Of course,
it is impossible to appraise the psychological impact of a relative decline of Russians from, say, 55 to 49 percent between two censuses;
most Russians are probably unaware of their share of the total population, except in a very vague sense.

Clearly, the Russians are and have been politically the dominant
group in the USSR and in the Russian Empire, despite their varying
relative share of the population. Furthermore, there is no indication
that their dominance has varied with their relative share of the population. In fact, a dominant group need not be in the majority; witness
the position of the West Pakistanis in the state of Pakistan as it formerly existed. In terms of the present-day boundaries, it has only
been sometime after 1926 that the Russians have comprised a majority
of the Soviet population (Table 7.5), and no appreciable change in their
influence can be related to this relative increase. Their dominance
relates primarily to political, historical, economic, and ideological
factors, not just to sheer numbers. Within the boundaries of the Russian Empire in 1897 their share was 44.3 percent; it rose to about
53 percent within the 1926 boundaries, largely because of the loss of
territory inhabited by non-Russians, and to 58.1 percent in 1939.
With the territory and population acquired during World War II, the
Russians declined relatively; Russians enumerated in the 1939 census
as a percent of the 1939 population in present-day boundaries com-

prised 51.3 percent of the population. Thus, the Russians have not
always been in the majority in the Russian Empire and the USSR, and
their proportion of the total population has varied considerably.

Because of the current differences in natural increase among
the various nationalities, there have been exaggerated statements as
to the future ethnic composition of the USSR. For example, after a
very brief discussion of relative fertility differentials among nationalities as measured by child-woman ratios, Alexandre Bennigsen
states, "If the trend continued, in the year 2000 the Soviet Union would
probably have a Turkic and Muslim majority and a Russian and even
a Slavic minority."[44] To test this notion, we will make the following
assumptions, which are very favorable for the relatively rapid growth
of the Turkic-Muslim population: the non-Turkic-Muslim population
of the USSR will not grow at all during the next 30 years; and the
Turkic-Muslim population, including the Tatars, will grow at 3.1
percent per year, its average growth between 1959 and 1970. If
these conditions prevailed, by the year 2000 the Turkic-Muslim population would increase from about 37 million, or 15 percent of the total
population in 1970, to about 92 million, or 31 percent of the total population in the year 2000. The Eastern Slavs would comprise 60 percent
of the USSR population and the Russians 43 percent. Thus, even if
these differential rates were realized, the Turkic-Muslims would
still not be close to comprising a majority of the Soviet population,
as Bennigsen has stated would probably occur, and although the USSR
would have a Russian minority, it would not have the Slavic minority
that he predicted.

It is, of course, an exercise in futility to attempt to predict the
growth of the population of the various groups to the end of the century, because in order to do this one would have to know in detail the
economic, social, and cultural conditions under which the various
groups will be living in the next 30 years. Judging from past and current economic and urban trends, it would seem reasonable to assume
that by the end of the century the USSR will be a highly industrialized
and urbanized society, and that these developments will affect the
growth of the population of all groups, although differentially. It is
probably not realistic to assume that the non-Turkic-Muslim population will not grow at all. For example, in the major areas of Slavic
settlement (RSFSR, the Ukraine, Belorussia) and in the Baltic republics where fertility is low, natural increase in 1972 was between 0.5
and 1 percent per year.[45] Natural increase will probably decline in
these areas because the net reproduction rate is near or below 1 in
most of these areas, and fertility may continue to decline slowly as
urbanization continues and educational levels increase. Current natural increase is the result of higher fertility in the past that affects
the current age distribution rather than the current level of fertility.

Therefore, even without a further decline in fertility, the population would probably be near replacement by the end of the century. Mortality will rise as the population becomes older. By the end of the century these areas will probably all be near or below replacement; highly urbanized areas and rural areas that have experienced much out-migration will probably have a natural decrease in population. In 1972 several oblasts to the north of Moscow experienced a natural decrease in population, largely because of the affect of rural depopulation on fertility. However, during the overall period there should be some population growth, and the Russians will probably continue to grow faster than other Slavic groups because of assimilation.

The assumption that Turkic-Muslim natural increase will continue at the rate of the past 11 years until the end of the century is also not realistic. Fertility is not uniformly high among all Turkic-Muslim groups, and some groups are experiencing declines, as might be expected. For example, Tatar fertility is less than half of the level of the major Central Asian groups and appears to be declining, although child-woman ratios can be compared only very crudely (Table 7.9). The Tatars are a large group, numbering about 6 million in 1970, that has experienced considerable modernization. Other Volga Turkic-Muslim groups also have fertility levels significantly lower than the Central Asian groups, and also appear to be declining. There is evidence of fertility decline among other Turkic-Muslim groups, as well. In the Azerbaydzhan SSR, for example, the crude birthrate declined from 43 per 1,000 in 1960 to 26 in 1972,[46] even though the child-woman ratio for the Azeri rose between 1959 and 1970, probably due largely to changes in infant mortality. Even the Central Asian groups will probably experience a substantial decline in fertility by the end of the century.

Educational levels are rising among both urban and rural Turkic-Muslim women in Central Asia, and the proportion married aged 16 to 19 has declined sharply. For example, among rural Uzbek women educational levels rose from 20 per 1,000 finishing ten years or more of school and 224 per 1,000 finishing seven years or more in 1959 to 88 and 333, respectively, in 1970. Most of the increase was among young women. The proportion of women aged 16 to 19 who were married dropped from 323 per 1,000 in 1959 to 219 in 1970. Roughly comparable changes in education and early marriage occurred among the other major groups in Central Asia, and these general trends are occurring among most Turkic-Muslims. Peter Mazur found a significant relationship between fertility differentials by nationality and education and the percentage of females aged 20 to 49 that were married.[47] In particular, there is a strong relationship between fertility and the percentage of women aged 16 to 19 that are married; consequently, changes in these variables should affect fertility.

294 NATIONALITY AND POPULATION CHANGE

As indicated in a previous chapter, the Turkic-Muslim population has also increased its level of urbanization, although not as substantially as most other groupings, and will continue to do so in the future. The essential point is that the Turkic-Muslims are modernizing and moving into the modernized sectors of the society, and this will result in a decline in fertility and natural increase. It is impossible to estimate accurately what proportion of the total Soviet population the Turkic-Muslim population will comprise by the end of the century, but clearly they will not be a majority nor will the Eastern Slavs be a minority, unless they suffer catastrophic population losses. The Russians will probably constitute less than half of the population, but will undoubtedly continue to be by far the largest nationality.

Ukrainians

Between 1897 and 1970 the Ukrainian population grew relatively slowly, 0.7 percent per year, or 68 percent, largely because of fertility decline, war, famine, and assimilation, and their proportion of the total population declined from 19 percent in 1897 to 17 in 1970 (Tables 7.5 to 7.8). In fact, the Ukrainian population actually grew slower than this rate, because the number of Ukrainians in 1897 was underestimated. As already indicated, in the 1897 census there are no data on nationality as such; there are data, however, on native language, which is generally a good approximation of nationality. Because a substantial number of Ukrainians considered Russian to be their native language, we have had to record them as Russians, not Ukrainians, thus underestimating the 1897 Ukrainian population.

In the 1896-1900 period, natural increase of the political units that comprise the present-day Ukraine averaged about 20 per 1,000 with crude birthrates in the 40s or 50s and crude death rates generally in the 20s. In 1926 the crude birthrate for the Ukrainian SSR was reported at 42 per 1,000, the crude death rate at 18, and crude natural increase at 24 per 1,000.[48] Therefore, under normal conditions it might be expected that the Ukrainian population would have grown by roughly 2 percent per year between 1897 and 1926 and there would have been roughly 8 million more Ukrainians than were reported in 1926. However, the growth of Ukrainians during this period averaged only 1.3 percent per year, a figure that is inflated by the underenumeration in 1897. Although the Ukraine was not a major battle area during World War I, the Ukrainians probably sustained their proportionate share of direct military deaths and a decline in fertility as a result of mobilization. The Ukraine, however, was a major area of military conflict during the Civil War as competing armies, including the Germans, attempted to control this grain-producing area; the result was hunger, economic disruption, and considerable loss of life. The famine of 1922-23, although centered in the Volga and Urals, also occurred in the southern Ukraine and the Crimea.[49] In short, the civil war period was very chaotic in the Ukraine and the loss of life was great. That the Ukrainians increased their share of the total Soviet population from 19 to 21 percent is largely because of their relatively high rate of natural increase and the underestimate of their population in 1897.

Between 1926 and 1959 the Ukrainian population increased only 4.1 percent, or 0.1 percent per year; in fact, within the 1926 boundaries of the USSR there was a 10 percent decline in the Ukrainian population between 1926 and 1939, or some 3 million people. The chief sources of this decline were a major famine from 1932 to 1934, considerable Russification, and collectivization. Losses from the famine must have been in the millions, although they are difficult to estimate with any precision.[50] As we have previously indicated, there was substantial Russification of Ukrainians between 1926 and 1959, which would also account for the loss of millions. During World War II, the Ukraine was occupied by the Germans and was a major area of battle, and the loss of life must have been substantial. Throughout the 1926-59 period natural increase declined in the Ukrainian SSR because the reported crude birthrate declined faster than the crude death rate. By 1960 the crude birthrate of the Ukraine had declined to 21 per 1,000, or by 50 percent since 1926; child-woman ratios for the Ukrainian population also indicate about a 50 percent decline in fertility between 1926 and 1959 (Table 7.9). Crude death rates declined from a reported 18 per 1,000 in 1926 to 7 in 1960; thus natural increase declined from 24 to 14 per 1,000.[51] If one assumes a linear decline in natural increase for the Ukraine between 1926 and 1959 and accepts a median natural increase rate of 19 per 1,000 as representative of the Ukrainian population, the deficit between the expected and observed population is some 28 million. Of course, this estimate is extremely crude, because the assumption of a linear decline is not realistic and the reporting of births and deaths was not complete. The essential point is that between 1926 and 1959 the Ukrainian population suffered great losses, even if they cannot be accurately estimated, and their share of the total Soviet population declined considerably (Table 7.5).

Between 1959 and 1970 the Ukrainian population increased 0.8 percent per year, or 14 percent. This relatively slow increase was mainly the result of a continued decline in natural increase but Russification probably continued to be an important source of population loss. Natural increase in the Ukrainian SSR declined to 6 per 1,000 in 1970; the crude birthrate declined to 15 per 1,000. These figures probably are fairly representative of the Ukrainian population in that 75 percent of the population of the republic in 1970 was Ukrainian and

87 percent of the Ukrainians lived in the republic. According to their child-woman ratio, Ukrainian fertility continued to decline since 1959 and has one of the lowest ratios in the USSR. Once again, if a median natural increase rate is accepted, there is a deficit of some 800,000; it is probably fair to say that losses from Russification were in the hundreds of thousands. In short, the Ukrainian population has completed the transition from high to low death and birthrates, with a pattern similar to that of the Russian population.

Belorussians

The Belorussians experienced the slowest population growth of the three Eastern Slav nationalities between 1897 and 1970, increasing by only about 60 percent, or 0.6 percent per year, largely because its territory was occupied in both world wars and thus they suffered disproportionately large war losses (Tables 7.7 and 7.8). Their natural increase rate was much above their growth rate, which reflects a substantial loss of population. In the period 1896-1900 natural increase in roughly the territory of present-day Belorussia was about 18 per 1,000,[52] and by 1926 it had increased to 26 per 1,000 within the 1926 boundaries of Belorussia.[53] By 1960 it had declined to 18 per 1,000 and by 1971 to 9 per 1,000.[54] Despite this relatively low natural increase in recent years, the Belorussian rate of growth was the highest between 1959 and 1970 because of the absence of war.

The Belorussian population also has gone through the demographic transition in a manner similar to the Russians and Ukrainians. Crude birthrates for the territory of Belorussia declined from 43 in the 1896-1900 period to 41 in 1926, 24 in 1960, and 16 in 1970. Child-woman ratios for Belorussians also reflect this decline, decreasing by about 50 percent between 1926 and 1970 (Table 7.9). Mortality declined from about 25 per 1,000 total population in the 1896-1900 period to 15 in 1926, 7 in 1960, and 8 in 1970. The vast majority of the Belorussians live in Belorussia in all census years (Appendix E), so these rates are probably representative of the Belorussian population.

Russification probably also accounts for the relatively slow growth of the Belorussian population; in 1926, 27.6 percent of the Belorussians spoke Russian as their native language, in 1959, 15.3 percent, and in 1970 about 19 percent. As mentioned before, in major areas of Belorussian settlement outside their republic there have been sharp declines in their numbers (Chapter 6). As a result of this slow growth of population, their relative proportion of the total Soviet population has declined (Table 7.5).

Tatars

The Tatars are the only Turkic-Muslim group that has undergone appreciable modernization, and this is reflected in their pattern of population growth. Unfortunately, data on natural increase for the Tatars are scant, but the pattern of growth can be inferred from the expected patterns of a modernizing population. The Tatars are the only group that grew faster, even though only slightly faster, than the Russians between 1897 and 1970 (Tables 7.7 and 7.8), largely because their population was not significantly affected by war losses, emigration, or assimilation.

In the 1897-1926 period, their growth was relatively slow, very probably because both fertility and mortality were high, as might be expected in this premodern period. By 1926 Tatar fertility was still high (Table 7.9). The only indication of the natural increase of the Tatar population are data for the Tatar ASSR, where, since 1926, Tatars have comprised slightly less than half of the population, with Russians accounting for most of the remainder. By 1940 natural increase for this republic was 11 per 1,000, with a crude birthrate of 37 and a crude death rate of 26.[55] Although the 1940 data can be considered only as an approximation of natural increase, they indicate that mortality had declined appreciably and fertility had probably begun to decline. By 1960 the crude birthrate had declined to 28 per 1,000 and the crude death rate to 8;[56] by 1971 the corresponding rates were 16 and 8.[57] By 1959 Tatar fertility was relatively low and apparently declined further by 1970, although fertility levels remain higher than the Eastern Slavs (Table 7.9). Thus, the Tatar population also exemplifies the transition from high to low birth- and death rates that occurs with modernization, although they have not completed the transition. Their population began to expand in the 1930s as a result of a decline in mortality and relatively high levels of fertility; and their growth in the postwar period has diminished somewhat because fertility decline exceeded mortality decline. A further decline in their growth rate can be expected, as their fertility will probably continue to decline.

They probably have suffered some loss through Russification. Although only 0.7 percent of the Tatars spoke Russian as their native language in 1926, by 1959 this figure had increased to 7.0 percent, and in 1970, 10 percent. As has been previously noted, there were relatively substantial population losses in conjunction with the deportation of the Crimean Tatars during the war, but since they comprise only a small proportion of the total Tatar population, these losses were relatively insignificant (Chapter 6).

Turkic-Muslims

    The Turkic-Muslim population grew relatively slowly until after
World War II and subsequently has grown at a very rapid rate (Tables
7.7 and 7.8), which reflects the fact that this grouping has moved
through only the first stage of the population transition. Mortality
has declined substantially, but fertility has generally remained high
to moderately high with a general tendency to decline. Before 1949
the decline in mortality probably was not great. There are no mortality data by ethnic group, and regional data for 1940 are generally underreported, particularly in Central Asia and the North Caucasus.
Reported crude death rates for the Turkic-Muslim republics along the
Volga, the Yakut ASSR, and Kazakhstan were in the 20s in 1940, and
they were somewhat lower in Central Asia, the North Caucasus, and
Azerbaydzhan SSR. [58] These rates, of course, were depressed by a
significant admixture of urban Russians and underreporting. After
World War II, mortality declined sharply in Turkic-Muslim areas,
and current crude death rates in these areas are generally below the
Union-wide average because the population is significantly younger
than the Union-wide average.
    Fertility among the various Turkic-Muslim groups grades from
high to relatively moderate, as measured by child-woman ratios
(Table 7.9). The Central Asian groups, the Kazakhs, the Azeri, and
some of the North Caucasus groups have high fertility, probably at
the preindustrial level. Gross reproduction rates for the Central
Asian republics approach 3, which means that even with a significant
number of Russians and other nonindigenous groups they average almost six children per woman in the reproductive years. Other Turkic-
Muslim groups along the Volga, in the North Caucasus, and in Siberia
have moderate levels of fertility and probably are experiencing a decline in fertility. The rise in the Turkic-Muslim child-woman ratios
between 1959 and 1970 probably is owing largely to a decline in infant
mortality. On the basis of age distribution alone, however, one would
expect a decline in child-woman ratios since 1959. Because of the
effect of the war, the proportion of the women aged 20 to 49 comprised
by women 20 to 29, the group with the highest fertility, has dropped
sharply. For the entire country it dropped nine percentage points,
whereas in the Azerbaydzhan SSR, it fell 23 percentage points, and in
the Central Asian republics from 10 to 15 percentage points. As we
have previously noted, however, child-woman ratios are only a crude
approximation of fertility, in that even though the rate for the Azeri
increased, probably because of a decline in infant mortality, crude
birthrates for the Azerbaydzhan SSR indicate a sharp decline in fertility. In summary, among the Turkic-Muslims there has been a great
decline in mortality, which requires relatively little socioeconomic

change, but fertility decline seems to be in its initial stages. Thus the population is growing very rapidly and their proportion of the total Soviet population is increasing (Table 7.5).

The slow growth before 1959 also can be partially explained by population losses as a result of war and collectivization. The draft riots among the Kazakhs in 1916 resulted in considerable loss of life and emigration. Between 1897 and 1926 the Bashkir population declined by about 0.5 million, largely because of the Soviet subjugation of the Bashkirs in 1920. The colonization of the Kazakh steppe and the settling of the nomads between 1926 and 1939 resulted in a decline of almost 1 million in the Kazakh population (Chapter 6). The growth of the Yakut population also has been appreciably affected by the settling of the nomads and mobilization during World War II. Between 1926 and 1959 the Yakut population declined from 240,709 to 236,655. However, there has been very little population loss through Russification; an insignificant proportion of the Turkic-Muslims speak Russian as their native language. Future trends in the Turkic-Muslim population have been discussed in the section of this chapter dealing with the Russians.

Jews

By all indicators, the Jewish population is the most modernized group in the Soviet Union, but the effect of modernization on the growth of the Jewish population cannot be determined because of substantial population losses and a lack of data. Between 1897 and 1970 the Jewish population declined by 50 percent, or by some 2 million people, because of emigration, war, genocide, Russification, and a decline in natural increase, and their proportion of the total population declined substantially (Tables 7.5 to 7.8).

The only data available on fertility are child-woman ratios for 1897, 1926, and 1970 (Table 7.9). In 1897 Jewish fertility was high in both urban and rural areas; the child-woman ratio for the total population was 1.533 and for urban areas, 1.423. The crude birthrate was probably upward of 50 per 1,000. These rates were significantly higher than the comparable Russian rates of 1.433 and 0.944, probably because the Jewish population was concentrated in the small towns and villages of the Jewish Pale where higher fertility is to be expected. By 1926 the Jewish child-woman ratio had declined by almost 50 percent to 0.795. There are no data on Jewish mortality, but since by 1926 more than half of the Jewish population lived in centers of 15,000 or more, the urban crude death rate of 17 per 1,000 for European USSR in 1926 was probably representative of the Jewish population. In 1897 their crude death rate probably was between 25 and 30 per 1,000, judging from the data for the gubernii where most of the Jews lived. Yet, between 1897 and 1926, there was a slight decline in the Jewish population. This decline partly was owing to the fact that more than a million Jews emigrated from Russia between 1898 and 1914 (Chapter 6). There probably were also significant war losses, because a large part of the Pale was behind the front lines and at least 600,000 Jews were evacuated from Poland and the Baltic area to other parts of Russia.[59] High mortality very probably resulted from this evacuation.

Between 1926 and 1959 the Jewish population declined by about 45 percent, or by about 1.8 million people. Both fertility and mortality continued to decline; by 1970 the child-woman ratio for the Jewish population in the RSFSR was an incredibly low 0.286 and only about 6 percent of the population was below age 10, which very probably reflects Russification and intermarriage, as well as declining fertility. Clearly, war losses and genocide account for the bulk of this loss, because the part of the Jewish Pale that is currently within the USSR was completely occupied during the war. The German policy of exterminating the Jews, in addition to losses associated with the war, must have virtually decimated the Jewish population in these areas (Chapter 6). Although he does not indicate the basis for his estimate, Kulischer claims that 2.5 million Soviet Jews were killed by the Germans,[60] a figure that seems plausible even if a small amount of natural increase is taken into account. There is no way to estimate accurately Jewish population losses, because there are no data on natural increase. However, if one assumes that fertility and mortality continued to decline between 1926 and 1959 and the Jewish population had a slow rate of natural increase during this period, say 0.5 percent per year, the difference between the observed and the expected Jewish population is about 2.5 million people. A complicating factor in estimating Jewish losses is immigration; hundreds of thousands of Jews fled or were evacuated from Eastern Europe with the movement of the German army into the USSR.[61] If one assumes a 1.0 percent increase per year because of immigration and slightly higher fertility and lower mortality, the corresponding deficit is 3.3 million. The true figure of Jewish population losses probably lies somewhere between these two estimates.

Part of the Jewish population loss can be attributed to Russification; in 1926 about 26 percent of the Jewish population spoke Russian as their native language; in 1939, about 55 percent; and in 1959, about 76 percent.[62] No other group in the USSR approached these levels, and clearly the Jews have undergone more Russification than any other group in the USSR.

Between 1959 and 1970 the Jewish population decreased by about 117,000, or by about 5 percent. It is difficult to ascertain the source of this decline. Emigration during this period was insignificant; the highly publicized Jewish emigration in recent years occurred primarily after the 1970 census was taken. The two major sources of decline are Russification and very probably natural decrease. In 1970, 78 percent of the Jewish population spoke Russian as their native language, so there must be significant Russification. There could also be a natural decrease of the Jewish population because of low fertility. There are no age data for the Jewish population in 1959, and in 1970 data are only available for the Jewish population residing in the RSFSR, or 38 percent of the total Jewish population. It is probably reasonable to assume that this population is fairly representative of the total Jewish population. Because the RSFSR has been a major area of Jewish in-migration and migrants tend to be younger than the total population from which they came, one would not expect the RSFSR Jewish population to be older than the total Jewish population. Whereas 12 percent of the total USSR population and the Russian population and 8 percent of the Uzbek population was over age 60 in 1970, an amazing 26 percent of the Jewish population in the RSFSR was over 60 years of age. This is indeed an old population, probably because of past low fertility and high levels of Russification among the younger segments of this population. Fertility must be at a relatively low level, because the Jewish population is the most urbanized group in the USSR and they have by far the highest educational levels. About 16 percent of the Russian population and 35 percent of the Uzbek population was under age 10 in 1970, but only about 6 percent of the Jewish population in the RSFSR was in this age group. It is very probable that the Jewish population is experiencing natural decrease, which in part explains its loss in population since 1959. Thus, the Jewish population was probably one of the first Soviet nationalities to go through the demographic transition, and currently it is probably suffering natural decrease largely as a result of low fertility and Russification.

Mobilized Europeans

Although the ethnic groups that comprise the Mobilized Europeans are similar according to most indicators of modernization, with respect to the stage of the demographic transition that they occupy they differ sharply, as do their rates of growth in all periods (Table 7.10). Consequently, the aggregate data are not representative of the nationalities within this grouping. Even though the aggregate data indicate that the Mobilized Europeans grew relatively rapidly between 1897 and 1970 (Tables 7.7 and 7.8), the Latvians and Estonians have increased so slightly that their average annual increase was close to zero (0.01); virtually all of the increase in this grouping was accounted for by the Georgians and Armenians.

TABLE 7.10

Average Annual Percentage Change in the Total Population by
Mobilized European Nationality: 1897-1970

Nationality	1897-1926	1926-59	1959-70	1897-1970
Latvians	0.3	-0.3	0.2	0.0
Estonians	0.5	-0.5	0.2	0.0
Georgians	1.0	1.2	1.7	1.2
Armenians	1.0	1.8	2.2	1.5

Sources: See Chapter 2, footnotes 2 and 3.

By the beginning of the century, fertility and mortality in Latvia
and Estonia had already begun to decline and were at levels comparable to Western European countries. In the period 1896-1900 the gubernii that comprise present-day Latvia and Estonia had the lowest fertility in European Russia; crude birthrates in Liflyand, Kurlyand, and
Estlyand averaged 29 per 1,000, whereas the average for European
Russia was 50 per 1,000. Crude death rates averaged 19 per 1,000
and were also significantly lower than the average for the 50 gubernii
of European Russia, which was 32 per 1,000; thus natural increase
was less than 1 percent per year and it continued to decline in the
prerevolutionary period. These gubernii had a much more urbanized,
literate population than the average for European Russia and the proportion of the women married by age 20 was much below the average
for European Russia.[63] Clearly, the Latvian and Estonian populations
were well into the demographic transition by the end of the nineteenth
century.
    By the period 1921-25 the crude birthrate in Latvia was 21.6
per 1,000 and the crude death rate was 14.4 per 1,000, which results
in a natural increase rate of about 7. That the Latvian population
grew somewhat slower in the 1897-1926 period than these crude natural increase rates would seem to imply is probably largely due to the
effects of World War I and perhaps to the differential natural increase
of the non-Latvian groups living in Latvia. By the period 1936-39,
crude birthrates in Latvia had declined to about 18 per 1,000 and by
1960 to 17 per 1,000; corresponding crude death rates were 14 and 10,
and by 1960 crude natural increase remained at 7. Between the early
1920s and World War II, the net reproduction rate was below 1,
and the natural increase that occurred was the result of the effect of
past higher fertility on the age distribution. The Latvian population
declined because of war losses and emigration; almost a third of the

population of Latvia was killed or emigrated during World War II. Despite considerable Russian in-migration, the net reproduction rate of Latvia was below 1 in 1959.[64]

By 1926 the crude birthrate in Estonia was about 18 and the crude death rate was 16 per 1,000; natural increase, thus, was 2 per 1,000. Prior to 1921 the death rate fluctuated considerably and in some years there was a natural decrease, but in general between 1921 and 1926 natural increase averaged about 4 per 1,000. By 1939 a natural decrease of 1 per 1,000 occurred in Estonia, and between 1926 and 1939 the Estonian population barely increased at all. Between January 1939 and about November 1944, the population of Estonia declined 18 percent, or over 200,000. By 1959 the crude birthrate had declined to 17 per 1,000 but natural increase rose to 6 per 1,000, because the crude death rate continued to decline. That fertility did not decline more after the war was the result of much in-migration, particularly of Russians. Although prior to World War II, Estonia was predominantly inhabited by Estonians, by 1959 Russians comprised 20 percent of the population. In-migrants are younger and therefore have higher fertility than the native Estonian population.[65] The low fertility of Latvians and Estonians is reflected in the child-woman ratios for these nationalities (Table 7.9).

Between 1959 and 1970 both the Estonian and Latvian populations increased only 0.2 percent per year. These populations have had a net reproduction rate below 1 since the 1930s, and this, coupled with the effect of war losses and emigration on the age distribution, has resulted in fertility and mortality levels that are now very probably below replacement. The slight rise in the child-woman ratios is very probably due to a decline in infant mortality. There has been very little Russification of Latvians and Estonians, because in both 1959 and 1970 over 95 percent of the Latvians and Estonians considered Latvian and Estonian their native languages. In 1970 the population of these republics had a slow rate of natural increase. Crude birthrates for Latvia and Estonia were 14 and 16 per 1,000, respectively, in 1970, and corresponding crude death rates were 11 per 1,000, which was higher than the USSR average because these are older populations.[66] Latvians comprised only 57 percent of the population of their republic in 1970 and Estonians, 68 percent of the population of their republic. The Latvian and Estonian populations are probably now very close to a zero population growth, and unless a rise in fertility occurs they will experience a natural decrease in the near future. In short, as expected, these highly modernized groups have gone through the demographic transition.

In contrast to the Latvians and Estonians, the Georgians and Armenians have grown rapidly since 1897 and their populations have expanded considerably. Apparently, only recently have they experi-

enced fertility decline, although their patterns of natural increase cannot be analyzed because of a general lack of data. The available data
for the early period do not seem reasonable and are inconsistent and
variable. Reported crude birthrates and crude death rates for the
gubernii of the Transcaucasus for the period 1894-98 are much below
those of European Russia, with Tiflis and Erivan gubernii, areas
where one might expect more complete reporting, having the highest
rates. For example, Baku and Yelisavetpol' gubernii and Dagestan
Oblast have reported crude birthrates in the low to mid-20s, less than
half the level of European Russia. Reported crude birthrates in Tiflis
and Kutais gubernii, which constitute a large portion of the Georgian
Republic, were 35 and 28 per 1,000, respectively, and corresponding
crude death rates were 22 and 17 per 1,000.[67] Yet, in 1897 the child-
woman ratio for the Georgian population was 1.73, much above the
Russian ratio. Clearly, there must have been underregistration of
births and deaths in this period. Erivan Guberniya reported a crude
birthrate of 37 and a crude death rate of 21. Very probably, both
birth- and death rates in Georgia and Armenia were much above
these levels, and approximated the normal rates for preindustrial
societies.

By 1926 the reported crude birthrate in Armenia was 54 per
1,000 and the crude death rate was 17 per 1,000, which would yield
a natural increase rate of 37 per 1,000.[68] However, deaths were
probably underreported, because the rural rate was reported as being
below the urban rate. About a half million Armenians fled from Turkey
into the USSR, mainly to Soviet Armenia, during the World War I period, but this immigration probably did not substantially affect these
rates because refugee migration is normally not age selective.[69] Lorimer estimates gross reproduction rates for Georgia and Armenia in
1926-27 at 3.06 and 3.89, respectively, with particularly high rates in
rural areas; corresponding net rates were 1.99 and 2.53. These
rates are much above the USSR average, and Frank Lorimer charac-
terizes the Transcaucasus as a region of extraordinarily high fertility.[70]

Although firm data are lacking to characterize natural increase
for the Georgians and Armenians, it is very probable that by 1926 fertility remained high at a preindustrial level and it was significantly
higher in Armenia than Georgia, and death rates were probably declining. However, it must be acknowledged that Georgian scholars
accept the low fertility rates of the prerevolutionary period and accept
as fact that Georgian fertility was much below that of European Russia. G. B. Pirtskhalava maintains that the crude birthrate in Georgia
was 31 per 1,000 in the 1876-1900 period and 29 per 1,000 in the 1900-
13 period, and that between 1897 and 1926 rural fertility increased by
6 percent. He presents an array of previously unpublished data without providing the source of the data or an explanation of the low fertility.[71]

Adequate data for the 1926-59 period are also lacking, but judging from available crude birthrates and death rates for the Georgian Republic, natural increase was relatively high and stable, with moderate levels of fertility and low mortality in at least the last half of this period. In 1940 the reported crude birthrate was 27 per 1,000; it declined to 24 in 1950 and remained about at that level until 1963, when it began to decline slowly. By 1970 it was 19 per 1,000. Crude birthrates, of course, do not take into account changes in the proportion of the population in the reproductive ages. Child-woman ratios for the Georgian population show a greater decline, even though infant mortality probably declined considerably (Table 7.9). The crude death rate declined even less; by 1949 it was reported to be 9 and in 1959 about 7.[72] Thus, throughout the 1950-59 period the natural increase rate averaged about 17 per 1,000, or somewhat below their growth rate between 1926 and 1959. Age data for the cohort born during the war indicate a sharp decline in fertility. In addition, in 1959, Georgians comprised only 64 percent of the population of the Georgian Republic, so the rates for the republic may not be representative of the Georgian population.

In 1940 fertility in the Armenian Republic, where Armenians comprised 88 percent of the population in 1959, was still relatively high and remained so until 1959. In 1940 the crude birthrate was 41 per 1,000, declined somewhat in the intervening years, and rose to 42 in 1959. Such fluctuations could result from changing age distribution or changes in the extent of reporting. Child-woman ratios for the Armenian population, however, show a decline in fertility between 1926 and 1959, even though infant mortality probably declined considerably (Table 7.9). The crude death rate was 15 per 1,000 in 1940, but declined to 10 in 1950, and to 8 in 1959. Between 1950 and 1959 natural increase averaged almost 3 percent. Once again, the natural increase rate was much below their growth rate for the years that data are available, probably because of the war and deficiencies in the reporting of births and deaths. It would seem that the Armenian population moved into the stage of the demographic transition of declining mortality and high and stable fertility.

Between 1959 and 1970 the natural increase rate declined in both the Georgian and Armenian republics, largely as a result of a decline in fertility. In Georgia, natural increase declined steadily from 18 to 12 per 1,000 between 1959 and 1970 and averaged 15 per 1,000, which was below their growth rate of 1.7 percent (Table 7.10). The natural increase rate for the Georgian Republic is probably not representative of the Georgian population; in 1970 they comprised 67 percent of the population of their republic. During this period reporting was probably fairly complete, as were the census enumerations. The crude birthrate declined slowly from 25 per 1,000 in 1960 to 19 per 1,000 in 1967 and then stabilized up to 1970. Child-woman ratios indicate a slight increase in fertility during this period, probably because of declining infant mortality (Table 7.9). The crude death rate changed very little, being 6.5 per 1,000 in 1960 and 7.3 per 1,000 in 1970. Thus, the Georgian population would seem to be entering the last stage of the demographic transition. Russification probably has not affected the growth of the Georgian population, because in 1970, about 98 percent of the Georgians considered Georgian to be their native language.[73]

In the Armenian Republic, where Armenians comprised 89 percent of the population in 1970, natural increase declined by about 50 percent from 33 to 17 per 1,000 between 1959 and 1970 and averaged 24 per 1,000, which was slightly above the overall growth rate of the Armenians during this period (Table 7.10). This decline was due primarily to a decline in fertility; crude birthrates declined steadily during this period from 40 to 22 per 1,000. Child-woman ratios also indicate a decline, but not as great, because this measure is essentially an average for the past ten years. Crude death rates remained at a low level and declined from 6.8 to 5.1 per 1,000, reflecting the fact that this is a very young population due to the past high fertility.[74] Obviously, the Armenian population is also approaching the last stage of the demographic transition. Russification among Armenians also has probably not been significant, in that in 1970 about 91 percent of the Armenians spoke Armenian as their native language.

Finnic Peoples

The Finnic peoples have sustained a very slow rate of population growth since 1897, largely because of emigration, Russification, war losses, and declining natural increase (Tables 7.7 and 7.8). Therefore, they have not experienced the expected rapid growth of their population that occurs in the stage of the demographic transition when mortality declines and fertility remains high. Between 1926 and 1959 and 1959 and 1970, the population of the Finns, Karelians, and Mordvinians actually declined. The Finns and Karelians declined by about a third between 1939 and 1959, because over 400,000 were evacuated to Finland from the Finnish territory that the USSR annexed during World War II, which primarily accounts for the decline in this grouping between 1926 and 1959 (Chapter 6). War losses probably also account for some of the decline. Between 1959 and 1970, the Karelians decreased 13 percent and the Finns, 9 percent, largely because of Russification. About 36 percent of the Finns in the USSR spoke Russian as their native language in 1959 and 43 percent in 1970; corresponding percentages for the Karelians were 29 and 37 percent. The Mordvinians declined 11 percent between 1939 and 1959 and 2 percent between 1959 and 1970, largely because of Russification and the effect of the war. In both 1959 and 1970 about 22 percent of the Mordvinians spoke Russian as their native language. Moreover, in 1970, 19 percent of all Finnic peoples considered Russian to be their native language, a figure that was about twice the national average for all non-Russians (Table 5.10).

The Udmurts, Mari, and Komi grew by 14 percent between 1926 and 1939, 4 percent between 1939 and 1959, and 14 percent between 1959 and 1970. These groups grew because their fertility was higher than the other Finnic groups; they are less urbanized and there was less Russification among them. In 1970, 9 percent of the Mari spoke Russian as their native language, 16 percent of the Komi, and 17 percent of the Udmurts, so some Russification undoubtedly occurred.

Natural increase for the Finnic peoples was probably low before World War II because both fertility and mortality were relatively high, increased appreciably after the war because mortality declined much more than fertility, and in recent years has fallen to a low level because of declines in fertility. There are no data to describe accurately natural increase for these groups, because available data are only for their republics and Russians comprise a majority of the population in these units. For example, in 1970 Russians comprised from 47 to 68 percent of the population of the republics of these groups. Nevertheless, data for these republics indicate that as late as 1940 both fertility and mortality were still high and that crude death rates had declined appreciably by 1950 and were at a low level in 1960. Crude birthrates had declined somewhat by 1960, but did not reach low levels until fairly recently. In 1940 crude birthrates ranged between 34 and 45 per 1,000 and in 1971 between 15 and 17. Child-women ratios indicate moderate to low levels of fertility, but they were affected by Russification and infant mortality (Table 7.9). Crude death rates ranged between 22 and 38 per 1,000 in 1940 and between 6 and 11 in 1971. Consequently, natural increase in these republics was generally below 1 percent in 1940, rose to slightly above 2 percent in 1960, and then declined to below 1 percent in 1971.[75] If these data are representative of the Finnic peoples, it would seem that only recently have they completed the transition from high to low birth- and death rates. In much of the postwar period their population was expanding, but their growth has been relatively slow in this period largely because of Russification.

Lithuanians

The Lithuanian population grew relatively slowly between 1897 and 1970, primarily because of a decline in the rate of natural increase and the effect of the war (Tables 7.7 and 7.8). Russification

has not appreciably affected the Lithuanian population; in 1970 about
98 percent of the Lithuanians spoke Lithuanian as their native language.
In the 1896–1900 period fertility and mortality were still moderately
high, although significantly lower than in the Russian gubernii, in
Kovno Guberniya, which occupied much of present-day Lithuania.
The crude birthrate was 35 and the crude death rate was 23. The
Catholic Lithuanian population was less modernized in terms of education and urbanization and less influenced by the Western European
countries than were the populations of Latvia and Estonia, where German and Swedish influence was strong.[76] By 1940 the crude birthrate
in the Lithuanian Republic, where Lithuanians comprised about 80
percent of the population in 1970 and earlier even a large percentage,
had declined to 23 per 1,000 and the crude death rate stood at 13.
Thus, even before World War II, the Lithuanian population had almost
completed the transition to low birth- and death rates. By 1960 fertility remained at this level, but mortality had declined by almost 50
percent and natural increase rose from 10 per 1,000 to 15. Their
slower rate of population growth can largely be accounted for by the
effects of the war, in particular the German occupation of the republic
(Table 7.8). Between 1960 and 1970 the crude birthrate declined to
18 and the crude death rate rose slightly to 9, and the natural increase
rate dropped to 9.[77] Child-woman ratios for 1959 and 1970 do not reflect a decline but indicate a relatively low level of fertility (Table 7.9).
Thus, in terms of fertility and mortality, the Lithuanians have been
one of the more modernized groups at least for the past three decades.

Moldavians and Romanians

The Moldavians and Romanians have maintained a relatively
rapid rate of population growth since 1897, despite the effects of their
territory being occupied in both world wars (Tables 7.7 and 7.8).
The rate of natural increase has been relatively high throughout the
1897–1970 period. In the period 1896–1900 the natural increase rate
in Bessarabia Guberniya, which occupied much of present-day Moldavia, was 19 per 1,000, with a crude birthrate of 44 and a crude
death rate of 25 per 1,000. By 1940 these rates had declined to 27
and 17 per 1,000, but the crude birthrate rose to 39 in 1950, which
probably indicates underreporting in 1940. By 1960 the rates were
29 and 6; and by 1970, 19 and 7 in the Moldavian Republic where
Moldavians currently comprise about two-thirds of the population.[78]
Therefore, in the postwar period, the Moldavian and Romanian population has had a fairly rapid rate of natural increase, which has been
declining in the past decade. The relatively slow growth during the
1926–59 period was largely due to the effects of the war. Thus, the
Moldavian and Romanian populations have experienced the decline in

birth- and death rates only recently, and have more than doubled their population since 1897 (Table 7.6).

NOTES

1. Walter F. Wilcox, ed., International Migrations, II (New York: National Bureau of Economic Research, 1931), p. 523; and Frank Lorimer, The Population of the Soviet Union: History and Prospects (Geneva: League of Nations, 1946), p. 39.

2. C. P. Blacker, "Stages in Population Growth," Eugenics Review 39 (October 1947): 88-101; Kingsley Davis, "The World Demographic Transition," Annals of the American Academy of Political and Social Science 273 (January 1945): 1-11; David M. Heer, "The Demographic Transition in the Russian Empire and the Soviet Union," Journal of Social History 1 (Spring 1968): 193-240; and Warren S. Thompson, Population and Peace in the Pacific (Chicago: University of Chicago Press, 1946), pp. 22-35.

3. Time, 6 May 1974, p. 41.

4. Lorimer, op. cit., pp. 114-15; and A. G. Volkov, "O Nekotorykh Prichinakh Snizheniya Koeffitsiyenta Rozhdayemosti," in Izucheniye Vosproizvodstva Naseleniya (Moscow: Izdatel'stvo "Nauka," 1968), p. 175.

5. M. K. Karakhanov, ed., Problemy Narodonaseleniya (Moscow: Izdatel'stvo Moskovskogo Universiteta, 1970), pp. 21, 334.

6. Frederick A. Leedy, "Demographic Trends in the USSR," in U.S. Congress, Joint Economic Committee, Soviet Economic Prospects for the Seventies, Joint Committee Print (Washington, D.C.: U.S. Government Printing Office, 1973), p. 440. This is an excellent study of the purely demographic aspects of fertility decline in the USSR since 1950.

7. D. I. Valentey, ed., Osnovy Teorii Narodonaseleniya (Moscow: Izdatel'stvo "Vysshaya Shkola," 1973), p. 270.

8. "Demograficheskaya Problema: Zanyatost' Zhenshchin i Rozhdayemost'," Voprosy Ekonomiki, no. 5 (May 1969), p. 158.

9. P. P. Zvindrin'sh, "Dinamika i Demograficheskiye Faktory Rozhdayemosti v Latvii," in Voprosy Demografii, ed. A. G. Volkov (Moscow: Statistika, 1970), p. 247.

10. Vestnik Statistiki, no. 12 (1973), p. 75.

11. A. A. Isupov, "Sostoyaniye i Osnovnyye Pokazateli Statistiki Naseleniya v Respublikakh Sredney Azii," in Problemy Narodonaseleniya, ed. M. K. Karakhanov (Moscow: Izdatel'stvo Moskovskogo Universiteta, 1970), p. 282.

12. Leedy, op. cit., p. 447.

13. Narodnoye Khozyaystvo SSSR v 1970 G., p. 51.

14. Vestnik Statistiki, no. 12 (1973), p. 79.

15. Narodnoye Khozyaystvo SSSR v 1969 G., p. 588.

16. For a discussion of population trends in Russia and the USSR in terms of the demographic transition, see Heer, op. cit.

17. Lorimer, op. cit., pp., 41, 133-37.

18. V. V. Pokshishevskiy, Geografiya Naseleniya SSSR (Moscow: Izdatel'stvo "Prosveshcheniye," 1971), p. 34.

19. Narodnoye Khozyaystvo SSSR v 1970 G., p. 47.

20. Vestnik Statistiki, no. 6 (1973), p. 90.

21. M. V. Kurman and I. V. Lebedinskiy, Naseleniye Bol'shogo Sotsialisticheskogo Goroda (Moscow: Statistika, 1968), p. 126.

22. D. Peter Mazur, "Fertility Among Ethnic Groups in the USSR," Demography 4, no. 1 (1967): 176.

23. A. G. Rashin, Naseleniye Rossii za 100 Let (Moscow: Gosudarstvennoye Statisticheskoye Izdatel'stvo, 1956), p. 218.

24. Lorimer, op. cit., pp. 81-82, 114.

25. Ibid., pp. 39-41.

26. Dana G. Dalrymple, "The Soviet Famine of 1932-1934," Soviet Studies 15 (January 1964): 260.

27. Lorimer, op. cit., pp. 40-41.

28. Vestnik Statistiki, no. 1 (1965), pp. 86-87.

29. For a summary of the assimilation question in the Soviet Union, see Vernon V. Aspaturian, "The Non-Russian Nationalities," in Prospects for Soviet Society, ed. Allen Kassof (New York: Praeger, 1968), pp. 143-98.

30. See Alexandre Bennigsen and Chantal Lemercier-Quelquejay, The Evolution of the Muslim Nationalities of the USSR and Their Linguistic Problems (London: Central Asian Research Centre, 1961).

31. Aspaturian, op. cit., pp. 158-64.

32. Brian D. Silver, "Ethnic Identity Change Among Soviet Nationalities: A Statistical Analysis" (Ph.D. diss., University of Wisconsin, 1972), pp. 25-40.

33. Brian D. Silver, "The Impact of Urbanization and Geographical Dispersion on the Linguistic Russification of Soviet Nationalities," Demography 11 (February 1974): 89-103. As the title of the article implies, Silver was particularly interested in the combined influence of urbanization and residence outside one's nationality homeland. His concern was to demonstrate statistically the positive relationship between these two characteristics and linguistic Russification, utilizing data from the 1959 Soviet census; he attempted no estimates of the actual number of persons who might have assimilated.

34. Karl W. Deutsch, Nationalism and Social Communication, 2d ed. (Cambridge, Mass.: Massachusetts Institute of Technology Press, 1966), Chaps. 5 and 6.

35. Raymond Breton, "Institutional Completeness of Ethnic Communities and the Personal Relations of Immigrants," American Journal of Sociology 70 (September 1964): 193-205.

36. Silver, "Ethnic Identity," op. cit., pp. 43-75. There are a few exceptions to the generalization that native-language schools are not provided outside one's nationality unit; these cases are enumerated by Silver. More important, Silver has focused attention upon the use of non-Russian languages as the medium of instruction, rather than as a subject of instruction.

37. See Ivan Dzyuba, Internationalism or Russification? 2d ed. (London: Weidenfeld and Nicolson, 1968), p. 187.

38. Ibid., pp. 187-88; and Yaroslav Bilinsky, "Assimilation and Ethnic Assertiveness Among Ukrainians of the Soviet Union," in Ethnic Minorities in the Soviet Union, ed. Erich Goldhagen (New York: Praeger, 1968), pp. 155-56.

39. Eugene M. Kulischer, Europe on the Move (New York: Columbia University Press, 1948), pp. 82-87.

40. B. Ts. Urlanis, Rozhdayemost' i Prodolzhitel'nost' Zhizni v SSSR (Moscow: Gosstatizdat, 1963), pp. 82-87.

41. Vestnik Statistiki, no. 1 (1967), pp. 86-96.

42. Urlanis, op. cit., p. 88.

43. Data on natural increase for the RSFSR were obtained from the various editions of Narodnoye Khozyaystvo SSSR published since 1960; Vestnik Statistiki, no. 1 (1965), p. 87; and Vestnik Statistiki, no. 12 (1966), p. 83. There were no data for 1961 and 1962; estimates were made for these years by assuming a linear decline between 1960 and 1963.

44. Alexandre Bennigsen, "Islamic, or Local Consciousness Among Soviet Nationalities?" in Soviet Nationality Problems, ed. Edward Allworth (New York: Columbia University Press, 1971), p. 174.

45. Vestnik Statistiki, no. 12 (1973), pp. 76-77.

46. Ibid.; and Narodnoye Khozyaystvo SSSR v 1970 G., pp. 50-51.

47. Mazur, op. cit., p. 172.

48. Rashin, Naseleniye Rossii za 100 Let, pp. 217-18; and Lorimer, op. cit., p. 81.

49. Kulischer, op. cit., p. 69.

50. Dalrymple, op. cit., p. 259.

51. Narodnoye Khozyaystvo SSSR v 1970 G., p. 50.

52. Rashin, Naseleniye Rossii za 100 Let, p. 217.

53. Lorimer, op. cit., p. 81.

54. Narodnoye Khozyaystvo SSSR v 1970 G., pp. 50-51.

55. Vestnik Statistiki, no. 1 (1965), pp. 88-89.

56. Ibid.

57. Vestnik Statistiki, no. 2 (1973), p. 77.

58. Vestnik Statistiki, no. 1 (1965), pp. 86-96.
59. Kulischer, op. cit., p. 31.
60. Ibid., p. 276.
61. Ibid., pp. 255, 264-65.
62. A. A. Isupov, Natsional'nyy Sostav Naseleniya SSSR (Moscow: Izdatel'stvo "Statistika," 1961), p. 34.
63. Rashin, op. cit., pp. 101, 167-68, 176, 187-88, 217-18, 308.
64. Zvidrin'sh, op. cit., pp. 236-41.
65. Tonu Parming, "Population Changes in Estonia, 1935-1970," Population Studies 26 (March 1972): 61-78.
66. Narodnoye Khozyaystvo SSSR v 1970 G., pp. 50-51.
67. V. Sh. Dzhaoshvili, Naseleniye Gruzii (Tbilisi: Izdatel'stvo "Metsniyereba," 1968), p. 17.
68. Lorimer, op. cit., p. 83.
69. Kulischer, op. cit., p. 51.
70. Lorimer, op. cit., pp. 92-93.
71. G. B. Pirtskhalava, "Dinamika i Nekotoryye Osobennosti Rozhdayemosti v Gruzii," in Materialy Vsesoyuznoy Nauchnoy Konferentsii po Problemam Narodonaseleniya Zakavkaz'ya (Erevan, 1968), pp. 43-44.
72. Dzhaoshvili, op. cit., p. 19.
73. Ibid.; Vestnik Statistiki, no. 12 (1973), p. 79; Narodnoye Khozyaystvo SSSR v 1967 G., pp. 40-41; and Narodnoye Khozyaystvo SSSR v 1970 G., p. 51.
74. Ibid.
75. Vestnik Statistiki, no. 12 (1973), pp. 76-79; and Vestnik Statistiki, no. 1 (1965), pp. 86-91.
76. Rashin, op. cit., pp. 101, 167, 187, 217, 308.
77. Vestnik Statistiki, no. 1 (1965), pp. 90-91; and Narodnoye Khozyaystvo SSSR v 1970 G., p. 51.
78. Rashin, op. cit., pp. 167, 187, 217; and Narodnoye Khozyaystvo SSSR v 1970 G., pp. 50-51.

CHAPTER

8

**FACTOR ANALYSIS
AND CORRELATION
ANALYSIS**

In this chapter two modes of statistical analysis will be utilized to describe and explain the complex nature of the relationships among variables indicative of modernization and those characteristic of the geographic distribution of the nationality groupings. In the first section the use of factor analysis provides both a means of detailing the linkages among the wide range of modernization and nationality variables and a convenient method of summarizing these interrelationships. Second, rank order correlations are used to supplement the factor analysis.

SUMMARY DISCUSSION

By subjecting matrices of socioeconomic and demographic variables to factor analysis, a number of statistical relationships emerged that largely substantiate the trends outlined in the preceding empirical chapters. Specifically, the results of the factor analysis demonstrated that the Russians were highly related with modernization and that the other nationality groupings were only moderately or even negatively associated with modernization. In any statistical investigation involving complicated geographic and socioeconomic changes, aberrant or spurious relationships may emerge. This was the case in our analysis, but fortunately the deviant results can be explained by other empirical evidence.

Because of problems of accuracy or availability, only data for 1926 and 1959 were utilized in the factor analysis. This in itself presents few problems, since, as is evident from earlier discussions, virtually all of the major social, economic, and demographic changes that occurred in Russia and the USSR between 1897 and 1970 actually took place in the span of 1926 to 1959. Furthermore, nationality groupings employed in the factor analysis varied slightly from those utilized in the remainder of this investigation; in this instance Jews are included with Mobilized Europeans and Tatars with Turkic-Muslims.

The conceptual background of this study hypothesized that the dominant group, the Russians, and certain other nationalities (such as Jews, Tatars, Estonians, Latvians, Armenians, and Georgians) could be expected to modernize to a greater extent than other nationalities of the Soviet Union. The results of the factor analysis revealed that the Russians, by 1959, were more highly associated with variables representing modernization than any other grouping. Most minority nationalities not expected to modernize extensively (Ukrainians, Belorussians, Turkic-Muslims, Lithuanians, and Moldavians and Romanians) had, by 1959, little (or even a negative) association with the indicators of advanced society. Paradoxically, however, the Mobilized Europeans (including Jews) had almost no positive relationship with modernization, and the Finnic peoples had a moderately high association with these variables.

Again, the spatial nuances of modernization may disguise or portray a false picture of the relationships between nationalities and socioeconomic change. In this case, other empirical data demonstrate clearly that the Mobilized Europeans did in fact modernize significantly between 1926 and 1959, whereas the Finnic peoples were characterized by low levels of advancement. Yet, the regions inhabited by the Mobilized Europeans were not among those in the vanguard of the dramatic economic development that took place in the USSR during the period 1926-59. Conversely, the Finnic peoples happened to reside in some regions (such as the Urals and Northwest) where tremendous urbanization and industrial growth took place. Thus, although the one grouping is in reality modernized and the other grouping relatively nonmodernized, their spatial association with the indicators of socioeconomic change was not in conformity with these facts.

In addition to the factor analyses, rank order (Spearman) correlation coefficients for 1926 and 1959 were calculated for the distributions of the ten mutually exclusive nationality groupings used in the earlier chapters and the regional levels of urbanization. This provided an additional perspective on the important linkages between nationalities and modernization (urbanization, as noted many times before, is perhaps the best single indicator of modernization), and also enabled an examination of the trends among Jews and Tatars, plus Mobilized Europeans excluding Jews and Turkic-Muslims excluding Tatars.

As might be expected, the results of the correlation analysis revealed that, by 1959, the Russians had by far the highest association with the critical urbanization variable, the Tatars were moderately associated with urbanization, and the Ukrainians, Turkic-Muslims, Lithuanians, and Moldavians and Romanians had very low or negative associations with this measure. Again, the Jews, Mobilized Europeans, and Finnic peoples had relationships with urbanization contrary to expected patterns, and in this instance the Belorussians also joined in the aberrant cases. As in the factor analysis, the geographic distributions of Jews and Mobilized Europeans are not entirely in conformity with spatial patterns of urbanization. Thus, although aggregate data demonstrate conclusively that these two groups are highly urbanized (the Jews, of course, are the most highly urbanized nationality in the USSR), this fact is disguised by spatially ordered correlations. Likewise, we know from earlier discussions that the Finnic peoples and Belorussians are not characterized by high levels of urbanization, yet the peculiarities of their geographic distributions afford them the appearance of a positive relationship with urbanization.

In general, then, factor analyses and rank order correlations tend to confirm hypothesized relationships concerning the association of Soviet nationalities with modernization. With respect to the four major questions of this study, the following statements can be made:

1. Because they are relatively advanced peoples, we would expect the regional settlement patterns of the Russians, Jews, Tatars, and Mobilized Europeans to have been relatively highly correlated with regional patterns in the degree of urbanization or modernization, with the remaining less advanced groupings experiencing relatively low correlations in this regard.

2. Although no grouping displayed consistently high correlations, the Russians, Jews, and Tatars, generally speaking, did experience the highest correlations by 1959. The Jews and the Mobilized Europeans had high correlations for 1926, but for the most part failed to conform to expected patterns by 1959, although the Jews actually had a higher relationship than the correlation analysis suggested. The less advanced groupings generally displayed, as expected, very low and, in some cases, even negative correlations.

3. The emergent patterns were, generally speaking, not the result of governmental policies aimed directly at their creation. However, governmental policies, especially those with regard to regional patterns of industrial investment, certainly had a profound indirect effect, especially as they influenced regional variations in industrialization and urbanization and, consequently, influenced the distribution and redistribution patterns of many groupings, especially Russians, Jews, and Tatars.

4. Many implications for Soviet society as a whole can be noted. Foremost is the fact that regional variations in the degree of urbaniza-

tion and industrialization generated a major redistribution of many groupings, thus changing the nationality composition of many regions. Outstanding in this regard were the Russians. Indeed, the well-known movement of Russians to non-Russian areas in association with the modern economic development of such areas received further support by means of statistical correlations. The implications of such a movement are enormous, and have been discussed in depth in Chapters 5, 6, and 10.

DETAILED DISCUSSION

Factor Analysis

The generation of vast amounts of data across a wide range of indicators often leaves the investigator with more information than can be reasonably utilized or explained. Factor analysis provides the means of examining simultaneously the complex interrelationships among a whole host of variables and of summarizing these statistical linkages in a convenient fashion (for a more detailed discussion of factor analysis, see Chapter 2). Thus, two matrices with dimensions 19 x 90 (19 regions and 90 variables) were subjected to factor analysis with the goal of obtaining a concise statistical expression of the relationships between modernization and nationality. Despite some procedural difficulties and problems of interpretation, the results of the factor analyses were valuable and provided important insights into the nature of this important socioeconomic phenomenon.

Because of numerous adjustments to the data for 1897 occasioned by changes in detailed ethnic allocations, the matrix for this census year could not be utilized in the factor analysis. Furthermore, data from the 1970 Soviet census were not available at the time these calculations were performed. Thus, this analysis was, of necessity, limited to an examination of data for 1926 and 1959. This is not a crucial shortcoming, as virtually all of the major socioeconomic and demographic changes that took place in Russia and the Soviet Union between 1897 and 1970 also occurred between 1926 and 1959.

A second problem with respect to the factor analyses was that at the time we performed the calculations, only eight nationality groupings were utilized (instead of the ten groupings employed in all other sections of this study). Initially, the Jews and Mobilized Europeans were combined, as were the Tatars and Turkic-Muslims. Subsequent events convinced us to separate these groupings, but retroactive changes in the factor analysis were not feasible.

Both factor analyses resulted in the clustering of certain variables relating to aspects of modernization, a cluster we termed the "modernization factor." The variables included and their relationship (loading) with the modernization factor are detailed in Table 8.1 (1926) and Table 8.2 (1959). As is evident from these two tables, the factor is defined by variables indicative of modernization: urbanization, industrial and tertiary work force, and in-migration (the variable percentage of the population aged 20 to 39 being representative of in-migration, which is age selective). Notice the high negative association of the agricultural work force variable with the modernization factor in both years. For both years the associations of the distribution of the eight nationality groupings with the regional distribution of the modernization factor are listed below the loadings for the variables themselves. The associations (loadings) of the nationality groupings with the modernization factor is indicative of the degree to which the geographic distributions of the nationalities are related to the spatial aspect of modernization. Because the factor analysis and correlation analysis sections will both deal primarily with the regional distribution of nationalities as compared to regional variations in urbanization, the reader is advised to refer to Appendixes E.2 and E.3 plus Table 8.3 in order to make the following discussion more comprehensible.

Factor Analysis: 1926

Because comparatively little modernization had taken place in the Soviet Union as of 1926, it is not unexpected that few nationality groupings demonstrated even a moderately high positive relationship with the modernization factor (Table 8.1). Specifically, the Russians were characterized by a weak negative loading on the 1926 modernization factor, mainly because at this time many major regions of Russian settlement, such as the Central Chernozem, Urals, Volga, and Volgo-Vyatsk, were not major urban-industrial areas. The emergence of any strong positive relationship on the part of the Russians was also influenced by the fact that few Russians resided in regions, such as the South, Transcaucasus, and West, which were, in the 1926 context, relatively highly urbanized. The low share of Russians in the West region, of course, is a reflection of the fact that this area was outside the USSR in 1926.

The association of Ukrainians, Belorussians, Turkic-Muslims, Finnic peoples, and Moldavians and Romanians with the modernization factor is quite low or even negative. These relationships are expected, and conform to patterns evidenced in aggregate data on levels of urbanization. The regions that constituted the homelands of these nationalities in 1926 very frequently were relatively nonmodernized, and inasmuch as the vast majority of these groups resided in their homelands, they were likewise comparatively underdeveloped.

TABLE 8.1

Modernization Factor: 1926

	Loading
Variable	
32. Level of urbanization	0.981
34. Percent of total population in cities of 100,000 plus	0.898
46. Percent of total population in tertiary work force	0.823
88. Percent of work force in tertiary sector	0.815
86. Percent of work force in agriculture	-0.793
45. Percent of total population in industrial work force	0.734
87. Percent of work force in industry	0.687
2. Distribution of urban population	0.516
89. Percent of total population aged 10–49 literate	0.508
Grouping—Distribution	
21. Russians	-0.068
22. Ukrainians	-0.087
23. Belorussians	0.001
24. Turkic-Muslims (including Tatars)	-0.049
28. Mobilized Europeans (including Jews)	0.513
29. Finnic peoples (excluding Estonians)	-0.030
30. Lithuanians	0.415
31. Moldavians and Romanians	0.140

Sources: 1926 Soviet census; and various foreign sources (see Chapter 2, footnotes 2 and 3).

The moderately high relationship of the Mobilized Europeans with the modernization factor is the result of the concentration of the constituent nationalities of this group (Jews, Estonians, Latvians, Georgians, and Armenians) in regions, which, for 1926, were highly urbanized (the Transcaucasus, West, Center, and South regions). The moderately high association of the Lithuanians with the modernization factor is a spurious one, caused by the concentration of the relatively nonmodernized Lithuanians in the comparatively modernized West region.

Factor Analysis: 1959

By 1959 the profound socioeconomic and demographic changes of the Soviet era had altered significantly the human landscape of the

TABLE 8.2

Modernization Factor: 1959

	Loading
Variable	
32. Level of urbanization	0.974
86. Percent of work force in agriculture	-0.905
34. Percent of total population in cities of 100,000 plus	0.883
46. Percent of total population in tertiary work force	0.837
44. Percent of total population in agricultural work force	-0.820
87. Percent of work force in industry	0.808
45. Percent of total population in industrial work force	0.787
38. Percent of total population aged 20-39	0.767
88. Percent of work force in tertiary sector	0.714
2. Distribution of urban population	0.595
Grouping—Distribution	
21. Russians	0.587
22. Ukrainians	0.231
23. Belorussians	0.375
24. Turkic-Muslims (including Tatars)	0.148
28. Mobilized Europeans (including Jews)	0.014
29. Finnic peoples (excluding Estonians)	0.471
30. Lithuanians	0.104
31. Moldavians and Romanians	-0.268

Sources: 1959 Soviet census (see Chapter 2, footnote 2); and Narodnoye Khozyaystvo SSSR v 1961 G., pp. 131-32, 462.

USSR. These dramatic alterations are highly visible in the relationships between the nationalities and the modernization factor (Table 8.2). Most important, by 1959 the Russians had become highly related to the modernization factor, much more so than any of the other nationalities. The principal reason for this change in the relationship between the distribution of the Russians and the variables indicative of modernization was the economic development of most of the traditional Russian regions and the spread of many Russians to those non-Russian regions where industrial growth was taking place (such as the Donetsk-Dnepr, Kazakhstan, and West).

The loadings of the non-Russian nationalities on the modernization factor are generally weak or negative, as is to be expected in most cases. For example, the Turkic-Muslims, not surprisingly,

TABLE 8.3

Level of Urbanization by Economic Region: 1926 and 1959

Region	1926	1959
Northwest	23.9	52.4
West	18.7	32.2
Center	17.6	53.0
Volgo-Vyatsk	5.2	29.2
Central Chernozem	7.3	21.4
Volga	11.3	41.6
Belorussia	8.8	21.1
Moldavia	11.5	15.2
Southwest	10.3	18.9
South	23.1	38.7
Donetsk-Dnepr	15.0	49.7
North Caucasus	19.8	37.9
Transcaucasus	18.0	36.6
Urals	9.6	47.4
West Siberia	9.8	47.0
East Siberia	8.8	37.4
Far East	16.3	47.4
Kazakhstan	5.5	34.3
Central Asia	13.5	26.9
USSR total	13.3	38.2

Sources: 1926 and 1959 Soviet censuses; and various foreign sources (see Chapter 2, footnotes 2 and 3).

had a low positive loading on this factor. It is interesting to note that in the factor analysis for 1959 another factor emerged that further indicated the comparatively low level of modernization of the Turkic-Muslims. This factor is shown in Table 8.4 and can be termed the "Turkic-Muslim fertility factor." As this table suggests, in 1959 there was a strong association between major areas of Turkic-Muslim settlement, high fertility, and relatively low literacy levels (although all regions had literacy rates of over 90 percent). This is but another reflection of the high fertility levels and low educational levels characteristic of the less modernized Turkic-Muslims.

The one non-Russian grouping hypothesized to be strongly associated with modernization, the Mobilized Europeans, stands out as contrary to expectations. By 1959 the Transcaucasus and West re-

TABLE 8.4

Turkic-Muslim Fertility Factor: 1959

Variable	Loading
53. Percent of total population comprised by Turkic peoples	0.946
51. Percent of total population comprised by Turkic-Muslims	0.935
24. Distribution of Turkic-Muslims	0.913
26. Distribution of Turkic peoples	0.910
35. Percent of total population aged 0.9 (that is, children)	0.870
84. Child-woman ratio	0.869
54. Percent of total population comprised by Muslims	0.867
39. Percent of total population aged 40-59	-0.854
27. Distribution of Muslims	0.848
89. Percent of total population aged 10-49 literate	-0.848
37. Percent of total population aged 0-19	0.831
41. Percent of total population aged 0-19 and 60 and over (that is, dependents)	0.720
47. Percent of total population comprised by Eastern Slavs	-0.717
85. Sex ratio	0.701

Source: 1959 Soviet census (see Chapter 2, footnote 2).

gions, the major areas of settlement for the non-Jewish Mobilized Europeans, had slipped to 11th and 13th place in level of urbanization among the 19 regions. Likewise, two of the principal regions of Jewish settlement, the Southwest and Belorussia, remained relatively low with respect to the level of urbanization and modernization. Despite the fact that within these homeland regions the Mobilized Europeans are fairly urbanized and modernized, the low levels of the regions as a whole in the Union-wide context influence the loadings.

Finally, the moderately high loading of the Finnic peoples on the modernization factor for 1959 presents another spurious case. Nearly half of the Finnic peoples happen to reside mainly in two regions (the Northwest and Urals), which, coincidentally, are regions that have undergone dramatic modernization. A glance at aggregate data on, for instance, the level of urbanization of the Finnic peoples indicates that they have not participated to any significant degree in this modernization. Yet, their mere presence in these areas is enough to produce a statistical aberration with regard to the modernization factor.

In summary, the results of the factor analyses of the 1926 and 1959 data matrices revealed that the modernization that took place in the Soviet Union during the 1930s and after World War II brought about a realignment of the distribution of Russians and largely bypassed most of the other nationality groupings. Although some nationalities, such as the Mobilized Europeans, are highly urbanized (as is apparent from aggregate data), highly educated, and integrated into the advanced work force, the fact that they remain comparatively concentrated in their homelands precludes their association within the spatial context with the variables indicative of modernization.

Correlation Analysis

Because the factor analyses were conducted with nationality groupings dissimilar from those employed in the remainder of this study, we calculated rank order (Spearman) correlation coefficients between the regional distribution of all ten nationality groupings and the regional variations in the level of urbanization (Table 8.5). In this regard, the level of urbanization is a good surrogate for the modernization factor; note in Tables 8.1 and 8.2 that the largest contributions to the modernization factor are made by the urbanization variables. Again, the focus in the correlation analysis is for the period 1926-59. The results of the correlations present patterns virtually identical to those obtained in the factor analyses. Although a similar correlation analysis could be undertaken for 1970 also, it would merely duplicate that for 1959, because regional distributions and regional variations in the level of urbanization did not change much between 1959 and 1970.

Correlation Analysis: 1926

As was the case in the factor analysis of 1926, the 1926 rank order correlations revealed a weak negative relationship between the Russians and the level of urbanization (-0.171) and similar associations for all other groupings with the exception of the Jews, Mobilized Europeans, and Lithuanians. The low level characteristic of the Russians on this measure can be explained, as before, by the fact that most areas where Russians lived remained rural, agricultural regions in 1926.

On the other hand, the Jewish rank correlation coefficient was relatively high (0.469) in 1926 and was exceeded only by that of the Mobilized Europeans. Outstanding regions contributing to the relatively high relationship between the distribution of Jews and regional variations in urbanization included the South, West, Donetsk-Dnepr, and Center, which were simultaneously four of the top six regions of Jewish settlement, with the first three being part of the "Pale," and

TABLE 8.5

Rank Correlation Coefficients Between the Regional Distribution of
a Grouping and Regional Variations in Urbanization: 1926 and 1959

Grouping	1926	1959
Russians	-0.171	0.692
Ukrainians	-0.022	0.280
Belorussians	0.038	0.445
Tatars	-0.161	0.443
Turkic-Muslims	-0.166	-0.032
Jews	0.469	0.118
Mobilized Europeans	0.655	0.098
Finnic peoples	-0.134	0.507
Lithuanians	0.441	0.138
Moldavians and Romanians	0.272	-0.308

Sources: 1926 and 1959 Soviet censuses; and various foreign
sources (see Chapter 2, footnotes 2 and 3).

four of the eight most urbanized regions; and the Volgo-Vyatsk,
Kazakhstan, and the Central Chernozem, which were the three least
urbanized regions and regions of meager Jewish settlement. Some
regions impeded the emergence of an even higher relationship in
1926. Foremost in this respect were the Southwest and Belorussia,
which were the two primary regions of Jewish settlement but were
not highly urbanized.

In 1926 the rank correlation coefficient involving the Mobilized
Europeans was the highest of any grouping (0.655). Major regions
enhancing this relatively high positive relationship, as before, included the Transcaucasus, the West, the North Caucasus, the Northwest, and Center, which were the five leading regions of Mobilized
European settlement, and, at the same time, five of the six most urbanized regions; and the Volgo-Vyatsk, Central Chernozem, and
Kazakhstan, which were the three least urbanized regions and regions
of very sparse Mobilized European settlement, with the first two regions along with Moldavia having the lowest shares of the population
of this grouping. All in all, the high relationship experienced by this
grouping in 1926 primarily reflects the fact that the two outstanding
regions of Mobilized European settlement, the Transcaucasus and the
West, were also two of the most urbanized regions at the same time.

The relatively high association (0.441) between the distribution
of the Lithuanians and regional variations in urbanization in 1926 was

especially owing to the fact that most of the Lithuanians resided in the West region, one of the most highly urbanized regions. As with the Finnic peoples in 1959, this situation was more one of coincidence than an actual reflection of a high degree of Lithuanian modernization. Although the West region was relatively highly urbanized at this time, this urbanization was more a reflection of the Latvians and Estonians than of the Lithuanians. Whereas the level of urbanization for the Mobilized European population, virtually all of whom were Latvians or Estonians, of the West region was 23.7 percent, the level for the entire West region was 18.7 percent, while that for the Lithuanians of the West region was only 6.5 percent. This reflects the fact that, as mentioned before, few Lithuanians resided outside Lithuania and, thus, did not reside in Latvia and Estonia, the prime areas of urbanization in the West region.

Other regions also enhanced a fairly high and positive rank correlation coefficient in 1926. For example, the Northwest and Center were both relatively highly urbanized and were the third and fourth most important regions of Lithuanian settlement. However, their importance as "major" areas of Lithuanian settlement is greatly exaggerated. It will be remembered that in all four census years, including 1926, the Lithuanians were the most concentrated grouping, with well over 90 percent of their population residing in the West region alone, especially in Lithuania or a roughly equivalent area. Therefore, the regions containing the next largest shares of the Lithuanian population actually comprised very small shares of the Lithuanian population. In short, all other 18 regions were insignificant regions of Lithuanian settlement. Indeed, neither the Northwest nor the Center region contained even 1 percent of the Lithuanian population in 1926. Thus, although these relatively highly urbanized regions had the third and fourth highest shares of the Lithuanian population, they were obviously not really major regions of Lithuanian settlement.

The correlation coefficients for the remaining six groupings were quite low. Not unexpectedly, the distribution of Turkic-Muslims in 1926 exhibited a weak negative relationship with the level of urbanization (-0.166). Major regions contributing to the absence of a high positive relationship included Central Asia, Kazakhstan, the Urals, and Volgo-Vyatsk, which were four of the six major regions of Turkic-Muslim settlement, but which were not highly urbanized (Kazakhstan was particularly outstanding in this area, ranking second with respect to the share of the Turkic-Muslim population and next to last with respect to level of urbanization); and the Northwest, West, South, and Center, which were four of the six most highly urbanized regions of the USSR, but were not regions of appreciable Turkic-Muslim settlement; indeed, three of the four regions (Northwest, West, and Center) were tied with some other regions with respect to having the lowest share of the Turkic-Muslim population.

Likewise, the Moldavians and Romanians showed no strong association with the urbanization variable in 1926 (0.272). The two main regions of Moldavian-Romanian settlement, the Southwest and Moldavia, were among the lesser urbanized regions in the USSR. Ukrainians, Belorussians, and Finnic peoples also shared low coefficients with respect to the regional levels of urbanization (-0.022, 0.038, and -0.134, respectively), again because the nationality homelands in which these three groups were concentrated in 1926 were only slightly urbanized.

In 1926 the distribution of the Tatars was not highly associated with regional variations in urbanization (-0.161). Major regions contributing to this low relationship were the Volga, Urals, Volgo-Vyatsk, and Kazakhstan, which were four of the top five regions of Tatar settlement, but which were also not highly urbanized (indeed, the Volgo-Vyatsk and Kazakhstan were the two least urbanized regions of the USSR at this time); and the Northwest, Transcaucasus, North Caucasus, and West, which comprised four of the five most urbanized regions, but contained relatively low shares of the Tatar population (indeed the West region was tied for last place in this respect). The only region that was simultaneously among the five most important regions of Tatar settlement and the five most highly urbanized regions was the South region. This one region, however, could not offset the great number of other regions that impeded a high positive relationship.

Correlation Analysis: 1959

As was the case with the factor analysis, the correlation patterns had changed significantly by 1959. In particular, the Russian rank order coefficient with urbanization (0.692) was the highest of any grouping in either year. This high relationship between the regional distribution of Russians and regional variations in the levels of urbanization, of course, reflects the high level of modernization attained by Russians in more recent years. Particularly outstanding regions involved in this 1959 relationship included the Center, Northwest, Urals, and Volga, each of which was both a major region of Russian settlement and a major region of urbanization in 1959. Indeed, these regions were simultaneously the four major regions of Russian settlement and four of the seven most urbanized regions in the USSR in 1959; furthermore, three of these regions (Center, Urals, and Northwest) were also three of the five most urbanized regions. The Center and Northwest regions occupied roughly similar positions in 1926, but the Urals and Volga regions changed dramatically in that, although they were major regions of Russian settlement in both 1926 and 1959, they were relatively highly urbanized only in 1959. Other regions

contributing to this strong relationship included West Siberia, which
was also a fairly significant region of Russian settlement and Soviet
urbanization in 1959; and Moldavia, Belorussia, and the Southwest,
each of which contained a very low share of the Russian population
and had a comparatively low level of urbanization.

Some regions did not correspond to this strong relationship,
but they are relatively few in number. They included the Central
Chernozem region, a region still fairly prominent with regard to
Russian settlement, but still among the least urbanized regions in the
USSR; and the Donetsk-Dnepr and Far East regions, which are relatively highly urbanized, comprising the remaining two of the five
most highly urbanized regions in the USSR, but do not contain relatively high shares of the Russian population, although it should be
remembered that the Donetsk-Dnepr region was the most prominent
region of Russian settlement outside the RSFSR in 1959.

With regard to the regions beyond the RSFSR, it is instructive
to note that a high correlation existed there also in 1959. In particular, based upon the nine regions outside the RSFSR, a rank correlation coefficient of 0.633 emerged between the percentage of the total
Russian population of the USSR residing in each region and the level
of urbanization of the region. This further demonstrates that modern
economic development in non-Russian areas usually entails an influx of
Russians. The Donetsk-Dnepr was particularly outstanding in this
respect, being the most urbanized region outside the RSFSR and, as
just mentioned, the prime region of Russian settlement beyond the
Russian Republic.

The relationship between the distribution of Ukrainians and
Belorussians and regional variations in the level of urbanization had
also improved somewhat by 1959. Major regions enhancing the relatively higher relationships in 1959 for Ukrainians included the Donetsk-
Dnepr, the South, the Urals, West Siberia, and the Far East, each
of which was both relatively highly urbanized and contained a relatively high share of the Ukrainian population, although the latter three
regions comprised a much smaller share of this population than did the
Donetsk-Dnepr and South regions. However, the 1959 relationship was
still quite low (0.280), primarily because of the Southwest region.
Although this region continued to be the prime region of Ukrainian
settlement, by 1959 only one other region (Moldavia) had a lower level
of urbanization. In addition, in 1959 the two most highly urbanized
regions in the USSR (the Center and Northwest regions) did not contain high proportions of the Ukrainian population.

The somewhat higher relationship for Belorussians in 1959
(0.445) reflects the fact that three of the five most highly urbanized
regions in that year (the Northwest, Donetsk-Dnepr, and Urals)
were simultaneously the three "most important" regions of Belorus-

sian settlement after Belorussia itself. It should be pointed out, however, that these three regions were "important" only in an ordinal
sense and were not close to Belorussia in actual numerical terms.
Belorussia contained more than 80 percent of the Belorussian population, whereas none of these three regions contained even 4 percent.
Thus, the fairly high relationship noted above is somewhat distorted.
Indeed, only two regions were less urbanized than Belorussia in 1959,
indicating that the distribution of Belorussians was still largely unrelated to regional variations in urbanization.

By 1959 a relatively high positive relationship also existed between the distribution of Tatars and regional urbanization (0.443).
Indeed, of the ten groupings, only two had a higher rank correlation
coefficient at this time. As was the case with the Russians, this
higher relationship in 1959 reflects the fact that the Volga and Ural
regions, the two main regions of Tatar settlement in all four census
years, had been transformed into relatively highly urbanized regions.
Thus, in 1959 the two most important regions of Tatar settlement
were also two of the most highly urbanized regions of the USSR, thus
enhancing a high positive relationship. Other regions promoting such
a relationship were the Center and West Siberia, both of which were
relatively highly urbanized and contained a relatively high share of the
Tatar population, although this share was quite low as compared to the
main regions of Tatar settlement; and Moldavia, the Southwest, Belorussia, and the Central Chernozem, which were the four least urbanized regions of the USSR and contained relatively low shares of the
Tatar population. Indeed, Moldavia, the Southwest, and the Central
Chernozem, along with the South region, were tied for last in this
respect.

The position of the South region involves a dramatic change, as
this region was one of the three main regions of Tatar settlement in
1926. This change was due, of course, to the deportation of the
Crimean Tatars. Combined with the fact that the South region was
still one of the more highly urbanized regions in 1959, though relatively speaking it was not as outstanding as it was in 1897 and 1926,
this situation tended to impede an even higher positive relationship
between the distribution of Tatars and regional variations in urbanization.

A number of other regions also tended to impede such a relationship. These included Central Asia, the Volgo-Vyatsk, and Kazakhstan,
which were the three most important regions of Tatar settlement after the Volga and Urals in 1959, but which were still not highly urbanized; and the Northwest, Donetsk-Dnepr, and Far East, which were
relatively highly urbanized, but did not contain relatively high shares
of the Tatar population. Nevertheless, in spite of these regions, a
relatively high and positive relationship still emerged in 1959, especially as compared to 1926.

In 1959 the expected low relationship between the distribution of Lithuanians and regional variations in urbanization was manifested in a low relationship (0.138). This was caused partly by the fact that the West region, still by far the prime region of Lithuanian settlement, was no longer one of the most urbanized regions in the USSR. In addition, according to our calculations, 15 of the 19 regions contained 0.0 percent of the Lithuanian population. Thus, because there was virtually no variation in the distribution of Lithuanians, it was impossible for there to be any strong covariation between such a distribution and regional variations in urbanization. The presence of so many regions with 0.0 percent of the Lithuanians, of course, partly reflects the fact that the 1959 and 1970 censuses did not list the population of every nationality in every political unit. But the fact remains that virtually all of the Lithuanians resided in the West region, which was not that highly urbanized. In fact, similar to 1926, most Lithuanians resided in the Lithuanian SSR, the least urbanized republic of the West region.

The situation with regard to Moldavians and Romanians in 1959 was even more exaggerated and a negative relationship existed (-0.308). Not only were Moldavia and the Southwest still the two main regions of Moldavian and Romanian settlement but they were also the two least urbanized regions of the USSR. Moldavia was outstanding in this regard, containing the vast majority of the Moldavian and Romanian population and, at the same time, being the least urbanized region in the USSR. It is no wonder that a negative relationship emerged. In addition, as with the Lithuanians, the majority of the regions contained 0.0 percent of the Moldavians and Romanians. Hence, there could be little covariation since there was little variation.

The absence of any significant relationship between Turkic-Muslims and urbanization (-0.032) on the regional scale continued to 1959. The four leading regions of Turkic-Muslim settlement (Central Asia, Kazakhstan, the North Caucasus, and the Transcaucasus) were not highly urbanized. Likewise, few members of this grouping were found in the more urbanized regions.

For the Finnic peoples, 1959 witnessed a strong positive relationship between their regional distribution and urbanization (0.507). This association was due (as was the case in the 1959 factor analysis) to the fact that six of the seven leading regions of Finnic settlement (Urals, Northwest, Volga, Center, Far East, and West Siberia) were simultaneously six of the seven most urbanized regions. However, it appears that this association was actually somewhat coincidental or spurious rather than being one involving an actual high degree of Finnic modernization. It will be remembered that the Finnic peoples have been concentrated in regions that are dominated by Russians; indeed, in 1926 and 1959 the rank correlation coefficients between the distribution of Russians and the distribution of the Finnic peoples were quite high (0.700 and 0.617, respectively). Consequently, because many of the Russian regions have become highly urbanized, this has meant that the relatively backward Finnic peoples generally reside in relatively highly urbanized regions. However, in the two outstanding regions of Finnic settlement (Urals and Northwest) involved in this high positive relationship between Finnic settlement and Soviet urbanization, the Finnic peoples were, in fact, not highly urbanized. Whereas the levels of urbanization for the total population of these two regions were 47.4 and 52.4 percent, respectively, the Finnic levels were only 17.1 and 24.8, respectively. Thus, although two of the main regions of Finnic settlement were also highly urbanized, the Finnic peoples of these regions were not highly urbanized. Therefore, the high rank correlation coefficient in 1959 between the regional distribution of the Finnic peoples and regional variations in urbanization is somewhat spurious and should not be interpreted as being indicative of a high degree of modernization on the part of the Finnic peoples. A more realistic situation was presented by the Volgo-Vyatsk region, which was the second leading region of Finnic settlement in 1959, but one of the least urbanized regions in the USSR. Indeed, in this region only 6.6 percent of the Finnic peoples resided in urban centers.

Finally, the rank order correlation coefficients for both the Jewish and Mobilized European populations on this measure declined from moderately high in 1926 to low in 1959 (0.118 and 0.098, respectively). Again, the continued concentration of these nationalities in their traditional regions of settlement, which had comparatively low levels of urbanization in 1959, was responsible for this low relationship. For example, although the highly urbanized Center and Northwest regions were now important regions of Jewish settlement, the highly rural Southwest region continued to be the leading region of Jewish settlement, despite the fact that its share of the Jewish population declined from nearly 40 percent in 1926 to less than 20 percent in 1959.

In general terms, the results of the correlation analysis confirmed those of the factor analysis, as well as providing information on the Jews and Tatars. Thus, we can point to these measures as further evidence that the hypothesized relationships between nationality and modernization did indeed hold true in almost all cases. The Russians, in particular, clearly were associated with the measures of modernization, once the major period of development had taken place in the USSR.

9

SUMMARY AND
CONCLUSIONS

SUMMARY

A universal approach and demographic, geographic, and ethnic concepts have been employed in an attempt to explain the demographic and geographic aspects of ethnic processes in the USSR and their impact on society. In general, the universality of these concepts was confirmed in the Soviet context, although the expected relationships did not always emerge, and these concepts proved to be useful in organizing and systematizing the data applied to them. The authors also feel that by integrating concepts from several fields, the explanation of not only ethnic processes but also of demographic and geographic processes in the USSR has been furthered. In short, there is considerable generality of these processes in the USSR, and the Soviet government appears to have been no more successful in controlling demographic and ethnic behavior than any other government. The authors do not maintain, however, that demographic and ethnic processes can be explained completely with general concepts. The determining conditions of the modernization process vary from country to country, which, of course, affects the relationships being tested, and demographic, geographic, and ethnic theory is not yet well developed. It must also be acknowledged that there are historical and cultural features unique to the Soviet Union that affect the processes being investigated, despite the overall generality of the processes.

The theme of this study is the impact of modernization on the population of the multinational Soviet state. The authors hypothesized that population trends among the various Soviet nationality groupings would conform to the patterns found in other modernizing, multinational states. Universal experience indicates that modernization affects various ethnic groups in multinational states to different degrees

and at different times, and this differential modernization is reflected
by demographic trends indicative of modernization. The more modernized groups would be characterized by higher levels of urbanization,
geographic mobility, employment in the nonagricultural work force,
higher education levels, and lower levels of fertility. On the other
hand, those ethnic groups that were less modernized would retain
many of the demographic characteristics of premodern societies,
which include continued rural residence, mainly agricultural employment, lower levels of educational attainment, and higher fertility.
These demographic conditions, of course, reflect the degree to which
a group is integrated into the modern sectors of society, and thus the
degree to which a group benefits from the economic development that
occurs with modernization. Specifically, it was hypothesized that the
dominant ethnic group, the Russians, and certain other ethnic groups
with cultural traits that facilitate early modernization, the Tatars,
Jews, and Mobilized Europeans, would be the more modernized groups
in Soviet society. We cannot, of course, completely determine in an
objective manner which groups would be expected to modernize, because there has been insufficient conceptual work on this subject. This
deficiency does not, however, undermine our assertion that ethnic
stratification along socioeconomic lines does occur in multinational,
modernizing states.

   With regard to urbanization, our hypothesis, in general, was
confirmed. The Russians and the Jews experienced the highest rates
and achieved the highest levels of urbanization in the USSR between
1897 and 1970. In terms of the world, they urbanized at an extremely
rapid rate. The Tatars and the Mobilized Europeans urbanized at
moderate rates. The Tatars, however, experienced very rapid urbanization during the Soviet era (1926-70), and have attained a high level
of urbanization, particularly relative to the "non-European" nationalities of the USSR. The relatively slower rate of urbanization of the
Mobilized Europeans can largely be accounted for by the fact that during the prewar period of rapid industrialization, Estonia and Latvia
were not part of the USSR, and Armenia and Georgia have not industrialized as rapidly as other parts of the USSR and the demand for
labor in rural areas has remained relatively high because of their
labor intensive system of agriculture. The Ukrainians, Belorussians,
and Lithuanians have urbanized at moderate rates, and their level of
urbanization is significantly below that of the Russians, Jews, Tatars,
and Mobilized Europeans. The Finnic peoples, Turkic-Muslims, and
Moldavians and Romanians generally have had low rates and levels of
urbanization. Once again it should be pointed out that urbanization is
very probably the best indicator of the modernization of a group, at
least in the beginning and intermediate stages of modernization.

In terms of geographic mobility, although the Soviet population has experienced appreciable interregional redistribution, only a relatively few nationality groupings have undergone substantial interregional migration and dispersal since 1897. As expected, the Russians, Jews, and Tatars have experienced the greatest redistribution. The Mobilized Europeans did not redistribute to the degree that we expected. The lack of dispersal of the Latvians and Estonians can be explained primarily by the high level of economic development and substantial job opportunities in their republics combined with a very slow rate of population growth. The Georgians and Armenians have not dispersed to the expected degree, probably because of the very labor-intensive system of agriculture, moderate levels of economic development, and participation in illegal activities. In addition, being relatively highly educated peoples, they have been better able to respond to job opportunities in the modern sectors of their homelands. As expected, the other groupings, being less modernized, experienced comparatively little redistribution.

As to the expected patterns of population growth, it was hypothesized that the more modernized groupings would go through the population transition first and would have the lowest birth- and death rates. The available empirical evidence only partially confirms these hypotheses. Mortality, which requires relatively little socioeconomic change, has gone down for all groups, although not at the same time and at the same rate. It would seem from available evidence that mortality probably declined among the more modernized groups first and spread to the less modernized groups at least by World War II.

The Jews, Estonians, and Latvians experienced an early decline in fertility and the Russians experienced a similar decline somewhat later. These groups have the lowest fertility in the USSR, and currently are below replacement in terms of net reproduction. The Georgians and Armenians, however, have experienced fertility decline relatively recently, and their fertility levels are at present still above those of the other more modernized groups. Tatar fertility did not decline as early as expected, even though at present it is probably fairly low. The fertility of the Ukrainians, Belorussians, Lithuanians, Moldavians and Romanians, and Finnic peoples is much lower than would be expected based on other indicators of modernization. Clearly, fertility is a very complex phenomenon and difficult to explain adequately, particularly in the USSR where fertility data are relatively scarce. However, an attempt to explain fertility in more detail will be made in a later volume.

Factor analysis and rank order correlation also tend to confirm the hypothesis. Although no grouping displayed consistently high correlations with regards to their regional distribution vis-a-vis regional variations in modernization, the Russians, Jews, and Tatars did have the highest correlations, although the Jewish situation required some qualification. The Mobilized Europeans, however, for the most part failed to conform to expected patterns, but the less advanced groupings displayed very low and, in some instances, even negative correlations.

Because Soviet nationality policy has been variable and in general loosely defined, it is difficult to test empirically or to isolate long-term from short-term effects. One aspect of Soviet nationality policy, however, can be tested: the equalization of economic development in terms of industrialization in less advanced, non-Russian areas. Despite Soviet claims to the contrary, this long-standing policy has not been achieved on a regional basis, and many of the industrial and other urban jobs in non-Russian areas have been taken by Russians and other "Europeans," so disparities are even greater than the available data would indicate. That there is considerable ethnic stratification along socioeconomic lines as measured by demographic and other indicators supports this contention. It should be acknowledged, however, that some governmental policies, particularly those dealing with economic development, have had an indirect effect on the population processes of Soviet nationalities.

CONCLUSIONS

If the processes described in the preceding empirical chapters were in fact related to ethnic stratification, then the results should be evidenced in aggregate data. We propose here to examine available census and other socioeconomic data that provide insights into this important question: has the modernization that has taken place in the USSR affected all nationalities to approximately the same extent, or have certain groups (as hypothesized) benefited to a greater degree than others? Specifically, indexes of urbanization, nonagricultural employment, and education will be adduced to analyze this question.

Urbanization

As stated earlier, urbanization is perhaps the single best indicator of modernization, and the level of modernization of any group in society is highly related to the degree to which that group has been integrated into advanced sectors. Furthermore, as noted in Chapter 5, the most recent Soviet census (1970) revealed wide disparities in the levels of urbanization among the nationalities (Tables 5.1 and 5.4). Thus, it is already apparent that no appreciable equalization with regard to this important index has taken place.

Perhaps the most significant aspect of the urbanization of the nationalities, however, is the fact that the difference in the level of urbanization between the Russians and the other groups actually has increased since 1897, in some instances dramatically so (Table 9.1). Thus, since the tsarist era, the Russians have become relatively more urbanized in relation to the other nationalities, with the sole exception of the Jews, who increased slightly their position vis-a-vis the Russians.

Another vantage point for the urbanization aspect is afforded by reference to absolute figures regarding the increase of nationalities in the cities. Since 1897 approximately twice as many Russians have been added to the urban population of the country than all the other nationality groupings combined (65.4 million Russians as opposed to 33.3 million non-Russians). This is a remarkable figure in light of the fact that the Russians have never accounted for more than a slight majority of the population; a group comprising roughly one-half of the population has accounted for about two-thirds of the total increase in the urban population.

Aggregate data on urbanization, therefore, substantiate the hypothesis that the Russians, as the dominant group in society, will take advantage of modernization to a more significant extent than will the minorities. Furthermore, at least two of the minorities that were expected to modernize early because of cultural traits, the Jews and Tatars, also rank high in the aggregate 1970 census data on urbanization (Tables 5.1 and 5.4), the Jews, of course, being the most urbanized group in the USSR. As mentioned, the Jews actually became slightly more urbanized than the Russians since 1897, and of all the other nationality groupings, the Tatars lost the least ground in relation to the Russians over this same period (Table 9.1).

Work Force

The participation of nationalities in the nonagricultural work force is another important index of modernization for which aggregate data are available. Again, because of the influence of ethnic stratification, the Russians would be expected to be represented in the advanced jobs to a disproportionately large degree. Likewise, as hypothesized earlier, those groups whose cultural traits emphasized achievement, education, and professional status would also be expected to enter the nonagricultural sectors in large numbers. In order to test these contentions, the number of each nationality employed as specialists with higher and secondary educations for the population aged 16 to 59 (work force ages) for each individual nationality was calculated (Table 9.2). By adjusting the Soviet data for age distribu-

TABLE 9.1

Percentage Point Difference in the Level of Urbanization of the Russians and Other Nationality Groupings: 1897–1970

	1897	1926	1959	1970	Change: 1897–1970
Russians (level)	13.0	16.1	46.0	56.3	—
Difference					
Ukrainians	-8.3	-8.8	-14.7	-16.2	-7.9
Belorussians	-10.8	-10.3	-19.8	-20.2	-9.4
Tatars	-4.1	-5.0	-9.1	-10.7	-6.6
Turkic–Muslims	-8.0	-9.8	-27.4	-33.5	-25.5
Jews	21.4	36.9	31.4	22.2	.8
Mobilized Europeans	-.7	3.9	-9.5	-10.0	-9.3
Finnic peoples	-11.3	-12.7	-25.6	-28.9	-17.6
Lithuanians	-10.7	-8.9	-18.6	-18.3	-7.6
Moldavians and Romanians	-8.9	-8.8	-35.7	-40.3	-31.4

Sources: See Chapter 2, footnotes 2 and 3.

335

tion, the influence of unequal numbers of very young or older persons is reduced. The specialist category, composed mainly of technicians, agronomists, and the like, is an important work force sector amounting to almost 17 million persons, or about 15 percent of the Soviet work force in 1970.

It is clear from the data regarding specialists that the Russians, Georgians, Latvians, Armenians, and Jews have entered the modernized work force in numbers considerably greater than their share of the total population would warrant. In 1970 the Russians alone accounted for over 62 percent of specialists (whereas the Russian share of the USSR population equaled approximately 53 percent). In 1970 the percentage of Russians in the work-force ages (16 to 59) employed as specialists was exceeded by only nine of the 40 nationalities for which data were available (Georgians, Latvians, Estonians, Buryats, Ossetians, Yakuts, Altays, Jews, and Circassians). Of these nine nationalities, only the Latvians, Estonians, Georgians, and Jews accounted for large absolute numbers of specialists; the other groups with percentages higher than the Russians are comparatively minor nationalities, and thus a small number of specialists results in a high rate.

Also of some note is the fact (Table 9.2) that for the 31 non-Russian nationalities for which data are available on specialists in both 1959 and 1970, the change for 23 of the nationalities in the rate of employment in this sector was lower than the change in the Russian level, indicating that these groups lost ground relative to the Russians in this important index. Prominent among the groups that became relatively farther behind the Russians in this regard were Ukrainians, Belorussians, Uzbeks, Kazakhs, Georgians, Azeri, Kirgiz, Tadzhiks, Tatars, indeed almost all of the major nationalities of the USSR.

The Soviet sociologist Yu. V. Arutyunyan recently has presented data on the nationality composition of the nonagricultural work force for the census years of 1926, 1939, and 1959.[1] These data (Table 9.3) present yet another perspective on the integration of Soviet nationalities into modern sectors of the economy. We have, however, adopted a somewhat different posture on the interpretation of these important data than did Arutyunyan, whose goal was to demonstrate that a significant leveling of society along ethnic lines had been accomplished. Rather than rely upon percentage increase figures to measure the progress of the nationalities (as Arutyunyan admitted, such indexes are affected by small base figures and, as he put it, the "law of diminishing rates"[2]), we decided instead to evaluate these data by comparing the levels and change in levels of nonagricultural work force participation of the indigenous nationalities vis-a-vis the total population. By utilizing these relative figures and the change therein, the critical question of differential modernization may at least be partially answered.

TABLE 9.2

Specialists with Higher and Secondary Education per 1,000 Population Aged 16 to 59 by Nationality: 1959 and 1970

Nationality	1959	1970	Change: 1959-70
Russians	72.8	134.9	62.1
Ukrainians	53.1	108.3	55.2
Belorussians	50.0	102.8	52.8
Uzbeks	30.3	75.7	45.4
Kazakhs	41.5	94.0	52.5
Georgians	97.7	148.8	51.1
Azeri	65.9	113.5	47.6
Lithuanians	49.9	119.1	69.2
Moldavians	24.5	56.9	32.4
Latvians	75.5	140.9	65.4
Kirgiz	38.5	84.0	45.5
Tadzhiks	32.7	67.5	34.8
Armenians	85.3	132.4	47.1
Turkmens	39.8	79.9	40.1
Estonians	85.5	161.2	75.7
Abkhaz	n.a.	105.8	n.a.
Balkars	41.8	108.9	67.1
Bashkirs	30.9	68.1	37.2
Buryats	64.0	156.5	92.5
Ingush	14.7	44.2	29.5
Kabardinians	48.5	91.3	42.8
Kalmyks	34.5	92.0	57.5
Karakalpaks	n.a.	107.3	n.a.
Karelians	53.0	102.1	49.1
Komi*	66.9	120.1	53.2
Mari	28.8	59.0	30.2
Mordvinians	25.9	61.7	35.8
Peoples of Dagestan	36.3	98.9	62.6
Ossetians	82.8	147.8	65.0
Tatars	43.1	87.0	43.9
Tuvinians	n.a.	88.3	n.a.
Udmurts	43.1	73.4	30.3
Chechens	5.2	32.0	26.8
Chuvash	44.1	82.1	38.0
Yakuts	70.4	140.4	70.0
Adyge	n.a.	120.3	n.a.
Altays	n.a.	176.7	n.a.
Jews	n.a.	402.6	n.a.
Karachay	n.a.	109.1	n.a.
Khakas	n.a.	96.1	n.a.
Circassians	n.a.	145.9	n.a.

n.a.: data not available

*Includes Komi-Permyaks.

Sources: 1959 specialist data from Narodnoye Khozyaystvo SSSR v 1959 G. (Moscow: Gosstatizdat, 1960), p. 617; 1970 specialist data from Tsentral'noye Statisticheskoye Upravleniye pri Sovete Ministrov SSSR, Narodnoye Obrazovaniye, Nauka i Kultura v SSSR (Moscow: Izdatel'stvo "Statistika," 1971), p. 240.

It is of some significance that in 1959 only the Russians and Armenians were characterized by higher levels of nonagricultural employment than the total population of their titular republics. For the remaining nationalities, all of which were relatively less integrated into the advanced economy than the total population of their republics, the gap was particularly wide in this respect in the Turkic-Muslim republics (Azerbaydzhan, Uzbek, Tadzhik, Kazakh, Kirgiz, Turkmen) and somewhat less in the non-Russian "European" republics (Ukraine, Belorussia, Georgia, Estonia, Latvia). More important, for six of the ten republics for which data were available in both 1926 and 1959, the relative gap between the indigenous and total populations increased.

The data from Arutyunyan's study indicate that nationalities other than the indigenous groups are taking a disproportionately large share of the jobs in the nonagricultural sectors. Since most nonagricultural jobs are located in cities, and inasmuch as our urban data demonstrate that cities in non-Russian areas are major areas of Russian settlement, we can point to the Russians (and also to Tatars, Jews, and Armenians) as the group that comprises the large balance between the indigenous and total populations in the advanced economy.

Available evidence, therefore, indicates that although all nationalities have been integrated into the modernized work force to some extent, the Russians and a few other groups have benefited to a greater degree than the minorities. Thus, while we would agree with Arutyunyan that "the attainment of real factual equality is possible only on the condition that the principal differences between the working class and the peasants, between mental and physical labor, between town and the countryside, are eliminated," we cannot agree with his contention that differences in the levels of ethnic integration have been virtually erased.[3]

Education

Perhaps the most impressive results achieved by the Soviet government in the modernization of nationalities have been in the field of education. These achievements are reflected in both levels of educational attainment and in the nationality composition of university and technical school enrollments (Tables 9.4 and 9.5). Yet, the familiar patterns of differential modernization remain, particularly with regard to the level of education of each nationality.

In 1970 the Russians enjoyed a higher level of educational attainment than any of the 17 major nationalities save the Georgians, Armenians, and Jews (Table 9.4). Furthermore, the percentage point change in the educational level of the Russians between 1959 and 1970 was higher than for all the other groups except the Lithuanians (whose 1970 level remains considerably below the Russians).

TABLE 9.3

Percentage of the Total and Indigenous Employed Population Engaged in Mental and
Physical Nonagricultural Work by Union Republic: 1926, 1939, and 1959

Republic	1926	1939	1959	Percentage Point Change: 1926–1959
Ukrainian				
Total	15.9	52.8	59.1	43.2
Indigenous	9.2	44.7	52.5	43.3
Belorussian				
Total	12.8	43.4	46.1	33.3
Indigenous	6.2	33.3	42.5	36.3
Georgian				
Total	21.8	40.9	53.4	31.6
Indigenous	16.7	33.3	47.7	31.0
Armenian				
Total	16.2	38.6	58.8	42.6
Indigenous	16.6	39.5	60.7	44.1
Azerbaydzhan				
Total	36.9	47.0	55.1	18.2
Indigenous	23.5	28.6	41.9	18.4
Kazakh				
Total	7.7	55.8	71.1	63.4
Indigenous	2.9	36.2	48.6	45.7
Uzbek				
Total	17.4	34.9	47.3	29.9
Indigenous	11.4	21.2	29.1	17.7
Turkmen				
Total	15.7	45.7	56.2	40.5
Indigenous	4.1	22.1	33.4	29.3
Tadzhik				
Total	6.0	n.a.	42.9	36.9
Indigenous	5.5	n.a.	26.2	20.7
Kirgiz				
Total	7.5	36.9	55.1	47.6
Indigenous	1.3	16.2	24.7	23.4
RSFSR				
Total	n.a.	n.a.	74.1	n.a.
Indigenous	n.a.	n.a.	76.2	n.a.
Estonian				
Total	n.a.	n.a.	73.3	n.a.
Indigenous	n.a.	n.a.	68.8	n.a.
Latvian				
Total	n.a.	n.a.	68.7	n.a.
Indigenous	n.a.	n.a.	63.4	n.a.

n.a.: data not available

Source: Yu. V. Arutyunyan, "Izmeneniye Sotsial'noy Struktury Sovetskikh Natsiy,"
Istoriya SSSR, no. 4 (July-August 1972), pp. 3-20.

Data on the composition of students in higher education, standard-ized for age, reveal significant improvements in the enrollment rates for non-Russians, improvements that will be translated into gains in the level of educational attainment for these nationalities in the future (Table 9.5). Although the Russians and other modernized nationalities are still (1970) relatively high in the indexes of enrollment in higher and specialized secondary schools, a number of comparatively non-modernized groups now exceed the level of the Russians. These fig-ures are evidence of an apparent Soviet attempt to integrate and mod-ernize the non-European nationalities through education, an attempt that has met with some success.

In all such comparisons, however, it must be borne in mind that the numerically smaller nationalities have an inherent advantage when

TABLE 9.4

Percent of Population Aged 10 and over Having Higher and Secondary Education (Complete and Incomplete) by Major Nationality: 1959 and 1970

Nationality	1959	1970	Percentage Point Change: 1959-70
Russians	37.8	50.8	13.0
Ukrainians	35.3	47.6	12.3
Belorussians	31.1	43.8	12.7
Uzbeks	31.1	41.2	10.1
Kazakhs	26.8	39.0	12.2
Georgians	47.4	57.8	10.4
Azeri	36.0	42.4	6.4
Lithuanians	20.8	35.3	14.5
Moldavians	21.2	33.8	12.6
Latvians	42.6	48.8	6.2
Kirgiz	29.9	40.0	10.1
Tadzhiks	29.9	39.0	9.1
Armenians	44.3	51.8	7.5
Turkmens	36.3	43.0	6.7
Estonians	35.8	46.2	10.4
Tatars (RSFSR)	32.9	44.2	11.3
Tatars (Uzbek SSR)	43.6	53.5	9.9
Jews (RSFSR)	76.4	82.4	6.0
Jews (Ukrainian SSR)	65.2	74.7	9.5

Source: 1970 census (see Chapter 2, footnote 2).

TABLE 9.5

Students in Higher Education Institutions and Specialized Secondary Schools per 1,000
Population Aged 16 to 24 by Nationality: 1959 and 1970

Nationality	Higher Education Institutions		Specialized Secondary Schools	
	1959	1970	1959	1970
Russians	100.2	146.1	94.2	144.7
Ukrainians	71.4	115.1	70.6	124.9
Belorussians	64.6	109.3	66.2	125.5
Uzbeks	81.0	134.4	46.5	86.3
Kazakhs	95.8	143.1	63.5	101.8
Georgians	138.7	211.6	61.6	113.1
Azeri	76.3	166.6	60.7	111.4
Lithuanians	92.6	147.1	111.2	166.6
Moldavians	48.7	85.2	38.6	86.0
Latvians	113.8	136.9	105.7	123.7
Kirgiz	89.6	158.0	54.9	93.4
Tadzhiks	63.6	111.1	34.8	70.0
Armenians	105.1	179.4	68.1	134.5
Turkmens	88.0	122.4	58.1	81.2
Estonians	133.2	157.5	138.4	136.4
Abkhaz	n.a.	174.3	n.a.	91.7
Balkars	108.4	208.3	81.3	166.7
Bashkirs	55.9	102.0	48.5	106.9
Buryats	184.3	259.8	115.9	146.1
Ingush	87.0	98.8	46.8	72.8
Kabardinians	75.6	155.9	64.8	104.9
Kalmyks	113.5	190.2	165.9	202.8
Karakalpaks	n.a.	166.6	n.a.	148.5
Karelians	59.8	109.5	59.8	164.3
Komi*	61.1	80.6	75.0	147.3
Mari	46.6	66.5	40.6	102.1
Mordvinians	35.7	79.2	32.9	107.9
Peoples of Dagestan	66.8	139.0	77.6	131.5
Ossetians	114.6	225.1	94.0	131.0
Tatars	61.6	105.5	55.2	119.9
Tuvinians	70.9	85.5	49.1	90.3
Udmurts	56.8	85.7	55.5	106.5
Chechens	44.6	61.4	46.3	74.4
Chuvash	53.6	80.7	49.4	105.9
Yakuts	98.6	161.2	81.7	126.0
Adyge	n.a.	203.6	n.a.	162.8
Altays	n.a.	137.8	n.a.	153.1
Jews	n.a.	512.4	n.a.	193.7
Karachay	n.a.	184.8	n.a.	73.9
Khakas	n.a.	124.9	n.a.	159.0
Circassians	n.a.	224.8	n.a.	122.6

n.a.: data not available.

*Includes Komi-Permyaks.

Sources: Narodnoye Khozyaystvo SSSR v 1964 G. (Moscow: Statistika, 1965), p. 691; and
Tsentral'noye Statisticheskoye Upravleniye pri Sovete Ministrov SSSR, Narodnoye Obrazovaniye,
Nauka i Kultura v SSSR (Moscow: Izdatel'stvo "Statistika," 1971), p. 196. Data on student enrollments for 1959 are not available. Accordingly, we have utilized figures for the 1962-63 school
year, the earliest available, and have standardized these on the 1959 population. In reality, therefore, the 1959 data presented here are slightly inflated, but the overall relationships remain valid.

341

rates per population are calculated. Thus, 1,000 Buryat students in universities results in a high rate when compared to the relatively small Buryat population, but the same number of Ukrainian students would be lost in the much larger Ukrainian population. This is especially true of the Russians, whose large size requires a massive enrollment to maintain or, as is the case, increase the level of students in higher education. In 1970, for example, the more than 2.7 million Russians in colleges and universities dwarfs the figure for any other nationality.[4]

Thus, aggregate data on the levels of urbanization, nonagricultural work force participation, and education further substantiate that the Russians and a select few nationalities have been integrated into modernized society to a greater extent than the balance of the groups. Because of the dominant position of Russians in society, and because of the achievement orientation and other cultural traits of such groups as the Tatars, Jews, Georgians, Armenians, Latvians, and Estonians, these nationalities entered the modernization process relatively early and thus today are characterized by demographic and socioeconomic levels typical of modernized society.

NOTES

1. Yu. V. Arutyunyan, "Izmeneniye Sotsial'noy Struktury Sovetskikh Natsiy," Istoriya SSSR, no. 4 (July-August 1972), pp. 3-20.

2. Ibid., pp. 15-16.

3. Ibid., p. 12.

4. Tsentral'noye Statisticheskoye Upravleniye pri Sovete Ministrov SSSR, Narodnoye Obrazovaniye, Nauka, i Kultura v SSSR (Moscow: Statistika, 1971), p. 196.

CHAPTER

10

IMPLICATIONS

THE IMPACT OF MODERNIZATION ON A
MULTINATIONAL STATE

Within the past century, and particularly since the advent of
Soviet power, dramatic economic, social, political, and demographic
changes have occurred across the territory of what is today the USSR.
Most, if not all, of these changes have in some way been determined
or shaped by the dimension of ethnicity. The crucial fact is that the
Soviet Union, like its predecessor, the Russian Empire, is a diverse
multinational state and, as in all other multinational states, a wide
range of problems exists in the USSR that are related to ethnicity.
Many of these problems, particularly social questions, are apparently
exacerbated by the very developmental processes that raised the Soviet Union to a world economic and military power.

The purpose in this final chapter will be to place the Russian and
Soviet case within the broader context of ethnic relations, in general,
and to assess the implications for the future of the nationality question in the USSR based upon universal experience. Implicit in this
approach, and we again hasten to stress our position in this regard,
is the underlying assumption that socioeconomic, demographic, and
ethnic processes in the Soviet Union are fundamentally very similar
to those same processes in all multinational states, Soviet propaganda
and some Western scholarship notwithstanding. It would be naive and
unscientific to impute uniqueness to the Russians as the dominant nationality in the USSR, or to the impact of their political–economic system upon society, unless strong evidence existed to substantiate such
a claim. It is our opinion that, to the contrary, the Russian and Soviet example tends to confirm the universal character of demographic
and socioeconomic processes in all multinational states.

343

The basic framework through which we propose to assess the implications of the impact of modernization upon the multinational Soviet state is that proposed and detailed by Tamotsu Shibutani and Kian Kwan; that is, the establishment and realignment of systems of ethnic stratification.[1] According to this formulation, all societies are characterized by the ranking of categories of people on the basis of a number of possible criteria, such as age, sex, natural ability, occupations, caste, family background, religion, or whatever. Ethnic background is a possible, and it appears common, criterion from which status is inferred in multinational societies.[2]

The ethnic dimension may be further reinforced when nationality coincides with other categories, such as occupation, class, or urban-rural residence. For example, Nathan Glazer and Daniel Moynihan noted that in New York City certain occupations or segments of society were identified with specific ethnic groups. Thus, in such a setting, government policies regarding teachers affect one ethnic group, events concerning the police force have a strong impact on another ethnic group, the welfare population consists mainly of yet other ethnic groups, and so on.[3] In instances such as these the ethnic dimension assumes greater importance, and ethnic groups function as economic interest groups. Milton Gordon recognized the critical nature of the coincidence of ethnicity with other social or economic characteristics among segments of the American population in his concept of "eth-class," which he defined as "the subsociety created by the intersection of the vertical stratifications of ethnicity with the horizontal stratifi-cations of social class."[4] More specifically, Gordon postulated four factors that are particularly important in delimiting the divisions in a multiethnic society: ethnic group, social class, rural or urban residence, and region of the country in which one resided:

> These four factors [ethnic group, social class, rural
> or urban residence, and region of the country lived
> in] do not function in isolation, or serially, but com-
> bine or intersect to form the basic large social units
> which make up American society and which bear and
> transmit the subcultures of America. While the
> factors are theoretically discrete, they tend to form
> in their combination " a functioning unity which has
> an integrated impact on the participating individual."[5]

The degree to which ethnicity coincides with other socioeconomic divi-sions and the extent to which mobility is possible between the sub-groups of society clearly are critical features of any multinational setting.

Systems of ethnic stratification are normally established when two or more nationalities come into contact. In cases of imperialist expansion, such as that which occurred during the growth of the Russian Empire or the extension of the United States to the Pacific, the ethnic group with the most advanced technology and sociopolitical organization is likely to establish hegemony. Ethnic stratification results from the gradual delineation of privilege and status according to the relative power of the various nationalities; the dominant group assumes the more privileged positions within society and the economy, while the minorities are relegated to lesser positions. Often, groups that are so inclined may assume intermediary roles between the dominant nationality and the lower ranking minorities. Differences in religion and skin color may serve to define further the divisions within the stratification system, and eventually the order becomes accepted through various sanctions and ideologies. If the stratification system is rigid, ethnicity will be strengthened by prolonged, inflexible discrimination, since the various groups will be compartmentalized and individuals within the groups will develop like interests.[6] Systems of ethnic stratification can and do change, although it appears that the evolution into a new order is normally a realignment and not an elimination of discrimination and differential status among nationalities.

The most important catalyst for change in ethnically stratified societies is modernization and economic development. During periods of economic growth, older patterns of stratification become inadequate, and change is required to adapt the system to the demands imposed by the modernization process. With the onset of economic development, considerations of efficiency and the maximum utilization of human resources require a loosening of the older, more rigid stratification systems, and the integration of all or most ethnic groups into advanced society eventually becomes necessary for sustained growth. Periods of change are disjunctive to stable systems of ethnic stratification, because consensus over the relative status of groups breaks down and ethnic tensions inevitably result; the situation, in military parlance, becomes fluid.[7]

The long-range impact of modernization upon ethnicity is a controversial subject that has been treated at some length by scholars concerned with nationality problems. For some time the prevailing opinion on this important subject was that propounded by Karl Deutsch, who, in Nationalism and Social Communication, hypothesized that modernization (or, as he termed it, "social mobilization") would result in the erosion of limited, narrow attachments to language, regional identifications, particularistic customs and the like, and a simultaneous expansion in broader affiliations. The prime mover in this process would be, according to Deutsch, the more intense and all-pervading communications channels characteristic of modernization. The ultimate result was envisioned as the gradual disintegration of nationality distinctiveness and an increase in assimilation.[8]

The contention that modernization would lead to a lessening of
ethnic identity and a reduction in interethnic conflict was disputed by
Walker Connor in the important article "Nation-Building or Nation-
Destroying?" in which he demonstrated with a number of empirical
cases that just the opposite had occurred in modernized and modernizing states throughout the world. Modernization and increased interethnic and intraethnic communications led, Connor stated, to heightened ethnic awareness and a reinforcement of the "us-them" dichotomy.[9]
In a summary of his article's findings, Connor noted that:

> The preponderant number of states are multiethnic.
> Ethnic consciousness has been definitely increasing,
> not decreasing, in recent years. No particular
> classification of multiethnic states has proven im-
> mune to the fissiparous impact of ethnicity: authori-
> tarian and democratic; federative and unitary; Asian,
> African, American, and European states have all
> been afflicted. Form of government and geography
> have clearly not been determinative. Nor has the
> level of economic development. But the accompani-
> ments of economic development—increased social
> mobilization and communication—appear to have
> increased ethnic tensions and to be conducive to
> separatist demands.[10]

The principal factors in any interpretation of modernization and
its impact upon ethnic groups in a multinational state are, in our
opinion, twofold. When considered jointly, these factors may contribute to an explanation of why, contrary to the hypotheses stated by
Deutsch, the process of economic development and social mobilization
almost always leads to heightened ethnic tensions rather than to an
erosion of nationality awareness and distinctiveness. One of these
two factors is the fact that systems of ethnic stratification do not
break down completely during the period of change wrought by modernization, but rather realign. This situation means, very simply, that
ethnic inequalities in the social, economic, and political spheres will
be perpetuated, and will continue to be the source of nationality antago-
nisms. The other factor is that the demographic and socioeconomic
changes that take place in conjunction with modernization will, in
themselves, lead to increased ethnic animosities. The influx of outsiders into nationality homelands in response to economic development, urban-rural dichotomies between nationalities, rising levels of
education among minority groups, and discrimination in employment
in the advanced sectors all promote discontent among ethnic groups.

The differential impact of modernization upon ethnic groups in a multinational state is owing largely, as hypothesized in an earlier chapter, to the relative power of the various nationalities in the pre-modern system of ethnic stratification and, in the case of certain groups, to aspects of culture that encourage their entry into the modern sector. As the system of ethnic stratification realigns to facilitate economic development, some concessions must be made to the minorities or other ethnic groups, and the socioeconomic levels of all groups will probably rise. The dominant ethnic group or groups, however, can be expected to preempt the most favorable positions within modernized society, and to benefit disproportionately from economic development; the dominant group may actually improve its position relative to the other ethnic groups as modernization progresses.

The impact of economic development also has a spatial aspect, and regional inequalities in development may, in a multinational state where different ethnic groups occupy separate nationality areas, translate into inequalities in the socioeconomic development of the groups. Economic development does not occur uniformly across the territory of any state, owing to regional differences in natural resource endowment, market potential, location relative to other regions, labor force characteristics, economic infrastructure, or other considerations. Thus, a group occupying the most favorable region for economic development quite naturally enjoys an advantage relative to nationalities in more backward areas.[11] Further, there might be a tendency for the dominant group to favor the development of their homeland at the expense of other nationality areas. These regional inequities are often the basis for ethnic discontent, as demonstrated by the rising animosities among the Bretons; Brittany is one of the more underdeveloped regions of France.[12]

Attempts by central governments to alleviate regional development inequalities by siphoning off funds from the more modernized nationalities that are expected to sacrifice some of their gains in the "fraternal" interest also result in ethnic tensions. In Yugoslavia, for example, the Croatians and Slovenians, whose nationality areas are the most economically advanced, demonstrated significant resentment against policies they believed exploited their position and retarded further progress in their republics.[13] In addition to causing resentment among the "haves," policies designed to equalize regional development usually sacrifice some economic efficiencies, as the less developed areas are frequently not the optimal location for industry. These policies, therefore, may result in slower growth of the country's total economy, which in itself contributes to ethnic tensions.

The second major factor that, in our opinion, contributes significantly to the increased ethnic tensions and seems to accompany

modernization are the demographic and socioeconomic changes that
occur in conjunction with economic development. Primary among
these changes are urbanization, migration, higher levels of education,
and the development of an advanced, nonagricultural work force. All
of these important aspects of population have an ethnic dimension in
multinational states. Perhaps the single most important aspect of
demographic change is urbanization, and the differential integration of
nationalities into urban society appears to be the best indicator of
continuing ethnic stratification. In advanced societies, the cities are
the areas of economic opportunities, cultural life, educational facilities, and a generally higher standard of living. The degree to which
each ethnic group is urbanized, therefore, serves as an important
index of the degree to which the group is modernized, is integrated
into advanced society, and shares in the benefits of modernization.
Also, cities have been linked to the erosion of ethnicity and to assimilation, and one might expect a strong emphasis to be placed upon the
urbanization of minority groups in order to facilitate their incorporation into the larger society. Yet, multinational states are characterized
normally by sharp differentials in the levels of urbanization, with the
dominant group or groups controlling the cities and the minorities remaining largely rural. The well-known contrast between city and rural
life may become an additional reinforcing element to ethnic distinctiveness in such situations.

Migration between nationality areas in response to expanding
economic opportunities will, as a general rule, lead to the mixing of
ethnic groups on a regional (macro) scale and perhaps on a neighbor-
hood (micro) scale. Perhaps the best example of this phenomenon was
the migration of blacks from the American South to cities in the North
in search of jobs in the expanding industrial sectors.[14] The implications of ethnic mixing are difficult to assess. Clearly, the contact and
communication between nationalities would seem to be a prerequisite
for understanding and reconciliation and an erosion of ethnic barriers.
In situations where ethnic mixing has occurred, however, hostilities
have often been the outcome. Shibutani and Kwan suggested that proximity may exacerbate ethnic tensions by bringing different groups into
direct competition in social and economic pursuits.[15] The consequences of the migration of outsiders into nationality areas, particularly when there are distinct racial or religious differences between
the groups, has led to violence and civil disorders in northern cities
in the United States, in southern France, in Nigeria, and a host of
other countries.

Interethnic friction may become particularly intense when outsiders migrate in large numbers to the nationality homeland of another group. Despite the fact that such claims are often disputed, individuals of one ethnic group may consider themselves as the true

owners or "charter members" of a region, and as such deserving of special consideration in jobs, education, language rights, and other fields. "They conceive of themselves as the people who 'really' belong in the area; others are either guests or unwanted intruders."[16] Many multinational states, such as Yugoslavia, Nigeria, Canada, Belgium, and the Soviet Union, have adopted a federal system of ethnic territorial units with varying degrees of local autonomy as a "solution" to the integration of nationalities.[17] Although this form of political organization may reduce tensions initially, it is not inconceivable that federal units, no matter how artificial they may appear, will become legitimate in the eyes of the nationalities, and encroachment upon the prerogatives of the "charter members" may be the source of heightened ethnic animosities.

The process of modernization requires the attainment of higher levels of education for the populace in order to provide the necessary skills for the expanding economy. Education, however, has been singled out by some authors as the most potentially disjunctive element in social change. Education, the argument goes, acquaints the individual with broader horizons, bolsters self-confidence, and increases aspirations and expectations. Furthermore, higher levels of education equip one for better job opportunities, and often leads to direct competition for skilled employment with the dominant group, which prior to economic development held a monopoly on the advanced socioeconomic sectors.[18] Thus, education presents a paradox, in that higher levels of education are necessary in order to integrate all groups fully into the modernizing society, yet that very step may contribute, in the absence of sufficient opportunities and rewards, to frustrations and resentment on the part of the minorities.

The final aspect of demographic and socioeconomic change that is likely to result in increased ethnic tensions is the development of the advanced, nonagricultural work force. Jobs in the modernized sectors are generally the best society has to offer, and of course pay higher wages. It is not surprising, then, that the dominant group will preempt these better jobs and that minorities will almost certainly be underrepresented in the nonagricultural occupations.

Modernization, therefore, presents an interesting paradox in its impact upon ethnic relations in multinational states. It has been hypothesized that modernization and its concomitants will lead to a diminution of nationality distinctiveness and a lessening of ethnic tensions. Such facets of modernization as urbanization and ethnic mixing will, it has been suggested, lead to an erosion of nationality awareness and will promote more general, less particularistic attachments. The facts say otherwise, as was so amply demonstrated by Connor.

We have suggested here that this seeming incongruity derives from the fact that the true promise of modernization has yet to be ful-

filled in multinational societies. Because the older systems of ethnic
stratification were not completely eradicated, but merely reshaped,
socioeconomic inequities persist and promote ethnic animosities.
Furthermore, the demographic trends that occur when modernization
takes place likewise lead to increased tensions. Thus, although modernization may indeed raise the standards of living for all, there almost certainly will continue to be distinct gaps between nationalities,
gaps that are a function of the position of these ethnic groups within
the stratified order.[19] It is precisely this differential integration
into the modernized sectors of the society that is a major source of
ethnic friction.

MODERNIZATION AND IMPLICATIONS FOR THE
NATIONALITY QUESTION IN THE SOVIET UNION

It is apparent that modernization in multinational states exacer-
bates ethnic animosities and leads to heightened tensions and ultimately to conflict. Given this premise, the changes in the ethnic
stratification system in Russia and the USSR are examined briefly and
the implications for the nationality question that arise from the process of modernization in the Soviet context are assessed.

The expansion of the Russian Empire under the tsars was a
classic example of the imperialist conquest and colonization model.
Smaller, technologically backward groups were overawed or defeated
militarily, and were then incorporated into the empire. The imperial
government made few concessions to the non-Russian nationalities,
and there could have been little doubt that the Russians as a nationality
were in the ascendancy. The system of ethnic stratification that developed in the Russian Empire naturally placed the Russians themselves in the most favored position. The imperial order was characterized by sufficient flexibility to coopt the nobility and other promis-
ing individuals from non-Russian groups, a practice common to most
systems of ethnic stratification.[20]

It is clear that the Russians, as the dominant group in the empire, benefited to a much larger degree than did the minorities. Russian settlers seized agricultural lands from nomadic groups, a practice that often led to uprisings and punitive expeditions not unlike the
sequence of events during the expansion of the United States.[21] Russians occupied disproportionately large shares of the populations of
cities in non-Russian regions, particularly in areas that had undergone the initial stages of economic development (such as the eastern
Ukraine and Baku).

The system of ethnic stratification with the Russians as the
dominant group has survived revolution, civil war, foreign invasion,

and the upheavals of the Stalinist model of rapid, forced industrialization and modernization. Clearly, the Soviet system embodies much
less rigid barriers to upward mobility for non-Russians than did the
ancien regime, but this may be a characteristic of any modernizing
or modernized society, for, as we have noted earlier, the powerful
forces of change associated with modernization demand some concessions and accommodations for the minorities. The system of ethnic
stratification in the Soviet Union today is the result of the evolution
from the older, more rigid tsarist system, and although the present
situation is no doubt more favorable for the minorities, there is little
doubt that the Russians remain the dominant and hence most privileged
nationality. The continued use of race or ethnic ideologies, such as
the well-known "Russian big brother" appeal to justify in some way
the favored position of the Russians, is indicative of the maintenance
of ethnic stratification in the Soviet Union.

The question of socioeconomic advancement and economic development of previously backward nationalities and non-Russian regions
has been discussed in previous chapters, but it would be appropriate
here to assess the implications behind the unequal nature of development in the Soviet period. It is clear from the data presented in earlier chapters that the Russians have benefited to a greater extent from
modernization than have the other nationalities of the Soviet Union,
with the possible exception of the Jews. Although impressive gains
in the economy and general conditions of life have been attained in all
areas of the Soviet Union, almost all non-Russian nationalities have
actually lost ground relative to the Russians in socioeconomic levels.
With regard to the important urbanization indicator, the difference
between the level of urbanization of the Russians and the various non-
Russian groupings increased, often dramatically so, during the period
1897-1970. In 1897, for example, the Russian level of urbanization
was eight percentage points higher than the Turkic-Muslims, but by
1970 the Russians were 33.5 percentage points higher.

The preceding section noted that regional inequalities are likely
to exist in multinational or, for that matter, homogeneous states.
In the Soviet context these regional inequalities principally are evidenced in non-Russian areas, particularly in the Muslim areas of
Central Asia. Although Soviet achievements in Central Asia have been
significant, these regions remain among the most backward in the
USSR. Central Asians frequently are reminded by Soviet authorities
about the higher levels of economic development and the better standard of living in their homelands as contrasted with neighboring Muslim countries, such as Afghanistan. That these gains are real is beyond dispute, even though Russians have benefited disproportionately
from the economic development that has occurred in Central Asia,
but other considerations mitigate the seemingly favorable comparisons

with non-Soviet countries. How does one evaluate these socioeconomic gains in light of the harsh reality of the continuing domination of non-Russian nationality territories by Russians? Can the dramatic increase in the number of skilled technicians in the Uzbek SSR or the number of hospital beds per capita in the Turkmen SSR ameliorate the lack of genuine ethnic self-determination among Uzbeks and Turkmens? It must be remembered that the Central Asian nationalities, as well as the other non-Russian nationalities of the USSR, are (at least within the span of the past few centuries) the original inhabitants of these territories, and are certain to consider the Russians as usurpers and outsiders. Referring to situations such as Central Asia, where the indigenous population may have benefited in material terms from outside domination, Shibutani and Kwan noted: "In many cases subjugated peoples have enjoyed material advantages as a result of the contact, but they have invariably dwelled upon the indignities."[22]

Furthermore, is it realistic to expect Central Asians to compare their lot with coreligionists in other countries, or would they instead contrast their position relative to the Russians? Would a Tadzhik in Dushanbe be happy that he is substantially better off than the average Afghan in Kabul, or would he be more likely to notice his standing relative to the Russians who control the capital of the Tadzhik Republic? One is reminded here of the invidious suggestion that blacks in the United States need only contrast their socioeconomic gains with blacks in Africa to "appreciate" their position in American society. The demographic changes related to modernization have also contributed to an increase in ethnic tensions in the USSR, just as these same trends have evoked hostilities in other multinational countries. The ethnic mixing that has resulted from economic development and migration has been owing largely to the influx of Russians into non-Russian regions.[23] Ethnic tensions in the Baltic region, for instance, have increased because of the continuing in-migration of Russians into that area.[24] In Lithuania this situation deteriorated into open hostility in the form of street fighting between young people and police and paratroops, and several deaths were reported.[25] The prominent Soviet Ukrainian dissident Ivan Dzyuba protested the Russification of the Ukraine, and was subsequently arrested for his efforts.[26]

Thus, it would appear that the nationality units of the USSR have taken on real meaning for the titular ethnic groups.[27] The perception of relative deprivation of the non-Russian nationalities may be heightened by the ethnic basis of the Soviet federation; these nationalities may expect certain advantages to accrue to them in their own ethnic homeland, and if many opportunities are instead preempted by Russians and other outsiders, tensions will almost certainly increase. Thus, that out of political expediency and counter to Marxist theory, Lenin established a federal structure may well be a factor that will continue to intensify ethnic tensions in the USSR.

Finally, there is some Soviet evidence to suggest that rising educational levels and employment in the advanced work force may lead to rising ethnic hostilities, just as has been the case in other multinational countries. In a study of ethnic relations in rural areas in the Tatar ASSR,[28] Arutyunyan discovered that professionals held higher levels of negative attitudes toward other nationalities (realistically interpreted as attitudes toward Russians) than did farm workers: "Despite the fact that professionals have the greatest success both in education and in overcoming the influences of traditional culture, they [the professionals] do not have a higher level of positive attitudes in cross-national relationships than do other segments of the population, but rather the contrary."[29] Arutyunyan links this phenomenon to a higher level of expectations among the more educated, expectations that, if not fulfilled, lead to frustrations.[30] Therefore, as the non-Russian nationalities become increasingly better educated and integrated into the advanced work force, ethnic tensions actually may be exacerbated.

The foregoing situations or trends are all clearly important for the future of nationality relations in the Soviet Union. The most profound and far-reaching impact upon society, occasioned by dramatic demographic forces, is, however, yet to come. This condition stems from the high levels of population growth in many Turkic-Muslim areas, especially Soviet Central Asia, and from the large Russian presence in advanced economic sectors of these regions.

Continued economic development in the USSR coupled with sharp ethnic and regional differentials in natural increase should result in a substantial further redistribution of population, much ethnic mixing, and increased ethnic tensions. Economic development is unevenly distributed within a country and ultimately results in a massive redistribution of a population. Areas of economic development are usually characterized by low natural increase, and less developed areas usually have higher natural increase. Migration equalizes the supply of and demand for labor on a regional basis, providing the necessary labor for areas of rapid economic development and relieving population pressures in the less developed parts of a country. In the USSR, areas of rapid economic development are located chiefly in Slavic areas, which are characterized by a low rate of natural increase and frequently labor shortages, and Turkic-Muslim areas are generally characterized by less economic development, labor surpluses, and a high rate of natural increase, particularly among the rural population that predominates. Moreover, in the cities of these areas, Russians and other in-migrants frequently take most of the more desirable jobs and the urban economy is unable to absorb the surplus indigenous labor. As the indigenous work force in these areas continues to expand at a rapid rate, the only meaningful alternative in a devel-

oped country such as the USSR will be out-migration to areas of economic development where jobs are available. Therefore, what should
occur in the next few decades in the USSR will be a significant redistribution of the Turkic-Muslim population to more developed areas of
the USSR, which are predominantly Slavic, and where they will take
relatively low-level jobs because of their lower levels of skill and
education. Analogous processes have affected the black population
of the United States in the past 50 years. Thus, we expect that in the
next few decades there will be an appreciable redistribution of the
Turkic-Muslim population, which will result in ethnic mixing and increased ethnic tensions. Central Asia is the best example of an area
where these processes are expected to occur.

The Central Asian Problem

Intense demographic pressures are developing in Central Asia
among the Turkic-Muslim population, which is primarily rural and
resides in irrigated oases with limited water and agricultural land resources. Between 1959 and 1970 the total Turkic-Muslim population
of Central Asia increased at an average rate of 3.4 percent per year,
or 44 percent, and the total Uzbek, Kirgiz, Tadzhik, and Turkmen
population increased by almost 4 percent per year. In 1970 only 21
percent of the Turkic-Muslim population lived in urban centers
(15,000 and over definition). This very rapid rate of population growth
of the relatively large Turkic-Muslim population, numbering more than
14 million or almost a half of all Soviet Turkic-Muslims, coupled with
the intense drive by the government to mechanize agriculture, will
surely result in a large surplus rural population, as there is already
a labor surplus in most rural areas of Central Asia.

The rapid population growth among the Turkic-Muslims of Central Asia has resulted in increasing pressures upon agricultural and
other resources. During the last decade, the population density in
Central Asia increased rapidly, particularly in comparison to the
past. Between 1913 and 1939 the number of rural inhabitants (official
definition) per sown hectare of agricultural land in Central Asia remained fairly stable, and apparently even declined slightly (1.6 and
1.5, respectively). By 1959 the density was still roughly the same
(1.6). However, by 1970 it had increased to 2.0.[31] Only the Transcaucasus republics had higher densities (see Table 6.9). Thus, a
density that remained essentially stable for at least roughly a half
century suddenly increased by 25 percent within approximately one
decade. These patterns suggest that the degree of population pressure
has increased significantly in rural areas of Central Asia and that
rural overpopulation may in fact now exist.

Additional data attest further to the existence of overpopulation in rural areas in Central Asia. First of all, according to V. I. Perevedentsev, Central Asia is now regarded as a labor-surplus region.[32] Even in 1959, it was estimated that the labor supply on collective farms in Kirgiziya during the peak working season exceeded demand by 22 percent, while in some other regions, especially in the RSFSR, a labor shortage existed.[33] The existence of a labor surplus in rural areas of Central Asia is further indicated by Ann Sheehy. She notes that "there has been a reducation in the the number of days worked by kolkhozniks (in Central Asia), particularly women, and that farms are often at a loss to know how to employ all the labor they have. In Andizhan Oblast, for instance, instead of the norm of one man per ten hectares of arable land, there are ten and often twenty."[34] In addition, although income per kolkhoznik is generally above the national average, income per family member on collective farms of all four Central Asian republics was below the Union-wide average in 1966.[35] Indeed, in the Uzbek, Kirgiz, and Tadzhik SSRs, incomes per family member were less than 80 percent of this average.[36]

The problem of rural overpopulation in Central Asia will be exacerbated in the future by the rapid rate of growth of the work force. In particular, Central Asia will have by far the most rapid increase in the number of workers and the number of new entrants to the work force of any region in the coming decades (Tables 10.1 and 10.2). In fact, the work force (here defined as the population aged 20 to 59) of Central Asia will roughly double between 1970 and 1990, while the number of new entrants to the work force (population aged 20 to 29) will almost triple. Furthermore, based upon our calculations, Central Asia alone will account for 14.2 percent of the increase in the total Soviet work force between 1970 and 1980 and for 40.2 percent between 1980 and 1990; in both periods, it will have by far the greatest absolute increase in the size of the work force of any region. It will also occupy similar positions with respect to the absolute increase in the number of new entrants to the work force. Indeed, between 1980 and 1990 when the number of new entrants to the work force will be declining in most Soviet regions, particularly the more industrialized ones, and by more than 2 million in the USSR as a whole, it will be increasing in Central Asia by nearly 2 million! Central Asia, thus, will be the leading Soviet region with respect to increasing number of workers.

Another important factor to consider in terms of rural population pressure is the mechanization of agriculture. Grey Hodnett has documented the desire of the Soviet government to be self-sufficient in cotton, to produce as much cotton as possible, and to lower the cost of producing cotton, which is now relatively high and has been increasing rapidly in recent years. In an attempt to lower production costs, the government has put strong emphasis and pressure on mechanizing the harvesting of cotton. Despite a number of problems, including the surplus of rural labor, considerable progress has been made in the last decade, and by the end of the 1960s, machine harvesting accounted for 33 percent of the Soviet cotton crop, which is primarily located in Soviet Central Asia. An equivalent percentage was reported for the Uzbek Republic in 1970. Considering the efforts of the Soviet government to mechanize cotton harvesting and to mechanize agriculture in general (the current five-year plan calls for an expenditure of about 35.5 billion rubles to mechanize Soviet agriculture), it seems highly likely that Central Asian agriculture will become much more mechanized in the next decade or so. If one assumes, as Hodnett does, that mechanized cotton harvesting releases 50 percent of the labor in the production of cotton, it is apparent that this campaign alone will release large numbers of rural workers and further intensify the labor surplus in rural areas of Central Asia.[37]

Consequently, it appears that as a result of population growth and the mechanization of agriculture, the main bloc of Turkic–Muslim peoples of the USSR, those of Central Asia, will be experiencing a significant increase in the degree of population pressure, and a major problem facing the Soviet economy in the future will be how to absorb the greatly increasing number of Central Asian workers.

How can this situation be alleviated? To investigate this question, we can turn to the conceptual model developed by Eugene Kulischer. According to Kulischer, societies faced with increased "economic density" or population pressure and a decline in living standards have three means of response: economic development (operationally defined here as economic development in rural areas of Central Asia); birth control; and emigration, that is, out-migration to other places, both within the country or to another country.[38]

Because Central Asian agriculture is so highly dependent upon irrigation, an investigation of the possibilities of "economic development" in rural areas of Central Asia naturally leads to the possibilities of increasing the amount of irrigated land. In the early 1960s Robert Lewis estimated the irrigation potential of Soviet Central Asia, including southern Kazakhstan (which includes the bulk of the irrigated acreage of Kazakhstan).[39] According to his estimates, 22 million acres are potentially irrigable at the rates of irrigation efficiency obtaining in the early 1960s, and roughly 50 million acres are suitable for irrigation only if the irrigation efficiency were significantly raised.[40] In 1970, the irrigated acreage of Central Asia and Kazakhstan, was somewhat more than 15 million acres.[41] Thus, using the unrealistic figure of 50 million, it appears that the irrigated acreage of Central Asia and southern Kazakhstan at the very maximum

could be approximately tripled. Between 1959 and 1970 the rural
population (census definition) of a roughly comparable area (Central
Asia plus Chimkent and Dzhambul oblasts of Kazakhstan) was, not
surprisingly, growing at a rate virtually equal to that of all Turkic-
Muslims as a whole, that is, approximately 3 percent per year.

If this rate were maintained in the future, it would mean that
the rural population of this area would triple in about 35 to 40 years;
that is, by the end of the first decade of the 21st century. Of course,
the rural population may not continue to maintain such a growth rate,
but it is also improbable that the amount of irrigated land could ever
be trebled, because the estimate of 22 million acres for the irrigable
acreage is more realistic. In fact, in recent years additions to the
irrigated acreage of Central Asia and Kazakhstan have not been pro-
ceeding at a very rapid rate. Between 1960 and 1970 the irrigated
acreage of this area increased by only 5.1 percent, or approximately
0.5 percent a year.[42] Clearly, a continuation of this rate would not
allow the irrigated acreage to keep pace with the growth of the rural
population. However, the current five-year plan calls for an increase
in the irrigated acreage of 1.6 million acres, or about 10 percent.[43]
Even this projected increase is only about half of the rate of increase
of the work force during the next decade.

It is interesting to note, however, that despite the higher wages
on the state farms associated with new irrigation projects, such as
the Golodnvaya Steppe, the Central Asian collective farmers apparently
are unwilling to relocate to these new enterprises. "Lack of housing
is partly to blame. Another factor is that the new lands need mainly
skilled agricultural workers such as machine operators, of whom
there is a shortage even in labor surplus areas. As a result, at least
in the early 1960's, some 20 to 40 per cent of the labor force in some
sovkhozes in the Hungry Steppe, the lower reaches of the Amu Darya,
and the Karakum Canal area came from outside Central Asia."[44]
Such a process is not unlike that involving in-migration from other
areas in pursuit of nonagricultural jobs in Central Asia.

Thus, it is highly questionable that increased irrigation in Central Asia will provide a main outlet for the local surplus labor. As
Sheehy notes, "the new sovkhozes set up as a result of various major
irrigation schemes now under way will be able to take a certain
amount of the surplus agricultural labor. But if the Hungry Steppe is
anything to go by, they will be highly mechanized and there will be a
limit to the numbers they can absorb."[45] In short, it appears that
even if the irrigated acreage of Central Asia is increased, the new
areas of agricultural development will not be able to absorb the excess
rural labor.

It is also unlikely that changing the agricultural system would
increase employment in rural areas. Hodnett maintains that it is

doubtful that the introduction of crop rotation and a more balanced
crop structure would create more jobs in rural areas, because other
crops in the USSR are less labor intensive than cotton and are more
susceptible to mechanization.[46]

Birth control also will not be a likely solution in the near future.
Although the Central Asian birthrate may decline, such a decline will
undoubtedly take many years to occur, particularly in rural areas,
and the effects of current high fertility on the age distribution will ensure a proportionately large number of women in the reproductive
years. For example, over 50 percent of the total Uzbek, Kirgiz,
Tadzhik, and Turkmen population was below age 15 in 1970, a percentage unequaled by any country in the world. Thus, there is a substantial fertility potential among these populations, and even if fertility
declined, rapid population growth can be expected. Furthermore,
even if the current birthrate plummeted overnight, the repercussions
of past high fertility levels will continue to be a burden in the next
few decades. As mentioned before, the indigenous Central Asian
work force will roughly double between 1970 and 1990, an increase
that will exceed that of any other Soviet region. Most important, this
increase will come from people who were already born as of the 1970
census.

Consequently, it would seem likely that rural out-migration
would be the most immediate and far-reaching response. Of course,
this response would not be novel in that most peoples of the world have
generally responded in the same manner when confronted with deteriorating rural living standards. As implied repeatedly, such a migration has been minimal to date. According to Sheehy,

> Probably the main reason the Central Asian kolkhoz-
> niks have not left the kishlak in greater numbers
> before now is that they are still able to make a living
> there. Those released from work on the kolkhoz can
> usually do quite well out of their private plots. There
> has also been a certain amount of resistance to mech-
> anization on the kolkhozes themselves, and since
> wage rates have risen faster than productivity, the
> wages of the individual kolkhoznik may have not
> dropped very much, even if he does work fewer
> days. But with mechanization remaining the order
> of the day (however irrational in the circumstances),
> with more and more youngsters reaching working
> age, and with wages bound to drop even if yields
> rise, it is doubtful that this situation can continue
> much longer.[47]

Hodnett suggests four reasons why there has been relatively little out-migration from rural Central Asian areas:

1. Cotton pickers are mainly women in Central Asia, and because of their low education and status they are less likely to migrate when they are released by mechanization of cotton harvesting;
2. The kolkhozniki have an overall lower educational level, including poor Russian-language training, and thus they have difficulty or perceive a difficulty in adjusting to urban life;
3. The possibility of surviving fairly comfortably on a private plot;
4. The relative desirability of living and working in the city.

In this connection, Hodnett points out that, according to a Soviet study, in 1968 the combined per capita income of kolkhozniki in the Uzbek Republic, including wages, social consumption, and income from private plots, was 87.4 percent that of workers and employees, not including the amenities of better housing in the rural areas. He further points out that he does not expect the low rate of out-migration to persist indefinitely.[48]

The last two reasons that Hodnett cites primarily explain why there has been relatively little out-migration from the rural areas of Central Asia. If economic conditions in the rural areas of the Uzbek Republic relative to the urban areas of the republic are roughly comparable throughout Central Asia, and they probably are, one of the chief motivations for migration, significant rural-urban differentials in the standard of living, does not exist in Central Asia. Clearly, economic conditions have not yet begun to deteriorate in the rural areas of Central Asia, but with the total work force doubling between 1970 and 1990 and growing faster in rural than urban areas not considering migration and the government drive for mechanization of agriculture, economic conditions will deteriorate, unless the Soviet government will tolerate supporting a large, rapidly increasing population on the land in the form of low labor productivity or essentially a large welfare population. In an economy with increasing labor shortages, it is not rational for farmers to subsist on small plots much like the agricultural system of Southeast Asia, where a substantial surplus of labor exists. Eventually average wages will decline and unemployment rise, unless the Soviet government chooses to pay more for cotton. The motivation behind mechanizing Central Asian agriculture is, of course, to lower the price of cotton.

With regard to Hodnett's first two reasons for the delay in migration, it is not realistic to view the rural population of Central Asia as an undifferentiated mass of uneducated Moslems, and there are indications that the status of women among the younger cohorts is improving rapidly as educational attainment increases. We have already indicated that the overall educational level of the indigenous population of Central Asia is significantly below that of the Russians, but this generalization does not apply to the younger cohorts, in Central Asia or generally elsewhere in the USSR. For example, in 1970, the cohort aged 20 to 29 for the total Uzbek population of the USSR had completed ten years or more years of education at almost the identical rate of the Russian population of the USSR (53.5 percent in contrast to 53.8 percent for the Russian population). In fact, both the urban and rural rates for the Uzbeks (65.5 and 47.9 percent) were somewhat higher than the Russian rates (59.2 and 35.5); that the totals were almost identical is because the Russian population is much more urbanized. Slightly higher rates prevail for the Uzbek population in the Uzbek Republic. The Kirgiz population of the USSR has only a slightly lower rate than the Uzbeks, and the Tadzhiks and Turkmen only somewhat lower, registering 44.6 and 47.3 percent for the total population ages 20 to 29 that had completed more than ten years of school.

Clearly, there has been a dramatic rise in educational attainment in both urban and rural areas of Central Asia, and higher levels of educational attainment facilitate the modernization of a group and erode the traditional way of life. The world-over migration is age and education selective; young people in rural areas who have completed high school and have higher education, particularly in those rural areas experiencing population pressures, have a high propensity to migrate and generally predominate in rural out-migration. Higher education levels also improve the status of women, if they participate in the process, and raise their propensity to migrate.

There are no education data by age, sex, and nationality in the 1970 census, but education data are available by sex and age for the rural, urban, and total populations of the republics. In the Uzbek Republic only less than 5 percent of the rural population is comprised of nationalities, such as Russians, Tatars, Jews, and Armenians, that might have higher educational levels than the Uzbeks and other Turkic-Muslim groups, so these data are probably representative of the rural Turkic-Muslim population in the Uzbek Republic. In 1970, about 8 percent of the female cohort aged 30 to 39 had finished ten years of school, whereas for the 20 to 29 cohort it was 27 percent and for the 16 to 19 cohort, 30 percent. Of course, students normally finish ten years of school at age 17, so the rate for the 16 to 19 cohort does not truly represent the trend in completing high school. For example, although 45 percent of the males in the 20 to 29 cohort had finished ten years of school, only 34 percent of the 16 to 19 cohort had. These data suggest that the female rate probably is still increasing rapidly. Equally as important as this rapid increase in female educational attainment is that the ratio between the percentages of men and women completing ten years of school for the 30 to 39 cohort was about three to one, for the 20 to 29 cohort less than two to one, and for the 16 to 19 cohort the difference was only four percentage points. Thus, female education participation rates are increasing rapidly and now are only slightly below male, which most certainly will affect the status of women and their mobility. Furthermore, 62 percent of the males 20 to 29 and 35 percent of the females in the rural areas of the Uzbek Republic had completed ten or more years of school in 1970. Education rates for the other republics show similar trends, and the percent of the females aged 16 to 19 who are married has also declined sharply in the Central Asian republics, further reflecting the dramatic cultural change that is occurring in this area.

Thus, the view that the Central Asian rural population is an uneducated, traditional Muslim population is a very static one and not representative of reality, and is applicable only to the older cohorts. There has been a dramatic rise in educational levels for both males and females, and if this trend continues, which it very likely will, by 1990 a significant proportion, probably more than half of the rural population, will have completed more than ten years of school, and the rates will be particularly high in the age groups that are most prone to migrate.

It is very probable, however, that under the economic conditions that now prevail, the educational levels and Russian-language competence of the older cohorts are influential in impeding migration, but if economic conditions in rural areas deteriorate rapidly, one can expect out-migration even among the more uneducated population, particularly since there are job opportunities for unskilled labor throughout the Soviet economy. In essence, the conclusion that can be drawn from surveying the world literature on migration is that people move primarily for jobs and economic improvement, and the young and the more educated have the highest propensity to migrate. Cultural factors, such as education and language differences, can impede migration, but they will not stop it. The migration history of the United States testifies to the fact that language differences are not a major obstacle to migration, as does the recent migration to northern Europe. Therefore, the poor Russian-language training and lower education levels of some segments of the population in rural Central Asia also will very probably not be a decisive factor in impeding migration, once economic conditions begin to deteriorate. Hodnett reports on the basis of his travels in Central Asia that "Soviet observers frequently suggest, on the contrary, that kolkhozniki—especially young people—gravitate naturally to the towns."[49]

Assuming that appreciable rural out-migration will occur in Central Asia in the next few decades, the next question concerns the destination or destinations of such a movement. Aside from other

rural areas of Central Asia, which, as discussed above, do not appear
to be able to absorb large numbers of workers, a number of other possible alternative destinations can be put forth: other countries, that
is, emigration; other rural areas of the USSR; local urban areas; and
distant urban areas of the USSR. Emigration is highly unlikely partly
because of governmental restrictions against such movements, both
on the part of the Soviet government and foreign governments. The
recent emigration of some Soviet Jews notwithstanding, it does not
appear that the Soviet government is on the verge of allowing mass
emigration from the USSR. Also, although many developed countries,
especially in Western Europe, have let in thousands of workers from
lesser developed countries in recent years, most developed countries
still have highly restrictive immigration policies.

But perhaps the major factor impeding the emigration of the
Central Asians is the fact that there are numerous areas within the
USSR that have labor shortages and can thus serve as major destinations. Indeed, with respect to the next hypothetical alternative, migration to other rural areas of the USSR, labor shortages do, in fact,
exist in other rural areas of the USSR, particularly in Russian areas.[50]
For example, whereas, as mentioned before, the collective farm labor
supply in Kirgiziya exceeded that of demand by 22 percent in 1959,
in West Siberia, Kazakhstan, the Northwest, Estonia, and East Siberia, the supply was only equal to 70 to 83 percent of the demand.[51]
However, substantial out-migration of young people is occurring from
these areas, primarily because of "dissatisfaction with the standard
of living there and the lack of cultural opportunities (clubhouses,
movies, theaters, concerts, sports facilities, etc.) and interesting
companions."[52] The government has, in addition to stressing the
mechanization of agriculture, undertaken a number of measures to
induce young people to remain on these farms, but, according to Murray Feshbach and Stephen Rapawy, "these measures seem not to have
slowed down the flow of out-migrants."[53] In addition, although labor
shortages exist in some rural areas, much of it is only seasonal in
nature and year-round job opportunities are not great. Thus, although
many Turkic-Muslims may migrate to rural areas experiencing a
labor shortage, especially in the RSFSR, it does not appear that these
areas will hold much attraction for such groups as Central Asians,
and these areas probably could not absorb an appreciable number of
workers.

Another possible alternative could be a movement to currently
unexploited agricultural areas. Such areas have provided a major
outlet in the past for Russians in the overpopulated rural areas of
central European Russia. The Russians have been quite fortunate in
that abundant agricultural land was still available within the country,
especially in the southern European steppe, Siberia, and northern

Kazakhstan. Thus, as mentioned earlier, a major response has been out-migration from rural districts of central European Russia to these areas.

Unfortunately, like rural inhabitants in underdeveloped countries in general, the Turkic-Muslim rural population does not have this "safety valve" that was available to rural inhabitants of Russia and the other portions of the world in the past. Although the sown acreage of the USSR has increased substantially in the last few decades, especially with the New Lands Program, which began in the mid-1950s and which greatly increased the sown acreage of northern Kazakhstan and West Siberia in particular, the chances of further increasing cultivated land in the USSR in the future do not seem appreciable. Indeed, the sown area has increased very little since this expansion. [54] It should also be remembered that the USSR has a fairly poor natural environment for agriculture, and that a great share of the extensive amount of land already put under the plow is of very marginal quality.

In short, the possibilities of increasing job opportunities in rural areas of the USSR are quite limited, as they are throughout the world. Indeed, the modernization process typically has involved a diminution of such opportunities, especially because of the increased mechanization of agriculture. The current five-year plan calls for allocating about 27.5 percent of total investment in agriculture, including 35.5 billion rubles in machinery and equipment. [55] Thus, it does not appear that the Central Asians will find employment opportunities to any great extent in other rural areas of the USSR.

This leads to the two final hypothetical alternative destinations: local and distant urban centers. As is obvious, the migration of the Central Asian nationalities to urban centers to date has not been great. Central Asia traditionally has been a region of very meager local rural-to-urban migration. For example, place-of-birth data from the 1897 census indicate that Central Asian cities generally had the lowest levels of in-migration in the Russian Empire, and, in fact, in many large cities of Central Asia in-migrants comprised under 10 percent of the population. In such cities as Kokand, Andizhan, and Namangan in-migrants comprised only between 2 and 4 percent of the population, and in Staryy Margelan, now Margilan, in-migrants accounted for only 0.3 percent of the population, the lowest percentage for any city with a population of 15,000 and over for which data were available in the empire in 1897. In comparison, in-migrants comprised roughly 50 percent of the total urban population of the empire, and many cities had levels in excess of 60 and 70 percent.

A low degree of rural-to-urban migration is still a characteristic trait of the Central Asian nationalities. According to 1970 census data, rural-to-urban migrants comprised a relatively low percentage of the total population of the Uzbeks, Tadzhiks, Kirgiz, and Turkmens, and, for that matter, of most of the major Turkic-Muslim nationalities. In particular, whereas rural-to-urban migrants in the two years preceding the census comprised 1.8 percent of the total population of the USSR, corresponding percentages for the four major Central Asian nationalities ranged from 1.1 percent for the Kirgiz to 0.5 percent for the Uzbeks, who are, of course, by far the largest Turkic-Muslim nationality.[56] A further reflection of their relatively low degree of rural-to-urban migration has been the fact that the rural growth accounted for more than two-thirds (67.9 percent) of the total population increase of the Turkic-Muslims between 1959 and 1970, as compared to a paltry 0.1 percent for the USSR as a whole.

It should be noted, however, that from another perspective the rural-to-urban migration of the Turkic-Muslims has been more significant in recent years. Because the urban population of the Turkic-Muslim peoples has been increasing very rapidly, a not insignificant rural-to-urban movement has apparently been taking place. Between 1959 and 1970, as mentioned earlier, the urban population of the Turkic-Muslims increased by 77.9 percent, or by 5.2 percent per year. Even though the urban natural increase rate of the Turkic-Muslims is relatively high in comparison to other nationalities, it probably did not account for much more than one-half of their total urban increase at best. Therefore, it appears that a substantial share of the present urban growth of the Turkic-Muslims is the result of rural-to urban migration.

Because the Turkic-Muslim nationalities are still typically very highly concentrated in their respective homelands, what rural-to-urban migration that has occurred undoubtedly has involved local urban centers rather than distant urban centers, especially those in Russian areas. This is reflected by the fact that between 1959 and 1970, over three-fourths (77.7 percent) of the increase in the number of urban (census definition) Uzbeks occurred within Uzbekistan.

As implied before, a major question concerning Soviet society in the future is whether or not these local cities in Turkic-Muslim regions will be able to accommodate the projected substantial increase in the number of out-migrants from nearby rural areas. In particular, what has the government been doing and what does it intend on doing with regard to investment in these cities in Turkic-Muslim areas, especially Central Asia? Will local rural-to-urban migration solve the problem of increased rural population pressure? The answer is somewhat mixed, but perhaps more negative than positive. First of all, on the positive side, three of the four Central Asian republics are scheduled to have a rate of industrial growth above the Union-wide average during the current five-year plan (1971-75).[57] In addition, the amount of capital investment in Central Asia increased by well over two times between 1960 and 1970, whereas the total amount

of Soviet investment only roughly doubled.[58] Thus, because the total
population of Central Asia increased by approximately 50 percent over
the same period, the per capita amount of capital investment in Central Asia increased.

However, from other perspectives the amount of capital investment in Central Asia is less impressive. First of all, per capita investment increased in all republics of the USSR, and by 1970 Central
Asia was still receiving a proportion of the Soviet capital investment
that was below its proportion of the total population (roughly 6 and 8
percent, respectively).[59] Furthermore, during the current five-year
plan (1971-75) the position of Central Asia with respect to investment
is not expected to improve dramatically. According to this plan, the
percentage increase in per capita new fixed capital investment in all
four Central Asian republics is to be less than the percentage increase
for the Soviet Union as a whole.[60] In fact, James H. Noren and E.
Douglas Whitehouse conclude that "investment per capita in most of
the minority republics is to grow somewhat slower than in 1966-70, or
at best, maintain the same rate of growth. . . . Scheduled cutbacks
in the rate of growth of investment are especially steep in Lithuania,
Belorussia, Armenia, and the Uzbek republic. . . . Therefore, since
the plans do not clearly favor the lagging republics, existing regional
disparities in levels of development should persist."[61] Thus, the
Soviet government does not appear to be undertaking any profound special measures toward helping the Central Asian cities to accommodate
the substantial increase in the number of out-migrants from nearby
rural areas. However, given the low level of industrial productivity
in Central Asia, the lack of more substantial investment in this region
does have some economic rationale.

From another perspective, Central Asian cities are again relatively deprived in comparison with Soviet cities in general. Although
data concerning total investment in cities are not available, data are
commonly available on the housing stock of all republic capitals and
other large cities in the RSFSR. Like most Soviet cities, the cities
of Central Asia have experienced a significant increase in their housing space in recent years as the Soviets have begun to pay increasing
attention to this sector. Although improvements have occurred, a
substantial housing shortage still plagues most Soviet cities. For
example, by the end of 1971, the amount of per capita useful urban
housing space in the USSR was roughly one-half that of the United
States (11.2 square meters versus 25 square meters, respectively).[62]

Most important for the discussion at hand, however, is the fact
that of the entire 15 republics, the six republics that are based on
Turkic-Muslim nationality had the six lowest values of per capita useful urban housing space.[63] In particular, the urban centers of the
Kirgiz, Tadzhik, and Uzbek republics had the three lowest values,

with Uzbekistan ranking the lowest of any republic in this regard![64] Similarly, Tashkent had the smallest amount of per capita useful housing space of all the individual cities investigated (8.3 square meters),[65] owing in part to the earthquakes of the 1960s. To put the matter in even better perspective, Moscow, a city not known for its plentiful housing supply, had the highest value of any city (13.9 square meters).[66]

Also, Central Asian cities have experienced a relatively small increase in the per capita amount of available living space. Between the end of 1959 and the end of 1970, the per capita figure for the entire Soviet urban population (census definition) increased from 8.6 to 11.0 square meters.[67] During a comparable period, the per capita figure for the urban population (census definition) of Central Asia increased from 8.2 to only 8.8 square meters.[68] Thus, Central Asian cities experienced both an absolute and percentage increase that was lower than the national increase, and, at present, the per capita amount of housing space in these cities approximates the national average of the early 1960s. Thus, based on the above index, the housing situation in Central Asian cities today is roughly comparable to that of Soviet cities in general about a decade earlier, which itself was not ideal, to say the least.

Given the restricted housing situation of Central Asian cities, one might expect another similarity to occur between Soviet Central Asia and underdeveloped countries. In these countries rural over-population has led to a mass migration to cities. However, because the housing supply in these cities has not been able to accommodate the rapidly increasing numbers of people, many people have responded by putting up shacks. As a result, extensive shantytowns are perhaps the major aspect of the urban landscape in underdeveloped countries. Although it is possible that a similar situation could emerge in Central Asia, it should be remembered that the Soviet Union is able to increase housing fairly rapidly, especially by means of the construction of prefabricated apartments. Thus, although the Soviet Union housing situation still leaves much to be desired, it is somewhat questionable whether extensive shantytowns would ever proliferate the urban landscape of Central Asia.

In order to investigate further the ability of Central Asian cities to accommodate a large influx of peoples from nearby rural areas, it might be worthwhile to make use of a study by A. J. Jaffe and J. N. Froomkin.[69] This study concerns, among other things, the rate of economic growth in the nonagricultural sector and the proportion of the male work force currently engaged in agriculture. In particular, given a certain rate of economic growth in the nonagricultural sector that is needed to maintain the agricultural work force at a constant size, or to decrease it by 15 percent per decade, that is, the rate of

nonagricultural growth that will be needed to absorb enough farmers
so that the size of the agricultural work force will remain the same
or be reduced appreciably.

In order to make such an estimate, assumptions have to be made
regarding the future increase in the work force, the future increase
in nonagricultural productivity, and the proportion of the male work
force currently engaged in agriculture. Accordingly, we made the
following assumptions for Soviet Central Asia:

1. There would be a 3 percent average annual increase in the
work force, which is in accordance with future estimates of the population aged 20 to 59 (Table 10.1).

2. The average annual increase in nonagricultural productivity
would be 4 percent, which is somewhat in accordance with the rate of
increase of industrial productivity in Central Asia between 1965 and
1970. Average annual rates among the four republics ranged from
roughly 6 percent for Kirgiziya to about 3 percent for Uzbekistan,
which contains the majority of industrial workers in Central Asia.[70]
This is perhaps a conservative estimate since the current five-year
plan envisages an increase of nearly 7 percent for Soviet industry as
a whole.[71] If such an ambitious target were actually reached in Central Asia, this would further diminish the number of local urban job
opportunities.

3. We assume a work force in which 40 percent of the male
workers are engaged in agriculture, a figure in accordance with data
from the 1970 census. In addition, as we have done above, we will
for the time being, assume an absence of in-migration, particularly
of Russians, from other regions.

If such assumptions are made, Central Asia would require an
average annual rate of growth in the nonagricultural sector of 8.8
percent to maintain the present number of farmers and 9.5 percent
to reduce the agricultural work force by 15 percent. If labor productivity in the nonagricultural sector of Central Asia rose to the planned
USSR average of about 7 percent per year, the corresponding average
annual growth rates would have to be 12.0 and 12.7 percent, respectively. Thus, based on the above assumptions, the rate of economic
growth in the nonagricultural sector of Central Asia would have to be
roughly 9 to 13 percent a year in order to absorb enough agricultural-
ists so that the local agricultural work force would maintain either its
current size or decline appreciably.

In order to estimate the rate of economic growth in the nonagricultural sector of Central Asia, we can, first of all, make use of industrial production data for the period 1965-70.[72] According to these
data, average annual industrial growth rates among the four republics

of Central Asia ranged from 12 percent for Kirgiziya to 8 percent for
Tadzhikistan and Turkmenistan to only 6 percent for Uzbekistan.
Since the bulk of the Central Asian industrial production probably
comes from Uzbekistan, we might then approximate a rate of, say,
8 percent a year. Indeed, according to the current Soviet five-year
plan, industrial production in the four republics is scheduled to increase annually by 10 percent in Turkmenistan, by 9 percent in Kirgiziya, by 8 percent in Uzbekistan, and by 6 percent in Tadzhikistan.[73]
Thus, the assumption of an average annual rate of 8 percent a year
in the nonagricultural sector does not seem out of line. Consequently,
because an average annual growth rate in the nonagricultural sector
of roughly 9 to 13 percent is required to absorb the local agricultural
surpluses, it appears that the nonagricultural sector of Central Asia
will have difficulty in absorbing the excess local agricultural labor.

Other conditions will also tend to impede a more substantial
local rural-to-urban migration in Central Asia. As we have just demonstrated, it would be difficult for the nonagricultural sector of Central Asia to absorb the excess local rural workers, even if they were
the only workers who could take advantage of the increased number
of jobs in the nonagricultural sector. Other factors impeding such a
migration have been discussed in greater detail elsewhere in this
study and need only be briefly discussed here. In particular, such
absorption will be even more difficult, because a great number of
these jobs will continue to be taken by outsiders, especially Russians.
Between 1959 and 1970 the Russian urban population of Central Asia
continued to grow rapidly, by 3.7 percent annually, which was exactly
the same rate as the corresponding rapid rate for Russians in all 14
republics outside the RSFSR in aggregate. In absolute terms, the
number of Russians in centers of 15,000 or more increased by almost
700,000. Although the in-migration of Russians is owing to a large
extent to the lack of job skills on the part of the indigenous labor
force, Russians no doubt also take many jobs that could be taken by
the indigenous peoples; for example, those in the textile mills that
do not require a high degree of skill. However, the rapidly increasing levels of educational attainment of the younger cohorts of the indigenous population should appreciably raise their qualifications for
urban jobs.

In addition, local rural-to-urban migration in Central Asia will
probably continue to be impeded by the fact that many of the major
nodes of modern activity in Central Asia are highly Russianized and
thus different in culture; especially important in this regard is the
frequent use of Russian as the on-the-job language, a language of
which the indigenous nationalities still have a generally poor command.

Furthermore, it has been noted that many small and medium-
sized old towns in Central Asia already have considerable reserves

of labor.[74] Consequently, it is possible that a great share of the increased industrial job opportunities would be taken by laborers already in the cities, thus further reducing the number of jobs available to the surrounding rural populace. Such a situation would not be unique to Central Asia. Indeed, Jaffe suggests that it happens quite often in developing areas in general.[75]

Of course, it is possible that job opportunities for the indigenous population could be expanded by changing some of these conditions, especially by limiting the in-migration of Russians and by increasing the training of the indigenous population in terms of both the Russian language and job skills. It does appear that steps are being made in some of these directions. For example, according to Sheehy, "great efforts are being made to improve the teaching of Russian in rural schools, and there are signs that the population is becoming more mobile. In November 1971 the Uzbek Central Committee and Council of Ministers also announced that the number of vocational training schools in the republic was to be doubled by 1975 to overcome the shortage of skilled workers."[76] However, the effectiveness of such measures is somewhat questionable. In particular, Sheehy expresses doubts that the party and ministries really want to impede the in-migration of Russians to any substantial degree.[77] Furthermore, she concludes that, "on the evidence available (and for a non-economist) it is difficult to say whether sufficient steps are being taken to deal adequately with the problem of Central Asia's labor surpluses, but to judge from remarks in the local press it would seem that those on the spot do not always think so."[78]

Therefore, although an increase in local rural-urban migration will most likely occur, it does not appear that Central Asian cities will be able to accommodate completely the projected mass outflow of indigenous peoples from nearby rural areas. Thus, it appears that about the only reasonable alternative available to a substantial number of these peoples will be migration to cities of other areas, the last of the alternative destinations under investigation.

These labor problems should be viewed from the perspective of the total Soviet economy, because pull factors are equally as important as push factors in the analysis of migration. Currently, there are labor shortages in most large cities and in many "European" areas of the USSR, both urban and rural, and these labor problems will intensify because of the past declines in fertility in these areas. Indeed, between 1980 and 1990 almost three-fourths of the net increase of the total Soviet work force (population aged 20 to 59), not considering migration, will occur in Central Asia, Kazakhstan, and the Transcaucasus, where the work force will be increasing at a rate of 2.5 percent per year. In the remainder of the USSR, the work force will grow at an average annual rate of 0.2 percent, and the work force will decline in the major industrial regions. Much of this slight increase will come from the non-European areas of the RSFSR, where fertility has remained significantly above Slavic and Baltic levels. In terms of new entrants to the work force (population aged 20 to 29), in the areas outside Central Asia, Kazakhstan, and the Transcaucasus there will be an increase of over 11 million potential workers between 1970 and 1980, but a decrease of 5 million between 1980 and 1990. Between 1970 and 1990 new entrants in Central Asia, Kazakhstan, and the Transcaucasus will increase by over 7 million. Virtually all of this increase will be contributed by the indigenous populations of these areas, because they constitute a large percentage of the population and Slavic fertility is also very low in the areas outside the RSFSR.

If the Soviet government wishes to sustain a high rate of economic development, it must economize its labor resources, because it will have an increasingly tight labor market. The current five-year plan calls for an increase in national income between 7 and 8 percent, and it is a relatively modest plan. Between 1970 and 1980 the total work force will increase by 1.7 percent per year and between 1980 and 1990, 0.7 percent. The Soviet economy perennially has suffered from relatively low labor productivity and rather moderate rates of increase in labor productivity. Between 1955 and 1967 the rate of growth of real national income per employed worker was 4.1 percent per year.[79] It is obvious that if this rate of increase in productivity is not drastically raised, the government will be unable to maintain the rate of economic growth into the future that it currently plans, particularly since the Soviet economy is now experiencing labor shortages. Past performance, therefore, would seem to cast doubt on the prospect of its raising labor productivity to the extent that it would require no additional labor, at least in the Slavic areas where the work force will be essentially stationary, if not declining, by the 1980s. Without in-migration, virtually the total increase in production from these areas would have to be based on the increases in labor productivity.

To sustain a high rate of economic growth, the government must rationalize its use of labor. Central Asia, Kazakhstan, and the Transcaucasus, where the bulk of the net increase in the work force will originate in the 1980s, have among the lowest rates of productivity of industrial fixed capital in the USSR. Therefore, it would not generally be rational, if it wants to maximize economic development, to concentrate the bulk of the industrial investment in these labor surplus areas. Moreover, since Soviet planners in terms of investment have given disproportionate emphasis to heavy industry, which is generally resource oriented, regions favorably endowed with resources for heavy industry have generally received investment priority. Central Asia and the Transcaucasus are relatively poorly endowed with resources for heavy industry, although Kazakhstan has significant deposits of coal and iron ore. These areas are also rather remote from the major areas of consumption in the USSR. There are also economies of agglomeration that favor locating industries in established industrial areas, and in some industries significant economies are realized by expanding an existing enterprise rather than building a new one. Therefore, given the goals of the Soviet government, it would not seem rational for it to concentrate investment and development in these peripheral areas, despite their labor surpluses. Of course, the Soviet government gives high priority to full employment and the provision of jobs in local areas whenever possible. However, if there were a serious conflict between economic growth and these employment policies it would mean that in the interest of building socialism, a higher goal, Soviet planners would opt for economic growth and a high priority for heavy industry.

When conditions such as now prevail in the USSR have occurred elsewhere, and frequently not of the intensity we expect in the next two decades in the USSR, migration has equalized the supply of and demand for labor on a regional basis, and as rural population pressures have intensified surplus rural workers have migrated to the more highly productive urban-industrial areas that were experiencing labor shortages. In the Soviet context, this appears also to be the most rational solution to their labor problems.

In many respects, the Central Asian situation is similar to that of underdeveloped countries in that cities in these countries are also having difficulties in absorbing the excess labor in surrounding rural areas. However, the Central Asians are in a decidedly better position than their Third-World counterparts in the sense that they reside within a developed country, and, in fact, one with appreciable labor shortages in many areas.[80] In short, because there are presently no restrictions on the interregional migration of the Central Asian nationalities, these nationalities, unlike millions in underdeveloped countries, can migrate to more industrialized areas where there is a demand for labor. Moreover, the relatively backward Central Asians are especially fortunate in that labor "shortages occur primarily in the construction, transport, light, and food industry branches, where the work is considered by many to be degrading and of low occupational prestige."[81] These are the types of jobs that migrants traditionally take. Thus, labor shortages exist in most branches of the economy and are particularly great in sectors that can utilize low-skilled labor, the type of labor for which the indigenous peoples of Central Asia are especially well qualified.

A more precise picture of the regions of destination is suggested by Tables 10.1 and 10.2. They reveal that, as mentioned before, Central Asia will be the outstanding region with regard to increase in

TABLE 10.1

Projected Increases in the Work Force by Economic Region: 1970–90

Region	Estimated Percentage Change in Population Aged 20–59			Estimated Percentage Change in Population Aged 20–29		
	1970–80	1980–90	1970–90	1970–80	1980–90	1970–90
Northwest	12.0	-1.9	9.9	24.7	-20.6	-0.9
West	9.0	2.5	11.7	6.4	2.9	9.5
Center	9.4	-4.7	4.2	32.4	-23.8	0.9
Volgo-Vyatsk	18.5	3.5	22.7	76.4	-19.6	41.7
Central Chernozem	13.6	1.0	14.7	77.0	-19.5	42.4
Volga	16.7	3.8	21.1	49.0	-15.7	25.6
Belorussia	18.9	6.5	26.6	53.7	-5.1	45.9
Moldavia	22.7	10.8	36.0	61.7	-3.9	55.3
Southwest	10.7	2.6	13.6	34.6	-2.6	31.2
South	10.2	1.1	11.5	19.4	-8.1	9.7
Donetsk-Dnepr	9.3	-1.1	8.2	30.7	-12.9	13.9
North Caucasus	14.9	6.9	22.9	61.2	-2.9	56.6
Transcaucasus	31.0	23.1	61.2	86.2	18.1	119.9
Urals	22.0	6.4	29.7	64.3	-15.4	39.0
West Siberia	22.5	3.5	26.8	66.1	-22.9	28.1
East Siberia	24.8	8.6	35.6	49.6	-13.9	28.9
Far East	17.5	4.4	22.7	9.8	-16.6	-8.4
Kazakhstan	31.1	22.2	60.2	64.8	13.9	87.8
Central Asia	41.2	38.8	96.0	102.1	39.8	182.4
USSR total	17.8	7.1	26.1	50.7	-5.2	42.8

TABLE 10.2

Projected Increases in the Work Force by Republic: 1970-90

Republic	Estimated Percentage Change in Population Aged 20-59			Estimated Percentage Change in Population Aged 20-29		
	1970-80	1980-90	1970-90	1970-80	1980-90	1970-90
RSFSR	16.1	2.3	18.8	48.9	-17.3	23.2
Ukrainian SSR	10.1	1.0	11.1	30.8	-7.4	21.1
Belorussian SSR	18.9	6.5	26.6	53.7	-5.1	45.9
Estonian SSR	6.1	-0.4	5.7	1.8	-2.5	-0.7
Latvian SSR	5.2	-1.2	4.0	-1.5	-2.0	-3.5
Lithuanian SSR	13.4	6.5	20.8	14.6	8.1	23.9
Uzbek SSR	42.4	39.9	99.2	103.9	40.1	185.6
Kirgiz SSR	37.2	30.5	79.1	102.6	27.5	158.3
Turkmen SSR	39.2	39.0	93.5	90.3	41.1	168.5
Tadzhik SSR	42.1	43.2	103.6	103.2	50.1	205.0
Kazakh SSR	31.1	24.5	63.2	64.8	13.9	87.8
Georgian SSR	18.5	10.4	30.8	52.1	5.7	60.7
Armenian SSR	39.3	23.0	71.3	95.8	8.8	113.0
Azerbaydzhan SSR	40.9	35.4	90.9	118.2	32.2	188.4
Moldavian SSR	22.7	10.8	36.0	61.7	-3.9	55.3
USSR total	17.8	7.1	26.1	50.7	-5.2	42.8

SOURCES AND CALCULATION PROCEDURES FOR
TABLES 10.1 AND 10.2

Sources and calculation procedures: In order to make projections of future changes in the size of the work force by regions and republics, age data from the 1970 Soviet census (see Chapter 2, footnote 2) were used in conjunction with U.S. government estimates of future age patterns for the USSR as a whole. These estimates can be found in Godfrey Baldwin, Estimates and Projections of the Population of the USSR, by Age and Sex: 1950 to 2000, in U.S. Department of Commerce, Bureau of Economic Analysis, International Population Reports, Series P-91, no. 23 (December 1972). The results of the Baldwin study have been presented in a more abbreviated form in Frederick A. Leedy, "Demographic Trends in the USSR," in U.S. Congress, Joint Economic Committee, Soviet Economic Prospects for the Seventies, Joint Committee Print (Washington, D.C.: Government Printing Office, 1973), pp. 428-84.

We are concerned here with projected trends in the size of the total work force and new entrants to the work force between 1970 and 1980 and between 1980 and 1990. The total work force is operationally defined here as the total population aged 20 to 59 for each region and republic. The population aged 20 to 59 for 1970 can be extracted from the 1970 census itself. The estimated population aged 20 to 59 in 1980 consists of those people who were aged 10 to 49 in 1970, while the estimated population aged 20 to 59 in 1990 consists of those aged 0 to 39 in 1970. In both cases mortality has been taken into account, and immigration to and emigration from the USSR are assumed as being of no significance. In particular, in order to estimate the population aged 20 to 59 in 1980 by region and republic, we have multiplied the population aged 10 to 49 for each region and republic in 1970 times a survival ratio of 0.97. This ratio is based upon the Baldwin estimates of the total USSR population aged 10 to 49 in 1970 and 20 to 59 in 1980. Similarly, to estimate the population aged 20 to 59 in 1990 by region and republic, we have multiplied the population aged 0 to 39 for each region and republic in 1970 by a survival ratio of 0.95. This ratio is based upon the Baldwin estimates of the total USSR population aged 0 to 39 in 1970 and 20 to 59 in 1990.

Similar procedures were used to estimate new entrants to the work force from 1970 to 1980 and 1980 to 1990. "New entrants" in each ten-year period are defined as those persons who were aged 20 to 29 at the end of each period. Thus, new entrants in 1980 consist of those people who were aged 10 to 19 in 1970, while new entrants in 1990 would be those aged 0 to 9 in 1970. Once again, in both cases mortality has been taken into account, and immigration to and emigration from the USSR are assumed as being of no significance. In particular, the number of new entrants to the work force between 1970 and 1980 by region and republic was estimated by multiplying the population aged 10 to 19 for each region and republic in 1970 by a survival ratio of 0.99. The number of new entrants between 1980 and 1990 was estimated by multiplying the population aged 0 to 9 in 1970 times a survival ratio of 0.98. In both periods the survival ratios are again based upon the Baldwin estimates of the Soviet population aged 10 to 19 in 1970 and 20 to 29 in 1980, on the one hand, and 0 to 9 in 1970 and 20 to 29 in 1990, on the other.

the labor supply. At the other end of the spectrum, major regions where the work force will barely increase or even decline include the most urbanized and industrialized regions of the USSR. Outstanding are the Northwest, West, Center, Donetsk-Dnepr, Volga, Urals, and West Siberia, most of which are predominantly Russian; of course, the labor shortages of these regions partly result from the fact that being so highly urbanized and industrialized, fertility is low and consequently the growth rate of the total population and local work force is also low. Hence, assuming that the demand for outside labor will be very great in these areas because labor productivity will probably not be raised rapidly enough to solve their labor problems, a large influx of Turkic-Muslims to cities in these regions may be expected.

As implied above, such a migration has been, to date, very meager. For example, although the number of urban (census definition) Uzbeks in the RSFSR more than doubled from 1959 to 1970, only about 52,000, or 2 percent of the entire Uzbek urban population in the USSR, resided in the RSFSR, with virtually the entire amount residing in Central Asia or nearby southern Kazakhstan and with the vast majority residing in Uzbekistan, in particular. Furthermore, in no case did Uzbeks comprise even 1 percent of the urban population of any of the very few political units of the RSFSR for which their urban population was indicated in the 1970 census.

This does not mean that this situation cannot change dramatically. Witness the large number of U.S. cities, for example, that had virtually no blacks nor Puerto Ricans a few decades ago but now have a substantial share of their population comprised by such groups. Or witness cities of Great Britain that previously had no Indians, Pakistanis, nor West Indians, or cities of Sweden that previously had no Yugoslavs. The historical precedent for groups leaving their cultural homelands is obvious. It should be remembered that there are even precedents for the migration of Turkic peoples, in particular; witness the current migration of the Turks from eastern Anatolia to cities of Western Europe, or, for that matter, the migration of Turkic peoples to Central Asia long ago.

It is obvious from most of these examples that when the economic crunch is on, people will migrate to other areas even if the movement is to an area with a different culture and less favorable climate. Consequently, although the cultural and climatic advantages of a homeland area may impede migration to another area, they do not completely stop it. Thus, it is difficult to to argue that the Central Asians will never migrate in substantial numbers to cities in the colder Russian areas to the north because of cultural and climatic considerations. Indeed, it bears repeating that the occurrence of such a migration in the USSR is promoted by the fact, that, unlike many of the above precedents, this type of migration is an internal

movement and not an international migration. Therefore, the Central
Asians are, for the moment at least, not subjected to the legal restrictions upon their migration that are placed upon the migration of
many groups from lesser developed areas of the world.

The implications of the migration of the Central Asians to Russian cities cannot be overemphasized. Little tension may now exist
between the Russians and the very few Uzbeks in, say, Omsk, but
what would the Russian feelings toward Uzbeks be if the latter came
to comprise 20 to 30 percent or more of the population of the city and
occupied the more menial positions in the economy? Similar experiences in world history certainly would not lead one to expect increased harmony between the two groups.

Of course, it is not inconceivable that restrictions could be
placed upon the migration of the Turkic-Muslims to Russian areas.
But past experience reveals very few instances where a government
has impeded the internal movements of a particular group. Indeed,
even the Soviet government has not been able to control completely
internal migration; net out-migration occurs from many areas with a
labor shortage (for example, West Siberia and rural Russian areas)
and a net in-migration is characteristic of some areas with a labor
surplus (for example, Central Asia and the North Caucasus), [82] and
large cities continue to grow despite policies to the contrary.

Russia and the USSR, however, also have been the scene of some
of the very few instances where governments have controlled internal
migration. Witness, for example, the restrictions placed upon Jewish
migration during the tsarist era, a subject discussed in greater depth
earlier, or the forced migration to labor camps. However, it is one
thing to control the movements of groups with only a very few million
people at the most (the Jewish population in the Russian Empire was
roughly 5 million), but it is another thing to control the internal movements of a population that now numbers roughly 15 million and could
conceivably number over 40 million by the end of the century if their
present rate of growth continues. If all Turkic-Muslims are considered, the numbers are even more staggering. Although the above discussion has focused upon the Central Asian nationalities, it should be
remembered that many other Turkic-Muslim nationalities will be subjected to increased population pressure in a similar manner, especially the Azeri and Kazakhs. Thus, the greatest share of the over 30
million Turkic-Muslims will be subjected to the same pressures that
will be placed upon the Central Asians. Given the future population
of the Turkic-Muslims, it would be almost unprecedented for a government to restrict the movements of such a population. Needless to say,
the relatively rapid growth of the Turkic-Muslims will have substantial repercussions on Soviet society as a whole.

Hodnett, however, has argued that appreciable out-migration from Central Asia will not occur:

> The second course of action is possible, but it would confound the expectations of most observers. As we have seen, one of the ways in which Central Asia does not fit the "plantation society" model is that the native population involved has lived for centuries in the region and is culturally rooted to the land. Despite Slavic immigration, it now seems unlikely that demographic forces will compel the natives to relinquish claim to Central Asia as their own. In any event, would the Soviet leaders want to create what John Armstrong has called an "internal proletariat of Central Asians working at jobs in the Urals and Siberia? Would the Central Asians be technically equipped to fill skilled jobs for which specialized training is not available in Central Asia? And would the Central Asians be willing to leave their native lands for inhospitable regions from which Russians themselves are now migrating to Central Asia? There is little evidence to date that the answer would be yes to any of these questions. [83]

The essential point to consider in evaluating Hodnett's argument is, as we have indicated, that when a growing population begins to exceed its econonic density in any geographic area, the options for that population are economic development, birth control, further declines in the standard of living, or out-migration. Historically the world over, the traditional solution has been out-migration when this has been possible, because the other options have been difficult or unpleasant. In Central Asia, for the reasons we have discussed, economic development sufficient to absorb the growing populations is not feasible, at least in the long run, and birth control in traditional rural areas is very difficult, and not an immediate solution because of the age distribution and the fact that the workers for the next two decades have already been born. It is safe to say that no one likes a declining standard of life. The basic mechanism is, of course, deteriorating economic conditions. As to being culturally rooted to the land for centuries, when the economic crunch occurs, this makes little difference. The Turks of Central Asia moved to their present homeland from another, and several million Turks have left Anatolia for Europe. Migrants throughout history have left homelands when conditions dictated a departure; one has only to think of the migration history of the United States. That Central Asia is part of a developed country with labor shortages facilitates this migration, because international restrictions on migration do not affect them. As to the prospect of their relinquishing claim to Central Asia, we agree that is not likely, because even if surplus Central Asian workers left Central Asia, they would still clearly be in the majority, particularly considering their rapid rate of population growth and the relatively small number of outsiders in the area. Furthermore, as we have indicated, the establishment of ethnic administrative units furthers their claim on their homelands.

With regard to the problem of an "internal proletariat," judging from world experience, it is probable that the Soviet government is unaware of the social disruption that normally occurs in a multinational country when economic development results in a massive redistribution of its population and ethnic mixing. In the past decade, there have been labor shortages, primarily for unskilled workers, in Western Europe, and apparently as a result of economic expediency, the governments opted for foreign immigration. One wonders if, in the face of the economic benefits, these governments even considered the social costs of the ethnic conflict that occurred or alternative measures such as more capital investment or other sources of labor. The drive to mechanize agriculture in Central Asia by the Soviet government is also an example of economic expediency in decision making.

Furthermore, a common pattern in most societies is that when a person completes high school, regardless of the quality of education, there are many jobs that are beneath his dignity or below his aspirations, and these are the jobs that uneducated migrants normally take in developed countries with high education levels. To date, in the USSR most of these jobs have been taken by relatively uneducated "Europeans," but as their educational levels rise and the new entrants to the work force decline in number in "European" areas of the USSR, the shortage of unskilled workers will probably intensify. Can the Soviet government afford to bottle up the "non-European nationalities" in their ethnic homelands, or to concentrate most investment in these areas, or does it even have the will or the means to do it by force. During World War II the government moved a few nationalities that were small in number, but although there was much collaboration with the Germans among the Ukrainians, this population was too large to be moved east. Can a multinational country experiencing relatively rapid economic growth and labor shortages expect to have its chief areas of economic development ethnically pure even in the short run? One has only to consider New York, or any other large American city, or the migration of blacks and Puerto Ricans in the United States to appreciate the processes involved.

We have demonstrated that given current rates of investment, cities in Central Asia could not absorb the surplus population even if

there were no in-migration from outside Central Asia. In short, the
economic costs to the Soviet government of avoiding an "internal proletariat" would be immense in terms of economic growth, and the
feasibility of bottling up large populations is remote. It seems doubtful that it would tolerate these costs, given its emphasis on economic
development, even if it appreciated the ethnic problems involved.

As to whether Central Asians would be "technically equipped to
fill skilled jobs for which specialized training is not available in Central Asia," we have indicated that there are many jobs for unskilled
laborers and that the education levels of the Central Asian population
are rising rapidly. Of course, there are jobs for which they are not
qualified, but there are not too many jobs even in a highly developed
society that require much more than ten years of school, and an increasing proportion of the indigenous population is attaining this level.

As to their unwillingness to move to inhospitable areas from
which Russians are migrating to Central Asia, this, of course, depends
on economic conditions in the more hospitable (warmer) and the inhospitable (colder) areas. Suffice it to say that the major migration
streams since World War II have been ethnic and from relatively warm
to cold areas, which includes Turks, Greeks, Algerians, Italians,
and Spanish to northern Europe and blacks and Puerto Ricans to the
north of the United States, as well as the migration from the West In-
dies to Europe and North America. Furthermore, there is no mass
exodus of Russians to Central Asia because only an insignificant percentage of the Russians live in Central Asia. Only about 15 percent of
the Russians live outside the RSFSR, and most of these are found in
areas of economic development rather than warm areas. There are
relatively few Russians in Central Asia or the Transcaucasus, whereas
in the eastern Ukraine and Kazakhstan they are numerous. It must be
admitted, however, that some people probably move deliberately to
warm areas, but as yet this does not seem to be a significant factor
in migration in the USSR.

Hodnett considers the most reasonable option to be "a structurally dependent pattern of development linking Central Asia to the rest
of the Soviet Union, but also generating local employment."[84] He,
however, sees problems in this solution in terms of cost considerations of small plants in overpopulated areas, which could lead to un-
controlled migration to local cities and unemployment, and other problems, such as ethnic tensions. We do not maintain that out-migration
to areas beyond Central Asia is the only solution to Central Asian
labor problems. Clearly, there probably will also be much migration
to local cities, which should impede Russian migration and may very
well result in ethnic tensions as competition for jobs in Central Asian
cities intensifies. The rising educational levels of the younger segments of the indigenous population very probably will stimulate rural

out-migration. There also could be more investment in Central Asia
that would provide jobs, but it is doubtful that it would be at a scale
that could absorb the impending surplus labor over a sustained period
of time. Recall that in the next two decades the number of jobs would
probably have to be more than doubled, considering the doubling of
the work force and the release of labor through mechanization. Thus,
even the development of a structurally dependent economy in Central
Asia probably would not preclude considerable out-migration.

One must, of course, differentiate between a probable policy and
a conceivable policy in the Soviet context. There are many conceivable
policies, but few realistic ones in terms of the goals of the Soviet government. It could be that the Soviet government will decide to keep all
Asians in their homelands or to direct the bulk of its investment to
areas of surplus population. However, it is doubtful that it will institute such policies, because it is not in its economic interest to do this,
and most governments give emphasis to economic considerations and
are usually unaware of the process involved or future social implications. As Hodnett points out "Until now Moscow has not come to grips
with the broader problem but has simply sought to lower production
costs and expand cotton output. . . . One possible explanation of this
behavior is that the top leaders responsible for the strategic policy
choices have not understood what they were doing."[85]

We have also pointed out that population policies in the USSR
appear to be no more successful than in any other country, primarily
because the government has been unwilling to expend the necessary effort or expense. This would also probably be applicable to a Central
Asian population policy. It has been unable to stem the flow from rural
Russian areas, or induce people to move to Siberia, or to limit the
growth of large cities, or to raise Slavic fertility. Once the demographic pressures build sufficiently, it will require great effort and
expense to control migration, and the government currently does not
appear to be aware of the severity of the problem.

We have outlined the Central Asian labor problem and analyzed
it in some detail, because we feel that it is crucial to the understanding of the future impact of demographic processes on Soviet society
particularly in terms of ethnic relations. In summation, our argument
is based on our working hypothesis that people throughout the world
tend to react in the same manner to the forces that affect their demographic behavior, regardless of the political systems under which
they live. The universal experience has been that when conditions
analogous to those now developing in the USSR have occurred, they
have ultimately been associated with much out-migration and ethnic
mixing in multinational states. We cannot precisely predict when significant out-migration will begin to occur, because we are unable to
determine precisely many factors, such as labor requirements in the

USSR, how rapidly population pressures will build in certain rural areas, or future investment priorities. We can, however, make the forecast with some certainty that there will be considerable out-migration from "non-European" areas and ethnic mixing and their attendant problems, unless conditions in the USSR change drastically. We see no peculiar conditions in the USSR that would counter the demographic and economic forces currently in operation. Some factors, such as peculiarities of culture or increased local investment or some effective policy or drastic increases in labor productivity in the USSR, might affect the determining conditions for and thus diminish rural out-migration for a while, but ultimately the expected patterns of population redistribution most likely will occur in the USSR.

SUMMARY

Nationality problems will almost certainly intensify and collectively become a dominant force shaping the future Soviet society. The chief source of ethnic friction is and will increasingly become the existence of a system of ethnic stratification in conjunction with demographic processes related to nationality and modernization. Economic development ultimately results in a massive redistribution of a country's population, a regional as well as a rural-urban redistribution, which in multinational states results in much ethnic mixing. The chief impetus for this redistribution is job opportunities and higher wages in industrializing areas. Migrants generally come from rural areas that are experiencing population pressure because of a higher rural natural increase and the mechanization of agriculture. They generally have lower educational levels and are unskilled, and are thus forced to take the more menial jobs. In absolute terms, they are economically better off, but not relative to the dominant group or groups. As they improve their educational levels, their aspirations grow, and they often become increasingly discontent because the dominant group is reluctant to share the socioeconomic advantages of development with them, especially if they belong to a different nationality or ethnic group. With the growth of aspirations and discontent, ethnicity increases apace, and the ethnic group becomes increasingly a vehicle for achieving socioeconomic interests. As they press their demands, ethnic tensions and conflicts increase proportionately. Thus, ethnic groups become economic interest groups, and economic and ethnic tensions tend to be synonymous. This general pattern is occurring in the USSR, and a major problem in Soviet society is the increasing conflict between the Russians, the dominant group, and the other nationalities. In short, the Russians and a few other nationalities are benefiting the most from economic development, and

most of the other nationalities are relatively socioeconomically disadvantaged, although their standard of living generally has been rising.

To the present time, Russians and such nationalities as the
Jews and Tatars have migrated in large numbers to the cities of most
non-Russian areas, where they control the advanced sectors of the
urban economy. Cities in Russian areas have remained largely ethnically homogeneous. However, population pressures are building in
many rural, non-Russian areas. Barring any substantial increase in
labor productivity in Russian areas or any unusual coercive measures,
it can be expected that in the next few decades with continued economic
development, there will be considerable out-migration from these non-
Russian areas to the industrial centers of the RSFSR where labor
shortages will become increasingly acute, particularly in the more
unskilled jobs. This reverse flow of migrants should result in considerable ethnic mixing in the Russian cities and increased ethnic friction, as has occurred elsewhere in the world. Thus, problems related
to ethnicity very probably will become a major force shaping Soviet
society in the coming decades.

We do not maintain, however, that ethnic stratification and
demographic processes related to nationality and modernization are
the only conditions that determine ethnic identity and friction, nor do
we maintain that these processes are beyond human control. We
agree with Walker Connor that there is much emotionalism and irra-
tionality in national feelings and identity, but there are conditions that
affect ethnic identity and tension. The rise in ethnic identity is a
worldwide phenomenon, but it is variable in time and space. We simply feel that ethnic stratification and certain demographic processes
loom large as important determining conditions in the explanation of
ethnic identity and tensions, even though they are difficult to measure
with precision. We also acknowledge the importance of other factors
in the explanation of this very complex phenomenon. Connor has a
good grasp of the situation when he stresses the importance of communications, transportation, and mobilization in reinforcing the "us-
them" dichotomy, which is the basis of ethnic identity, and the importance of the idea of popular sovereignty with respect to self-determination.[86] This is particularly important in the Soviet context
where self-determination is the policy, but a very limited form of
autonomy is the practice, despite the creation of an ethnically based
federal structure.

We also do not deny that these conditions and thus their effects
could be ameliorated by government action. Clearly, if Lenin's policy of economic equalization and autonomy were rigorously applied
or other major efforts to integrate the nationalities were adopted,
one might expect a lessening of ethnic tensions, even though the Soviet
government claims that the nationality question has been solved. Fi-

nally, we would like to emphasize once again that the Soviet government and the Russians as the dominant group are not the worst example in terms of ethnic relations. In fact, the Soviet government from the beginning has been more attentive to nationality problems than most governments of multinational states, very probably out of necessity; there has been a considerable economic leveling in Soviet society; and there is a great potential for upward social and economic mobility than in many other societies. What we have done in this study is simply to describe and analyze the ethnic and demographic processes that occur to a greater or lesser degree in multinational, modernizing states, and to highlight the importance of ethnic problems in such states. In short, our message is that in terms of demographic and ethnic processes there are no major surprises in the USSR.

NOTES

1. Tamotsu Shibutani and Kian M. Kwan, Ethnic Stratification: A Comparative Approach (New York: Macmillan, 1965).

2. Ibid., pp. 27-55.

3. Nathan Glazer and Daniel Patrick Moynihan, Beyond the Melting Pot: The Negroes, Puerto Ricans, Jews, Italians, and Irish of New York City, 2d ed. (Cambridge, Mass.: Massachusetts Institute of Technology Press, 1970), pp. lxxxiii-lxxxv.

4. Milton M. Gordon, Assimilation in American Life: The Role of Race, Religion, and National Origins (New York: Oxford University Press, 1964), p. 51.

5. Ibid., p. 47.

6. Shibutani and Kwan, op. cit., pp. 139-250.

7. Ibid., pp. 343-46.

8. Karl W. Deutsch, Nationalism and Social Communication, 2d ed. (Cambridge, Mass.: Massachusetts Institute of Technology Press, 1966), pp. 123-64. This is necessarily an abbreviated description of Professor Deutsch's very extensive formulation of the relationships between modernization and nationality. Importantly, it should be noted that the hypothesized reduction in nationality distinctiveness with modernization may be, according to Deutsch, short-circuited if the rate of assimilation is exceeded by the rate of social mobilization. Both of these critical aspects of change are determined by a complex of factors that essentially involve aspects of communication and social and economic opportunity. See also Karl Deutsch, "Social Mobilization and Political Development," American Political Science Review 55 (September 1961): 493-514.

9. Walker Connor, "Nation-Building or Nation-Destroying?" World Politics 24 (April 1972): 319-55.

10. Ibid., p. 332.

11. For example, Jack C. Fisher has examined regional economic development disparities in Yugoslavia largely in terms of the different historical, cultural, and political influences resulting from foreign domination. See his Yugoslavia: A Multinational State (San Francisco: Chandler, 1966).

12. Henry Kamm, "Troubled Brittany Expects Little Help from Paris," New York Times, 24 April 1974, p. 8.

13. Gary K. Bertsch, "The Revival of Nationalisms," Problems of Communism 22 (November-December 1973): 1-15.

14. Karl E. and Alma F. Taeuber, Negroes in Cities (Chicago: Aldine, 1965), pp. 1-14.

15. Shibutani and Kwan, op. cit., pp. 372-401.

16. Ibid., p. 219. See also Walker Connor, "Nationalism Reconsidered" (Paper presented at the Annual Meeting of the Northeast Political Science Association, 1971), pp. 16-17.

17. Cynthia H. Enloe, Ethnic Conflict and Political Development (Boston: Little, Brown, 1973), pp. 84-107.

18. Shibutani and Kwan, op. cit., pp. 328-29, 361-83.

19. This is, of course, one mode of the political scientist's concept of "relative deprivation." See Ted Robert Gurr, Why Men Rebel (Princeton, N.J.: Princeton University Press, 1970).

20. Marc Raeff, "Patterns of Russian Imperial Policy Toward the Nationalities," in Soviet Nationality Problems, ed. Edward Allworth (New York: Columbia University Press, 1971), pp. 22-42. For the general case, see Shibutani and Kwan, op. cit., pp. 334-36.

21. For a most interesting example of Russian conquest of a nomadic people and subsequent colonization of the territory, see Alton S. Donnelly, The Russian Conquest of Bashkiria, 1552-1740 (New Haven, Conn.: Yale University Press, 1968).

22. Shibutani and Kwan, op. cit., p. 5.

23. Robert A. Lewis, "The Mixing of Russians and Soviet Nationalities and Its Demographic Impact," in Soviet Nationality Problems, ed. Edward Allworth (New York: Columbia University Press, 1971), pp. 117-67.

24. "Latvians Chided for Nationalism," New York Times, 21 March 1971, p. 17; and Bernard Gwertzman, "Protest on Soviet Laid to Latvians," New York Times, 27 February 1972, p. 11.

25. "200 Lithuanians Reported Jailed," New York Times, 14 June 1972, p. 1.

26. "Ukrainian Writer Pardoned After Renunciation," New York Times, 14 November 1973, p. 8.

27. See Richard Pipes, "'Solving' the Nationality Problem," Problems of Communism 26 (September-October 1967): 128. Professor Pipes states: "National governments, even when impotent, are

known from historical experience to arouse strong feelings of loyalty among both their officials and subjects. . . . The fact that the Uzbek Republic is a Soviet creation, and that its government enjoys no meaningful authority, probably does not make it any less real for the Uzbeks."

28. Yu. V. Arutyunyan, "Konkretno-Sotsiologicheskoye Issledovaniye Natsional'nykh Otnosheniy," Voprosy Filosofii, no. 12 (1969), pp. 129-39.

29. Ibid., p. 135.

30. Ibid., p. 136.

31. Data for 1913 come from "Tsentral'noye Statisticheskoye Upravleniye pri Sovete Ministrov SSR," in Strana Sovetov za 50 Let (Moscow: Statistika, 1967), pp. 314, 315, 328-31, 334, 335. The 1939 ratio is based upon the 1940 sown area, which can be found in the above source, and the 1959 ratio is based upon the 1960 sown area. The sown areas for 1960 and 1970 can be found in Narodnoye Khozyaystvo SSSR v 1970 G., p. 300.

32. For example, see V. I. Perevedentsev, "Sovremennaya Migratsiya v SSSR," in Narodonaseleniye i Ekonomika (Moscow: Izdatel'stvo "Ekonomika," 1967), p. 104.

33. V. I. Perevedentsev, "Migratsiya Naseleniya i Ispol'zovaniye Trudovykh Resursov," Voprosy Ekonomiki, no. 9 (September 1970), p. 35.

34. Ann Sheehy, "Some Aspects of Regional Development in Soviet Central Asia," Slavic Review 31 (September 1972): 589-60.

35. Gertrude E. Schroeder, "Regional Differences in Incomes and Levels of Living in the USSR," in The Soviet Economy in Regional Perspective, ed. V. N. Bandera and Z. L. Melnyk (New York: Praeger, 1973), pp. 177-80.

36. Ibid., p. 178.

37. Grey Hodnett, "Technology and Social Change in Soviet Central Asia: The Politics of Cotton Growing," in Soviet Politics and Society in the 1970's, eds. Henry W. Morton and Rudolph L. Tokes (New York: Free Press, 1974), pp. 65-79, 88.

38. Eugene M. Kulischer, Europe on the Move (New York: Columbia University Press, 1948), p. 319.

39. Robert A. Lewis, "The Irrigation Potential of Soviet Central Asia," Annals of the Association of American Geographers 52 (March 1962): 99-114.

40. Ibid., p. 112.

41. Narodnoye Khozyaystvo SSSR v 1970 G., p. 348.

42. Ibid.

43. Central Intelligence Agency, USSR Agricultural Atlas (Washington, D.C.: Government Printing Office, 1974), p. 24.

44. Sheehy, op. cit., p. 561.

45. Ibid., p. 562.

46. Grey Hodnett, op. cit., p. 90.

47. Sheehy, op. cit., pp. 561-62.

48. Grey Hodnett, op. cit., pp. 93-94.

49. Ibid., p. 93.

50. For example, see Murray Feshbach and Stephen Rapawy, "Labor Constraints in the Five-Year Plan," in U.S. Congress, Joint Economic Committee, Soviet Economic Prospects for the Seventies, Joint Committee Print (Washington, D.C.: Government Printing Office, 1973), pp. 512-13.

51. Perevedentsev, op. cit.

52. Norton T. Dodge, "Recruitment and the Quality of the Soviet Agricultural Labor Force," in The Soviet Rural Community, ed. James R. Millar (Urbana, Ill.: University of Illinois Press, 1971), p. 210.

53. Feshbach and Rapawy, op. cit., pp. 490 and 512-14.

54. W. A. Douglas Jackson, "The Virgin and Idle Lands Reappaised," Annals of the Association of American Geographers 52 (March 1962): 69-79; and Chauncy D. Harris, "USSR Resources for Agriculture," Focus 20 (December 1969): 1-7.

55. Central Intelligence Agency, op. cit., p. 4.

56. Vestnik Statistiki, no. 2 (1973), p. 87.

57. James H. Noren and E. Douglas Whitehouse, "Soviet Industry in the 1971-75 Plan," in U.S. Congress, Joint Economic Committee, Soviet Economic Prospects for the Seventies, pp. 223-24.

58. Narodnoye Khozyaystvo SSSR v 1970 G., p. 488.

59. Ibid. These investment figures are for both total investment and total investment excluding investment in collective farms.

60. Noren and Whitehouse, op. cit.

61. Ibid.

62. Willard S. Smith, "Housing in the Soviet Union—Big Plans, Little Action," in U.S. Congress, Joint Economic Committee, Soviet Economic Prospects for the Seventies, pp. 406, 422.

63. Ibid., p. 422.

64. Ibid.

65. Ibid.

66. Ibid.

67. Ibid.

68. The urban populations are from the 1959 and 1970 censuses (early 1959 and 1970). The housing data are for the end of 1959 and the end of 1970. Respectively, these data can be found in Narodnoye Khozyaystvo SSSR v 1961 G., p. 615; and Narodnoye Khozyaystvo SSSR v 1970 G., p. 546.

69. A. J. Jaffe and J. N. Froomkin, "Economic Development and Jobs—A Comparison of Japan and Panama, 1950 to 1960," Estadistica 24 (September 1966): 577-92.

70. Narodnoye Khozyaystvo SSSR v 1970 G., pp. 159, 164.

71. Noren and Whitehouse, op. cit., pp. 220-23.

72. Narodnoye Khozyaystvo SSSR v 1970 G., p. 141.

73. Noren and Whitehouse, op. cit., p. 224. The table on p. 224 bears a misprint in that "1950" should be "1970."

74. Sheehy, op. cit., p. 560.

75. A. J. Jaffe, People, Jobs, and Economic Development (Glencoe, Ill.: Free Press, 1959), p. 15.

76. Sheehy, op. cit., p. 563.

77. Ibid.

78. Ibid.

79. Abram Bergson, "Development Under Two Systems: Comparative Productivity Growth Since 1950," World Politics 23 (July 1971): 588.

80. Feshbach and Rapawy, op. cit., pp. 485-91.

81. Ibid., p. 486.

82. Perevedentsev, "Sovremennaya Migratsiya v SSSR," op. cit., p. 104.

83. Grey Hodnett, op. cit., pp. 105-07.

84. Ibid.

85. Ibid., p. 105.

86. Connor, op. cit., pp. 319-55.

Appendix A contains a listing of the individual nationalities, as listed in each of the Russian and Soviet censuses, which comprise each of the ten mutually exclusive nationality groupings investigated in this study. (For sources, see Chapter 2, footnote 2.) The component nationalities are listed in the transliterated form of how they generally appear in the corresponding census itself. If there is a common English version of a nationality, it is noted in parentheses in noun-plural form (for example, Russians). Groups that were listed in the 1926 census but had a population of zero are not included in this appendix.

It should be added that it was sometimes difficult to decide into which grouping, if any, certain nationalities should be placed (for example, the Abkhaz, who are 50 percent Christian and 50 percent Muslim). In such cases the decision had to be arbitrary (for example, the Abkhaz are included in the Turkic-Muslim grouping). Such problems usually only involved small nationalities. Therefore, the population figures derived for each grouping were not strongly affected and, thus, are basically correct.

Russians

1897 census components

   Velikorusskiy (Russians)

1926 census components

   Russkiye (Russians)

1959 and 1970 census components
   Russkiye (Russians)

Ukrainians

1897 census components

   Malorusskiy (Ukrainians)

1926 census components

   Ukraintsy (Ukrainians)

1959 and 1970 census components

   Ukraintsy (Ukrainians)

Belorussians

1897 census components

   Belorusskiy (Belorussians)

1926 census components

   Belorussy (Belorussians)

1959 and 1970 census components

   Belorusy (Belorussians)

Tatars

1897 census components

   Tatarskoye (Tatars) (excluding
   most Tatars in the Transcaucasus region who are Azeri and
   belong to the Turkic-Muslim
   grouping)

1926 census components

   Tatary (Tatars)

1959 and 1970 census components

   Tatary (Tatars)

Turkic-Muslims

1897 census components

   Abkhazskoye (Abkhaz)
   Arabskiy (Arabs)
   Avarsko-Andiyskoye (Avars)
   Avganskiy (Afghans)
   Bashkirskoye (Bashkirs)
   Chechenskoye (Chechens)
   Cherkesskoye (Circassians)
   Chuvashskoye (Chuvash)
   Darginskoye (Dargins)
   Ingushskoye (Ingush)
   Kabardinskoye (Kabardinians)
   Karachayevskoye (Karachay)
   Kara-kalpakskoye (Karakalpaks)
   Kara-kirgizskoye (Kara-Kirgiz)
   Karapapakhskoye (Karapapakhs)
   Kashgarskoye (Kashgars)
   Kazi-Kumukskoye i ostal. lez-
     gin. nar.
   Kipchakskoye (Kipchaks)
   Kirgiz-kaysatskoye
   Kistinskoye
   Kumykskoye (Kumyks)
   Kurdskiya (Kurds)

Kyurinskoye (Lezgians)
Lezginskiya bez raspredeleniya
Meshcheryakskoye (Mishars)
Nogayskoye (Nogays)
Persidskiy (Persians)
Sartskoye (Sarts)
Tadzhikskoye (Tadzhiks)
Talyshinskoye (Talysh)
Taranchinskoye (Taranchy)
Tatarskoye (i.e., Tatars in the
  Transcaucasus region who
  were mainly Azeri)
Tatskoye (Tats)
Teptyarskoye (Teptyars)
Turetskoye (Turks)
Turkmenskoye (Turkmens)
Tyurkskiya nar. bez raspre-
  deleniya
Udinskoye (Udins)
Uzbekskoye (Uzbeks)
Yakutskoye (Yakuts)

1926 census components

   Abkhazy (Abkhaz)
   Afgantsy (Afghans)
   Aguly
   Akhvakhtsy
   Altaytsy (Altays)
   Andii
   Araby (Arabs)
   Archintsy
   Avary (Avars)
   Bagulaly
   Balkary (Balkars)
   Barabintsy
   Bashkiry (Bashkirs)
   Batsbii
   Bel'tiry
   Beludzhi
   Berberi (Berbers)
   Beskesek-abaza
   Botlikhtsy
   Buduki
   Bukhartsy

Chamalaly
Checheny (Chechens)
Cherkesy (Circassians)
Chernevye tatary
Chuvashi (Chuvash)
Dargintsy (Dargins)
Didoi
Dolgany
Dungane
Dzheki
Dzhemshidy
Gagauzy (Gagauz)
Godoberintsy
Ingushi (Ingush)
Irani (Iranians)
Ishkashimtsy
Iyezidy
Kabardintsy (Kabardinians)
Kachintsy
Kapuchiny
Karachai (Karachay)
Karagas
Karaimy
Karakalpaki (Karakalpaks)
Karapapakhi (Karapapakhs)
Karatai
Kashgartsy
Kaytaki
Kazaki (Kazakhs)
Khakasy (Khakas)
Khaputsy
Khazara (Khazars)
Khemshiny
Khinalugi
Khunzaly
Khvarshiny
Kipchaki (Kipchaks)
Kirgizy (Kirgiz)
Kizil'tsy
Koybaly
Kryasheny
Kryzy
Kubachintsy
Kumandintsy
Kumyki (Kumyks)

Kurama
Kurdy (Kurds)
Laki (Laks)
Lezgi (Lezgians)
Mishari (Mishars)
Nagaybaki
Nogaytsy (Nogays)
Oyraty (Oyrots)
Persy (Persians)
Rutuly
Sagaytsy
Sart-Kalmyki (Sart-Kalmyks)
Shortsy
Shugnantsy
Soyoty
Tabasarany
Tadzhiki (Tadzhiks)
Talyshi (Talysh)
Taranchi (Taranchy)
Taty (Tats)
Tavlintsy
Telengety
Teleuty
Teptyari (Teptyars)
Tindii
Tsakhury
Turkmeny (Turkmens)
Tyurki (Azeri)
Tyurki ferganskiye i samar-
   kandskiye
Tyurki osmanskiye
Ubykhi
Uygury (Uygurs)
Uzbeki (Uzbeks)
Vakhantsy
Yagnobtsy
Yakuty (Yakuts)
Yazgulyamtsy

1959 and 1970 census components

Abaziny (Abaza)
Abkhazy (Abkhaz)
Adygeytsy (Adyge)
Afghantsy (Afghans)

Aguly
Altaytsy (Altays)
Araby (Arabs); not listed in
  1970 census
Avartsy (Avars)
Azerbaydzhantsy (Azeri)
Balkartsy (Balkars)
Bashkiry (Bashkirs)
Beludzhi
Chechentsy (Chechens)
Cherkesy (Circassians)
Chuvashi (Chuvash)
Dargintsy (Dargins)
Dolgany; not listed in 1959 cen-
  sus
Dungane
Gagauzy (Gagauz)
Ingushi (Ingush)
Iraniantsy (Iranians)
Kabardintsy (Kabardinians)
Karachayevtsy (Karachay)
Karaimy
Karakalpaki (Karakalpaks)
Kazakhi (Kazakhs)
Khakasy (Khakas)
Kirgizy (Kirgiz)
Kumyki (Kumyks)
Kurdy (Kurds)
Laktsy (Laks)
Lezginy (Lezgians)
Nogaytsy (Nogays)
Rutul'tsy
Shortsy
Tabasarany
Tadzhiki (Tadzhiks)
Taty (Tats)
Tofalary; listed as Tofy in 1970
  census
Tsakhury
Turki; not listed in 1970 census
Turkmeny (Turkmens)
Tuvintsy (Tuvinians)
Uygury (Uygurs)
Uzbeki (Uzbeks)
Yakuty (Yakuts)

Jews

1897 census components

  Yevreyskiy (Jews)

1926 census components

  Yevrei (Jews)
  Yevrei gorskiye (Mountain
    Jews)
  Yevrei gruzinskiye (Georgian
    Jews)
  Yevrei krymskiye (Crimean
    Jews)
  Yevrei sredne-aziatskiye
    (Central Asian Jews)

1959 and 1970 census components

  Yevrei (Jews)

Mobilized Europeans

1897 census components

  Armyanskiy (Armenians)
  Estonskoye (Estonians)
  Gruzinskiy (Georgians)
  Imeretinskoye
  Latyshskoye (Latvians)
  Mingrel'skoye (Mingrelians;
    Megrelians)
  Svanetskoye

1926 census components

  Adzhartsy (Adzhars)
  Armyane (Armenians)
  Esty (Estonians)
  Gruziny (Georgians)
  Latyshi (Latvians)
  Lazy
  Megrely (Mingrelians;
    Megrelians)
  Svany

1959 and 1970 census components

Armyane (Armenians)
Estontsy (Estonians)
Gruziny (Georgians)
Latyshi (Latvians)

Finnic Peoples

1897 census components

Cheremisskoye (Cheremises;
 Mari)
Chudskoye
Finskoye (Finns)
Izhorskoye
Karel'skoye (Karelians)
Loparskoye (Lapps)
Mordovskoye (Mordvinians;
 Mordva)
Permyatskoye (Permyaks; Komi-
 Permyaks)
Votyatskoye (Votyaks; Udmurts)
Zyryanskoye (Zyryans; Komi)

1926 census components

Besermyane
Finny (Finns)
Finny leningradskiye (Finns of
 Leningrad)
Izhory
Karely (Karelians)
Lopari (Lapps)
Mariytsy (Mari)
Mordva (Mordvinians)
Permyaki (Permyaks; Komi-
 Permyaks)
Vepsy
Vod'
Votyaki (Votyaks; Udmurts)
Zyryane (Zyryans; Komi)

1959 and 1970 census components

Finny (Finns)
Izhortsy
Karely (Karelians)
Komi
Komi-Permyaki (Komi-
 Permyaks)
Mariytsy (Mari)
Mordva (Mordvinians)
Saamy (Lapps)
Udmurty (Udmurts)
Vepsy

Lithuanians

1897 census components

Litovskoye (Lithuanians)
Zhmudskoye (Zhmuds)

1926 census components
Litovtsy (Lithuanians)
Zhmud' (Zhmuds)

1959 and 1970 census components

Litovtsy (Lithuanians)

Moldavians and Romanians

1897 census components
Moldavanskiy i Rumynskiy
 (Moldavians and Romanians)

1926 census components

Moldavane (Moldavians)
Rumyny (Romanians)

1959 and 1970 census components

Moldavane (Moldavians)
Rumyny (Romanians)

I. Distribution Variables (variables 1-31)

II. Composition Variables (variables 32-58)

1. Total population
2. Urban population
3. Rural population
4. Ages 0-9
5. Ages 10-19
6. Ages 0-19
7. Ages 20-39
8. Ages 40-59
9. Ages 20-59
10. Ages 60 and older
11. Ages 0-19 and 60 and older
12. Females aged 20-49
13. Males
14. Females
15. Total work force
16. Agricultural work force
17. Industrial work force
18. Tertiary work force
19. Literate population aged 10-49
20. Eastern Slavs
21. Russians
22. Ukrainians
23. Belorussians
24. Turkic-Muslims (including Tatars)
25. Iranian language
26. Turkic language
27. Muslim religion
28. Mobilized Europeans (including Jews)
29. Finnic peoples (excluding Estonians)
30. Lithuanians
31. Moldavians and Romanians

32. Urban population
33. Urban population in size class 15,000-99,999
34. Urban population in size class 100,000 and over
35. Ages 0-9
36. Ages 10-19
37. Ages 0-19
38. Ages 20-39
39. Ages 40-59
40. Ages 60 and older
41. Ages 0-19 and 60 and older (obverse is ages 20-59)
42. Females aged 20-49
43. Total work force
44. Agricultural Work force
45. Industrial work force
46. Tertiary work force
47. Eastern Slavs
48. Russians
49. Ukrainians
50. Belorussians
51. Turkic-Muslims (including Tatars)
52. Iranian language
53. Turkic language
54. Muslim religion
55. Mobilized Europeans (including Jews)
56. Finnic peoples (excluding Estonians)
57. Lithuanians
58. Moldavians and Romanians

III. Level of Urbanization Variables (variables 59-82)

59. Ages 0-9
60. Ages 10-19
61. Ages 0-19
62. Ages 20-39
63. Ages 40-59
64. Ages 20-59
65. Ages 60 and older
66. Ages 0-19 and 60 and older
67. Females aged 20-49
68. Males
69. Females
70. Literate population aged 10-49
71. Eastern Slavs
72. Russians
73. Ukrainians
74. Belorussians
75. Turkic-Muslims (including Tatars)
76. Iranian language
77. Turkic language
78. Muslim religion
79. Mobilized Europeans (including Jews)
80. Finnic peoples (excluding Estonians)
81. Lithuanians
82. Moldavians and Romanians

IV. Specialized Variables (variables 83-90)

83. Percent of females aged 20-49
84. Child-woman ratio [(population aged 0-9 ÷ females aged 20-49) x 100]
85. Sex ratio [(males ÷ females) x 100]
86. Percent of work force in aggriculture
87. Percent of work force in industry
88. Percent of work force in tertiary sector
89. Percent of literate population aged 10-49
90. Population density (population ÷ square kilometers)

APPENDIX C:
VARIABLES FOR URBAN
POPULATION MATRICES:
1897, 1926, and 1959

I. Distribution Variables (variables 1-29)

1. Urban population
2. Urban population in size class 15,000-99,999
3. Urban population in size class 100,000 and over
4. Ages 0-9
5. Ages 10-19
6. Ages 0-19
7. Ages 20-39
8. Ages 40-59
9. Ages 20-59
10. Ages 60 and older
11. Ages 0-19 and 60 and older
12. Females aged 20-49
13. Males
14. Females
15. Total industrial work force
16. Total tertiary work force
17. Literate population aged 10-49
18. Eastern Slavs
19. Russians
20. Ukrainians
21. Belorussians
22. Turkic-Muslims (including Tatars)
23. Iranian language
24. Turkic language
25. Muslim religion
26. Mobilized Europeans (including Jews)
27. Finnic peoples (excluding Estonians)
28. Lithuanians
29. Moldavians and Romanians

II. Composition Variables (variables 30-50)

30. Urban population in size class 100,000 and over
31. Ages 0-9
32. Ages 10-19
33. Ages 0-19
34. Ages 20-39
35. Ages 40-59
36. Ages 60 and older
37. Ages 0-19 and 60 and older (obverse is ages 20-59)
38. Females aged 20-49
39. Eastern Slavs
40. Russians
41. Ukrainians
42. Belorussians
43. Turkic-Muslims (including Tatars)
44. Iranian language
45. Turkic language
46. Muslim religion
47. Mobilized Europeans (including Jews)
48. Finnic peoples (excluding Estonians)
49. Lithuanians
50. Moldavians and Romanians

III. Specialized Variables (variables 51-55)

51. Percent of females aged 20-49
52. Child-woman ratio [(population aged 0-9 ÷ females aged 20-49) x 100]
53. Sex ratio [(males ÷ females) x 100]

54. Percent of the total nonagricul- 55. Percent of literate popula-
    tural work force in industry   tion aged 10-49

APPENDIX D:
VARIABLES FOR RURAL
POPULATION MATRICES:
1897, 1926, and 1959

I. Distribution Variables (variables 1-26)

1. Rural population
2. Ages 0-9
3. Ages 10-19
4. Ages 0-19
5. Ages 20-39
6. Ages 40-59
7. Ages 20-59
8. Ages 60 and older
9. Ages 0-19 and 60 and older
10. Females aged 20-49
11. Males
12. Females
13. Total agricultural work force
14. Literate population aged 10-49
15. Eastern Slavs
16. Russians
17. Ukrainians
18. Belorussians
19. Turkic-Muslims (including Tatars)
20. Iranian language
21. Turkic language
22. Muslim religion
23. Mobilized Europeans (including Jews)
24. Finnic peoples (excluding Estonians)
25. Lithuanians
26. Moldavians and Romanians

II. Composition Variables (27-46)

27. Ages 0-9
28. Ages 10-19
29. Ages 0-19
30. Ages 20-39

31. Ages 40-59
32. Ages 60 and older
33. Ages 0-19 and 60 and older
34. Females aged 20-49
35. Eastern Slavs
36. Russians
37. Ukrainians
38. Belorussians
39. Turkic-Muslims (including Tatars)
40. Iranian language
41. Turkic language
42. Muslim language
43. Mobilized Europeans (including Jews)
44. Finnic Peoples (excluding Estonians)
45. Lithuanians
46. Moldavians and Romanians

III. Specialized Variables (variables 47-50)

47. Percent of females aged 20-49
48. Child-woman ratio [(population aged 0-9 ÷ females aged 20-49) x 100]
49. Sex ratio [(males ÷ females) x 100]
50. Percent of literate population aged 10-49

COMPONENT VARIABLES AND ADDITIONAL
VARIABLES THAT CAN BE GENERATED

The tables of Appendix E include the following variables:

1. Regional distribution (in percent) of the ten groupings for all four census years (Appendixes E.1 to E.4)
2. Regional redistribution (in percentage point change) of the ten groupings for all six intercensal periods (Appendixes E.5 to E.10)
3. Total and urban populations of each region for all four census years (Appendixes E.11 and E.12, respectively)
4. Urban population of the ten groupings for all four census years (Appendix E.13)
5. Regional distribution (in percent) of the urban population of the ten groupings for all four census years (Appendixes E.14 to E.17)

On the basis of many of these tables in combination with Table 7.6 of the text (total population by grouping), it is possible to generate a host of other nationality variables by economic region and for the entire USSR. We have already generated many of these variables, but have decided not to include them in this book because of the tremendous volume of tables involved. Instead, we will briefly describe some of the additional major variables that can be generated from the information published in this book and how these variables can be derived. As will be seen, the procedures are not difficult.

It should be pointed out that the following procedures are not applicable in certain instances. It will be remembered that 1897 data for Belorussians, Tatars, Turkic-Muslims, Finnic peoples, Lithuanians, and Moldavians and Romanians contain a number of inconsistencies, as do data for Moldavians and Romanians in 1926 (Chapter 6). The regional distribution percentages presented for these groupings in these years are corrections of previous percentages derived by the allocation procedures used in this study. The urban figures presented in Appendixes E.12 to E.17 are based upon the allocation procedures and have not been corrected for the groupings and years just mentioned. Therefore, the following procedures concerning urban and rural populations should not be undertaken for these groupings in the years indicated or in the intercensal periods involving such years. However, because these errors primarily involve 1897, all of the following variables can still be generated for all groupings in the Soviet era, except for those involving Moldavians and Romanians in 1926. It should be added that minor inconsistencies may appear in the calculation of the following variables, primarily resulting from the utilization of rounded numbers.

Despite these problems, our work has now made it possible to derive a host of demographic variables for major Soviet nationality groupings over a considerable period of time. Indeed, by following the procedures discussed below and using data that are completely included within this volume, it is possible to generate roughly 100 additional tables with the dimensions of ten groupings by 19 regions (for example, nationality composition of the urban population in 1926, redistribution of the rural population by nationality grouping between 1959 and 1970, and so on). The additional variables that can be derived include the following.

REGIONAL TOTAL, URBAN, AND RURAL POPULATIONS
(INCLUDING URBAN REDISTRIBUTION, AND RURAL
DISTRIBUTION AND REDISTRIBUTION)
BY NATIONALITY GROUPING

The total population of a given grouping for a given region in a given year can be calculated by multiplying the total USSR population (Table 7.6) of that grouping by the percent (in decimal form, of course) of its population residing in that region (Appendixes E.1 to E.4). For example, if the total USSR population of Grouping X in 1970 was 1 million and 20 percent of its population resided in the West region, its total population in this region would be 200,000.

Similarly, the urban population (15,000 and over definition) of a given grouping for a given region in a given year can be calculated by multiplying the total USSR urban population (Appendix E.13) of that grouping by the percent of its urban population residing in that region (Appendixes E.14 to E.17). Thus, for example, if the total USSR urban population of Grouping X in 1970 was 400,000 and 30 percent of its urban population resided in the West region, its urban population in this region would be 120,000.

Finally, the rural population of a given grouping for a given region in a given year can be calculated simply by subtracting its urban population from its total population in that region, both of which were derived following the procedures in the two previous paragraphs. For example, in 1970 the total and urban populations of Grouping X in the West region were, as calculated above, 200,000 and 120,000, respectively. Hence, the rural population of Grouping X in the West region

in 1970 would be 80,000 (200,000 - 120,000). Based upon these calculations, the regional distribution (in percent) of the rural population
for each grouping in each year can also be calculated, resulting in
tables similar to those for the total and urban populations (Appendixes
E.1 to E.4 and E.14 to E.17).

In addition, the regional redistribution (in percentage point
change) of the urban and rural populations for each grouping can then
be calculated, resulting in tables similar to those for the total population (Appendixes E.5 to E.10). Also, one can estimate the total USSR
rural population of a grouping in a given year either by summing the
regional rural populations or by subtracting data in Appendix E.13
(urban population) from those in Table 7.6 (total population).

REGIONAL TOTAL, URBAN, AND RURAL POPULATION
CHANGE BY NATIONALITY GROUPING

Based on the estimates of the total, urban, and rural populations
of a given grouping in a given region in a given year, it is then possible to compute the absolute amount of and rate of intercensal population
change for each of these populations for each region. For example,
if the total population of Grouping X in the West region in 1959 was
160,000, this means that its total population in this region grew by
40,000 (from 160,000 to 200,000, the value of 200,000 being derived
in the previous section) or by 25 percent between 1959 and 1970; if
its urban population in the West region in 1959 was 70,000, this means
that its urban population in this region grew by 50,000 (70,000 to
120,000) or by 71.4 percent between 1959 and 1970; a similar procedure can, of course, be used to calculate rural population change also
(here, 90,000 to 80,000, or a decline of 11.1 percent). In addition,
it is possible then to compute average annual rates of change in each
case. Of course, rates of growth for the total, urban, and rural populations of each grouping for the USSR as a whole can be calculated by
using Table 7.6 and Appendix E.13.

REGIONAL TOTAL, URBAN, AND RURAL
NATIONALITY COMPOSITION

Based again on the estimates for the total, urban, and rural
populations of a given grouping in a given region in a given year, it
is also possible to compute the nationality composition of the region,
that is, the percentage of the total, urban, and rural populations of
each region comprised by each grouping. The total and urban populations of each region in each year can be found in Appendixes E.11

and E.12; the rural population can be calculated simply by subtracting the urban population in Appendix E.12 from the total population in Appendix E.11. The corresponding total, urban, and rural populations for each grouping can be derived by following procedures in the section preceding the previous section.

Thus, for example, if the total population of the West region in 1970 was 6 million (Appendix E.11), this means that Grouping X comprised 3.3 percent of the total population of that region in 1970 (200,000, as calculated above, divided by 6 million); if the population of Grouping Y in the West region in 1970 was 3 million, then it would comprise 50 percent of the total population of that region (3 million divided by 6 million).

Once again, similar procedures could be applied to compute the nationality composition of the urban and rural populations in each region in each year. For example, if the total urban population of the West region was 3 million (Appendix E.12), then Grouping X would comprise 4 percent of the urban population of that region, since the urban population of Grouping X in the West region in 1970 was, as calculated above, 120,000. In addition, the simple technique of percentage point change could be applied to describe changes in the nationality composition of the total, urban, and rural populations of a given region.

Also, the nationality composition of the urban and rural populations for the USSR as a whole (the composition for the total population is already shown in Table 7.5) can be easily calculated by using the information in Table 7.6 and Appendixes E.11 to E.13.

REGIONAL LEVELS OF URBANIZATION
BY NATIONALITY GROUPING

Based on the estimates for the total and urban populations of a given grouping in a given region in a given year, it is also possible to compute the level of urbanization of a given grouping in each region. For example, we have seen that the total and urban populations of Grouping X in the West region in 1970 were 200,000 and 120,000, respectively. Accordingly, the level of urbanization of Grouping X in the West region in 1970 would be 60 percent. Once again, the technique of percentage point change could be applied to assess the rate of urbanization of a given grouping in a given region.

Note: The abbreviations for the regions and groupings found in the tables of Appendix E follow the sequences used elsewhere in this book. See, for example, Map 2.1 for the regions and the list on p. 47 for the groupings.

APPENDIX E.1

Regional Distribution by Nationality Grouping: 1897

Region	USSR Tot.	Russ.	Ukr.	Belo.	Tat.	T.M.	Jews	M.E.	Finn.	Lith.	M.R.
NW	6.4	10.4	0.0	2.7	0.3	0.1	1.5	4.0	28.1	0.5	0.0
W	4.6	0.6	0.0	6.0	0.2	0.0	11.0	42.4	0.2	97.7	0.0
C	12.2	25.6	1.7	5.0	0.6	0.0	1.9	0.5	4.7	0.1	0.0
VV	4.9	8.7	0.0	0.0	9.9	4.0	0.1	0.0	23.4	0.0	0.0
CC	6.6	12.2	5.7	0.1	0.6	0.0	0.3	0.0	2.3	0.0	0.0
V	7.8	11.4	2.2	0.1	45.0	2.3	0.3	0.3	16.2	0.0	0.0
B	5.2	0.6	1.5	81.2	0.3	0.0	21.1	2.9	0.1	1.0	0.0
M	1.2	0.2	1.7	0.0	0.0	0.3	4.2	0.0	0.0	0.0	70.0
SW	14.0	1.6	46.6	2.9	0.4	0.0	43.5	0.0	0.1	0.0	14.0
S	3.0	1.3	7.4	0.4	6.4	0.1	8.4	0.2	0.0	0.0	14.0
DD	6.3	2.6	23.9	0.9	3.1	0.1	5.5	0.1	0.0	0.0	1.3
NC	5.0	5.0	7.3	0.4	3.6	8.1	0.6	1.5	0.1	0.1	0.5
TC	3.7	0.4	0.1	0.1	0.6	12.4	0.5	47.3	0.0	0.2	0.0
U	7.3	11.9	0.4	0.1	18.0	10.7	0.2	0.2	23.0	0.0	0.0
WS	1.6	3.0	0.4	0.1	4.0	0.5	0.2	0.0	0.6	0.1	0.0
ES	1.7	2.5	0.1	0.0	2.6	1.3	0.5	0.1	0.2	0.0	0.0
FE	0.3	0.3	0.2	0.0	0.1	0.3	0.0	0.0	0.0	0.0	0.0
K	3.9	1.4	0.5	0.0	3.3	25.1	0.1	0.1	0.7	0.0	0.0
CA	4.4	0.2	0.1	0.0	0.7	34.8	0.1	0.1	0.2	0.0	0.0

Sources: 1897 Russian census and various foreign sources (see Chapter 2, footnotes 2 and 3).

APPENDIX E.2

Regional Distribution by Nationality Grouping: 1926

Region	USSR Tot.	Russ.	Ukr.	Belo.	Tat.	T.M.	Jews	M.E.	Finn.	Lith.	M.R.
NW	6.2	10.9	0.1	0.8	0.7	0.0	3.3	2.9	29.6	0.5	0.0
W	3.4	0.4	0.0	2.6	0.0	0.0	7.6	38.7	0.0	95.6	0.0
C	12.6	25.4	0.5	1.3	1.8	0.0	5.7	0.8	4.3	0.3	0.0
VV	4.3	7.1	0.0	0.0	5.1	4.3	0.3	0.0	18.1	0.0	0.0
CC	6.6	11.7	4.7	0.2	0.1	0.0	0.5	0.0	0.0	0.0	0.0
V	7.4	10.8	1.4	0.2	50.5	2.9	0.7	0.2	21.4	0.0	0.0
B	4.6	0.5	0.4	82.9	0.1	0.0	15.8	0.2	0.0	2.6	0.0
M	1.2	0.3	0.9	0.0	0.0	0.4	3.7	0.0	0.0	0.0	70.0
SW	12.8	0.6	44.3	2.8	0.1	0.0	38.4	0.1	0.0	0.1	17.0
S	2.7	1.1	5.8	0.4	6.2	0.2	10.0	0.3	0.0	0.1	11.2
DD	7.1	2.2	26.4	0.6	0.6	0.0	8.3	0.2	0.0	0.2	0.6
NC	5.5	5.0	8.7	0.8	0.8	8.1	1.5	3.2	0.1	0.1	0.5
TC	3.5	0.4	0.1	0.1	0.4	11.7	1.5	51.3	0.0	0.0	0.0
U	7.1	11.0	0.8	1.0	26.0	6.4	0.5	0.3	21.8	0.1	0.0
WS	3.7	6.1	2.0	2.7	2.0	1.0	0.4	0.6	2.9	0.2	0.1
ES	2.2	3.3	0.3	2.4	1.4	1.6	0.6	0.4	0.8	0.0	0.0
FE	0.9	0.9	1.0	0.7	0.2	0.3	0.1	0.1	0.1	0.1	0.2
K	3.7	1.7	2.4	0.4	2.8	22.3	0.1	0.1	0.8	0.0	0.1
CA	4.5	0.6	0.3	0.1	1.3	40.8	1.0	0.5	0.1	0.0	0.0

Sources: 1926 Soviet census and various foreign sources (see Chapter 2, footnotes 2 and 3).

Regional Distribution by Nationality Grouping: 1959

Region	USSR Tot.	Russ.	Ukr.	Belo.	Tat.	T.M.	Jews	M.E.	Finn.	Lith.	M.R.
NW	5.5	8.7	0.9	3.4	1.0	0.0	8.7	0.4	14.4	1.1	0.0
W	2.9	0.9	0.2	1.3	0.1	0.0	3.1	29.1	0.6	98.4	0.0
C	11.9	20.5	1.0	1.2	3.6	0.1	14.9	0.4	3.2	0.1	0.0
VV	4.0	5.5	0.2	0.0	4.4	3.8	0.9	0.0	28.1	0.0	0.0
CC	4.2	7.3	0.8	0.0	0.0	0.0	0.3	0.0	0.0	0.0	0.0
V	6.0	8.3	0.8	0.3	34.5	0.0	2.1	0.0	13.6	0.0	0.0
B	3.9	0.6	0.4	84.4	0.2	2.2	7.1	0.1	0.0	0.4	0.0
M	1.4	0.3	1.1	0.1	0.0	0.0	4.5	0.0	0.0	0.0	85.0
SW	9.7	1.1	47.8	0.7	0.0	0.5	18.8	0.0	0.0	0.0	8.0
S	2.4	1.4	7.7	0.7	0.0	0.0	8.4	0.0	0.0	0.0	5.6
DD	7.9	3.8	30.8	1.9	0.8	0.1	11.9	0.0	0.0	0.0	0.6
NC	5.6	7.9	1.0	0.5	0.6	0.0	2.5	2.5	0.0	0.0	0.0
TC	4.6	0.8	0.2	0.1	0.7	7.5	4.4	66.5	0.1	0.0	0.2
U	8.9	12.0	1.5	1.5	32.1	14.5	2.9	0.0	34.2	0.0	0.0
WS	4.9	7.6	1.2	0.9	2.9	5.8	1.0	0.0	1.5	0.0	0.0
ES	3.3	4.9	0.6	0.7	2.1	0.8	0.6	0.0	0.6	0.0	0.0
FE	2.1	3.1	1.2	0.7	1.0	1.9	1.1	0.0	1.5	0.0	0.0
K	4.5	3.5	2.0	1.4	3.9	0.0	1.3	0.2	1.0	0.0	0.7
CA	6.5	2.0	0.7	0.3	12.0	47.9	5.6	0.7	1.1	0.0	0.0

Source: 1959 Soviet census (see Chapter 2, footnote 2).

APPENDIX E.4

Regional Distribution by Nationality Grouping: 1970

Region	USSR Tot.	Russ.	Ukr.	Belo.	Tat.	T.M.	Jews	M.E.	Finn.	Lith.	M.R.
NW	5.3	8.7	1.1	3.4	1.1	0.0	8.8	0.3	14.2	1.3	0.5
W	2.8	1.0	0.3	1.8	0.1	0.0	3.1	25.3	0.6	97.7	0.0
C	11.1	19.5	1.2	1.7	3.5	0.2	15.1	0.5	2.6	0.1	0.2
VV	3.5	4.9	0.2	0.1	4.0	2.8	0.8	0.0	26.2	0.0	0.0
CC	3.7	6.7	0.6	0.2	0.0	0.0	0.5	0.0	0.0	0.0	0.0
V	5.9	8.4	0.8	0.6	33.2	1.9	2.3	0.0	12.9	0.0	0.1
B	3.7	0.7	0.5	80.7	0.2	0.0	7.0	0.1	0.1	0.3	0.1
M	1.5	0.3	1.2	0.1	0.0	0.4	4.6	0.0	0.0	0.0	84.4
SW	9.1	1.1	47.3	1.1	0.0	0.0	17.4	0.0	0.0	0.0	7.1
S	2.6	1.7	8.6	0.9	0.1	0.1	8.1	0.1	0.1	0.0	5.4
DD	7.8	4.2	30.7	2.3	0.8	0.0	11.0	0.1	0.0	0.0	0.6
NC	6.0	8.1	1.0	1.0	1.0	8.1	3.2	0.1	0.4	0.0	0.4
TC	5.1	0.7	0.2	0.1	0.6	14.7	4.6	69.8	0.0	0.0	0.1
U	8.4	11.6	1.2	1.5	31.6	4.9	2.8	0.0	33.5	0.0	0.0
WS	4.4	7.3	0.8	0.7	2.8	0.7	1.3	0.1	3.3	0.0	0.0
ES	3.4	5.1	0.5	0.7	2.0	1.8	0.8	0.0	2.1	0.0	0.0
FE	2.1	3.4	0.9	0.6	1.0	0.1	1.1	0.0	1.1	0.0	0.1
K	5.4	4.3	2.3	2.2	4.9	15.5	1.3	0.2	1.9	0.5	1.0
CA	8.2	2.3	0.7	0.4	12.7	48.9	6.1	0.7	0.9	0.0	0.0

Source: 1970 Soviet census (see Chapter 2, footnote 2).

APPENDIX E.5

Regional Redistribution by Nationality Grouping: 1897–1926

Region	USSR Tot.	Russ.	Ukr.	Belo.	Tat.	T.M.	Jews	M.E.	Finn.	Lith.	M.R.
NW	-0.2	0.5	0.1	-1.9	0.4	-0.1	1.8	-1.1	1.5	0.0	0.0
W	-1.2	-0.2	0.0	-3.4	-0.2	0.0	-3.4	-3.7	-0.2	-2.1	0.0
C	0.4	-0.2	-1.2	-3.7	1.2	0.0	3.8	0.3	-0.4	0.2	0.0
VV	-0.6	-1.6	0.0	0.0	-4.8	0.3	0.2	0.0	-5.3	0.0	0.0
CC	0.0	-0.5	-1.0	0.1	-0.5	0.0	0.2	0.0	-2.3	0.0	0.0
V	-0.4	-0.6	-0.8	0.1	5.5	0.6	0.4	-0.1	5.2	0.0	0.0
B	-0.6	-0.1	-1.1	1.7	-0.2	0.0	-5.3	-2.7	-0.1	1.6	0.0
M	0.0	0.1	-0.8	0.0	0.0	0.1	-0.5	0.0	0.0	0.0	0.0
SW	-1.2	-1.0	-2.3	-0.1	-0.3	0.0	-5.1	0.1	-0.1	0.1	3.0
S	-0.3	-0.2	-1.6	0.0	-0.2	0.1	1.6	0.1	0.0	0.1	-2.8
DD	0.8	-0.4	2.5	-0.3	-2.5	-0.1	2.8	0.1	0.0	0.2	-0.7
NC	0.5	0.0	1.4	0.4	-2.8	0.0	0.9	1.7	0.0	0.0	0.0
TC	-0.2	0.0	0.0	0.0	-0.2	-0.7	1.0	4.0	0.0	-0.2	0.0
U	-0.2	-0.9	0.4	0.9	8.0	-4.3	0.3	0.1	-1.2	0.1	0.0
WS	2.1	3.1	1.6	2.6	-2.0	0.5	0.2	0.6	2.3	0.1	0.1
ES	0.5	0.8	0.2	2.4	-1.2	0.3	0.1	0.3	0.6	0.1	0.0
FE	0.6	0.6	0.8	0.7	0.1	0.0	0.1	0.1	0.1	0.0	0.2
K	-0.2	0.3	1.9	0.4	-0.5	-2.8	0.0	0.0	0.1	0.1	0.1
CA	0.1	0.4	0.2	0.1	0.6	6.0	0.9	0.4	-0.1	0.0	0.0

Sources: 1897 Russian census, 1926 Soviet census, and various foreign sources (see Chapter 2, footnotes 2 and 3).

APPENDIX E.6

Regional Redistribution by Nationality Grouping: 1926–59

Region	USSR Tot.	Russ.	Ukr.	Belo.	Tat.	T.M.	Jews	M.E.	Finn.	Lith.	M.R.
NW	-0.7	-2.2	0.8	2.6	0.3	0.0	5.4	-2.5	-15.2	0.6	0.0
W	-0.5	0.5	0.2	-1.3	0.1	0.0	-4.5	-9.6	0.6	2.8	0.0
C	-0.7	-4.9	0.5	-0.1	1.8	0.1	9.2	-0.4	-1.1	-0.2	0.0
VV	-0.3	-1.6	0.2	0.0	-0.7	-0.5	0.6	0.0	10.0	0.0	0.0
CC	-2.4	-4.4	-3.9	-0.2	-0.1	0.0	-0.2	0.0	0.0	0.0	0.0
V	-1.4	-2.5	-0.6	0.1	-16.0	-0.7	1.4	-0.2	-7.8	-2.2	0.0
B	-0.7	0.1	0.0	1.5	0.1	0.0	-8.7	-0.1	0.0	-2.2	0.0
M	0.2	0.0	0.2	0.1	0.0	0.1	0.8	0.0	0.0	0.0	15.0
SW	-3.1	0.5	3.5	-2.1	-0.1	0.0	-19.6	-0.1	0.0	-0.1	-9.0
S	-0.3	0.3	1.9	0.3	-6.2	-0.1	-1.6	-0.3	0.0	-0.1	-5.6
DD	0.8	1.6	4.4	1.3	0.2	0.0	3.6	-0.2	0.0	-0.2	0.0
NC	0.1	2.9	-7.7	-0.3	-0.2	-0.6	1.0	-0.7	-0.1	-0.1	-0.5
TC	1.1	0.4	0.1	0.0	0.3	2.8	2.9	15.2	0.1	0.0	0.2
U	1.8	1.0	0.7	0.5	6.1	-0.6	2.4	-0.3	12.4	-0.1	0.0
WS	1.2	1.5	-0.8	-1.8	0.9	-0.2	0.6	-0.6	-1.4	-0.2	-0.1
ES	1.1	1.6	0.3	-1.7	0.7	0.3	0.0	-0.4	-0.2	0.0	0.0
FE	1.2	2.2	0.2	0.0	0.8	-0.3	1.0	-0.1	1.4	-0.1	-0.2
K	0.8	1.8	-0.4	1.0	1.1	-7.4	1.2	0.1	0.2	0.0	0.6
CA	2.0	1.4	0.4	0.2	10.7	7.1	4.6	0.2	1.0	0.0	0.0

Sources: 1926 and 1959 Soviet censuses and various foreign sources (see Chapter 2, footnotes 2 and 3).

APPENDIX E.7

Regional Redistribution by Nationality Grouping: 1897-1959

Region	USSR Tot.	Russ.	Ukr.	Belo.	Tat.	T.M.	Jews	M.E.	Finn.	Lith.	M.R.
NW	-0.9	-1.7	0.9	0.7	0.7	-0.1	7.2	-3.6	-13.7	0.6	0.0
W	-1.7	0.3	0.2	-4.7	-0.1	0.0	-7.9	-13.3	0.4	0.7	0.0
C	-0.3	-5.1	-0.7	-3.8	3.0	0.1	13.0	-0.1	-1.5	0.0	0.0
VV	-0.9	-3.2	0.2	0.0	-5.5	-0.2	0.8	0.0	4.7	0.0	0.0
CC	-2.4	-4.9	-4.9	-0.1	-0.6	0.0	0.0	0.0	-2.3	0.0	0.0
V	-1.8	-3.1	-1.4	0.2	-10.5	-0.1	1.8	-0.3	-2.6	0.0	0.0
B	-1.3	0.0	-1.1	3.2	-0.1	0.0	-14.0	-2.8	-0.1	-0.6	0.0
M	0.2	0.1	-0.6	0.1	0.0	0.2	0.3	0.0	0.0	0.0	15.0
SW	-4.3	-0.5	1.2	-2.2	-0.4	0.0	-24.7	0.0	-0.1	0.0	-6.0
S	-0.6	0.1	0.3	0.3	-6.4	0.0	0.0	-0.2	0.0	0.0	-8.4
DD	1.6	1.2	6.9	1.0	-2.3	-0.1	6.4	-0.1	0.0	0.0	-0.7
NC	0.6	2.9	-6.3	0.1	-3.0	-0.6	1.9	1.0	-0.1	-0.1	-0.5
TC	0.9	0.4	0.1	0.0	0.1	2.1	3.9	19.2	0.1	-0.2	0.2
U	1.6	0.1	1.1	1.4	14.1	-4.9	2.7	-0.2	11.2	0.0	0.0
WS	3.3	4.6	0.8	0.8	-1.1	0.3	0.8	0.0	0.9	-0.1	0.0
ES	1.6	2.4	0.5	0.7	-0.5	0.6	0.1	-0.1	0.4	0.0	0.0
FE	1.8	2.8	1.0	0.7	0.9	-0.3	1.1	0.0	1.5	0.0	0.0
K	0.6	2.1	1.5	1.4	0.6	-10.2	1.2	0.1	0.3	0.0	0.7
CA	2.1	1.8	0.6	0.3	11.3	13.1	5.5	0.6	0.9	0.0	0.0

Sources: 1897 Russian census, 1959 Soviet census, and various foreign sources (see Chapter 2, footnotes 2 and 3).

Regional Redistribution by Nationality Grouping: 1959–70

Region	USSR Tot.	Russ.	Ukr.	Belo.	Tat.	T.M.	Jews	M.E.	Finn.	Lith.	M.R.
NW	-0.2	0.0	0.2	0.0	0.1	0.0	0.1	-0.1	-0.2	0.2	0.5
W	-0.1	0.1	0.1	0.5	0.0	0.0	0.0	-3.8	0.0	-0.7	0.0
C	-0.8	-1.0	0.2	0.5	-0.1	0.1	0.2	0.1	-0.6	0.0	0.2
VV	-0.5	-0.6	0.0	0.1	-0.4	-1.0	-0.1	0.0	-1.9	0.0	0.0
CC	-0.5	-0.6	-0.2	0.2	0.0	0.0	0.2	0.0	0.0	0.0	0.0
V	-0.1	0.1	0.0	0.3	0.0	-0.3	0.2	0.0	-0.7	0.0	0.1
B	-0.2	0.1	0.1	-3.7	-1.3	0.0	-0.1	0.0	0.1	-0.1	0.1
M	0.1	0.0	0.1	0.0	0.0	-0.1	0.1	0.0	0.0	0.0	-0.6
SW	-0.6	0.0	-0.5	0.4	0.0	0.0	-1.4	0.0	0.0	0.0	-0.9
S	0.2	0.3	0.9	0.2	0.1	0.0	-0.3	0.1	0.1	0.0	-0.2
DD	-0.1	0.4	-0.1	0.4	0.0	0.0	-0.9	0.1	0.0	0.0	0.0
NC	0.4	0.2	0.0	0.5	0.4	0.6	0.7	0.2	0.4	0.0	0.4
TC	0.5	-0.1	0.0	0.0	-0.1	0.2	0.2	3.3	-0.1	0.0	-0.1
U	-0.5	-0.4	-0.3	0.0	-0.5	-0.9	-0.1	0.0	-0.7	0.0	0.0
WS	-0.5	-0.3	-0.4	-0.2	-0.1	-0.1	0.3	0.1	1.8	0.0	0.0
ES	0.1	0.2	-0.1	0.0	-0.1	-0.1	0.2	0.0	1.5	0.0	0.0
FE	0.0	0.3	-0.3	-0.1	0.0	0.1	0.0	0.0	-0.4	0.0	0.1
K	0.9	0.8	0.3	0.8	1.0	0.6	0.0	0.0	0.9	0.5	0.3
CA	1.7	0.3	0.0	0.1	0.7	1.0	0.5	0.0	-0.2	0.0	0.0

Sources: 1959 and 1970 Soviet censuses (see Chapter 2, footnote 2).

APPENDIX E.9

Regional Redistribution by Nationality Grouping: 1926–70

Region	USSR Tot.	Russ.	Ukr.	Belo.	Tat.	T.M.	Jews	M.E.	Finn.	Lith.	M.R.
NW	-0.9	-2.2	1.0	2.6	0.4	0.0	5.5	-2.6	-15.4	0.8	0.5
W	-0.6	0.6	0.3	-0.8	0.1	0.0	-4.5	-13.4	0.6	2.1	0.0
C	-1.5	-5.9	0.7	0.4	1.7	0.2	9.4	-0.3	-1.7	-0.2	0.2
VV	-0.8	-2.2	0.2	0.1	-1.1	-1.5	0.5	0.0	8.1	0.0	0.0
CC	-2.9	-5.0	-4.1	0.0	-0.1	0.0	0.0	0.0	0.0	0.0	0.0
V	-1.5	-2.4	-0.6	0.4	-17.3	-1.0	1.6	-0.2	-8.5	0.0	0.1
B	-0.9	0.2	0.1	-2.2	0.1	0.0	-8.8	-0.1	0.1	-2.3	0.1
M	0.3	0.0	0.3	0.1	0.0	0.0	0.9	0.0	0.0	0.0	14.4
SW	-3.7	0.5	3.0	-1.7	-0.1	0.0	-21.0	-0.1	0.0	-0.1	-9.9
S	-0.1	0.6	2.8	0.5	-6.1	-0.1	-1.9	-0.2	0.1	-0.1	-5.8
DD	0.7	2.0	4.3	1.7	0.2	0.0	2.7	-0.1	0.0	-0.2	0.0
NC	0.5	3.1	-7.7	0.2	0.2	0.0	1.7	-0.5	0.3	-0.1	-0.1
TC	1.6	0.3	0.1	0.0	0.2	3.0	3.1	18.5	0.0	0.0	0.1
U	1.3	0.6	0.4	0.5	5.6	-1.5	2.3	-0.3	11.7	-0.1	0.0
WS	0.7	1.2	-1.2	-2.0	0.8	-0.3	0.9	-0.5	0.4	-0.2	-0.1
ES	1.2	1.8	0.2	-1.7	0.6	0.2	0.2	-0.4	1.3	0.0	0.0
FE	1.2	2.5	-0.1	-0.1	0.8	-0.2	1.0	-0.1	1.0	-0.1	0.0
K	1.7	2.6	-0.1	1.8	2.1	-6.8	1.2	0.1	1.1	0.5	0.9
CA	3.7	1.7	0.4	0.3	11.4	8.1	5.1	0.2	0.8	0.0	0.0

Sources: 1926 and 1970 Soviet censuses and various foreign sources (see Chapter 2, footnotes 2 and 3).

APPENDIX E.10

Regional Redistribution by Nationality Grouping: 1897–1970

Region	USSR Tot.	Russ.	Ukr.	Belo.	Tat.	T.M.	Jews	M.E.	Finn.	Lith.	M.R.
NW	-1.1	-1.7	1.1	0.7	0.8	-0.1	7.3	-3.7	-13.9	0.8	0.5
W	-1.8	0.4	0.3	-4.2	-0.1	0.0	-7.9	-17.1	0.4	0.0	0.0
C	-1.1	-6.1	-0.5	-3.3	2.9	0.2	13.2	0.0	-2.1	0.0	0.2
VV	-1.4	-3.8	0.2	0.1	-5.9	-1.2	0.7	0.0	2.8	0.0	0.0
CC	-2.9	-5.5	-5.1	0.1	-0.6	0.0	0.2	0.0	-2.3	0.0	0.0
V	-1.9	-3.0	-1.4	0.5	-11.8	-0.4	2.0	-0.3	-3.3	0.0	0.1
B	-1.5	0.1	-1.0	-0.5	-0.1	0.0	-14.1	-2.8	0.0	-0.7	0.1
M	0.3	0.1	-0.5	0.1	0.0	0.1	0.4	0.0	0.0	0.0	14.4
SW	-4.9	-0.5	0.7	-1.8	-0.4	0.0	-26.1	0.0	-0.1	0.0	-6.9
S	-0.4	0.4	1.2	0.5	-6.3	0.0	-0.3	-0.1	0.1	0.0	-8.6
DD	1.5	1.6	6.8	1.4	-2.3	-0.1	5.5	0.0	0.0	0.0	-0.7
NC	1.0	3.1	-6.3	0.6	-2.6	0.0	2.6	1.2	0.3	-0.1	-0.1
TC	1.4	0.3	0.1	0.0	0.0	2.3	4.1	22.5	0.0	-0.2	0.1
U	1.1	-0.3	0.8	1.4	13.6	-5.8	2.6	-0.2	10.5	0.0	0.0
WS	2.8	4.3	0.4	0.6	-1.2	0.2	1.1	0.1	2.7	-0.1	0.0
ES	1.7	2.6	0.4	0.7	-0.6	0.5	0.3	-0.1	1.9	0.0	0.0
FE	1.8	3.1	0.7	0.6	0.9	-0.2	1.1	0.0	1.1	0.0	0.1
K	1.5	2.9	1.8	2.2	1.6	-9.6	1.2	0.1	1.2	0.5	1.0
CA	3.8	2.1	0.6	0.4	12.0	14.1	6.0	0.6	0.7	0.0	0.0

Sources: 1897 Russian census, 1970 Soviet census, and various foreign sources (see Chapter 2, footnotes 2 and 3).

APPENDIX E.11

Total Population by Economic Region: 1897-1970

Region	1897	1926	1959	1970
NW	8,002,979	10,341,034	11,474,054	12,888,896
W	5,725,779	5,638,518	6,001,694	6,848,442
C	15,245,585	21,049,713	24,789,349	26,720,545
VV	6,181,344	7,255,893	8,253,038	8,347,817
CC	8,285,760	11,035,835	8,697,909	8,929,242
V	9,712,792	12,433,500	12,454,354	14,287,358
B	6,468,422	7,640,980	8,054,648	9,002,338
M	1,534,261	2,035,581	2,884,477	3,568,873
SW	17,558,515	21,448,191	20,254,509	21,948,629
S	3,759,355	4,599,128	5,066,132	6,380,614
DD	7,846,363	11,978,274	16,548,405	18,797,274
NC	6,225,625	9,268,453	11,785,606	14,548,637
TC	4,595,096	5,861,528	9,504,810	12,295,312
U	9,105,907	11,847,333	18,613,230	20,409,372
WS	1,975,600	6,257,867	10,159,437	10,703,400
ES	2,097,908	3,624,449	6,960,535	8,127,557
FE	422,564	1,559,354	4,346,803	5,116,386
K	4,825,013	6,179,050	9,309,847	13,008,726
CA	5,473,973	7,601,154	13,667,813	19,790,716
USSR total	125,042,841	167,655,835	208,826,650	241,720,134

Sources: See Chapter 2, footnotes 2 and 3.

412

Urban Population by Economic Region: 1897–1970

Region	1897	1926	1959	1970
NW	1,736,473	2,469,953	6,013,233	7,950,265
W	836,750	1,057,003	1,930,000	3,016,593
C	1,846,177	3,699,813	13,131,619	17,043,796
VV	115,061	375,964	2,410,329	3,454,095
CC	609,060	804,484	1,862,925	2,985,379
V	835,750	1,402,387	5,184,212	7,508,654
B	444,088	673,415	1,698,213	3,077,590
M	205,725	233,796	438,971	817,979
SW	1,337,458	2,214,145	3,825,116	5,999,627
S	854,477	1,060,185	1,958,645	2,898,768
DD	828,645	1,798,739	8,230,656	11,212,489
NC	628,515	1,832,747	4,469,115	6,461,650
TC	527,067	1,052,878	3,481,326	5,128,182
U	508,433	1,131,841	8,821,227	11,200,409
WS	127,872	610,859	4,775,992	6,008,902
ES	78,172	319,969	2,600,304	3,651,661
FE	61,767	254,233	2,061,140	2,757,278
K	121,238	340,388	3,189,383	5,343,052
CA	618,312	1,024,298	3,678,486	6,107,215
USSR total	12,321,040	22,357,097	79,760,892	112,623,584

Sources: See Chapter 2, footnotes 2 and 3.

Urban Population by Nationality Grouping: 1897–1970*

Grouping	1897	1926	1959	1970
Russians	7,222,151	12,806,572	53,887,927	73,898,414
Ukrainians	1,134,961	2,608,100	10,807,145	15,512,560
Belorussians	123,519	351,257	1,765,680	3,160,269
Tatars	206,191	325,943	1,875,559	2,729,437
Turkic-Muslims	749,968	1,061,573	3,621,293	6,747,478
Jews	1,482,712	2,166,964	1,556,505	1,661,791
Mobilized Europeans	598,276	1,222,370	2,668,082	3,927,947
Finnic peoples	48,944	126,914	496,308	784,042
Lithuanians	36,963	140,946	505,874	923,265
Moldavians and Romanians	53,562	148,930	169,464	373,508
USSR total	12,321,040	22,357,097	79,760,892	112,623,584

*Data for all four years are based upon summations of data for the 19 economic regions. Therefore, the data in this table for 1959 and 1970 differ slightly from those used throughout the text of this book. It will be remembered that the data used in the text for 1959 and 1970 were based upon census summary volume totals for the USSR, not upon the summation of data for the 19 economic regions. The estimated urban populations based upon census summary tables in 1959 and 1970 are R (52,482,667 and 72,642,212); U (11,645,090 and 16,330,420); B (2,073,783 and 3,266,084); T (1,834,501 and 2,702,966); TM (3,988,044 and 7,095,286); J (1,754,740 and 1,689,354); ME (2,871,392 and 4,279,696); F (638,087 and 900,989); L (638,087 and 1,013,612); and MR (239,283 and 450,494). Corresponding rural populations can be calculated by subtracting these urban populations from the total populations in Table 7.6 (do not use those in the footnote of Table 7.6!).

Sources: See Chapter 2, footnotes 2 and 3.

APPENDIX E.14

Regional Distribution of Urban Population by Nationality Grouping: 1897

Region	USSR Tot.	Russ.	Ukr.	Belo.	Tat.	T.M.	Jews	M.E.	Finn.	Lith.	M.R.
NW	14.1	20.7	0.8	5.9	3.4	0.0	2.0	6.1	63.9	14.1	0.0
W	6.8	2.4	0.1	17.9	1.6	0.1	12.5	42.7	3.4	72.4	0.0
C	15.0	23.9	2.4	3.2	2.7	0.0	2.2	0.3	3.8	0.0	0.0
VV	0.9	1.5	0.0	0.1	1.2	0.0	0.1	0.0	0.9	0.0	0.0
CC	4.9	7.6	3.8	0.5	0.3	0.0	0.5	0.1	1.2	0.0	0.0
V	6.8	10.1	0.7	0.7	25.9	0.6	0.5	0.8	6.8	0.0	0.0
B	3.6	1.1	0.4	58.1	1.3	0.1	16.5	0.3	0.9	3.6	0.0
M	1.7	0.8	2.9	0.2	0.2	0.0	4.9	0.2	0.0	0.0	44.9
SW	10.9	4.9	34.4	5.7	3.2	0.4	33.1	0.2	2.7	0.0	12.5
S	6.9	5.1	11.9	1.5	18.6	0.2	14.7	1.3	0.0	0.0	41.5
DD	6.7	3.9	32.5	3.5	4.8	0.2	9.4	0.3	0.0	0.0	0.0
NC	5.1	6.0	7.7	2.1	5.8	2.4	1.4	5.1	2.6	3.4	0.0
TC	4.3	1.2	0.7	0.5	0.5	19.2	0.8	41.7	1.1	4.3	1.0
U	4.1	6.1	0.7	0.0	17.7	1.6	0.3	0.1	7.3	0.0	0.0
WS	1.0	1.5	0.3	0.0	2.4	0.4	0.3	0.0	2.1	0.3	0.0
ES	0.6	0.9	0.1	0.0	0.7	0.3	0.3	0.0	0.1	0.0	0.0
FE	0.5	0.6	0.2	0.1	0.4	0.0	0.1	0.0	0.4	0.2	0.1
K	1.0	0.9	0.2	0.0	5.5	5.3	0.1	0.0	1.5	0.0	0.0
CA	5.0	0.8	0.8	0.0	3.6	69.3	0.3	0.7	1.3	1.7	0.0

Sources: 1897 Russian census and various foreign sources (see Chapter 2, footnotes 2 and 3).

APPENDIX E.15

Regional Distribution of Urban Population by Nationality Grouping: 1926

Region	USSR Tot.	Russ.	Ukr.	Belo.	Tat.	T.M.	Jews	M.E.	Finn.	Lith.	M.R.
NW	11.0	16.3	0.6	5.6	3.0	0.7	4.9	3.4	75.9	5.3	0.0
W	4.7	0.5	0.0	2.4	0.0	0.0	7.8	38.0	0.0	87.0	0.0
C	16.5	26.4	0.9	6.3	6.8	0.3	7.5	1.8	2.9	2.6	0.0
VV	1.7	2.8	0.0	0.2	0.9	0.3	0.3	0.1	1.8	0.0	0.0
CC	3.6	5.4	3.3	0.9	0.3	0.0	0.7	0.1	0.0	0.0	0.0
V	6.3	9.3	1.2	0.8	25.8	0.7	1.0	0.3	5.5	0.0	0.0
B	3.0	0.7	0.2	61.2	0.6	0.1	12.8	0.2	0.5	1.0	0.0
M	1.0	0.5	0.8	0.0	0.0	0.4	2.9	0.0	0.0	0.0	45.1
SW	9.9	1.3	31.4	1.9	0.7	0.0	31.1	0.2	0.0	0.0	32.7
S	4.7	3.3	8.2	1.5	11.1	0.6	12.6	1.0	0.0	0.8	22.1
DD	8.0	4.5	34.7	4.6	2.8	0.2	10.5	0.6	0.0	1.3	0.0
NC	8.2	8.6	14.4	8.9	3.9	4.0	2.8	9.3	1.4	1.3	0.0
TC	4.7	1.5	0.6	0.6	2.3	20.1	1.8	42.4	0.8	0.0	0.0
U	5.1	8.0	0.3	0.3	18.1	1.0	0.5	0.1	4.5	0.0	0.0
WS	2.7	4.2	0.7	1.4	4.7	0.3	0.5	0.3	3.9	0.4	0.0
ES	1.4	2.1	0.2	0.7	2.3	0.4	0.6	0.2	0.8	0.2	0.0
FE	1.1	1.4	0.9	0.8	0.6	0.0	0.1	0.1	0.4	0.2	0.2
K	1.5	1.4	0.8	1.0	9.4	8.9	0.1	0.1	0.8	0.0	0.0
CA	4.6	1.9	0.7	0.9	6.9	62.0	1.4	1.8	0.8	0.0	0.0

Sources: 1926 Soviet census and various foreign sources (see Chapter 2, footnotes 2 and 3).

Regional Distribution of Urban Population by Nationality Grouping: 1959

Region	USSR Tot.	Russ.	Ukr.	Belo.	Tat.	T.M.	Jews	M.E.	Finn.	Lith.	M.R.
NW	7.5	9.7	1.9	7.8	1.9	0.0	9.7	0.7	20.6	2.4	0.0
W	2.4	1.0	0.3	2.6	0.2	0.0	2.9	25.8	1.2	97.3	0.0
C	16.5	22.6	2.4	3.7	7.0	0.4	16.9	1.0	5.3	0.0	0.0
VV	3.0	4.0	0.3	0.0	2.7	2.0	0.9	0.0	10.7	0.0	0.0
CC	2.3	3.3	0.6	0.0	0.0	0.0	0.2	0.0	0.0	0.0	0.0
V	6.5	8.1	1.2	0.9	23.5	1.6	2.3	0.0	13.6	0.0	0.0
B	2.1	0.6	0.5	64.4	0.2	0.0	6.3	0.1	0.0	0.3	0.0
M	0.6	0.2	0.8	0.1	0.0	0.5	3.9	0.0	0.0	0.0	73.3
SW	4.8	1.2	25.2	1.3	0.0	0.0	16.0	0.0	0.0	0.0	6.8
S	2.5	1.6	7.9	1.2	0.0	0.1	8.7	0.0	0.0	0.0	9.2
DD	10.3	5.2	46.0	5.6	1.3	0.0	12.2	0.0	0.0	0.0	4.9
NC	5.6	6.9	1.8	1.3	1.0	5.2	2.9	4.0	0.0	0.0	0.0
TC	4.4	1.2	0.5	0.4	1.3	22.6	4.2	66.8	0.0	0.0	2.1
U	11.1	13.4	2.8	3.5	31.0	5.1	3.4	0.0	33.8	0.0	0.0
WS	6.0	7.8	1.7	1.9	4.3	0.9	1.2	0.0	3.8	0.0	0.0
ES	3.3	4.2	1.0	1.2	2.4	1.1	0.5	0.0	1.0	0.0	0.0
FE	2.6	3.2	1.5	1.4	1.4	0.0	0.9	0.0	3.7	0.0	0.0
K	4.0	3.4	2.2	2.0	5.3	16.6	1.2	0.2	2.6	0.0	3.8
CA	4.6	2.5	1.2	0.6	16.5	44.0	5.7	1.4	3.7	0.0	0.0

Source: 1959 Soviet census (see Chapter 2, footnote 2).

APPENDIX E.17

Regional Distribution of Urban Population by Nationality Grouping: 1970

Region	USSR Tot.	Russ.	Ukr.	Belo.	Tat.	T.M.	Jews	M.E.	Finn.	Lith.	M.R.
NW	7.1	9.4	1.8	6.0	1.7	0.2	9.1	0.6	19.3	1.7	2.1
W	2.7	1.1	0.4	2.8	0.2	0.0	2.9	23.7	1.1	97.4	0.0
C	15.2	21.4	2.4	3.8	6.2	0.5	16.4	0.9	4.3	0.0	0.0
VV	3.1	4.1	0.2	0.2	2.5	2.4	0.8	0.0	14.5	0.0	0.0
CC	2.7	3.9	0.5	0.4	0.0	0.0	0.5	0.0	0.0	0.0	0.0
V	6.7	8.5	1.2	1.2	24.8	1.6	2.7	0.0	12.4	0.0	0.0
B	2.7	0.8	0.7	67.5	0.2	0.0	6.8	0.1	0.0	0.3	0.0
M	0.7	0.3	1.0	0.2	0.0	0.5	4.2	0.0	0.0	0.0	76.9
SW	5.3	1.3	29.4	1.5	0.0	0.0	15.5	0.0	0.0	0.0	6.4
S	2.6	1.7	8.6	1.2	0.1	0.1	8.0	0.1	0.0	0.0	7.0
DD	10.0	5.4	42.9	4.6	1.2	0.0	11.5	0.3	0.0	0.0	3.0
NC	5.7	6.9	1.5	1.2	1.2	7.5	3.5	3.8	0.8	0.0	1.7
TC	4.6	0.9	0.4	0.3	1.1	20.9	4.6	69.2	0.0	0.0	0.0
U	9.9	12.4	2.0	2.8	30.8	4.5	2.7	0.0	34.3	0.0	0.0
WS	5.3	7.3	1.1	1.1	3.5	0.3	1.5	0.0	3.1	0.0	0.0
ES	3.2	4.3	0.8	1.0	2.0	1.2	0.7	0.0	1.9	0.0	0.0
FE	2.4	3.2	1.2	1.0	1.2	0.1	1.0	0.0	2.5	0.0	0.0
K	4.7	4.2	2.6	2.5	6.1	15.7	1.3	0.3	3.4	0.6	2.9
CA	5.4	2.7	1.1	0.6	17.0	44.6	6.2	1.1	2.3	0.0	0.0

Source: 1970 Soviet census (see Chapter 2, footnote 2).

PUBLIC DOCUMENTS

Baldwin, Godfrey. Estimates and Projections of the Population of the
    USSR, by Age and Sex: 1950 to 2000. U.S. Department of
    Commerce. Bureau of Economic Analysis. International Popu-
    lation Reports, Series P-91, no. 23, December 1972.

Davis, Kingsley, and Hertz, Hilda. "Patterns of World Urbanization
    for 1800-1950." United Nations. Bureau of Social Affairs.
    Report on the World Social Situation Including Studies of Urbani-
    zation in Underdeveloped Areas (ST/SOA/33), 1957.

DeWitt, Nicholas. Education and Professional Employment in the
    USSR. Washington, D.C.: Superintendent of Documents, 1961.

Feshbach, Murray, and Rapawy, Stephen. "Labor Constraints in the
    Five-Year Plan." U.S. Congress. Joint Economic Committee.
    Soviet Economic Prospects for the Seventies. Joint Committee
    Print. Washington, D.C.: Government Printing Office, 1973.

Glavnoye Upravleniye Geodezii i Kartografii pri Sovete Ministrov
    SSSR. Malyy Atlas SSSR. Moscow, 1973.

Leedy, Frederick A. "Demographic Trends in the USSR." U.S.
    Congress. Joint Economic Committee. Soviet Economic Pros-
    pects for the Seventies. Joint Committee Print. Washington,
    D.C.: Government Printing Office, 1973.

New Zealand. Department of Statistics. Population Census, 1961.
    Vol. 8.

Noren, James H., and Whitehouse, Douglas E. "Soviet Industry in
    the 1971-75 Plan." U.S. Congress. Joint Economic Committee.
    Soviet Economic Prospects for the Seventies. Joint Committee
    Print. Washington, D.C.: Government Printing Office, 1973.

Russian Empire. Tsentral'nyy Statisticheskiy Komitet Ministerstva
    Vnutrennikh Del. Pervaya Vseobshchaya Perepis' Naseleniya
    Rossiyskoy Imperii, 1897 G., 89 vols.

Smith, Willard S. "Housing in the Soviet Union—Big Plans, Little Action." U.S. Congress. Joint Economic Committee. Soviet Economic Prospects for the Seventies. Joint Committee Print. Washington, D.C.: Government Printing Office, 1973.

United Nations. Bureau of Social Affairs. Report on the World Social Situation Including Studies of Urbanization in Underdeveloped Areas (ST/SOA/33), 1957.

_____. Department of Economic and Social Affairs. Demographic Yearbook—1971.

_____. Growth of the World's Urban and Rural Population, 1920-2000 (ST/SOA/Series A/44), 1969.

_____. Department of Social Affairs. Population Division. The Determinants and Consequences of Population Trends (ST/SOA/SER. A/17), 1953.

USSR. Prezidium Verkhovnogo Soveta. SSSR: Administrativno-Territorial'noye Deleniye Soyuznykh Respublik, 1971. Moscow: Izdatel'stvo "Izvestiya Sovetov Deputatov Trudyashchikhsya SSSR," 1971.

_____. Tsentral'noye Statisticheskoye Upravleniye pri Sovete Ministrov SSSR. Itogi Vsesoyuznoy Perepisi Naseleniya 1959 Goda, 16 vols.

_____. Itogi Vsesoyuznoy Perepisi Naseleniya 1970 Goda, 7 vols.

_____. Narodnoye Khozyaystvo SSSR v 1959 G. Moscow: Gosstatizdat, 1960.

_____. Narodnoye Khozyaystvo SSSR v 1961 Godu. Moscow: Gosstatizdat, 1962.

_____. Narodnoye Khozyaystvo SSSR v 1964 G. Moscow: Statistika, 1965.

_____. Narodnoye Khozyaystvo SSSR v 1967 G. Moscow: Statistika, 1968.

_____. Narodnoye Khozyaystvo SSSR v 1969 G. Moscow: Izdatel'stvo "Statistika," 1970.

_____. Narodnoye Khozyaystvo SSSR v 1970 G. Moscow: Izdatel'stvo "Statistika," 1971.

_____. Narodnoye Obrazovaniye, Nauka i Kultura v SSSR. Moscow: Izdatel'stvo "Statistika," 1971.

_____. Strana Sovetov za 50 Let. Moscow: Statistika, 1967.

_____. Tsentral'noye Statisticheskoye Upravleniye SSSR. Vsesoyuznaya Perepis' Naseleniya 1926 Goda, 66 vols.

U.S. Department of Commerce. Bureau of the Census. The Methods and Materials of Demography, by Henry S. Shryock, Jacob S. Siegel, and Associates. Vol. I. Washington, D.C.: Government Printing Office, 1971.

Yugoslavia. Savezni Zavod za Statistiku. Statisticki Godisnjak Jugoslavije, 1973. Beograd, 1973.

BOOKS

Allworth, Edward, ed. Central Asia: A Century of Russian Rule. New York: Columbia University Press, 1967.

_____, ed. Soviet Nationality Problems. New York: Columbia University Press, 1971.

Apter, David E. The Politics of Modernization. Chicago: University of Chicago Press, 1965.

Bennigsen, Alexandre, and Lemercier-Quelquejay, Chantal. Islam in the Soviet Union. London: Pall Mall Press, 1967.

_____. The Evolution of the Muslim Nationalities of the USSR and Their Linguistic Problems. London: Central Asian Research Centre, 1961.

Berard, Victor. The Russian Empire and Czarism. London: David Nutt, 1905.

Black, C. E. The Dynamics of Modernization. New York: Harper & Row, 1966.

Bloom, Solomon F. The World of Nations: A Study of National Implications in the Work of Karl Marx. New York: AMS Press,
1967; originally published in New York: Columbia University
Press, 1941.

Boldyrev, V. A. Ekonomicheskiy Zakon Naseleniya pri Sotsializme.
Moscow: Izdatel'stvo "Mysl'," 1968.

Brezhnev, Leonid I. O Pyatidesyatiletii Soyuza Sovetskikh Sotsialisticheskikh Respublik. Moscow: Izdatel'stvo Politicheskoy
Literatury, 1973.

Burmistrova, T. Yu. Teoriya Sotsialisticheskoy Natsiy. Leningrad:
Izdatel'stvo Leningradskogo Universiteta, 1970.

Chamberlain, Neil W. Beyond Malthus. New York: Basic Books,
1970.

Clark, Colin. The Conditions of Economic Progress. London:
Macmillan, 1951.

Conquest, Robert. The Nation Killers: The Soviet Deportation of
Nationalities. 2d ed. New York: Macmillan, 1970.

_____. Soviet Nationalities Policy in Practice. New York: Praeger,
1967.

Davitaya, F. F. Gruziya. Moscow: Izdatel'stvo "Mysl'," 1967.

Demko, George J. The Russian Colonization of Kazakhstan: 1896-
1916. The Hague: Mouton & Co., 1969.

Deutsch, Karl W. Nationalism and Social Communication. Rev. ed.
Cambridge, Mass.: Massachusetts Institute of Technology
Press, 1966.

Dixon, W. J., ed. BMD Biomedical Computer Programs: X-Series
Supplement. Berkeley, Calif.: University of California Press,
1970.

Dobb, Maurice. Soviet Economic Development Since 1917. Rev. ed.
New York: International Publishers, 1966.

Dol'skaya, A. A. Sotsialisticheskiy Zakon Narodonaseleniya. Moscow: Sotsekgiz, 1959.

Donnelly, Alton S. The Russian Conquest of Bashkiria, 1552-1740. New Haven, Conn.: Yale University Press, 1941.

Dublin, Louis I.; Lotka, Alfred J.; and Spiegelman, Mortimer. Length of Life. Rev. ed. New York: Ronald Press, 1949.

Duncan, Otis Dudley, ed. William F. Ogburn on Culture and Social Change. Chicago: University of Chicago Press, 1964.

Dunn, Stephen P. Cultural Processes in the Baltic Area Under Soviet Rule. Berkeley, Calif.: University of California Press, 1966.

Dzhaoshvili, V. Sh. Naseleniye Gruzii. Tbilisi: Izdatel'stvo "Metsniyereba," 1968.

Dzyuba, Ivan. Internationalism or Russification? 2d ed. London: Weidenfeld and Nicolson, 1968.

Eisenstadt, S. N. Modernization: Protest and Change. Englewood Cliffs, N.J.: Prentice-Hall, 1966.

Eldridge, Hope T., and Thomas, Dorothy Swaine. Demographic Analyses and Interrelations. Vol. 3. Population Redistribution and Economic Growth: United States, 1870-1950. Philadelphia: American Philosophical Society, 1964.

Enloe, Cynthia H. Ethnic Conflict and Political Development. Boston: Little, Brown, 1973.

Erlich, Alexander. The Soviet Industrialization Debate, 1924-1928. Cambridge, Mass.: Harvard University Press, 1960.

Fainsod, Merle. Smolensk Under Soviet Rule. New York: Vintage Books, 1958.

Fisher, Jack C. Yugoslavia: A Multinational State. San Francisco: Chandler, 1966.

Glass, D. V. Population Policies and Movements in Europe. London: Frank Cass and Co., 1967.

Glazer, Nathan, and Moynihan, Daniel Patrick. Beyond the Melting Pot: The Negroes, Puerto Ricans, Jews, Italians, and Irish of New York City. Cambridge, Mass.: Massachusetts Institute of Technology Press, 1970.

Goldscheider, Calvin. Population, Modernization, and Social Structure. Boston: Little, Brown, 1971.

Gordon, Milton M. Assimilation in American Life: The Role of Race, Religion, and National Origins. New York: Oxford University Press, 1964.

Gregory, James S. Russian Land, Soviet People. New York: Pegasus, 1968.

Groves, Harold M. Education and Economic Growth. Washington, D.C.: National Education Association, 1961.

Gurr, Ted Robert. Why Men Rebel. Princeton, N.J.: Princeton University Press, 1970.

Hagen, Everett E. On the Theory of Social Change: How Economic Growth Begins. London: Tavistock, 1962.

Harbison, Frederick, and Myers, Charles A. Education, Manpower, and Economic Growth. New York: McGraw-Hill, 1964.

Harris, Chauncy D. Cities of the Soviet Union. Chicago: Rand McNally, 1970.

Hawthorn, Geoffrey. The Sociology of Fertility. London: Collier-Macmillan, 1970.

Hempel, Carl G. Aspects of Scientific Explanation. New York: Free Press, 1965.

Hetzler, Stanley A. Technological Growth and Social Change. London: Routledge and Kegan Paul, 1969.

Honda, Tatsuo. Population Problems in Post War Japan. Vol. 2. Tokyo: Institute of Population Problems, 1967.

Hoselitz, Bert F. Sociological Aspects of Economic Growth. New York: Free Press, 1960.

Hrushevsky, Michael. A History of Ukraine. New Haven, Conn.: Yale University Press, 1941.

Isupov, A. A. Natsional'nyy Sostav Naseleniya SSSR. Moscow: Izdatel'stvo "Statistika," 1961.

Jackson, Keith, and Harre, John. New Zealand. New York: Walker, 1969.

Jaffe, A. J. People, Jobs, and Economic Development. Glencoe, Ill.: Free Press, 1959.

Karakhanov, M. K., ed. Problemy Narodonaseleniya. Moscow: Izdatel'stvo Moskovskogo Universiteta, 1970.

Kholmogorov, A. I. Internatsional'nyye Cherty Sovetskikh Natsiy. Moscow: Mysl', 1970.

Khorev, B. S. Problemy Gorodov. Moscow: Izdatel'stvo "Mysl'," 1971.

Koropeckyj, I. S. Locational Problems in Soviet Industry Before World War II. Chapel Hill, N.C.: University of North Carolina Press, 1971.

Kozlov, V. I. Dinamika Chislennosti Narodov. Moscow: Mysl', 1969.

Kozyrev, Yu. N., ed. Voprosy Marksistsko-Leninskoy Teorii Narodonaseleniya. Moscow: Izdatel'stvo Moskovskogo Universiteta, 1969.

Kulischer, Eugene M. Europe on the Move. New York: Columbia University Press, 1948.

Kurman, M. V., and Lebedinskiy, I. V. Naseleniye Bol'shogo Sotsialisticheskogo Goroda. Moscow: Statistika, 1968.

Lang, David Marshall. A Modern History of Soviet Georgia. New York: Grove Press, 1962.

Leasure, William J., and Lewis, Robert A. Population Changes in Russia and the USSR: A Set of Comparable Territorial Units. San Diego, Calif.: San Diego State College Press, 1966.

Lenin, V. I. Questions of National Policy and Proletarian Internationalism. Moscow: Progress Publishers, 1970.

Lerner, Daniel. The Passing of Traditional Society: Modernizing the Middle East. New York: Free Press, 1958.

Lorimer, Frank. The Population of the Soviet Union: History and Prospects. Geneva: League of Nations, 1946.

Low, Alfred D. Lenin on the Question of Nationality. New York: Bookman Associates, 1958.

Lyashchenko, Peter I. History of the National Economy of Russia to the 1917 Revolution. New York: Macmillan, 1949.

Lydolph, Paul A. Geography of the U.S.S.R. 2d ed. New York: John Wiley, 1970.

McClelland, David C. The Achieving Society. Princeton, N.J.: Van Nostrand, 1961.

Marx, Karl. Capital. Vol. 1. New York: International Publishers, 1967.

Mavor, James. An Economic History of Russia. Vol. 2. 2d ed., rev. New York: Russel and Russel, 1925.

Meining, D. W. Southwest: Three Peoples in Geographical Change, 1600-1970. New York: Oxford University Press, 1971.

Moore, Wilbert E. The Impact of Industry. Englewood Cliffs, N.J.: Prentice-Hall, 1965.

Nagel, Ernest. The Structure of Science. New York: Harcourt, Brace, and World, 1961.

Narody Yevropeyskoy Chasti SSSR. Vol. 1. Moscow: Izdatel'stvo "Nauka," 1964.

Naulko, V. I. Geografichne Rozmishchennya Narodiv v URSR. Kiev: Naukova Dumka, 1966.

Odud, A. L. Moldavskaya SSR. Moscow: Gosudarstvennoye Izdatel' stvo Geograficheskoy Literatury, 1955.

Parker, W. H. An Historical Geography of Russia. Chicago: Aldine, 1969.

Pavlovsky, George. Agricultural Russia on the Eve of the Revolution. New York: Howard Fertig, 1968; originally published in London: George Routledge and Sons, 1930.

Petersen, William. Population. London: Macmillan, 1970.

Pipes, Richard. The Formation of the Soviet Union. Rev. ed. New
York: Atheneum, 1968.

Pokshishevskiy, V. V. Geografiya Naseleniya SSSR. Moscow:
Izdatel'stvo "Prosveshcheniye," 1971.

Quine, Willard Van Orman. From a Logical Point of View. New
York: Harper & Row, 1963.

Rakowska-Harmstone, Teresa. Russia and Nationalism in Central
Asia. Baltimore: Johns Hopkins Press, 1970.

Rashin, A. G. Naseleniye Rossii za 100 Let. Moscow: Gosudarstvennoye Statisticheskoye Izdatel'stvo, 1956.

Robinson, Geroid Tanquary. Rural Russia Under the Old Regime.
Rev. ed. Berkeley, Calif.: University of California Press,
1972; originally published in New York: Macmillan, 1932.

Rummel, R. J. Applied Factor Analysis. Evanston, Ill.: Northwestern University Press, 1970.

Schapiro, Leonard. The Communist Party of the Soviet Union. New
York: Vintage Books, 1964.

Seton-Watson, Hugh. The Russian Empire, 1801-1917. Oxford:
Oxford University Press, 1967.

Shabad, Theodore. Basic Industrial Resources of the U.S.S.R.
New York: Columbia University Press, 1969.

Shibutani, Tamotsu, and Kwan, Kian M. Ethnic Stratification: A
Comparative Approach. New York: Macmillan, 1972.

Slesarev, G. A. Metodologiya Sotsiologicheskogo Issledovaniya
Problem Narodonaseleniya SSSR. Moscow: Izdatel'stvo "Mysl',"
1965.

Smulevich, B. Ya. Kritika Burzhuaznykh Teorii i Politiki Narodonaseleniya. Moscow: Sotsekgiz, 1959.

Stalin, J. V. Works. Moscow: Foreign Languages Publishing House,
1953.

Taeuber, Irene B. The Population of Japan. Princeton, N.J.:
Princeton University Press, 1958.

Taeuber, Karl E., and Alma F. Negroes in Cities. Chicago: Aldine, 1965.

Thompson, Warren S. Population and Peace in the Pacific. Chicago:
University of Chicago Press, 1946.

Treadgold, Donald. The Great Siberian Migration. Princeton, N.J.:
Princeton University Press, 1957.

Urlanis, B. Ts. Rost Naseleniya v SSSR. Moscow: Statistika, 1966.

_____. Rozhdayemost' i Prodolzhitel'nost' Zhizni v SSSR. Moscow:
Gosstatizdat, 1963.

Valentey, D. E., ed. Marksistsko-Leninskaya Teoriya Narodonaseleniya. Moscow: Izdatel'stvo "Mysl'," 1971.

_____, ed. Osnovy Teorii Narodonaseleniya. Moscow: Izdatel'stvo
"Vysshaya Shkola," 1973.

_____. Problemy Narodonaseleniya. Moscow: Vysshaya Shkola,
1961.

_____. Reaktsionnyye Teorii Narodonaseleniya Perioda Obshchego
Krizisa Kapitalizma. Moscow: Izdatel'stvo Sotsialno-Ekono-
micheskoy Literatury, 1963.

_____; Pokshishevskiy, V. V.; and Khorev, B. S., eds. Problemy
Urbanizatsii v SSSR. Moscow: Izdatel'stvo Moskovskogo Universiteta, 1971.

Vorob'yev, N. Ya. Vsesoyuznaya Perepis' Naseleniya 1926 G. Moscow: Gosudarstvennoye Statisticheskoye Izdatel'stvo, 1957.

Ward, David. Cities and Immigrants. New York: Oxford University
Press, 1971.

Weber, Adna Ferrin. The Growth of Cities in the Nineteenth Century.
Ithaca, N.Y.: Cornell University Press, 1963; originally published in New York: Macmillan, 1899.

Willcox, Walter F., ed. International Migrations. Vol. 2. New York: National Bureau of Economic Research, 1931.

Wrigley, E. A. Population and History. New York: McGraw-Hill, 1969.

Wuorinen, John H. Nationalism in Modern Finland. New York: Columbia University Press, 1931.

Yarmolinsky, Avrahm. The Jews and Other Minor Nationalities Under the Soviets. New York: Vanguard Press, 1928.

ARTICLES, JOURNALS, PROCEEDINGS,
MAGAZINES, AND NEWSPAPERS

Abramsky, Chimen. "The Biro-Bidzhan Project, 1927-1959." The Jews in Soviet Russia Since 1917. Edited by Lionel Kochan. London: Oxford University Press, 1970.

Abu-Lughod, Janet. "Migration Adjustment to City Life: The Egyptian Case." American Journal of Sociology 67 (July 1961): 22-32.

Allworth, Edward. "Restating the Soviet Nationality Question." Soviet Nationality Problems. Edited by Edward Allworth. New York: Columbia University Press, 1971.

Anderson, C. Arnold. "The Modernization of Education." Modernization: The Dynamics of Growth. Edited by Myron Weiner. New York: Basic Books, 1966.

Armstrong, John A. "The Ethnic Scene in the Soviet Union." Ethnic Minorities in the Soviet Union. Edited by Erich Goldhagen. New York: Praeger, 1968.

Arutyunyan, Yu. V. "Izmeneniye Sotsial'noy Struktury Sovetskikh Natsiy." Istoriya SSSR, no. 4 (July-August 1972), pp. 3-20.

_____. "Konkretno-Sotsiologicheskoye Issledovaniye Natsional'nykh Otnosheniy." Voprosy Filosofii, no. 12 (1969), pp. 129-39.

_____. "Opyt Sotsial'no-Etnicheskogo Issledovaniya." Sovetskaya Etnografiya, no. 4 (1968), pp. 3-13.

Aspaturian, Vernon V. "The Non-Russian Nationalities." Prospects for Soviet Society. Edited by Allen Kassof. New York: Praeger, 1968.

Beijer, G. "Modern Patterns of International Migration Movements." Migration. Edited by J. A. Jackson. Cambridge, Mass.: Cambridge University Press, 1969.

Bennigsen, Alexandre. "Islamic, or Local Consciousness Among Soviet Nationalities?" Soviet Nationality Problems. Edited by Edward Allworth. New York: Columbia University Press, 1971.

Bergson, Abram. "Development Under Two Systems: Comparative Productivity Growth Since 1950." World Politics 23 (July 1971).

Bertsch, Gary K. "The Revival of Nationalisms." Problems of Communism 22 (November-December 1973): 1-15.

Bilinsky, Yaroslav. "Assimilation and Ethnic Assertiveness Among Ukrainians of the Soviet Union." Ethnic Minorities in the Soviet Union. Edited by Erich Goldhagen. New York: Praeger, 1968.

_____. "Education of the Non-Russian Peoples in the USSR, 1917-1967: An Essay." Slavic Review 27 (September 1968): 411-37.

_____. "The Soviet Education Laws of 1958-1959 and Soviet Nationality Policy." Soviet Studies 14 (October 1962): 138-57.

Blacker, C. P. "Stages in Population Growth." Eugenics Review 39 (October 1947): 88-101.

Blake, Judith. "Demographic Science and the Redirection of Population Policy." Public Health and Population Change. Edited by Mindel C. Sheps and Jeanne Clare Ridley. Pittsburgh: University of Pittsburgh Press, 1965.

Breton, Raymond. "Institutional Completeness of Ethnic Communities and the Personal Relations of Immigrants." American Journal of Sociology 70 (September 1964): 194-205.

Bronson, David W., and Krueger, Constance B. "The Revolution in Soviet Farm Household Income, 1953-1967." The Soviet Rural Community. Edited by James R. Millar. Urbana, Ill.: University of Illinois Press, 1971.

Bruk, S., and Kozlov, V. "Voprosy o Natsional'nosti i Yazyke v
Predstoyashchey Perepisi Naseleniya." Vestnik Statistiki, no.
3 (1968), pp. 32-37.

Carlsson, Gosta. "The Decline of Fertility: Innovation or Adjustment Process." Population Studies 20 (November 1966): 149-74.

Central Intelligence Agency. USSR Agricultural Atlas. Washington,
D.C.: Government Printing Office, 1974.

Clem, Ralph S., and Gordon, Steven I. "Nationality Classification
for Geographic Research." Proceedings of the Middle States
Division, Association of American Geographers (1972).

Coale, Ansley J. "Population and Economic Development." The Population Dilemma. Edited by Philip M. Hauser. 2d ed. Englewood Cliffs, N.J.: Prentice-Hall, 1969.

Connor, Walker. "Nation-Building or Nation-Destroying?" World
Politics 24 (April 1972): 319-55.

Dalrymple, Dana G. "The Soviet Famine of 1932-1934." Soviet
Studies 15 (January 1964): 250-84.

Davis, Kingsley. "Population Policy: Will Current Programs Succeed?" Science 158 (November 10, 1967): 730-39.

_____. "The Theory of Change and Response in Modern Demographic
History." Population Index 29 (October 1963): 346-67.

_____. "The Urbanization of the Human Population." Cities. New
York: Knopf, 1970.

_____. "The World Demographic Transition." Annals of the Ameri-
can Academy of Political and Social Sciences 273 (January
1945): 1-11.

Day, Lincoln H., and Day, Alice Taylor. "Family Size in Industrialized Countries: An Inquiry into the Social-Cultural Determinants of Levels of Childbearing." Journal of Marriage and the
Family 31 (May 1969): 242-51.

"Demograficheskaya Problema: Zanyatost' Zhenshchin i Rozhdayemost'." Voprosy Ekonomiki, no. 5 (May 1969), pp. 157-59.

Deutsch, Karl. "Social Mobilization and Political Development." American Political Science Review 55 (September 1961): 493-514.

Dienes, Leslie. "Investment Priorities in Soviet Regions." Annals of the Association of American Geographers 62 (September 1972): 437-54.

Dodge, Norton T. "Recruitment and the Quality of the Soviet Agricultural Labor Force." The Soviet Rural Community. Edited by James R. Millar. Urbana, Ill.: University of Illinois Press, 1971.

Dorn, Harold F. "Mortality." The Study of Population. Edited by Philip M. Hauser and Otis Dudley Duncan. Chicago: University of Chicago Press, 1959.

Duncan, Otis Dudley, and Hodge, Robert W. "Education and Occupational Mobility." American Journal of Sociology 68 (May 1963): 629-44.

Dzhunusov, M. S. "Natsiya kak Sotsial'no-Etnicheskaya Obshchnost' Lyudei." Voprosy Istorii, no. 4 (April 1966), pp. 16-30.

Esipov, N. S. "O Zakone Narodonaseleniya Sotsialisticheskogo Obshchestva." Voprosy Marksistsko-Leninskoy Teorii Narodonaseleniya. Edited by Yu. N. Kozyrev. Moscow: Izdatel'stvo Moskovskogo Universiteta, 1969.

Ettinger, S. "The Jews in Russia at the Outbreak of the Revolution." The Jews in Soviet Russia Since 1917. Edited by Lionel Kochan. London: Oxford University Press, 1970.

Field, Neil C. "Land Hunger and the Rural Depopulation Problem in the USSR." Annals of the Association of American Geographers 53 (December 1963): 465-78.

Friedlander, Dov. "Demographic Responses and Population Change." Demography 6 (November 1969): 359-81.

"Germans Join in $1-Billion Pact to Equip a Soviet Steel Plant." New York Times. 23 March 1974, p. 1.

Gibbs, Jack P., and Martin, Walter T. "Urbanization, Technology, and the Division of Labor: International Patterns." American Sociological Review 27 (October 1962): 667-77.

Glass, D. V. "Population Growth and Population Policy." Public Health and Population Change. Edited by Mindel C. Sheps and Jeanne Clare Ridley. Pittsburgh: University of Pittsburgh Press, 1965.

Grunbaum, Adolph. "Causality and the Science of Human Behavior." Readings in the Philosophy of Science. Edited by Herbert Feigl and May Brodbeck. New York: Appleton-Century-Crofts, 1953.

Gwertzman, Bernard. "Protest on Soviet Laid to Latvians." New York Times. 27 February 1972, p. 11.

Harris, Chauncy D. "Urbanization and Population Growth in the Soviet Union, 1959-1970." Geographical Review 61 (January 1971): 102-24.

_____. "USSR Resources for Agriculture." Focus 20 (December 1969): 1-7.

Hauser, Philip M. "Observations on the Urban-Folk and Urban-Rural Dichotomies as Forms of Western Ethnocentrism." The Study of Urbanization. Edited by Philip M. Hauser and Leo F. Schnore. New York: Wiley, 1967.

_____. "World Population Growth." The Population Dilemma. Edited by Philip M. Hauser. 2d ed. Englewood Cliffs, N.J.: Prentice-Hall, 1969.

Heer, David M. "Economic Development and Fertility." Demography 3, no. 2 (1966): 423-44.

_____. "The Demographic Transition in the Russian Empire and the Soviet Union." Journal of Social History 1 (Spring 1968): 193-240.

Hodnett, Grey. "The Debate over Soviet Federalism." Soviet Studies 18 (April 1967): 458-81.

_____. "What's in a Nation?" Problems of Communism 16 (September-October 1967): 2-15.

_____. "Technology and Social Change in Soviet Central Asia: The Politics of Cotton Growing." Soviet Politics and Society in the 1970's. Edited by Henry W. Morton and Rudolph L. Tokes. New York: Free Press, 1974.

Hoselitz, Bert F. "The Role of Cities in the Economic Growth of Un-
    derdeveloped Countries." Journal of Political Economy 61
    (June 1953): 195-208.

Hume, David. "Liberty and Necessity." An Enquiry Concerning Hu-
    man Understanding. I. Enquiries Concerning the Human Under-
    standing and Concerning the Principles of Morals. Edited by
    L. A. Selby-Bigge. 2d ed. Oxford: Clarendon Press, 1902.

Hurvitz, Nathan. "Sources of Middle Class Values of American Jews."
    Social Forces 37 (December 1958): 117-23.

Isupov, A. A. "Sostoyaniye i Osnovnyye Pokazateli Statistiki Nase-
    leniya v Respublikakh Sredney Azii." Problemy Narodonasele-
    niya. Edited by M. K. Karakhanov. Moscow: Izdatel'stvo
    Moskovskogo Universiteta, 1970.

Izvestiya. 19 April 1970, p. 1.

Jackson, W. A. Douglas. "The Virgin and Idle Lands of Western
    Siberia and Northern Kazakhstan: A Geographic Appraisal."
    Geographical Review 46 (January 1956): 1-19.

_____. "The Virgin and Idle Lands Reappraised." Annals of the As-
    sociation of American Geographers 52 (March 1962): 69-79.

Jaffe, A. J. "Differential Fertility in the White Population in Early
    America." Journal of Heredity 31 (September 1940); 407-11.

_____. "Population, Working Force, and Economic Growth: A Pre-
    liminary Outline." Centro Latinoamericano de Demografia
    (CELADE), S.474/26. Santiago, Chile. June 1970, 26 pp.

_____. "Urbanization and Fertility." American Journal of Sociology
    48 (July 1942): 48-60.

_____, and Azumi, K. "The Birth Rate and Cottage Industries in Un-
    derdeveloped Countries." Economic Development and Cultural
    Change 9 (October 1960): 52-63.

_____, and Froomkin, J. N. "Economic Development and Jobs—A
    Comparison of Japan and Panama, 1950 to 1960." Estadistica
    24 (September 1966): 577-92.

_____, and Wolfbein, Seymour L. "Internal Migration and Full Em-
      ployment in the U.S." Journal of the American Statistical Asso-
      ciation 40 (September 1945): 351-63.

Jensen, Robert G. "Soviet Subtropical Agriculture: A Microcosm."
      Geographical Review 54 (April 1964): 185-202.

Kamm, Henry. "Troubled Brittany Expects Little Help from Paris."
      New York Times. 24 April 1974, p. 8.

Kohn, Hans. "Soviet Communism and Nationalism: Three Stages of
      a Historical Development." Soviet Nationality Problems. Edited
      by Edward Allworth. New York: Columbia University Press,
      1971.

Kuznets, Simon. "Introduction: Population Redistribution, Migra-
      tion and Economic Growth." Demographic Analyses and Inter-
      relations, by Hope T. Eldridge and Dorothy Swaine Thomas.
      Vol. 3. Population Redistribution and Economic Growth:
      United States, 1870-1950. Philadelphia: American Philosophical
      Society, 1964.

_____. "Quantitative Aspects of the Economic Growth of Nations. II.
      Industrial Distribution of National Product and Labor Force."
      Economic Development and Cultural Change, supplement to 5
      (July 1957): 3-111.

_____, and Thomas, Dorothy S. "Internal Migration and Economic
      Growth." Selected Studies of Migration Since World War II.
      Proceedings of the Milbank Memorial Fund. New York, 1958,
      pp. 196-211.

"Latvians Chided for Nationalism." New York Times. 21 March
      1971, p. 17.

Leasure, J. William, and Lewis, Robert A. "Internal Migration in
      Russia in the Late Nineteenth Century." Slavic Review 27 (Sep-
      tember 1968): 375-94.

_____. "Internal Migration in the USSR: 1897-1926." Demography
      4, no. 2 (1967): 479-96.

Lee, Everett S. "A Theory of Migration." Demography 3, no. 1
      (1966): 47-57.

_____. "Migration in Relation to Education, Intellect, and Social
Structure." Population Index 36 (October–December 1970): 437–
43.

Lenin, V. I. "Kriticheskiye Zametki po Natsional'nomu Voprosu."
Sochineniya. Vol. 20. 4th ed. Moscow: Gosudarstvennoye
Izdatel'stvo Politicheskoy Literatury, 1948.

_____. "O Prave Natsiy na Samoopredeleyine." Sochineniya. Vol. 20.
4th ed. Moscow: Gosudarstvennoye Izdatel'stvo Politicheskoy
Literatury, 1948.

Lewis, Oscar. "Further Observations on the Folk–Urban Continuum
and Urbanization with Special Reference to Mexico City." The
Study of Urbanization. Edited by Philip M. Hauser and Leo F.
Schnore. New York: Wiley, 1967.

Lewis, Robert A. "The Irrigation Potential of Soviet Central Asia."
Annals of the Association of American Geographers 52 (March
1962): 99–114.

_____. "The Mixing of Russians and Soviet Nationalities and Its
Demographic Impact." Soviet Nationality Problems. Edited by
Edward Allworth. New York: Columbia University Press,
1971.

_____, and Rowland, Richard H. "Urbanization in Russia and the
USSR: 1897–1966." Annals of the Association of American Geographers 59 (December 1969): 776–96.

_____, and Rowland, Richard H. "Urbanization in Russia and the
USSR: 1897–1970." The City in Russian History. Edited by
Michael F. Hamm. Lexington, Ky.: University Press of Ken-
tucky, forthcoming.

Lieberson, Stanley. "The Impact of Residential Segregation on Ethnic Assimilation." Social Forces 40 (October 1961): 52–57.

McKeown, Thomas. "Medicine and World Population." Public Health
and Population Change. Edited by Mindel C. Sheps and Jeanne
Clare Ridley. Pittsburgh: University of Pittsburgh Press,
1965.

Mazur, D. Peter. "Fertility Among Ethnic Groups in the USSR."
Demography 4, no. 1 (1967): 172–95.

Meyer, Alfred G. "The Comparative Study of Communist Political Systems." Slavic Review 26 (March 1967): 3-12.

Moore, Wilbert E. "Changes in Occupational Structures." Social Structure and Mobility in Economic Development. Edited by Neil J. Smelser and Seymour Martin Lipset. Chicago: Aldine, 1966.

Nove, Alec, and Newth, J. A. "The Jewish Population: Demographic Trends and Occupational Patterns." The Jews in Soviet Russia Since 1917. Edited by Lionel Kochan. London: Oxford University Press, 1970.

Ogburn, William F. "Social Trends." William F. Ogburn on Culture and Social Change. Edited by Otis Dudley Duncan. Chicago: University of Chicago Press, 1964.

_____. "Technology and Cities: The Dilemma of the Modern Metropolis." Sociological Quarterly 1 (July 1960): 139-53.

Ornstein, Jacob. "Soviet Language Policy: Continuity and Change." Ethnic Minorities in the Soviet Union. Edited by Erich Goldhagen. New York: Praeger, 1968.

Parming, Tonu. "Population Changes in Estonia, 1935-1970." Population Studies 26 (March 1972): 61-78.

Perevedentsev, V. I. "Migratsiya Naseleniya i Ispol'zovaniya Trudovykh Resursov." Voprosy Ekonomiki, no. 9 (September 1970), pp. 34-43.

_____. "O Vliyanii Etnicheskikh Faktorov na Territorial'noye Pereraspredeleniye Naseleniya." Izvestiya Akademii Nauk SSSR, Seriya Geograficheskaya, no. 4 (1965), pp. 31-39.

_____. "Sovremennaya Migratsiya v SSSR." Narodonaseleniye i Ekonomika. Moscow: Izdatel'stvo "Ekonomika," 1967.

Pipes, Richard. "'Solving' the Nationality Problem." Problems of Communism 16 (September-October 1967): 125-31.

Pirtskhalava, G. B. "Dinamika i Nekotoryye Osobennosti Rozhdayemosti v Gruzii." Materialy Vsesoyuznoy Nauchnoy Konferentsii po Problemam Narodonaseleniya Zakavkaz'ya. Erevan, 1968.

Pokshishevskiy, V. V. "Etnicheskiye Protsessy v Gorodakh SSSR i Nekotoryye Problemy ikh Izucheniya." Sovetskaya Etnografiya, no. 5 (1969), pp. 3-15.

_____. "Urbanizatsiya i Etnograficheskiye Protsessy." Problemy Urbanizatsii. Edited by D. I. Valentey, V. V. Pokshishevskiy, and B. S. Khorev. Moscow: Izdatel'stvo Moskovskogo Universiteta, 1971.

Popper, Karl R. "The Nature of Philosophical Problems and Their Roots in Science." Plato's Meno. Edited by Malcolm Brown. New York: Bobbs Merrill, 1971.

Price, Charles. "The Study of Assimilation." Migration. Edited by J. A. Jackson. Cambridge, Mass.: Cambridge University Press, 1969.

Rabut, Odile. "Les Etrangers en France." Population, no. 3 (May-June 1973), pp. 620-24.

Raeff, Marc. "Patterns of Russian Imperial Policy Toward the Nationalities." Soviet Nationality Problems. Edited by Edward Allworth. New York: Columbia University Press, 1971.

Redfield, Robert. "The Folk Society." American Journal of Sociology 52 (January 1947): 243-308.

Rodgers, Allan. "The Locational Dynamics of Soviet Industry." Annals of the Association of American Geographers 64 (June 1974): 226-40.

Rosen, Bernard C. "Race, Ethnicity and the Achievement Syndrome." American Sociological Review 24 (February 1959): 47-60.

Rutgayzer, V. "Torzhestvo Leninskoy Natsional'noy Politiki v Ekonomicheskom Stroitel'stve." Kommunist, no. 18 (December 1968), pp. 24-35.

Schaefer, Fred K. "Exceptionalism in Geography: A Methodological Examination." Annals of the Association of American Geographers 43 (September 1953): 226-49.

Schnaiberg, Allan. "The Modernizing Impact of Urbanization: A Causal Analysis." Economic Development and Cultural Change 20 (October 1971): 80-104.

Schroeder, Gertrude E. "Regional Differences in Incomes and Levels
of Living in the USSR." The Soviet Economy in Regional Perspective. Edited by J. N. Bandera and Z. L. Melnyk. New
York: Praeger, 1973.

Shabad, Theodore. "Soviet Lists Plans to Expand Iron and Steel Industry." New York Times. 3 April 1971, p. 2.

_____. "Soviet Starting Production in Largest Blast Furnace." New
York Times. 20 February 1973, p. 43.

Sheehy, Ann. "Some Aspects of Regional Development in Soviet Central Asia." Slavic Review 31 (September 1972): 555-63.

Shkaratan, O. I. "Etno-Sotsial'naya Struktura Gorodskogo Naseleniya
Tatarskoy ASSR." Sovetskaya Etnografiya, no. 3 (1970), pp.
3-16.

Silver, Brian D. "The Impact of Urbanization and Geographical Dispersion on the Linguistic Russification of Soviet Nationalities."
Demography 11 (February 1974): 89-103.

_____. "Levels of Sociocultural Development Among Soviet National-
ities: A Partial Test of the Equalization Hypothesis." American Political Science Review 68 (December 1974).

Smelser, Neil J. "Mechanisms of Change and Adjustment to Change."
Industrialization and Society. Edited by Bert F. Hoselitz and
Wilbert E. Moore. The Hague: UNESCO-Mouton, 1966.

Smith, Hedrick. "Estonians Retain Identity but Mix More with Russians." New York Times. 28 December 1973, p. 2.

_____. "Moscow Allows Armenia Its Nationalism." New York Times.
20 December 1971, p. 8.

_____. "Pravda Assailing Soviet Georgians." New York Times.
19 November 1973, p. 6.

Smulevich, B. Ya. "K Voprosu o Zakone Narodonaseleniya." Narodonaseleniye i Ekonomika. Moscow: Izdatel'stvo "Ekonomika,"
1967.

"Soviet Officials Outfox Crafty Fruit Smugglers." New York Times.
15 January 1974, p. 2.

Spengler, Joseph J. "Demographic Factors and Early Modern Economic Development." Daedalus 97 (Spring 1968): 433-46.

_____. "Values and Fertility Analysis." Demography 3, no. 1 (1966), 109-30.

Strodtbeck, Fred L.; McDonald, Margaret R.; and Rosen, Bernard C. "Evaluation of Occupations: A Reflection of Jewish and Italian Mobility Differences." American Sociological Review 22 (October 1957): 546-53.

Szporluk, Roman. "Nationalities and the Russian Problem in the U.S.S.R.: An Historical Outline." Journal of International Affairs 27, no. 1 (1973): 22-40.

Taeuber, Irene B. "Demographic Modernization: Continuities and Transition." Demography 3, no. 1 (1966): 90-108.

"The Great Russian Ripoffsky." Newsweek, 20 August 1973, pp. 38, 43.

Tilly, Charles. "The Modernization of Political Conflict in France." Perspectives on Modernization. Edited by Edward B. Harvey. Toronto: University of Toronto Press, 1972.

Time, 6 May 1974, p. 41.

"200 Lithuanians Reported Jailed." New York Times. 14 June 1972, p. 15.

"Ukrainian Writer Pardoned After Renunciation." New York Times. 14 November 1973, p. 8.

Vardys, V. Stanley. "Geography and Nationalities in the USSR: A Commentary." Slavic Review 31 (September 1972): 564-70.

Vestnik Statistiki, no. 1 (1965), pp. 86-96.

Vestnik Statistiki, no. 12 (1966), p. 83.

Vestnik Statistiki, no. 1 (1967), pp. 86-96.

Vestnik Statistiki, no. 11 (1971), p. 84.

Vestnik Statistiki, no. 2 (1973), pp. 77, 87-89.

Vestnik Statistiki, no. 6 (1973), p. 90.

Vestnik Statistiki, no. 12 (1973), pp. 75-79.

Volkov, A. G. "O Nekotorykh Prichinakh Snizheniya Koeffitsiyenta Rozhdayemosti." Izucheniye Vosproizvodstva Naseleniya. Moscow: Izdatel'stvo "Nauka," 1968.

Weinberg, Ian. "The Concept of Modernization: An Unfinished Chapter in Sociological Theory." Perspectives on Modernization. Edited by Edward H. Harvey. Toronto: University of Toronto Press, 1972.

Weiner, Myron. "Political Demography: An Inquiry into the Political Consequences of Population Change." Rapid Population Growth: Consequences and Policy Implications. Edited by Roger Revelle. Baltimore: Johns Hopkins Press, 1971.

Wirth, Louis. "Urbanism as a Way of Life." American Journal of Sociology 44 (July 1938): 1-24.

Zvindrin'sh, P. P. "Dinamika i Demograficheskiye Faktory Rozhdayemosti v Latvii." Voprosy Demografii. Moscow: Statistika, 1970.

                              UNPUBLISHED MATERIALS

Clem, Ralph S. "Population Change and Nationality in the Soviet Union, 1926-1970." Ph.D. dissertation, Columbia University, 1975.

Connor, Walker. "Nationalism Reconsidered." Paper presented at the Annual Meeting of the Northeast Political Science Association, 1971.

Jaffe, A. J. "Manpower and Other Economic Contributions by Migrants: The United States Experience." Paper presented at the Conference on Labor and Migration, Brooklyn College, New York, March 13-14, 1970.

Silver, Brian D. "Ethnic Identity Change Among Soviet Nationalities: A Statistical Analysis." Ph.D. dissertation, University of Wisconsin, 1972.

331, 334; nonagricultural work
force, 334-38; population growth,
277-94; privileged position of,
115, 117, 120, 351; specialists
in work force, 336; urbanization,
high, 130, 131, 133, 141-59, 315,
325, 327, 329, 331; urbanization
of, in non-Russian areas, 130,
131-32, 133, 144-59, 160-62,
165-66, 181, 294, 298, 322, 326,
368, 382
Russification, 108, 109, 132, 133,
156-57, 159, 161, 175, 181, 195,
219-20, 222, 245, 257-58, 259,
267, 282-84, 285-86, 287-88, 295,
296, 297, 299, 300, 301, 303, 306,
307-08, 352 (see also, assimilation)
Russo-Finnish War, 257
Russo-Japanese War (1904-05), 107

St. Petersburg (Leningrad), 73
Sakhalin, 94, 102, 107
Samarkand, 105
Saratov, 285; Oblast, 283
Sarts, 45, 46
Saudi Arabia, 67
Schroeder, Gertrude, 120
self-determination, Lenin's views
on, 111-12, 113
Sevastopol', 39, 145, 148
Severo-Osetin ASSR, 144
Shamil, Imam, 104
shantytowns, 366
Shaumian, 97
Sheehy, Ann, 153, 155, 355, 357,
358, 369
Shibutani, Tamotsu, and Kian
Kwan, 344, 348, 352
Shortsy, 170
Siberia, 68, 71, 73, 76, 77, 101,
102, 113, 118, 130, 144, 153,
237, 268, 289, 298, 362, 377,
380; East, 36, 60-61, 62, 64, 66,
68, 78, 213, 222, 286, 362; West,

36, 65, 69, 71-72, 75, 76, 78,
117, 213, 214, 220, 222, 285,
286, 287, 326, 327, 328, 362,
363, 375, 376
Sibir', 101
Silver, Brian, 92, 120, 156
Simferopol', 148
Singapore, 173
Slavs, 100, 156, 269, 287, 293,
353, 354, 370, 377; Eastern, 167
Slovenians, 347
Smolensk, 103
"social communication," 85
Social Democrats, Marxist, 110-11,
112; factions within, 110-11
"social mobilization," 93
Soligorsk, 165
South, the, 36, 147, 151, 161, 162,
176, 193, 200, 215, 216, 219, 224,
261, 262, 317, 318, 322, 324, 325,
326, 327
South Africa, 84
South America, 11
Southwest, the, 36, 65, 151, 162,
176, 200, 216, 254, 246, 261, 262,
321, 323, 325, 326, 327, 328, 329
Soviet nationality policies, 107-08,
110-22; assimilation, 115-16; cen-
tralism, Stalin and, 115; industrial
equalization, 116-22; industrial lo-
cation principles, 117
Soviet Union (see, USSR)
Sovietization, 282
Spanish (people), 379
Spearman rank correlation coeffi-
cients, 54, 314, 322
Stalin, J. V., 75, 97, 113-14, 115,
270
Staryy Margelan (Margilan), 363
Stavropol Kray, 285
steel, 67-68, 74, 75, 76, 78
Suvalk Guberniya, 260
Svetlogorsk, 165
Sweden, 86, 89, 375
Swedes, 101, 103

ABOUT THE AUTHORS

ROBERT A. LEWIS is professor of geography, Columbia University. His research has been concentrated on population change in Russia and the USSR since the end of the nineteenth century and its impact on society. At present, he is studying the redistribution of population in the USSR, with special reference to nationality problems. Dr. Lewis holds a Ph.D. from the University of Washington.

RICHARD H. ROWLAND, Ph.D. in geography, Columbia University, is assistant professor of geography at California State College, San Bernadino. Although he studies all aspects of Soviet population, his research has largely focused on urbanization and migration in the USSR. He currently is studying, in collaboration with Robert Lewis, population redistribution in the USSR since the end of the nineteenth century.

RALPH S. CLEM is assistant professor in the Department of International Relations, Florida International University, Miami. He was awarded the Ph.D. in geography from Columbia University. Although a student of population change in the USSR, his publications have dealt primarily with the demography of Soviet nationalities. Dr. Clem is the author of The Soviet West: Interplay Between Nationality and Social Organization (Praeger, 1975). Currently, he is doing research on a comparative study of neocolonialism in the United States and the Soviet Union.

SOVIET ASIA: BIBLIOGRAPHIES
The Iranian, Mongolian, and Turkic Nationalities
Edward Allworth

THE SOVIET WEST: Interplay Between Nationality and
Social Organization
Ralph S. Clem

SEX ROLES IN SOVIET RUSSIA: A Study of the Impact of
Industrialization on the Status of Women
Michael Paul Sacks

SOVIET MANPOWER: Supply and Demand, 1950-1980
Murray Feshbach

THE NATIONALITY QUESTION IN SOVIET CENTRAL ASIA
edited by Edward Allworth

THE SOVIET TREATMENT OF JEWS
Harry G. Shaffer